Optimizing Digital Solutions for Hyper-Personalization in Tourism and Hospitality

Nuno Gustavo
Estoril Higher Institute for Tourism and Hotel Studies, Portugal

João Pronto
Estoril Higher Institute for Tourism and Hotel Studies, Portugal

Luísa Carvalho
Polytechnic Institute of Setúbal, Portugal & CEFAGE, University of Évora, Portugal

Miguel Belo
Lisbon University, Portugal & Portuguese National Funding Agency for Science, Research, and Technology, Portugal

A volume in the Advances in Hospitality, Tourism, and the Services Industry (AHTSI) Book Series

Published in the United States of America by
    IGI Global
    Business Science Reference (an imprint of IGI Global)
    701 E. Chocolate Avenue
    Hershey PA, USA 17033
    Tel: 717-533-8845
    Fax: 717-533-8661
    E-mail: cust@igi-global.com
    Web site: http://www.igi-global.com

Library of Congress Cataloging-in-Publication Data

Names: Gustavo, Nuno, 1978- editor. | Pronto, Joao Miguel, 1970- editor. |
    Carvalho, Luísa Cagica, 1970- editor. | Belo, Miguel, 1991- editor.
Title: Optimizing digital solutions for hyper-personalization in tourism
    and hospitality / Nuno Gustavo, Joao Miguel Pronto, Luisa Carvalho, and
    Miguel Belo, Editor.
Description: Hershey : Business Science Reference, [2022] | Includes
    bibliographical references and index. | Summary: "This book contributes
    in an objective way for leveraging digital solutions to optimize the
    concept of hyper personalization in the tourist experience, emphasizing
    the importance of hyperpersonalization models, processes, strategies and
    issues within tourism and hospitality fields with a particular focus on
    digital IT solutions"-- Provided by publisher.
Identifiers: LCCN 2021035508 (print) | LCCN 2021035509 (ebook) | ISBN
    9781799883067 (hardcover) | ISBN 9781799883074 (paperback) | ISBN
    9781799883081 (ebook)
Subjects: LCSH: Tourism--Technological innovations. | Hospitality
    industry--Technological innovations. | Tourism--Marketing. | Hospitality
    industry--Marketing. | Tourism--Management. | Hospitality
    industry--Management.
Classification: LCC G156.5.I5 O68 2022 (print) | LCC G156.5.I5 (ebook) |
    DDC 910.285/55--dc23
LC record available at https://lccn.loc.gov/2021035508
LC ebook record available at https://lccn.loc.gov/2021035509

This book is published in the IGI Global book series Advances in Hospitality, Tourism, and the Services Industry (AHTSI) (ISSN: 2475-6547; eISSN: 2475-6555)

Advances in Hospitality, Tourism, and the Services Industry (AHTSI) Book Series

Maximiliano Korstanje
University of Palermo, Argentina

ISSN:2475-6547
EISSN:2475-6555

MISSION

Globally, the hospitality, travel, tourism, and services industries generate a significant percentage of revenue and represent a large portion of the business world. Even in tough economic times, these industries thrive as individuals continue to spend on leisure and recreation activities as well as services.

The Advances in Hospitality, Tourism, and the Services Industry (AHTSI) book series offers diverse publications relating to the management, promotion, and profitability of the leisure, recreation, and services industries. Highlighting current research pertaining to various topics within the realm of hospitality, travel, tourism, and services management, the titles found within the AHTSI book series are pertinent to the research and professional needs of managers, business practitioners, researchers, and upper-level students studying in the field.

COVERAGE

- Travel Agency Management
- International Tourism
- Cruise Marketing and Sales
- Customer Service Issues
- Service Training
- Sustainable Tourism
- Health and Wellness Tourism
- Service Design
- Leisure & Business Travel
- Hotel Management

IGI Global is currently accepting manuscripts for publication within this series. To submit a proposal for a volume in this series, please contact our Acquisition Editors at Acquisitions@igi-global.com or visit: http://www.igi-global.com/publish/.

Titles in this Series

For a list of additional titles in this series, please visit: http://www.igi-global.com/book-series/advances-hospitality-tourism-services-industry/121014

Global Perspectives on Literary Tourism and Film-Induced Tourism
Rita Baleiro (University of the Algarve, Portugal & CiTUR, Portugal) and Rosária Pereira (University of the Algarve, Portugal & CinTurs, ortugal)
Business Science Reference • © 2022 • 371pp • H/C (ISBN: 9781799882626) • US $215.00

Planning and Managing the Experience Economy in Tourism
Rui Augusto Costa (GOVCOPP, University of Aveiro, Portugal) Filipa Brandão (GOVCOPP, University of Aveiro, Portugal) Zelia Breda (GOVCOPP, University of Aveiro, Portugal) and Carlos Costa (GOVCOPP, University of Aveiro, Portugal)
Business Science Reference • © 2022 • 407pp • H/C (ISBN: 9781799887751) • US $195.00

Food Safety Practices in the Restaurant Industry
Siti Nurhayati Khairatun (Universiti Putra Malaysia, Malaysia) Ainul Zakiah Abu Bakar (Universiti Putra Malaysia, Malaysia) Noor Azira Abdul Mutalib (Universiti Putra Malaysia, Malaysia) and Ungku Fatimah Ungku Zainal Abidin (Universiti Putra Malaysia, Malaysia)
Business Science Reference • © 2022 • 334pp • H/C (ISBN: 9781799874157) • US $215.00

Prospects and Challenges of Community-Based Tourism and Changing Demographics
Ishmael Mensah (University of Cape Coast, Ghana) and Ewoenam Afenyo-Agbe (University of Cape Coast, Ghana)
Business Science Reference • © 2022 • 300pp • H/C (ISBN: 9781799873358) • US $195.00

Challenges and New Opportunities for Tourism in Inland Territories Ecocultural Resources and Sustainable Initiatives
Gonçalo Poeta Fernandes (CITUR, Polytechnic Institute of Guarda, Portugal)
Business Science Reference • © 2022 • 295pp • H/C (ISBN: 9781799873396) • US $195.00

Rebuilding and Restructuring the Tourism Industry Infusion of Happiness and Quality of Life
André Riani Costa Perinotto (Universidade Federal do Delta do Parnaíba, Brazil) Verônica Feder Mayer (Federal Fluminense University, Brazil) and Jakson Renner Rodrigues Soares (Universidade da Coruña, Spain & Universidade Estadual do Ceará, Brazil)
Business Science Reference • © 2021 • 330pp • H/C (ISBN: 9781799872399) • US $195.00

Handbook of Research on the Impacts and Implications of COVID-19 on the Tourism Industry
Mahmut Demir (Isparta University of Applied Sciences, Turkey) Ali Dalgıç (Isparta University of Applied Sciences, Turkey) and Fatma Doğanay Ergen (Isparta University of Applied Sciences, Turkey)

701 East Chocolate Avenue, Hershey, PA 17033, USA
Tel: 717-533-8845 x100 • Fax: 717-533-8661
E-Mail: cust@igi-global.com • www.igi-global.com

Table of Contents

Detailed Table of Contents

Section 1
Digitalisation in Tourism and Hospitality: New Trends

Chapter 1

Nuno Gustavo, Estoril Higher Institute for Tourism and Hotel Studies, Portugal
Elliot Mbunge, University of Eswatini, Eswatini
Miguel Belo, Estoril Higher Institute for Tourism and Hotel Studies, Portugal
Stephen Gbenga Fashoto, University of Eswatini, Eswatini
João Miguel Pronto, Estoril Higher Institute for Tourism and Hotel Studies, Portugal
Andile Simphiwe Metfula, University of Eswatini, Eswatini
Luísa Cagica Carvalho, Instituto Politécnico de Setúbal, Portugal
Boluwaji Ade Akinnuwesi, University of Swaziland, Swaziland
Tonderai Robson Chiremba, University of Swaziland, Swaziland

This chapter aims to review the tech evolution in hospitality, from services to eServices, that will provide hyper-personalization in the hospitality field. In the past, the services were provided by hotels through diligent staff and supported by standardized and weak technology that was not allowed to provide personalized services by itself. Therefore, the study applied K-means and FCM clustering algorithms to cluster online travelers' reviews from TripAdvisor. The study shows that K-means clustering outperforms fuzzy c-means in this study in terms of accuracy and execution time while fuzzy c-means converge faster than K-means clustering in terms of the number of iterations. K-means achieved 93.4% accuracy, and fuzzy c-means recorded 91.3% accuracy.

Chapter 2

Elliot Mbunge, University of Eswatini, Eswatini
Benhildah Muchemwa, University of Eswatini, Eswatini

Social media platforms play a tremendous role in the tourism and hospitality industry. Social media platforms are increasingly becoming a source of information. The complexity and increasing size of tourists' online data make it difficult to extract meaningful insights using traditional models. Therefore, this scoping and comprehensive review aimed to analyze machine learning and deep learning models applied to model tourism data. The study revealed that deep learning and machine learning models are used for forecasting and predicting tourism demand using data from search query data, Google trends, and social media platforms. Also, the study revealed that data-driven models can assist managers and policymakers in mapping and segmenting tourism hotspots and attractions and predicting revenue that is likely to be generated, exploring targeting marketing, segmenting tourists based on their spending patterns, lifestyle, and age group. However, hybrid deep learning models such as inceptionV3, MobilenetsV3, and YOLOv4 are not yet explored in the tourism and hospitality industry.

Chapter 3

Nil Sonuç, İzmir Katip Çelebi University, Turkey
Merve İşçen, İzmir Katip Çelebi University, Turkey

This chapter aims to review the evolution of digitalisation and its effects on the tourism and hospitality industry. A holistic perspective is adopted providing a review and analysis of digitalisation in the tourism and hospitality sector comprising both supply and demand sides for the originality of the content. The supply side, as well as the demand side, is analysed through a literature review of academic resources, policy documents published by international organisations and related websites. The existing literature and the industrial practices are reviewed to find out and classify the state of proposal and implementation of innovative technologies and the trends followed by suppliers and the demand side to use them. Furthermore, the effects of digitalisation on managerial processes on the supply side (actors, entrepreneurs, businesses, destinations) and decisional and behavioural processes on the demand side (consumer, tourists) are taken into consideration to provide a holistic perspective of digitalisation and its effects on the given sector.

Chapter 4

Hussein Salimo Jamal, Estoril Higher Institute for Tourism and Hotel Studies, Portugal

Based on the growing evolution of intelligent technology and automation in the provision of services, this chapter analyzes its incorporation into the 4- and 5-star national hotels and its consequent impact on decision and consumer choice. In this sense, the authors proceeded to characterize the technologies with greater appetence concerning the reality of the hotel industry. Furthermore, they investigated the appreciation made by the guests, researched trends, advantages, inconveniences, changes in behavior and procedures, given the COVID-19 pandemic.

Chapter 5

Lakhvinder Singh, Government College, Kaithal, India
Dinesh Dhankhar, Kurukshetra University, India

Digitalization has forced the accommodation sector to use information and communication technology (ICT) to excel in their business performance. Hence, it is of paramount importance to scan the pros and cons associated with use of ICT marketing in the accommodation sector. This chapter considers this fact and focuses on opportunities and challenges associated with the use of ICT-based marketing in the accommodation sector of Gurugram (Haryana) region of India. The phenomena of ICT marketing is exhaustively assessed and highlighted through different components such as introduction, ICT as emerging concept, application of ICT tools in the marketing accommodation sector, opportunities associated with using ICT-based marketing, challenges faced during applying ICT marketing in the accommodation sector, followed by a conclusion. This study has been considered as a modification and addition to the existing body of knowledge in the accommodation sector. Moreover, the tourism and accommodation marketers also apprehend practical implications to augment their services for survival in a competitive business environment.

Section 2
Smart Tourism and Co-Creation

Chapter 6

    Ana Sousa, COMEGI, Universidade Lusíada - Norte, Portugal
    Clara Madeira, COMEGI, Universidade Lusíada - Norte, Portugal
    Paula Rodrigues, COMEGI, Universidade Lusíada - Norte, Portugal
    Carlos Martins, COMEGI, Universidade Lusíada - Norte, Portugal

Policymakers and business practitioners increasingly recognize the importance of sustainability in the development of smart tourism destinations, which require clear directions and specific guidelines. The authors used the Bibliometrix R-package and VOS Viewer software to perform a bibliometric analysis of 59 articles between 1900-2020 retrieved from the Web of Science (WoS) Core Collection database. They compiled a bibliographic coupling, identified the key authors, journals, documents, and the most relevant universities. The findings detail four clusters: (1) smart tourism, (2) sustainable tourism, (3) technology, and (4) smart specialization. This work contributes to a better understanding of the concepts and aspires to provide useful information for those academics and destination marketing organizations (DMOs) attempting to analyze and deepen their knowledge within this research field. Simultaneously, it also aims to provide insights concerning the future development of sustainability and smart tourism in the social sciences' academic literature.

Chapter 7

    Murat Ödemiş, Tourism Faculty, Gümüşhane University, Turkey

Tourism businesses and touristic destinations that want to reach a highly competitive position in the world should fulfill the required infrastructure investments and acquire a service concept that is consistent with the smart tourism strategy in order to turn into smart tourism. In order to compete with rival destinations, it has become a prerequisite for Turkey's world-famous destinations such as Istanbul, Antalya, Izmir, and Cappadocia to embrace digital transformation and smart tourism concepts. Accordingly, the concepts of smart tourism, smart city, and smart tourism destinations will be explained, and smart tourism applications in Turkey's touristic destinations will be explored in this chapter within the framework of current academic studies. It is aimed to ascertain how well these specified destinations adhere to the concept of smart tourism.

It is known that businesses are looking for different ways to reach customers, both technologically and through employees, in order to protect their existing customers as well as to gain new customers. However, today, due to the personable approaches of services, there is a need to create a bond between the business and the customer. In this context, value is an original understanding that people have, and businesses aim to create value together by reaching more customers through personalized services. Thus, the importance of studies aimed at understanding this phenomenon based on multilateral profit relationship is increasing day by day. In the current study, the approach of creating value together is discussed, and the understanding of the creation of value together in air transportation operating in the service sector is examined.

Section 3
Consumer Behaviour, Brand, and Digital Marketing

Customer brand identification is described by the customer's perception and feeling about a brand. It brings value and meets the customer's needs. The four drivers of CBI are brand self-similarity, brand social benefits, brand identity, and memorable brand experiences. The purpose of this study is to understand the influence of CBI (and, consequently, its drivers) on customer loyalty and its perception of hotel brands. Although the importance of CBI has already been recognized in some studies, its effects on customer loyalty in the hospitality context are still relatively unexplored. A survey was used to understand and confirm that CBI and all four of its dimensions significantly influence customer loyalty. This means, in the hotel industry, customers tend to look for brands that are distinct from their competitors, have an identity of their own, and close to their values. It was also possible to conclude that the client tends to behave more favorably towards the brand, spreading positive word of mouth and recommending brands that meet CBI conditions.

Chapter 10

This chapter aimed to explicate CRM concept along with its distinct dimensions. Following the explanation of the denotation, evolution, and types of the CRM concept, the benefits of CRM, success factors, and possible causes for downfall are discussed. Another section of the chapter considers the role and evolution of CRM in the digitization process. This part introduces the reader to the concepts of E-CRM and SCRM that arose during the process, as well as the success conditions and essential aspects of these approaches. This section examines the relationship between customer satisfaction and loyalty in the tourism sector, the impact of CRM on business performance, and CRM applications in the context of destination management. In the last part, CRM practices and approaches in Turkey were discussed in terms of destination management and tourism businesses, and some applications and modules employed in the digitalization process are included.

Chapter 11

Gabriel Vieira Mendes Figueiredo, Pontifícia Universidade Católica de São Paulo, Brazil
João Pinheiro de Barros Neto, Pontifícia Universidade Católica de São Paulo, Brazil

Brazil has enormous, underexplored tourism potential. To identify how digital marketing can boost tourism, the authors chose to examine the city of Paraty—a touristic microcosm of Brazil. Digital marketing is a low-cost marketing strategy that can reach potential tourists anywhere. Its use by tourism entrepreneurs has proven effective and able to generate significant return on investment. This exploratory study aimed to develop hypotheses. The authors used questionnaires and interviews to assess the perception of local tourism entrepreneurs regarding the affordances and advantages of digital marketing tools, techniques, and strategies. They found that entrepreneurs' adoption of digital marketing brought several benefits, including low investment costs and significant returns. However, the research revealed the need for training, mainly for small entrepreneurs to explore the numerous opportunities of the web in their businesses. Public authorities can also play a more leading role in combining and steering efforts to promote tourism.

Chapter 12

João Ferreira do Rosário, Escola Superior de Comunicação Social, Instituto Politécnico de Lisboa, Portugal
Maria de Lurdes Calisto, CiTUR, Portugal
Ana Teresa Machado, Escola Superior de Comunicação Social, Instituto Politécnico de Lisboa, Portugal
Nuno Gustavo, Estoril Higher Institute for Tourism and Hotel Studies, Portugal

This chapter presents an importance-performance analysis to evaluate the ability of a destination's attributes to attract tourists through tourism stakeholder perceptions. In this case, one of Europe's larger destination cities, Lisbon, was considered. It departs from the proposition that tourists are not the most knowledgeable about a destination while the evaluation of a destination's competitiveness from the supply side perspective is scarce. This stakeholder feedback approach to identifying a destination's attributes to attract tourists showed that only 7 of the 40 attributes (five of them related to accessibility and technological infrastructures as municipality responsibility) fall in the IPA grid Concentrate Here quadrant, results that are consistent with the recently received Best City Destination and Best City Break World Travel Awards. This research shows the relevance of multiple stakeholders' feedback to evaluate a city's attributes, including the feedback about the city's need to improve its technological offer through an integrated digital strategy.

The chapter explores shared accommodation platforms such as Airbnb and the primary motivations for its customers. This research will be based on the deductive process, which is focused on primary and secondary research. This research aims to analyze the motivation towards either the Airbnb platform or traditional hotel from different perspectives, such as economic, environmental, and social. Additionally, after secondary data research, the questionnaire has been constructed to understand the main concepts of the P2P platform and its customers' needs. The investigation tried to notice what are the motivations which drive individuals to use P2P accommodation service. Through the survey, it was possible to see the motivations mainly related to the economic factor and environmental. Primarily due to the lower price of Airbnb, there is a more significant intent to book through this specific platform.

Chapter 14

This study aims to investigate which hotels' attributes are most valued by the guests of the main markets of Porto. The guests' knowledge, preferences, and needs are crucial data that impact customer satisfaction. As a people-to-people industry, the hotel industry must consider the heterogeneity of its markets and invest in improving its services, considering the aspects they value. However, is the heterogeneity pronounced that much? Or are there any similarities between markets? Guests do not have similar satisfaction levels, so to guarantee the best experience for the most significant number of customers, these should be studied by market segments, once individual study would be impracticable. Through the comments made on the Booking.com, following the assumption that guests comment on what they value, the attributes that guests of different nationalities refer to Porto hotels have been collected. From the analysis of all the collected data, it can be concluded that all the main markets' value attributes and the fundamental differences are based on the hierarchy of these attributes.

In recent years, online reputation management has become increasingly crucial in the hotel industry, as online reviews have become one of the most critical factors in choosing accommodation. Consequently, hotels have adapted themselves to this new reality and define strategies focused on online reputation management, whose primary goal is to monitor and correct unwanted situations verified on the internet. Regarding its importance, several investigations about online reputation management have been made, but mostly about their impact on consumer satisfaction and decision-making. This investigation shows that hotels in Lisbon adopt adequate strategies in both four and five-star hotels, and their classification (star rating) did not influence the strategies chosen by them. Additionally, hotels with the same classification have similar strategies, in contrast to some investigations in the literature. Finally, the method of data collection chosen for the current investigation was the online survey, since it allows the collection of a significant volume of data in a short period.

Preface

As hyper-personalization has yet to be perfected, developing hyper-personalized strategies presents a critical challenge; due to this, optimizing hyper-personalization and designing new processes and business models take center stage in tourism and hospitality to reach new levels of customer service and experience. These main challenges for the following years include aspects such as the introduction and development of new solutions supported in the internet of things, software interfaces, artificial intelligence solutions, back-end and front-end management tools, and other emergent business intelligence strategies.

Optimizing Digital Solutions for Hyper-Personalization in Tourism and Hospitality serves as an essential reference source that emphasizes the importance of hyper-personalization models, processes, strategies, and issues within tourism and hospitality fields with a particular focus on digital IT solutions. More than a simple starting point for a critical reflection on the state of the art of this sector, this book aims to contribute in an objective way to leveraging digital solutions to optimize the concept of hyper-personalization in the tourist experience.

The content of this book covers research topics that include digital tourism and hospitality, consumer behavior, customer journey, and smart technologies and is ideal for professionals, executives, hotel managers, event coordinators, restaurateurs, travel agents, tour directors, policymakers, government officials, industry professionals, researchers, students, and academicians in the fields of tourism and hospitality management, marketing, and communications.

The book consists of 15 chapters which the editors decided to organize in three sections: "Digitalisation in Tourism and Hospitality: New Trends"; "Smart Tourism and Co-Creation"; and "Consumer Behaviour, Brand, and Digital Marketing." It can be said that the boundaries between each of these sections are rather blurred as the chapters are to a greater or lesser extent interrelated. It is considered, however, that this structure will render the book's consultation more effective insofar as the first section on new trends promoted by technology and ICT in hospitality and tourism. The second section discuss the opportunities created by smart tourism strategies and co-creation. The last part, which is perhaps more controversial, is merely aimed at grouping together the chapters which cover the consumer behaviour, brand and digital marketing, given the specificities which are usually attributed to these topics.

In the first chapter, "Emphasizing the Digital Shift of Hospitality Towards Hyper-Personalization: Application of Machine Learning Clustering Algorithms to Analyze Travelers," Gustavo et al. start by referring to the impacts and challenges of COVID-19 on the tourism sector. In this context, the authors argue that one possible solution could be based on emphasizing the digital shift of hospitality, namely in regarding the optimization of its operational standard procedures, while underlining health as the main driver of guests' satisfaction. Moreover, studying how digital solutions can ensure hygiene and cleanliness in various touchpoints in customer's experience based on operational efficiency should be critical for the next few years, contributing to the importance of rethinking and rebuilding hospitality towards a more sustainable, resilient, and innovative sector for the future.

In Chapter 2, entitled "Deep Learning and Machine Learning Techniques for Analyzing Travelers' Online Reviews: A Review," Elliot Mbunge and Benhildah Muchemwa discuss the role played by social media platforms in the tourism and hospitality industry. Social media platforms are increasingly becoming a source of information. The complexity and increasing size of tourists' online data make it difficult to extract meaningful insights using traditional models. This study revealed that deep learning and machine learning models are used for forecasting and predicting tourism demand using data from search query data, Google trends and social media platforms. Also, the study revealed that data-driven models can assist managers and policymakers in mapping and segmenting tourism hotspots and attractions and predicting revenue that is likely to be generated, exploring targeting marketing, segmenting tourists based on their spending patterns, lifestyle, and age group.

Chapter 3 addresses the topic of "Digitalisation in Tourism and Hospitality Industry: Perspectives of Supply and Demand Sides" in which Nil Sonuç and Merve İşçen provides a comprehensive classification of digitalisation in the tourism industry. For the demand side, the existing studies related to the implication and effects of digitalisation in tourism demand are mentioned including the aspects of new generation consumer needs and behaviours. Additionally, the specific methods used for marketing such as neuromarketing in tourism and suggestions are made accordingly for further studies. However, as the tourism sector is becoming more participative, cooperative and co-creative, the transition between both sides is sometimes inevitable.

In Chapter 4, "Intelligent Technology and Automation in Hospitality: The Case of Four- and Five-Star Units Operating in Portugal," by Hussein Salimo Jamal, analyzes the incorporation of Intelligent Technology and Automation in the 4- and 5-star National Hotel and its consequent impact on decision and consumer choice. In this sense, the author characterized the technologies with greater appetence concerning the reality of the Hotel industry. Furthermore, the chapter investigated the appreciation made by the guests, researched trends, advantages, inconveniences, changes in behavior and procedures, given the Covid-19 pandemic.

Section 1 closes with the chapter "Opportunities and Challenges of ICT-Based Marketing in the Accommodation Sector: A Study Of Gurugram (Haryana), India" in which Lakhvinder Singh and Dinesh Dhankhar introduces the context of the contemporary world, where ICT has become a crucial infrastructure including computer, maps, multimedia, internet, mobile that provides lot of opportunities to enrich customer experience and add to firms' profit maximization also. The accommodation segment of tourism sector deals with providing goods or services to enable pleasure, leisure and business activities away from the home environment to visitors. The Indian accommodation industry is growing with high pace comparative to past decades. The chapter provide a perspective about the application of information and communication technology (ICT) based marketing in accommodation industry in India.

Section 2 incorporates three chapters more concerned with smart tourism and co-creation. Thus, Chapter 6, "Smart and Sustainable Tourism Destination: A Bibliometric Analysis," authored by Ana Sousa, Clara Madeira, Paula Rodrigues and Carlos Martins, presents a bibliometric review about smart tourism destination in the last six years. This chapter conducted a bibliometric analysis to explore trends and patterns in the tourism field. Results indicate that the sustainability approach or concern to smart tourism is, in fact, very recent, with an outcome of 59 papers from Web of Science analysed. This bibliometric review offers support for the need for an interdisciplinary view, based on dialogue, participation, and a critical vision among the stakeholders and destination marketing organisations (DMOs).

The seventh chapter, "Smart Tourism Destinations: A Literature Review on Applications in Turkey's Touristic Destinations," by Murat Ödemiş, refers that smart tourism holds a position among the essential concepts and applications in the course of adaptation to digital transformation of tourism businesses and touristic destinations, expecting to boost and maintain their competitive advantages. The chapter analyse the case of Turkey to embrace digital transformation and smart tourism concept.

Section 2 concludes with Chapter 8, "The Phenomenon of Value Co-Creation and Its Place in Air Transport," assigned by Fatma Selin Sak, Özlem Atalık and Evrim Genç Kumtepe. It introduces the topic of co-creation and emphasizes the common value creation between the manufacturer and the customer. The value of a product created together depends on several variables based on consumers' knowledge of the product in airport operations. This chapter provide a better understanding by emphasizing the importance of the understanding of creating such an important value in air transport together with business and customer partnerships.

Section 3 addresses the topics related to consumer behaviour, brand, and digital marketing. Thus, in Chapter 9, "Customer Brand Identification and Its Influence on Customer Loyalty in the Hotel Industry," Catarina Basílio e Nuno Gustavo examines the relationship between Customer Brand Identification and customer loyalty, starting by individually evaluating the behavior of the four dimensions of CBI. The chapter presents initially, a theoretical contextualization of each concept was carried out, which allowed the formulation of the hypotheses to be studied. Then, the methods used in the investigation, the structure of the survey, and procedures for evaluating the results were explained. Finally, the results were exposed and analyzed, and the conclusions presented.

In the following chapter entitled "Customer Relationship Management in Tourism in the Digitalization Process the Case of Turkey," İsmail Çalık explicates the customer relationship management (CRM) concept along with its distinct dimensions. Following the explanation of the denotation, evolution and types of the CRM concept, the benefits of CRM, success factors and possible causes for failure are discussed. Another part of the book chapter considers the role and evolution of CRM in the digitization process. The chapter provides CRM examples in the Turkish tourism industry.

In the eleventh chapter, "Digital Marketing as a Driver of Tourism: Case Study in Paraty, Rio de Janeiro, Brazil," Gabriel Figueiredo and João Neto explores the affordances of digital marketing strategies to help increase the income of small and medium-sized tourism entrepreneurs in Paraty, in the state of Rio de Janeiro, Brazil. Based on social media and in-person visits to the city, the authors perception is that only the largest agencies have been engaged in digital marketing. Many locals and small business owners who live off tourism still lack an online presence and largely depend on the high season and word-of-mouth advertising to earn their income.

In the next chapter, "Importance-Performance Analysis of Tourism Destination Attractiveness: Technology and Other Influencing Factors," by João Rosário, Maria de Lurdes Calisto, Ana Teresa Machado and Nuno Gustavo, the authors aims at assessing Lisbon's competitiveness to attract tourists using the importance-performance analysis (IPA) based on the perceptions of tourism stakeholders working in several areas of tourism business in Lisbon, like hotels, restaurants, travel agencies, and others, whose activity depends on the tourist's attraction to the city. The results reveal that all 40 attributes studied are considered as important, while globally there exists a positive perception of the city attributes performance.

In Chapter 13, "Living Room Instead of Hotel Room: The Underlying Motivation of Peer-to-Peer Booking in Airbnb and Hotels," Artur Martea contributes to the investigation of the shared accommodation system and how people's choice to use it changes or not the growth and evolution of hotel giants on the market. The literature review suggests the intention to be closer to locals. The social factor is as well a base concept of Airbnb, as the focus of Airbnb is to deliver a local experience and to live like a local. And conclude that Airbnb is still very well positioned in the hospitality industry, where the price is still the main motivator for people to use the platform.

The subsequent chapter, "The Hierarchization of Product Attributes Hotel Manager in the Decision and Purchase Process of Consumers: The Case of Outbound Markets of Porto," by Inês Guerra Alves, aimed to approach a current and pertinent theme for the hotel universe. After analyzing several investigations already carried out, this chapter concludes that the improvement of the product offered, customer satisfaction, and the heterogenization of the needs of hotel product customers are topics addressed by several authors. These themes represent one of the current and past concerns of the hotel industry, the attraction of customers and their loyalty. However, this concern is currently on a larger scale, thanks to the significant increase in competition caused by globalization and the significant increase in online reviews that began to impact consumer purchase decision-making.

Section 3 ends with the chapter entitled "The Importance of Online Reputation Management in Four- and Five-Star Hotels: Case of Lisbon," where Catarina Silva and Miguel Belo aims to answer the following starting question: "What are the strategies adopted by the four and five-star hotels in the city of Lisbon, given the importance of online reputation management in the hotel industry?". Once the hotels' strategies are known, it is intended to analyze each category's behavior and understand if the hotel classification influences the chosen approaches. In general, this investigation concluded that the hotels under analysis in the city of Lisbon have, for the most part, adequate strategies in managing their online reputation and that there is a very similar behavior within each category. Concerning the comparison between the two categories under analysis, only discrepancies were found about the speed of response, although this did not translate into a problematic case. Finally concludes that the hotel classification did not influence the strategies adopted by the hotels in this investigation.

To conclude, we would like to thank the authors whose collaboration has made this project possible and express our hope that readers will find this publication inspiring and useful.

Nuno Gustavo
João Pronto
Luísa Carvalho
Miguel Belo

Section 1
Digitalisation in Tourism and Hospitality: New Trends

Chapter 1
Emphasizing the Digital Shift of Hospitality Towards Hyper–Personalization:
Application of Machine Learning Clustering Algorithms to Analyze Travelers

Nuno Gustavo
Estoril Higher Institute for Tourism and Hotel Studies, Portugal

João Miguel Pronto
Estoril Higher Institute for Tourism and Hotel Studies, Portugal

Elliot Mbunge
University of Eswatini, Eswatini

Andile Simphiwe Metfula
University of Eswatini, Eswatini

Miguel Belo
Estoril Higher Institute for Tourism and Hotel Studies, Portugal

Luísa Cagica Carvalho
(iD) https://orcid.org/0000-0002-9804-7813
Instituto Politécnico de Setúbal, Portugal

Stephen Gbenga Fashoto
University of Eswatini, Eswatini

Boluwaji Ade Akinnuwesi
University of Swaziland, Swaziland

Tonderai Robson Chiremba
University of Swaziland, Swaziland

ABSTRACT

This chapter aims to review the tech evolution in hospitality, from services to eServices, that will provide hyper-personalization in the hospitality field. In the past, the services were provided by hotels through diligent staff and supported by standardized and weak technology that was not allowed to provide personalized services by itself. Therefore, the study applied K-means and FCM clustering algorithms to cluster online travelers' reviews from TripAdvisor. The study shows that K-means clustering outperforms fuzzy c-means in this study in terms of accuracy and execution time while fuzzy c-means converge faster than K-means clustering in terms of the number of iterations. K-means achieved 93.4% accuracy, and fuzzy c-means recorded 91.3% accuracy.

DOI: 10.4018/978-1-7998-8306-7.ch001

INTRODUCTION

In 2019, travel and tourism's direct, indirect, and induced impact accounted for US$8.9 trillion contributions to the world's GDP (10.3%), 330 million jobs (10% of global employment), US$1.7 trillion visitor exports (6.8% of total exports, 28.3% of global services exports) and US$948 billion of capital investment (4.3% of total investment) (World Travel & Tourism Council (WTTC), 2020). However, in the light of the novel global coronavirus (COVID-19), as an ongoing outbreak of viral pneumonia around the world that is highly transmissible between humans, many governments imposed severe although necessary restrictions for individuals and businesses to contain the spread of the pandemic (e.g. quarantines, travel restrictions or lockdown of cities). As a result, brutal economic and social impacts were felt around the world, especially in the tourism and hospitality industry. The effects of COVID-19 were acute on international tourism demand, plunging by 74.0% in 2020 over the previous year on a global level (UNTWO, 2021). In Portugal, where tourism and hospitality account for 10.4% of the national GDP and 9.9% of the national employment (WTTC, 2018), international tourism demand decreased by 74.9% (INE, 2020).

In the light of the outbreak of such global pandemic, the described acute impacts felt in the tourism and hotel sector, particularly in small businesses, the hygiene and cleanliness of hotels have been emphasized among the main drivers of hotel guests' satisfaction, considering a virus that is highly transmissible between humans. Therefore, efforts must be made to deal with this paradigm shift. One possible solution could be based on emphasizing the digital shift of hospitality, namely in regarding the optimization of its operational standard procedures, while underlining health as the main driver of guests' satisfaction. Studying how digital solutions can ensure hygiene and cleanliness in various touchpoints in customer's experience based on operational efficiency should be critical for the next few years, contributing to the importance of rethinking and rebuilding hospitality towards a more sustainable, resilient, and innovative sector for the future.

RETHINKING HOSPITALITY FOR TOMORROW

Previous research has shown that small tourism and hospitality businesses have been particularly affected by the pandemic, being pushed for mass lay-offs, temporarily closing, becoming more financially fragile with cash on hand of only one month, and/or seeking support from the government, with problematic difficulties in recovering business (Bartik et al., 2020; Sobaih et al., 2021). Considering that small and medium enterprises constitute 95.4% of the Portuguese entrepreneurial tissue (European Commission, 2019) and that 59.5% of the hospitality is composed of independent hotels (Deloitte, 2020), protecting and securing jobs in Small Hospitality Businesses (SHBs) seems to be of utmost importance for the socio-economic response to COVID-19 in Portugal.

Indeed, micro, small and medium-sized tourist companies are decapitalized financially and in human resources, with no capacity of investment to turn around their businesses on a standalone basis (Gössling et al., 2021). These companies have been facing other challenges for years, like low managerial skills, low technical and, digital skills, which will be exacerbated by the post-pandemic current and future challenges. Moreover, previous research has recognized that tourism firms' innovation efforts are often made individually and independently by various tourism stakeholders, although collaborative networks have been recognized as a competitive advantage for tourism companies' innovativeness (Martínez-Román, 2015).

On the other hand, the unprecedented circumstances of this crisis also create the unique opportunity of rethinking and rebuilding hospitality for the future, towards a more sustainable, resilient, and innovative sector (Organisation for Economic Co-operation and Development (OECD), 2021). In fact, despite crises representing a potential change trigger, so far, the response has been limited to stabilizing existing structures, diminishing the possibility of collective mobilization (Masco, 2017). As climate change increases the frequency of pandemics and outbreaks, pandemics are expected to become more common in the future (World Economic Forum, 2019). Moreover, in today's globalized world, developments in transportation, the growing population, and the increasing number of travelers rapidly accelerate the rate of the spread of infectious diseases (Yu, Seo & Hyun, 2021). Therefore, although crises have not been a significant transition event for hospitality (Hall et al., 2020), lessons must be learned and measures should be taken, meaning that hotels must adopt permanent measures to be well prepared for dealing with future pandemics (Deloitte, 2021). Otherwise, we will simply experience one crisis after another (Lew, 2020). The impacts from infectious diseases seem to be particularly acute on sectors such as tourism and hospitality, as showed by Hung et al. (2018) or Lee et al. (2012) in regard H1N1, by Chien and Law (2003), Doumbey (2004), Henderson and Ng (2004), Hung et al. (2018), Kim et al. (2005), Kline et al. (2014), Lo et al. (2006), Tew et al. (2008), Tse et al. (2006) or Wen et al. (2005) in the case of SARS.

This new reality will also significantly change the dynamics and processes of the markets, as well as the strategies and management models of companies and organizations of the sector (Sigala, 2020). This does not mean necessarily that the tourism activity will lose its economic and social relevance. On the contrary, the consequences associated with COVID-19 demonstrated its centrality and social significance, giving it a reinforced meaning, which will be materialized in more sustainable growth in the post-pandemic period. Tourism has a strategic role in the world's economy, being a major GDP contributor to several countries, a circumstance that gives it a unique centrality in the research and debate field in the post-pandemic period. Commissioner Breton, who claimed that tourism should stand first in line: "I will be fighting to make sure tourism will be the biggest beneficiary of this [recovery plan] - with around 20 [to] 25 percent" (Nicolás, 2020).

Alongside the traditional models and concepts of tourism management, new solutions are needed, reflecting an increasingly dynamic, global, and integrated world. As in so many other areas of business, tourism management needs to incorporate new matrices and principles in its dynamics, like the network economy, the sharing economy, and the digital economy. While hospitality businesses always needed to stay adaptive, flexible, and innovative enough to deal with ever-changing markets (Gustavo, 2018), as SHBs are even more exposed to even more problematic pandemics' effects, the implementation of strategies for enhancing SHBs' resilience and therefore performance is important (Sobaih et al., 2021). However, there are no specific proposals for small tourism businesses (Dias et al., 2021), in which SHBs are included. Therefore, for the next years, rather than simply focus on recovering activity, the critical challenge for SHBs is to innovate and optimize standard operating procedures towards a more resilient hospitality economy post-COVID-19 (McKinsey, 2020; OECD, 2021), while emphasizing the importance of health.

For academics, as Sigala (2020) points out, COVID-19 hospitality research should attempt to go beyond replicating existing knowledge for measuring and predicting tourism impacts within the COVID-19 context, responding to the call for transformative research by advancing our knowledge for informing, fostering, shaping or even leading such crises-enabled transformations. In this line, tourism research should assume more responsibility in informing, driving, and leading sustainable futures, enabling to reimagine and reset tourism while inspiring and motivating tourism businesses (Gössling et al., 2021).

In parallel, in response to a pandemic highly transmissible between humans, it is expected that the post-pandemic environment will emphasize health safety and wellness among the main drivers of hotel guests' satisfaction, with greater levels of consciousness and awareness of individuals regarding health measures (Meng, 2020). This paradigm shift implies that pre-pandemic standard aspects such as room condition, F&B, or service staff will no longer be able to ensure guests' satisfaction. It is expected that hospitality services should now embrace the new macro environment and guests' perception of health risk in their model, vision, and standard operational procedures, in line with the emphasized importance of promoting and preventing health for the twenty-first-century individual (Gustavo, 2018).

To advance tourism research, a study conducted by Wen et al. (2020) have suggested the adoption of an inter-disciplinary approach that bridges the gap between medical / health science and tourism, claiming that the spread of COVID-19 and associated mobility constraints sparked public concerns about general cleanliness, hygiene, and healthcare accessibility. The importance of this matter cannot be underestimated: actionable implications are needed to help tourists, tourism practitioners, and industry policymakers deal with outbreaks and their effects. In this sense, the authors highlight the need for collaborative research projects for enabling medical and health experts and tourism and hospitality professionals to come together and apply relevant knowledge to the post-COVID-19 environment.

Even in a pre-pandemic world, hospitality businesses already needed to move towards higher-order customer engagement, using co-creativity to generate value and using the service-dominant logic to manage customer experiences through online platforms and customer interfaces (Chathoth et al., 2016). Furthermore, new technologies, cultural changes in customers, and fiercer competition led hotels to consider outsourcing specialist service activities, reducing the level of vertical integration and focusing on their core competencies (Espino-Rodríguez & Padrón-Robaina, 2005). Expertise decision centralization and strategic alliances seem to be important to improve innovation and decision-making process involved in the development of integrated solutions, as it provides better grounding for coordination between departments, being closely linked to product-service innovation (Vendrell-Herrero, Gomes, Bustinza & Mellahi, 2020). The smart hospitality framework requires a fully integrated ecosystem that fully integrates technological tools such as business intelligence and customer relationship management, using big data to enhance decision making as well as strengthen competitiveness and improve strategies performance (Buhalis & Leung, 2018).

For the future, Sigala (2020) places technology at the core of solutions for combating the COVID-19 and re-opening tourism and the economy. It seems true that one possible way to optimize SHBs' standard operating procedures is by developing and integrating new digital solutions (He, Meadows, Angwin, Gomes & Child, 2020). In Higgins-Desbiolles' perspective (2020), leading tech and disrupting companies could be thought of as emissaries of a better future. In turn, Kandampully, et al. (2016) argue that technology seems to have a special ability to transform existing processes through creativity and innovation towards a people-technology hybrid business model, providing online platforms to fundamentally change the processes in which they deliver services (Ostrom et al., 2015) while establishing and maintaining a more personalized customer relationship (Rust & Huang, 2014).

In fact, in response to COVID-19, hospitality businesses have already upgraded their cleaning procedures, either by adopting new standards and restraining staff (e.g. upgrading cleaning procedures, promoting hygiene certifications accredited by health expert associations, training professionals to obtain relevant health certifications or re-engineering operations to make them contactless), or by implementing various digital solutions, including mobile apps (for check-in, check-out, room keys, mobile payments, bookings-purchases), self-service kiosks, in-room technologies for entertainment, robots (for reception and concierge services or food delivery), artificial intelligence-enabled websites and chatbox for customer communication and services and digital payments (e.g. digital wallets, PayPal, credit cards). In addition, the new operating environment enforced by COVID-19 measures require firms to adopt new technologies and applications to ensure the management of crowds and number of people gathered in public spaces human disinfectors and hand sanitizer equipment, applications identifying and managing people's health identity and profiles (Sigala, 2020).

Moreover, Pillai and collaborators (2021) already introduced and explained the role of Hospitality 5.0 technologies in assisting hotels in creating a technological shield that facilitates physical distancing and providing a competitive advantage during the pandemic and post-pandemic times. In this study, the authors suggest the adoption of "high-tech and low-touch" Hospitality 5.0 technologies such as contactless technology can be a critical means to alleviate risk in customer journeys, demonstrating how contactless technologies influence hygiene, cleanliness, and safety while contributing to eliminating human error, increasing service efficiency and stabilizing service quality.

FROM SERVICES TO eSERVICES IN HOSPITALITY

The present chapter aims to describe the cocktail systems that allow the Hotels to achieve the Hyper-Personalization of Services, i.e., the path from Services to e-Services in the Hotel Industry.

Let's clarify from the very beginning: to have communications that provide sharing data/information between different systems, it's always needed interfaces systems. The Interface standard nowadays is the XML Language, i.e. eXtended Markup Language. It's so powerful that the communications between systems inside the hotel are XML based, but the communications from the Hotel systems to the outside systems, as Financial Government and OTA's – Online Travel Agencies, use XML Language as well.

To Achieve Hyper-Personalization in Hotels, it's necessary the combination of several systems, inside and outside of the Hotel, that allows the personalized communication between the hotel staff and services and the e-Lookers (potential Customers), eBookers (Customers), Guest (Customers that stays in the Hotel Rooms at the Hotel), and e-Lookers (ex-Guest or potential Customers).

The heart of the Hotel Systems, the PMS – Property Management Systems, interact with the servers that provide services to the Guest:

1. **IPTV System:** To provide personalized communication with the Room TV's, it means that the TV system (the TV are usually connected to Coax, RJ45 Cable or HDMI Cable) needs to connect with the PMS to provide Channels and Contents in the mother language of "that" Guest, as Channels from "the same country that that Guest", personalized Films and Promotions. Nowadays, this kind of IPTV system can provide "screen mirroring" contents of Guest smartphones. So, when the Guest wants to see their content like Netflix, HBO, Disney +, personal pictures, and films... the IPTV System provides the screen sharing from the smartphone's Guest to the IPTV systems. The IPTV System, when connected with PMS via XML Interfaces, displays the total amount of money that "that" Guest dispended, at that moment, in all services provided by the Hotel, like SPA and F&B movements. To add value, some IPTV systems, have the capability of system checkout, with a payment gateway included.

2. **Unified Communication server**: To provide Guest Phone communication to the Hotel services, and to the outside of the Hotel. Nowadays, this kind of Unified Communication, uses Sip-Trunk

protocols, within the Internet Hotel Private connection. Some Unified Communication Systems provide video-calls integrated with the Hotel Services, as Concierge, Guest Service, SPA, Reception, etc., from the Phone Guest Room to the hotel services described.

3. **Guest Internet System**: To acknowledge Internet Guest access to the Guest, within a captive portal, when each Guest needs to populate their credentials (username and password). This kind of system also provides Internet connections to the Meeting users and to the Restaurant and bars customers, that do not belong to the Guest clusters. This kind of service, needs interaction with the PMS, via XML Webservices, to validate the Guest credentials, as the Meeting Rooms Users or Customers that do not use the Hotels Rooms. There are lots of Hotels that provide different Internet Speeds to the Guest and the Meeting Room Users. It's possible to provide different Internet Speeds to Guests of dissimilar rooms typology.

4. **Channel Manager (CM)**: To interact with the OTA (Online Travel Agencies) Reservation Systems, and with the own hotel website reservation system. Must be a standard, the capability of each potential Guest provided own authentication, to get, if needed, personalized commercial content. Soon, the Hotels must upgrade their websites, to have as a standard, the capability of each potential Guest, if needed, provided their authentication, to get personalized commercial content. If I'm going 10 times in the 3 last years to the Estorilix Hotel, why do I have the same price to the Junior Suite, that Nuno Gustavo, that seeks, at the same time, in the Website hotel, the price to the same kind of room typology, and never, ever, had at this Estorilix Hotel? There are lots of Travel Agencies and Airlines that use this kind of personalization, at the very begging of the travel journey. But, unlikely, there are only a few hotel chains that use this kind of personalization.

5. **eXtended – Business Intelligence (X-BI)**: Systems that provided, in real-time, commercial and financial information vs budget information, that can be linked to:
   a. Partners, CEO, and Managing Director's Team - this kind of platform allows Partners and their closed staff, to project execution and monitoring in real-time, strategic knowledge of the Hotels enterprises.
   b. Operations Managers, General Managers, Revenue, Financial, Commercial, Marketing, Human Resources, Information Systems, Maintenance, and their closed staff, to project execution and monitoring in real-time, local operations, increasing better decisions, detecting quickly data malfunctions in the general systems that provide data information to the Business Intelligent platform.

6. **Customer Relationship Management (CRM)**: Systems that provide the empowerment of the Hyper-Personalization at the Hotels! There are lots of CRM Systems, as the generalists' vs the CRM designed by and to Hoteliers, with obvious advantages to both sides of the "coin". There are lots of CRM Books, in and outside of the Hospitality Industry. CRM needs to interact, via XML Webservice, with the PMS System, and the CRM needs, as well, to interact, via XML Webservice, with different systems as Outlook, BI Portal, SMS/eMail Gateways, Social Media Systems, and so on. The more platforms connected via XML Interface Webservice, the more powerful is the CRM system, and more closely is to the Hiper-Personalization into the Hotel or Hotel Chain. So, the CRM systems must be linked to:
   a. Marketing staff Systems, like Marketing Automation Systems and e-Mail/SMS Gateways; this kind of platform allows the marketing staff to project, execute, monitoring and measure, in real-time, Marketing Campaigns. Always via XML Webservices Interfaces.

    b.   Commercial Staff systems, like Outlook and BI portals, that lets the Commercial staff manage the entire journey of "that Customer", from the Customer-first approach, (eMail, phone call, website communication…) to the check-in.

    c.   Operations Staff Systems, as the PMS, SPA, POS, Events, and Golf Systems, to populate the interactions of the Guest, during the "stay journey", based on the previous guest interactions, if exists, or based in the "cluster behavior where that Guest belongs". To the Operation Staff, the Hoteliers need to decide if the PMS is the main application to interact with, or if they change the interactions to the CRM. Meanwhile, the XML web service interface is always required!

    d.   Guest own mobile devices as smartphones, tablets, laptops, smart-watch, Gaming gateways, and so on, connected with the CRM, PMS, POS, Events, and Golf Systems, via XML web services interface, providing the necessary connectivity that allows the Hyper-Personalization that the Hoteliers need to increase their revenue, as a result of a better quality of the hotel service, and then, a good percentage of Guest will spend a large amount of money, at upselling and cross services, increasing, in this way, the Hotel's famous GOP – Gross Operating Profit.

In this Guest Mobile approach, that increased exponentially the Hyper-Personalization Services, the Guest is allowed to:

1.   **Pre-Check-In and validate their own personal data**: Starting from the very beginning of the Hyper-Personalization journey, upselling their Room typology, adding meal options, subscribing to SPA Services, schedules for the breakfast, lunch, or dinner. It is also possible, for the Guest, to acknowledge the GDPR Hotel Options. This kind of service also provides to a large cluster of Guest, the confidence of knowing the booking is confirmed by the Hotel Services.

2.   **Check-In:** In this process, the Guest does not need to sign a significant set of papers, as he can validate, either on his mobile phone or on a tablet provided by the Hotel, the details of his reservation, digitally signing on the selected equipment. This digital functionality simplifies and improves data quality in the check-in process, and the Check-In process in-self. There are a lot of Hoteliers, that are adding another facility in the Check-In process: the Self-Check-In capability! Of course, there are much more hoteliers that consider that this hi-tech capability de-virtualizes the hotel service. If the Hoteliers consider applying this kind of solution, they need to implement XML interfaces between the Self-Check-In Kiosk, the PMS, the Key-Card machine (or smartphone mobile key-card solution), the ID-Card Reader machine, and the Payment Gateway.

3.   **e-Mobility, Room Guest entry**: In their Room, during the stay, with their smartphone, without the traditional Room key card, minimizing the Guest contact with hotel furniture. This kind of solution also provides to the hotelier, the capability of understanding, in real-time, if the Guest is, or not, in their Room, improving in this way the speed and the quality of service of Housekeeping, Food and Beverage, Reception, Guest Service and Maintenance, if necessary. This smartphone mobile key-card solutions, nowadays, in the new normal of hospitality, providing a modern and safe approach that the Guest tend to appreciate.

4.   **Internet Guest Solutions**: Via the captive portal, is an "old way" to manage the Internet Guest, that allows the hoteliers to interact with the Guest, in a secure way, in cases of captive portals with a digital and secure certificate. This kind of solution allows the hoteliers to implement IoT solutions, to better understands where the Guest are, in the Hotel area, to better communicate with the

Guest. i.e., this kind of solution, allows the Hotel, for instance, to send push notifications to the selected Guest that are not at the Swimming Pool Bar, to send them promotion of Daiquiri, because the Terrace Bar has already an occupancy of 80%, and the Swimming Pool Bar has only 35% of occupancy.

5. **Hotel Services Portal**: To provide to the guest the capability of buying hotel services, in complement to the staff interaction, and, of course, increasing the Hyper-Personalization at the Hotel, because the Hotel knows, in real-time, the needs of each Guest, the times of service, the complaints and specific requests of each guest, whether for food and beverages or other hotel services, as well as the specific allergies and preferences of each guest! These solutions, can also, if request by the Hoteliers, managed satisfaction surveys, and the ability to manage the relationship with the social networks of guests who decided to identify themselves at the hotel, during or after their stay at the hotel.

APPLICATION OF MACHINE LEARNING CLUSTERING ALGORITHMS TO ANALYZE TRAVELERS' ONLINE REVIEWS

Despite that the tourism industry is projected to grow significantly by creating jobs (Fotiadis et al., 2021); cultural exchange, and economic growth, especially in the modern digital era where traveling and touring are increasingly becoming indispensable basic needs. This is necessitated by the increasing use of social media platforms which facilitate sharing and exchange of information and experiences. Social media platforms witnessed increasing numbers of users exponentially; derivatively the number of tourists who use the internet is increasing correspondingly. Moreso, the relaxation of travel restrictions and controls over freedom of movement of populations in many countries and accessibility of information dissemination platforms facilitate the mobility of travelers (Khorsand et al., 2020). Travelers use information from social media platforms such as Facebook, Flicker, Twitter, YouTube, and Instagram, and online marketing websites such as TripAdvisor, Google trends, Baidu Index and Expedia to inform their decision-making process concerning the destination, budgeting, safety, and security, accommodation, service delivery ratings, and the length of travel. These digital platforms allow travelers to share their experiences, feedback, and reviews which subsequently become a crucial source of information in the tourism industry (Nilashi et al., 2019a). Most importantly, understanding and predicting the travelers' choice preferences on hotels using data generated from social media platforms is paramount for developing recommender engines. However, social media data tend to have different formats (structured and unstructured), voluminous, veracity, and variety which results in cost, time-consuming, difficult to process and draw meaningful insights using traditional methods (Bigne et al., 2021; Luo et al., 2021; Tsai et al., 2020).

To counter these impediments, empirical studies by (Chang et al., 2020; Khorsand et al., 2020) show that deep learning and machine learning models play a salient role in analyzing travelers' online reviews and extract meaningful insights to enhance travelers' decision-making and planning process. Notably, (Mostafa, 2020) applied Naive Bayes, support vector machine, and decision tree to develop Traveler Review Sentiment Classifier to analyze traveler's reviews on Egyptian Hotels and provide a classification of each sentiment based on hotel features. The classifier analyzed 11458 online reviews from TripAdvisor and Expedia. Also, (Nilashi et al., 2019b) applied adaptive neuro-fuzzy inference systems (ANFIS) and classification and regression trees(CART) to analyze travelers' online reviews on TripAdvisor. (Ma et al., 2018) applied deep learning approaches to assess the information value of user-provided photos embedded in online hotel reviews from Yelp and TripAdvisor. TripAdvisor is a digital platform that allows travelers to socialize and share their opinions and experiences on several aspects of hotels. K-nearest neighbors (KNN), Naïve Bayes, decision tree, logistic regression; support vector machine, neural network, random forest, and gradient boosting were applied in a study conducted by (Khorsand et al., 2020) to forecast hotel user ratings based on user-generated data from TripAdvisor.

Machine learning clustering algorithms discover classes without supervision on a large unlabeled data saves much time especially in the tourism industry where several online marketing websites such as TripAdvisor (Taecharungroj & Mathayomchan, 2019), Hotels, and other social media platforms such as Facebook, Flicker (Giglio et al., 2019), Twitter, YouTube, and Instagram collect volumes of data. Travelers share their experiences, feedbacks, or reviews on social networks. social media data and machine learning clustering algorithms play a salient role in developing recommender systems that could be used to enhance travelers' decision-making and planning process in the tourism industry. Therefore, this study aimed to apply K-means and Fuzzy C-means clustering algorithms to group different TripAdvisor travelers' responses into different clusters.

Machine learning is a subset of artificial intelligence that provides systems with the ability to automatically learn without being explicitly programmed (Elujide et al., 2021). Machine learning models utilize different training methods such as supervised learning, unsupervised learning, and hybrid training function to train the model (Fashoto et al., 2021). Supervised machine learning algorithms use labeled data to predict future events. While unsupervised machine learning uses unlabeled data; and algorithms extract features on their own. Clustering algorithms are the most widely used unsupervised machine learning technique for discovering interesting insights from underlying complex online tourism data. Unsupervised learning is applied when there is input data without corresponding output variables associated with it (Mbunge et al., 2017). The purpose of unsupervised learning is to understand and model the underlying distribution of data to learn more about it (Mbunge et al., 2015.). Therefore, data clustering thrives to find similar objects, points, or patterns from a given dataset with respect to the given data labels or features (Renjith et al., 2020a). Thus, clustering algorithms classify a set of objects into homogeneous groups or clusters consisting of similar data points (Lu et al., 2019). Clustering algorithms have been applied in various fields including marketing (Ghosal et al., 2020), telecommunications (Alkhayrat et al., 2020), insurance (Majhi, 2019), healthcare, banking, and retailing because they often operate in high dimensional spaces, flexibility, and robustness when dealing with noisy, incomplete and sampled data, their performance can vary substantially for different applications and types of data (Rodriguez et al., 2019). Clustering algorithms are generally classified into three groups namely, hierarchical, partitioning, and density-based clustering. K-means, Fuzzy C-means, K-medoid are the most utilized partitioning clustering algorithms (Renjith et al., 2019). Therefore, in this study, we applied K-means clustering and Fuzzy C-means clustering algorithms to analyze travelers' online reviews from TripAdvisor.These algorithms are explained in the following sections.

K-means clustering algorithm is one of the simplest approaches to unsupervised learning algorithms (Rodriguez et al., 2019). The algorithm classifies into a fixed number of clusters. The concepts revolve around defining k-centers, one center for each cluster. These centers should be placed cunningly because of different location causes the different result. The step which follows finding k- centers is to take each point belonging to a given data set and associate it to the nearest center (Majhi, 2019). Similar computations have to be done to find k-new centroids as the barycenter of the clusters resulting from the previous step. After we have these k new centroids, we assign the same points from the data set to the new centers which clear generates a loop. The centers keep on changing positions until they get to a point when they don't change again. The whole concept behind K-means is completed when the centers are stable that is they do not shift anymore (Renjith et al., 2019).

The fuzzy C-means clustering (FCM) algorithm differs from K-means because it enables one data point to belong to two different clusters. The FCM method was developed by Dunn (Dunn, 2008) and improved by Bezdek, to permits a single piece of data to belong to more than one cluster by assigning a degree of membership to each data point (Majhi, 2019). This is done by determining the distance of the entity from the center of the cluster. Thus, an entity that is closer to the centroid of the cluster will have a higher degree of membership to the particular cluster (Renjith et al., 2019).

METHOD

Travel online reviews were collected from TripAdvisor and can be accessed on the UCI Machine learning data repository (https://archive.ics.uci.edu/ml/datasets/). The dataset was populated by crawling TripAdvisor.com. Reviews on destinations in 10 categories mentioned across East Asia were considered. Each traveler rating was mapped as Excellent (4), Very Good (3), Average (2), Poor (1), and Terrible (0), and the average rating is used against each category per user. Python libraries such as Pandas, Numpy, Matplotlib, SciPy, sci-kit-learn were used to apply K-means and Fuzzy C means clustering algorithms. The dataset had no missing values. However, data was normalized using Min-Max scaling.

Table 1. Description of the travel online reviews dataset

S/N	Attribute	Description	Type
1	User ID	Unique identifier of the user	Nominal
2	Category 1	Average user feedback on art galleries	Nominal
3	Category 2	Average user feedback on dance clubs	Nominal
4	Category 3	Average user feedback on juice bars	Nominal
5	Category 4	Average user feedback on restaurants	Nominal
6	Category 5	Average user feedback on museums	Nominal
7	Category 6	Average user feedback on resorts	Nominal
8	Category 7	Average user feedback on parks/picnic spots	Nominal
9	Category 8	Average user feedback on beaches	Nominal
10	Category 9	Average user feedback on theaters	Nominal
11	Category 10	Average user feedback on religious institutions	Nominal

RESULTS

Comparison of Clustering Algorithms Models

The clustering algorithms models on K-means and fuzzy c-means were employed in this study. The elbow method which can also be referred to as the knee-point method is also used to determine the optimal value of K in this study (Stephen et al., 2013) (Wiharto & Suryani, 2020). Figure 1 shows the value of the optimal value of K. The study makes use of a social media dataset in the tourism domain. In this study, we follow the recommendation of (Gbenga et al., 2021) and Fahad, et al. (2017) which requires that it is important to consider some performance measures such as accuracy, execution time, memory usage, number of iterations, and so on to determine the effectiveness and efficiency of algorithms or pseudo-code for describing the optimal solution in design paradigm. In this study, we considered accuracy, execution time, and the number of iterations for the performance measures.

Figure 1. Elbow method for optimal K

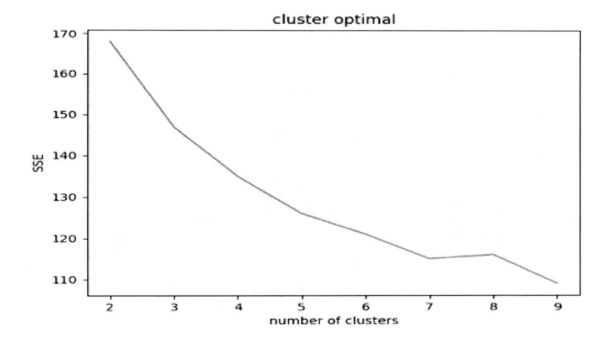

Figure 2 shows the clustered data points when the optimal value of k=5 and Figure 3 presents the clustered data points when the optimal value of k=5. The characters C1, C2, C3, C4, and C5 represent cluster1 (purple) cluster 2 (red), cluster 3 (green), cluster 4 (orange), and cluster 5 (blue) respectively in Figures 4 and 5.

Figure 2. Optimal clusters of K-means clustering

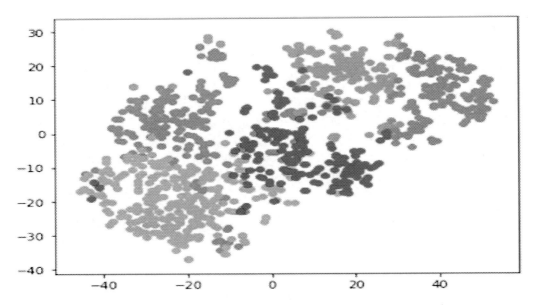

Figure 3. Optimal clusters of fuzzy C-means clustering

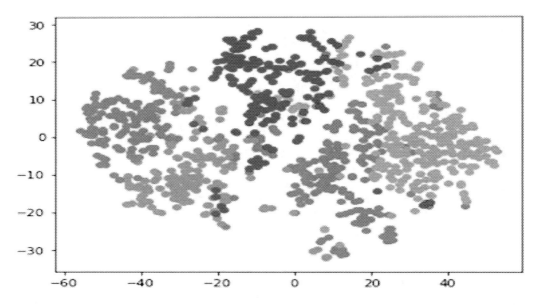

Table 2 is a summary of the performance measures on K-means and Fuzzy C-means clustering on the optimal value of k=5 obtained through the use of elbow method presented in figure 4 in python carried out on online traveler's reviews dataset from trip advisor.

Table 2. Performance measure

Measure	K-means	Fuzzy C-means
Accuracy (%)	**93.4**	91.3
Execution time(s)	**17.6**	25.01
Number of iterations	5	**4**

K-means clustering outperforms Fuzzy C-Means in this study in terms of accuracy and execution time while Fuzzy C-Means converge faster than K-means clustering in terms of the number of iterations. The findings of authors (Renjith et al., 2019) and (Renjith et al., 2020b) show that if the optimal value of K is less than 4, the performance of K-means and Fuzzy C-means clustering is expected to be poor but if the optimal value of K is greater than or equal to 4 the performance of, K-means and Fuzzy C-means are expected to be better. Our results support this claim.

CONCLUSION

In conclusion, interdisciplinary efforts must be made to address this multidimensional problem, aiming for a sector of hospitality that is digital-driven and sustainable-orientated, which would bridge the business-customer relationship. These efforts may be undertaken through projects of interdisciplinary nature that promote important aspects such as the digital transition of hospitality, the adoption of sustainable practices, and the development of more sustainable business models (OECD, 2021), while also contributing to preparing plans for supporting the sustainable long-term structural and transformational changes to hospitality (Sigala, 2020). Moreover, such efforts would also be a socioeconomic response to COVID-19, contributing to protecting hotel businesses and secure jobs through science, technology, innovation, and transfer knowledge, by seeking the innovation and resilience of hospitality businesses for the future.

Hyper-Personalization, in this new normal in the Hotel industry, is a new way of modern Hotel Services, with real-time processes shared between the Guest and the Hoteliers, with a fundamental collaboration of a huge amount of XML web services interfaces. To achieve this new kind of Hotel Services, it's mandatory to implement XML web services interfaces, that provide the necessary "glue" that interconnects the inevitable growing set of hotel systems, hardware plus software solutions that increase the quality of Hotel Services. Curiously, it has been this complex growing web of systems connections that have simplified and smooth the processes arising from the hotel service, with guests, whether repeated or new ones.

The exponential growth of social media platforms plays a tremendous role in the tourism and hospitality industry. Policymakers and managers rely on accurate tourism forecasting and prediction to make informed decisions. The mobility of tourists around the globe results in data shared on social media and transformed data to be voluminous, veracity, veracity, variety, and value. Due to tremendous amounts of structured and unstructured data generated by social media platforms, datasets are increasingly becoming large in scale which results in cost, time-consuming, difficult to process and summarize to get interesting patterns and traveler's relevant information. Having clustering algorithms discover classes without supervision on a large unlabeled data saves much time and trouble especially in the tourism industry where several online marketing websites such as TripAdvisor. By applying machine learning clustering algorithms in the tourism and hospitality industry, managers can predict revenue that is likely to be generated, explore targeting marketing, as well as segmenting tourists based on their spending patterns, lifestyle age group and provide services to customers based on their profiles.

In this study, we applied K-means and FCM clustering algorithms to cluster online travelers' data which consists of reviews, feedback, and rating information, from TripAdvisor. Our study shows that K-means clustering outperforms Fuzzy C-Means in this study in terms of accuracy and execution time while Fuzzy C-Means converge faster than K-means Clustering in terms of the number of iterations. Future work can measure the performance of more clustering algorithms using the same dataset.

CONFLICTS OF INTEREST

The authors declare no conflict of interest.

ACKNOWLEDGMENT

We would like to thank Dr. Shini Renjith for making the Travel Reviews dataset used in this study available online for free on the UCI Machine learning repository.

REFERENCES

Alkhayrat, M., Aljnidi, M., & Aljoumaa, K. (2020). A comparative dimensionality reduction study in telecom customer segmentation using deep learning and PCA. *Journal of Big Data, 7*(1), 1–23. doi:10.1186/s40537-020-0286-0

Bartik, A. W., Bertrand, M., Cullen, Z., Glaeser, E. L., Luca, M., & Stanton, C. (2020). The impact of COVID-19 on small business outcomes and expectations. *Proceedings of the National Academy of Sciences.* 10.1073/pnas.2006991117

Bigne, E., Ruiz, C., Cuenca, A., Perez, C., & Garcia, A. (2021). What drives the helpfulness of online reviews? A deep learning study of sentiment analysis, pictorial content and reviewer expertise for mature destinations. *Journal of Destination Marketing & Management, 20,* 100570. doi:10.1016/j.jdmm.2021.100570

Buhalis, D., & Leung, R. (2018). Smart hospitality—Interconnectivity and interoperability towards an ecosystem. *International Journal of Hospitality Management, 71,* 41–50. doi:10.1016/j.ijhm.2017.11.011

Chang, Y. C., Ku, C. H., & Chen, C. H. (2020). Using deep learning and visual analytics to explore hotel reviews and responses. *Tourism Management, 80,* 104129. doi:10.1016/j.tourman.2020.104129

Chathoth, P. K., Ungson, G. R., Harrington, R. J., & Chan, E. S. W. (2016). Co-creation and higher order customer engagement in hospitality and tourism services. *International Journal of Contemporary Hospitality Management, 28*(2), 222–245. doi:10.1108/IJCHM-10-2014-0526

Chien, G. C. L., & Law, R. (2003). The impact of the severe acute respiratory syndrome on hotels: A case study of Hong Kong. *International Journal of Hospitality Management*, 22(3), 327–332. doi:10.1016/S0278-4319(03)00041-0 PMID:32287842

Deloitte. (2020). *The end of an era: Rethink what's normal. Portuguese Hospitality Atlas 2020 – 15th edition*. https://www2.deloitte.com/content/dam/Deloitte/pt/Documents/AtlasHotelaria/ATLAS2020_en.pdf

Deloitte. (2021). *The future of hospitality: Re-engaging consumers post pandemic*. https://www2.deloitte.com/content/dam/Deloitte/ca/Documents/consumer-industrial-products/ca-future-of-hospitality-pov-aoda-en.pdf

Dias, A. L., González-Rodríguez, M. R., & Patuleia, M. (2021). Retaining tourism lifestyle entrepreneurs for destination competitiveness. *International Journal of Tourism Research*, 23(4), 701–712. Advance online publication. doi:10.1002/jtr.2436

Dombey, O. (2004). The effects of SARS on the Chinese tourism industry. *Journal of Vacation Marketing*, 10(1), 4–10. doi:10.1177/135676670301000101

Dunn, J. C. (2008). *A Fuzzy Relative of the ISODATA Process and Its Use in Detecting Compact Well-Separated Clusters*. Https://Doi.Org/10.1080/01969727308546046 doi:10.1080/01969727308546046

Elujide, I., Fashoto, S. G., Fashoto, B., Mbunge, E., Folorunso, S. O., & Olamijuwon, J. O. (2021). Application of deep and machine learning techniques for multi-label classification performance on psychotic disorder diseases. *Informatics in Medicine Unlocked*, 23, 100545. doi:10.1016/j.imu.2021.100545

Espino-Rodríguez, T. F., & Padrón-Robaina, V. (2005). A resource-based view of outsourcing and its implications for organizational performance in the hotel sector. *Tourism Management*, 26(5), 707–721. doi:10.1016/j.tourman.2004.03.013

European Commission. (2019). *Annual report on European SMEs 2018/2019 Research & Development and Innovation by SMEs*. https://op.europa.eu/en/publication-detail/-/publication/cadb8188-35b4-11ea-ba6e-01aa75ed71a1/language-en

Fashoto, S. G., Mbunge, E., Ogunleye, G., & den Burg, J. Van. (2021). *Implementation of machine learning for predicting maize crop yields using multiple linear regression and backward elimination*. https://mjoc.uitm.edu.my

Fotiadis, A., Polyzos, S., & Huan, T. C. T. C. (2021). The good, the bad and the ugly on COVID-19 tourism recovery. *Annals of Tourism Research*, 87, 103117. doi:10.1016/j.annals.2020.103117 PMID:33518847

Gbenga, S., Member, F., & Sani, S. (n.d.). *Design and Implementation of MOLP Problems with Fuzzy Objective Functions Using Approximation and Equivalence Approach*. Academic Press.

Ghosal, A., Nandy, A., Das, A. K., Goswami, S., & Panday, M. (2020). A Short Review on Different Clustering Techniques and Their Applications. *Advances in Intelligent Systems and Computing*, 937, 69–83. doi:10.1007/978-981-13-7403-6_9

Giglio, S., Bertacchini, F., Bilotta, E., & Pantano, P. (2019). Using social media to identify tourism attractiveness in six Italian cities. *Tourism Management*, 72, 306–312. doi:10.1016/j.tourman.2018.12.007

Gössling, S., Scott, D., & Hall, C. M. (2021). Pandemics, tourism and global change: A rapid assessment of COVID-19. *Journal of Sustainable Tourism*, *29*(1), 1–20. doi:10.1080/09669582.2020.1758708

Gustavo, N. (2018). Trends in Hospitality Marketing and Management: facing the 21st century challenges. In L. Cagica & P. Isaías (Eds.), *Handbook of Research on Entrepreneurship and Marketing for Global Reach in the Digital Economy* (pp. 311–337). IGI Global. doi:10.4018/978-1-5225-6307-5

Hall, C. M., Scott, D., & Gössling, S. (2020). Pandemics, transformations and tourism: Be careful what you wish for. *Tourism Geographies*, *22*(3), 1–22. doi:10.1080/14616688.2020.1759131

He, Q., Meadows, M., Angwin, D., Gomes, E., & Child, J. (2020). Strategic Alliance Research in the Era of Digital Transformation: Perspectives on Future Research. *British Journal of Management*, *31*(3), 589–617. doi:10.1111/1467-8551.12406

Henderson, J. C., & Ng, A. (2004). Responding to crisis: Severe acute respiratory syndrome (SARS) and hotels in Singapore. *International Journal of Tourism Research*, *6*(6), 411–419. doi:10.1002/jtr.505

Higgins-Desbiolles, F. (2020). Socialising tourism for social and ecological justice after COVID-19. *Tourism Geographies*, *22*(3), 610–623. doi:10.1080/14616688.2020.1757748

Hung, K. K. C., Mark, C. K. M., Yeung, M. P. S., Chan, E. Y. Y., & Graham, C. A. (2018). The role of the hotel industry in the response to emerging epidemics: A case study of SARS in 2003 and H1N1 swine flu in 2009 in Hong Kong. *Globalization and Health*, *14*(1), 1–7. doi:10.118612992-018-0438-6 PMID:30482214

Instituto Nacional de Estatística (INE). (2020). *Atividade Turística: Dezembro 2020*. https://www.ine.pt/xportal/xmain?xpid=INE&xpgid=ine_destaques&DESTAQUESdest_boui=415204526&DESTAQUESmodo=2

Kandampully, J., Bilgihan, A., & Zhang, T. (2016). Developing a people-technology hybrids model to unleash innovation and creativity: The new hospitality frontier. *Journal of Hospitality and Tourism Management*, *29*, 154–164. doi:10.1016/j.jhtm.2016.07.003

Khorsand, R., Rafiee, M., & Kayvanfar, V. (2020). Insights into TripAdvisor's online reviews: The case of Tehran's hotels. *Tourism Management Perspectives*, *34*, 100673. doi:10.1016/j.tmp.2020.100673

Kim, S. S., Chun, H., & Lee, H. (2005). The effects of SARS on the Korean hotel industry and measures to overcome the crisis: A case study of six Korean five-star hotels. *Asia Pacific Journal of Tourism Research*, *10*(4), 369–377. doi:10.1080/10941660500363694

Kline, S., Almanza, B., & Neal, J. (2014). Hotel guest room cleaning: a systematic approach. In B. Almanza, R. Ghiselli, & K. Mahmood (Eds.), *Food Safety: Researching the Hazard in Hazardous Foods* (pp. 303–322). CRC Press Taylor and Francis.

Lee, C. K., Song, H. J., Bendle, L. J., Kim, M. J., & Han, H. (2012). The impact of nonpharmaceutical interventions for 2009 H1N1 influenza on travel intentions: A model of goal-directed behavior. *Tourism Management*, *33*(1), 89–99. doi:10.1016/j.tourman.2011.02.006 PMID:32287736

Lew, A. (2020). *How to Create a Better Post-COVID-19 World*. https://medium.com/new-earth-consciousness/creating-a-better-post-covid-19-world-36b2b3e8a7ae

Lo, A., Cheung, C., & Law, R. (2006). The survival of hotels during disaster: A case study of Hong Kong in 2003. *Asia Pacific Journal of Tourism Research, 11*(1), 65–80. doi:10.1080/10941660500500733

Luo, Y., He, J., Mou, Y., Wang, J., & Liu, T. (2021). Exploring China's 5A global geoparks through online tourism reviews: A mining model based on machine learning approach. *Tourism Management Perspectives, 37,* 100769. https://doi.org/10.1016/j.tmp.2020.100769

Ma, Y., Xiang, Z., Du, Q., & Fan, W. (2018). Effects of user-provided photos on hotel review helpfulness: An analytical approach with deep leaning. *International Journal of Hospitality Management, 71,* 120–131. https://doi.org/10.1016/j.ijhm.2017.12.008

Majhi, S. K. (2019). Fuzzy clustering algorithm based on modified whale optimization algorithm for automobile insurance fraud detection. *Evolutionary Intelligence, 14*(1), 35–46. doi:10.1007/S12065-019-00260-3

Martínez-Román, J. A., Tamayo, J. A., Gamero, J., & Romero, J. E. (2015). Innovativeness and business performances in tourism SMEs. *Annals of Tourism Research, 54,* 118–135. doi:10.1016/j.annals.2015.07.004

Masco, J. (2017). The Crisis in Crisis. *Current Anthropology, 58*(S15), S65–S76.

Mbunge, E., Makuyana, R., Chirara, N., & Chingosho, A. (n.d.). Fraud Detection in E-Transactions using Deep Neural Networks-A Case of Financial Institutions in Zimbabwe Cite this paper Fraud Detection in E-Transactions using Deep Neural Networks-A Case of Financial Institutions in Zimbabwe. *International Journal of Science and Research, 17*(2). doi:10.21275/ART20176804

Mbunge, E., Vheremu, F., & Kajiva, K. (2017). A Tool to Predict the Possibility of Social Unrest Using Sentiments Analysis-Case of Zimbabwe Politics 2017-2018. *International Journal of Science and Research, 6.* doi:10.21275/ART20177198

McKinsey. (2020). *Beyond coronavirus: The path to the next normal.* https://www.mckinsey.com/industries/healthcare-systems-and-services/our-insights/beyond-coronavirus-the-path-to-the-next-normal

Meng, Y. (2020). *The hospitality way of survival after Covid-19 crisis.* Retrieved from the École Hôtelière de Lausanne website: https://hospitalityinsights.ehl.edu/hospitality-covid19-crisis

Mostafa, L. (2020). Machine Learning-Based Sentiment Analysis for Analyzing the Travelers Reviews on Egyptian Hotels. *Advances in Intelligent Systems and Computing, 1153,* 405–413. doi:10.1007/978-3-030-44289-7_38

Nicolás, E. S. (2020, April 22). EU pledges help, as tourism faces €400bn hit. *EU Observer.* https://euobserver.com/coronavirus/148137

Nilashi, M., Yadegaridehkordi, E., Ibrahim, O., Samad, S., Ahani, A., & Sanzogni, L. (2019a). Analysis of Travelers' Online Reviews in Social Networking Sites Using Fuzzy Logic Approach. *International Journal of Fuzzy Systems, 21*(5), 1367–1378. doi:10.1007/S40815-019-00630-0

Nilashi, M., Yadegaridehkordi, E., Ibrahim, O., Samad, S., Ahani, A., & Sanzogni, L. (2019b). Analysis of Travelers' Online Reviews in Social Networking Sites Using Fuzzy Logic Approach. *International Journal of Fuzzy Systems, 21*(5), 1367–1378. https://doi.org/10.1007/s40815-019-00630-0

Organisation for Economic Co-operation and Development (OECD). (2021). *Rebuilding tourism for the future: COVID-19 policy responses and recovery*. https://www.oecd-ilibrary.org/social-issues-migration-health/rebuilding-tourism-for-the-future-covid-19-policy-responses-and-recovery_bced9859-en

Ostrom, A. L., Parasuraman, A., Bowen, D. E., Patrício, L., Voss, C. A., & Lemon, K. (2015). Service research priorities in a rapidly changing context. *Journal of Service Research*, *18*(2), 127–159. doi:10.1177/1094670515576315

Phillips, C. A., & Langston, M. A. (2019). A robustness metric for biological data clustering algorithms. *BMC Bioinformatics*, *20*(15), 1–8. doi:10.1186/S12859-019-3089-6

Pillai, S. G., Kavitha, H., Seo, W. S., & Kim, W. G. (2021). COVID-19 and hospitality 5.0: Redefining hospitality operations. *International Journal of Hospitality Management*, *94*(3). Advance online publication. doi:10.1016/j.ijhm.2021.102869

Renjith, S., Sreekumar, A., & Jathavedan, M. (2019). Evaluation of partitioning clustering algorithms for processing social media data in tourism domain. *2018 IEEE Recent Advances in Intelligent Computational Systems, RAICS 2018*, 127–131. doi:10.1109/RAICS.2018.8635080

Renjith, S., Sreekumar, A., & Jathavedan, M. (2020a). An extensive study on the evolution of context-aware personalized travel recommender systems. *Information Processing & Management*, *57*(1), 102078. https://doi.org/10.1016/J.IPM.2019.102078

Renjith, S., Sreekumar, A., & Jathavedan, M. (2020b). Performance evaluation of clustering algorithms for varying cardinality and dimensionality of data sets. *Materials Today: Proceedings*, *27*, 627–633. https://doi.org/10.1016/J.MATPR.2020.01.110

Rodriguez, M. Z., Comin, C. H., Casanova, D., Bruno, O. M., Amancio, D. R., Costa, L. da F., & Rodrigues, F. A. (2019). Clustering algorithms: A comparative approach. *PLoS One*, *14*(1), e0210236. https://doi.org/10.1371/JOURNAL.PONE.0210236

Rust, R. T., & Huang, M.-H. (2014). The service revolution and the transformation of marketing science. *Marketing Science*, *33*(2), 206–221. doi:10.1287/mksc.2013.0836

Sharma, G. D., Thomas, A., & Paul, J. (2021). Reviving tourism industry post-COVID-19: A resilience-based framework. *Tourism Management Perspectives*, *37*, 100786. https://doi.org/10.1016/j.tmp.2020.100786

Sigala, M. (2020). Tourism and COVID-19: Impacts and implications for advancing and resetting industry and research. *Journal of Business Research*, *117*, 312–321. doi:10.1016/j.jbusResearch2020.06.015

Sobaih, A. E., Elshaer, I., Hasanein, A. M., & Abdelaziz, A. S. (2021). Responses to COVID-19: The role of performance in the relationship between small hospitality enterprises' resilience and sustainable tourism development. *International Journal of Hospitality Management*, *94*, 102824. doi:10.1016/j.ijhm.2020.102824

Stephen, F. G., Olumide, O., & Jacob, G. A. (2013). Application of Data Mining Technique for Fraud Detection in Health Insurance Scheme Using Knee-Point K-Means Algorithm. *Australian Journal of Basic and Applied Sciences*, *7*(8), 140–144.

Taecharungroj, V., & Mathayomchan, B. (2019). Analysing TripAdvisor reviews of tourist attractions in Phuket, Thailand. *Tourism Management, 75*, 550–568. https://doi.org/10.1016/J.TOURMAN.2019.06.020

Tew, P. J., Lu, Z., Tolomiczenko, G., & Gellatly, J. (2008). SARS: Lessons in strategic planning for hoteliers and destination marketers. *International Journal of Contemporary Hospitality Management, 20*(3), 332–346. doi:10.1108/09596110810866145

Tsai, C. F., Chen, K., Hu, Y. H., & Chen, W. K. (2020). Improving text summarization of online hotel reviews with review helpfulness and sentiment. *Tourism Management, 80*, 104122. https://doi.org/10.1016/j.tourman.2020.104122

Tse, A. C. B., So, S., & Sin, L. (2006). Crisis management and recovery: How restaurants in Hong Kong responded to SARS. *International Journal of Hospitality Management, 25*(1), 3–11. doi:10.1016/j.ijhm.2004.12.001

United Nations. (2020). *Shared responsibility, global solidarity: Responding to the socio-economic impacts of COVID-19.* https://unsdg.un.org/sites/default/files/2020-03/SG-Report-Socio-Economic-Impact-of-Covid19.pdf

United Nations World Tourism Organization (UNWTO). (2021). *UNWTO World Tourism Barometer and Statistical Annex, January 2021.* https://www.e-unwto.org/DOI/abs/10.18111/wtobarometereng.2021.19.1.1?journalCode=wtobarometereng

Vendrell-Herrero, F., Gomes, E., Bustinza, O. F., & Mellahi, K. (2018). Uncovering the role of cross-border strategic alliances and expertise decision centralization in enhancing product-service innovation in MMNEs. *International Business Review, 27*(4), 814–825. doi:10.1016/j.ibusrev.2018.01.005

Wen, J., Wang, W., Kozak, M., Liu, X., & Hou, H. (2020). Many brains are better than one: The importance of interdisciplinary studies on COVID-19 in and beyond tourism. *Tourism Recreation Research.*

Wen, Z., Huimin, G., & Kavanaugh, R. R. (2005). The impacts of SARS on the consumer behaviour of Chinese domestic tourists. *Current Issues in Tourism, 8*(1), 22–38. https://DOI.org/10.1080/13683500508668203

Wiharto, W., & Suryani, E. (2020). The Comparison of Clustering Algorithms K-Means and Fuzzy C-Means for Segmentation Retinal Blood Vessels. *Acta Informatica Medica, 28*(1), 42. https://doi.org/10.5455/AIM.2020.28.42-47

World Economic Forum. (2019). *Outbreak readiness and business impact protecting lives and livelihoods across the global economy.* http://www3.weforum.org/docs/WEF HGHI_Outbreak_Readiness_Business_Impact.pdf

World Travel & Tourism Council (WTTC). (2018). *Travel & tourism economic impact 2018 Portugal.* https://www.sgeconomia.gov.pt/ficheiros-externos-sg/wttc_portugal2018-pdf.aspx

World Travel & Tourism Council (WTTC). (2020). *Global economic impact & trends 2020.* https://wttc.org/Portals/0/Documents/Reports/2020/Global%20Economic%20Impact%20Trends%202020.pdf?ver=2021-02-25-183118-360

Yu, J., Seo, J., & Hyun, S. S. (2021). Perceived hygiene attributes in the hotel industry: Customer retention amid the COVID-19 crisis. *International Journal of Hospitality Management, 93*, 102768. doi:10.1016/j.ijhm.2020.102768

Chapter 2

Deep Learning and Machine Learning Techniques for Analyzing Travelers' Online Reviews:
A Review

Elliot Mbunge

University of Eswatini, Eswatini

Benhildah Muchemwa

University of Eswatini, Eswatini

ABSTRACT

Social media platforms play a tremendous role in the tourism and hospitality industry. Social media platforms are increasingly becoming a source of information. The complexity and increasing size of tourists' online data make it difficult to extract meaningful insights using traditional models. Therefore, this scoping and comprehensive review aimed to analyze machine learning and deep learning models applied to model tourism data. The study revealed that deep learning and machine learning models are used for forecasting and predicting tourism demand using data from search query data, Google trends, and social media platforms. Also, the study revealed that data-driven models can assist managers and policymakers in mapping and segmenting tourism hotspots and attractions and predicting revenue that is likely to be generated, exploring targeting marketing, segmenting tourists based on their spending patterns, lifestyle, and age group. However, hybrid deep learning models such as inceptionV3, MobilenetsV3, and YOLOv4 are not yet explored in the tourism and hospitality industry.

DOI: 10.4018/978-1-7998-8306-7.ch002

INTRODUCTION

The exponential growth of social media platforms plays a tremendous role in the hotel and tourism industry. Social media platforms such as TripAdvisor, Expedia, Facebook, YouTube, and Twitter together with electronic word of mouth (eWOM) are increasingly becoming a source of information in the tourism industry (Luo & Xu, 2021). Tourists share their experiences and opinions on social media platforms. These platforms provide tourists and travelers with a vast amount of information that subsequently influence their decision-making process. Travelers' user-generated data provides online reviews and ratings on information such as tourist destinations, security and safety, hospitality services, among others. Such travelers' online reviews and ratings could be utilized to improve services delivery, budgeting, improve customer experience, market segmentation, tourists forecasting, hotel room price and demand forecasting, predict tourists' behavior and make informed decisions. Owing to the dynamic business environment exacerbated by the outbreak of the coronavirus disease 2019 (COVID-19) pandemic (Chitungo et al., 2021; Mbunge, 2020), the hotel and tourism industry need to incorporate emerging technologies such as deep learning and machine learning techniques to address emerging challenges and exploring new opportunities by analyzing travelers' online reviews. Also, analyzing ever-increasing travelers' online reviews using conventional methods such as collaborative filtering recommender systems is highly computational intensive (Calheiros, Moro, & Rita, 2017), not scalable in the context of big data especially when online reviews become voluminous, variety, velocity, variability and veracity. To extract and utilize meaningful insights hidden in travelers 'online reviews, there is a need for incorporating deep learning and machine learning techniques to predict tourists' behavior, tourists forecasting, demand forecasting, and for developing recommender systems for hotel recommendations and identification of deceptive reviews in e-tourism platforms.

In the tourism and hospitality industry, technology is evolving drastically, moving from generalized analysis to customers using traditional methods to the application of deeper and wider computing technologies. This is evidenced by the integration of emerging technologies such as deep learning and machine learning in the tourism and hospitality industry. Deep learning (DL) is a subfield of machine learning (ML) that involves the application of computing models inspired by biological neurons. Deep learning models are composed of multiple processing layers that learn representations of data with multiple levels of abstraction, to extract meaningful information from the dataset (Mbunge, Simelane, Fashoto, Akinnuwesi, & Metfula, 2021). DL models extract features through multiple layers of nonlinear processing units using either supervised or unsupervised learning (Mubarak, Cao, & Ahmed, 2021). Deep learning models have been greatly recognized in voice and speech recognition (Tu, et al., 2019), visual and object recognition, segmentation, image classification and detection since their inception from artificial neural networks (ANNs). Such deep learning models include convolutional neural networks (CNN), long short-term memory (LSTM) among others. However, there has been significant progress made towards the application of DL and ML in the tourism and hospitality industry. Both machine learning and deep learning use basic principles of artificial neural networks. ANNs are biologically inspired neurons that extract features using training function either supervised or unsupervised learning algorithm (Fashoto, Mbunge, Ogunleye, & den Burg, 2021). The most prominent supervised learning algorithm called BackPropagation has been applied in several ANNs to minimize network's errors through gradient descent (Mbunge, Vheremu, & Kajiva, 2017).

However, the BackPropagation algorithm in ANNs is severely affected by the local minima problem (Choi, Ju-Hong, & Deok-Hwan, 2008). To improve the performance of ANNs while minimizing local minima problem, (Atakulreka & Daricha, 2007) state that the ANN should be trained more than once, while other scholars proposed new ways to eliminate local minima problem such as the introduction of new training algorithms (Kawaguchi & Yoshua, 2019), momentum, least-squares methods (Mubarak et al., 2021), adaptive learning rate among others. However, due to the advancement of technology and complexity of ANNs, machine learning algorithms such as support vector machines, linear regression, Bayesian networks, random forest, logistic regression, k-nearest neighbors, and decision trees were developed which further led to the introduction of deep learning. The distinct characteristic of deep learning models which makes them different from ANNs lies in their architecture (Mbunge et al., 2015). For instance, deep learning models have more complex hidden layers with adaptive activation functions such as sigmoid function, Hyperbolic tangent, SoftMax, softplus, rectified linear unit (Ying, et al., 2019), absolute value rectification, Maxout (Goodfellow, David, Mehdi, Aaron, & Yoshua, 2013) among others, and also DL supports pre-training of deep auto-encoder unlike the previous simple ANNs. Deep learning algorithms and models include deep belief networks (DBNs), convolutional neural networks (CNNs), restricted Boltzmann machines (RBMs), Deep Boltzmann machines (DBM) and recursive autoencoders among others. The most prominent deep learning neural network is called the convolutional neural networks. The CNNs consist of many feed-forward artificial neural networks and has been successfully implemented in visual imagery classification (Dubey & Jain, 2019). CNNs are made up of multiple layers such as a fully connected layer, pooling layer, convolutional and non-linearity layers.

To the best of our knowledge, there are limited reviews reported on the application of deep learning and machine learning techniques for analyzing travelers' online reviews. Therefore, this study aims to provide a pioneering comprehensive review of deep learning and machine learning techniques for analyzing travelers' online reviews in different application domains within the tourism and hospitality industry. The study sought to address the following research objectives:

- Identify and explain deep learning and machine learning used to analyzing travelers' online reviews.
- Determine the performance of deep learning and machine learning models applied to analyze travelers' online reviews.
- Identify and group variables or attributes relevant for analyzing travelers' online reviews using deep learning and machine learning techniques.
- Identify the most frequently used data sources for analyzing travelers' online reviews.
- Recommend and propose future work based on the findings and limitations of the previous studies that applied deep learning and machine learning models to analyze travelers' online reviews.

Therefore, the following section provides a comprehensive methodology used to carry out the study. Section 3 presents the results and major findings, and Section 4 discusses the results as well as limitations of the deep learning and machine learning models and points at possible future work. Finally, the last section presents the conclusion of the study.

MATERIALS AND METHOD

The study applied a systematic literature review guided by the preferred reporting items for the systematic reviews and meta-analyses (PRISMA) model. The literature search was guided by the search strategy, and the selection of relevant articles was informed by the inclusion and exclusion criteria as stipulated in the PRISMA model.

1. Search Strategy

We searched previously published studies from electronic databases such as Web of Science, Scopus, Google Scholar, PubMed, ScienceDirect, IEEE Xplore Digital Library, ACM Digital Library, and Springer Link. The literature searching was based on the following search keywords: *"Deep learning"* OR *"Machine Learning"* OR *"Hybrid learning"* AND *"Tourism"* OR *"Travelers' online Review"* OR *"Tourism demand forecasting"* OR *"Hotel demand prediction"*

2. Study Selection

The searches yielded a total of 300 articles from electronic databases. The selected articles were screened based on the following: title and abstract. We selected published peer-reviewed articles available from 2019 to 2021 (July). Incomplete articles, opinion pieces, and non-peer-reviewed articles, and articles without English translations were excluded from the study. To ensure that all relevant articles were included in the study, the authors performed a citations chain for each article retrieved. Duplicates articles were removed from a pool of articles.

3. Selecting Primary Sources and Quality Assessment

After the selection of relevant articles, authors further assessed articles' abstracts independently, and 34 articles were considered for review eligibility. We further assessed full-text articles for eligibility and removed 10 articles. Only 24 articles were considered in this study. The study included articles that mainly applied deep learning and machine learning techniques to analyze tourism data.

RESULTS

The results of the selected deep learning and machine learning models are presented in Table1. For each model, the purpose of the model, performance accuracy, dataset and variable used as well as limitations were captured.

Table 1. Deep learning and machine learning models applied to the tourism industry

Reference	Model	Purpose	Accuracy	Dataset and variables used	Dataset Source	Limitations
Crivellari and Beinat (2020)	LSTM to predict the next location in the sequence	Human mobility	70.13%	Mobile phone call detailed records, timestamp, the position of the device	Real-world dataset of roamers in Italy	The study did not consider other important variables such as integrating time information, nationality, and age in the sequence
Polyzos et al (2020)	LSTM to predict tourism demand	Prediction	LSTM performed better than baseline models.	Tourists' arrivals, hotel prices, season and events.	National Travel & Tourism Office and Australian Bureau of Statistics	The study did not examine different potential dates for a thorough solution, whereby the drop-in arrivals would be forecasted.
Y. Li and Cao (2019)	LSTM to predict tourism flow	Prediction	LSTM outperformed Autoregressive integrated moving average (ARIMA), and back-propagation neural network	Timestamp and travel data	Small wild goose pagoda	The dataset used was small hence the reason to split it into 67% training and 33% testing.
Piccialli et al (2020)	Sequence to Sequence Neural networks	Prediction	86.89%	Patterns of visits, their characteristics, time spent inside the museum, spatial features, and behavior.	National Archaeological Museum of the city of Naples.	The study is limited to tourists with Bluetooth devices in a detectable area, and then the sensor records the media access control number of such devices and the current timestamp. Once the device becomes unreachable, it lost tracking ability.
Law et al (2019)	LSTM- tourism demand forecasting	Forecasting	LSTM model performed better than baselines models.	Dining data, lodging, transportation, Tour, weather, shopping, recreation	Google Trends and Baidu Index	The study experienced two limitations: feature engineering and lag order selection.
Kanjanasupawan et al (2019)	LSTM to predict tourist behavior	Prediction	96%	Posts, location, and users	Destination360 website	The model was trained with a limited dataset.
Hao et al (2021)	CNN-based deep learning approach to predict tourists' perception and prescription	Prediction	The model improved sentiment predictive performance with minimal domain knowledge and human effort.	Data was extracted from microblogs	Social media platforms	Data extracted was limited to online sentiments and excluded other important variables such as integrating time information, nationality, and age in the sequence.
Zhang et al (2020)	LSTM to forecast daily tourist flow	Forecasting	42%	Food, sightseeing, festival events,	Natural World Heritage site, Baidu Index	The study did not include geographic big data concerning tourism can also be introduced as input variables of LSTM for tourism demand forecasting

Continued on following page

Table 1. Continued

Reference	Model	Purpose	Accuracy	Dataset and variables used	Dataset Source	Limitations
Höpken et al (2020)	ARIMA and ANN to predict tourists' arrival	Prediction	ARIMA achieved 73.73% while ANN achieved 78.9%	Tourist arrivals, search traffic data on web search engines	Google Trends, Baidu Index	Cosine similarity used has limited capabilities for matching semantically identical search terms when constructing the aggregated search index. The dataset used was small.
J. W. Bi et al (2021)	Hybrid deep learning-based model to forecast tourism demand in time series imaging.	Forecasting	The proposed model outperformed SVM, ARIMA and NN	Weather, seasonality change, key events, seasonal factors, local recurring patterns and temporary relations.	Jiuzhaigou and Mount Siguniang	The proposed model is univariate and does not consider other exogenous variables and search engine data. The proposed model is computationally intensive as compared to the shallow learning algorithm.
Lv et al (2019)	SAEN Deep learning to predict tourism demand	Forecasting	SAEN achieves better forecasting results than Li's model, ARIMA and BPNN	Weather, Travel agent rank, ticket search and events.	Search query data and Baidu Index	The web search query data was done manually and often depends on simple correlation relationships, which is inefficient.

Continued on following page

Table 1. Continued

Reference	Model	Purpose	Accuracy	Dataset and variables used	Dataset Source	Limitations
Kulshrestha et al (2020)	Bayesian BILSTM approach to forecasting tourism demand	Forecasting	BBiLSTM performs better than the LSTM, SVR, RBFNN, and ADLM	Tourist arrivals, price, tourist income and transportation cost.	Singapore tourism dataset	The study utilized Singapore as a single test case, and quarterly data with only two explanatory variables. For better generalization capability and robustness, more destination countries, yearly or monthly data, and more explanatory variables like marketing expenditure, and the number of hotels in the destination country can be tested.
Guizzardi et al (2021)	A smart approach to tourism demand forecasting	Forecasting	The model performed better than traditional time series forecasting methods.	Rates, accommodation, arrival dates, duration of stay and hotel	Online reviews from Expedia	The limitation of the study findings lies in the choice of a single destination (a business destination). Other destinations may have a smaller number of high category hotels, and public data from OTAs might not be able to realistically predict expected occupancy. The study did not dig deeper into the possible use of different big data sources in increase forecasting accuracy: for example, search engine queries and website traffic data, social media mentions or mobile phone data, could show synergies with our index that could lead to a further increase in forecasting accuracy

Continued on following page

Table 1. Continued

Reference	Model	Purpose	Accuracy	Dataset and variables used	Dataset Source	Limitations
H. Li et al (2020)	Machine learning models to forecast tourism demand with multisource big data	Forecasting	ARIMAX improved the forecasting accuracy when forecasting 1 to 6 weeks ahead.	Weekly tourist arrivals, travel guide, weather, altitude, tourist attractions, weekly review volume and weekly average review rating.	Search query data and online reviews (Ctrip and Qunar)	The model constructed tourism demand forecasting models tended to incorporate only internet big data and a lagged tourism demand variable without considering other important influencing factors in tourism demand. The study also only considered one type of social media data, namely online review data, to forecast tourism demand.
Miah et al (2020)	big data analytics for tourist behaviour analysis	Behaviour		Geotagged photo data, date, and time.	Social media platforms such as Flickr	The study used an incomplete dataset, profile of those posting photos and a single site as the data source.
Xie et al (2021)	Optimized machine learning approach	Forecasting	The optimized model produced the best forecasting performance	Destination details, ticket prices, cruise sites and past customer feedback.	Search query data from Baidu and economic indexes.	The model was limited to the Chinese cruise tourism market and also other important economic indexes, other types of data sources such as web-based text and social media were not considered.
(Ahani, Nilashi, Ibrahim, Sanzogni, & Weaven, 2019)	SVM, CART, ANFIS and NN to segment the market and travel choice prediction in Spa hotels.	Segmentation	Mybrid SOM, HOSVD, CART and Text mining method discovered nine dissimilar segments	Commentary on prior hotels frequented by the user, stay date, traveling type, multi-dimensional ratings, overall rating, user review distribution, user experience, user reviews, hotel description, and user information	Social media platform and Google Trends	The dataset used by the study was extracting available customer data from TripAdvisor which only included general preferences of spa hotel customers
Jiao et al (2020)	Spatiotemporal autoregressive model	Forecasting	The model generates the most accurate results in over 70% of the cases.	Tourist arrivals, time, price, and place	World Bank and UNWTO	The study did not include exogenous explanatory variables.

Continued on following page

Table 1. Continued

Reference	Model	Purpose	Accuracy	Dataset and variables used	Dataset Source	Limitations
Y. Zhang et al (2020)	LSTM	Forecasting	The model achieved higher forecasting accuracy than dynamic linear modeling	Tourism arrival volume, weather, food, and transportation.	Google Trends and Baidu Index	Other important variables such as economy, climate change, and leisure time were not included in the study. The model forecasting was not stable due to limited dataset size, therefore a large number of parameters for optimization in the future to improve forecasting stability.
Park et al (2021)	Seasonal autoregressive integrated moving average (SARIMA)	Forecasting	SARIMA outperformed the benchmark models	Monthly tourist arrivals, trending events, ratings, and news hits.	Hong Kong Tourism Board and	The study did not include sentiment analysis with topic modeling to assess the association between latent sentiment toward a particular news topic and potential tourist behaviors.
Al Shehhi and Karathanasopoulos, (2020)	SARIMA, SVM, ANFIS and deep belief network model	Forecasting	ANFIS model outperformed other models.	Average daily hotel room rates, price, trends, and seasonality.	Smith Travel Research	The models used time-series data only.
Sánchez-Medina and C-Sánchez, (2020)	Machine learning models (random forest, SVM, ANN, GA)	Forecasting		Demographic data, booking details (day, month of booking), check-in data (day, time) and price	Gran Canaria	The model used data from Gran Canaria, therefore, there is a need to incorporate unstructured texts from additional information sources such as articles from blogs, Internet forums, and user-generated content.
Nilashi et al (2021)	Classification and Regression Trees (CART)	Decision making	The model achieved 86% accuracy	Cleanliness, service, value, rooms, location, sleep quality, and check-in/ front desk and travelers' ratings	TripAdvisor	The study used only k-means and CART; other clustering algorithms were excluded to compare the performance of the model.
Kanjanasupawan et al (2019)	Convolutional LSTM (CLSTM) and LSTM	Prediction	CLSTM outperformed LSTM in both accuracy and loss values	Features, users, posts and groups of locations	Destination360	The model was compared only with LSTM, hence the need to compare it with other models.

Table 1 shows that deep learning models such as Convolutional Neural Networks, long-short-term memory, and machine learning models such as support vector machines, Decision trees, K-Nearest Neighbors and Ensemble methods have been mostly used in the tourism industry. These models are explained in the following subsections.

Convolutional Neural Networks

CNN is a deep neural feed-forward network that works on the principle of weight sharing, spatial feature extraction capability, and less computational costs (Jiang & Fan, 2020). CNN architecture was initially designed to process visual imagery (Militante & Dionisio, 2020). The recent improvements in CNN architectures in detecting objects have seen the great performance of several CNN-based models in detecting face masks (Mbunge et al., 2021). CNN-based models adopt the architecture of artificial neural networks (ANNs). It can be thought of as a classifier that extracts and processes hierarchical features for imagery data. This network usually uses activation function and training algorithms to adaptively learn spatial hierarchies of image features (Yamashita, Nishio, Do, & Togashi, 2018). Thus, images are given as input labels and training is done automatically, as shown in Figure 1. In CNN, the first layer is the input image. Instead of having an input layer and output layer only, CNNs have more additional types of layers or building blocks called convolutional layer, pooling layer, and fully-connected layer (Elujide et al., 2021). Scholars such as Hao et al (2021) applied a CNN-based deep learning approach to predict tourists' perception and prescription.

Figure 1. Convolutional neural networks
Source: Mahdianpari et al., 2018

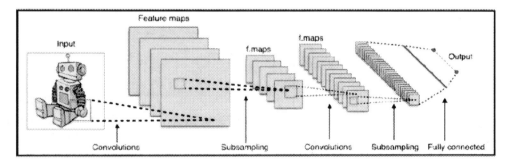

Long Short-Term Memory Network

Long short-term memory network is a hierarchal representational deep learning model which consists of several non-linear layers that contribute to learning the representations from the input data (Mubarak et al., 2021). It is now mostly utilized in deep learning and learning analytics to analyze students' data in education. LSTM analyses students log data created in form of time series. LSTM was introduced by Hochreiter and Schmidhuber (Hochreiter & Schmidhuber, 1997) as an extension of recurrent neural network (RNN). RNNs are not efficient to learn a pattern from long-term dependency because of the gradient vanishing and the exploding gradient problems (Bengio, Simard, & Frasconi, 1994). Therefore,

LSTM was introduced to address these limitations of recurrent neural networks by adding additional interactions per module (or cell). Cells are memory blocks of LSTM that have two states transferred to the next cell state (C_t); the hidden state and cell state (C_{t-1}), as shown in Figure 2. Long Short-term memory networks process a complete sequence of data at once by capturing information temporarily but cannot remember the full input context (Ali, Joshua Thomas, & Nair, 2021). Most recently, the bidirectional Long Short-term Memory network (Bi-LSTM), which is an extension of LSTM has been utilized to train two LSTM models namely: forward LSTM and reverse LSTM (Dong, 2019). Long Short-term memory network is organized in form of a chain structure, with each repeating cell having a different structure (see Figure 2).

Figure 2. Structure of long short-term memory
Source: Le et al., 2019

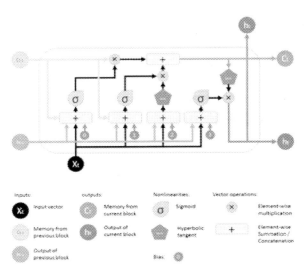

The procedure of developing a Long short-term memory network is to remove irrelevant information and will be omitted from the cell in that step. The sigmoid function (σ) plays an important role in removing and excluding irrelevant information, which takes the output of the last LSTM unit (h_{t-1}) at time $t-1$ and the current input (X_t) at time t, as shown in Figure 2. Additionally, the sigmoid function determines which part from the old output should be eliminated (Le, Ho, Lee, & Jung, 2019). Several scholars applied LSTM in the tourism and hospitality industry as shown in Tables 2 and 3.

Support Vector Machines

The support vector machine (SVM) is a supervised learning method that generates input-output mapping functions from a set of labelled training data (Akman, Karaman, & Kuzey, 2020). Support Vector Machines apply a simple linear method to the data but in a high-dimensional feature space non-linearly related to the input space. The adoption and use of Support Vector Machines do not involve complex computations, and it is this simplicity that has made it popular in many learning problems. A Support Vector Machine can be trained for classification, regression or novelty detection. Support Vector classifiers can handle outliers and because they can allow misclassifications, they can handle overlapping classifications. However, the more complex the data, the more Classifiers ant handle. This is where support vector machines are an upgrade. Support Vector Machines use kernel functions to systematically find support vector classifiers in higher dimensions. Kernel functions only calculate the relationships between every pair of points as if they are in the higher dimensions, they don't do the transformation, this is called the Kernel Trick. The Kernel trick reduces the amount of computation required for Support Vector machines by avoiding the math that transforms the data from low to high dimensions and it makes calculating relationships in the infinite dimensions used by the Radial Kernel possible. In the tourism industry, Ahani et al (2019) applied SVM, decision trees (CART), ANFIS and NN to segment the market and travel choice prediction in Spa-hotels.

Decision Trees

A decision tree is a classifier expressed as a recursive partition of the instance space. The decision tree consists of nodes that form a rooted tree, meaning it is a directed tree with a node called "root" that has no incoming edges (Miah et al., 2017). Decision trees are constructed by analyzing a set of training examples for which the class labels are known. They are then applied to classify previously unseen examples. If trained on high-quality data, decision trees can make very accurate predictions. A decision tree classifies an item by formulating and posing a series of questions based on the features of that item. Each question is contained in a node, and every internal node point to one child node for each possible answer to its question. Decision trees can be based on yes or no questions, numbers, and rankings. Classification can be categorical or numeric. Other decision trees combine numeric data and yes-no data. The top of the tree is called the Root node. Nodes in the middle of the tree are called internal nodes. They have arrows pointing to them and arrows pointing away from them (Kalipe, Gautham, & Behera, 2018). The last nodes are called leaf nodes. These nodes have arrows pointing to them, but none pointing away from them. Decision trees are sometimes more interpretable than other classifiers such as neural networks and support vector machines because they combine simple questions about the data in an understandable way (Nilashi et al., 2021).

Ensemble Methods

An ensemble consists of a set of individually trained classifiers (such as neural networks or decision trees) whose predictions are combined when classifying novel instances (Xie et al., 2021). These are a combination of machine learning techniques and different base classifiers (Nilashi, Bagherifard, Rahmani, & Rafe, 2017). Research has proven that a good ensemble is one where all the classifiers in the ensemble are both accurate and make their errors on different parts of the input space. Two popular methods for creating accurate ensembles are Bagging and Boosting. These methods rely on resampling techniques to obtain different training sets for each of the classifiers. In the tourism industry, Nilashi et al (2017) developed recommender systems based on ensemble methods. Also, Cankurt (2016) applied ensemble methods to forecast tourism demand.

DISCUSSION OF RESULTS

This section focuses on the discussion of deep learning and machine learning models for analyzing Travelers' Online Reviews. The study revealed that DL and ML models are used for tourism demand forecasting, predicting tourists' behavior, hotel room price forecasting and tracking tourists' mobility and segmentation. These models are explained below.

Tourism Demand Forecasting Models

The application of deep learning and machine learning for tourism demand forecasting continues to attract attention. The extant literature on tourism demand forecasting is divided into three broad categories: AI-based models, time series and econometric (J.-W. Bi, Han, & Li, 2020). Time series-based tourism demand forecasting models utilizes historical tourism data to forecast future trends. For instance, Jiao et al (2020) applied a spatiotemporal autoregressive model to forecast tourism demand using data from World Bank and UNWTO; and the model achieved 70% forecasting accuracy. However, most times series models such as autoregressive integrated moving average assume a linear relationship between the future and past time steps values. This affects the accuracy of the model when solving complex non-linear problems. To solve this problem, deep learning models that have been used for tourism demand forecasting perform better than baseline models. For instance, LSTM has been used for tourism demand forecasting using data from Google Trends and Baidu Index and performed better than ARIMA and ARIMAX (Law et al., 2019). Also, J. W. Bi et al (2021) applied a hybrid deep learning-based model to forecast tourism demand in time series imaging using data from Jiuzhaigou and Mount Siguniang. The model outperformed support vector machines, ARIMA and neural networks. However, deep learning-based tourism demand forecasting requires more computational resources and a huge dataset to produce accurate results and mitigate the overfitting problem. The study also revealed that tourism demand forecasting models shown in Table 1, mostly used data from Google Trends, Search query data and Baidu Index. However, the variables used by these models differ, as shown in Table 2.

Table 2. Tourism forecasting model and variables

Tourism forecasting model	Variables Used
LSTM	Dining data (food and restaurant), lodging (hotel and price), transportation (ferry or flight), Tour, weather, shopping, recreation (bar, show, nightlife, casino) (Law et al., 2019).
	Food, sightseeing and festival events (B. Zhang et al., 2020).
	Tourism arrival volume, weather, food, and transportation (Y. Zhang et al., 2020).
ARIMAX	Weekly tourist arrivals, travel guide, weather, altitude, tourist attractions, weekly review volume and weekly average review rating (H. Li et al., 2020).
ARIMA	Tourist arrivals, time, price and place (Jiao et al., 2020).
Bayesian BILSTM	Tourist arrivals, price, tourist income and transportation cost (Kulshrestha et al., 2020).
Hybrid deep learning model	Weather, seasonality change, key events, seasonal factors, local recurring patterns and temporary relations (J. W. Bi et al., 2021).
SAEN Deep learning	Weather, Travel agent rank, ticket search and events (Lv et al., 2018).

Tourists' Behavior Prediction Models

Several deep learning modes have been utilized for prediction purposes in the tourism and hospitality industry, as shown in Table 1. For instance, Y. Li & Cao (2018) applied long short-term memory to predict tourism flow using data from the Small wild goose pagoda. The model outperformed the Backpropagation neural network and autoregressive integrated moving average model. Also, Piccialli et al (2020) applied Sequence to Sequence neural network to predict the occupancy of locations of a sophisticated space using data from the National Archaeological Museum of the city of Naples. The model achieved 86.89% prediction accuracy. However, their study was limited to tourists with Bluetooth devices in a detectable area, and then the sensor records devices' MAC number and the current timestamp. Once the device becomes unreachable, the model loses tracking ability. Kanjanasupawan et al (2019) used LSTM to predict tourist behavior using data from the Destination360 website which consists of posts, location, and users. Their model achieved 96% prediction accuracy. Also, Hao et al (2021) implemented a CNN-based deep learning approach to predict tourists' perception and prescription using data from social media platforms. The model improved sentiment predictive performance with minimal domain knowledge and human effort. However, their study excluded econometric data and other important variables such as time information, nationality, and age in the sequence. Höpken et al (2020) applied artificial neural networks and ARIMA to predict tourists arrival using data from Google Trends and Baidu Index. ARIMA achieved 73.73% while ANN achieved 78.9% because of several factors including the limited dataset used. Also, Kanjanasupawan et al (2019) used a convolutional neural network with LSTM to predict tourist behavior using data from Destination360. The model utilized data with features such as users' online activities, posts and groups of locations, as shown in Table 3.

Table 3. Prediction model and variables used

Prediction model	Variables Used
LSTM	Timestamp and travel data (Y. Li & Cao, 2018).
	Posts, location, and users (Kanjanasupawan et al., 2019).
	Features, users, posts and groups of locations (Kanjanasupawan et al., 2019).
Sec2Sec Neural Network	Patterns of visits, their characteristics, time spent inside the museum, spatial features, and behaviour (Piccialli et al., 2020).
CNN-based deep learning approach	Data was extracted from microblogs (Hao et al., 2021).
ARIMA and ANN	Tourist arrivals and search traffic data on web search engines (Höpken et al., 2020).

Hotel Room Price Forecasting

Forecasting hotel room prices have been increasingly attracting the attention of researchers in the hospitality sector. For instance, practitioners and policymakers plan and invest in hospitality based on revenue predictions (Arefieva, Egger, & Yu, 2021). This depends on several factors prevailing in the market which may lead to change in hotel room prices. Even though there are limited studies in this aspect, Al Shehhi & Karathanasopoulos (2020) applied seasonal autoregressive integrated moving average, support vector machines, adaptive network fuzzy interference system and deep belief network model. Modelling data used consists of average daily hotel room rates, price, trends, and seasonality, from Smith Travel Research. Their study revealed that ANFIS outperformed other baseline models.

Tourists Segmentation and Mobility

Table 1 shows that some deep learning and machine learning models are applied to segment tourists' destination and their mobility. For instance, Crivellari & Beinat (2020) applied LSTM to predict the next location in the sequence using mobile phone call detailed records, timestamp, the position of the device (coverage area of the principal antenna). Also, Ahani et al (2019) utilized support vector machines, decision trees (CART), adaptive neuro-fuzzy inference systems and neural networks to segment the market and travel choice prediction in Spa-hotels. The following section discusses the data sources used with deep learning and machine learning models to analyse tourism data.

Data Sources

The increasing access and usage of the internet and social media platforms continue to change and sharpen the tourism and hospitality industry globally. This study revealed that online data generated from various tourism online data sources such as TripAdvisor, Google trends, Baidu Index, Destination360 website, Instagram, Flickr and Expedia plays a tremendous role in the application of deep learning machine learning models in the tourism industry. For instance, (Kanjanasupawan et al., 2019) used data from Destination360, Nilashi et al (2021) extracted data from TripAdvisor, while Y. Zhang et al (2020), Ahani et al (2019), Xie et al (2021), H. Li et al (2020), Guizzardi et al (2021), Lv et al (2018), Höpken et al (2020) and (Law et al., 2019) used data from Google Trends, Search query data and Baidu Index. Destination360 is a social platform where travelers share and exchange their travelling experiences worldwide. Travelers' posts are ordered by the groups of locations globally, thus this specifies the sequence of places (Ahani et al., 2019). Travelers that use the Destination360 platform use their name, therefore every action, behavior and clicks can be tracked on the platform. Inactive users with few posts, usually less than 4 posts, forums, and other related information are deactivated from the platform (Ahani et al., 2019). This study revealed that some DL and ML algorithms used search query data. Such data are unique from social media data. Searches are usually conducted in private and by a much larger population compared to social media discussions. However, search query data suffer from several pitfalls (H. Li et al., 2020). For example, search query data are not as rich as social media data, as they can only indicate tourists' level of interest in a tourism product or destination but have limited ability. Also, search query data, Google trends and social media data may have extraneous and noisy data which may affect the performance of deep learning algorithms (Mbunge, Jiyane, & Muchemwa, 2022) and machine learning models (X. Li, Law, Xie, & Wang, 2021). In such situations, data processing and shrinkage methods are required to reduce prediction and forecasting errors.

CONCLUSION AND FUTURE WORK

Social media platforms generate huge amounts of data that can be utilized by policymakers, managers in the tourism and hospitality industry to make informed decisions. Such data can be analyzed using deep learning and machine learning models to extract meaningful insights such as demand forecasting, tourists' mobility and segmentation, analyzing tourists' behaviour and hotel room price forecasting. As tourism data from various digital platforms become voluminous, veracity, veracity, variety and value, it becomes difficult to extract meaningful insights using traditional methods and may lead to biased analysis, hence the need for deep learning and machine learning models. These models can also be used to predict revenue that is likely to be generated, explore targeting marketing, as well as segmenting tourists based on their spending patterns, culture, lifestyle and age group. Also, Arefieva et al (2021) alluded that data-driven models such as deep learning models can assist managers and policymakers to map tourism hotspots and attractions through social media platforms. Therefore, in this study, authors analyzed deep learning and machine learning used to extract meaningful insight from tourism data from various digital platforms. The study revealed that online data sources such as TripAdvisor, Google trends, Baidu Index, Destination360 website, Instagram, Flickr and Expedia play a tremendous role in the tourism and hospitality industry. Data generated from these platforms have been used for predicting tourists' behavior, demand forecasting, hotel room price forecasting and tourists' segmentation and mobility. In addition, the study revealed that LSTM deep learning model is the most frequently used for predicting and forecasting tourism demand. However, wider and deeper hybrid deep learning models such as inceptionV3 and V4 as well as MobilenetsV3, YOLOv3 and V4 are not yet explored in the tourism and hospitality industry.

Declaration of Competing Interest

Authors declare no competing interest.

Funding

This research received no specific grant from any funding agency in the public, commercial, or not-for-profit sectors.

REFERENCES

Ahani, A., Nilashi, M., Ibrahim, O., Sanzogni, L., & Weaven, S. (2019). Market segmentation and travel choice prediction in Spa hotels through TripAdvisor's online reviews. *International Journal of Hospitality Management*, *80*, 52–77. doi:10.1016/j.ijhm.2019.01.003

Akman, E., Karaman, A. S., & Kuzey, C. (2020). *Visa trial of international trade: evidence from support vector machines and neural networks*. Https://Doi.Org/10.1080/23270012.2020.1731719 doi:10.1080/23270012.2020.1731719

Al Shehhi, M., & Karathanasopoulos, A. (2020). Forecasting hotel room prices in selected GCC cities using deep learning. *Journal of Hospitality and Tourism Management*, *42*, 40–50. doi:10.1016/j.jhtm.2019.11.003

Ali, A. M., Joshua Thomas, J., & Nair, G. (2021). *Academic and Uncertainty Attributes in Predicting Student Performance*. Springer. doi:10.1007/978-3-030-68154-8_72

Arefieva, V., Egger, R., & Yu, J. (2021). A machine learning approach to cluster destination image on Instagram. *Tourism Management, 85*, 104318. doi:10.1016/j.tourman.2021.104318

Bengio, Y., Simard, P., & Frasconi, P. (1994). Learning Long-Term Dependencies with Gradient Descent is Difficult. *IEEE Transactions on Neural Networks, 5*(2), 157–166. doi:10.1109/72.279181 PMID:18267787

Bi, J.-W., Han, T.-Y., & Li, H. (2020). *International tourism demand forecasting with machine learning models: The power of the number of lagged inputs.* Https://Doi.Org/10.1177/1354816620976954 doi:10.1177/1354816620976954

Bi, J. W., Li, H., & Fan, Z. P. (2021). Tourism demand forecasting with time series imaging: A deep learning model. *Annals of Tourism Research, 90*, 103255. doi:10.1016/j.annals.2021.103255

Calheiros, A. C., Moro, S., & Rita, P. (2017). Sentiment Classification of Consumer-Generated Online Reviews Using Topic Modeling. *Journal of Hospitality Marketing & Management, 26*(7), 675–693. doi:10.1080/19368623.2017.1310075

Cankurt, S. (2016). Tourism demand forecasting using ensembles of regression trees. *2016 IEEE 8th International Conference on Intelligent Systems, IS 2016 - Proceedings*, 702–708. 10.1109/IS.2016.7737388

Chitungo, I., Mhango, M., Mbunge, E., Dzobo, M., Musuka, G., & Dzinamarira, T. (2021, November 2). Utility of telemedicine in sub-Saharan Africa during the COVID-19 pandemic. A rapid review. *Human Behavior and Emerging Technologies*, hbe2.297. Advance online publication. doi:10.1002/hbe2.297

Crivellari, A., & Beinat, E. (2020). LSTM-Based Deep Learning Model for Predicting Individual Mobility Traces of Short-Term Foreign Tourists. *Sustainability 2020, 12*(1), 349. doi:10.3390/su12010349

Dong, H. (n.d.). *The Application of Artificial Neural Network, Long short-term Memory Network and Bidirectional Long short-term Memory Network in the Grades Prediction.* Academic Press.

Dubey, A. K., & Jain, V. (2019). Comparative Study of Convolution Neural Network's Relu and Leaky-Relu Activation Functions. *Lecture Notes in Electrical Engineering, 553*, 873–880. doi:10.1007/978-981-13-6772-4_76

Elujide, I., Fashoto, S. G., Fashoto, B., Mbunge, E., Folorunso, S. O., & Olamijuwon, J. O. (2021). Application of deep and machine learning techniques for multi-label classification performance on psychotic disorder diseases. *Informatics in Medicine Unlocked, 23*, 100545. doi:10.1016/j.imu.2021.100545

Fashoto, S. G., Mbunge, E., Ogunleye, G., & den Burg, J. Van. (2021). *Implementation of machine learning for predicting maize crop yields using multiple linear regression and backward elimination.* Retrieved from https://mjoc.uitm.edu.my

Guizzardi, A., Pons, F. M. E., Angelini, G., & Ranieri, E. (2021). Big data from dynamic pricing: A smart approach to tourism demand forecasting. *International Journal of Forecasting, 37*(3), 1049–1060. doi:10.1016/j.ijforecast.2020.11.006

Hao, J.-X., Wang, R., Law, R., & Yu, Y. (2021). How do Mainland Chinese tourists perceive Hong Kong in turbulence? A deep learning approach to sentiment analytics. *International Journal of Tourism Research, 23*(4), 478–490. doi:10.1002/jtr.2419

Hochreiter, S., & Schmidhuber, J. (1997). Long Short-Term Memory. *Neural Computation*, *9*(8), 1735–1780. doi:10.1162/neco.1997.9.8.1735 PMID:9377276

Höpken, W., Eberle, T., Fuchs, M., & Lexhagen, M. (2020). *Improving Tourist Arrival Prediction: A Big Data and Artificial Neural Network Approach.* Https://Doi.Org/10.1177/0047287520921244 doi:10.1177/0047287520921244

Jiang, M., & Fan, X. (2020). *Retinamask: A Face Mask Detector.* ArXiv.

Jiao, X., Li, G., & Chen, J. L. (2020). Forecasting international tourism demand: A local spatiotemporal model. *Annals of Tourism Research*, *83*, 102937. doi:10.1016/j.annals.2020.102937

Kalipe, G., Gautham, V., & Behera, R. K. (2018). Predicting Malarial Outbreak using Machine Learning and Deep Learning Approach: A Review and Analysis. *Proceedings - 2018 International Conference on Information Technology, ICIT 2018*, 33–38. 10.1109/ICIT.2018.00019

Kanjanasupawan, J., Chen, Y. C., Thaipisutikul, T., Shih, T. K., & Srivihok, A. (2019). Prediction of tourist behaviour: Tourist visiting places by adapting convolutional long short-Term deep learning. *Proceedings of 2019 International Conference on System Science and Engineering, ICSSE 2019*, 12–17. 10.1109/ICSSE.2019.8823542

Kulshrestha, A., Krishnaswamy, V., & Sharma, M. (2020). Bayesian BILSTM approach for tourism demand forecasting. *Annals of Tourism Research*, *83*, 102925. doi:10.1016/j.annals.2020.102925

Law, R., Li, G., Fong, D. K. C., & Han, X. (2019). Tourism demand forecasting: A deep learning approach. *Annals of Tourism Research*, *75*, 410–423. doi:10.1016/j.annals.2019.01.014

Le, H., Ho, Lee, & Jung. (2019). Application of Long Short-Term Memory (LSTM) Neural Network for Flood Forecasting. *Water (Basel)*, *11*(7), 1387. doi:10.3390/w11071387

Li, H., Hu, M., & Li, G. (2020). Forecasting tourism demand with multisource big data. *Annals of Tourism Research*, *83*, 102912. doi:10.1016/j.annals.2020.102912

Li, X., Law, R., Xie, G., & Wang, S. (2021). Review of tourism forecasting research with internet data. *Tourism Management*, *83*, 104245. doi:10.1016/j.tourman.2020.104245

Li, Y., & Cao, H. (2018). Prediction for Tourism Flow based on LSTM Neural Network. *Procedia Computer Science*, *129*, 277–283. doi:10.1016/j.procs.2018.03.076

Luo, Y., & Xu, X. (2021). Comparative study of deep learning models for analyzing online restaurant reviews in the era of the COVID-19 pandemic. *International Journal of Hospitality Management*, *94*, 102849. doi:10.1016/j.ijhm.2020.102849 PMID:34785843

Lv, S. X., Peng, L., & Wang, L. (2018). Stacked autoencoder with echo-state regression for tourism demand forecasting using search query data. *Applied Soft Computing*, *73*, 119–133. doi:10.1016/j.asoc.2018.08.024

Mbunge, E. (2020). Integrating emerging technologies into COVID-19 contact tracing: Opportunities, challenges and pitfalls. *Diabetes & Metabolic Syndrome*, *14*(6), 1631–1636. doi:10.1016/j.dsx.2020.08.029 PMID:32892060

Mbunge, E., Jiyane, S., & Muchemwa, B. (2022). Towards emotive sensory Web in virtual health care: Trends, technologies, challenges and ethical issues. *Sensors International*, *3*, 100134. doi:10.1016/j.sintl.2021.100134

Mbunge, E., Makuyana, R., Chirara, N., & Chingosho, A. (n.d.). Fraud Detection in E-Transactions using Deep Neural Networks-A Case of Financial Institutions in Zimbabwe Cite this paper Fraud Detection in E-Transactions using Deep Neural Networks-A Case of Financial Institutions in Zimbabwe. *International Journal of Scientific Research*, *17*(2). Advance online publication. doi:10.21275/ART20176804

Mbunge, E., Simelane, S., Fashoto, S. G., Akinnuwesi, B., & Metfula, A. S. (2021). Application of deep learning and machine learning models to detect COVID-19 face masks - A review. *Sustainable Operations and Computers*, *2*, 235–245. doi:10.1016/j.susoc.2021.08.001

Mbunge, E., Vheremu, F., & Kajiva, K. (2017). A Tool to Predict the Possibility of Social Unrest Using Sentiments Analysis-Case of Zimbabwe Politics 2017-2018. *International Journal of Science and Research (IJSR). ISSN*, *6*. Advance online publication. doi:10.21275/ART20177198

Miah, S. J., Vu, H. Q., Gammack, J., & McGrath, M. (2017). A Big Data Analytics Method for Tourist Behaviour Analysis. *Information & Management*, *54*(6), 771–785. doi:10.1016/j.im.2016.11.011

Militante, S. V., & Dionisio, N. V. (2020). Deep Learning Implementation of Facemask and Physical Distancing Detection with Alarm Systems. *Proceeding - 2020 3rd International Conference on Vocational Education and Electrical Engineering: Strengthening the Framework of Society 5.0 through Innovations in Education, Electrical, Engineering and Informatics Engineering, ICVEE 2020*. 10.1109/ICVEE50212.2020.9243183

Mubarak, A. A., Cao, H., & Ahmed, S. A. M. (2021). Predictive learning analytics using deep learning model in MOOCs' courses videos. *Education and Information Technologies*, *26*(1), 371–392. doi:10.100710639-020-10273-6

Nilashi, M., Bagherifard, K., Rahmani, M., & Rafe, V. (2017). A recommender system for tourism industry using cluster ensemble and prediction machine learning techniques. *Computers & Industrial Engineering*, *109*, 357–368. doi:10.1016/j.cie.2017.05.016

Nilashi, M., Samad, S., Ahani, A., Ahmadi, H., Alsolami, E., Mahmoud, M., Majeed, H. D., & Abdulsalam Alarood, A. (2021). Travellers decision making through preferences learning: A case on Malaysian spa hotels in TripAdvisor. *Computers & Industrial Engineering*, *158*, 107348. doi:10.1016/j.cie.2021.107348

Park, E., Park, J., & Hu, M. (2021). Tourism demand forecasting with online news data mining. *Annals of Tourism Research*, *90*, 103273. doi:10.1016/j.annals.2021.103273

Piccialli, F., Giampaolo, F., Casolla, G., Di Cola, V. S., & Li, K. (2020). A Deep Learning approach for Path Prediction in a Location-based IoT system. *Pervasive and Mobile Computing*, *66*, 101210. doi:10.1016/j.pmcj.2020.101210

Polyzos, S., Samitas, A., & Spyridou, A. E. (2020). *Tourism demand and the COVID-19 pandemic: an LSTM approach*. Https://Doi.Org/10.1080/02508281.2020.1777053 doi:10.1080/02508281.2020.1777053

Sánchez-Medina, A. J., & C-Sánchez, E. (2020). Using machine learning and big data for efficient forecasting of hotel booking cancellations. *International Journal of Hospitality Management, 89*, 102546. doi:10.1016/j.ijhm.2020.102546

Xie, G., Qian, Y., & Wang, S. (2021). Forecasting Chinese cruise tourism demand with big data: An optimized machine learning approach. *Tourism Management, 82*, 104208. doi:10.1016/j.tourman.2020.104208

Yamashita, R., Nishio, M., Do, R. K. G., & Togashi, K. (2018). Convolutional neural networks: An overview and application in radiology. *Insights Into Imaging, 9*(4), 611–629. Advance online publication. doi:10.100713244-018-0639-9 PMID:29934920

Zhang, B., Li, N., Shi, F., & Law, R. (2020). *A deep learning approach for daily tourist flow forecasting with consumer search data.* Https://Doi.Org/10.1080/10941665.2019.1709876 doi:10.1080/10941665.2019.1709876

Zhang, Y., Li, G., Muskat, B., & Law, R. (2020). *Tourism Demand Forecasting: A Decomposed Deep Learning Approach.* Https://Doi.Org/10.1177/0047287520919522 doi:10.1177/0047287520919522

Chapter 3
Digitalisation in the Tourism and Hospitality Industry:
Perspectives of the Supply and Demand Sides

Nil Sonuç
 https://orcid.org/0000-0002-7572-9192
İzmir Katip Çelebi University, Turkey

Merve İşçen
 https://orcid.org/0000-0003-2305-5824
İzmir Katip Çelebi University, Turkey

ABSTRACT

This chapter aims to review the evolution of digitalisation and its effects on the tourism and hospitality industry. A holistic perspective is adopted providing a review and analysis of digitalisation in the tourism and hospitality sector comprising both supply and demand sides for the originality of the content. The supply side, as well as the demand side, is analysed through a literature review of academic resources, policy documents published by international organisations and related websites. The existing literature and the industrial practices are reviewed to find out and classify the state of proposal and implementation of innovative technologies and the trends followed by suppliers and the demand side to use them. Furthermore, the effects of digitalisation on managerial processes on the supply side (actors, entrepreneurs, businesses, destinations) and decisional and behavioural processes on the demand side (consumer, tourists) are taken into consideration to provide a holistic perspective of digitalisation and its effects on the given sector.

DOI: 10.4018/978-1-7998-8306-7.ch003

INTRODUCTION

Digitalisation in the tourism and hospitality industry with its evolutionary nature comprises the fact of being an innovation driving hyper-personalisation and requiring expertise in the creation of high-quality service. Under the subtitles concerning the supply side in this chapter, a comprehensive classification of digitalisation in the tourism industry is probed. For the demand side, the existing studies related to the implication and effects of digitalisation in tourism demand are mentioned including the aspects of new generation consumer needs and behaviours. Additionally, the specific methods used for marketing such as neuromarketing in tourism and suggestions are made accordingly for further studies. However, as the tourism sector is becoming more participative, cooperative and co-creative, the transition between both sides is sometimes inevitable. Consequently, this comprehensive analysis of digitalisation in the tourism and hospitality sector is aimed to inspire and contribute to the evolution of further academic studies.

BACKGROUND

Innovative information and communication technology has an evolutionary effect on many sectors and industries. One of the most representative industries of the world economy, tourism has got and will get its share inevitably (Buhalis & Law 2008, Buhalis & O'Connor 2005, Ip et al, 2011, Law et al. 2014). Tourism 1.0, 2.0, 3.0, 4.0 and 5.0; the versions augment at a pace that humans can hardly reach. The production industry has been first to acquaint with the mentioned chronological development of information and communication technologies and their effects. The innovations such as internet technologies, smart robots and tools have created both pleasing and terrifying effects on humankind.

The aspect pleasing the managers include the increasing profitability and quality (Law et al., 2009), as the smart technologies never get tired and work with zero defects. The unpleasing angle includes the insufficiency of online security measures and the replacement of the workforce resulting in growing unemployment. Covering an important portion of the service industry, the importance of face-to-face communication on the co-creation of quality touristic experiences is still undeniable for tourism and hospitality. The cancellation of the use of robots at a hotel (The Henn-na) in Japan for certain period shows that robots have not yet reached the level required for tourism services and human contact still has high validity and acceptance.

In this chapter, the content and evolutionary phase of innovative technologies for the tourism sector are described. The innovative technologies used by hotels (Gonzalez et al, 2019), travel agencies, tour guides, museums, destinations and the tourists are described and exemplified. Additionally, the effects of technology on the management (Leung & Law, 2005) of touristic establishments, destinations and the employees (Jeong et al., 2016) on the supply side are examined. Additionally, on the demand side, the creation of experiences of tourists in relationship with the internet and other related technologies (Gretzel & Jamal, 2009) are also implied. The suggestions and proposals of co-advancement of digital technology and tourism harmoniously are determined accordingly. As indicated by Buhalis (2000: 56), the future success in tourism and hospitality depends on the ability to produce a good synergy of "the information technologies, intellect and management vision".

The concept of digitalisation, which emerges with the continuous development of information technologies, is very important in the tourism industry as in every field. Digitalisation that occurs in tourism businesses plays an important role not only for businesses but also in sharing tourist experiences (Huang et al., 2017). Tourists can also communicate directly with the business, determine the choice of hotel or agency, and share their experiences through these digital platforms. Today, many local and foreign tourists make a detailed research on the internet about the destinations and tourism businesses before they engage in tourism activities, and as a result of this research, they decide to participate in tourism activities or not (Taş et al, 2018). In many parts of the world, tourism enterprises offer virtual reality applications that enable users to experience places they have not been before. Virtual reality programs offer tourists the opportunity to see and hear about the activities, food and beverages and souvenirs before going to their chosen destination (Sarı and Kozak, 2005: 250). Therefore, the interaction opportunities provided by the internet and digital technologies allow tourists to be included in the marketing processes of services in tourism enterprises (Gülmez et al., 2014). ET (Eye-tracking) is mentioned as a method used in the neuromarketing aspect of tourism pricing psychology in an analysis of OTA (Online travel agency) (Boz et al., 2017). Similar studies mention the importance of multidisciplinary neuromarketing measurement methods of tourism demand with the increasing impact of digitalisation on consumer preferences by analyzing the consumer reactions to advertisements (Hernández-Méndez & Muñoz-Leiva 2015, Noone & Robson 2014).

Especially with the increase in the number of Generation Z tourists, digitalisation has become inevitable in tourism businesses and in this context, the concept of super-smart tourist called Tourist 5.0 has started to be discussed (Bahar et al., 2019: 72). Super smart tourists, that is, Generation Z tourists are at the forefront with their adaptation to technology and their hedonistic behaviour due to the period they were born (Kon, 2017). Since it is largely driven by information technologies, the Internet and Social Media, demands, needs and consumption habits vary when compared to other generations (Haddouche & Salomone, 2018: 69). Previous studies mentioned young tourists' travel behaviours in areas such as last-minute decision-making, reading recommendations (eWOM), focusing on low-cost travel tools (Haddouche & Salomone, 2018) also communication via mobile and web-based applications, and sharing data about their personalized experiences.

EVOLUTIONARY ANALYSIS OF DIGITALISATION IN TOURISM AND HOSPITALITY INDUSTRY- SUPPLY SIDE

"When digital transformation is done right, it is like a caterpillar turning into a butterfly, but when done wrong, all you have is a really fast caterpillar"

George Westermann (Research Scientist on the Digital Economy)

"When a snake sheds its skin it changes; when a caterpillar becomes a butterfly, it transforms"

Business Transformation Academy

Means of communication among people have led to enormous transformations since the Paleolithic period. They have evolved from drawing pictures on the walls of caves followed by later periods with hieroglyphs, cuneiform writing on clay tablets, writing on papyrus and parchment (Pergaminae Chartae), pen and paper and other materials and press into a very different era today with digital world allowing synchronous communication through screens of mobile devices. Similarly, the world has witnessed many revolutionary periods since the appearance of human on earth such as the agricultural revolution, industrial revolution and technology revolution. Each period has had transformational effects on the socio-cultural, environmental and economic dimensions.

The conceptual and theoretical foundations of digitalisation are developing as well as the practical world. While causing devastating impacts on the environment, the concentration of population in the urban centres has increased the speed of both life and digital convertibility. The complex interconnectedness of all happenings in human life necessitates more responsibility for sustainability. If the power of digitalisation is used correctly as a tool to facilitate sustainability, then the true transformation may be expected to occur for the world. Tourism and hospitality is an integral part of the healthy life and well-being of society. Adoption of and adaptation to digitalisation brings the tourism and hospitality industry transformational paths on both macro and micro dimensions. Digitalisation and sustainability requirements force responsible professionals to reconstitute all the actors of the tourism and hospitality industry together with the strategic policy and decision-making structures in tourism, hospitality and destination management including human resources management, product development, service quality management, marketing and distribution channels management which will result in desired inevitable transformation.

Digitisation is defined as the material process of converting analogue streams of information into digital bits; while *digitalisation* is defined as the way many domains of social life are restructured around digital communication and media infrastructures (Brennen & Kreiss, 2016: 1). *Digital transformation* refers to the economic and societal effects of digitisation and digitalisation (OECD, 2020).

Digitalisation began in the tourism industry approximately in the 1970s when flight tickets were distributed and sold electronically. In the 1990s, people began to book their trips via the Internet. Today the online and mobile technologies offer various comparable options for trip booking decisions in a co-creative business environment where buyers also share experiences that shape the positioning of the brands and destinations. The current state of ever-growing and even in some respects disrupting digital technology challenges the businesses and destinations in the tourism and hospitality industry for providing competitive and higher quality products and services with the pressure of innovativeness and hyper-personalisation resulting in the customization of the products and services than ever before. This part will first continue with the focus of digitalisation on smart destination management, followed by the analysis of digitalisation and its close relationship with the tourism and hospitality industry.

Smart Destination Management

Many studies and research efforts for description and categorisation of smart tourism, smart cities and smart destinations prove that smart tourism is still in the era of conceptualisation (Johnson et al. 2021, Ivars-Baidal et al. 2021, Buhalis & Amaranggana 2014, Del Chiappa & Baggio 2015). The emphasis on the lacking theoretical and conceptional evolutionary phase of the smart tourism management at the destination level is interestingly similar to the sustainability in the 1990s (Ivars-Baidal & Vera-Rebollo 2019, as cited in Ivars-Baidal et al 2021).

Boes et al. (2016) analyzed and reported with a holistic approach and with the precision of open information to all partners that, value co-creation and inclusive ecosystems requires a certain period for developing competitive smart tourism destinations. The authors also divided the criteria of smart destinations as 'hard' and 'soft' smartness, the former mostly associated with the interconnectedness of all the members of the smart ecosystem and the latter characterized with 4 criteria constructed together upon the "revolutionary" technology which are 'innovation, human capital, social capital and leadership'. This study, comprising at the same time a good literature review of smart tourism destinations as well, proves that the interconnectedness of human expertise with digitalisation is inevitable for competitive strategic sustainable management. Without knowledge and intervention of human capital, digitalisation alone has no meaningful results.

European Capital of Smart Tourism Initiative (ECSTI) defines smart tourism destination as: "A destination facilitating Access to tourism and hospitality products, services, spaces and experiences through ICT-based tools. It is a healthy social and cultural environment, which can be found through a focus on the city's social and human capital. It also implements innovative, intelligent solutions and fosters the development of entrepreneurial businesses and their interconnectedness" (EU, 2019). Put in practice by the ECSTI, "European Capital of Smart Tourism" (ECST) is an award comprising 'digitalisation' prominently among other criteria of smart destinations. 'Accessibility', 'sustainability', 'digitalisation' and 'cultural heritage and creativity' are the four criterias in this respect (EU 2020, EC 2021). In 2019, Copenhagen was awarded ECST for digitalisation criteria. Moving posters, VR goggles of Copenhagen Visitor Center as well as the city's app providing data for authorities asking consent of the user are the examples of successful digital applications. Ljubliana, awarded ECST in 2019 for sustainability and in 2020 for digitalisation, exhibits the locations of tap water with the digital application of official tourism web site (Cleverciti, 2021). ECST of 2019 Helsinki satisfies guests with its smart public transport system, putting the trial of driverless buses in practice, additionally. Also, Lyon as ECST of 2019, provides the guests with Lyon City Card which enables free public transport and entrance to 23 attractions.

A more up-to-date research analysed 18 destinations from the Region of Valencia, including its capital (the city of Valencia to develop certain criteria for smart destination management. The indicators reached by this study were: *"Governance, sustainability, accessibility, connectivity, intelligence, information system, online marketing, the evolution of tourism activity"* (Ivars-Baidal et al 2021). Here, 'connectivity' is the most directly related indicator comprising of the connectivity to the internet at the destination and the availability of Wi-Fi at the facilities and public places. Governance and sustainability signify the managerial and participative part emphasizing the need for strategic planning on the issue. The 8 indicators form a holistic strategic managerial model.

Digitalisation and its Evolutionary Impacts on Tourism and Hospitality Industry

The expectation from digitalisation's effects on tourism is to create contactless and more individualized experiences for tourists (Gretzel et al., 2020). Examples include reduced crowds, improved queue management, QR codes instead of restaurant menus and smartphone-based guides instead of audio guides for more contact-free visits (Ivars-Baidal et al 2021). Shell oil stations in Turkey, for instance, has started a series of advertisements promoting sustainability provided thanks to digitalisation. Themes of sustainable practices supported by digitalisation such as contactless toilets, cleaned and sanitized with the ozone technology even special version for children; other contactless services for protecting public health, increasing accessibility, supporting gender mainstreaming/employment of women are emphasized on the video-ads (Shell, 2021). Similar digital and sustainable implications may be possible for the tourism and hospitality industry at hotels, parks, museums and all the public places that tourists visit.

Especially after the COVID-19 pandemic, which affected negatively the tourism and hospitality industry, destinations try to find ways to improve green and digital practices. Smart tourism responds to those new challenges in trends of supply and demand sides by meeting the new expectations for the products and services, providing equal opportunity and access for visitors, sustainable development of local talent and heritage in the destination (EC, 2021).

Digital and technological inventions go beyond the imagination. The tourism and hospitality industry providing many services with comfort and quality such as accommodation, transportation, security will continue to get its share from these inventions without any doubt. Isn't it enthralling to hear the news such as the first 3D printed house is inhabited in the Netherlands by a couple (Boffey, 2021) or, the English Channel is crossed on a fly board by Franky Zapata for the first time (Rascouet, 2019)? Would the world be more accessible and green if autonomous vehicles or driverless cars began to circle? (Emeraldpublishing, 2020) Similarly, how does it make you feel when you can control everything including the security systems and electricity of the rooms/flats on your smartphone with IoT technology? Alternatively, would you be more than pleased if you could visit just by wearing VR glasses the destination before you buy your next trip? Would you not be enchanted just touching the augmented reality app's invisible screen available in your hotel room to change your view and in-room atmosphere and feel in a relieving lakeside in the Alpes? (Revfine, 2019) Revfine (2019) shows key digital trends in the hospitality industry on its website with very comprehensive content. This informative content also includes example videos to watch about the usage of digital tools and services for the tourism and hospitality industry such as the Internet of Things (IoT), AI-driven robots, recognition technology (facial recognition, fingerprint or retina scanning), virtual reality (VR), augmented reality[1], chatbots & AI (Artificial Intelligence, mobile technology, reputation management.

COVID-19 pandemic has also increased the need and urge for eliminating and avoiding the crowds especially in closed places leading the preferences of people to contactless services, however, it is not the only reason; it has only had a speeding effect on the evolutionary process of digitalisation.

Another reason for the transition to digitalisation for the tourism and hospitality industry is to protect natural and cultural heritages and transmit them to future generations. The Lascaux Caves in France is a good example of it. Found in 1940 but closed to visit since 1963 for protection, Lascaux is a World Heritage Site. Called "Exaltemps" a dark room inside Chapelle Sixtine in Paris is reserved for a guided virtual reality visit of 235 m galleries of Lascaux Caves in 45 minutes. Visitors putting the rucksack and wearing virtual reality casks, feel as if they are inside the cave as they are guided through the virtual twin of the Lascaux provided through the cooperation of local public authority and a private ICT company. So, twin that, even the unevenness of ground is felt by visitors. In each visit, max 6 people are accepted and they can communicate with each other during the visit via their avatars (Cite de l'Architecture, 2021).

Few thousand years ago people developed tools that provided them with a life that required less muscle strength. In the 1960s, 6 axis robots decreased the need for physical strength in many areas including the automotive industry. Industry 4.0 goes far beyond these developments, meaning that, by converting the jobs that digital technologies can facilitate and produce results that are more effective and people will have time to develop more creative ways of business (Endüstri40, 2019). The Digital era becomes a more brain than brawn era for human. Big data, transforming the business management processes into a co-creative and co-integrated (e) ecosystem, is considered at the heart of all digital information circulation. All sustainable and smart tourism industry assumptions of big data work in harmony with the evolution of ICT, (e)Security, (e)Tourism on the condition that it is specifically analysed and classified by human intelligence intervention shortly symbolized (HI) Big Data ('HI' meaning 'via Human Intelligence'). Figure 1 shows the (HI)Big data-centred (e)Ecosystem of (e)Tourism.

Figure 1. Big data via Human Intelligence (HI) at the heart of digitalisation in (e)Tourism (e)Ecosystem
Source: Prepared by Authors.

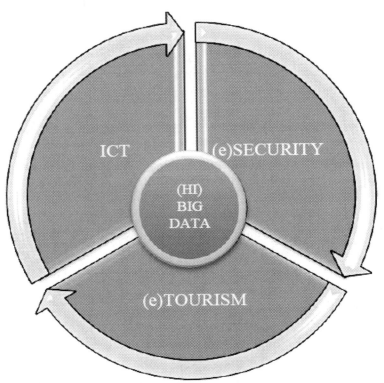

Possessing an enormous amount of data does not show that you are the ruler of the market. The correct analysis and management of the data (Endüstri40, 2019) are essential to creating the correctly perceived value of the brand in the eye of the consumer (LeHub, 2017). This can only be available with strategic talent management and education for software creation and usage (Ruel & Njoku, 2020). Additionally, the use of big data for smart tourism and destination management (Li et al., 2018) especially for the adaptation to the impacts of climate change (Pérez & Barreiro, 2019) is still retarded on the awareness levels of actors and the implementation level (Ivars-Baidal et al 2021). The evolution of Artificial Intelligence (AI) and automated digital technologies has been a facilitator for people and businesses in tourism and hospitality to succeed in the mentioned similar tasks. Created by human, will AI overcome the HI is an issue evoking curiosity.

Digitalisation has leaded people to abandon the usage of 1.0 technologies of computers that required a sedentary living sitting on a chair. It has additionally provided the possibility to work mobile with 2.0 devices (Patin, 2020). Web 1.0 is referred to as a web of *information* or *percipience*, 2.0 as the web of *verbalization*, 3.0 as the web of *affiliation*, 4.0 as a web of *integration* and 5.0 as the web of the *decentralized smart communicator* (Khanzode & Sarode, 2016). Another study classifies the web 0.0 as *desktop-era*, web 1.0 as *early web*, web 2.0 as *post PC era* and *Social web*, 3.0 as *semantic web*, web 4.0 as *mobile* and *symbiotic web*, web 5.0 as *Emotional/Sensitive Web* and 6.0 web as *Independent existence* (Król, 2020: 35). Also, Marketing 1.0 is centred on offer, 2.0 on the client, 3.0 on experience, 4.0 on data

(LeHub, 2017). Shortly, as the numbers beginning from 1.0 increase, the level of social connectivity and similarly data connectivity increases on the virtual level of a digital ecosystem.

Homo-digitus (translated from the French original word 'Homo-numéricus') become the concept for the changing human and the inter-personal relationships, ways of thinking, dreaming, creating, working, reaching the knowledge and producing and distributing the bits of knowledge and experiences of the World (Patin, 2020). The disrupting revolutions of digitalisation bring new business paths while suppressing some others. Time will show which of the innovations will survive and which of them will be history. Table 1 shows a list of digital tools that benefited the tourism and hospitality industry in the evolutionary era.

Table 1. The evolution of digitalisation in tourism and hospitality industry

Years	Digitised Services or Digital Inventions	Examples
1970s	CRSs (Computer/Central Reservation Systems)	SabreSonic orAltea, Navitare
	PMSs (Property Management Systems)	Opera, eZee FrontDesk, MSI CloudPM
	POS (Point of Sales Systems)	Hard/Softwares at Restaurants
1980s	GDSs (Global Distribution Systems)	Amadeus, Sabre, Galileo, Worldspan, Apollo, Pegasus
1990s	Internet	World Wide Web (www), HTML, Own web sites of tourism and hospitality service providers, Email
	Mobile phones	Nokia, Blackberry
	Destination city cards	London city card, Lyon city card
	Search Engines and SEO (Search Engine Optimisation)	Google, Yahoo
	OTAs (Online Travel Agencies)	Viator, Expedia, Priceline, Travelocity, Orbitz, Yahoo Travel, Lastminute.com, Opodo
	Contactless payment	secure payment method using a debit or credit card, smartcard, or another payment device by using RFID technology and near-field communication
2000s	Growth of ICTs, e-commerce	Information Points, Digital TV, Social Media, 3G, GPRS, WIFI, Smart Mobile Phones, Virtual reality, PDA's, Game consoles, Digital Radio
	Travel Metasearch Engines	Trivago, Kayak, Skyscanner
	Social networking and VTCs (Virtual travel community: web 2.0/travel 2.0 portals)	Tripadvisor, Flyertalk, Wayn, igougo.com
	Sharing economy platforms/Peer to peer market places	Airbnb, Couchsurfing, Stayz, HomeAway, Flipkey, Travelling Frogs, Aura, Tripping

Continued on following page

Table 1. Continued

Years	Digitised Services or Digital Inventions	Examples
2010s co-creative, interconnected, smart era	Cloud PMSs/Softwares: Revenue and/or (e)-marketing management integrated systems	IDeaS, Travog, OLSET
	Big Data	Cloud Technologies
	DMSs (Destination Management Systems)	Visitbritain.com
	Tourism data aggregators	Cirkwi
	mCommerce (Mobile Commerce), Wireless Technologies	Mobile Applications for Booking
	eWOM/	Untied.com (for complaints/no more available at present)
	Social Media/generic social networks	Facebook, Instagram, Twitter, LinkedIn, Youtube, Whatsapp
	Location-based apps on mobile phones	Apps for public transportation, places to visit, weather forecast, itinerary planning/ location search (GIS/GPS)
	Teleconferencing, Online meetings (Especially following the COVID-19 pandemic)	Zoom, Skype, Microsoft Teams, Google meet, Private business software solutions
	Contactless payment	Special Credit Cards
	Digital technologies used at the front desk or online services	Robot Technology, AI (Artificial Intelligence), Chatbots (e.g. Siri, Alexa, and others), Facial recognition, Voiceover technology
	Inventions used for Digitalisation of Cultural Heritage Tourism Management, Museums, Tourism and Destination Marketing	VR (Virtual Reality), AR (Augmented Reality, XR Applications, Holograms, 3D Scanning modelling and printing, 360° photos and videos
	In-room applications at hotels	IoT (Internet of Things)
	Virtual technologies and platforms	Virtual reality, virtual meetings, delivery Apps, visual games, virtual tourism, virtual health care
2020 and ahead: hyper-connectivity & hyper-personalization	More modernised, practical, secure apps	Access to XML and JSON connectors instead of SOAP-based APIs
	Efficient messaging to send data to wearable devices	Google Glass, highly anticipated iWatch
	Booking handsfree on location in real-time	By using personal voice and a digital wallet or mobile payment system
	One step booking capabilities	Multimodal systems
	Blockchain technology (Secure sharing of digital marketing information)	Winding Tree: Elimination of Intermediaries & Commission ShoCard and SITA: Digital ID Trippki: Loyalty Program Through Blockchain
	Digital currencies (Bitcoin and others)	For investments (finance) For payment (Accepted by cheapair.com since 2013, by Expedia for accommodation payments)

Source: Compiled from multiple sources by the Authors

The era of digitalisation in the tourism and hospitality industry is described as moving from "operators" towards "aggregators" (Bennane & Haouata, 2019). As an example of a so-called *tourism data aggregator*, Cirkwi is shortly described as a specific search engine serving the e-tourism and hospitality industry. There is a system of paid membership to reach this database. It enables the professionals and entrepreneurs of the tourism industry to produce new tourism products such as the French Federation of Trekking has organised IGNRANDO, which offers alternative trekking itineraries, on their website. The data provided by tourism data aggregators is not limited to creating new itineraries. The purpose is to help the tourism professionals for proficiency in the new era of digitalisation (Pellegrin, 2018).

Perception of digitalisation's impacts may not always be positive for all the members of society. Transformational innovations may even become disruptive especially when they remove opportunities of employment for people. Artificial intelligence and robotic technology not only eliminated labour from the production line, but they also have begun to replace labour in the service industry. Many jobs in tourism and hospitality are threatened as digitalisation improve. In hotels for example, besides its advantages such as software of HR, front office, marketing, cost, accounting and management; robotic devices enabling self-check-in and out services may decrease the need for front desk personnel. The museums have already begun to serve with the audio guides, which eliminate again the job of tour guides. However, as in each industrial revolution, suppression of obsolete jobs means the birth of novel jobs that require people with new intelligence, talent, knowledge and skills. For the era of digitalisation, this can be translated or conceptualised as the need for the skilful human resource as an individual, who is specifically experienced about the tourism and hospitality profession and able to combine it with the ICT practicability.

The challenges of adopting digital technologies that tourism and hospitality businesses, especially SMEs face are given as high costs of training, costs of adopting new technologies and their uncertain ROI when compared to its benefits such as online presence and acknowledgement internationally, increase in service quality and competitiveness and visitor satisfaction (Dredge et al., 2018).

Even if the tourism and hospitality industry is considered more labour-intensive and more resistant to change, the studies show that the adoption and adaptation levels of digitalisation have increased. It is emphasized that the perceptions of the consumer change according to the presence of COVID-like precarious situations. Even though the traditional concepts such as personal human care and hospitality are always at a premium in sentimental value, especially after COVID-19, robot services were highly appreciated in terms of the qualities of reliability, efficiency, and novelty. (Kim et al., 2021).

Cyber- is a prefix used with many words like cyber-marketing, cyber-clients, cyber-security. Merriam Webster defines it as "of, relating to, or involving computers or computer networks (such as the Internet)". According to their decisional and buying processes, 'cyber clients' are categorised with such conceptions as "looker, moderate booker, booker" (Del Chiappa et al., 2016); "Serial shoppers, Internet lookers, Internet bookers" (Duthion & Mandou, 2016); "bookers, lookers" (Garín-Muñoz et al., 2020). Called online shoppers by the EC report DESI, in 2019, the people preferred mostly to buy clothes and sports goods (%65) which were followed by travel and holiday accommodation (54%), household goods (46%), tickets for events (41%), and finally books, magazines and newspapers, which were chosen by every third European (33%). Only 17% bought computer hardware, while 16% purchased medicines. People aged 25-54 were the most frequent buyers of travel and holiday accommodation (57%), household goods (52%), and tickets for events (43%) (DESI, 2020: 61). If co-creation and interconnectedness are required in the new era of digitalisation, then this chapter continues with the demand, which is the other important contributing actor. Both supply and demand sides are indeed involved in the new web of production and consumption tourism and hospitality, and they are difficult to separate, however, each single party deserves comprehensive and deeper analysis.

EVOLUTION OF DIGITALISATION IN TOURISM AND HOSPITALITY INDUSTRY- DEMAND SIDE

With digitalisation, consumer needs have changed and traditional purchasing preferences have been replaced by online consumption preferences with the "e-" prefix (e-commerce, e-purchase, etc.) (Keskin & Küçükali, 2017). The spread of digitalisation and changing consumer preferences have pushed businesses to adapt to new technologies.

Table 2. Industrial revolutions and the evolution of tourist characteristics

	Industry 1.0	Tourism 1.0	Tourist 1.0
18th Century	The first industrial society was formed with the invention of the steam engine, Mass production started with mechanization.	Tourist transportation started with the invention of steam engines, The first package tour was introduced, The first travel agency was established.	The wealthy, scientists and young nobles living in Europe started to participate in trips for educational purposes, Tourists participating in the excursions began to collect information about the places they went.
	Industry 2.0	**Tourism 2.0**	**Tourist 2.0**
20th Century	The use of mobile machinery (car, truck) has increased as oil has become an important source of energy, Mass production based on the division of labour started with electrical energy.	With the increase in the use of mobile machines, affordable travel has emerged. With the development of railway, road and sea transportation, touristic trips have increased. Modern travel guides (handbooks) released.	Many trips have taken place due to immigration. With the increase in leisure time, the middle class also started to participate in tourism activities. Demand for beach holidays has increased. Apart from tours, individual trips have started. Travelled with guidebooks. Package tour holidays preferred. Tourists created their private trips through travel agencies.
	Industry 3.0	**Tourism 3.0**	**Tourist 3.0**
The End of 20th Century	Focused not only on products but also on services, With the development of the Internet, communication between people has increased, Automation programs began to be used with the widespread use of computers, Information and communication technologies have started to develop, Usage of smart mobile phones, laptops and tablet computers.	The communication network in tourism enterprises has accelerated, The period of automation and innovation has begun, Computerized reservation networks are developed, The concept of sustainable tourism and green hotel management has emerged, Creation of Web promotion sites.	Due to the World War II, people were in displaced and when they returned, they shared own experience of the places they have been with their surroundings, There has been a trend towards different types of alternatives such as cheap package tours, cultural tourism and adventure tourism, Sustainable tourism businesses have started to be preferred, Tourists have started to demand tourism products that will show their status.
	Industry 4.0	**Tourism 4.0**	**Tourist 4.0**
Today: First Two Decades of 21st Century	Big data, the internet of things, artificial intelligence have emerged, Information technologies and digitalisation have affected the way they do business, Technological devices such as robots, transponders, tablet computers become economical in businesses.	Promotion and marketing of tourism businesses done through internet channels, Social media applications such as YouTube, Instagram, Facebook, Twitter widely used by the tourism industry, Smartphone applications developed in the tourism industry.	Social media platforms have become a useful medium for people to get ideas before their trip by interacting with other individuals who had travelled before to that destination More money is spent on experiencing new trips, Various resources are used to plan the complete tourism experience, Tourism products with social sensitivity are demanded, Mobile applications and new generation technologies actively used.

Source: Compiled by the Authors.

Nearly 3 billion people actively use social media and mobile technologies today, and mobile users tend to research every phenomenon they may encounter before they experience it (Pamukçu & Tanrısever, 2019). Digitalisation has created a change in tourist preferences and experiences as well as in the tourism industry so much so that tourists discover the places they visit through digital technologies and share their experiences in virtual environments through digital technologies (Pamukçu & Tanrısever, 2019).

The development of digitalisation increases the service expectations of tourists from tourism enterprises, and the attractiveness of the places visited is formed in line with the experiences offered by tourism enterprises to tourists. In this direction, tourism enterprises should be able to understand tourist expectations and behaviours and create experiences in line with these expectations (Hong, 2009). To better understand the change in tourist behaviour from past to present, the evolution of the tourist concept in the past should be analysed. Industrial revolutions and the changing tourist characteristics are very briefly listed for this purpose in Table 2.

New inventions and technologies that have entered human life with the Industry 1.0 and Industry 2.0 revolutions have revolutionized all industries, as well as changed human behaviour and purchasing preferences. The transition to urban life with the 1st industrial revolution has led people to leave their places of residence and explore different places (Atar, 2019). As seen in Table 1, individuals tended to travel with new technologies. The new inventions that came into our lives with the 1st Industrial Revolution have created different needs in individuals. At that time, Tourist 1.0 was mostly formed of individuals with high income and social status and tended to gather information about the places they went by travelling for educational purposes.

Digitalisation has also changed tourist characteristics. Middle-class individuals have started to participate in tourism activities that appeal to the rich class. The emergence of free time has led people to spare more time and money for themselves (Çelik, 2020). Especially with the increase in population and welfare, the demand for tourism has grown by being stimulated by consumer preferences (Sarı Çallı, 2015).

20th century perspective was not only service-oriented but also production-oriented. New technologies developing with globalization have affected almost the whole world. In the 20th century, with the development of Industry 3.0, tourists started to prefer more sustainable tourism businesses by turning to different tourism alternatives.

Tourist behaviour and expectations have completely changed with information and communication technologies and digitalisation. With Industry 4.0, it is seen that tourists benefit from technology in every area from the stage of deciding on a vacation to the feedback stage (Çakmak & Demirkol, 2017:222). Especially since the 2000s, it has been determined that tourists have completely adopted the use of the internet and used online technologies intensively in travel-related transactions (Xiang et al., 2015a). Travellers, called Tourist 4.0, first referred to the Internet to search for information (Chung & Koo, 2015).

Today, the majority of travel-related research, reservations and payments are made through digital channels. The vast majority of visitors use the internet, mobile devices and other digital technologies even during the travel period because they find it easy and accessible (Huang et al., 2017).

With the development of digital technologies, visitor travel stages have been redefined as *dreaming, researching, booking, experiencing and sharing* (World Tourism Organization 2011, Veloso et al. 2019). Tourists benefit from digital tourism technologies at every moment of their holidays. The use of travel-related websites, social media and smartphones increases progressively (Huang et al., 2017).

Mobile technologies have a direct impact on personalizing tourist experiences, as they are easy to access, ubiquitous, and facilitate travellers' access to information (Gretzel et al. 2006, Palumbo et al.

2014). Tourists state that they find smartphones useful for visiting more places and having rich experience and as a result, high satisfaction (Dan et al., 2012).

According to the study of Adobe (2014), 45% of tourists use mobile technologies to make travel reservations, 81% to search for travel destinations, 71% to compare prices, and 87% to look at maps and find directions. Tourists also tend to adopt mobile technologies for reasons such as health and safety services, transportation, location-based services, payment, ordering food (Tan et al. 2007, Okumus & Bilgihan 2014, Morosan & DeFranco 2016). Tourists find mobile technologies valuable because they reduce time and effort and can provide information (Lyu & Hwang, 2015). The fact that internet access is easy, thanks to mobile devices, enables tourists to trust and prefer tablets and smartphones (Murphy et al., 2016).

Internet-based social media technologies emerge as a platform where tourists can share their travel experiences. Information shared on social media channels is an important source of information that affects the purchasing behaviour of potential tourists (Kang & Schuett, 2013). Today, younger generations, especially generation Y tourists, prefer social media as a source of information search in their travel planning (Xiang et al., 2015b).

Tourism consumers visit social media applications 10-11 times a day the purpose of using these applications is for communication (Arat & Dursun, 2016). According to Carter (2017), 29% of tourists use Facebook, 14% use TripAdvisor, and 6% Twitter before planning their trip. Most of the tourists post vacation photos, update status and evaluate hotels on social media not only before but also after the vacation (Carter, 2017). In this case, most of the social media applications serve as a source of information for potential tourists by helping tourists to share their personal experiences with travel (Xiang & Gretzel, 2010).

Websites are one of the first platforms tourists prefer to search for information, and therefore the content of the website constitutes a critical part of the tourist decision-making process (Huang et al. 2017). Tourists prefer websites because of the ease of obtaining detailed information, comparing alternatives, booking and payment (Sarı, 2003). The travel preferences of tourists are shaped according to the price, transportation, accommodation, promotional photos, ratings and comments on the websites as shows a study (Çiçek et al., 2013). Therefore, the beneficial perception of a website by tourists encourages the visits to that destination, and website reviews provide strategic benefits such as customer retention, positive return on investment and competitive leadership (Romanazzi et al., 2011).

Generations X, Y (Millenials) and Z (iGen/Gen Z): Tourist Behavior in the Digital Age

The age range of the generations vary and they are approximate, despite the existence of academic studies on this field. The important issue is their common characteristics towards the use of digitalisation in the tourism and hospitality industry market. In addition, according to social sciences, it is possible to collect generations that are suitable for travel in four groups: Baby Boomers, Generation X, Generation Y and Generation Z (Szromek et al. 2019, Dolot 2018).

The baby boom generation travels to various parts of the world due to their social position, financial opportunities and more leisure time (Hysa et al., 2021). In addition, the main reasons for holiday preferences are; having fun, enjoying travelling, needing change and increasing their motivation (Naidoo et al., 2015). In terms of technology use, Boomers use computers to plan their trips and make reservations, and 70% of them actively use smartphones in their travels (Mullis, 2018). Tourists in this generation keep their smartphones with them to communicate, take pictures, discover new restaurants and different activities. Moreover, 80% of Boomers record their vacation memories and share them digitally via text message, Facebook and digital photo albums (www.aarp.org). Today, 60% of Baby Boomers stated that they appreciate travel brands' digital applications (online check-in, room entry via smartphone instead of a key, etc.) and that these applications affect their purchasing decisions and the quality of their travel experience (Reed, 2019). In addition, 72% of Baby Boomers conduct travel research through online travel agencies (OTA) (Vivion, 2016).

The children of Baby Boomers form Generation X. The oldest today considered to be 56, individuals of generation X (Williams & Page 2011, McCrindle 2018) were affected negatively by the political conflicts and economic restructuring but grew up in a peaceful world (Dabija et al. 2018, Çöp et al. 2020). This generation, who cares about work-life balance, is eager to visit new places and are interested in cultural activities. 71% of Generation X prefer to participate in different activities and 70% prefer museums, historical places, art and cultural trips (Skift, 2019). Generation X tourists make value-oriented shopping because their needs are intense but financially limited, and they look at travel advisors, discount prices and packages when purchasing a tourism product (Benckendorff et al., 2010). They usually travel with their families and therefore they are cautious about risks and crises (Peltomäk, 2015). From the digitalization point of view, these people are known as individuals who were born in the period when technology was developed and the internet was first used (Engizek & Sekerkaya, 2016). For this reason, Generation X individuals partially dominate today's technologies (Karakan, 2020). OTAs, tourist reviews and digital applications are effective in the purchasing decisions of 71% of Generation X (Vivion, 2016). Apart from this, the travel opportunities in the Facebook application is the most effective (with 70%) among all other social media platforms for generation X (Reed, 2019).

While making a travel plan, they do their research according to the reviews of other tourists and the informative content of the brands. They generally prefer hotels and resorts and can spend a third of their budget on them (Mullis, 2018). Tourists in this generation are very adaptable to modern digital technologies, so they do not hesitate to use digital technologies when planning their travels (Hysa et al., 2021).

The next generation, the Generation Y individuals are those who grew up with technology, can take risks, are extroverted, entrepreneurs, impatient and open to development (Karakan, 2020). The beginning of this generation is associated with the development of digital technologies and their widespread use globally. These individuals, who are highly dependent on digital technologies, are also called Millennials, GenNext, net Generation, GenMe, Google generation and Digital generation (Luttrell & McGrath, 2015). Millennials are extremely active and willing to travel to different places (Hysa et al., 2021). They usually make their travel plans based on online reviews (Sweetescape, 2019). The individuals of this generation support apps such as TripAdvisor, Yelp, Expedia, Google Maps, Hotels.com, etc. (Starĉević & Konjikušić, 2018), receive advice from social networks such as Facebook, Twitter, Instagram and Pinterest (Future Foundation, 2016) and share their travel experiences via those networks (Karakan, 2020).

Generation Z, which is accepted to have been born after 1995 (Seemiller, 2017; Cilliers, 2017), stands out with their hedonistic behaviours and adaptation to technology, depending on the period they were born (Kon, 2017). Driven by the ICT, the internet and social media, their demands and consumption habits differ from other generations (Haddouche and Salomone, 2018: 69). Generation Z is open to innovations and eager to explore new places, not just technology. Since they are not in the business professionally yet, they undertake various touristic activities even if they are lacking in financial matters (Hysa et al., 2021).

Generation Z individuals are called "digital natives" because they adopt technology at an early age. Studies have shown that 64% of Generation Z are constantly online, and 57% do not feel safe when they do not have a mobile phone. In addition, Generation Z travellers influence family travel decisions, choose destinations through their social media accounts, and interact with their smartphones during the journey (European Travel Commission 2020, Thinkdigital 2020).

Finally, we have to emphasize that similar to the approximation of their age ranges, the travel behaviours of the different generations can vary according to the different cultures and localisations. Even if digitalisation has created virtual networking and the availability of a huge amount of data, deeper demand analysis is always a need. Here, we have focused only on some common characteristics of them from the perspective of travel behaviours.

Neuromarketing and Tourism

Neuromarketing has emerged as a combination of marketing and neuroscience. The purpose of neuroscience is to understand deeply the functioning of the human brain. Neuromarketing is a new field of consumer research and marketing that uses the latest technologies to examine the neurophysiological processes that occur when making individual decisions (Tanasic, 2017). This concept is a marketing method based on measuring parameters such as where consumers pay attention to their purchasing behaviour, what they are afraid of, what they love, the advertisement they watch or how much of the picture they see is remembered (Yücel & Coşkun, 2018).

The concept of neuromarketing has become a topic of interest for tourism researchers in the early 2010s. While some researchers have studied tourism and neuroscience conceptually, some researchers have conducted tourism research with different neuroscience methods. Some tourism researchers have used the concept of neurotourism (Sop, 2018). In this context, neurotourism is a discipline that combines neuroscience and tourism. Within the science of management, tourism management is a traditional discipline and recreational activities contribute greatly to economic development (Giudici et al., 2017). The concept of neurotourism is a concept that has emerged to investigate tourist behaviour with neural methods and in addition to understanding the decision-making processes of tourists and tries to understand the reasons for satisfaction and loyalty of tourists (Özdemir Akgül & Sezgin, 2019).

Boz (2015), investigated the emotional causes and consequences of tourists' purchasing behaviour in accommodation establishments in terms of psychoneurobiochemicals. He prepared 30 different holiday package advertisements with different discounts and visuals in his study. He examined the purchasing and decision-making processes of tourists with techniques such as eye-tracking, EEG, HR and GSR. For example, eye-tracking technique was used in the case of the first holiday package advertisement. Results of the study show that the points gathering the most attention are the article with 50% discount in case of payment in advance. As a result, the discount rate rather than the discount amount attracted more attention. Also, men focused on the discounted areas more than women, while women pay more attention to articles promoting holiday packages. Finally, the study concluded that discounts on touristic products have a serious emotional impact on purchasing and preference.

Hernández-Méndez & Muñoz-Leiva (2015), used eye-tracking method, which is one of the neuromarketing techniques, to determine the effectiveness of online advertising on tourists in the tourism and hospitality industry. Facebook, Tripadvisor and blog ads were shown to the participants. As a result of the research, the participants focused on the pictures rather than the texts on the poster, because, famous people were included in the advertisement poster. Apart from this, regarding the variables of classification, comparing participants' time to hang on the banner, gender, experience level and type of advertisement there were no significant differences.

A study on perception of pricing of the holidays of different travel websites showed that tourists do not pay attention to the website logo, they mostly focus on the discount text, then focus on the areas that promote the hotel and the areas containing the search engine (Boz et al., 2017).

Another study using the eye-tracking method for testing the decision-making processes of tourists for choosing among web pages of different hotel groups suggested that limiting the use of text (about price, location) and using more visuals on web pages can maximize the overall user experience (Pan & Zhang, 2016).

CONCLUSION

"It is not the strongest of the species to survive, nor the most intelligent but, the one most responsive to change".

Charles Darwin

The collaborative efforts of governments and the private sector for the interconnected digitalisation and sustainability goals of tourism shape the new global tourism. The training and education for new tourism jobs require knowledge of the industry and digital ICT skills simultaneously. World Tourism Organization (2019: 15) emphasizes the importance of education and labour relations for adapting to digitalisation in tourism, reporting that, today's skills will not match the jobs of tomorrow and newly acquired skills may quickly become obsolete.

The Digital web of marketing and the presence of tourism is another important area to challenge businesses. The need for deeper research analysing diverging demand and its personalization urges the tourism and hospitality industry.

Finally, the survival of tourism and hospitality businesses depend on their qualified human resources having both ICT and tourism expertise, their assertive presence through the web of the digital world, the practicality of the mobile services they offer and their escalatory brand reputation through the supportive user-generated content.

FUTURE RESEARCH DIRECTIONS

As digitalisation in tourism and hospitality industry develops, the concern for hyper-personalisation increase. Specific targets may be analysed for understanding the demand and propose digital marketing solutions. Especially the 'more-digital-ever' generation; 'The Gen Alpha' is the closest client of the tourism and hospitality industry for the future research directions.

Another promising research area is the AI & HI relationship and interaction. In June 2021, China has paid wages for the first time with digital yen. The digital currency, finance and tourism industry is another research area.

Additionally, multidisciplinary studies including both tourism and ICT expertise such as neuro-tourism are expected to bring valuable results.

REFERENCES

Adobe. (2014). *2014 Mobile Consumer Survey Results*. https://www.mycustomer.com/sites/default/files/attachments/Adobe%20mobile_survey_report_ie%5B1%5D%5B1%5D.pdf

Arat, T., & Dursun, G. (2016). Seyahat ve Konaklama Tercihi Açısından Sosyal Paylaşım Sitelerinin Kullanımı. *Selçuk Üniversitesi Sosyal Bilimler Meslek Yüksekokulu Dergisi, 19*(41), 112-128.

Atar, A. (2019). Dijital Dönüşüm ve Turizme Etkileri. M. Sezgin, S. Özdemir Akgül, & A. Atar. In *Turizm 4.0 (Dijital Dönüşüm)* (pp. 100–111). Detay.

Bahar, M., Yüzbaşıoğlu, N., & Topsakal, Y. (2019). Akıllı Turizm ve Süper Akıllı Turist Kavramları Işığında Geleceğin Turizm Rehberliğine Bakış. *Journal of Travel and Tourism Research, 14*, 72–93.

Benckendorff, P., Moscardo, G., & Pendergast, D. (2010). *Tourism and Generation Y*. CABI Publishing.

Bennane, Y., & Haouata, S. (2019, April). L'industrie touristique en évolution: De l'ère des opérateurs à l'ère des agrégateurs touristiques. In *Congrès international sur le tourisme et le développement durable*. Destinations et Produits Touristiques, Compétitivité et Innovation.

Boes, K., Buhalis, D., & Inversini, A. (2016). Smart tourism destinations: Ecosystems for tourism destination competitiveness. *International Journal of Tourism Cities, 2*(2), 108–124. doi:10.1108/IJTC-12-2015-0032

Boffey, D. (2021). *3D printing: Dutch couple become Europe's first inhabitants of a 3D-printed house*. https://www.theguardian.com/technology/2021/apr/30/dutch-couple-move-into-europe-first-fully-3d-printed-house-eindhoven

Boz, H. (2015). *Balıkesir Üniversitesi Sosyal Bilimler Enstitüsü Anabilim Dalı. In Turistik ürün satın alma karar sürecinde itkiselliğin rolü: Psikonörobiyokimyasal analiz*. Doktora Tezi.

Boz, H., Arslan, A., & Koç, E. (2017). Neuromarketing aspect of tourısm pricing psychology. *Tourism Management Perspectives, 23*, 119–128. doi:10.1016/j.tmp.2017.06.002

Brennen, J. S., & Kreiss, D. (2016). Digitalisation. *The international encyclopedia of communication theory and philosophy*, 1-11.

Buhalis, D. (2000). Tourism and Information Technologies: Past, Present and Future. *Tourism Recreation Research, 25*(1), 41–58. doi:10.1080/02508281.2000.11014899

Buhalis, D., & Amaranggana, A. (2014). Smart tourism destinations enhancing tourism experience through personalisation of services. In I. Tussyadiah & A. Inversini (Eds.), *Information and communication technologies in tourism 2015* (pp. 377–389). Springer.

Buhalis, D., & Law, R. (2008). Progress in information technology and tourism management: 20 years on and 10 years after the internet-the state of etourism research. *Tourism Management, 29*(4), 609–623. doi:10.1016/j.tourman.2008.01.005

Buhalis, D., & O'Connor, P. (2005). Information Communication Technology Revolutionizing Tourism. *Tourism Recreation Research, 30*(3), 7–16. doi:10.1080/02508281.2005.11081482

Çakmak, T. F., & Demirkol, Ş. (2017). Teknolojik Gelişmelerin Turist Rehberliği Mesleğine Etkileri Üzerine Bir Swot Analizi. *Bingöl Üniversitesi Sosyal Bilimler Enstitüsü Dergisi, 7,* 221-235.

Carter, E. (2017). *Social Media, Mobile, and Travel: Like, Tweet, and Share Your Way Across the Globe.* https://www.webfx.com/blog/social-media/social-media-mobile-travel/

Çelik, E. (2020). Osmanlı Topraklarına Yeni Bir Gezi Türü: 19. ve 20. Yüzyılda Cruise Gezileri. *Cumhuriyet Tarihi Araştırmaları Dergisi, 16*(32), 401–430.

Chung, N., & Koo, C. (2015). The Use of Social Media in Travel Information Search. *Telematics and Informatics, 32*(2), 215–229. doi:10.1016/j.tele.2014.08.005

Çiçek, E., Pala, U., & Özcan, S. (2013). Destinasyon Tercihlerinde Web Sitelerinin Önemi: Yerli Turistler Üzerine Bir Araştırma. *Sosyoteknik Sosyal ve Teknik Araştırmalar Dergisi, 3*(5), 1–14.

Cilliers, E. J. (2017). The Challange of Teaching Generation Z. *The International Journal of Social Sciences (Islamabad), 3*(1), 188–198.

Cleverciti. (2021). *9 European smart tourism destinations to watch and learn from.* https://www.cleverciti.com/en/resources/blog/9-european-smart-tourism-destinations-to-watch-and-learn-from

Çöp, S., İbiş, S., & Kızıldemir, Ö. (2020). Seyahat Motivasyonlarının X, Y ve Z Kuşaklarına Göre Farklılıklarının İncelenmesi Üzerine Bir Araştırma. *Uluslararası Toplum Araştırmaları Dergisi, 16*(30), 2530–2550.

Dabija, D.-C., Bejan, B. M., & Tipi, N. (2018). Generation X Versus Millenials Communication Behaviour on Social Media When Purchasing Food Versus Tourist Services. *Ekonomie a Management, 21*(1), 191–205. doi:10.15240/tul/001/2018-1-013

Dan, W., Park, S., & Fesenmaier, D. R. (2012). The Role of Smartphones in Mediating the Touristic Experience. *Journal of Travel Research, 51*(4), 371–387. doi:10.1177/0047287511426341

de l'Architecture, C. (2021). *Visite de la grotte de Lascaux 1/1, le jumeau virtuel À partir du 8 juillet 2021.* https://www.citedelarchitecture.fr/fr/evenement/visite-de-la-grotte-de-lascaux-11-le-jumeau-virtuel

Del Chiappa, G., Alarcón-Del-Amo, M.-D.-C., & Lorenzo-Romero, C. (2016). Internet and User-Generated Content Versus High Street Travel Agencies: A Latent Gold Segmentation in the Context of Italy. *Journal of Hospitality Marketing & Management, 25*(2), 197–217. doi:10.1080/19368623.2014.1001933

Del Chiappa, G., & Baggio, R. (2015). Knowledge transfer in smart tourism destinations: Analyzing the effects of a network structure. *Journal of Destination Marketing & Management, 4*(3), 145–150. doi:10.1016/j.jdmm.2015.02.001

DESI. (2020). *European Commission, Digital Economy and Society Index Thematic Chapters.* https://innogrowth.org/wp-content/uploads/2020/07/DESI-2020.pdf

Dolot, A. (2018). *The Characteristics of Generation Z. E-mentor.* Warsaw School of Economics.

Dredge, D., Phi, G., Mahadevan, R., Meehan, E., & Popescu, E. S. (2018). *Digitalisation in Tourism: In-depth analysis of challenges and opportunities. Virtual Tourism Observatory.* Aalborg University.

Duthion, B., & Mandou, C. (2016). *L'innovation dans le tourisme: culture numérique et nouveaux modes de vie*. De Boeck Supérieur.

EC. (2021). *European Commission, European Capitals of Smart Tourism*. https://smart-tourism-capital. ec.europa.eu/european-capitals-smart-tourism_en#about-the-award

Emerald Publishing. (2020). *Driverless cars and their impact on our future*. https://www.emeraldgroup-publishing.com/opinion-and-blog/driverless-cars-and-their-impact-our-future

Endüstri40. (2019). *Endüstri Mitleri ve Kavram Yanılgıları*. https://www.endustri40.com/endustri-4-0-mitleri-ve-kavram-yanilgilari/

Engizek, N., & Sekerkaya, A. (2016). X ve Y Kuşak Kadınlarının Karar Verme Tarzları Bakımından İncelenmesi. *Mustafa Kemal Üniversitesi Sosyal Bilimler Enstitüsü Dergisi*, *13*, 242–271.

EU (2019). *Initiative of European Capital of Smart Tourism. Guide for Applicants*. SmartTourismCapital.eu

EU (2020). *Compendium of Best Practices '2019-2020 European Capital of Smart Tourism Competitions'*. Report commissioned by European Union and prepared by Scholz & Friends Agenda Berlin GmbH European Office.

European Travel Commission. (2020). *Study on Generation Z Travellers*. Brussel: ETC Market Intelligence.

Future Foundation. (2016). *Millennial Traveller Report: Why Millennials Will Shape*. https://www. thinktur.org/media/Expedia-Millennial-Traveller-Report.pdf

Garín-Muñoz, T., Perez-Amaral, T., & Lopez, R. (2020). Consumer engagement in e-Tourism: Micro-panel data models for the case of Spain. *Tourism Economics*, *26*(6), 853–872. doi:10.1177/1354816619852880

Giudici, E., Dettori, A., & Caboni, F. (2017). Neurotourism: Futuristic Perspective or Today's Reality? In *20th Excellence in Services International Conference* (pp. 335-346). Academic Press.

Gonzalez, R., Gasco, J., & Llopis, J. (2019). ICTs in hotel management: A research review. *International Journal of Contemporary Hospitality Management*, *31*(9), 3583–3609. doi:10.1108/IJCHM-07-2017-0470

Gretzel, U., Fesenmaier, D. R., & O'Leary, J. T. (2006). The Transformation of Consumer Behaviour. D. Buhalis, & C. Costa. In *Tourism Business Frontier* (pp. 1–18). Elsevier. doi:10.1016/B978-0-7506-6377-9.50009-2

Gretzel, U., Fuchs, M., Baggio, R., Hoepken, W., Law, R., & Neidhardt, J. (2020). e-Tourism Beyond COVID-19: A call for transformative research. *Journal of Information Technology & Tourism*, *43*, 1–21.

Gretzel, U., & Jamal, T. (2009). Conceptualizing the creative tourist class: Technology, mobility, and tourism experiences. *Tourism Analysis*, *14*(4), 471–481. doi:10.3727/108354209X12596287114219

Gülmez, M., Kavacık, S. Z., Kaçmaz, Y. Y., & Özyurt, P. M. (2014). Turistlerin Turizme Yönelik İnternet Kullanım Alışkanlıkları Üzerine Bir Araştırma. *Turizm ve Araştırma Dergisi*, *3*(1), 5–18.

Haddouche, H., & Salomone, C. (2018). Generation Z And The Tourist Experience: Tourist Stories And Use Of Social Networks. *Journal of Tourism Futures*, *4*(1), 69–79. doi:10.1108/JTF-12-2017-0059

Hernández-Méndez, J., & Muñoz-Leiva, F. (2015). What type of online advertising is most effective for eTourism 2.0? An eye tracking study based on the characteristics of tourists. *Computers in Human Behavior, 50*, 618–625. doi:10.1016/j.chb.2015.03.017

Hong, W.-C. (2009). Global Competitiveness Measurement for the Tourism Sector. *Current Issues in Tourism, 12*(2), 105–132. doi:10.1080/13683500802596359

Huang, C. D., Goo, J., Nam, K., & Yoo, C. W. (2017). Smart Tourism Technologies in Travel Planning: The Role of Exploration. *Information & Management, 54*(6), 757–770. doi:10.1016/j.im.2016.11.010

Hysa, B., Karasek, A., & Zdonek, I. (2021). Social Media Usage by Different Generations as a Tool for Sustainable Tourism Marketing in Society 5.0 Idea. *Sustainability, 13*(3), 2–27. doi:10.3390u13031018

Ip, C., Leung, R., & Law, R. (2011). Progress and development of information and communication technologies in hospitality. *International Journal of Contemporary Hospitality Management, 23*(4), 533–551. doi:10.1108/09596111111130029

Ivars-Baidal, J. A., Celdrán-Bernabeu, M. A., Femenia-Serra, F., Perles-Ribes, J. F., & Giner-Sánchez, D. (2021). Measuring the progress of smart destinations: The use of indicators as a management tool. *Journal of Destination Marketing & Management, 19*, 100531. doi:10.1016/j.jdmm.2020.100531

Jeong, M., Lee, M., & Nagesvaran, B. (2016). Employees' use of mobile devices and their perceived outcomes in the workplace: A case of luxury hotel. *International Journal of Hospitality Management, 57*, 40–51. doi:10.1016/j.ijhm.2016.05.003

Johnson, A. G., Rickly, J. M., & McCabe, S. (2021). Smartmentality in Ljubljana. *Annals of Tourism Research, 86*, 103094. doi:10.1016/j.annals.2020.103094

Kang, M., & Schuett, M. A. (2013). Determinants Of Sharing Travel Experiences in Social Media. *Journal of Travel & Tourism Marketing, 30*(1-2), 93–107. doi:10.1080/10548408.2013.751237

Karakan, H. İ. (2020). Y Kuşağı ve Turizm. Ç. Ertaş, & B. Kanca. In *Turizmin Geleceği: Yeni Deneyimler* (pp. 33–52). Detay.

Keskin, K., & Küçükali, U. F. (2017). Sanallaşmanın Toplum Hayatına Etkileri. *İnsan ve Toplum Bilimleri Araştırmaları Dergisi, 6*(1), 396-418.

Khanzode, C. A., & Sarode, R. (2016). Evolution of the world wide web: from web 1.0 to 6.0. *International Journal of Digital Library Services, 6*(2), 1-11.

Kim, S. S., Kim, J., Badu-Baiden, F., Giroux, M., & Choi, Y. (2021). Preference for robot service or human service in hotels? Impacts of the COVID-19 pandemic. *International Journal of Hospitality Management, 93*, 102795. doi:10.1016/j.ijhm.2020.102795

Kon, B. (2017). *Humanica. Kuşakları Anlamak ve Yönetmek.* https://www.humanica.com.tr/kusaklari-anlamak-yonetmek/

Król, K. (2020). Evolution of online mapping: From Web 1.0 to Web 6.0. *Geomatics, Landmanagement and Landscape, 1*, 33–51. doi:10.15576/GLL/2020.1.33

Law, R., Buhalis, D., & Cobanoglu, C. (2014). Progress on information and communication technologies in hospitality and tourism. *International Journal of Contemporary Hospitality Management, 26*(5), 727–750. doi:10.1108/IJCHM-08-2013-0367

Law, R., Leung, R., & Buhalis, D. (2009). Information technology applications in hospitality and tourism: A review of publications from 2005-2007. *Journal of Travel & Tourism Marketing, 26*(5/6), 599–623. doi:10.1080/10548400903163160

LeHub. (2017): *Connaisses-vous la nouvelle définition du marketing?* https://lehub.laposte.fr/dossiers/connaissez-vous-nouvelle-definition-marketing

Leung, R., & Law, R. (2005). An analysis of information technology publications in leading hospitality journals. *FIU Hospitality Review, 23*(2), 55–65.

Li, J., Xu, L., Tang, L., Wang, S., & Li, L. (2018). Big data in tourism research: A literature review. *Tourism Management, 68*, 301–323. doi:10.1016/j.tourman.2018.03.009

Luttrell, R., & McGrath, K. (2015). Millenials: Who are they? Where have they been? Where are they going? In *The Millenial Mindset: Unraveling Fact From Fiction* (pp. 3–21). Rowman & Littlefield.

Lyu, S., & Hwang, J. (2015). Are The Days of Tourist Information Centers Gone? Effects of the Ubiquitous Information Environment. *Tourism Management, 48*, 54–63. doi:10.1016/j.tourman.2014.11.001

McCrindle, M. (2018). *The ABC of XYZ: Understanding the Global Generations*. McCrindle Research.

Morosan, C., & DeFranco, A. (2016). It's About Time: Revisiting UTAUT2 to Examine Consumers' Intentions to Use NFC Mobile Payments in Hotels. *International Journal of Hospitality Management, 53*, 17–29. doi:10.1016/j.ijhm.2015.11.003

Mullis, M. (2018). *Generational Travel Differences: 4 Insights And 4 Surprises*. https://www.wexinc.com/insights/blog/wex-travel/generational-travel-differences/

Murphy, H. C., Chen, M.-M., & Cossutta, M. (2016). An Investigation of Multiple Devices and Information Sources Used in the Hotel Booking Process. *Tourism Management, 52*, 44–51. doi:10.1016/j.tourman.2015.06.004

Naidoo, P., Ramseook-Munhurrun, P., Seebaluck, N., & Janvier, S. (2015). Investigating the Motivation of Baby Boomers For Adventure Tourism. *Social and Behavioral Sciences, 175*, 254–251. doi:10.1016/j.sbspro.2015.01.1197

Noone, B., & Robson, S. (2014). Using Eye Tracking to Obtain a Deeper Understanding of What Drives Online Hotel Choice. *Cornell Hospitality Report, 14*(18). www.chr.cornell.edu

OECD. (2020). *OECD Tourism Trends and Policies 2020, Chapter 2, Preparing tourism services for the digital future*. https://www.oecd-ilibrary.org/sites/f528d444-en/index.html?itemId=/content/component/f528d444-en

Okumus, B., & Bilgihan, A. (2014). Proposing a Model to Test Smartphone Users' Intention to Use Smart Applications When Ordering Food in Restaurants. *Journal of Hospitality and Tourism Technology, 5*(1), 31–49. doi:10.1108/JHTT-01-2013-0003

Özdemir Akgül, S., & Sezgin, M. (2019). Konaklama İşletmelerinde Yeni Bir Yaklaşım Nöroturizm: Yerli ve Yabancı Turist Algısı Üzerine Bir Araştırma. *Journal of Recreation and Tourism Research*, 70-80.

Palumbo, F., Dominici, G., & Basile, G. (2014). The Culture on the Palm of Your Hand: How to Design a User Oriented Mobile App for Museums. In Management of cultural products: e-relationship marketing and accessibility perspectives (pp. 224-243). IGI Global.

Pamukçu, H., & Tanrısever, C. (2019). Turizm Endüstrisinde Dijital Dönüşüm. M. Sezgin, S. Özdemir Akgül, & A. Atar. In *Turizm 4.0 (Dijital Dönüşüm)* (pp. 2–22). Detay.

Pan, B., & Zhang, L. (2016). An Eyetracking Study on Online Hotel Decision Making: The Effects of Images and Umber of Options. *Travel and Tourism Research Association: Advancing Tourism Research Globally, 27*.

Patin, S. (2020). *Les enjeux du numérique en sciences sociales et humaines: vers un Homo numericus?* https://hal.archives-ouvertes.fr/hal-03173567

Pellegrin, H. (2018). *Cirkwi: L'agrégateur de données spécifiques au Tourisme.* https://www.tom.travel/2018/03/07/cirkwi-lagregateur-de-donnees-specifiques-tourisme/

Peltomäk, S. M. (2015). *Crises in the Tourism Industry and Their Effects on Different* (Master Thesis). HAAGA-HELIA University of Applied Sciences.

Pérez, Y. P., & Barreiro, D. B. (2019). Using big data to measure tourist sustainability: Myth or reality? *Sustainability, 11*(20).

Rascouet, A. (2019). *French 'Flying Man' Succeeds in Cross-Channel Attempt.* https://www.bloomberg.com/news/articles/2019-08-04/french-flying-man-finally-succeeds-in-cross-channel-attempt

Reed, D. (2019). *Most Travelers, Including Baby Boomers, Are Cool With Digital Travel Technology, But Younger Ones Crave More.* https://www.forbes.com/sites/danielreed/2019/11/05/a-large-majority-of-travelers-including-baby-boomers-are-cool-with-digital-travel-technology-but-younger-travelers-crave-even-more/?sh=4740dfdc22d0

Revfine. (2019). *Key Digital Trends in the Hospitality Industry.* https://www.revfine.com/digital-trends-hospitality-industry/

Romanazzi, S., Petruzzellis, L., & Iannuzzi, E. (2011). "Click & experience. Just virtually there." The Effect of a Destination Website on Tourist Choice: Evidence from Italy. *Journal of Hospitality Marketing & Management, 20*(7), 791–813. doi:10.1080/19368623.2011.605037

Ruel, H., & Njoku, E. (2020). AI redefining the hospitality industry. *Journal of Tourism Futures*.

Sarı, Y. (2003). *Bölgesel Düzeyde Hazırlanan Web Sitelerinin Turizm Talebine Etkisinin Araştırılması: Muğla Bölgesinde Bir Uygulama. Doktora Tezi.* Muğla Üniversitesi, Sosyal Bilimler Enstitüsü, İktisat Ana Bilim Dalı.

Sarı, Y., & Kozak, M. (2005). Turizm Pazarlamasında İnternetin Etkisi: Destinasyon Web Siteleri İçin Bir Model Önerisi. *Akdeniz İ.İ.B.F. Dergisi, 9*, 248–27.

Sarı Çallı, D. (2015). Uluslararası Seyahatlerin Tarihi Gelişimi ve Son Seyehat Trendleri Doğrultusunda Türkiye'nin Konumu. *Turizm ve Araştırma Dergisi*, *4*(1), 5–28.

Seemiller, G. (2017). *Generation Z: Educating and Engaging the Next Generation of Students.* https://journals.sagepub.com/doi/pdf/10.1002/abc.21293

Shell. (2021). *Video ads of Shell Oil Company in Turkey for sustainable contactless technologies.* https://www.shell.com.tr/suruculer/engin-akyurek-shellde-kalitesinin-verdigi-guvenle-shell-hep-ileride.html

Skift. (2019). *Travel Marketing Across Generations in 2020: Reaching Gen Z, Gen X, Millennials, and Baby Boomers.* https://skift.com/2019/12/11/travel-marketing-across-generations-in-2020-reaching-gen-z-gen-x-millennials-and-baby-boomers/

Sop, S. A. (2018). Nöropazarlama Yaklaşımının Turizm Araştırmalarındaki Konumu Üzerine Kavramsal Bir Değerlendirme. In *The Second International Congress on Future of Tourism Innovation, Entrepreneurship and Sustainability* (pp. 318-324). Mersin: Mersin Üniversitesi Yayınları.

Starĉević, S., & Konjikušić, S. (2018). Why Millenials as Digital Travelers Transformed Marketing Strategy in Tourism Industry. In *The Third International Scientific Conference, Tourism in Function of Development of the Republic of Serbia: Tourism in the Era of Digital Transformation* (pp. 221-240). Vrnjačka Banja.

Sweetescape. (2019). *Gen X, Millennials, and Gen Z: Travel Habits of the Generations.* https://www.sweetescape.com/en/blog/ideas/travel-habits

Szromek, A. R., Hysa, B., & Karasek, A. (2019). The Perception of Overtourism from the Perspective. *Sustainability*, *11*(24), 2–19. doi:10.3390u11247151

Tan, E. M.-Y., Goh, D. H.-L., Theng, Y.-L., & Foo, S. (2007). An Analysis of Services for the Mobile Tourist. In *The International Conference on Mobile Technology, Applications and Systems* (pp. 490-494). 10.1145/1378063.1378142

Tanasic, B. R. (2017). Impact of Sensory Branding On The Decision-Making Process of Tourism Product Purchase. *Journal of Research in Engineering and Innovation,* 109-125.

Taş, M., Akkaşoğlu, S., & Akyol, C. (2018). Turizm İşletmelerinde Bilgi Sistemi Kullanımı Kapsamında Seyahat Acentesi Web Sitelerinin İncelenmesi. *Akademik Bakış Dergisi*, 207-221.

Thinkdigital. (2020). https://www.thinkdigital.travel/talking-to-gen-z/

Veloso, B., Leal, F., Malheiro, B., & Burguillo, J. C. (2019). On-line Guest Profiling and Hotel Recommendation. *Electronic Commerce Research and Applications*, *34*, 2–33. doi:10.1016/j.elerap.2019.100832

Vivion, N. (2016). *What stats reveal about travel behaviors by generation.* https://www.sabre.com/insights/what-stats-reveal-about-travel-behaviors-by-generation/

Williams, K. C., & Page, R. A. (2011). Marketing to the Generations. *Journal of Behavioral Studies in Businesses*, *3*(1), 36–53.

World Tourism Organization. (2011). *Technology in Tourism.* https://www.e-unwto.org/doi/pdf/10.18111/9789284414567

World Tourism Organization. (2019). *The Future of Work and Skills Development in Tourism – Policy Paper*. UNWTO.

Xiang, Z., Dan, W., O'Leary, J., & Fesenmaier, D. R. (2015a). Adapting to the Internet: Trends in Travelers' Use of the Web for Trip Planning. *Journal of Travel Research, 54*(4), 511–527. doi:10.1177/0047287514522883

Xiang, Z., & Gretzel, U. (2010). Role of Social Media in Online Travel Information Search. *Tourism Management, 31*(2), 179–188. doi:10.1016/j.tourman.2009.02.016

Xiang, Z., Magnini, V. P., & Fesenmaier, D. R. (2015b). Information Technology and Consumer Behavior in Travel and Tourism: Insights From Travel Planning Using the Internet. *Journal of Retailing and Consumer Services, 22*, 244–249. doi:10.1016/j.jretconser.2014.08.005

Yücel, A., & Coşkun, P. (2018). Nöropazarlama Literatür İncelemesi. *Fırat Üniversitesi Sosyal Bilimler Dergisi*, 157-177.

KEY TERMS AND DEFINITIONS

AI (Artificial Intelligence): The intelligent software of the digital era approaching human intelligence and used for digital touristic services such as robots, chatbots, (facial) recognition technologies and expected to continue inventing superior digital services.

Chatbots: The online and mobile services that give the impression of being similar to human with their voice and/or visual appearance and mimics, which is developed by the AI.

Digital Generation: The new generation of individuals born in the technological age, well-educated and familiar with digital applications.

E-Tourism: The virtual platform of the operational area of the tourism industry in the digital era.

IoT (Internet of Things): The digital systems enabling connectivity of devices to control the sustainability inside living areas such as energy-saving and security by smart systems.

Neurotourism: Adapting the methods used in neuroscience to tourism industry marketing research.

Smart Tourism: The digital interconnectedness of all the web of the tourism industry including activities, resources, actors and e-tourism products and services in a selectively and specifically targeted way.

User-Generated Content: The experiences and comments of e-tourists streaming through digital media channels.

ENDNOTE

[1]   The related video on revfine is jitter after certain minutes; it is fully available on https://vimeo.com/179645420

Chapter 4

Intelligent Technology and Automation in Hospitality:
The Case of Four- and Five-Star Units Operating in Portugal

Hussein Salimo Jamal

Estoril Higher Institute for Tourism and Hotel Studies, Portugal

ABSTRACT

Based on the growing evolution of intelligent technology and automation in the provision of services, this chapter analyzes its incorporation into the 4- and 5-star national hotels and its consequent impact on decision and consumer choice. In this sense, the authors proceeded to characterize the technologies with greater appetence concerning the reality of the hotel industry. Furthermore, they investigated the appreciation made by the guests, researched trends, advantages, inconveniences, changes in behavior and procedures, given the COVID-19 pandemic.

INTRODUCTION

Creating value in hotels implies anticipating guests' needs, meeting them and assertively taking advantage of the potential of new technologies (Ivanovv et al., 2017). In this sense, the new technological wave based on the potential of the fifth generation (5G) and the analysis of emotional data raises the possibilities of technology to a different level, but also generates new challenges on the creation of experiences, the use and privacy of data, which the hotel industry cannot ignore (Zsarnoczky, 2017).

Innovating, regardless of the scope of innovation, creates differences between those who innovate and those who do not, and this difference is only profitable if the market values it. This aspect is critical considering that the Internet of Everything (IoE) will continue to reinvent industries, but if some technologies in terms of acceptance by guests are peaceful and even a requirement, others such as robots, artificial intelligence, biometrics, or autonomous vehicles, are still controversial (Lukanova & Galina, 2019). Many of the fears and criticisms presented result from the lack of knowledge about the possibilities of technologies, namely, about automation and artificial intelligence, and focus on replac-

DOI: 10.4018/978-1-7998-8306-7.ch004

ing workstations with machines or the possibility of misuse of data. Regardless of the type of fear, 5G exponentially increases the amount of data connected (Dahlman, 2018). This fifth generation of mobile network technology is presented as two hundred times faster than the fourth generation (4G), with a much shorter latency period, an extremely high-reliability rate and capacity for one million devices per square kilometer. In addition to the promise of speed, strength, reliability and intelligence, the fifth generation's most significant impact is expected to be on the devices' ubiquitous connectivity. It is essential to point out that this new generation is not just a technology that aims to improve the communication capacity of devices that make the provision of services more accessible and more interactive, as it will allow an unprecedented growth in data communication capacity, opening up the ports to hitherto unimaginable services and applications (IIA, 2019). For this revolution in the way we live, work and travel, the possibility of intelligent technology, interacting with each other, and having the ability to learn has contributed significantly. In this brave "new world," systems and devices with artificial intelligence are already able to recognize, interpret, process, simulate human emotions, perform facial or voice analysis and decode feelings (Piteira et al., 2019).

All these new smart technologies allow changing how hotel services are provided by customizing the guest experience (Bilgihan et al., 2016). Thus, given a future that has already arrived in technological terms, the hotel industry will once again have to reinvent itself (Tanti and Buhalis, 2016). In recent decades, we are talking about a sector that has suffered a series of financial crises, terrorist attacks, and natural disasters and is currently facing one of its most significant challenges – "learning" to deal with the impact of the COVID-19 pandemic (Seyitoglu and Ivanov, 2020). Because of tourism, the hotel industry is related to the movement of people and goods, and whose transport acts as a vector for the distribution of infectious agents, such as viruses and bacteria, on a regional and global scale. When an infectious agent reaches the human population in a pandemic way, its combat involves closing borders, sanitary fences, social distance, and the imposition of confinement, which affects all parts of the hospitality value chain. Therefore, knowing the relationship between pandemics and travel is essential to understand the systemic effects that this and new viruses can generate (Gössling et al., 2020; Dube et al., Chikodzi, 2020).

For Gursoy and Chi (2020), the pandemic, by creating the need to minimize contacts, came to promote digital support technology, payments for mobile equipment, touchless elevators, keyless locks, voice-controlled equipment and service robots, as well, foster the emergence of new inventions.

"In this sense, the investment in information and communication technologies is assumed as a strategic axis of intervention, aimed at enhancing, reinventing and adapting the national offer to the profile of an increasingly high-tech tourist" (Gustavo & Belo: 55).

The 4- and 5-star hotels operate in a very demanding and competitive market, in which there is a permanent need to provide a quality service with differentiation through innovation. Nevertheless, given the wide variety of technologies available on the market, it is not always easy for those who must decide which technology to incorporate, knowing which ones will be valued by guests and contribute to a practical improvement in satisfaction. The literature review shows that incorporating some technologies in the hotel industry has had great acceptance for the comfort and independence it generates for guests, but other technologies, such as artificial intelligence, automation, robotics and biometrics, are still controversial. The focus of the discussion is essentially based on the controversy of the humanization of the appearance of robots, the dehumanization of automated services, the issues of protection and destination of data collected about guests. However, other aspects also need reflection, particularly the issue of safety in the case of driverless cars or personalized services based on technologies, which allow changing the physical attributes of the room, such as color, sound, or smell (Melián-González, and Bulchand-Gidumal, 2016).

In this environment of technological evolution, in addition to a national and transnational environment that is still impossible to predict given the pandemic, it is plausible to say that we are facing a new global economic and social order, which forces us to rethink business strategies in the hotel business, reception procedures and preventive measures to maximize the ability to handle a case of an infected guest or employee, or even an outbreak. The new "Clean & Safe" seal is essential as a guideline and procedure guide (Turismo de Portugal, 2020b). However, its generalization reduces the character of differentiation, and in periods of more outstanding registration of contagions, it may not work as attractive enough.

For Buhalis and Foerste (2015), even before the pandemic, the focus of the new guest relationship paradigm was technology, particularly mobile phones and smartphones, equipment that the authors considered critical devices, due to their flexibility and usability anytime and anywhere. It should be noted that maximizing guest value through personalization is widely recognized in the literature, considering that it drives loyalty and the intention to return. However, it is necessary to know guests' perception, if only because neither technological innovation create value, are helpful, or are ethically accepted (Mohd-Any et al., 2014).

Effectively, when hotels offer the opportunity to integrate services operated by mobile devices, they generate the possibility of providing only those services that fit the guests' preferences, profiting from services and creating direct and personalized interactions. Furthermore, this personalization of services allows collecting information about the guest's behavior as a consumer, which must be analyzed and applied to improve the present and future experience (Chathoth et al., 2016).

Consequently, the growing popularity of technology has allowed guests to engage more and more interactively with the services provided by hotels, whether through virtual agents, chatbots or bright rooms (Melián-González et al., 2019). This aspect is crucial for its uniqueness, as these interactions are difficult to replicate in different contexts, representing an asset in differentiation, value creation and enhanced competitiveness.

Thus, and having as a premise the growing incorporation of Intelligent Technology and Automation in the World Hospitality, this study aims to simultaneously address the vision of the 4- and 5-star National Hospitality sector, but also that of the guests, responding to the following starting question: "What is the level of importance of the new Intelligent and Automation Technologies for the guest in the provision of hotel services?"

The inclusion of the vision of entities and personalities linked to the hotel industry presents itself as a means of deepening and enriching the study, namely, due to the new trends in the organization of spaces, redesign of areas, renovation of furniture, replacement of materials, all in its offspring of the new rules and technologies for hygiene and cleaning. In addition, the era of low-contact experiences will demand new safety criteria from the hotel industry, new ways of providing services, new business models in which the vast existing and developing area involving Intelligent Technologies and Automation will play an essential role (Gursoy et al., 2020).

LITERATURE REVIEW

Regarding the studies, it should be noted that priority was given to measuring the adhesion of guests to intelligent technologies, but the scarcity of scientific literature was evident. Despite the growing interest in the subject, this is a recent subject, and, therefore, there are many news and reports from engineering and information technology companies. However, a remarkable lack of work already carried out on its application in hospitality and the degree of guests' membership. Considering the above, the criterion that prevailed in selecting reference studies was aimed at contributing to the construction of information gathering instruments, which does not reflect the breadth of the bibliographic review. Thus, in the study by Ivanov et al. (2018) - Consumers' attitudes towards the introduction of robots in accommodation establishments, the instrument used was a questionnaire applied and validated to 393 Iranian consumers to know their position as guests regarding the incorporation of service robots in the hotel industry, which are the tasks that they accept to be performed by robots and which ones they want to continue to be performed by humans. In terms of observations, it is interesting to highlight that they were identified by Ivanov et al. (2018) two groups of consumers regarding their attitude towards robots, the high-techies and the high-touches. High-techies are pretty receptive to this technology, while high-touches prefer human interaction. Given these results, the authors consider it prudent that the hotel industry does not replace human workers with robots because they would lose high-touche customers, but robots are used to improve human employees' performance (Ivanov et al., 2018). This option would also not face resistance from employees. The results also show that respondents better accept the performance of robots in cleaning activities, handling luggage, delivering products, providing information, receiving orders and processing payments. Another exciting aspect is that receiving an order given by a robot was not well accepted and that respondents prefer robots to deal with activities that place the human in a dominant position in the human-robot interaction. One of the cases given as an example is a robot performing guard functions. The authors also reinforce the importance of a balance between work carried out by humans and work carried out using robotics and highlight that greater or lesser adherence to robots is also related to cultural, gender and age group issues (Ivanov et al., 2018).

In the study carried out by Park (2018) "Comparing Self-Service Technologies and Human Interaction Services in the Hotel Industry", the instrument used was the questionnaire survey. A total of 320 questionnaires were collected, but only 275 were validated. It is interesting to highlight the recommendation that before adopting Self-Service Technologies (SST), hotels should consider guest information as support for decision making and that there should be a balance between Self-Service Technologies (SST). -Service Technologies (SST) and Human Interaction Services (HIS). Guests who receive service from HIS experience higher levels of interactive quality and loyalty. This suggests, in contrast to the current trend of moving from HIS to SST, that hotel organization should not ignore the importance of HIS in the perception of service.

In the study by Djelassia et al. (2018), "How self-service technology experience evaluation affects waiting time and customer satisfaction?" The instrument used in the moderated mediation model was the questionnaire, with 714 questionnaires having been validated. Each respondent rated only one Self-Service Technology (SST) to avoid respondent fatigue and ensure adequate responses. Despite not having been established quotas for data collection, the respondents showed an outstanding balance of distribution in terms of sociodemographic variables. The survey's main objective was to assess how the experience of Self-Service Technologies (SST) affects waiting time and customer satisfaction. This purpose justified the concentration on psychological consequences and showed that the more the user attributes the success of the experience to him/her, the lower the satisfaction. On the other hand, the greater the attribution of success to the technology, the higher the satisfaction rate.

In the study by Kattara and El-Said (2014) "Customers' preferences for new Technology-based Self-Services (SST) versus Human Interaction Services (HIS) in hotels", the authors analyzed the differences in guest preferences between the use of Self- Service Technologies (SST) and human service and human Interaction Services (HIS) in 5-star hotels in Egypt. In terms of instruments, they used a mixed approach based on interviews and questionnaires. The questionnaire was designed for this purpose and based on information collected in the interview. The 5-star Sharm El-Sheikh hotels distributed a total of 200 questionnaires. The sampling technique was random and aimed to choose 5 guests from each hotel in the sample. A total of 122 questionnaires were collected, and 106 were validated. They concluded that guests prefer to contact an employee rather than rely on technology in most services. Of the nine service alternatives, seven were preferred as HIS. An important fact is that the preference between SST and HIS varies between the different phases of the occupation cycle. Preference for fast and easy service is the main reason to use SST. The authors highlight the importance of human contact in service provision as a source of competitive advantage in hospitality. However, they also point out that both SST and HIS formats have their consumers and that it is necessary to build synergies with the strengths of both formats.

In the study by Nakanishi et al. (2018), "Can a Humanoid Robot Engage in Heartwarming Interaction Service at a Hotel?", the instrument used was a questionnaire. 67 Japanese guests were invited to participate in the study. A total of 64 accepted to participate that met the criterion of staying between one and six nights. However, 11 questionnaires were not validated for being incomplete, so the study focused only on the responses of 53 guests. Interviews were also conducted with respondents to assess the merits, demerits and expectations about the experience with service robots with a human appearance. The authors concluded that using a human-looking service robot promotes a touching interaction and increases guest satisfaction, emphasizing females. However, the conversation between two service robots in a corridor did not meet the guests' pleasure. The difference in terms of satisfaction of guest interaction with a voice-controlled loudspeaker and interaction with a human-looking service robot was analyzed, with most preferences falling on interaction with the robot. The interaction only with the voice presented itself as a feeling of more significant intrusion.

In the study by Jaremen et al. (2016), "The Concept of Smart Hotels as an Innovation in the Hospitality Industry Market – Case Study of Puro Hotel in Wrocław", the main instrument was the personal interview with the management of the Puro Hotels group to get to know the characteristics of a smart hotel, what are the incorporated technologies and the resulting advantages? In 2015 there were around 300 hotels in Poland, mainly four and five stars, considered leaders in terms of the application of innovative technological solutions, one of them being the Puro Hotels network. The investor's idea was to establish a network of smart hotels based on simple solutions and a self-service system. Mainly focused on the younger generation of guests, natives of the "age" of the Internet and social media. When the design phase began, investors asked internet users to provide them with valuable guidelines for developing a hotel designed according to guests' expectations. Potential guests were invited to report their needs and preferences on the hotel's Facebook profile, analyzed comments, and, whenever appropriate, considered. As a result, the Puro hotel chain implemented innovative solutions. Also, according to Jaremen et al. (2016), implementing the idea of intelligent organization in the operation of hotels has a positive impact on the image. It distinguishes them from their competitors, confirmed by the numerous awards they have received in various competitions.

In the study carried out by Yu (2019) on the perception of guests in placing robots as employees at the front line of a hotel, Humanlike robots as employees in the hotel industry: Thematic content analysis of online reviews, the author concludes that it is essential to reconsider the differences between human-looking and machine-like robots, given that what is expected and required of each is different. As an analysis tool, the author used the Data Mining technique to select the two most viewed videos on

YouTube about robots in the hotel industry. A total of 1,163 comments were analyzed for video 1 and 458 comments for video 2. Of the 1,621 comments, a total of 1,569 were subject to content treatment using the NVivo 11 software.

In the study carried out by Lee et al. (2021), "Exploring hotel guests' perceptions of using robot assistants", the authors analyzed the opinion of 494 guests about the expected behavior regarding the incorporation of service robots in a hotel based on an explanatory video. Data were collected in two different periods, May 2017 and January 2018, using an online panel of random anonymous consumers through monetary compensation, with the acceptance criterion being the statement of stay in more than one hotel in the last twelve months. The research aimed to analyze functional and emotional aspects, identified as functional - performance expectation, facilitating conditions and perceived importance, and emotional aspects - capacity for innovation, social presence, and hedonic motivation. The authors pointed out that functional aspects can prevent hotel guests from using the robot service because it does not meet expectations and those emotional aspects should be considered when adopting the robot service, as guests can become attached emotionally. In this context, the authors identified four guest profile clusters: The ordinary, Enthusiastic adopter, Tech laggard, and Value seeker. According to the results obtained, The Ordinary and the Enthusiastic adopter are very similar and demonstrate a positive perception of using the robot. Value seekers, focusing on efficiency factors, are primarily young male travelers with a degree. Finally, tech laggards do not show much interest in the adoption of robots by a hotel.

In terms of contribution to the previously presented studies, it is essential to note that the analysis of the study by Ivanov et al. (2018) – "Consumers' attitudes towards the introduction of robots in accommodation establishments", because it allowed a better understanding of consumer behavior towards the incorporation of robotics in hotels to provide services. Given the clarity of the study, it was possible to assess which functions were best accepted, as well as their appearance. In the study carried out by Park (2018) Comparing Self-Service Technologies and Human Interaction Services in the Hotel Industry, the appreciation of guests' opinions as support for decision-making by the hotel directors/administration stands out. There must be a balance between Self-Service Technologies (SST) and Human Interaction Services (HIS) for the authors. As the authors refer, dissociating the hospitality industry from human care can be unnatural, so a balance is needed. Djelassia et al. (2018) studied how self-service technology evaluation affects waiting time and customer satisfaction? The moderated mediation model evaluated how the experience with Self-Service Technologies (SST) affects waiting time and customer satisfaction, showing that the more a customer feels responsible for the performance of the service, the lower their satisfaction. In terms of contribution, it is a reminder that it is not enough to innovate for the sake of innovating. Not all technologies are valued in the same way, which implies that if some represent an added value and contribute to the creation of value, others can only be reduced to costs and waste. In the study by Kattara and El-Said (2014) Customers' preferences for new Technology-based Self-services (SST) versus Human Interaction Services (HIS) in hotels, the authors studied the guests' preferences for the type of service performed in the register. SST and HIS record, having concluded that the preference between SST and HIS varies between the different phases of the occupation cycle and that human contact in the provision of services in the hotel industry is a source of competitive advantage. In the study by Nakanishi et al. (2018), Can a Humanoid Robot Engage in Heartwarming Interaction Service at a Hotel? The contribution focuses on the advantages and disadvantages of the humanized appearance of robots. Proponents of robot humanization point out that this appearance facilitates interaction, while opponents argue that a puppet-like robot or machine can also be sociable, interactive and exciting without having a human appearance. Most of those who do not accept the so-called "human robots" use them as arguments to create stereotypes and discrimination. In the study by Jaremen et al. (2016), The Concept of Smart Hotels as an Innovation in the Hospitality Industry Market – Case Study of Pure Hotel in Wrocław, it is interesting to verify the importance of creating solutions in harmony with the wishes and expectations of the customers. The strategy adopted of listening to the market, listening to the consumer and meeting them in anticipation of the competition again proves to be a winning bet. About the study carried out by Yu (2019) Humanlike robots as employees in the hotel industry: Thematic content analysis of online reviews, it appears that what is expected and required of a service robot differs according to its appearance. This aspect intersects some conclusions made by Ivanov et al. (2018) and challenges that need further investigation. One of the problems of human appearance is the association of greater credibility and confidence in providing certain services according to gender, age group, beauty, or physical strength. The study conducted by Gursoy et al. (2020), Covid-19 Research for Hospitality Industry: Customer Sentiments, contributed to understanding the evolution of consumer sentiment in this new era of the pandemic and how to adapt/adopt strategies accordingly.

The study conducted by Lee et al. (2021), "Exploring hotel guests' perceptions of using robot assistants", highlights the possibility of different behaviors by guest profile. In addition, it reflects on the hypothetical use of robots and warns about the importance of choosing the name for the robot due to its impact in terms of marketing. For these reasons, all these works, by addressing important specificities that allowed the creation of a broad view of the problem under study, contributed to constructing the analysis model and instruments for collecting information.

In the study conducted by Pillai et al. (2021) "COVID-19 and hospitality 5.0: Redefining hospitality operations", the authors, drawing on previous work on how hospitality has responded to other hygiene and cleanliness epidemics and pandemics, analyzed the role contactless technology can play in guest safety. One of the study's limitations is its conceptual nature and the fact that ethical issues such as privacy and data transparency in the adoption of contactless, automated and intelligent technologies are not explored. One of the future clues is to increase research on the balance between technology-based service delivery and human-presence care (box 1). Once the study is completed, it is intended that it will be possible to contribute to a better understanding of the Portuguese reality of 4- and 5-star hotels on the incorporation of technology and its impact on the consumer's decision and choice process.

METHODS

It was considered a general objective to analyze the reality of the 4- and 5-star National Hospitality regarding the incorporation of Intelligent Technology and Automation in providing services and its consequent impact on the decision process and consumer choice. The importance of knowing the consumer and realizing what influences their behavior leads to the need to try to answer specific questions, which is why it was relevant to define specific objectives as:

- Characterize the incorporation of Intelligent Technology and Automation in providing services in 4- and 5-star National Hotels.
- Assess the appreciation by guests of the incorporation of Intelligent Technology and Automation in providing services in the 4- and 5-star National Hotels.
- Search for trends and assess the advantages and disadvantages of incorporating Intelligent Technology and Automation in providing services in the 4- and 5-star National Hotels.

- Identify changes in behavior and procedures, either by the hotel industry or by guests of the 4- and 5-star National Hotel, before and after the declaration of Covid-19 as a pandemic.

The line of thought that supported the definition of specific objectives is based, on the one hand, that to analyze the reality of the 4- and 5-star National Hotel industry given the incorporation of Intelligent Technology and Automation in the provision of services and facilities, it is essential to proceed with its characterization, but also research trends and assess advantages and disadvantages. Nevertheless, on the other hand, to know the impact on the consumer's decision and choice process, it is essential to investigate the value made by the guests and identify the changes in their behavior.

Concerning the changes introduced by the hotel industry after the declaration of a pandemic, some are by legal imposition, such as the distance, the reduction of the allowed capacity, given the installed capacity and all sanitation and cleaning procedures. Others are by option strategic for differentiation, value creation and strengthening competitiveness.

Research is a systematic process of knowledge construction whose main goals are to generate new knowledge and corroborate or refute pre-existing knowledge. In this sense, this study aims to obtain a more profound knowledge of the Intelligent and Automation Technologies used in Hospitality National 4 and 5 stars, how they are perceived by guests and what is their strategic framework. To achieve this purpose, a methodological approach was chosen in line with a descriptive study, with a qualitative and a quantitative component, since in principle, they are not antagonistic and allow for greater depth and understanding of the results (Creswell, 2014).

The choice of a descriptive study is justified, considering that this type of study aims to assess different aspects, dimensions or components of a phenomenon or phenomena to be investigated without interfering. They are often characterized as studies that seek to determine opinions and behavior. Its value is based on the premise that problems can be solved and practices improved by describing and analyzing the results obtained and observed (Vilelas, 2017). For this purpose, it was decided to favor a quantitative approach through questionnaire surveys.

It was considered essential to determine the number of 4- and 5-star hotels operating in Portugal and the number of guests. According to information available on the website Hotéis de Portugal – hotels.pt, 459 4-star units and 139 5-star units were identified, totaling 598 units to be contacted, which is 2019, according to Turismo de Portugal, received 11,091,100 guests. As it is not possible for operational reasons to ensure its representativeness, by typology, Nuts II, nationality and gender, the cumulative number of guests of 11,091,100 was considered as the population, which for a confidence level of 95% and a margin of error 5%, a sample of 385 questionnaires was found.

For the construction of the questionnaire to be applied to the guests of the 4- and 5-star National Hospitality, the option fell on the elaboration of closed questions and, whenever appropriate, using the Likert scale to expand the possibilities of answers (Hill and Hill, 2008). The questionnaire was prepared on an online platform (Google Forms), and a link was provided for completion. When preparing the questions, bibliographical research and the need to verify the research hypotheses and the contribution of exploratory interviews were considered. Without underestimating the contributions of other authors present in the bibliography (table 1) were considered as reference models of Buhalis and Leung (2018), Belanche et al. (2020) and Seyitoglu and Ivanov (2020) and for a better systematization of the problem under study, five dimensions of analysis were built: Behavioral; Social distancing; Security and Privacy; Experience and Demographics and Cultural.

Table 1. Reference studies for the construction of the questionnaire model

Author	Study
Belanche et al. (2020)	Service robot implementation: a theoretical framework and research agenda
Buhalis and Leungb (2018)	Smart hospitality—Interconnectivity and interoperability towards an ecosystem
Chathoth et al. (2016)	Co-creation and higher order customer engagement in hospitality and tourism services
Duffy (2003)	Anthropomorphism and the social robot.
Gonçalves et al. (2020)	Understanding the customer experience with smart services.
Gössling et al. (2020)	Pandemics, tourism and global change: a rapid assessment of COVID-19.
Gursoy and Chi (2020)	Effects of COVID-19 pandemic on hospitality industry: review of the current situations and a research agenda.
Ivanov and Webster (2017)	Adoption of robots, artificial intelligence and service automation by travel, tourism and hospitality companies – a cost-benefit analysis.
Jaremen et al. (2016)	The Concept of Smart Hotels as an Innovation on the Hospitality Industry Market – Case Study of Puro Hotel in Wrocław.
Kansakar et al. (2019)	Technology in the Hospitality Industry: Prospects and Challenges.
Kattara (2014)	Customers' preferences for new technology-based self-services versus human interaction services in hotels.
Kaushik and Kumar (2018)	Investigating consumers' adoption of SSTs – a case study representing India's hospitality industry.
Kuo et al. (2017)	Investigating an innovative service with hospitality robots.
Lopatovska et al. (2018)	Talk to me: Exploring user interactions with the Amazon Alexa.
López et al. (2014)	BellBot. A hotel assistant system based on mobile robots.
Luís-García et al. (2003)	Big Data in Hotel Revenue Management: Exploring Cancellation Drivers to Gain Insights Into Booking Cancellation Behavior.
Lukanova and Ilieva (2019)	Robots, Artificial Intelligence and Service Automation in Hotels.
Melián-González et al. (2019)	Predicting the intentions to use chatbots for travel and tourism.
Nakanishi et al. (2018)	Can a Humanoid Robot Engage in Heartwarming Interaction Service at a Hotel?
Nayyar et al. (2018)	Virtual Reality (VR) & Augmented Reality (AR) technologies for tourism and hospitality industry.
Park (2018)	Comparing Self-Service Technologies and Human Interaction Services in the Hotel Industry.
Yu (2019)	Humanlike robots as employees in the hotel industry: Thematic content analysis of online reviews.
Seyitoglu and Ivanov (2020)	Service robots as a tool for physical distancing in tourism.
Tussyadiah and Park (2018)	Consumer Evaluation of Hotel Service Robots.
Wilson and Laing (2018)	Wearable Technology: Present and Future.
Wu and Cheng (2018)	Relationships between technology attachment, experiential relationship quality, experiential risk and experiential sharing intentions in a smart hotel.
Yu (2019)	Humanlike robots as employees in the hotel industry: Thematic content analysis of online reviews.

Table 2 presents the dimensions, variables and indicators for the questionnaire by the five dimensions: Behavioral, Social distancing; Security and Privacy; Experience and Demographics and Cultural previously presented.

Table 2. Dimensions, sub-dimensions and variables for the questionnaire

Dimensions	Sub-dimensions	Variables	Author
Behavioral	Characterization of Consumption.	Stay motivation (P1); Length of stay (P2)	Swarbrooke and Horner (2002); Turismo de Portugal (2020a)
	Appreciation of Intelligent Technology and Automation in the hotel industry.	Degree of importance (P7)	Gössling et al. (2020); Gursoy and Chi (2020); Seyitoglu and Ivanov (2020)
	Assessment of empathy with appearance.	Appearance: Human (P 9.1); Doll (P 9.2)	Belanche et al. (2020); Duffy (2003); Kuo et al. (2017); López et al. (2014); Nakanishi et al. (2018)
	Change of opinion on Robots and Virtual Assistants with the Pandemic.	Opinion: No change (P 8.1); With change (P 8.2)	Gössling et al. (2020); Gursoy and Chi (2020); Jiang and Wen, 2020)
	Analysis of sentiment about the sector.	Expectations: Affirmations (P 11)	Gössling et al. (2020)
Social distancing	Services and Facilities.	Preferences: Check-in/ Check-out (P 3)	Kattara (2014); Kaushik and Kumar (2018); Lukanova and Ilieva (2019); Pinillos et al. (2016) and Yu, (2019)
		Preferences: Access Control (P4)	Costa and Gonçalves (2018); Gonçalves et al. (2020); Gursoy and Chi, (2020); Iannacci (2018); Jarremen et al. (2016); Melián-González et al. (2019); Park, (2018); Wilson and Laing, (2018)
Security and Privacy	Characterization of confidence in the provision of data by guests.	Degree of Concern (P10)	Chathoth et al. (2016); Popat and Sharma (2013)
Experience	Reception with face-to-face reception; Assistance by virtual assistants; Room with voice-controlled equipment, Voice-controlled access; Access controlled by Tablet or Smartphone; Receptionist Robots; Robots for Cleaning Service; Robots for Delivery Services; Wearable Technology (bracelets); Virtual Reality Devices.	Importance (P 5) Performance (P6)	Buhalis and Leungb (2018); Ivanov and Webster (2017); Kansakar et al. (2019); Kaushik and Kumar (2018); Lopatovska, et al. (2018); Meuter et al. (2000); Nayyar et al. (2018); Seyitoğlu and Ivanov (2020); Tanti and Buhalis, (2016); Tori et al. (2006); Tussyadiah and Park (2018); Wu and Cheng (2018); Yu (2019)
Demographic and Cultural	Demographic and sociocultural profile.	Nationality (P12); P. Country of Residence (P13); Age (P14); Gender (P15); Qualifications (P16)	Creswell (2014), Hill and Hill (2008); Ivanov et al. (2018)

Table 3 presents the questions prepared for the questionnaire, the type of response and the scale used.

Table 3. Structure of the questionnaire

Question	Answer	Scale
1. What is the most frequent reason for staying at a 4- and 5-star hotel in Portugal.	a) Leisure; b) Work or Business; c) both	-
2. What is the frequency of the duration of stays at the 4 and 5 star Portuguese Hotels.	a) 1 night; b) 2 to 4 nights; c) 5 to 10 nights; d) more than 10 nights.	Not frequent at all; Slight frequent; Frequent; Very frequent
3. From the following Check-in and Check-out modalities, indicate how often they are used.	a) Kiosks; b) Hotel App on Smartphone/Tablet; c) Face-to-face service	Never; Rarely; Sometimes; Regularly; Always
4. From the following access control modalities, indicate the degree of frequency of use.	a) key; b) Card; c) Password; d) Smartphone/Tablet; e) Voice Command f) Biometrics; e) Wearable Technology (bracelets)	Never; Rarely; Sometimes; Regularly; Always
5. What is the degree of importance you attach to the following services and facilities in a Hotel?	a) Reception with face-to-face reception; b) Assistance by virtual assistants; c) Bedroom with TV, lighting and voice-controlled shutters; d) Voice-controlled accesses; e) Smartphone/Tablet controlled access, f) Receptionist robots; g) Robots for Cleaning Service h) Robots for Delivery Services; i) Wearable Technology (bracelets); j) Virtual Reality Devices.	Minimum; Slight; Moderate; Great; Maximum
6. How do you consider the performance of the following services and facilities in a Hotel?	a) Reception with face-to-face reception; b) Assistance by virtual assistants; c) Bedroom with TV, lighting and voice-controlled shutters; d) Voice-controlled accesses; e) Smartphone/Tablet controlled access, f) Receptionist robots; g) Robots for Cleaning Service h) Robots for Delivery Services; i) Wearable Technology (bracelets); j) Virtual Reality Devices.	Very bad; Bad; Reasonable; Well; Very good
7. The Intelligent Technology and Automation, allows social distancing. How important is it when choosing a hotel unit?	-	Not important at all; Slight important; Important; Very important
8. Has your opinion on the generalization of Robots in Hospitality and Virtual Assistants changed with the Pandemic and with the consequent need for social distance?	a) Yes b) No	-
9. In a Hotel, what is the appearance you prefer in a Robot that you have to interact with?	a) With Human appearance b) With Puppet appearance	-
10. Considering the increased collection of personal data by the Hotel, what is your level of concern in terms of privacy and security?	-	Not worried at all; Slight worried; Worried; Very worried
11. Which statement best characterizes your expectations for the Hospitality industry?	a) Many units will not open again; b) You will start to recover but very slowly; c) It will only reach the 2019 numbers again in 2023; d) In the summer of 2021 it will be in a reasonable dynamic; e) Everything will depend on effective support from the State; f) Only large chains and smaller hotels will survive.	-
12. Nationality, 13. Main Country of Residence and 14. Age	open question	-
15. Gender	a) Female; b) Male.	-
16. Qualifications	a) Basic Education; b) Secondary education c) Degree and postgraduate d) Master's and f) Doctorate	-

After validation of the questionnaire by pre-test, it was translated into English and subject to a new pre-test. The pre-test represents one of the ways to improve research instruments. It aims to assess the consistency and clarity of the questions and consists of testing the instruments on a small part of the universe, or of the sample, before being definitively applied to ensure that the research obtains results free from errors. According to Lakatos and Marconi (2017), measuring at 5 or 10% of the sample size is sufficient. The third stage corresponded to the necessary steps to collect the information, either in the scope of the questionnaire survey, or in the scheduling and confirmation of face-to-face interviews, or online. Finally, the fourth stage corresponded to the process of collecting, analyzing and processing information. The data collected in the questionnaire survey are analyzed using the Statistical Package for Social Sciences (SPSS) version 26 software with the support, whenever necessary, of Microsoft Excel.

RESULTS

Sample

Table 4. Sociodemographic variables

Variables	Categories	N	%
Gender	Female	181	46.8
	Male	206	53.2
	Total	387	100.0
Education	Basic school	1	0.3
	High school	62	16.0
	Superior degree	222	57.4
	Masters	92	23.8
	Doctoral	10	2.5
	Total	387	100.0
Country of residence	Angola	4	1.0
	Belgium	1	0.3
	Brazil	8	2.1
	France	1	0.3
	Guinea	1	0.3
	Hong Kong	1	0.3
	Italy	4	1.0
	Japan	1	0.3
	Netherlands	2	0.5
	Portugal	346	89.2
	Qatar	1	0.3
	Spain	9	2.3
	Switzerland	1	0.3
	United Kingdom	7	1.8
	Total	387	100.0

Data were collected between the 7th and 20th of December 2020, and 387 questionnaires were validated, representing a 95% confidence level and a 5% margin of error. The most frequent gender is male (53.2%), with a mean of 32.39 years old and a range between 18 and 68 years old. Concerning academic qualifications, the most frequent degree is a bachelor's degree, with 57.4%. Portugal is the primary elected country of residence (89.2%) (table 4).

Most respondents (67.5%) stated that leisure was the most frequent reason for their stay in 4- and 5-star hotels. Only 9.8% do it for work or business reasons (Figure 1).

Figure 1. "What is the most frequent reason for your stays at the 4- and 5-star Portuguese Hotels?

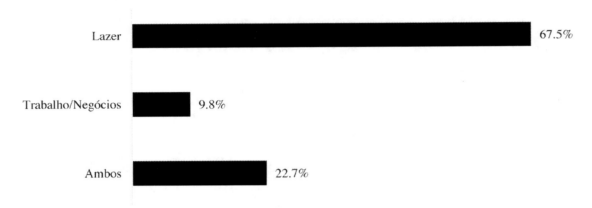

In figure 2, we observe that the highest frequency of respondents in 4- and 5-star hotels are between 1 and 4 nights, where 42.9% said one night was frequent and very frequent, and 70.3% reported two to four nights.

The "In-person Service" modality was the one with the highest frequency of use in terms of Check-in and Check-out (84.2%). On the other hand, the "kiosks" and the "Hotel App" were never used by 71.4% and 42.4% of users, respectively (*Figure 3*).

Figure 4 shows the access control modalities in a hotel, with the "card" still being used more frequently (many times and always), with 90.6%, followed by the "key" with 23.8%. On the other hand, the "biometrics" and "voice command" modalities were never or rarely used, 97.6% and 96.4%, respectively.

Figure 2. "How often do you stay at the 4- and 5-star Portuguese Hotels?"

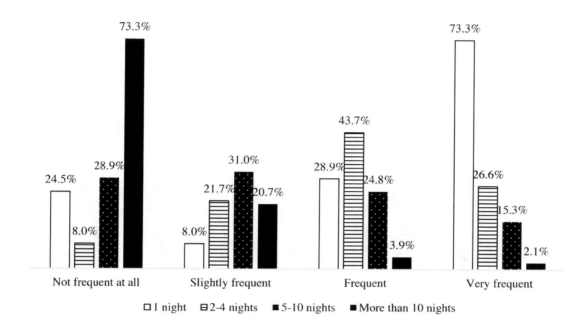

Figure 3. "For the following Check-in and Check-out modalities, indicate your degree of frequency of use?"

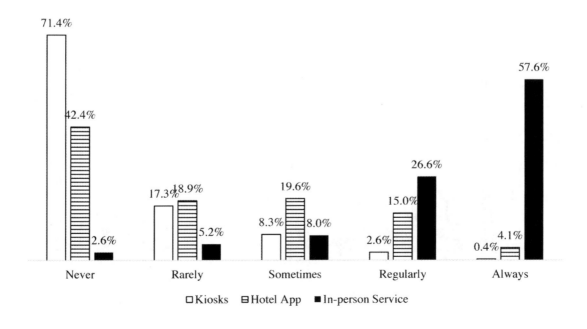

Figure 4. "From the following access control modalities in a Hotel, indicate your degree of frequency of use?"

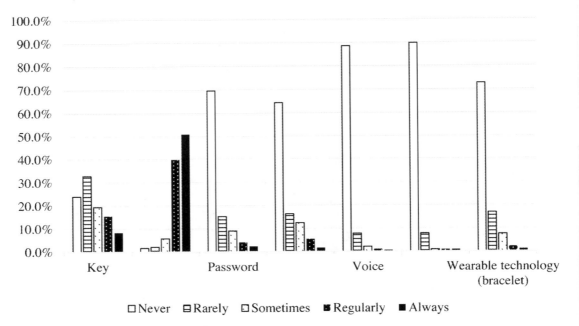

Figure 5. "From the following access control modalities in a hotel, indicate your degree of frequency of use?"

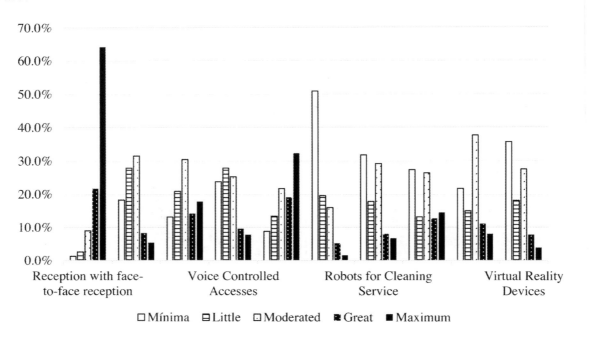

Regarding the services and facilities offered by the hotels, we can see that 85.8% of the respondents gave great and high importance to "Reception with face-to-face service". On the other hand, concerning "Accesses controlled by Smartphone/Tablet", it is observed that only 51.4% are of this opinion. On the other hand, among the services and facilities to which users give little or little importance are "Receptionist robots" and "Virtual Reality Devices", with 70.5% and 53.8%, respectively (Figure 5).

Respondents were asked to assess the performance of the services and facilities provided by the 4- and 5-star hotels. Thus, it was found that 87.9% said that the "Reception with face-to-face service" was good/very good, as well as 47.8%, who performed the same assessment for the performance of "Accesses controlled by SmartPhone/Tablet" (Figure 6). With a performance evaluation of poor/reasonable, there is the "Service by virtual assistants" (46.0%) and the "Virtual Reality Device" (29.7%).

Figure 6. "How do you rate the performance in the following services and facilities in a hotel?"

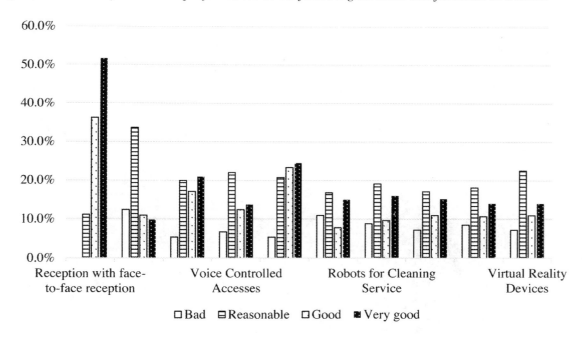

Regarding the importance given to automation and intelligent technology, 40.3% of respondents said that it was important for choosing a hotel unit, while 33.9% mentioned that it was not very important. For only 19.1%, this technology is very important when choosing a hotel (Figure 7).

Figure 7. "What is the degree of importance you attributed to automation and intelligent technology when choosing a hotel unit?"

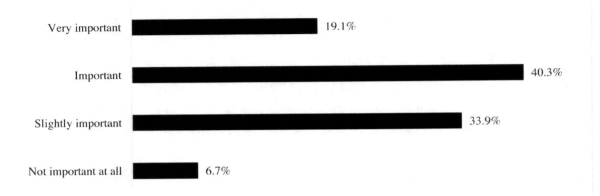

Figure 8 shows the respondents' opinion on whether the generalization of Robots and Virtual Assistants in the hotel industry has changed with the pandemic and with the need for social distance, noting that 54.8% said yes, that this change was registered.

Figure 8. "Has your opinion about the generalization of Robots in Hospitality and Virtual Assistants changed with the pandemic and consequently the need for social distance?"

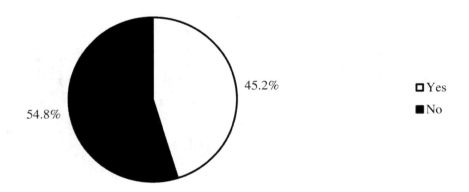

Most respondents (65.1%) believed that they preferred interacting with a robot with a puppet appearance. Only 34.9% refer to human appearance (Figure 9).

Figure 9. "In a hotel what do you prefer to look like in a robot you have to interact with?"

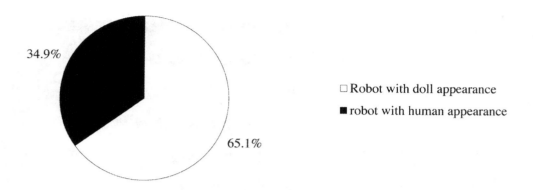

Privacy and security are factors that we sought to analyze. Thus, 69.2% of respondents expressed concern about the growing need for hotels to request personal data. On the other hand, only 7.0% said they were not concerned about this issue of personal data (Figure 10).

Figure 10. "Taking into account a greater collection of personal data by the hospitality, what is your level of concern in terms of privacy and security?"

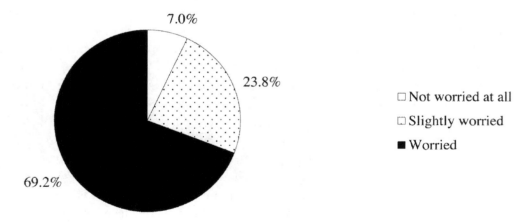

"Everything will depend on the effective support from the governments" was the statement that gathered the most significant consensus (24.8%) to characterize the respondents' experience in the hotel industry. With 23.7%, the statement "Only large chains and smaller hotels will survive" also stood out. It should be noted that only 2.8% believed that "Many units will not open again" (Figure 11).

Figure 11. "Which statement best characterizes your experience for the hospitality?"

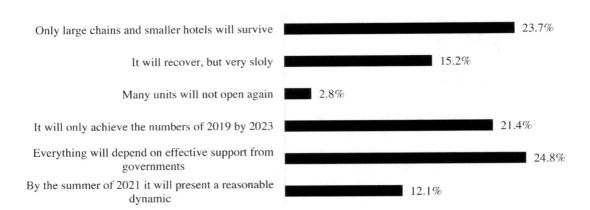

Only large chains and smaller hotels will survive	23.7%
It will recover, but very sloly	15.2%
Many units will not open again	2.8%
It will only achieve the numbers of 2019 by 2023	21.4%
Everything will depend on effective support from governments	24.8%
By the summer of 2021 it will present a reasonable dynamic	12.1%

CONCLUSION

Discussion

The sample in question consists mainly of men, graduates, with an average age of 32 years, Portuguese nationality and whose primary country of residence in Portugal. Being the main reason for staying at the 4- and 5 stars Hotelaria Portuguesa, leisure is the natural highlight attributed to the duration of 2 to 4 nights. Despite the weak positive correlation between the sociodemographic variables, it appears that by gender, the male elements have more extraordinary evidence in Work/Business than the female gender. The higher the age, the greater the incidence in the Work/Business reason. The most frequent foreign nationalities due to Work/Business are American, Angolan and Brazilian.

Given the reality observed in 4- and 5-star Portuguese Hotels, the frequency attributed to the Check-in and Check-out modality is expected, to the detriment of other modalities such as Kiosks, which are still practically non-existent in Portugal, or the App does Hotel on Smartphone/Tablet.

Concerning access control, the card is the leading technology installed, and the importance given to reception with face-to-face reception is evident, which is in line with the study by Kattara and El-Said (2014), in which the authors concluded that guests prefer to get in touch with an employee than rely on technology in most hotel services. For these authors, the preference for fast and easy service is the main reason for using technology-based self-services (SST), making the relevance of adapting the technology incorporation strategy to the Hotel positioning emerge (Seyitoglu and Stanislav, 2020). However, if the market does not value a particular innovation, its incorporation hardly acts as a competitive advantage. This aspect was highlighted by Interviewee 1 (Appendix 3) and by Cheraghalizadeh and Tümer (2017), among others.

Guests residing in countries such as Angola, Belgium, Brazil and Spain are the ones who most value the use of Smartphones for access control. However, in voice command technology, it is more valued by guests with higher academic qualifications.

Although most respondents acknowledge that they have changed their opinion about the generalization of Robots in Hospitality and Virtual Assistants in the face of the pandemic and, consequently, the need for social distance, only 40.3% considered Intelligent Technology Automation is essential and 19.1% very important.

Incorporating robots remains complex, which is why this study considered three realities: the receptionist robot, the cleaning service robot and the delivery service robot.

The receptionist robot is undoubtedly the most controversial, with most respondents assigning minimal importance. However, the role of the receptionist is significant because it is with him that the guest has the first contact, and it is he who transmits the first image of the hotel. If it does not comply with what guests expect or if the service is not well done, the negative impacts can be irreversible. In this sense, the reception has a human interaction function beyond the fulfillment of entry or exit procedures. As Interviewee 1 explains, in general, "only guests who hate talking to people will prefer Check-in without human intervention". However, technology can and should work as a complement, freeing hotel employees from more basic tasks with less added value. That is, even in hotels whose positioning is not focused on the incorporation of technology to replace human presence, part of the Check-in can be done by pre-filling the guest's data in a hotel application so that when the interaction with the receptionist occurs, it is shorter and more focused on the services the hotel can offer, as well as on other initiatives that aim to increase guest satisfaction with the hotel. This human interaction is highly valued and is almost inseparable from the guests' perception of quality hospitality in Hospitality, which may justify the results obtained. It is essential to mention that the sample comprises guests who frequent 4- and 5-star hotels and that, traditionally, the concept of quality service is intrinsically linked to face-to-face service. In contrast, technology-based self-services (SST) are associated with speed and 24-hour availability.

Regarding receptionist robots, there is still a long way for the market to recognize them as necessary, which does not mean that they are a reason for attraction and notoriety. In Portugal and the case of Hotel Evolution, it works as if it were a Hotel mascot. The appreciation of robots is closely related to the profile of the guests (Lee et al., 2021), with the cultural environment and the emotion that characterizes Hospitality.

The cleaning service robot involves a different reality than the receptionist robot, so it is already more valued by respondents. This type of robot does not need to interact with the guest but correctly performs its functions. Especially in the field of sanitation and decontamination, technology in general, and robots in particular, can represent an essential tool that protects the health of employees and guests and has a crucial effect on the perception of safety. In the same line of thought fits the robot for Delivery Services or baggage storage. As mentioned by Interviewee 2, despite the disadvantage of reducing the personalization and exclusivity of the service that human contact brings, the use of technology allows optimizing tasks, reducing operating time and costs. If, before the pandemic, the implementation of technology for some units was just a wish, now, at least in terms of sanitation and social distancing, it has become a necessity.

The remaining services and facilities presented in the study, according to respondents, do not have a high performance and therefore do not represent a priority. In short, they are considered relatively unimportant to respondents (Server, 2015).

The 4- and 5-star hotels operate in a very competitive and demanding market, in which the creation of value involves anticipating the needs of guests, meeting them and assertively taking advantage of the potential of new intelligent and automation technologies. However, given the wide variety of technologies available on the market and the new paradigms generated by the pandemic, it is not always easy for decision-makers to know which technologies are most valued by guests and contribute to a practical improvement in satisfaction. This reality substantiated the construction of the problem under study and the development of this work.

Based on the literature review, it was possible to infer that the possibility of intelligent technology and automation, being able to interact with each other and having the ability to learn, allows changing how hotel services are provided by personalizing the guest experience (Bilgihan et al., 2016; Tanti, and Buhalis, 2016). In addition to this "new world", the pandemic created the need to minimize contacts, promoted digital support technology, payments for mobile equipment, touchless elevators, keyless locks, voice-controlled equipment, service robots, and fostering the emergence of innovations, with the focus on technologies being considered as a strategic axis in the face of increasingly high-tech tourism (Gustavo and Belo, 2019; Gursoy and Chi, 2020).

Still, within the scope of the bibliographical review, the analysis of studies already carried out allowed interesting lines of reflection, namely, the study by Ivanov et al. (2018), allowed a better understanding of consumer behavior regarding the incorporation of robotics in the hotel industry, the A study by Park (2018) highlighted the importance of a balance between Self-Service Technologies (SST) and Human Interaction Services (HIS), given that dissociating hospitality from human care can be unnatural, the study by Djelassia et al ., (2018) warned that the more a customer feels responsible for the performance of the Self-Service Technologies (SST) service, the lower their satisfaction. In terms of contribution, it is a reminder that it is not enough to innovate for the sake of innovating. Not all technologies are valued in the same way by guests, which leads to the incorporation of technology, either representing an added value and a contribution to the creation of value, or it can only translate into costs and waste. In the study by Kattara and El-Said (2014), the authors concluded that the preference between OSH and HIS varies between the different phases of the occupation cycle and that human contact in the provision of services in the hotel industry is a source of advantage competitive. On the appearance of robots, opinions are divided on which appearance allows for better interaction. One of the arguments most used by opponents of robots with human-like appearance is the creation of stereotypes and discrimination, as explained by Nakanishi et al. (2018). About the study carried out by Yu (2019), it is verified that what is expected and demanded of a service robot differs according to its appearance. This question is crucial and crosses some conclusions presented by Ivanov et al. (2018). One of the problems of human appearance is the association of greater credibility and confidence in providing certain services according to gender, age group, beauty, or physical strength. Jaremen et al. (2016) highlight the importance of creating technological solutions aimed at satisfying the desires and expectations of guests and alerts to the need to listen to the market, listen to the consumer, and meet them in anticipation of the competition. The study by Gursoy et al. (2020) contributed to understanding the evolution of consumer sentiment in this new era of the pandemic and how to adapt/adopt strategies accordingly. Finally, the study carried out by Lee et al. (2021) on the expected behavior of guests regarding the incorporation of service robots in hotels highlights the possibility of different attitudes per profile, which forces us to consider the marketing strategy, in decision-making on investment in intelligent and automation technology.

Face-to-face service meets most preferences, the access card continues to be the most used means, but most of them are naturally faced with access control via Smartphones/Tablets. The pandemic changed respondents' opinion towards greater acceptance of the generalization of Robots in Hospitality and Virtual Assistants, but the incorporation of Intelligent Technology and Automation was not significantly valued as essential by most respondents. Safeguarding the privacy and security of data collected by the hotel industry is one of the concerns expressed mainly by respondents. The apprehension about the future is another important fact.

In terms of contribution to the Business and Scientific Community, this investigation essentially represents a tool for reflection and acquisition of knowledge about the relevance and usefulness of incorporating Intelligent Technology and Automation in Hospitality. It is essential to highlight that in a changing world, and a new national and international context under the pandemic, a considerable increase in competitive aggressiveness and new geostrategic arrangements is expected, impacting tourism and Portugal's nationalities' attraction. In this sense, the national hotel offer in the investment decision on the typology and valences of the technology to be incorporated must consider the opinion of its guests and its potential market, a reality only possible through the development of studies and research work.

LIMITATIONS

By methodological option based on operational reasons, the sample was built based on the number of guests of the 4- and 5-star National Hotels in 2019, and the collection procedure was online and random, with Portuguese nationality reaching 90.3% of the responses. In this sense, and given the weight of nationality in consumer behavior and age, in the adherence to different technologies, the lack of representation by sociodemographic strata represents a limitation.

FUTURE DIRECTIONS

Future investigations would be interesting to expand the sample and inquire about the national 4- and 5-star hotel industry about incorporating Intelligent Technology and Automation and the investment perspective.

REFERENCES

Belanche, D., Casaló, L. V., Flavián, C., & Schepers, J. (2020). Service robot implementation: A theoretical framework and research agenda. *Service Industries Journal*, *40*(3-4), 203–225. doi:10.1080/02642069.2019.1672666

Bilgihan, A., Smith, S., Ricci, P., & Bujisic, M. (2016). Hotel guest preferences of in-room technology amenities. *Journal of Hospitality and Tourism Technology*, *7*(2), 118–134. doi:10.1108/JHTT-02-2016-0008

Buhalis, D., & Foerste, M. (2015). SoCoMo marketing for travel and tourism: Empowering co-creation of value. *Journal of Destination Marketing & Management*, *4*(3), 151–161. doi:10.1016/j.jdmm.2015.04.001

Buhalis, D., & Leung, R. (2017). Smart hospitality—Interconnectivity and interoperability towards an ecosystem. *International Journal of Hospitality Management*, *71*, 41–50. doi:10.1016/j.ijhm.2017.11.011

Chathoth, P. K., Ungson, G. R., Harrington, R. J. & Chan, E. S. (2016). Co-creation and higher order customer engagement in hospitality and tourism services. *International Journal of Contemporary Hospitality Management, 28*(2), 222-245.

Cheraghalizadeh, R., & Tümer, M. (2017). The effect of applied resources on competitive advantage in hotels: Mediation and moderation analysis. *Journal of Hospitality and Tourism Management, 31*, 265–272. doi:10.1016/j.jhtm.2017.04.001

Costa, A., & Gonçalves, B. (2018). *Assistentes Pessoais Inteligentes com Reconhecimento de Voz*. Instituto Superior Tecnico.

Creswell, J. W. (2014). *Research design: Qualitative, quantitative, and mixed methods approaches* (4th ed.). SAGE Publications, Inc.

Dahlman, E. (2018). *What Is 5G? Em: 5G NR: the Next Generation Wireless Access Technology*. Academic Press. Elsevier.

Djelassi, S., Diallo, M. F., & Zielke, S. (2018). How self-service technology experience evaluation affects waiting time and customer satisfaction? A moderated mediation model. *Decision Support Systems, 111*, 1–10. doi:10.1016/j.dss.2018.04.004

Dube, K., Nhamo, G., & Chikodzi, D. (2020). COVID-19 cripples global restaurant and hospitality industry. *Current Issues in Tourism*, 1–5.

Duffy, B. R. (2003). Anthropomorphism and the social robot. *Robotics and Autonomous Systems, 42*(3-4), 177–190. doi:10.1016/S0921-8890(02)00374-3

Gonçalves, L., Patrício, L., Teixeira, J. G., & Wunderlich, N. V. (2020). Understanding the customer experience with smart services. *Journal of Service Management, 31*(4), 1–22. doi:10.1108/JOSM-11-2019-0349

Gössling, S., Scott, D., & Hall, C. M. (2020). Pandemics, tourism and global change: A rapid assessment of COVID-19. *Journal of Sustainable Tourism*, 1–20.

Gretzel, U., Werthner, H., Koo, C., & Lamsfus, C. (2015). Conceptual foundations for understanding smart tourism ecosystems. *Computers in Human Behavior, 50*, 558–563. doi:10.1016/j.chb.2015.03.043

Gursoy, D., & Chi, C. G. (2020). Effects of COVID-19 pandemic on hospitality industry: Review of the current situations and a research agenda. *Journal of Hospitality Marketing & Management, 29*(5), 527–529. doi:10.1080/19368623.2020.1788231

Gursoy, D. (2020). *Covid-19 Research for Hospitality Industry: Customer Sentiments. COVID-19 Study 5 Report: Restaurant and Hotel Industry, Washington State*. School of Hospitality Business Management.

Gustavo, N., & Belo, M. (2019). O Novo Ambiente Competitivo dos Negócios Turísticos. In *Tourfly. Inovação e Futuro: Contributos para o Desenho da Oferta Turística na Área Metropolitana de Lisboa* (pp. 35–55). ESHTE – Escola Superior de Hotelaria e Turismo do Estoril.

Iannacci, J. (2018). Internet of Things (IoT); Internet of Everything (IoE); Tactile Internet; 5G – A (Not So Evanescent) Unifying Vision Empowered by EH-MEMS (Energy Harvesting MEMS) and RF-MEMS (Radio Frequency MEMS). *Sensors and Actuators. A, Physical, 272*, 187–198. doi:10.1016/j.sna.2018.01.038

Institute of Internal Auditors (IIA). (2019). *Global Perspectives and Insights. 5G e a Quarta Revolução Industrial, EUA*. Institute of Internal Auditors.

Ivanov, S. (2020). The impact of automation on tourism and hospitality jobs. *Information Technology & Tourism, 22*, 205-215.

Ivanov, S., Webster, C., & Seyyedi, P. (2018). Consumers' attitudes towards the introduction of robots in accommodation establishments. *Tourism (Zagreb), 66*(3), 302–317.

Ivanov, S., & Webster, C. (2017). Adoption of robots, artificial intelligence and service automation by travel, tourism and hospitality companies – a cost-benefit analysis. Sofia University "St. Kliment Ohridski".

Ivanov, S., Webster, C., & Berezina, K. (2017). Adoption of robots and service automation by tourism and hospitality companies. *Revista Turismo & Desenvolvimento, 27/28*, 1501–1517.

Jaremen, D. E., Jędrasiak, M., & Rapacz, A. (2016). The Concept of Smart Hotels as an Innovation on the Hospitality Industry Market – Case Study of Puro Hotel in Wrocław. *Economic Problems of Tourism, 36*, 65–75. doi:10.18276/ept.2016.4.36-06

Jiang, Y. & Wen, J. (2020). Effects of COVID-19 on hotel marketing and management: A perspective article. *International Journal of Contemporary of Hospitality Management*, 1-17.

Kansakar, P., Munir, A., & Shabani, N. (2019). Technology in the Hospitality Industry: Prospects and Challenges. *IEEE Consumer Electronics Magazine, 8*(3), 60–65. doi:10.1109/MCE.2019.2892245

Kattara, H. S., & El-Said, O. A. (2014). Customers' preferences for new technology-based self-services versus human interaction services in hotels. *Tourism and Hospitality Research, 13*(2), 67–82. doi:10.1177/1467358413519261

Kaushik, A. K., & Kumar, V. (2018). Investigating consumers' adoption of SSTs – a case study representing India's hospitality industry. *Journal of Vacation Marketing, 24*(3), 275–290. doi:10.1177/1356766717725560

Kim, B. Y. & Oh, H. (2004). How do hotel firms obtain a competitive advantage? *International Journal of Contemporary Hospitality Management, 16*, 65-71.

Kuo, C.-M., Chen, L.-C., & Tseng, C.-Y. (2017). Investigating an innovative service with hospitality robots. *International Journal of Contemporary Hospitality Management, 29*(5), 1–44. doi:10.1108/IJCHM-08-2015-0414

Lakatos, E. M., & Marconi, M. A. (2017). *Metodologia do Trabalho Científico* (4th ed.). Editora Atlas.

Lanka, E., Lanka, S., Rostron, A. & Singh, P. (n.d.). Why We Need Qualitative Research in Management. *Revista de Administração Contemporânea. Journal of Contemporary Administration, 25*(2), 1-8.

Law, R., Buhalis, D., & Cobanoglu, C. (2014). Progress on information and communication technologies in hospitality and tourism. *International Journal of Contemporary Hospitality Management, 26*(5), 727–750. doi:10.1108/IJCHM-08-2013-0367

Lee, Y., Leeb, S., & Kim, D.-Y. (2021). Exploring hotel guests' perceptions of using robot assistants. *Tourism Management Perspectives, 37*, 100781. doi:10.1016/j.tmp.2020.100781

Lopatovska, I. (2018). Talk to me: Exploring user interactions with the Amazon Alexa. *Journal of Librarianship and Information Science*, 1–14.

López, J., Pérez, D., Zalama, E., & Gómez-García-Bermejo, J. (2014). BellBot. A hotel assistant system based on mobile robots. *International Journal of Advanced Robotic Systems*, 1–11.

Lukanova, G., & Galina, I. (2019). Robots, Artificial Intelligence and Service Automation in Hotels. In E. P. Limited (Ed.), *Robots, Artificial Intelligence, and Service Automation in Travel, Tourism, and Hospitality* (pp. 157–183). Emerald Publishing Limited. doi:10.1108/978-1-78756-687-320191009

Melián-González, S., Gutiérrez-Taño, D., & Bulchand-Gidumal, J. (2019). Predicting the intentions to use chatbots for travel and tourism. *Current Issues in Tourism*, 1–19.

Meuter, M. L., Ostrom, A. L., Roundtree, R. I., & Bitner, M. J. (2000). Self-Service Technologies: Understanding Customer Satisfaction with Technology-Based Service Encounters. *Journal of Marketing*, *64*(3), 50–64. doi:10.1509/jmkg.64.3.50.18024

Mohd-Any, A. A., Winklhofer, H., & Ennew, C. (2014). Measuring Users' Value Experience on a Travel Website (e-Value): What Value Is Cocreated by the User? *Journal of Travel Research*, *54*(4), 496–510. doi:10.1177/0047287514522879

Nakanishi, J. (2018). *Can a Humanoid Robot Engage in Heartwarming Interaction Service at a Hotel?* ACM. doi:10.1145/3284432.3284448

Nayyar, A., Mahapatra, B., Le, D., & Suseendran, G. (2018). Virtual Reality (VR) & Augmented Reality (AR) technologies for tourism and hospitality industry. *IACSIT International Journal of Engineering and Technology*, *7*(2.21), 156–160. doi:10.14419/ijet.v7i2.21.11858

Park, S. (2018). *Comparing Self-Service Technologies and Human Interaction Services in the Hotel Industry* (Masters Thesis). University of Central Florida.

Pillai, S. G., Haldorai, K., Seo, W. S., & Kim, W. G. (2021). COVID-19 and hospitality 5.0: Redefining hospitality operations. *International Journal of Hospitality Management*, *94*, 102869. doi:10.1016/j.ijhm.2021.102869 PMID:34785847

Pinillos, R., Marcos, S., Feliz, R., Zalama, E., & Gómez-García-Bermejo, J. (2016). Long-term assessment of a service robot in a hotel environment. *Robotics and Autonomous Systems*, *79*, 1–60. doi:10.1016/j.robot.2016.01.014

Piteira, M., Aparicio, M., & Costa, C. J. (2019). A Ética na Inteligência Artificial: Desafios. Institute of Electrical and Electronics Engineers.

Popat, K. A., & Sharma, P. (2013). Wearable Computer Applications. *International Journal of Engineering and Innovative Technology*, *3*(1), 213–217.

Seyitoğlu, F., & Ivanov, S. (2020). A conceptual framework of the service delivery system design for hospitality firms in the (post-)viral world: The role of service robots. *International Journal of Hospitality Management*, *91*, 1–10. doi:10.1016/j.ijhm.2020.102661 PMID:32952262

Swarbrooke, J., & Horner, S. (2002). *O Comportamento Do Consumidor no Turismo* (1st ed.). Aleph.

Tanti, A., & Buhalis, D. (2016). *Connectivity and the Consequences of Being (Dis)connected.* Information and Communication Technologies in Tourism. doi:10.1007/978-3-319-28231-2_3

Turismo de Portugal. (2020a). *Travel BI.* Available at: https://travelbi.turismodeportugal.pt/pt-pt/Paginas/PowerBI/hospedes.aspx

Turismo Portugal. (2020b). *Selo "Clean & Safe". Empreendimentos Turísticos. Requisitos a cumprir.* Turismo de Portugal.

Tussyadiah, I. P., & Park, S. (2018). Consumer Evaluation of Hotel Service Robots. *Information and Communication Technologies in Tourism,* 308-320.

Vilelas, J. (2017). *Investigação. O processo de Construção do Conhecimento* (2nd ed.). Edições Sílabo.

Wilson, S., & Laing, R. (2018). *Wearable Technology: Present and Future.* University of Leeds.

Wu, H.-C., & Cheng, C.-C. (2018). Relationships between technology attachment, experiential relationship quality, experiential risk and experiential sharing intentions in a smart hotel. *Journal of Hospitality and Tourism Management, 37,* 42–58.

Yu, C.-E. (2019). Humanlike robots as employees in the hotel industry: Thematic content analysis of online reviews. *Journal of Hospitality Marketing & Management, 29*(1), 22–38.

Zsarnoczky, M. (2018). The Digital Future of the Tourism & Hospitality Industry. *Boston Hospitality Review,* 1-9.

Chapter 5

Opportunities and Challenges of ICT–Based Marketing in the Accomodation Sector:
A Study of Gurugram (Haryana), India

Lakhvinder Singh

https://orcid.org/0000-0002-0778-1132
Government College, Kaithal, India

Dinesh Dhankhar

Kurukshetra University, India

ABSTRACT

Digitalization has forced the accommodation sector to use information and communication technology (ICT) to excel in their business performance. Hence, it is of paramount importance to scan the pros and cons associated with use of ICT marketing in the accommodation sector. This chapter considers this fact and focuses on opportunities and challenges associated with the use of ICT-based marketing in the accommodation sector of Gurugram (Haryana) region of India. The phenomena of ICT marketing is exhaustively assessed and highlighted through different components such as introduction, ICT as emerging concept, application of ICT tools in the marketing accommodation sector, opportunities associated with using ICT-based marketing, challenges faced during applying ICT marketing in the accommodation sector, followed by a conclusion. This study has been considered as a modification and addition to the existing body of knowledge in the accommodation sector. Moreover, the tourism and accommodation marketers also apprehend practical implications to augment their services for survival in a competitive business environment.

DOI: 10.4018/978-1-7998-8306-7.ch005

INTRODUCTION

Information and Communication Technology (ICT) has changed the global businesses environment by a wide range of tools, methodologies and functions, facilitating the strategic management and supporting firms to achieve a long term competitive advantage (Nikoli & Lazakidoi,2019). In the contemporary world, ICT has become a crucial infrastructure including computer, maps, multimedia, internet, mobile that provides lot of opportunities to enrich customer experience and add to firms' profit maximization also. Modern day tourists use this emerging technology to plan travel holidays, book hotel rooms, booking of air tickets, cruise and ground transportation and similarly help companies to effectively handle various business operation such as marketing (Buhalis, 2003; Verma & Shukla, 2019; Conyette, 2015).

The accommodation segment of tourism sector deals with providing goods or services to enable pleasure, leisure and business activities away from the home environment to visitors. The Indian accommodation industry is growing with high pace comparative to past decades. It is contributing highly in foreign exchange earnings and strengthening India economically. The input to foreign exchange of Indian accommodation sector has been enormous and foreign direct investment (FDI) inflow in Indian hotel and tourism industry was also reached to thousands of US dollars during last couple of years (Indian Brand Equity Foundation, 2021).

Therefore, number of foreign players also shown their very strong attendance in the country's accommodation industry space like Starwood, Accor, Marriott, Cabana Hotels, Premier Trav) el Inn (PTI), Mandarin Oriental, Hamptonc Inns, Cabana Hotels, Banana Tree, Amanda, Satinwoods is some of foreign accommodation firms. The Indian accommodation companies such as ITC, Asia Hotels, East India Hotels (EIH), Bharat Hotels, Leela venture and Indian Hotels Company (IHCL) etc. have also not lagged behind. Operating in a highly competitive market, accommodation players can only succeed if it is continuously providing the quality services and is concerned about the customer satisfaction and ways to improve the satisfaction level. The infrastructure particularly technology adoption is the key to sustaining the growth in accommodation sector of India.

The application of information & communication technology (ICT) based marketing in accommodation industry in India will increase substantially over the next decade as India is evolving as the one of the favourite tourist spot on the globe. With the increasing demand of India as a destination, number of hotels is also increasing. The main marketing tool of the Indian accommodation industry is going to be through ICT based marketing in both graded and non-graded properties. In present era, travelling is no more than enjoying luxury. This became possible only by dynamic technological developments in area of marketing through the use of information & communication technology (Buhalis,2003). This has brought about many novelties in ICT based marketing of the hotel products. Financial and other support were extended by different State Governments and Ministry of Tourism, India. The 'Digital India' campaign of the Government of India is another crucial move towards growth and progress of accommodation in the country. In these situations, the researcher felt the relevance to study the effectiveness of ICT based marketing in accommodation business and its impact on the service quality. To meet out the present challenges and to be ready for the emerging challenges regarding service performance before the accommodation industry, the ICT based marketing practices should be fair enough. Thus, this research problem has been chosen keeping in mind the well-versed significance of the accommodation industry so that the forthcoming researches may at least test the service performance in accommodation industry. The current chapter thus based on presenting opportunities and challenges in application of information & communication (ICT) based marketing in accommodation sector by taking Gurugram region of India as study area.

BACKGROUND

The present study confined to Gurugram region of Haryana located in northern India. The area is among the emerging and major metropolitan area of the country and has close proximity to capital of India, Delhi. It is now emerging as a hotel and tourism business hub. The choice of study area was attributable to concentration of the area in terms of number of accommodation firms, nearness to IGI (Indira Gandhi International Airport), development of the area as a business hub for multiple of national and international MNCs. The selection of accommodation firms for the study was made through the convenience sampling method. A total of 139 hotels were included in this total sample size. The list of accommodation properties was taken from the official website of ministry of tourism, India. The selected accommodation properties for the study, were contacted to draw the information regarding, application of ICT based marketing in this business, opportunities associated with its use and barriers faced in using this dynamic technology in the business. More reliable and balanced data collection was censured by asking both open and close ended questions.

The present study will provide a big insight to researchers, tourists, top management of the accommodation industry and other organizations of the concerned field. In other way, the present study, as the researcher visualizes, will not only be intellectually arousing for academics but will also prove considerable value to the whole accommodation industry.

MAIN FOCUS OF THE CHAPTER

ICT Based Marketing as an Emerging Concept

Starting with the usage in the internal functions of firms, computers are now widely used in accommodation industry. Airlines were first to use computers in central reservation systems (CRSs) and global distribution systems (GDSs) which enabled hotel companies and associated travel agencies to access schedule and pricing information and to request reservation for clients (Gretzel & Fesenmaier, 2006). Drawing analogy from internet technology and other communication technologies now business in accommodation sector is beyond imagination and the firms are implementing ICT based marketing to remain competitive in this globalised era. Marketing through information & communication technology is an application of computer software, hardware and telecommunication devices to manipulate, store, protect, convert send and receive the information (Olifer & Olifer, 2006) has brought both the hotelier and the traveler very close. The outcome of ICT based marketing adoption has definitely increased the guest experience and it is going to mature more in the coming decades.

A mainstream of the online accommodation booking portals of India are advanced, equipped and are proposing a total experience for both group and individual travellers. The extensive range of assistance to travellers' promises usefulness of ICT based marketing tools in travel planning, booking and stay. The contributions made by major e-accommodation portals as cited in figure 1. The accommodation and hotel industry in India have promptly accepted to ICT based marketing based systems to offer better and advanced services and the use of this technology have uncovered new avenues for this sector (Barnes & Hinton, 2007).

Hotels have taken benefits of ICT based marketing regarding the technology-based systems to upgrade their operations such as receptionist operations, front office, restaurant operations etc. Also, the ICT based marketing has become the trustworthy source of purchasing accommodation and other travel services. It helps travellers both in avoiding them the extra cost of booking and saving the time expended in negotiating and visiting an offline conventional booking store. Facilities like customized deals, easy annulment processes, ticket status tracking and standby customer service etc., ease the excursion of a travel hunter have become a surge. Accommodation companies throughout the globe are resorting to user-friendly interfaces to ease the experiences of consumer - better and easier navigation, better interactivity etc. these days. Dominating players in the industry are using trip advisors, social networking portals, and travel blogs to establish a brand name by motivating tourists to share their travel and is increasing the faith regarding usefulness of portals in customers and is increasing the number of loyal customers also.

Figure 1.
(Source: E-Travel Marketing India, 2015)

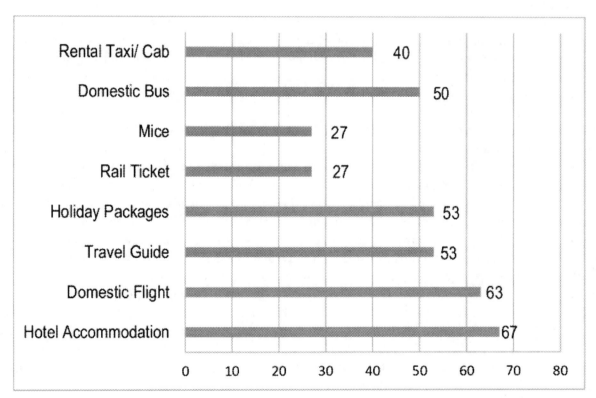

Also, in order to survive and grow in the accommodation industry, firms require focusing on the improving guest satisfaction and retention and ICT based marketing is providing better services for customer satisfaction. Therefore, ICT based marketing are extremely important for the accommodation industry.

ICT Based Marketing Applications in Accommodation Sector

The increased acceptability of ICT based marketing tools in accommodation industry has brought both customers and firms on the same platform. It has totally replaced the traditional business methods where there is one-to-one contact based on social procedures. ICT based marketing have grown at a high pace by reshaping the traditional marketing functions; integrating the hotel operations; providing tools for marketing research; improving overall efficiency of business; and partnership building; enhancing services while providing the strategic and tactical opportunities. Buhalis & Law (2008) has stated that the transformational effect of communication technologies has been visible causing the development of ICT based marketing tools and services that enable interface between providers of accommodation services, customers and partners on a digital and global level.

The accommodation industry has adopted the ICT based marketing and many firms have already developed their web portals to provide the product/services information to the customers in order to promote their products and services globally in a time effective and cost reducing manner and to gain a share of online market. Many tools of ICT based marketing have already boomeranged in other industries, thus individual evaluation of the ICT based marketing based tools and a practice in accommodation sector is necessitated.

The use of electronic platform is good idea to consider different marketing tools until one finds out what works for the organisation. It pertains to the informative services or description/features that are available in the web portal and includes the strategies and solutions to make it user friendly, such as navigation and search required in finalising a purchase, information retrieval and getting the critical feedback. The availability of value added services and reservation facilities in order to attract customers to the electronic marketplace are considered important. The assessment of ICT based marketing specific dimensions, i.e. mobile number, e-mail, website etc., that forms the customer contact information dimension also important tools of ICT based marketing. Such types of applications are in extensive use by guests to check-in data and information about various destinations and for sharing their overall experiences (Tussyadiah & Fesenmaier, 2009). Many factors are there behind this development such as more advanced software and hardware, advances in 'easy-to-use' tools for sharing and creating new content, a faster network edge, higher e-savvies in the population, and the upsurge of wireless and handy platforms. Further use of ICT based marketing is believed to be extensive in scope, because it is not only limited to promotions and marketing online, but also comprises marketing done via wireless media (SMS) and e-mail. It also comprises digital customer data and numerous other business management tasks. Further, it compasses that use of electronic devices (like computers) like tablets, smart phones, personal computers, cell phones, game consoles also to involve with stakeholders. In developing countries like India, many accommodation organizations use ICT based marketing channels to bring enhancement their business profitability. Majority of the accommodation firms have marked their attendance on this emerging phenomenon and promoting their products by posting quick updates and advertising the product/services offers via ICT based marketing based business applications.

Regarding application ICT based marketing in general policy and awareness, majority of accommodation firms in Gurugram have specific plans were found to exist to target leisure, corporate, and group markets. Large number of accommodation firms followed the practice of referring and recognizing to top referral sources, search engines, and associated service providers. Firms compared their websites with the websites of the comparative hotels, and had designed plans for ICT based marketing specific services/products, thus gaining a favourable chance for revealing customers to more diverse services and products offered. Investigating online consumer-generated reviews was not a common practice among hotels in Gurugram. Most of the accommodation firms in Gurugram constantly monitored keyword searches over search engines and about equal percentage of firms checked the counter for the number of visitors to the website to evaluate the site's popularity and quality of contents. This was indispensable to discover website guests' habits and ultimately ensure that the website visits into the buying. Moreover, accommodation firms in sufficient number used promotional SMSs and emails, web banners, and online directory to marketing their products and services.

Figure 2.

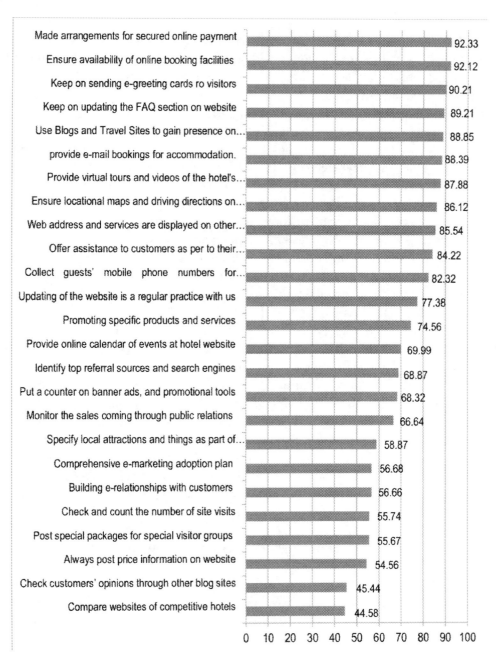

Use of ICT based marketing application in sale information and communication in accommodation firms of Gurugram indicating sufficient evidences of e-existence efforts in displaying the likeable information about their services, products, prices, and offers on their website, in totality to applying online channels to have the presence on the web. Literature has established that a noteworthy part of the population generally looks around blogs, wikis, search engines, tag clouds and social bookmarks. Accommodation firms also already started linking hotel's portal to city web pages. Another good practice followed by the accommodation firms was maintaining and updating continuously the current events in the online calendar scheduled at the hotel. Most of the accommodation firms updated price related information online on regular basis. Accommodation firms ensured ICT based marketing based special packages different segment group of visitors such as honeymooners, corporate groups and leisure travellers. Bundling local attractions packages on websites was common among accommodation firms in Gurugram. Providing online location maps and driving directions was provided by accommodation firms in large numbers on their websites alongside online videos of the hotel's facilities and online virtual tours by firms. Catchy information and details of hotel services were also provided by inserting FAQs on the website was the common practice.

Transaction through applying ICT based marketing, irrespective of the hotel grading, location or the services provided, accommodation firms ensured accessibility of e-mail facility for room bookings, and all kind of queries. In fact, this does not cost anything to the hotel. Also, standardised software packages were now available in the market whereby online booking has been automatized and secured online payment gateways were available. Call centres of the Accommodation firms are now more concerned with website-interactivity-related practices thus mediating dialogue between the hotel and the customer/s. An e-customization-related practice such as customizing of prices, services and products, various targeted market groups packages was the main focus of accommodation firms.

Enhancement of enhancing e-image and e-relationship by using ICT based marketing was noticed a common practice among accommodation firms in study area. Front office and public relations employees were especially trained in helping the usage of website chat services in the guest conversations. This clears many of the doubts in the minds of the customers. They are provided assistance and guidance for special offers/best buys. The objective is to increase the e-relationship and make longer the e-image with home guests, so that the ICT based marketing hard work does not come to an end once an e-transaction occurs. Such practices bring in innovations in notices of guests increasing the image of the hotel and raising the awareness of others utilizing booking methods and conventional contacts. That is why almost all accommodation firms have started putting Web address and its available services over all stationary items and even on flyers, tent cards bill etc. Maintaining relationships with e-mails with existing customers was common practice. Sending hotel news and e-greeting on special occasions has become a buzzword. Collecting mobile phone numbers of guests for promotional SMS, if they agree, and tracking responses was common among accommodation firms. Executives in their interviews supported the idea that e-mailing was the fastest and perhaps most personalised method of getting the customer response and hence effective.

Opportunities of Using ICT Based Marketing in Accommodation Sector

The purpose of using ICT based marketing is to utilise advanced electronic information communication in the most effective way to manage all processes and activities with the objective of attracting, finding, retaining and winning the customers. Compared to conventional marketing methods, scope and options have thus widened. Services offered through ICT based marketing platforms are increasing day by day and consequences and antecedents of its adoption are therefore crucial for organizations.

While accommodation industry in India has been trying hard to grow their revenues over the past few years and the techniques like search engine optimization, web portal design, paid search marketing on search engines and bulk e-mailing and many more have been flourishing, many of the hoteliers are at a loss with the new ICT based marketing channels. The speedy commercialization and expansion of ICT based marketing applications are advantageous to the hotel and other tourism-related companies are encouraged to accept these fruitful technologies, but Indian firms in the sector still appear in the nascent stage. It is expected that using ICT based marketing in accommodation is helps to is to enhance operational efficiency, improve service quality and decrease costs and to provide a global platform too (Sahadev & Islam, 2005).

Researchers comprehend that using ICT based marketing not only empowers customers to purchase or look for their 'made to order' accommodation offerings, but also, assist suppliers in administration, budding and dispensing their produce within short span of time and throughout the globe by availing the efficient tools (Buhalis & Law, 2008). It is advantageous for accommodation industry firms to apply applications through ICT based marketing that help their managerial decision-making and daily operations. This precipitates into the compulsory usage of ICT based marketing tools and applications by accommodation sector to remain competitive in the dynamic market.

The adoption of ICT based marketing plays a leading role in enhancing the image of the organization among its customers. They show that customers who perceive the organization as ICT based marketing -oriented tend to talk about it favourably, thus spreading positive word-of-mouth communications about it (Xiang et al.,2008). The effective use of ICT based marketing can improve not only the performance and functionality, but can also improve firm level productivity and innovation by allowing for more cost effective and fluid communication with all stakeholders, improving logistics, overcoming distance, helping firms understand their competitive positioning and enhancing transparency. Scaglione et al. (2009) analysed revenue per available room before and after hotels adopted websites. They found that website exploitation correlated positively to hotel performance and reportedly found a positive link between external web content and firm performance. In the context of e-business reported that it is helping to foster productivity enhancement. While, cost reduction considered as an important impact of ICT based marketing and higher customization and improvements are also argued in organizational learning.

Hotel employees pointed out that the main reason to use ICT based marketing was to increase product awareness. Reminding the consumers about the product repeatedly was considered a good practice; they mentioned that consumers will buy only products they recognize about. The usage of ICT based marketing can increase product awareness, and can provide stimuli whenever there is a need of the product. Realization of a wider and bigger set of audience was another reason to use it. Generating customer calls was another main reason of using information and communication tools. When done right, email marketing lets the accommodation industry reach the right person, at the right time with the right offer. Email has become prime mode of communication these days. It is instant. Whenever something is sent out to customers, our office is flooded of telephone calls.

It is also beneficial in a situation when accommodation firms are dealing with a bigger website audience, you can easily disseminate information about your company, foster good client relationships, increase profit and gains, improve product image, enhance product awareness, and many other positive points. Hence most of the hotels who have website, you need to actively exert effort in increasing the traffic to the site, and this can be done through ICT based marketing tools.

Savings in promotional budget was another objective as quoted by respondents. Reaching out to clients on an individual basis can be a costly and time-consuming process. ICT based marketing helps accommodation firms to save time by reaching out to your wider audience, while still delivering a message that's personal and relevant to them. Ease of use was another objective relevant to hoteliers behind using ICT based marketing in their business. The digit of online transactions has increased reliably in accommodation industry. Most hotel customers are now turning to the Internet and researching their needs before making a destination choice as Internet transacting is more convenient and cost-effective on the part of consumers. This type of marketing channels also helpful to handle all the marketing functions in a suitable and convenient manner. Accessible to consumers of the information and communication based applications 24/7, was also the main reason for adopting ICT based marketing based strategies. Another objective for using the ICT based marketing in hotels was the building customer relationships. For building strong customer relationships, marketers need to communicate on continuous basis with the customers who matter maximum to business. It `provides the hoteliers the ability to stay at the top-of-mind and keep customers involved during the whole year.

Figure 3.

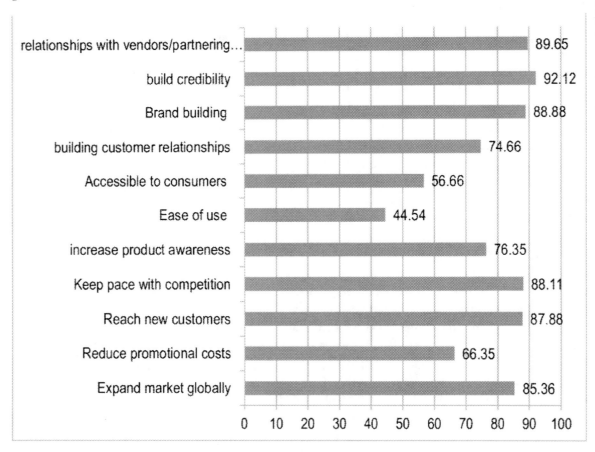

Brand building has also been the objective of using the ICT based marketing tools by the hotels. One can support brand recognition with potential and new clients, and encompass reach when customers share or forward messages with the friends. The use of more and more of information and communication devices has been another reason for hotels resorting to this technology. With messaging over mobile devices instant messaging has become one of the best tools for hoteliers. ICT based marketing gives the ability to organize the audience into lists and communicate with people based on interest, purchase behavior, location, and to stay top-of-mind and build credibility among customers. Using ICT based marketing to maintain relationships and build personal connections has been a key to our success. Besides building relationships with customers, there was a dire need to maintain relationships with vendors and partnering businesses. Two-way ICT based marketing gives hoteliers the ability to maintain communication with all audiences. Managers were specific to point out to this objective as major reason to adopt ICT based marketing in accommodation sector.

The above figure indicates that for most of accommodation properties in Gurugram was noted major opportunities of using ICT based marketing as its contribution to develop the market at global level. Through the firms can grasp the global markets without many efforts. Moreover, reduction in promotional costs, reaching new customers, keeping pace with competition, increasing the product awareness, easing the of use customer friendly, making business accessible to consumers, building customer relationships, for brand building, for building credibility and building relationships with vendors/partnering businesses were also observed as major advantages of using ICT based marketing in accommodation sector.

Challenges with Using ICT Based Marketing in Accommodation Sector

Earlier studies in the field of ICT based marketing noticed that despite all the benefits that can be achieved by ICT based marketing, many tourism and hotel businesses have failed to embrace ICT based marketing and the Internet. They further contemplated that the internal organizational ready to adopt e-business as the major arguments as perceived by managements of the accommodation firms. Continuing with organizational barriers among non-adopters, they attributed non-usage of ICT based marketing and internet to lack of technological and financial resources, the negative attitude of management such as lack of their support and less risk-taking propensity, and the lack of IT knowledge.

The main barriers to adopt this technology are simply the concern that the Internet or the website would not lead to more efficiency, lower costs or more revenues and the feeling that the Internet or a website is not suitable for a particular business (Sigala,2003). The uncertainty about real business value and web existence with an emphasis to determine the return of the investment as the major obstacle to using ICT based marketing.

The lack of adequate infrastructure to handle online payments limited online reservations as major barriers not to adopt ICT based marketing. A number of challenges that reduce the uptake of ICT based marketing by tourism and accommodation firms such as lack of training and capital limited understanding of the potential of technology, and a lack of clear business strategies. Moreover, the reluctance to adopt comprehensive technology are hidden costs of ICT based marketing adoption, such as training and upgrading software, as well as the precautions about time commitments and the problems of relying on external expertise. Hollenstein (2004) cornered ICT based marketing adoption is often impeded by information barriers such as uncertainties with respect to the performance and the future development of these technologies. Thus, studies have cited a number of reasons for not adopting the ICT based marketing by the accommodation firms. Consequently, it will be in the fitness of things if the reasons are brought out systematically under circumstances prevalent in Indian economy.

Figure 4.

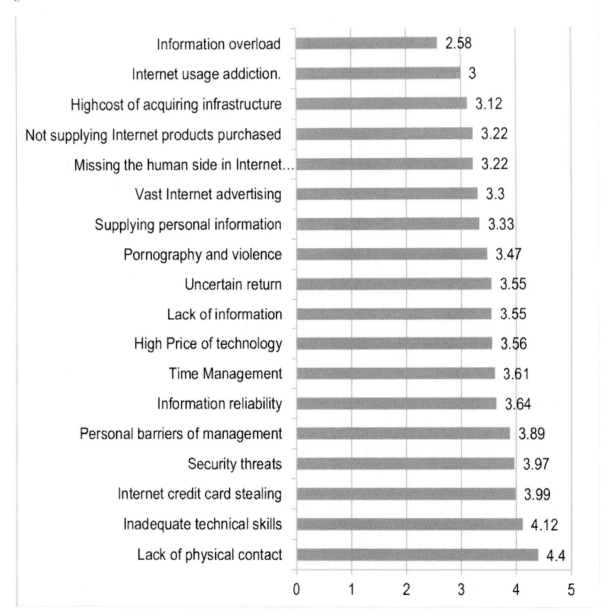

Manager respondents noted that there were enough financial resources available for ICT based marketing applications, but lack of knowledge about the importance of tools and the lack of experts was the major reason for using ICT based marketing to a limited extent. In fact, the respondents reported that the gestation period from the start of an ICT based marketing application to the finish when it gets fully integrated into the system was almost two years and that is why owners and managers have a fear of failure of the new technique at any stage. The most illogical stand reported by managers was that most of the guests were the corporate guests operating through travel agents and tour operators, having contacts with the hotels. Thus, they were dependent on agents and little bothered about costs and convenience.

Additionally, the hotel management systems and practices (booking and reservations, and food and beverage and accounting too) are obsolete and relatively inefficient; the hotel sector is not effectively linked to most of the global computer based reservation systems that can deliver up to 30% of the room sales for a typical four star hotel; accommodation prices are controlled and a dual pricing structure exists for domestic and international tourists with international tourists paying up to three times as much as domestic tourists. Hurdles integral in the execution of various ICT based marketing practices in the accommodation industry were look over through the literature and were put before the respondents for their view on a five-point scale starting from extreme barrier to not a barrier.

The most critical challenge facing hotels using ICT based marketing tools was identified as the Lack of physical contact with the customers. Hotels lacked technical skills – competent persons to use ICT based marketing tools, perceived security threats where by credit card data stealing was foremost. Managements/owners still had a lot of personal barriers, did not believe in the effectiveness of ICT based marketing, and were doubtful of information reliability besides the high price of technology and uncertain returns. Employees specified time constraints and lack of appropriate information to be posted on the sites. They were further scared of pornography and violence and leakage of personal information. Information overload was perceived to be high if ICT based marketing was adopted. Managers showed concern that it will be harassment for them if the promised product is not supplied to the customers. They also felt a threat that by resorting to ICT based marketing tools, their traditional marketing tactics was likely to suffer a lot. In line with other studies, sufficient evidences went on to say that ultimately the human side in purchase gets missing. Thus, overall ICT based marketing was considered too expensive to implement. Furthermore, further spending was needed to supplement training, advice and support. In the same manner, accommodation firms slightly agreed on the hotels that they do not have staff enriched with essential skills which are mandatory for the broad execution of the ICT based marketing. Interviews revealed that probably the biggest barrier owners face are those minute, irritating, uncertainty questions that keep popping into their head.

SOLLUTION AND RECOMMENDATION

The deliberations of current study showed that a positive association is there between ICT based marketing and success of accommodation service providers in study area. On the basis of outcomes, it can also be concluded that technological competence, managerial support, firm operational level. Though benefits of using information & communication technology (ICT) in marketing include capability to penetrate the markets globally, decrease in the advertising costs, enhancement in sales profitability and sales volume of firms as well, on the basis of outcomes, it can be said that not all the hotels uniformly make use of maximum of the common ICT-marketing features.

It was observed on the basis of outcomes of the current research that not all employees of accommodation are well versed with how to apply various digital marketing practices in successful manner. This makes it complicated probably for employees to effectively utilise ICT marketing practices. It was also observed that a number of the respondents were not even well-known with some of the ICT marketing applications and their features. Therefore, on the basis of results, it is strongly suggested that the hospitality firms necessarily invest in employees professional training so that they can be equipped with necessary skills to utilise ICT applications for marketing in an effective manner.

The present study recognised that observed that those accommodation firms where their managers are more active about ICT enabled marketing tended to exploit more strategic marketing practices comparative to other marketing tools. Hence, it can be said that deficiency of advice and required support from the top management is possibly the reason for some firms not fully getting the benefits of using ICT in marketing.

The current study on the basis of its findings also provides implications for academia and industry professional for better use of information & communication technology in the field of tourism and hospitality. The implication from the study can be a comprehensive ICT based -marketing plan should be there including; proper identification of the internet market by examining what is being searched on internet about India. By means of online and offline methodologies one must find out the factors responsible for bringing visitors to India, focussing on customers' e-satisfaction on priority basis.

A rich e-content with high quality should be designed that focuses on the needs of customer such as particular or special packages, lean season advertisings, packaging local activities, event-related getaways, and beginning of other marketing initiatives to provide customization, either it is the hotel website, or even email marketing campaigns or SMS. Tourism and hospitality organizations should have powerful e-existence, availability should be on all online channels including the effective social media like Facebook & Twitter and commencing advertising campaigns with SMSs and email.

The tourism firm's official website should be equipped with sufficient information about the hotel's services, outlets, branches etc. Accommodation service providers should resort to continuous status evaluation of guests and competitors; and finally, top management and independent hotels owners are advised to make the viability analysis of the potential of ICT in marketing.

On the basis of outcomes of the study it can be said that technological competence impact effective application and use of ICT based marketing practices. Conclusively present study also maintains the theory of the E-Value Model by Salwani et al., (2009), which stated that marketing through different ICT tools increases business profitability and variation in marketing efficiency of firms by both internal and external operational activities.

FUTURE RESEARCH DIRECTION

Though the study conducted with cautions but, it came across certain limitations, such as it is limited only to accommodation sector of tourism industry and Gurugram region of India only. Other segments such as travel intermediately, transportation and others were not included in this study. This has a negative consequence of failure in the quest to generalise the findings of the research to the entire tourism sector. Regardless of these few limitations, however, the researcher has managed to reach useful conclusions by taking all necessary precautions. Further the present research leads to some good outcomes that might be of interest to future researchers. It is suggested on the basis of researcher's experience that future research could repeat this study and observe the impact of ICT applications and business profitability in different tourism and hospitality firms. There is also a great scope for future researchers to find out the impact of social sites marketing (Twitter, Facebook, and Pinterest etc.) on the tourism sector.

CONCLUSION

ICT based marketing has a growing impact on accommodation industry of developing countries like India. With innovative forms of ICT based marketing applications, a novel type of experience has emerged in the current business era. The present study examined the ICT based marketing applications, opportunities and challenges associated with its usages in accommodation sector.

Outcomes regarding application of ICT based marketing presented through managers' responses for various ICT based marketing practices applied by accommodation firms. Investigating online consumer-generated reviews towards use of ICT based marketing in general policy and awareness was a common practice among accommodation firms. Hence, the study claimed that a significant relationship of ICT based marketing usage with increasing number of potential customers to the firms. With analysis of opportunities, more and more sale information and e-existence practices were being applied by the accommodation firms these days. This shows a clear trend on the part of accommodation firms getting ICT based marketing savvy. Scrutinizing results demonstrated that accommodation is vigilant in their e-existence efforts in displaying the likeable information about their services, products, prices, and offers on their website, in totality to applying online channels to have the presence on the web. Also, the transaction through ICT based marketing platform, the various department i.e. front office and public relations employees were especially trained in helping the usage of website chat services in the guest conversations. This clears many of the doubts in the minds of the customers. They are provided assistance and guidance for special offers/best buys. In order to increase the e-relationship and make longer the e-image with home guests, e-transaction results in sustainable growth. Such practices bring in innovations in notices of guests increasing the image of the hotel and raising the awareness of others utilizing booking methods and conventional contacts. That is why almost all accommodation firms have started putting Web address and its available services.

On analysis of opportunities, outcomes indicate that for most of accommodation firms using ICT based marketing as it provide them to develop the market at global level. Through the internet firms can grasp the global markets size with increased number of customers in a cost-effective manner and drawing positive word of mouth through enhanced customer experience. The study discovered major challenges to ICT based marketing adoption are costs effective, it is slow and still complex, ICT based marketing depends upon the size of the hotel, managements and owners lack advantage, usage is still little, hotels deficiency of staff training, insufficient number of educated staff, and security and safety concerns, and hotels operating at local level atmosphere the heat superfluously. These outcomes are in agreement and supported that developing nations like India faced difficulty of applying the ICT based marketing to avail technology benefits.

REFERENCES

Barnes, D., & Hinton, M. (2007). Searching for e-business performance measurement system. *The Electronic Journal of Information System*, *10*(1), 134–142.

Buhalis, D. (2003). *E-Tourism: Information Technology for Strategic Tourism Management*. London: Financial Times / Prentice-Hall.

Buhalis, D., & Law, R. (2008). Progress in information technology and tourism management: 20 years on and 10 years after the Internet. *Tourism Management, 29*(1), 609–623. doi:10.1016/j.tourman.2008.01.005

Card, J. A., Chen, C. Y., & Cole, S. T. (2003). Online Travel Products Shopping: Differences between Shoppers and Nonshoppers. *Journal of Travel Research, 42*(2), 133–139. doi:10.1177/0047287503257490

Conyette, M. (2015). 21 Century Travel using Websites, Mobile and WearableTechnology Devices. *Athens Journal of Tourism, 2*(2), 105–116. doi:10.30958/ajt.2-2-3

E-Travel Marketing India. (2015). *Annual Report 2015 E-Travel Marketing India: A Path to Purchase.* Octane Marketing Private Limited. Retrieved from https://octaneresearch.in/research/e-travel-marketing-india/

Gretzel, U., Fesenmaier, D. R., Fromica, S., & O'Leary, J. T. (2006). Searching for the future: Challenges faced by destination marketing organizations. *Journal of Travel Research, 45*(1), 116–126. doi:10.1177/0047287506291598

Hollenstein, H. (2004). Determinants of the adoption of Information and Communication Technologies (ICT); an empirical analysis based on firm-level data for the Swiss business sector. *Structural Change and Economic Dynamics, 15*(3), 315–342. doi:10.1016/j.strueco.2004.01.003

India Brand Equity Foundation. (2021). *Indian Tourism & Hospitality Sector Report.* A report Published by Indian Brand Equity Foundation (IBEF). Retrieved from https://www.ibef.org/download/Tourism-and-Hospitality-February2021.pdf

Nikoli, G., & Lazakidou, A. (2019). The Impact of Information and Communication Technology on the Tourism Sector. *Almatourism-Journal of Tourism, Culture and Territorial Development, 10*(19), 45–68.

Olifer, N., & Olifer, V. (2006). *Computer Networks, Principles, Technologies and Protocol for Network Design.* John Wiley and Sons Ltd.

Sahadev, S., & Islam, N. (2005). Why hotels adopt ICTs: A study on the ICT adoption propensity of hotels in Thailand. *International Journal of Contemporary Hospitality Management, 17*(5), 391–401. doi:10.1108/09596110510604814

Salwani, I. S., Marthandan, G., Norzaidi, M. D., & Chong, S. C. (2009). E- Commerce usage and business performance in the Malaysian tourism sector: Empirical analysis. *Information Management & Computer Security, 17*(2), 166–185. doi:10.1108/09685220910964027

Scaglione, M., Schegg, R., & Murphy, J. (2009). Website adoption and sales performance in Valais' hospitality industry. *Technovation, 29*(1), 625–631. doi:10.1016/j.technovation.2009.05.011

Sigala, M. (2003). Developing and Benchmarking Internet Marketing Strategies in the Hotel Sector in Greece. *Journal of Hospitality & Tourism Research (Washington, D.C.), 27*(4), 375–401. doi:10.1177/10963480030274001

Tussyadiah, I. P., & Fesenmaier, D. R. (2009). Mediating the tourist experiences Access to Places via Shared Videos. *Annals of Tourism Research, 36*(1), 24–40. doi:10.1016/j.annals.2008.10.001

Verma, A., & Shukla, V. (2019). Analyzing the influence of IoT in Tourism Industry. *International Conference on Sustainable Computing in Science, Technology & Management*, 2083-2093. 10.2139srn.3358168

Xiang, Z., Wober, K., & Fesenmaier, D. R. (2008). Representation of the online tourism domain in search engines. *Journal of Travel Research*, *47*(2), 137–150. doi:10.1177/0047287508321193

ADDITIONAL READING

Benckendorff, P. J., Sheldon, P. J., & Fesenmaier, D. R. (2014). *Tourism Information Technology* (2nd ed.). CABI. doi:10.1079/9781780641850.0000

Cantoni, L., & Xiang, Z. (2013). *Information and Communication Technologies in Tourism 2013*. Springer. doi:10.1007/978-3-642-36309-2

Hu, X., & Yang, Y. (2020). Determinants of consumers' choices in hotel online searches: A comparison of consideration and booking stages. *International Journal of Hospitality Management*, *86*(1), 1–41. doi:10.1016/j.ijhm.2019.102370

Khatri, I. (2019). Information Technology in Tourism & Hospitality Industry: A Review of Ten Years' Publications. *Journal of Tourism and Hospitality Education*, *9*(1), 74–87. doi:10.3126/jthe.v9i0.23682

Liu, S. Q., & Mattila, A. S. (2016). Using comparative advertising to promote technology- based hospitality services. *Cornell Hospitality Quarterly*, *57*(2), 162–171. doi:10.1177/1938965516630424

KEY TERMS AND DEFINITIONS

CRS: Computer reservation systems, or central reservation systems (CRS), are computerized systems used to store and retrieve information and conduct transactions related to air travel, hotels, car rental, or other activities.

Digital India: The 'Digital India' campaign of the Indian Government is crucial move to come out with innovative ideas and practical solutions to transforming nation and creating opportunities for all citizens by harnessing digital technologies.

GDS: A global distribution system (GDS) is a computerised network system owned or operated by a company that enables transactions between travel industry service providers, mainly airlines, hotels, car rental companies, and travel agencies.

ICT: Information and Communication Technologies (ICTs) is a broader term for Information Technology (IT), which refers to all communication technologies, including the internet, wireless networks, cell phones, computers, software, middleware, video-conferencing, social networking, and other media applications and services.

Marketing: Marketing is the activity, set of institutions, and processes for creating, communicating, delivering, and exchanging offerings that have value for customers, clients, partners, and society at large.

Social Media: Social media refers to websites and applications that are designed to allow people to share content quickly, efficiently, and in real-time. While many people access social media communication tool such as Twitter, Facebook, and Pinterest, etc.

Tourism: Tourism, the act and process of spending time away from home in pursuit of recreation, relaxation, and pleasure, while making use of the commercial provision of services.

Section 2
Smart Tourism and Co-Creation

Chapter 6
Smart and Sustainable Tourism Destinations:
A Bibliometric Analysis

Ana Sousa
COMEGI, Universidade Lusíada - Norte, Portugal

Clara Madeira
COMEGI, Universidade Lusíada - Norte, Portugal

Paula Rodrigues
https://orcid.org/0000-0003-2967-2583
COMEGI, Universidade Lusíada - Norte, Portugal

Carlos Martins
COMEGI, Universidade Lusíada - Norte, Portugal

ABSTRACT

Policymakers and business practitioners increasingly recognize the importance of sustainability in the development of smart tourism destinations, which require clear directions and specific guidelines. The authors used the Bibliometrix R-package and VOS Viewer software to perform a bibliometric analysis of 59 articles between 1900-2020 retrieved from the Web of Science (WoS) Core Collection database. They compiled a bibliographic coupling, identified the key authors, journals, documents, and the most relevant universities. The findings detail four clusters: (1) smart tourism, (2) sustainable tourism, (3) technology, and (4) smart specialization. This work contributes to a better understanding of the concepts and aspires to provide useful information for those academics and destination marketing organizations (DMOs) attempting to analyze and deepen their knowledge within this research field. Simultaneously, it also aims to provide insights concerning the future development of sustainability and smart tourism in the social sciences' academic literature.

DOI: 10.4018/978-1-7998-8306-7.ch006

INTRODUCTION

Previously to the current pandemic context of COVID-19, tourism was growing steadily and for some countries, it was one of the main sources of GDP. So, it has become one of the most important sectors worldwide being connected with social and economic development. To promote a sustainable development in the tourism sector a great effort has been made in technology and innovation, with consequences at the organization level and the new consumer-tourist demands (Sigalat-Signes, Calvo-Palomares, Roig-Merino, & García-Adán, 2020). Tourism and hospitality have faced several changes and digitalization is one of the most important ones. Digital innovations and technological devices influence the development of several industries such as information and communications technologies (ICT), manufacturing, and service industries. Tourism and hospitality depend on the cooperation of several stakeholders and the benefits of digital solutions allowed to better respond to consumer demands and remain competitive in a rapidly changing market (Zsarnoczky, 2018). In the last years, we testified the proliferation of web and social platforms which, in turn, contributed to the notion of an individual's life in a smart environment (Zeng, Tim, Yu, & Liu, 2020). As Ismagilova, Hughes, Dwivedi, and Raman (2019) suggest, on one hand, technology has promoted the advance of social, environmental, economic and cultural progress. However, on the other, smart cities should be capable of supporting these dimensions with resource to technology. According to López de Ávila (2015, p. 32) a smart city is defined as a "tourism-oriented and innovative space accessible to all, which is consolidated on a cutting-edge technological infrastructure, which must guarantee sustainable territorial development while facilitating visitor interaction and integration with the environment, increasing the quality of their experience in the destination and the quality of life of the residents". The concept of a smart city underlies the notion of an intelligent tourist destination (Ivars-Baidal, Celdrán-Bernabeu, Mazón, & Perles-Ivars, 2019), focusing on tourism development as the economic driving force and being called smart tourism destinations. Big Data Analytics (BDA), new trends in tourism, cloud-based booking sites, and new forms for sharing experiences via digital platforms, opened a window for special tailor-made offers (Vecchio, Mele, Ndou, & Secundo, 2018), which go beyond mass tourism. Smart tourism depends on the adoption of these technologies that enable to collect and analyze a vast amount of data and create personalized, or hyper-personalized, experiences. More and more, consumers are looking for a touristic and hospitality experience based on a personalized offer. Destinations that can provide great personal travel experiences to tourists, increase their success, and this can be done through smart tourism destination. Additionally, today there is a pronounced need for the development of more sustainable economic activities. One of the purposes of a smart tourism destination consists of the creation of a smart experience, described as an experience facilitated by technologies, and improved by personalization (Buhalis & Amaranggana, 2015). This implies the interconnection between communities, service providers, and tourists through dynamic platforms. Within smart tourism destination technology plays a major role since it is used to support tourist value and experience co-creation, and at the same time, create wealth for the organisations and destinations (Boes, Buhalis, & Inversini, 2015). Based on information from tourist's surrounding contexts, marketers can influence consumer's decision-making process, by promoting the interaction between the consumer and the supplier (e.g., the peer-to-peer communication used in Airbnb and Uber) (Buhalis & Foerste, 2015).

To address the growth academic importance of smart tourism destination in the last six years, this research conducted a bibliometric analysis to explore trends and patterns in the tourism field. Results indicate that the sustainability approach or concern to smart tourism is, in fact, very recent, with an outcome of 59 papers from Web of Science. To analyse the main topics of the selected articles, we developed a documents bibliographic coupling network with VOSviewer. This resulted in a map of 14 documents distributed among four clusters. This review aspires to provide useful information for those academics and practitioners attempting to analyse and deepen their knowledge within this research field. This bibliometric review offers support for the need for an interdisciplinary view, based on dialogue, participation, and a critical vision among the stakeholders and destination marketing organisations (DMOs). This interdisciplinary view will allow designing more personalised experiences for the tourists as well as for the inhabitants, generating revenues and a sustainable touristic identity. Simultaneously it also aims to provide insights concerning the future development on smart tourism destination towards a more sustainable management in the social sciences' academic literature.

BACKGROUND

Smart Tourism

The term "Smart" has been described as "a prefix to technological terms to indicate special capabilities, intelligence and/or connectivity, as in smart phone or smart card. It has also been associated with resource optimisation through advanced technologies (Gretzel, Koo, Sigala, & Xiang, 2015) or the interconnection and synchronization of different technologies (Höjer & Wangel, 2015)" (Gretzel, Werthner, Koo, & Lamsfus, 2015, p. 559). Another important concept is Internet of Things (IoT) since it plays a key role in filling the gap between physical and mobile engagement and providing interconnectivity among people, systems and products (Gretzel, Ham, & Koo, 2018; Porter & Heppelmann, 2014). Its use has been popularised to describe various urban areas, named "smart cities" and, thenceforth, extended to "smart tourism". Thus, the concept of smart tourism combines instrumented infrastructure and interconnected systems, which will support Destination Management Organisations (DMOs) decisions based on collective knowledge. This information will be of great interest for the tourism industry and help to offer more tourist personalised experiences and, at the same time, real-time monitoring (Xiang, Stienmetz, & Fesenmaier, 2021).

Smart Tourism Destinations

Bringing competitiveness and market a destination is challenging since it evolves several stakeholders most of the time with competitive interests (Buhalis, 2000; Papadopoulos & Hamzaoui-Essoussi, 2015). These mediate tourists' travel experiences, which are multidimensional in nature, by taking part in the tourism context to reflect the experience as a whole (including before, during, and after the trip) (Wang, Park, & Fesenmaier, 2012). Thus, an inclusive stakeholder's approach is highly recommended (Dinnie, 2008) which means considering the participation of representatives from government, commerce, non-profit organisations, tourism and the media. These organisations must share a value-based platform and present an authentic and compelling story to the world. This story should be supported by a set of values that resonate both domestically and internationally.

The concept of Smart Tourism Destinations (STD) emerges from the development of Smart Cities as well as Information and Communications Technology (ICTs), which gained importance being considered as significant drivers of destination competitiveness (Buhalis & Amaranggana, 2015; Del Chiappa &

Baggio, 2015). Gradually technology has evolved, being implanted in most of the tourism organisations supporting the improvement of tourist experiences (Buhalis & Amaranggana, 2015). The exchange that takes place between tourists and tourist destinations promoted through ICTs is described as the digital tourism ecosystem (Benckendorff, Xiang, & Sheldon, 2019; Gelter, Lexhagen, & Fuchs, 2020) and challenges the role DMOs. DMOs are responsible for managing all elements of a tourist destination (e.g., attractions, accommodation, marketing), guaranteeing its competitiveness and, at the same time, keeping sustainability as a pillar in their business strategy and core operation.

Ivars-Baidal et al. (2019) describe some of these challenges, such as the need for new management models, namely a systemic model for STDs. The authors suggest that despite the growing importance of technology and data management, the efficiency of the STDs will mostly depend on the governance, specifically: "the STD model should be adapted to the needs and resources and the territorial and tourist context of each destination; prioritise and reinforce new capacities in the DMOs in order to facilitate the application of smart solutions and further the analysis and exploitation of data, in collaboration with the tourism companies in the destination; and the development of a systemic management approach, which allows feedback from all strategic–relational, instrumental and applied levels" (Ivars-Baidal et al., 2019, p. 1595). Thus, STDs should make use of the smartness concept to analyse patterns and trends. The access to traveller's data is useful to offer personalised services that meet or even exceed each different type of tourist (Boes et al., 2015). However, to provide this personalised experience, DMOs must overcome some barriers. One of the obstacles concerns the gap between the amount of available data and the capacity of the infrastructures to manage the information and transform it into knowledge. Another barrier respects information privacy laws and the reticence to share the data of tourist service users (Habegger et al., 2014). By overcoming these problems, DMOs should have a systemic perspective and invest in personalisation of traveller's experiences. Considering the service industry personalisation refers to "a state where consumers increasingly expect service that moulds to them" (Buhalis & Amaranggana, 2015, pp. 379-380). Rosenbaum, Ramirez, Campbell, and Klaus (2021) suggest that hyper-personalization appears to be the next step in connectivity between customers and suppliers, encompassing both customization and personalization alternatives. The authors suggest that consumers believe that "hyper-personalized products are worth premium prices, regardless of their desire to own these products" (Rosenbaum et al., 2021, p. 446). Within the context of hospitality, Kornova and Loginova (2019) call attention to the service as a personification tool that identifies supply and demand and is capable of transforming consumer behaviour. Hyper-personalization is described as an excessive degree of human subjectivation of its importance, demanding from hospitality service providers the most personalized tools in order to meet customer's needs and influencing his loyalty. The biggest benefit from personalization as experienced by travellers is that the consumption of the service is exactly the way they want it, in terms of convenience and promptly. On the other side, the DMOs, beyond the adoption of new technologies, are also capable of using them to improve guest satisfaction, promoting an increased comfort at an emotional and physical level. The global nature of the STD models (including for example, innovation, sustainability, accessibility, technological infrastructure), as well as the transformation of consumer behaviour demands, brings the necessity to have professionals that own both high-tech and traditional methods of communication.

Another interesting perspective about STD falls on the tourist consumer behaviour, more specifically on engaging tourists in responsible and sustainable practices (Juvan & Dolnicar, 2014). Considering the significant growth of tourism and its negative impacts on sustainability and the wellbeing of local communities, it is important to promote measures beyond limiting the number of tourists. Thus, we have to understand the drivers that make tourists act in a more environmentally friendly way (Juvan &

Dolnicar, 2017). A sustainable tourist is described as a tourist "who respects the local culture, conserves the natural environment, and reduces interference of the local environment" (Lee, Jan, & Yang, 2013, p. 457). Shen, Sotiriadis, and Zhou (2020, p. 3) suggest that smart tourists should be "become co-creators of sustainable tourism experiences and co-managers of tourism resources in the sustainable management of tourism assets and resources at the destination". The authors support that smart tourist behaviour should be evaluated along three stages of the tourism experience, namely before-consumption (BC), during-consumption experience (DC) and post-consumption (PC). During these stages, smart tourists could be influenced by social networking sites (SNSs) to adopt sustainable behaviour. This implies that tourists adopt the point of view of local communities, respecting the uniqueness and difference of each destination and reducing the environmental footprint by being a guardian of natural resources (Shen et al., 2020).

Sustainable Tourism

The principles of sustainable tourism development are relevant to all forms of tourism, from mass to niche tourism, in all types of destinations. To guarantee long-term tourism sustainability, it is fundamental that a proper balance exists between its environmental, economic, and socio-cultural dimensions (UNWTO, 2021). This implies that governments, DMOs, business managers, and tourists should preserve the socio-cultural authenticity of host communities by preserving traditional values and cultural heritage. It is also important to guarantee the participation of all relevant stakeholders, ensuring long-term economic operations, including stable employment and income-earning opportunities and social services to host communities (UNWTO, 2021). Although governments and the World Tourism Organisation (UNWTO) advocate sustainable development as one of their main concerns, and several journals are focussing on sustainable tourism showing the importance of the topic, facts suggest the lack of sustainability of tourism at a global scale (Hall, 2019; Rutty, Gössling, Scott, & Hall, 2015; Scott, Gössling, Hall, & Peeters, 2016; Scott, Hall, & Gössling, 2016). Cities such as Barcelona, Venice, Amsterdam, among others, are recognised as popular tourist destinations struggling to cope with mass tourism, demanding from policymaker's responses to the hypothetical success of tourism (Hall, 2019). To address issues concerning the relationship between sustainable tourism and smart city/destinations, Ivars-Baidal, Vera-Rebollo, Perles-Ribes, Femenia-Serra, and Celdrán-Bernabeu (2021) suggest the convergence between smartness and sustainability evidenced by the "presence of indicators that specify, measure and apply their principles to cities and tourist destinations" (p. 3). Some of the criteria that include these indicators are reducing transport impact, climate change, solid and water management, and landscape and biodiversity protection. However, the authors call attention to the lack of studies analysing the contribution of ICTs to sustainable tourism (Ali & Frew, 2013). Considering the growing importance of ICTs in the service sector, Huovila, Bosch, and Airaksinen (2019) questioned the three main pillars of sustainability due to today's hyper digitalized society. Smart sustainability shows the synergies between smart city/destination and sustainable tourism (Ribes & Baidal, 2018). Considering the range of existing indicators and the lack of suitable ones that help policymakers in the construction of sustainable tourism, Ivars-Baidal et al. (2021) studied indicators that can contribute to real progress towards sustainable practices within a smart tourism context. The authors conclude that despite the potential that smart cities and destinations have to offer, much work has to be done in sustainability measures. Supporting Merrick's (2019) ideas, it is important to promote a systemic understanding of urban spaces to avoid city silos. Ivars-Baidal et al. (2021) findings suggest a clear dissociation between urban and tourism indicators. The analyses carried out showed problems regarding the integration of tourism indicators into smart city platforms "which epitomize the integral management of cities through technologies and data" (p. 12). Moreover, the initiatives carried out in many cities "require greater soundness and methodological harmonization, two aspects which can be improved under the smart sustainability" (Ivars-Baidal et al., 2021, p. 13). In conclusion, it is critical to develop specific tourism indicators that can be integrated into urban space management and create synergies between tourism activity and the urban quality of life.

The achievement of sustainable tourism is a continuous process that involves the maintenance of a high level of tourist satisfaction and experience, and at the same time raising their awareness about sustainability issues and promoting sustainable tourism practices amongst them. This cannot be done without constant evaluation of impacts, introducing the necessary preventive and/or corrective measures whenever necessary.

According to the literature review, we found that smart tourism is inseparable from sustainability. While the smart approach lacks a holistic and long-term view, the sustainability approach overlooks governance issues. Both can complement each other in the design and development of touristic activities (Ivars-Baidal et al., 2021; Ribes & Baidal, 2018). Considering the absence of studies that combine these two fields of knowledge (Ali & Frew, 2013), we aim to fill this gap by developing bibliometric analysis of sustainability and smart tourism since it provides visual mapping and observation of the most prominent themes. Escobar and Margherita (2021) also support the link between sustainability and smart tourism, highlighting that tourism actions should go beyond the safeguard of the environment, including the pillars of economic and socio-cultural aspects. Although sustainability is considered the base of the smart concept (Gretzel, 2020), and it is possible to find literature underlining the relevance of sustainability in smart tourism (González-Reverté, Díaz-Luque, Gomis-López, & Morales-Pérez, 2018; Ribes & Baidal, 2018; Shafiee, Ghatari, Hasanzadeh, & Jahanyan, 2019) to the best of the authors' knowledge this is the first study conducting a bibliometric analysis considering both concepts.

METHODOLOGY

Bibliometric Analysis

To study the longitudinal performance of the scientific production of sustainability and smart tourism, we resorted to a bibliometric analysis using bibliometric and SNA. This methodology has been increasingly used in order to explore trends and the understanding of emerging concepts (Garrigos-Simon, Narangajavana-Kaosiri, & Lengua-Lengua, 2018; Milán-García, Uribe-Toril, Ruiz-Real, & de Pablo Valenciano, 2019).

Bibliometric employ statistical and mathematical tools to several bibliographic indicators in order to depict the state-of-the-art of specific fields (Zupic & Čater, 2015). Our analyses include yearly, geographical, journal and individual production, enabling the identification of main affiliations and authors within the research field. We also develop statistics on citations, which can reflect the quality of the articles and demonstrate key areas studied so far. To run the statistical bibliometric results, we used the Bibliometrix package that is available in the software R-Program (version 3.2.3). To complement the statistics, we resorted to SNA. This tool structures interactions of all kinds, providing easy interpretations of the respective relationships. (Serrat, 2009; Tabassum, Pereira, Fernandes, & Gama, 2018). Additionally, it identifies strong groups within the networks, named clusters (Kamińska, 2018). Hence, through the use of VOSviewer (version 1.6.15) (van Eck & Waltman, 2010), we developed a bibliographic coupling map, in order to understand how the dissemination of the literature flows (Kessler, 1963). Furthermore, we tried to thematically categorise each cluster of the bibliographic coupling network and assess the content of the articles, such that we could provide useful information on the results achieved so far and on the theoretical guidelines for upcoming research. This step sustains the sum up of the most relevant literature about smart and sustainable tourism by recognising patterns of study and gaps to pursue in future investigations, complementing the bibliometric review (Gaur & Kumar, 2018; Sassmannshausen & Volkmann, 2018).

The combination of these methods embodies a clear, systematic, and reproducible review process, while expressing both quantitative and qualitative analysis (Glänzel, 2003; Serrat, 2009; Zupic & Čater, 2015). Thus, empirical analysis of this research on the topics smart and sustainable tourism aims at: (i) perceive the dimension and respective evolution of the literature production, (ii) recognise the key authors and most important affiliations, (iii) determine core themes, and (iv) recap main conclusions.

The findings reflect the contribution of scientific production of smart tourism and sustainability to theoretical debates, methodological sophistication, and practical implications regarding the theme.

Data Collection

The dataset that support our bibliometric review consists of 59 scientific documents from 2015-2020 retrieved from the online platform Web of Science Core Collection (Ferreira, Fernandes, & Ratten, 2016). The search focused the combination "smart tourism" AND ("sustainability" OR "sustainable"), looking for the terms on title, abstract, author keywords and keywords plus. Also, a filter was added to the type of document, considering only articles, book chapters and reviews. Due to the topic's novelty, a timespan filter was not applied since we wanted to assess the global production from its first scientific approach until now. It is noteworthy that research on both topics has been developed, namely in literature reviews. However, the convergence of these is much needed to boost new paths of knowledge. After pre-processing all the data to simplify the data exploitation, we checked for duplicates, which were not found, proceeding then to the analysis of the results. Table 1 presents the main indicators from the dataset collected. We observe that 59 documents belong to 31 sources and were written on average by three authors. This means that documents written in collaboration are predominant (92%). The average number of citations per document is approximately nine.

Table 1. Main information of the collected data

Description	Results
Documents	59
Sources	31
Period	2015 – 2020
Average citations per documents	9.37
Authors	158
Authors of single-authored documents	5
Authors of multi-authored documents	153
Single-authored documents	5
Multi-authored documents	54
Authors per document	2.68
Collaboration Index	2.83

The following sections will proceed with the bibliometric review and the content analysis.

RESULTS AND DISCUSSION

Figure 1 shows the yearly evolution of scientific production of smart tourism and sustainability from 2015 until 2020. The simultaneous approach of sustainability and smart tourism is very recent. As it is possible to observe, the combination of these topics in the literature dates from 2015, showing the novelty of the themes. One possible explanation relies on the fact that smart tourism is an emerging scientific field, whose works are still, tendentially, conceptual and do not explore, yet, specific brunches of smart tourism, such as sustainability. To identify these gaps among literature of smart tourism and sustainability so far, further bibliometric statistics are developed.

Figure 1. Annual scientific production, 2015-2020

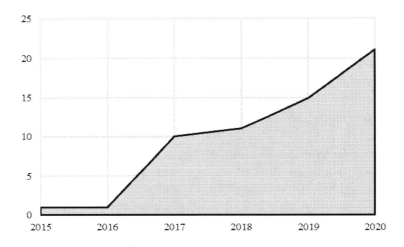

To understand the geographical dissemination of the scientific output, we observed the most relevant affiliations according to the number of citations (see Table 2).

University research centres are an important issue to analyse due to its role in promoting scientific production and enhance the researchers' activities. Moreover, the research centres can act as a key player supporting collaboration across the disciplines, with private sector, and government laboratories. We selected the most important universities based on the number of publications per affiliations. Affiliations are described as the universities and research centres in which the authors are allocated (Ponomariov & Boardman, 2010). Considering the affiliations of all co-authors of each article it is possible to observe that Europe, more specifically in the Mediterranean area (Spain, Portugal, and Greece), brings the major contribution (OECD, 2020). This might be explained by the highest importance of tourism sector for these countries. On the other side, Asian countries such as South Korea, Taiwan and China recognised by its reputation on technological interconnectivity in its cities, represent another important geographical group on the scientific production of the studied fields (Joo & Tan, 2020).

Table 2. Most relevant affiliations

Universities	Country	Number of Affiliations
Kyung Hee University	South Korea	11
University of Malaga	Spain	9
University of Alicante	Spain	7
University of Algarve	Portugal	6
National Technical University of Athens	Greece	4
University of Alcala de Henares	Spain	4
Beijing Normal University	China	3
Dankook University	South Korea	3
Matej Bel University	Slovakia	3
National Taiwan University	Taiwan	3
Tarbiat Modares University	Iran	3

The analysis of the most reputable journals is of extreme usefulness for academics and interested researchers who seek to understand the topics under investigation. Therefore, we present the most productive and influential journals within the context of smart and sustainable tourism (see Table 3).

Table 3. Ranking of five most productive and influential journals (sorted by publications and citations) 2015-2020

Journal	Publications	Citations	Impact Factor	Main Theme
Sustainability	28	129	2.58	Energy; Environmental Science; Social Sciences
IEEE Access	1	256	3.75	Computer Sciences; Engineering; Material Science
Science of the Total Environment	1	58	6.55	Environmental Science
Habitat International	1	23	4.31	Environmental Science; Social Sciences
Tourism Management Perspectives	1	14	3.65	Business; Management; Accounting

We noticed that Sustainability has a dominant position with 28 articles (90, 32%) and 129 citations. The remaining journals (30) show a much lower production with 1 paper in average. Despite the reduced number of articles, journals such as IEEE Access (256), Science of the Total Environment (58), Habitat International (23), and Tourism Management Perspectives (14) demonstrate a high rate of citations. Although the Journal of Regional Research is also considered a productive journal, we decided not to include since it shows a lower number of citations (less than 10 citations). These results might be explained by the interdisciplinary of the topics covered by various academic areas (see Table 2). In terms of impact factor Science of Total Environment shows the highest impact factor (6.55) followed by Habitat International (4.31) and IEEE Access (3.75). We observed that environmental sciences is a cross topic among the most relevant journals.

Table 4 and 5 present the top cited documents and authors, respectively. As it is possible to observe, Jara, Sun, Song and Bie are the authors with more citations, corresponding to the article entitled "Internet of Things and Big Data Analytics for Smart and Connected Communities" that belong to the IEEE access. Jara et al's higher number of citations is explained since this author also collaborated in another article. Subsequently, the authors of the article entitled "Advances and Challenges in Sustainable Tourism Toward a Green Economy" with 58 citations, which belongs to Science of the Total Environment, are also some of the most relevant scientific producers.

Table 4. Ranking of five most influential documents (2015-2020)

Documents	Title	Total Citations	Total Citations per Year
Sun, Song, Jara, and Bie (2016)	Internet of Things and Big Data Analytics for Smart and Connected Communities	256	51.20
Pan et al. (2018)	Advances and Challenges in Sustainable Tourism Toward a Green Economy	58	19.33
Encalada, Boavida-Portugal, Cardoso Ferreira, and Rocha (2017)	Identifying Tourist Places of Interest Based on Digital Imprints: Towards a Sustainable Smart City	23	5.75
Kim and Kim (2017)	The Role of Mobile Technology in Tourism: Patents, Articles, News, and Mobile Tour App Reviews	23	5.75
Romão and Neuts (2017)	Territorial Capital, Smart Tourism Specialization and Sustainable Regional Development: Experiences From Europe	23	5.75

Table 5. Ranking of five most influential authors (2015-2020)

Authors	Total Citations	m Index
Jara, Antonio J	260	0.33
Sun, Yunchuan	256	0.17
Song, Houbing	256	0.17
Bie, Rongfang	256	0.17
Pan, Shu-Yuan	58	0.25
Gao, Mengyao	58	0.25
Kim, Hyunook	58	0.25
Shah, Kinjal J	58	0.25
Pei, Si-Lu	58	0.25
Chiang, Pen-Chi	58	0.25

Social Network Analysis: Bibliographic Coupling Network

In order to complement the previous findings, we developed a bibliographic coupling mapping in VOSviewer, trough SNA. Social networks are usually modelled through graph theory, which applies mathematical and statistical tools to the representation and analysis of graphs. A graph represents relationships through nodes joined by lines (Martino & Spoto, 2006; Tabassum et al., 2018; Wasserman et al., 1994). The bibliographic coupling technique depicts the links between two documents (the nodes of this specific network) that share the same reference, enabling to draw the intellectual structure regarding the scientific production on smart and sustainable tourism (Egghe & Rousseau, 2002; Kessler, 1963). Then, the map returns clusters, that are tighter and shorter sub-networks with densely connected groups of nodes with sparser connections between them (Martino & Spoto, 2006). The concepts related to networks are described in Table 6, according to VOSviewer language (van Eck & Waltman, 2010).

Table 6. Terminology of networks based in VOSviewer language

Concepts	Description
Item or Node	The objects of interest. Items may for example be publications, researchers, or terms
Link	A connection or a relation between two items
Network	Set of nodes connected by their links
Cluster / Community	Set of connected nodes included in a network. One node belongs only to one cluster
Link strength[1]	Attribute of each link, expressed by a positive numerical value. In the case of co-authorship links, the higher the value, the higher the number of publications the two researchers have co-authored
Weight attribute: total link strength	The cumulative strength of the links of an item with other items

Starting with 59 documents, the criteria to stablish the network were: 1) Fractional counting method, to reduce the influence of documents with many authors (Perianes-Rodriguez, Waltman, & van Eck, 2016). With this method, the link strength of each node is divided by the number of adjacent nodes that collaborated with it in a same document; 2) Minimum number of citations of six; 3) Association as the normalization method of the network layout (Eck & Waltman, 2009; van Eck & Waltman, 2010).

Moreover, we selected the largest set of connected items (automatically by VOSviewer), which results in 14 nodes divided in 4 clusters. After carefully reading the titles, abstracts and the content of the document when needed, we named each cluster according to its core theme: (1) smart tourism, (2) sustainable tourism, (3) technology, and (4) smart specialization (see Figure 2 and Table 7).

Table 7. Clusters of bibliographic coupling network

Cluster	Document	Theme
1	Encalada et al. (2017), Romão and Neuts (2017), Luque Gil, Zayas Fernández, and Caro Herrero (2015)	Smart Tourism
2	Pan et al. (2018), Shafiee et al. (2019), Ribes and Baidal (2018)	Sustainable Tourism
3	Yoo, Kwon, Na, and Chang (2017), Polese, Botti, Grimaldi, Monda, and Vesci (2018), González-Reverté et al. (2018), Pradhan, Oh, and Lee (2018)	Technology
4	Kim and Kim (2017), Del Vecchio and Passiante (2017), Pencarelli (2020), Shen et al. (2020)	Smart Specialization

Figure 2. Visualization of the largest set of connected items of bibliographic coupling network, based on citations

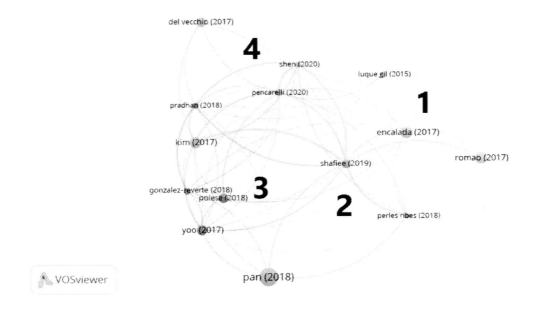

Content analysis

Noting the clusters identified previously through the mapping process (Table 7), we analysed the content of the documents as a way to deepen and extend the results found across the bibliometric study (Gaur & Kumar, 2018; White & Marsh, 2006). This method is recognised as a systematic and thorough approach to cover main trends and gaps in the literature (Krippendorff, 2018). Thus, complementarily to the information from WoS, the categories of core themes, methodological approach, and conclusions were added and determined to each of the 14 articles based on the reading of the respective content (see Table 8).

Table 8. Analysis of 14 most influential articles

Cluster	Articles	Number of citations	Type of Methodology	Main Conclusions
Smart Tourism	Encalada et al. (2017)	23	Quantitative	• There is a gap regarding the factors that can describe spatial patterns of city tourists. • This study analysed the spatial distribution of tourists in Lisbon based on data collected from a social network (Panoramio, based on visits between 2008 and 2014), and explored several relations between the observed pattern and a set of variables related to the city tourism offer. • Findings showed patterns on the city's tourist consumption, namely the city most visited areas as well as their location in the urban context.
	Romão and Neuts (2017)	23	Quantitative	• This study analyses the "link between the utilization of natural and cultural resources, along with other immaterial characteristics of the territorial capital of heterogeneous European regions, defining their innovation abilities characteristic of the smart development processes, in relation to tourism specialization and performance, aiming at the identification of the impacts of this global set of factors on sustainable development of European regions" (Romão & Neuts, 2017, p. 70). • Findings show a development gap among European regions, and the specialization in tourism does not mitigate this problem. • Considering the positive results obtained for the selected regions in terms of CO_2 emissions, technological and industrial development should be concerned with savings on energy consumption and energy production based on renewable sources to ensure an environmentally friendly process of industrial development.
	Luque Gil et al. (2015)	7	Conceptual	• The successful development of models of smart tourism destinations should be personalized to each case and supported on: Territorial Intelligence systems; a multidisciplinary approach; and co-creation management. • All physical and human elements have to be integrated, which is a huge challenge, considering the multiplicity of elements and individual needs.
Sustainable Tourism	Pan et al. (2018)	58	Conceptual	• Develop sustainable tourism requires an integrated and multi-disciplinary approach. • Create strategies, integrating local, national, and international policies and promoting green and innovative practices through environmental education.
	Shafiee et al. (2019)	14	Qualitative	• Smart tourism destinations depend on the fulfilment of several requirements such as a high internet penetration rate, the use of ICT, the existence of smart infrastructures, the development of social networks and the rate of global changes. • Need for a great integration between the economic, social, environmental, and technological strategies and substructures.
	Ribes and Baidal (2018)	6	Conceptual	• It was verified a strong connection between the concepts of sustainability and smartness, with common elements like the long-term vision and planning, innovation, public-private cooperation, and the involvement of the stakeholders. • A synergetic model of smart sustainability was developed, based on a governance framework that applies technology to five fundamental pillars.

Continued on following page

Table 8. Continued

Cluster	Articles	Number of citations	Type of Methodology	Main Conclusions
Technology	Yoo et al. (2017)	17	Quantitative	• The authors examined which factors affect the adoption of smart tourism applications that incorporate game elements. • Findings showed that applications offer tourists emotional pleasure (through gaming elements) and cognitive information. • Enjoyment or gaming factors are important for the tourists' experience with gamified tourism applications and expect that the game attributes from gamified smart tourism applications are different from general games.
	Polese et al. (2018)	16	Qualitative	• Regarding actors: different stakeholder groups in the Salerno smart tourism ecosystem tend to have relationships and also to establish collaborations that are mostly informal and not related to the offering of a bundle of services or discounts. • Concerning technology, ICTs are crucial elements for optimizing b&b (bed & breakfast) management and also facilitating the creation and maintenance of sustainable relationships between host and guests. • By confirming the relationship between value co-creation and sustainability, the mechanisms of resources integration identified bring advantages in terms of: (1) economic advantage (b&bs owners obtain innovation because they improve their service); (2) social well-being (by strengthening links with system actors); (3) environmental benefit (the network involves the development of the entire territory).
	González-Reverté et al. (2018)	7	Quantitative	• Tourists have different individual behaviours regarding their use of mobile devices, meaning that a single digital tourist does not exist. This brings important challenges for DMOs who should provide unique characteristics to their territories by offering different solutions and adapt the strategy to satisfy the different needs of their visitors.
	Pradhan et al. (2018)	7	Quantitative	• This study analysed the negative impact of smart devices on traveller's experiences. • Findings showed that the perceived benefits of smart devices have a greater impact on usage intention than do perceived risks. • Findings also show that the constructs of TRI (optimism, insecurity, and discomfort) influence travellers' perception experience.
Smart Specialization	Kim and Kim (2017)	23	Qualitative	• Advances in mobile technology can provide several and appropriate information to tourists, enabling them to make decisions that maximize their own well-being. • Destinations and firms can use refined and accumulated data to make accurate predictions and to respond effectively.
	Del Vecchio and Passiante (2017)	16	Conceptual	• Tourism is an important sector for Apulia and could represent a strategic industry for its growth and its smart specialization. • The symbioses between a smart specialization strategy and tourism growth will depend on the region's ability to encompass both the opportunities provided by information and communications technology (ICT) and these be linked to improve the sector competitiveness.
	Pencarelli (2020)	8	Conceptual	• New ICT have changed the way companies promote and provide services, and it has strongly impacted the tourist involvement in the co-creation processes • The ideal system of tourism should be based on a Smart Tourism perspectives like sustainability, circular economy, quality of life, and social value. • The enrichment of the tourist experience lays on a strategy of co-creation in both the physical and the digital world.
	Shen et al. (2020)	6	Quantitative	• Social networking sites influence tourist's experience at all stages (with incidence on the first two) on adopting sustainable and responsible behaviour.

Now we proceed with the discussion of the documents associated to the clusters. This discussion focuses on the investigation carried out by the authors and main conclusions.

Cluster 1 – Smart Tourism

The first cluster in Smart Tourism covers studies about the importance of Big Data analytics as a technology with the potential to develop Smart City services (Encalada et al., 2017), the contribution of the environmental dimension, and smart specialization to spatial sustainability (Romão & Neuts, 2017) and territorial intelligence (Luque Gil et al., 2015).

Encalada et al. (2017, p. 2) suggest that for cities "becoming smart implies reinforcing a city's uniqueness rather than allowing it to become impersonal and homogenized". The authors recognised a gap regarding the factors that can describe spatial patterns of city tourists. Thus, Encalada et al. (2017) carried out a study which analysed the spatial distribution of tourists in Lisbon based on data collected from a social network (Panoramio, based on visits between 2008 and 2014), and explored several relations between the observed pattern and a set of variables related to the city tourism offer. Findings showed patterns on the city's tourist consumption, namely the city most visited areas as well as their location in the urban context. The investigation carried out by Romão and Neuts (2017) also highlights the importance of smart specialization as a critical factor for regional innovation strategies (Foray et al., 2012) and sustainable development. The authors combine these concepts by analysing the utilization of territorial sensitive resources (natural and cultural resources). More specifically, the study focuses on analysing the "link between the utilization of natural and cultural resources, along with other immaterial characteristics of the territorial capital of heterogeneous European regions, defining their innovation abilities characteristic of the smart development processes, in relation to tourism specialization and performance, aiming at the identification of the impacts of this global set of factors on sustainable development of European regions" (Romão & Neuts, 2017, p. 70). Findings show a development gap among European regions, and the specialization in tourism does not mitigate this problem. Considering the positive results obtained for the selected regions in terms of CO_2 emissions, Romão and Neuts (2017) suggest that technological and industrial development should be concerned with savings on energy consumption and energy production based on renewable sources to ensure an environmentally friendly process of industrial development. Lastly, the study of Luque Gil et al. (2015), on its turn, explore, through a bibliometric review, the concept and the objectives of Territorial Intelligence and determine its tools and elements integrated in this approach. Moreover, the researchers aim to understand the relationship between Territorial Intelligence and the new "Smart Tourism Destination", identifying synergistic opportunities and challenges. Conclusions show the successful development of models of smart tourism destinations should be personalized to each case and supported on: Territorial Intelligence systems; a multidisciplinary approach; and co-creation management. All physical (climate, geography, infrastructures, etc.) and human elements (services, human resources, stakeholders, tourists, locals, etc.) have to be integrated, which is a huge challenge, considering the multiplicity of elements and individual needs.

Cluster 2 – Sustainable Tourism

The second cluster focuses on the modelling of Sustainable Tourism and on the conceptualization of some terms around sustainability, smartness, and community.

Shafiee et al. (2019) present a model of Sustainable Smart Tourism Destinations, whose successful implementation depends on the fulfilment of several requirements such as a high internet penetration rate, the use of ICT (Information and Communications Technology), the existence of smart infrastructures, the development of social networks and the rate of global changes. On the other side, Ribes and Baidal (2018) analyses and compares the concepts of sustainability and smartness from a theoretical and a managerial viewpoint, concerning the touristic destinations frame, in order to foster a new model of Smart Sustainability. It was verified a strong connection between the two concepts, with common elements like the long-term vision and planning, innovation, public-private cooperation, and the involvement of the stakeholders. The authors create a synergetic model focused on smart sustainability, based on a governance framework that applies technology to five fundamental pillars: planning, the efficient management of resources; monitoring, transparency and participation, public-private cooperation, knowledge, innovation; and communication, awareness raising and the improvement of the tourist experience. Even though, it cannot be interpreted linearly. Finally, Pan et al. (2018) approach tourism sustainability through a cross-disciplinary perspective. First, the authors focus on barriers and challenges of sustainability, such as energy and pollution, complementing the analysis with the understanding of key concepts like green infrastructures, agriculture, and smart technologies. They find that the development of a more sustainable tourism requires an integrated and multi-disciplinary approach, e.g., crossing government and tourism industry strategies, integrating local, national, and international policies and promoting green and innovative practices through environmental education.

Cluster 3 – Technology

The third cluster analyses the importance of Technology and its relationship with Smart and Sustainable Tourism. Within the tourism sector, Polese et al. (2018) explores the main element-steps for managing and optimizing value co-creation and sustainability and thus for transitioning from innovation to social innovation. The authors confirm the importance of ICT as an element that leverages the b&b management and acts as a facilitator of the creation and maintenance of sustainable relationships between host and guests. Pradhan et al. (2018) analysed the negative impact of smart devices on traveller's experiences. Findings showed that the perceived benefits of smart devices have a greater impact on usage intention than do perceived risks. Moreover, the authors also conclude that the constructs of TRI (optimism, insecurity, and discomfort) influence traveller's perception experience. Yoo et al. (2017) also contributed to this discussion by examining which factors affect the adoption of smart tourism applications that incorporate game elements. The findings showed that applications offer tourists "emotional pleasure (through gaming elements) and cognitive information" (Yoo et al., 2017, p. 14). Additionally, the authors also highlighted that enjoyment or gaming factors are important for the tourists' experience with gamified tourism applications and expect that the game attributes from gamified smart tourism applications are different from general games. Finally, the study of González-Reverté et al. (2018, p. 1) examines "the association between tourists' perceived risk of mobile device usage and several variables that demonstrate the perceived usefulness of mobile devices: utility, hedonic value and future intention of use". Based on the evidence of a relationship between tourists perceived risk and their use of mobile phones, the authors carried out a survey on two Catalonian destinations (Calella and Sitges) addressed to domestic and international tourists visiting the destination during their summer holiday. Findings show that tourists have different individual behaviours regarding their use of mobile devices, meaning that a single digital tourist does not exist. This brings important challenges for DMOs who should provide unique characteristics to their territories by offering different solutions and adapt the strategy to satisfy the different needs of their visitors.

Cluster 4 – Smart Specialization

This cluster addresses the topics that intersect the themes of smart tourism and sustainability considering the specialization approach. The study of Shen et al. (2020) examined the perceptions of Chinese tourist consumers about the contribution of social networking sites (SNSs) for sustainable behaviour during the three stages of the travel cycle: before, during, and after their experience. The authors found that social networking sites influence tourist's experience at all stages (with incidence on the first two) on adopting sustainable and responsible behaviour. Del Vecchio and Passiante (2017) developed a study focused on Apulia (Italy) and showed how tourism could promote smart regional growth. The smart specialization "is a place-based strategy that invites the European regions to identify and follow a development path that is based on their specific vocations leverages the appropriate key enabling technologies, and focuses particularly on entrepreneurial development" (Del Vecchio & Passiante, 2017, p. 163). Tourism is an important sector for Apulia and could represent a strategic industry for its growth and its smart specialization. The authors highlight that the symbioses between a smart specialization strategy and tourism growth will depend on the region's ability to encompass both the opportunities provided by information and communications technology (ICT) and these be linked to improve the sector competitiveness. The work of Pencarelli (2020) focus on the relationship between technology and the tourism industry. The authors analysed on one hand what was the impact of the digital revolution on tourism, and, on the other, examined the points in common and differences between tourism 4.0 and smart tourism. Pencarelli (2020) point out some differences between Tourism 4.0 and Smart Tourism. While the first refers merely to the new ICT, Smart Tourism refers to the efficient and effective use of these ICT with a sustainable and long-term approach toward the quality of life of guests and residents. Not only new ICT have changed the way companies promote and provide services, but also it has strongly impacted the tourist involvement in the co-creation processes. Thus, their ideal system of tourism should be based on a Smart Tourism perspectives like sustainability, circular economy, quality of life, and social value. They also highlight that the enrichment of the tourist experience lays on a strategy of co-creation in both the physical and the digital world. Kim and Kim (2017) draw attention to the role of mobile technology in promoting smart and sustainable tourism from the technology and customer perspectives. The authors suggest that it is difficult to assess the serial relationship from mobile technology to mobility to sustainability, due to the influence of different factors such as a destination's tourist type, demographics, and Geographic's. Furthermore, the advances in mobile technology might be fruitful in generating adequate information to tourists, which will help in their decision-making process and wellbeing.

SOLUTIONS AND RECOMMENDATIONS

Our study conducted a bibliometric analysis of 59 documents retrieved from the WoS Core Collection on smart and sustainable tourism topics. To the best of our knowledge, this is the first study analysing the interconnection of the smart tourism and sustainability, demonstrating the need to develop more research on both fields. Additionally, we performed a content analysis on both fields, assessing the main themes, examining the current tendencies, and identifying the barriers to smart tourism development without compromising sustainability.

We identified two main clusters concerning the affiliations of the authors: one belongs to Mediterranean Europe (Spain, Portugal, and Greece) and Asia (Taiwan, China, and South Korea) within the period of 2015-2020. These differences can be explained by the importance of tourism in the Mediterranean countries and the relevance of technology in some Asian communities (e.g., Tokyo, Hong Kong). Tools such as bibliometric coupling map of the selected documents allowed us to identify four clusters: smart tourism, sustainable tourism, technology, and smart specialization. The content analysis of the most cited articles enables the identification of the issues approached, the chosen methodology, and the main findings.

FUTURE RESEARCH DIRECTIONS

We recognise the importance of disclosing the limitations of our study so that future research can rectify accordingly. First, the selected themes are considered hot topics, meaning that it is difficult to keep the bibliometric reviews updated. Second, although we carefully selected and analysed the documents from the output database, there might be some relevant works that were not included due to several issues such as the novelty and the bureaucratic process of publication, and the use of different keywords. To address these limitations, future research should include several databases (i.e., Scopus, b-on, abi/inform, and Scielo, recent years), and other languages besides English. Third, the quality of the articles may not be reflected on the respective number of citations because of the auto-citations; the fact that highly ranked journals tend to be cited by more authors; and the higher tendency that earlier articles must be more cited in comparison to more recent ones. To overcome this restriction, future research could build on this study by including the Emerging Sources Citation Index.

CONCLUSION

This study aimed to review the existing literature thoroughly to provide valuable insights on sustainability and smart tourism. It is recognised that smart tourism has its roots in sustainability. However, several challenges needed to be addressed, such as further develop the socio-economic pillar initiatives to increase the responsible behaviour of the tourist at a destination. To achieve this goal, it is essential that policymakers, DMOs and business managers integrate a multidisciplinary approach. Technology can act as a promoter or a barrier to smart tourism considering respectively developed and developing countries. Therefore, for a destination to be considered smart, it requires several characteristics to be part of it, such as the use of big data to increase stakeholders' knowledge about tourism demand, high internet penetration rate, the use of ICT, the existence of smart infrastructures, and the development of social networks. Most importantly, the public and private sectors and civil society must be involved in the development of shared governance models that are effective for tourism. Several destinations, for example, Gothenburg, Málaga, Breda, Ljubljana, Karlsruhe, Helsinki, Lyon, Copenhagen, Linz, are interesting examples of smart destinations since they promote the continuous exchange between visitors and the government's tourism services, maximise the accessibility, and hospitality for disabled travellers, include the use of technology and ICT to offer targeted suggestions of attractions for visitors or personalized experiences. At the same time, it is fundamental to ensure the sustainability of local communities through the preservation of their cultural heritage and environment.

Nonetheless, this investigation is helpful to policymakers, DMOs, academics, and researchers that aim to be knowledgeable on these topics and develop smart tourism destinations strategies that secure and maximize sustainability.

REFERENCES

Ali, A., & Frew, A. (2013). *Information and communication technologies for sustainable tourism*. Routledge. doi:10.4324/9780203072592

Benckendorff, P. J., Xiang, Z., & Sheldon, P. J. (2019). *Tourism information technology*. Cabi. doi:10.1079/9781786393432.0000

Boes, K., Buhalis, D., & Inversini, A. (2015). Conceptualising Smart Tourism Destination Dimensions. In A. I. I. Tussyadiah (Ed.), *Information and communication technologies in tourism 2015* (pp. 391–403). Springer International Publishing.

Buhalis, D. (2000). Marketing the competitive destination of the future. *Tourism Management, 21*(1), 97–116. doi:10.1016/S0261-5177(99)00095-3

Buhalis, D., & Amaranggana, A. (2015). Smart Tourism Destinations Enhancing Tourism Experience Through Personalisation of Services. In Information and Communication Technologies in Tourism 2015. Springer. doi:10.1007/978-3-319-14343-9_28

Buhalis, D., & Foerste, M. (2015). SoCoMo marketing for travel and tourism: Empowering co-creation of value. *Journal of Destination Marketing & Management, 4*(3), 151–161. doi:10.1016/j.jdmm.2015.04.001

Del Chiappa, G., & Baggio, R. (2015). Knowledge transfer in smart tourism destinations: Analyzing the effects of a network structure. *Journal of Destination Marketing & Management, 4*(3), 145–150. doi:10.1016/j.jdmm.2015.02.001

Del Vecchio, P., & Passiante, G. (2017). Is tourism a driver for smart specialization? Evidence from Apulia, an Italian region with a tourism vocation. *Journal of Destination Marketing & Management, 6*(3), 163–165. doi:10.1016/j.jdmm.2016.09.005

Dinnie, K. (2008). *Nation branding. Concepts, issues, practice*. Butterworth-Heinemann.

Eck, N. J. v., & Waltman, L. (2009). Vosviewer: A Computer Program for Bibliometric Mapping. *Econometrics: Computer Programs & Software eJournal.*

Egghe, L., & Rousseau, R. (2002). Co-citation, bibliographic coupling and a characterization of lattice citation networks. *Scientometrics, 55*(3), 349–361. doi:10.1023/A:1020458612014

Encalada, L., Boavida-Portugal, I., Cardoso Ferreira, C., & Rocha, J. (2017). Identifying tourist places of interest based on digital imprints: Towards a sustainable smart city. *Sustainability, 9*(12), 2317. doi:10.3390u9122317

Escobar, S. D., & Margherita, E. G. (2021). Outcomes of Smart Tourism Applications On-site for a Sustainable Tourism: Evidence from Empirical Studies. In A. M. A. Musleh Al-Sartawi (Ed.), *The Big Data-Driven Digital Economy: Artificial and Computational Intelligence* (pp. 271–283). Springer International Publishing. doi:10.1007/978-3-030-73057-4_21

Ferreira, J. J. M., Fernandes, C. I., & Ratten, V. (2016). A co-citation bibliometric analysis of strategic management research. *Scientometrics*, *109*(1), 1–32. doi:10.100711192-016-2008-0

Foray, D., Goddard, J., Beldarrain, X. G., Landabaso, M., McCann, P., Morgan, K., . . . Ortega-Argilés, R. (2012). Guide to research and innovation strategies for smart specialisations. Brussels: S3P-European Union.

Garrigos-Simon, F. J., Narangajavana-Kaosiri, Y., & Lengua-Lengua, I. (2018). Tourism and sustainability: A bibliometric and visualization analysis. *Sustainability*, *10*(6), 1976.

Gaur, A., & Kumar, M. (2018). A systematic approach to conducting review studies: An assessment of content analysis in 25 years of IB research. *Journal of World Business*, *53*(2), 280–289. doi:10.1016/j.jwb.2017.11.003

Gelter, J., Lexhagen, M., & Fuchs, M. (2020). A meta-narrative analysis of smart tourism destinations: Implications for tourism destination management. *Current Issues in Tourism*, 1–15. doi:10.1080/13683500.2020.1849048

Glänzel, W. (2003). *Bibliometrics as a research field: A course on theory and application of bibliometric indicators*. Course Handouts.

González-Reverté, F., Díaz-Luque, P., Gomis-López, J. M., & Morales-Pérez, S. (2018). Tourists' risk perception and the use of mobile devices in beach tourism destinations. *Sustainability*, *10*(2), 413. doi:10.3390u10020413

Gretzel, U. (2020). Guiding principles for good governance of the smart destination. *Travel and Tourism Research Association: Advancing Tourism Research Globally*, *42*, 1–10.

Gretzel, U., Ham, J., & Koo, C. (2018). Creating the city destination of the future: the case of smart Seoul. In Managing Asian Destinations. Perspectives on Asian Tourism (pp. 199-214). Singapore: Springer. doi:10.1007/978-981-10-8426-3_12

Gretzel, U., Koo, C., Sigala, M., & Xiang, Z. (2015). Special issue on smart tourism: Convergence of information technologies, experiences, and theories. *Electronic Markets*, *25*(3), 175–177. doi:10.100712525-015-0194-x

Gretzel, U., Werthner, H., Koo, C., & Lamsfus, C. (2015). Conceptual foundations for understanding smart tourism ecosystems. *Computers in Human Behavior*, *50*, 558–563. doi:10.1016/j.chb.2015.03.043

Habegger, B., Hasan, O., Brunie, L., Bennani, N., Kosch, H., & Damiani, E. (2014). Personalization vs. privacy in big data analysis. *International Journal of Big Data*, 25–35. doi:10.29268tbd.2014.1.1.3

Hall, C. M. (2019). Constructing sustainable tourism development: The 2030 agenda and the managerial ecology of sustainable tourism. *Journal of Sustainable Tourism*, *27*(7), 1044–1060. doi:10.1080/09669582.2018.1560456

Höjer, M., & Wangel, J. (2015). Smart sustainable cities: definition and challenges. In *ICT innovations for sustainability* (pp. 333–349). Springer. doi:10.1007/978-3-319-09228-7_20

Huovila, A., Bosch, P., & Airaksinen, M. (2019). Comparative analysis of standardized indicators for Smart sustainable cities: What indicators and standards to use and when? *Cities (London, England)*, *89*, 141–153. doi:10.1016/j.cities.2019.01.029

Ismagilova, E., Hughes, L., Dwivedi, Y. K., & Raman, K. R. (2019). Smart cities: Advances in research— An information systems perspective. *International Journal of Information Management*, *47*, 88–100. doi:10.1016/j.ijinfomgt.2019.01.004

Ivars-Baidal, J. A., Celdrán-Bernabeu, M. A., Mazón, J.-N., & Perles-Ivars, Á. F. (2019). Smart destinations and the evolution of ICTs: A new scenario for destination management? *Current Issues in Tourism*, *22*(13), 1581–1600. doi:10.1080/13683500.2017.1388771

Ivars-Baidal, J. A., Vera-Rebollo, J. F., Perles-Ribes, J., Femenia-Serra, F., & Celdrán-Bernabeu, M. A. (2021). Sustainable tourism indicators: What's new within the smart city/destination approach? *Journal of Sustainable Tourism*, 1–24. doi:10.1080/09669582.2021.1876075

Joo, Y., & Tan, T.-B. (2020). *Smart cities in Asia: an introduction.* doi:10.4337/9781788972888

Juvan, E., & Dolnicar, S. (2014). The attitude–behaviour gap in sustainable tourism. *Annals of Tourism Research*, *48*, 76–95. doi:10.1016/j.annals.2014.05.012

Juvan, E., & Dolnicar, S. (2017). Drivers of pro-environmental tourist behaviours are not universal. *Journal of Cleaner Production*, *166*, 879–890. doi:10.1016/j.jclepro.2017.08.087

Kamińska, A. (2018). *The application of methods of social network analysis in bibliometrics and webometrics. Measures and tools.* Academic Press.

Kessler, M. M. (1963). Bibliographic coupling between scientific papers. *American Documentation*, *14*(1), 10–25. doi:10.1002/asi.5090140103

Kim, D., & Kim, S. (2017). The role of mobile technology in tourism: Patents, articles, news, and mobile tour app reviews. *Sustainability*, *9*(11), 2082. doi:10.3390u9112082

Kornova, G., & Loginova, E. (2019). Service opportunities in the development of the hospitality services market in terms of the new industrialization. *Advances in Social Science, Education and Humanities Research, 240*, 496-499.

Krippendorff, K. (2018). *Content analysis: An introduction to its methodology.* Sage publications.

Lee, T. H., Jan, F.-H., & Yang, C.-C. (2013). Conceptualizing and measuring environmentally responsible behaviors from the perspective of community-based tourists. *Tourism Management*, *36*, 454–468. doi:10.1016/j.tourman.2012.09.012

López de Ávila, A. (2015). *Informe destinos turísticos inteligentes: construyendo el futuro.* Technical report. https://www.segittur.es/opencms/export/sites/segitur/.content/galerias/descargas/proyectos/Libro-Blanco-Destinos-Tursticos-Inteligentes-ok es.pdf

Luque Gil, A. M., Zayas Fernández, B., & Caro Herrero, J. L. (2015). The Smart Tourism Destination and the Territorial Intelligence: Problems and opportunities. *Investigaciones Turísticas*, (10), 1–25.

Martino, F., & Spoto, A. (2006). Social Network Analysis: A brief theoretical review and further perspectives in the study of Information Technology. *PsychNology Journal*, 4, 53–86.

Merricks, W. J. (2019). Politicising smart cities standards. In C. Coletta, L. Evans, L. Heaphy, & R. Kitchin (Eds.), *Creating smart cities* (pp. 33–48). Routledge.

Milán-García, J., Uribe-Toril, J., Ruiz-Real, J. L., & de Pablo Valenciano, J. (2019). Sustainable Local Development: An Overview of the State of Knowledge. *Resources*, 8(1), 31. doi:10.3390/resources8010031

OECD. (2020). *Main Science and Technology Indicators, Volume 2020 Issue 1*. OECD.

Pan, S.-Y., Gao, M., Kim, H., Shah, K. J., Pei, S.-L., & Chiang, P.-C. (2018). Advances and challenges in sustainable tourism toward a green economy. *The Science of the Total Environment*, 635, 452–469. doi:10.1016/j.scitotenv.2018.04.134 PMID:29677671

Papadopoulos, N., & Hamzaoui-Essoussi, L. (2015). Place Images and Nation Branding in the African Context: Challenges, Opportunities, and Questions for Policy and Research. *Africa Journal of Management*, 1(1), 54–77. doi:10.1080/23322373.2015.994423

Pencarelli, T. (2020). The digital revolution in the travel and tourism industry. *Information Technology & Tourism*, 22(3), 455–476. doi:10.100740558-019-00160-3

Perianes-Rodriguez, A., Waltman, L., & van Eck, N. J. (2016). Constructing bibliometric networks: A comparison between full and fractional counting. *Journal of Informetrics*, 10(4), 1178–1195. doi:10.1016/j.joi.2016.10.006

Polese, F., Botti, A., Grimaldi, M., Monda, A., & Vesci, M. (2018). Social innovation in smart tourism ecosystems: How technology and institutions shape sustainable value co-creation. *Sustainability*, 10(1), 140. doi:10.3390u10010140

Ponomariov, B. L., & Boardman, P. C. (2010). Influencing scientists' collaboration and productivity patterns through new institutions: University research centers and scientific and technical human capital. *Research Policy*, 39(5), 613–624. doi:10.1016/j.respol.2010.02.013

Porter, M. E., & Heppelmann, J. E. (2014). How smart, connected products are transforming competition. *Harvard Business Review*, 92(11), 64–88.

Pradhan, M. K., Oh, J., & Lee, H. (2018). Understanding travelers' behavior for sustainable smart tourism: A technology readiness perspective. *Sustainability*, 10(11), 4259. doi:10.3390u10114259

Ribes, J. F. P., & Baidal, J. I. (2018). Smart sustainability: A new perspective in the sustainable tourism debate. *Investigaciones Regionales-Journal of Regional Research*, (42), 151–170.

Romão, J., & Neuts, B. (2017). Territorial capital, smart tourism specialization and sustainable regional development: Experiences from Europe. *Habitat International*, 68, 64–74. doi:10.1016/j.habitatint.2017.04.006

Rosenbaum, M. S., Ramirez, G. C., Campbell, J., & Klaus, P. (2021). The product is me: Hyper-personalized consumer goods as unconventional luxury. *Journal of Business Research*, *129*, 446–454. doi:10.1016/j.jbusres.2019.05.017

Rutty, M., Gössling, S., Scott, D., & Hall, C. M. (2015). The global eff ects and impacts of tourism: an overview. In S. G. C. M. Hall & D. Scott (Eds.), *The Routledge handbook of tourism and sustainability* (pp. 36–63). Routledge.

Sassmannshausen, S. P., & Volkmann, C. (2018). The scientometrics of social entrepreneurship and its establishment as an academic field. *Journal of Small Business Management*, *56*(2), 251–273. doi:10.1111/jsbm.12254

Scott, D., Gössling, S., Hall, C. M., & Peeters, P. (2016). Can tourism be part of the decarbonized global economy? The costs and risks of alternate carbon reduction policy pathways. *Journal of Sustainable Tourism*, *24*(1), 52–72.

Scott, D., Hall, C. M., & Gössling, S. (2016). A review of the IPCC Fifth Assessment and implications for tourism sector climate resilience and decarbonization. *Journal of Sustainable Tourism*, *24*(1), 8–30.

Serrat, O. (2009). *Social Network Analysis*. Academic Press.

Shafiee, S., Ghatari, A. R., Hasanzadeh, A., & Jahanyan, S. (2019). Developing a model for sustainable smart tourism destinations: A systematic review. *Tourism Management Perspectives*, *31*, 287–300. doi:10.1016/j.tmp.2019.06.002

Shen, S., Sotiriadis, M., & Zhou, Q. (2020). Could smart tourists be sustainable and responsible as well? The Contribution of Social Networking Sites to Improving Their Sustainable and Responsible Behavior. *Sustainability*, *12*(4), 1470. doi:10.3390u12041470

Sigalat-Signes, E., Calvo-Palomares, R., Roig-Merino, B., & García-Adán, I. (2020). Transition towards a tourist innovation model: The smart tourism destination: Reality or territorial marketing? *Journal of Innovation & Knowledge*, *5*(2), 96–104. doi:10.1016/j.jik.2019.06.002

Sun, Y., Song, H., Jara, A. J., & Bie, R. (2016). Internet of things and big data analytics for smart and connected communities. *IEEE Access: Practical Innovations, Open Solutions*, *4*, 766–773. doi:10.1109/ACCESS.2016.2529723

Tabassum, S., Pereira, F., Fernandes, S., & Gama, J. (2018). Social network analysis: An overview. *Wiley Interdisciplinary Reviews. Data Mining and Knowledge Discovery*, *8*(5), e1256. doi:10.1002/widm.1256

UNWTO. (2021). *Sustainable Development*. https://www.unwto.org/sustainable-development

van Eck, N. J., & Waltman, L. (2010). Software survey: VOSviewer, a computer program for bibliometric mapping. *Scientometrics*, *84*(2), 523–538. doi:10.100711192-009-0146-3 PMID:20585380

Vecchio, P. D., Mele, G., Ndou, V., & Secundo, G. (2018). Creating value from Social Big Data: Implications for Smart Tourism Destinations. *Information Processing & Management*, *54*(5), 847–860. doi:10.1016/j.ipm.2017.10.006

Wang, D., Park, S., & Fesenmaier, D. R. (2012). The role of smartphones in mediating the touristic experience. *Journal of Travel Research*, *51*(4), 371–387. doi:10.1177/0047287511426341

Wasserman, S., Faust, K., Press, C. U., Granovetter, M., Cambridge, U. o., & Iacobucci, D. (1994). *Social Network Analysis: Methods and Applications*. Cambridge University Press. doi:10.1017/CBO9780511815478

White, M. D., & Marsh, E. E. (2006). Content analysis: A flexible methodology. *Library Trends*, *55*(1), 22–45. doi:10.1353/lib.2006.0053

Xiang, Z., Stienmetz, J., & Fesenmaier, D. R. (2021). Smart Tourism Design: Launching the annals of tourism research curated collection on designing tourism places. *Annals of Tourism Research*, *86*, 103154. doi:10.1016/j.annals.2021.103154

Yoo, C., Kwon, S., Na, H., & Chang, B. (2017). Factors affecting the adoption of gamified smart tourism applications: An integrative approach. *Sustainability*, *9*(12), 2162. doi:10.3390u9122162

Zeng, D., Tim, Y., Yu, J., & Liu, W. (2020). Actualizing big data analytics for smart cities: A cascading affordance study. *International Journal of Information Management*, *54*, 102156. doi:10.1016/j.ijinfomgt.2020.102156

Zsarnoczky, M. (2018, Spring). The Digital Future of the Tourism & Hospitality Industry. *Boston Hospitality Review*, 1-9.

Zupic, I., & Čater, T. (2015). Bibliometric methods in management and organization. *Organizational Research Methods*, *18*(3), 429–472. doi:10.1177/1094428114562629

KEY TERMS AND DEFINITIONS

Hyper-Personalization: Is described as an excessive degree of human subjectivation of its importance.
Smart Cities: Tourism-oriented and innovative space accessible to all, based on technological infrastructure.
Smart Sustainability: The synergies between smart city/destination and sustainable tourism.
Smart Tourism: Creation of a smart experience, described as an experience facilitated by technologies, and improved by personalization.

ENDNOTE

[1] Link strength and total link strength are terms used in VOSviewer program.

Chapter 7
Smart Tourism Destinations:
A Literature Review on Applications in Turkey's Touristic Destinations

Murat Ödemiş
Tourism Faculty, Gümüşhane University, Turkey

ABSTRACT

Tourism businesses and touristic destinations that want to reach a highly competitive position in the world should fulfill the required infrastructure investments and acquire a service concept that is consistent with the smart tourism strategy in order to turn into smart tourism. In order to compete with rival destinations, it has become a prerequisite for Turkey's world-famous destinations such as Istanbul, Antalya, Izmir, and Cappadocia to embrace digital transformation and smart tourism concepts. Accordingly, the concepts of smart tourism, smart city, and smart tourism destinations will be explained, and smart tourism applications in Turkey's touristic destinations will be explored in this chapter within the framework of current academic studies. It is aimed to ascertain how well these specified destinations adhere to the concept of smart tourism.

INTRODUCTION

Destinations should constantly adapt and enhance their touristic goods and services to today's conditions in order to deliver a great experience to its tourists in the tourism sector, where competition is becoming increasingly fierce. On the other hand, technology can be argued to have a substantial impact on the tourism experience. As a result, encouraging the use of technology in tourism will hasten the evolution of the tourism experience (Liberato et al., 2018, p. 19). Service innovation, strategy, management, marketing, and competitiveness are all under tremendous stress in today's smart settings, forcing industry structures, processes, and practices to alter and transform (Buhalis, 2020, p. 270). The tourism industry is one of the sectors under pressure from smart environments' mandated change and transformation. The concept and application of smart tourism arose from the need to adapt the tourism industry to this change and transformation. The concept of smart tourism is one of the tourism-based concepts and practices used for making tourism activities much more effective, making cities and destinations smart, and

DOI: 10.4018/978-1-7998-8306-7.ch007

increasing tourist satisfaction, and has emerged with the need to ensure the adaptation and integration of internet and mobile technologies, which are among the technological developments of today, to tourism activities. In the tourism industry, smart tourism is mostly used for the tourism businesses, cities, and touristic destinations. The adaptation of touristic destinations to information technologies is significantly more challenging than that of tourism businesses due to the complex structure of touristic destinations, which is one of the most fundamental parts of the tourism system. However, in order to remain up with the fierce competition in the market, many touristic locations have recognized the need to turning into smart tourism destinations and have begun to take steps to do so, albeit slowly.

In terms of operational and economic elements, the tourism industry is one of the industries where information technologies are heavily exploited. As a result, it is no surprise that the concept of smart tourism destinations is swiftly gaining traction in the tourism sector. It is feasible to argue that smart tourism destination apps are crucial for destinations where one attraction is clearly dominant or where there are many attractions and where linking and marketing activities between these attractions are arduous (Koo et al., 2016).

Within the context of existing academic study on these destinations, the potential of Istanbul, Ankara, Antalya, and other popular or unpopular destinations in Turkey to be smart touristic destinations and their smart tourism applications will be studied in this chapter. Existing smart tourism applications in these destinations will be assessed for their level of success and flaws. Taking into account the diverse implementations of smart tourism destinations around the world, recommendations for popular and less popular tourist attractions in Turkey that have the potential to become smart tourism destinations will be made.

BACKGROUND

Smart Tourism Concept

It is vital to be smart to keep alive in the tourism sector especially in today's environment. From the creation of information to its dissemination, it is critical to be as smart as possible. Smartness enables stakeholders with disparate interests to collaborate to improve overall performance and competitiveness, as well as develop solutions and value for all. As a result, it enables real-time shaping of products, actions, processes, and services. Smartness is frequently associated with speed or the ability to produce swift outcomes. As a consequence, researchers have been working on the topic in order for smartness to find a place in tourism sector applications (Jasrotia & Gangotia, 2018, p. 48). The word smart is often brought as a prefix to technological terms to denote intelligence and/or connectivity, as is expressed in a smart phone or smart card (Gretzel et al., 2015c, p. 559). It can be said that the effectiveness of technological and other tools on tourism activities is tried to be emphasized with the title of smart used in the concept of smart tourism.

Table 1. Smart tourism vs. e-tourism

	Smart tourism	**E-Tourism**
Phase of Travel	During the travel	Before and after the travel
Environment	Digital and physical environment	Digital environment
Core Technology	Sensors and smartphones	Websites
Source of Life	Big data	Information
Structure	Ecosystem	Value chain/intermediaries

Source: (Vasavada & Padhiyar, 2016, p. 57)

Table 1 offers a comparison of the concepts of smart tourism and e-tourism. Some characteristics of smart tourism differ from those of e-tourism. Smart tourism, on the other hand, is reliant on the digital infrastructure built by e-tourism. Mobile connectivity is also a feature of smart tourism. It also connects the digital and physical worlds to supply a new collection of data covering the entire destination. Smart tourism aims to maximize efficiency and sustainability by providing co-creation and personalization of tourism experiences (Gretzel et al., 2015a, p. 46). The common features of smart tourism and e-tourism concepts and practices are the need for well-structured information technology infrastructures in order to achieve success in both.

One of the subjects that has recently received a lot of attention in the scientific literature is the transition from e-tourism to smart tourism. One could argue that smart tourism is the next step in the evolution of e-tourism. Smart tourism strategies in use in numerous places throughout the world (for example, in Amsterdam, Barcelona, and Seoul) as well as in national policies of countries (for example, in Spain) have grown increasingly vital (Gajdošík, 2018, p. 27). The integration of information technologies and tourism is referred to as smart tourism. In smart tourism, people create social ecosystems by exchanging information via mobile devices connected to the internet. Within the scope of the activities carried out during the information exchange are e-commerce, virtual reality, augmented reality and destination image creation. Smart tourism has accelerated and intensified information exchange, allowing for a digital redesign of tourism's social reality. Public culture has become a structure that can easily adapt to new situations and exhibit responses due to information technology. It is likely that destination managers and marketing specialists' efficacy in the flow of information and commerce, in influencing tourists' experiences of the destination, and in defining the place's image, has reduced nowadays. As a result, today's travel agencies and appealing travel brochures aren't as efficient in establishing a destination's image as they once were. Personal statements and reviews on social media, shared destination recommendations, remarks, and photos; in other words, user-created information has become far more effective in attracting potential visitors. Today, augmented reality technologies furnish environments that allow visitors to travel freely (Hunter et al., 2015, p. 104). Continuous advancements in information and communication technologies (ICTs) in the coming years can help to improve communication and cooperation between tourists and destination stakeholders, as well as offer tourists a high-quality tourism experience and boost destination stakeholders' business success rates. Making tourism destinations smart can further the integration between production and consumption and strengthen the links between producers and consumers (Jovicic, 2019, p. 279).

Figure 1. Components and layers of smart tourism
Source: (Gretzel et al., 2015b, p. 181)

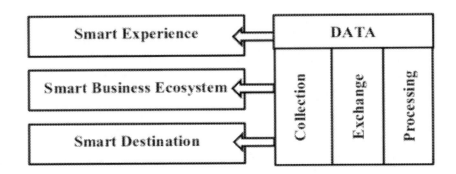

Smartness has now pervaded and penetrated every facet of life, even if people are often unaware of it or do not give it much thought. As a basis, its application in cities and tourism is not exceptional (Matos et al., 2019, p. 358). The notion of smart tourism arose as a result of the profound effects of smart technologies on the quick modification of traditional tourist roles and experiences' authentic characteristics (Mehraliyev et al., 2020, p. 78). Smart tourism concept can be defined as the type of tourism that is supported by integrated endeavors in a destination to gather and use data obtained from physical infrastructure, social connections, government/organizational resources and human bodies or minds through advanced technologies (Gretzel et al., 2015b, p. 181). The primary motivation for tourism service providers to improve smart tourism is to enhance the visitor experience. Understanding new tourists, their demands, and the smart tourism techniques that attract them have recently become highly significant. Tourists in the digital age have distinct requirements and behaviors than tourists in the pre-internet or pre-social media era. Information technology, self-service, and customized booking tools are helpful for future travelers. In addition, modern tourists care about accessing information technologies more easily and getting more value from the money and time they spend. Furthermore, they place a higher value on enlarged diversity, flexibility, customisation, and security (Wang et al., 2016, p. 310).

Smart tourism refers to smart services presented to tourists in order to suit their demands while visiting areas that they have never visited before and hence are unfamiliar with. The demand for individualized tourism services has intensified as domestic and international tourism movements have expanded, particularly among free and independent visitors. Accordingly, the number of online travel agencies that paved the way for the emergence of smart tourists has magnified day by day. Smart tourism travel businesses deliver much more than just flight tickets and reservation services. Other services offered by travel agencies in this context comprise comparison services, customized vacation packages, and an online community where people who use travel services can share their experiences (Park et al., 2016, p. 1321). One issue worth mentioning is that smart tourism does not always imply the presence of advanced technology that satisfies the needs of tourists, but rather the interdependence of various actors (Johnson & Samakovlis, 2018, p. 602).

The philosophy of smart tourism ensures that tourists' expectations are better met as a result of the individualized benefits rendered to them. In terms of data collection and developing more competitive products, this status presents new problems for tourism businesses and destination management organizations. It is imperative to yield information exchange and cooperation among all tourism stakeholders and to take an active part in the value creation process of the relevant stakeholders. Integration of information technologies with the stakeholders guided by destination management organizations that attach due importance to innovation can heighten the current potential and competitiveness of the tourism destination. Smart tourism is not the eventual goal but with the help of technology, cooperation and innovation, smart tourism can ensure tourists with a better tourism experience, raise the well-being of local people, enhance the efficiency and competitiveness of businesses and destinations, and achieve large-scale sustainable competitive advantage (Gajdošík, 2018, p. 41).

Smart tourism's technical infrastructure is a multifaceted structure with complex and dynamic interconnections that support not only the interaction of the person with the physical environment, such as the ubiquitous infrastructure, mobile and context-sensitive information systems, but also the interaction of the community and society with travelers, directly or indirectly. The smart tourism system's operation is based on processes including data collection, exchange, and processing created by various constituents of the consumer, business, and destination systems as a whole. The acquisition and creation of vast volumes of data about touristic consumers is enabled by networks and mobility, which have a substantial impact on touristic consumers' travel planning. Thus, tourism managers may understand where future and existing tourists reside, the information they use in travel planning, and the contacts that travelers exchange before, during, and after their travels thanks to modern technologies that give numerous metrics related to travel. These analytical business techniques allow for a smart tourist design that advances consumer intelligence, streamlines business processes, and allows for the adoption and execution of new initiatives that will help it become more profitable (Xiang & Fesenmaier, 2017, p. 303). Smart tourism can also be characterized as a tourism information service supplied to visitors. Comprehensive data about travelers can be obtained during smart tourism applications. Tourist demographic data, tourism resource data, tourism management data, and tourism marketing data are all gathered in this context. By making the best use of this data, the services offered to tourists can be improved (Li et al., 2017, p. 300).

The production of digital artifacts that support new processes, systems, and experiences that facilitate the reshaping of tourism activities should be the emphasis of smart tourism design. Smart tourism design is about more than just optimizing visitor experiences. It also concentrates on how to support and integrate tourism resources successfully (attractions, restaurants, parks, etc.). The creation of new measurement tools that will assure the efficacy of destination management will be aided by recent advancements in information technology and big data analytics. By recording tourist behaviors, services, and experiences both online and offline, these measuring tools can help destination administrators get a sense of the quality of the goods and services they grant (Xiang et al., 2021).

In a study, accessibility and information services have been identified as key drivers of smart tourist technologies. Plus, the research results show that accessibility and information criteria are effective in the preference of tourists to visit a destination. Tourists benefit from city guide applications, mobile payments, google maps, and map locations of touristic spots while deciding on a destination, according to research. Furthermore, when travelers grow more familiar with smart tourism technologies, they seek more detailed information about smart tourism destinations. According to other results of the research, installing high-end smart tourism technology infrastructures has been found to have a considerable impact on travelers' tourist experiences. As a result, the use of high-level smart tourism technologies by tourists will positively affect their tourism experience. Smart tourism technology enables travelers to have unforgettable travel experiences and encourage tourists desiring to repeat these experiences to participate in tourism activities (Azis et al., 2020, p. 615-616).

The construction of a smart tourism system will be valuable to the success of smart tourism apps. This smart tourism system, it can be claimed, should be built around five key features. Information exchange centers, visitors, government, natural areas, and businesses are some of these factors. Tourists frequently utilize the information exchange center to conduct searches, purchase tickets, make bookings, and communicate socially, among other things. The information exchange center is responsible for providing the tourists with the information and processed results that can meet these demands of the tourists. In addition, the information exchange center must constantly monitor natural resources. Visitor statistics may also be required at the information exchange center for analysis and archiving. These figures may be shared with authorized governmental organizations in order to serve as a source and guidance for the development of future tourist policy and planning. Businesses in the tourism industry, such as hotels, restaurants, and entertainment facilities, can ask the information exchange center to send adverts and promotional content to travelers. Based on the input they receive from tourists through the information exchange center, businesses can make arrangements for the quality and quantity of services they offer (Zhu et al., 2014).

Mobile technology is one of the variables that has a major impact on the development of smart tourism. The use and applications of smart phones, which are among the mobile technologies, contribute significantly to the improvement of smart tourism (Dorcic et al., 2019, p. 83). All forms of mobile technology and social media, as well as the digital footprints they generate, are included in smart tourism. It is also important to assess how transmedia narratives influence smart tourism's political impact on actions and functions (search engines, social media and software applications). As a result, in order to thrive in smart tourism applications, it is vital to understand the irrefutable role of technology in deciding how individuals connect to and react to one another, as well as how they act. While smart tourism technologies have a productive and temporary feature, the social, cultural and economic effects of information technologies on tourism are much more profound. Smart tourism represents a newly discovered source of soft power (Hunter et al., 2015, p. 108).

Some concepts have evolved from e-tourism to smart tourism, from e-destination to smart destination, and from digital tourist to smart tourist during the development of cycle of the smart tourism term. Smart tourism, which is among these concepts, is explained under this title, and the concept of smart destination is discussed in the next headings. If the characteristics of the smart tourist concept are mentioned, smart tourists can be expressed as an open type of tourist who does not hesitate to share this data with other smart stakeholders as long as they are sure of the potential use of their data such as basic personal information, preferences, social media profile information, location and movements, expenditures. Smart travelers recognize the value of the benefits they will receive and consider it common practice to render personal information, particularly with tourism firms, in the knowledge that their confidentiality and security will be respected. Hence, smart visitors understand the value of their data and the need to secure it, and they can share their personal and preferences information with tourism businesses in order to obtain specific information and offers. Using smart technologies, smart visitors aim to improve and enrich their experiences. They can use smart technology because they have the confidence, will, aptitude, and conditions to do so. Smart visitors, on the other hand, prefer smart technologies that are advantageous, easy to use, and offer additional functions. Smart tourists actively use smart technologies not only to increase their own experiences, but also to create real-time dynamic interactions with stakeholders in smart destinations and to create experiences together. Smart tourists must have trust in stakeholders in their interaction and experience-building procedures. If smart visitors sense they still have authority over the experiences that are tailored to their requirements and desires utilizing smart technologies, their trust in stakeholders will strengthen. Consequently, to create added value, smart tourists can voluntarily allow other agents to be involved in the experience creation process through smart technologies, provided they have control (Femenia-Serra et al., 2019).

It should be noted there are several challenges with smart tourism system applications. One of the misunderstood points about the smart tourism system is that it is not just an information technology design project. At the same time, the smart tourism system entails the fulfillment of the aforesaid project and, as a result, economically efficient and informatics support for the travel and tourism business. Future applications should be taken into account during the design phase and current adaptations should be made during the implementation process. The system, for example, can be adjusted to meet changing tourist expectations and requirements. If unified standards for the measurement and evaluation of smart tourism are not established, the management of the smart tourism system will become difficult. For example, a unified data exchange format can be created to facilitate communication between smart tourism systems in different cities. The main investor of smart tourism systems is the state. In case the state cannot adequately support the smart tourism project financially, the project may be interrupted or stopped. On the other hand, the state's being too active or taking responsibility in the smart tourism project will create an obstacle for smart tourism to come out of the state monopoly and to open up to the foreign market. If the project's profit does not meet expectations, it may be discontinued. As a result, it is imperative to allow private entrepreneurs to make prudent tourism investments (Zhu et al., 2014).

The reliance on the visitor experience and technology is one of the most major issues in smart tourism. Tourists' experiences from smart tourism depend on having smart devices running applications that will enable them to benefit from smart services. In addition, in order for smart devices to work continually, they must have access to electricity sources. Tourists who do not have smart devices or do not want to use smart devices during their travels have question marks about the scope of the experience they will have during their travels. Investments in infrastructure services necessary for the development of smart tourism are insufficient. Making investments that assure the control of the data usage system, i.e. the protection and confidentiality of citizen and tourist data, is particularly critical (Savić & Pavlović, 2018, p. 83).

Smart Tourism Destinations

Developments in ICTs help cities and destinations to build strategies and conduct initiatives in order to achieve their sustainability goals. Cities have recently discovered the capability to employ ICTs to develop new policies and strategies aimed at achieving sustainability goals (Shafiee et al., 2019, p. 289). It can be announced that with the discovery of this potential, smart city and smart tourism applications have begun to gain momentum in cities and destinations.

It can be asserted that smart tourism destinations are cities or locations where contemporary technological tools, innovations, and approaches are employed to submit tourists with an enjoyable experience while also generating revenue for businesses and destinations. Smart cities can be viewed as a first step toward creating smart tourism destinations. Smart tourism destinations are fundamentally smart cities that leverage information technology and innovation to satisfy tourists and give them a diversity of perspectives. It is necessary to correctly understand the concept of smart tourism destinations, which is becoming increasingly important today, and to make sustainable plans for the development of smart cities that will enable the formation of smart tourism destinations in the future and to carry out these plans effectively (Jasrotia & Gangotia, 2018, p. 53). Smart cities bring various services to their citizens and try to find solutions to social problems by using ICTs and the internet. Smart cities, for example, can notify its inhabitants about the location of public transit vehicles in real time using transportation apps available on smart phones. By guiding inhabitants and tourists to public transportation vehicles, pollution and traffic concerns can be minimized (Çelik & Topsakal, 2017, p. 150).

The emergence of the smart tourism concept is based entirely on the smart city concept. Sustainable tourism is at the heart of smart tourism, and touristic destinations prioritize sustainability as a strategic aim in the tourism planning process. One of the highlights is the involvement of stakeholders such as the government, educational institutions, the corporate sector, and public institutions in the formulation and management of sustainable measures through efficient technologies. Within the scope of these initiatives, there are broad (infrastructure works carried out in various sectors) and infrastructure works carried out on a narrow scale. Airlines, waterways, smart airports with surface transportation systems, smart hotels, and smart transportation are among some of the research conducted for the growth of the tourism sector in the limited sense (Khan et al., 2017, p. 4). Smart cities place a premium on efficiency and sustainability. The core technology applications that smart cities should create are big data and open data, sensors in municipal infrastructure such as public transit and public services, free wi-fi, and mobile connectivity services. Smart destinations are extensions of smart cities. In addition, smart destinations include touristic infrastructure such as touristic attractions and tour buses (Gretzel et al., 2015a, p. 43).

Table 2. Evolution of the tourism destination concept

Traditional Approach to Tourism Destination	Systematic Approach to Tourism Destination	Smart Tourism Destination
Geographical Dimension Aggerating of attraction features and services; disregard for destination collaboration and the role of tourists among destination players	Geographical Dimension Communication between tourists, service providers, and locals of the location; continual engagement with the macro-environment; non-linear relationships between stakeholders	Geographical Dimension Interconnected digital and physical platforms; collaboration between governmental institutions, the private sector, and consumers; participative governance; creative and knowledgeable individuals; collaborating to create value; tailored services

Source: (Jovicic, 2019, p. 280)

The evolution of the tourism destination concept is shown in Table 2. Destinations are thought of as geographical locations that are the subject of touristic visits, according to the traditional perspective. From the late 1990s to the present, theorists have underlined the necessity of numerous destination stakeholders who perform the required part in destination management as an understanding of the complexity and consequences of tourism has grown. The theory of smart destinations has emerged as a result of the digital revolution since it allows stakeholders to continuously innovate in their performance and activities while also allowing all stakeholders to access all types of information. The technology dimension and information communication technologies are not the only topics addressed by the smart destination approach. The smart experience and smart business ecosystem, which are the main elements of smart destinations, also include sociocultural, psychological, strategic management, educational and other components (Jovicic, 2019, p. 280). Smart tourism destinations are inextricably linked to the digital business ecosystem, which is one of these pillars. In the business ecosystem, a clear connection has been developed between actual and virtual components. Knowledge must permeate this ecosystem in order for innovation and consensus to emerge (Chiappa & Baggio, 2015).

In fact, it can be alleged that the term "smart tourism" refers to smart tourism destinations, which are an integral component of smart cities (Yalçınkaya et al., 2018, p. 311). Smart destinations are those in which technology, innovation, sustainability, accessibility, and inclusion techniques are implemented before, during, and after travel, in other words, throughout the entire tourist process. In addition, smart tourism destinations design tourism around elements like multilingualism, destination-specific cultural features, and seasonality, taking into account both locals and tourists (UNWTO, 2021). Smart tourism destination is described as *"an innovative tourist destination, built on an infrastructure of state-of-the-art technology guaranteeing the sustainable development of tourist areas, accessible to everyone, which facilitates the visitor's interaction with and integration into his or her surroundings, increases the quality of the experience at the destination, and improves residents' quality of life"* (Lopez de Avila, 2015). So, smart tourism means smart destinations. When applying smart destination principles to urban and rural areas, they take into account not only citizens but also tourist mobility, resource availability, resource sustainability and quality of life/visit (Çelik & Topsakal, 2017, p. 154). It is critical to turn the theoretical propositions and principles of smart tourism destinations into actual, usable, and worthwhile solutions, or 'smart solutions,' in order to use them from a community-oriented standpoint (Femenia-Serra & Ivars-Baidal, 2021, p. 366).

Figure 2. Structure of smart tourism destination
Source: (Boes et al., 2016, p. 119)

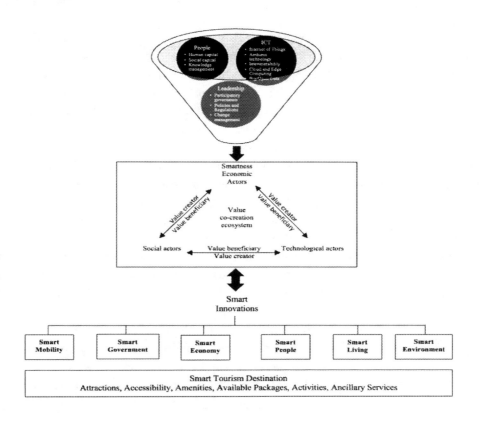

Human capital, which lays the foundation of social capital structures, as well as leadership, entrepreneurship, and innovation, are the core building blocks of smart tourism destinations. Technology applications and information communication technologies assist and empower these key building components. Internet of things, cloud computing and other advanced ICT infrastructures play an influential role in the development of a smart tourism destination (Boes et al., 2015, p. 400-401). Vision, leadership, strategic management, patience, and ongoing review and change are all critical components towards becoming a smart tourism destination. It is critical to think of a smart tourism destination as an ecosystem. Setting a vision and defined goals in order to innovate in this ecosystem will aid in the development of smart tourism destinations that are collectively responsible. Current developments in technology have increased the importance of resource integration in creating common value for all actors in the smart tourism destination ecosystem. This complicates the management of smart tourism destinations. This syst][em's interconnected and interoperable technology systems, as well as knowledgeable people, promote tourism destinations' long-term competitive advantage. Destination managers should combine all components of smartness and integrate the solid (visible presence of technology) and soft (leadership, innovation, social capital and human capital) constituents of smartness in an interoperable manner in order for destinations to take full advantage of the opportunities allowed by smartness (Boes et al., 2016).

It is seen that technological innovations have the potential to bring together all the stakeholders in the tourism service ecosystem (Buhalis, 2020, p. 270). In order to make tourism destinations smart, the stakeholders must be dynamically linked through a technical platform that allows for real-time sharing of tourism-related information. This platform contains a variety of touchpoints that can be accessed via end-user devices. This platform will aid in the design and facilitation of real-time tourism experiences, as well as the micro- and macro-level management of tourism resources. Smart tourism destinations benefit from embedded technological environments, responsive processes at the micro and macro levels, end-user devices positioned at various touchpoints, and ultimately, participatory stakeholders dynamically utilizing the platform. The major goal of changing into smart tourism destinations is to boost the tourism experience, improve resource management productivity in order to bolster destination competitiveness and touristic consumer experience, and assure tourism destination sustainability (Buhalis & Amaranggana, 2014, p. 557). Smart tourism applications will permit touristic attractions to engage with ICT and enable their customers to improve their personal experiences and satisfaction in the tourism business, which is becoming increasingly competitive. Thus, touristic destinations will be able to retain their existing customers and maintain and improve their competitive position by increasing their market share.

One of the most prominent risks in the tourism industry is that parties have opposing interests. Tourism service providers may need to employ centralized information platforms in order to make healthier judgments in smart tourism locations. Instant data transmission creates a big database from which customer patterns and trends can be identified. Smart tourism locations should ensure efficient use of this data to produce the entire services at the right time to match the preferences of their visitors. As a result, smart tourism destinations will be able to endow individualized services tailored to each different tourist type, exceeding existing tourist expectations and improving their overall tourist experience. The fact that tourists have such an experience will also affect their evaluation criteria of their tourism travels. Smart tourism apps, it can be asserted, will become increasingly weighty over time and will have a broader impact on the tourism industry. Smart tourism makes a significant contribution to touristic locations' competitiveness. However, it is possible for destinations to encounter some issues in the process of developing smartness (Buhalis & Amaranggana, 2015, p. 378).

Ensuring the development of smart destinations and improving destinations based on accessibility, technology, innovation and sustainability constitute the responsibility areas of today's tourism management approach. Efficient use of information and resources is notable in a destination strategy that will cover different elements such as competition (competitive advantage, competitive positioning and comparative), business pattern (sustainability and orientation), technology (provision and distribution), consumer (satisfaction, improvement and trends) and procurement (differentiation, innovation, certification and qualification) (Liberato et al., 2018, p. 21). Smart innovation approaches, in particular, play a critical role in the construction of smart tourism destinations. Intelligent innovation, which can include social innovation elements, can enable destination management organizations in smart tourism cities to manage assets and resources and expand their authority and influence beyond marketing. Smart innovation applications developed in smart tourism locations can help overcome the challenges that come with short- and medium-term sustainable development programs (Coca-Stefaniak, 2019, p. 515).

Smart tourism destination management is usually carried out with the help and leadership of government authorities, and it necessitates the involvement of citizens and social activists. Recognizing the importance of smartness and accepting the latest developments in technology, governments, private sector and other institutions and organizations have started to include smartness in the policies and strategies they have developed to ensure dynamic development and economic growth. In this sense, governments should not only incorporate knowledge-based tourist understanding into the regulations and policies they develop, but also propagate uniform smart tourism techniques and practices across the country in the context of long-term sustainability (Shafiee et al., 2019, p. 296).

Cities now have better environment for the formation of smart tourism because advanced technology companies have an innovative workforce, communications and built infrastructure, public transportation links, and an energy system, and they do have characteristics such as much more tourists concentrated in small spatial areas and less seasonality when measured in terms of volume. In essence, smart city applications address issues including transportation congestion, energy use, and crowding. As a result, smart city applications and smart tourism are becoming increasingly relevant in regions grappling with issues such as high tourist mobility and over-tourism. When measured in terms of connection, mobility, built infrastructure, and governance prospects, however, the applicability of smart tourism in smaller residential areas, such as rural destinations or tourism districts, appears to be somewhat problematic. In order for smart tourism to be implemented in rural areas and regions, it is eminent to determine smart tourism indicators suitable for the needs and development conditions of these settlements. In addition, Case studies are required to identify potential issues and possibilities that may emerge when smart tourism principles are implemented in rural areas. Each rural location or region has the ability to cater to a variety of smart tourism experiences and synergies. As a result, each region should create a smart tourist development strategy according to its own smart tourism goals (Gretzel, 2018).

Smart tourism destinations mean more than a technology-based system. Meanwhile, it can be described as a system of comprehensive organizational and administrative operations that includes the facilitation of resource sharing processes, the development of collaborative strategies, and the presentation of the destination by individual regional actors. Tourist experiences can be produced together in smart tourism destinations. Tourists can now participate as active stakeholders in smart platforms thanks to tourism's smartness. Tourists are more aware and capable since they can utilize social media to activate their marketing operations, participate in content development, and actively employ end-user devices. This may lessen tourists' uncertainties throughout the decision-making process, as well as the risk of their tourism experiences not living up to their expectations (Buonincontri & Micera, 2016). Thanks to the managers of smart tourism destinations creating tourism experiences with tourists by collaborating and sharing information; tourists have the opportunity to experience new experiences throughout their travels. This is one of the key characteristics that distinguishes smart tourist destinations from other holiday destinations (Savić & Pavlović, 2018, p. 84).

In smart tourism destinations, some customized services are intended to have a favorable impact on tourists' travel experiences. These tailored services are served in three stages: before, during, and following the visitors' travel. Planning should be based on real-time information based on the user profile so that tourists may make more informed decision before their visit. In order to enable tourists to discover destinations throughout their travel, it is recommended to provide access to real-time information, directly personalized services, and to receive feedback from tourists for the services provided. Finally, a feedback mechanism should be built after the visitors' travel that allows them to evaluate their entire tourism experience, and long-term cooperation of the tourists should be ensured to relive this experience. As a result, smart tourism destinations will benefit from access to real-time data in order to obtain data on users, instant feedback in terms of determining the opinions of tourists on the resources delivered, a dynamic platform that allows data exchange between different stakeholders for the integration of services, and existing data. Furthermore, it promotes the provision of personalized tourism services by allowing businesses to accurately anticipate the wants and desires of visitors in order to establish differentiated offerings and a dynamic recommendation system (Buhalis & Amarangana, 2015, p. 387). In smart tourism applications, tourist experiences can be improved by using NFC, QR, IoT, ICT, AR, VR, AI, more high-speed wi-fi, mobile applications, smart portable devices, smart sensors and cameras and similar technologies (Ağraş et al., 2020, p. 227). Tourists ensure that a vast flow of data is generated by sensors, micro-devices, and cameras in urban and non-urban regions that intrigue them throughout their travels, decision-making, and communication processes. While tourist data contributes significantly to the development of smart destinations, it also allows tourism businesses to customize their products and services (Ardito et al., 2019, p. 1806).

Smart tourism destinations should have smart technology compatible components, especially stakeholders. To make smart tourism destinations a reality, environmental awareness and green practices must be embraced and disseminated, particularly in tourism enterprises, because they have evolved into a major social issue that is increasingly recognized as requiring significant attention. For this reason, it is critical that the businesses in the destinations are both technologically and environmentally responsible. However, smart technologies must be implemented, and public institutions and non-governmental groups must take the lead in waste conservation in order to preserve the environment through the use of renewable energy sources. Nonetheless, there is no denying that a well-educated workforce has a considerable impact on the creation and maintenance of smart destinations. As a result, it is critical to educate and raise staff awareness about smart tourism within the context of comprehensive quality understanding (Yalçınkaya et al., 2018, p. 314-315).

The main benefits of smart tourism and smart tourism destinations concepts and practices for tourism businesses, cities and destinations are as follows:

- They respond to the expectations of tourists in the expectation of a tourism product integrated with technological developments in line with the current developments in ICT of touristic consumers,
- They provide destinations and organizations with a low-cost, easily accessible database about users, mostly through mobile technologies and social media platforms.,

- The employment of technological equipment in tourism operations improves client satisfaction and experience while also saving money,
- Cities with social, economic, and environmental difficulties can use smart tourism apps to improve their social, physical, and information technology infrastructures and to come up with solutions to their current problems.
- Smart tourism has the potential to become an economic development tool in cities,
- They enable small developing communities to strive for growth, even if they will never be able to become truly smart tourism destinations,
- Smart tourism destinations serve as a model for other destinations and a source of inspiration.

When the smart city or smart destination examples in Europe are examined, it is seen that some cities or destinations have been given the title of smart tourism capital in different years. In 2019, Helsinki (Finland) and Lyon (France) were selected as European Smart Tourism Capitals. In the same year, the European Smart Tourism Awards were awarded in the categories of sustainability to Ljubljana (Slovenia), accessibility to Málaga (Spain), digitalization to Copenhagen (Denmark), and cultural heritage and creativity to Linz (Austria). In 2020, Málaga (Spain) and Gothenburg (Sweden) were awarded the title of European Smart Tourism Capitals for their success in smart tourism planning. In the same year, awards were presented in the categories of sustainability to Gothenburg (Sweden), accessibility to Breda (Netherlands), digitalization to Ljubljana (Slovenia), and cultural heritage and creativity to Karlsruhe (Germany). The seven cities shortlisted in the 2022 European Smart Tourism Capitals competition are Bordeaux (France), Copenhagen (Denmark), Dublin (Ireland), Florence (Italy), Ljubljana (Slovenia), Palma (Spain) and Valencia (Spain) (European Commission, 2021).

STUDIES RELATED TO SMART TOURISM APPLICATIONS OF DESTINATIONS IN TURKEY

Turkey is a distinguished tourism destination. Many prominent and well-known touristic destinations are found in Turkey. Destinations such as Istanbul, Antalya, Izmir, Nevşehir (Cappadocia), Muğla (Fethiye, Bodrum, Marmaris) can be given as examples. Despite their significant tourism potential, however, these places' current competitive position is not where it should be. It may be highlighted that among these tourism destinations like Istanbul, Antalya, Izmir destinations, and Ankara, the capital of Turkey, which is also not among the popular tourism destinations, have the ICTs infrastructure development opportunities, innovative development opportunities, social and human capital that smart tourism destinations should have. Among the biggest shortcomings of these destinations in becoming smart tourism destinations, ICTs infrastructure services that will enable smart tourism applications to be implemented are not yet fully ready. Under this title, the results of the research attempting to reveal the scope, success level, strengths and deficiencies of the smart tourism applications of touristic destinations in Turkey are given in detail.

In this direction, Çelik & Topsakal (2017) conducted research and the smart tourism applications of the Antalya destination were studied. Considering the studies carried out to transform Antalya into a smart tourism destination, it has been detected that Antalya is just at the bottom of the ladder. In the study, smart tourism applications of destinations were reviewed in terms of attractiveness, accessibility, facilities, current packages, activities and ancillary services of destination components. According to the results, it has been determined that myAntalya, antalyakart, ICF Airport Mobile applications are being implemented within the scope of smart tourism destination dimensions of smart life and smart mobility within the scope of accessible destination component. With the available packages destination component, myAntalya application is utilised within the scope of smart people and smart mobility and smart tourism destination dimensions. Within the scope of activities destination component and smart mobility smart tourism destination dimension, there is myAntalya application. Finally, within the scope of ancillary services destination component and smart life smart tourism destination dimension in Antalya, it is observed that smart tourism applications are carried out through myAntalya and www.antalya.bel. tr. Likewise, it was found out that no application exists within the scope of the destination components of attractiveness and possibilities in Antalya.

Ataman's (2018) thesis study surveyed the potential of Edremit Bay to be a smart tourism destination and concrete suggestions have been made to develop this potential. In the study, it has been specified that Edremit, which has rich tourism potential, has not been sufficiently evaluated. The number of tourists in the region, the overnight stay and the average length of stay of the tourists is relatively low. The deficiency of ICTs in the region's tourism resources has a detrimental effect on the region's tourism development. Promotional activities are also lacking due to a lack of adequate ICT infrastructure. The holistic presentation of the tourism product, which is the biggest feature of smart tourism destinations, cannot be done in Edremit Bay due to the lack of a holistic policy understanding. In the study, a slogan and logo for Edremit were created and an imaginary website was designed in order to transform the Edremit Bay into a smart destination. In order to promote Edremit and to improve the services provided to tourists, social media channels were created on social media platforms such as facebook, twitter, instagram and youtube, where the slogan developed for Edremit is also used, along with a mobile application. In addition, In the study, indoor-outdoor kiosks were placed in district centers, points of tourism resources and public transportation points, and a system was designed to deliver smart services for tourists. Apart from these, within the scope of smart services that tourists can use during their stay at the destination, smart cards, physical and virtual travel guides, visual images such as puzzles, mobile games and documentaries were created. In the study, city tours, nature tours, archaeological discoveries, historical tours, gastronomic routes, festival time tours, blue cruise and water sports, virtual museum, observation decks tours were designed as smart destination experiences.

In the study of Erdem et al. (2019), Istanbul destination was evaluated as a smart tourism destination. Istanbul's smart tourism destination applications were contemplated within the scope of sustainability of the destination and quality of life of local people (a), accessibility of the destination (b), technological solutions and application of technological solutions to tourism, connectivity and sensor networks (c) and application of innovation, management and information systems to tourism (d) dimensions. In this direction, it has been determined that applications such as Istanbul Traffic Control Center, Smart Signaling, Vehicle Tracking System, Geographical Information System, Electronic Inspection System and Environmental Control Center (waste management place) have been implemented in Istanbul. Apart from these applications, there are steps taken in the context of establishing companies to operate in the field of smart city and information technologies within the scope of Istanbul Metropolitan Municipality and transforming Istanbul into a smart tourism destination. Although it was mentioned in these studies that there are smart applications, it was affirmed that these smart services and applications are insufficient in terms of transforming Istanbul into a smart tourism destination. In the study, it is emphasized that applications such as internet of things, cloud computing and end-user service providers should be employed in order to transform Istanbul into a smart tourism destination.

A study was conducted by Duran and Uygur (2019) on smart tourism practices in Ankara, the capital of Turkey. In the study, smart tourism applications of Ankara destination were examined in terms of destination components and smart tourism destination dimensions. According to the results, Ankara destination generally exhibits smart city characteristics, except for the smart environment dimension. However, it has been determined that Ankara has important deficiencies in terms of the features that a smart tourism destination should have. According to the results in this direction, applications made in Ankara within the scope of attractiveness destination component and also smart people and smart transportation, smart tourism destination dimensions are EGO, 360° Virtual Tour, ABB Traffic applications. Within the scope of accessibility destination component and also smart life and smart transportation smart tourism destination dimensions, there are EGO, Cultural Activities, ABB, ASKİ, ABB Cemetery Information System, Ankara Kurban (sacrificial worship), Blue Table (request, suggestion and demands), ABB Traffic applications. An application within the scope of facilities destination component and smart environment smart tourism destination dimension has not been determined. Within the scope of the the existing packages destination component and also smart people and smart transportation smart tourism destination dimensions; EGO, 360° Virtual Tour, ABB Traffic applications are available. There are EGO, ABB Traffic, Cultural Activities applications within the scope of the activities destination component and also smart transportation, smart tourism destination dimension in Ankara. Finally, it has been determined that there are Cultural Activities, 360° Virtual Tour, www.ankara.bel.tr applications within the scope of ancillary services destination component and smart life smart tourism destination dimension.

Ayyıldız & Ayyıldız (2020) conducted a study and tried to measure the smart tourism potential of Kuşadası and the applicability of smart tourism. When the studies on Kuşadası are questioned in terms of being a smart tourism destination, it is seen that the performed studies and applications are still new. It has been discovered that smart tourism applications in the destination are not widespread on the basis of cities, but instead on the basis of hotels and agencies. According to the results obtained in the study, it was revealed that Kuşadası could not yet become a smart destination due to its infrastructure deficiencies. It may be declared that the transformation of Kuşadası into a smart city may accelerate the development of tourism in the destination and supplement its market share. In this context, the participants in the research announced that institutions in the sector should cooperate and a mobile city guide application should be created that will enable use on smart phones. Two of the travel agencies that use smart tourism applications carry out Smart Ephesus tours and these agencies want to surge their technological equipment by investing more in smart tourism in the future. Besides, it has been determined that three chain hotels in Kuşadası use the smart phone application, and this service contributes to personalization of the services provided to the hotel guests and raised the satisfaction of the guests. On the other side, it is stated that Kuşadası Chamber of Commerce has projects to transform Kuşadası into a smart tourism destination in the study.

In a study conducted by Şimşek & Cinnioğlu (2020) on eight hotel businesses located in Istanbul's Beyoğlu destination, the Smart Beyoğlu Project was explored. It was aimed in the study to get the opinions and suggestions of the hotel officials about the project, to calculate the advantages and disadvantages of using QR codes, and also to identify in which areas four and five star hotels in smart destinations use QR codes. It has been determined that the Smart Beyoğlu project brings a different attractiveness to the destination, and tourists can easily obtain information about the region and businesses thanks to this project. In addition, while it was expressed that the project was not used effectively and efficiently and showed a slow development, it was concluded in the study that the project infrastructure should be improved, and promotional activities should be expanded. Moreover, it was identified that in order to widen customer satisfaction, data matrix application was used in hotel brochures to present information about restaurant promotion, location information, hotel transportation and campaigns. Yet, according to the results of the study, the hotels in Beyoğlu cannot benefit from the QR code application sufficiently because they use QR codes in a limited area. Another result of the research is that it is advantageous to use the QR code as it does not have a cost burden. Finally, in the study, it was found that tourists generally approached positively to QR code applications.

In the study carried out by Ağraş et al. (2020) to designate the applicability of smart tourism in Istanbul, it was ended that Istanbul's smart city infrastructure is not sufficient and other obligatory criteria have not yet been met. However, it is stated that Istanbul can meet the criteria of smart city and smart tourism within a period of 10 years. According to the results, there are projects for the development of the infrastructure and superstructure of Istanbul, Investments in the development of tourism and social areas continue and it has been determined that Istanbul is taking firm steps towards becoming a smart city. It is mentioned that there is a need for comprehensive and planned R&D studies and more robust investments to extend infrastructure and superstructure investments in Istanbul. It is pronounced that smart tourism studies should be supported by public authorities and large enterprises should be pioneers in this sense. As a result of that, this position may positively affect Istanbul's smart city image and smart tourism perception. It needs to be uttered that since these are investments that require substantial financing and time, it is still early for the smart tourism concept to find the opportunity to apply in Turkey considering the current conditions. However, it has been specified that smart tourism can be applied, albeit limited, in some destinations in Turkey such as Antalya, Bodrum, Izmir and Cappadocia. In addition, it was emphasized that investments should be made to create qualified human resources that can produce and use these technologies. In the study, it is articulated that smart tourism technologies can make Istanbul's tourism understanding innovative and dynamic. In this sense, some suggestions have been made such as tourism businesses and locals should be informed, smart tourism standards should be established, technological and other infrastructures should be strengthened, consumers and businesses should be protected by making legal arrangements for smart tourism, public institutions should lead investments, public and private sector enterprises should cooperate for the development of smart tourism.

In a study conducted by Ünal & Bayar (2020), it was intended to figure out the effects of the smart products of the destination and the applications made by the destination on destination choices and travel intentions of domestic tourists between the ages of 18-30 visiting the destination of Istanbul. It was concluded that each of the dimensions of attitude, behavior, belief and smart destination selection regarding the smart applications and products of touristic destinations affected the destination travel intentions of tourists in a high and positive way.

The research of Kafa et al. (2020) assessed the opinions of tourism business managers in Eskişehir destination regarding smart tourism tools and applications. It is aimed to estimate the smart technological systems and tools used in tourism enterprises. According to the results of the research, business managers consider smart tourism technologies necessary for the sector and they think that these technologies augment the competitiveness of destinations in the market. In the other respects, almost all tourism establishments in Eskişehir have modules and applications supported by smart systems, but the use of these smart systems in these businesses is not sufficient. The reasons why tourism businesses in Eskişehir cannot benefit from smart systems sufficiently are indicated as problems arising from economic constraints, insufficient infrastructure and market conditions.

Erkmen & Güler (2020) analyzed smart tourism practices in Edirne and some results were obtained in this study. In order to sustain the increasing tourism activity in Edirne in recent years, tourism enterprises, local and central institutions in the city have been trying to benefit from technology effectively. E-commerce applications supported by official institutions and 16 touchscreen kiosks placed by Edirne Municipality in different points of Edirne for the use of local and foreign tourists can be shown among these initiatives. In addition, the 'www.edirnevisit.com' website and some applications have been developed for use on android and IOS phones. In these applications, the logo of Edirne Municipality is also included. These applications serve in different languages such as Turkish, English and Bulgarian. The purpose of creating the said kiosk and applications is to promote Edirne in the best way possible. In these kiosks and applications, information such as digital city map, information about historical and touristic places, hotels, places to eat, a monthly calendar of events in the city, minibus routes, locations and numbers of taxi stands are included. Event information belonging to official institutions can be shared from kiosks and applications. Information about minibus routes can be obtained from the relevant website of Edirne Municipality. In addition, local and foreign tourists visiting the city can convey their suggestions and complaints to these institutions via the WhatsApp Suggestions and Complaints line created by Edirne Governorship and Edirne Municipality in 2017. With the QR code application made by the Edirne Governor's Office, it is possible to read books at the bus-stops via smart phones and tablets. Apart from these, carried out jointly by Edirne Keşan Municipality and Bulgaria, the "Geographic Information System" application allows people to access the information of the businesses in the region interactively. A tourism portal belonging to Uzunköprü is being prepared by Edirne Uzunköprü Municipality, which contains information about historical, cultural and touristic artifacts in the district and which can be used mobile by tourists.

FUTURE RESEARCH DIRECTIONS

With the introduction of addressing the shortcomings in physical and information technology infrastructures, smart tourism is predicted that the much more practicable will become in hotels, cities, and destinations in the long term. This situation may make it easier to conduct research in the future to determine the standard levels of effective tourism operations in hotels, cities, and destinations.

Smart tourism is projected to continue to evolve and alter in the next years, both philosophically and in terms of hotel, city, and destination applications. New developments in information and communication technologies in the near future may cause the current standards of smart tourism to be reviewed. This situation may enable the determination of higher standards for smart tourism and may require the adaptation of new digital tools into smart tourism applications. As a result, potential advances in ICTs in the coming years will dramatically improve the smartness of hotels, cities, and destinations. Similarly, given today's dizzying pace of technology advancements, the concept of smart tourism has not yet accomplished its conceptual evolution, and it may be feasible to restructure the concept in the future in response to new breakthroughs. Apart from smart tourism, this situation may pave the way for the formation of additional concepts that symbolize an advanced degree of smart tourism based on current situations.

After a thorough assessment of the Turkey destinations covered in this chapter, it may be proposed that the number of smart tourism studies conducted in these areas be expanded. In addition, the inadequacies in Turkey's smart tourism applications should be compared to competent, smart tourism applications elsewhere in the world and it is also seen to be vital to give specific suggestions for addressing these flaws.

CONCLUSION

Touristic destinations are built in such a way that they can accommodate a wide range of resources and capabilities, as well as a wide range of interest groups and stakeholders. To merge this structure into smart tourism, it is essential to force these interest groups together, foster cooperation among them, identify the fundamental physical and technological infrastructure, and best utilize these physical and technological infrastructure resources in accordance with smart tourism goals. The adaptation of touristic destinations to smart tourism seems to be more demanding due to the challenge of bringing together stakeholders with varied interests and aligning current digital and physical resources to a unified aim. In terms of constructing the physical and technological infrastructure required by the smart tourism destination, however, fostering cooperation among stakeholders is crucial. Meanwhile, in order to transform touristic destinations into smart tourism destinations, particular conditions must be met. For instance, destinations must have sufficient financial power to accelerate the development of their physical and technological infrastructure, local residents should be open to education and learning, social awareness should be high, stakeholders should give greater importance to the general interests of the society before their own interests, and public institutions should lead in terms of bringing stakeholders together. Therefore, in addition to creating a city infrastructure that is compatible with technological advancements, other social and physical elements are required for an ideal smart tourism destination.

When Turkey's transformation levels of touristic destinations into smart tourism destinations are evaluated in general in line with the studies carried out, it may be remarked that Antalya, Istanbul, Ankara, Edirne, Eskişehir, Edremit Bay and Kuşadası destinations, investigated in studies, are at the beginning of the road in terms of turning into smart tourism destinations. In general, these locations' smart tourism infrastructure investments are inadequate, and the value of smart tourism is just now getting to be acknowledged in key destinations. It can be said that the level of adaptation of tourism enterprises to the concept of smart tourism is higher, and the rate of transformation into smart tourism is much slower due to the complex structure of destinations and the low rate of development of infrastructure investments.

It may be recommended that technological infrastructure should remarkably be improved under the leadership of public investments and with the support of the private sector in order for Turkish touristic destinations to quickly adapt to the concept of smart tourism, within the framework of a destination management organization model to be created. Similarly, stakeholders such as government entities, locals, and tourism businesses should work together to develop successful strategic plans for the transformation into a smart tourism destination. They really should measure and analyze the efficacy of strategies on a regular basis, and the destination management organizations in issue should carry out practical training and awareness-raising campaigns in order to build a human resources infrastructure capable of making the most use of technical and mobile tools, as well as other economic resources. In addition, by examining the successful examples of smart tourism destinations in the world, it may be possible to determine the strengths and weaknesses of touristic destinations in Turkey and to realize changes and innovations to improve the identified weaknesses. It can be suggested that touristic destinations and tourism enterprises should make more efforts to create a smart tourism service concept that meets the expectations of visitors or tourists by regularly measuring the satisfaction levels of touristic consumers about smart tourism experiences. Finally, the realization of investments and practices that will enable the transformation of touristic destinations in Turkey and in the world into smart tourism destinations within the framework of the basic philosophy of protecting the environment is considered important in terms of the sustainability of the smart tourism concept.

REFERENCES

Ağraş, S., Ayyıldız, A., & Aktürk, E. (2020). Akıllı turizmin Türkiye'deki büyük şehirlerde uygulanabilirliği: İstanbul örneği [Applicability of smart tourism in major cities in Turkey: The case of Istanbul]. *Bartın Üniversitesi İktisadi ve İdari Bilimler Fakültesi Dergisi, 11*(21), 207–231.

Ardito, L., Cerchione, R., Vecchio, P. D., & Reguseo, E. (2019). Big data in smart tourism: Challenges, issues and opportunities. *Current Issues in Tourism, 22*(15), 1805–1809. doi:10.1080/13683500.2019.1612860

Ataman, H. (2018). *Akıllı turizm ve akıllı destinasyonlar: Edremit Körfezi'ne yönelik bir uygulama* [Smart tourism and smart destinations: an application intended for the Gulf of Edremit] [Unpublished master dissertation]. Balikesir University Institute of Social Sciences, Department of International Trade and Marketing, Balikesir, Turkey.

Ayyıldız, A. Y., & Ayyıldız, T. (2020). Pazarlama fırsatı olarak akıllı turizm: Kuşadası örneği [Smart tourism as a marketing opportunity: the case of Kuşadası]. *Business & Management Studies: An International Journal, 8*(1), 599–623. doi:10.15295/bmij.v8i1.141

Azis, N., Amin, M., Chan, S., & Aprilia, C. (2020). How smart tourism technologies affect tourist destination loyalty. *Journal of Hospitality and Tourism Technology, 11*(4), 603–625. doi:10.1108/JHTT-01-2020-0005

Boes, K., Buhalis, D., & Inversini, A. (2015). Conceptualising smart tourism destination dimensions. In I. Tussyadiah & A. Inversini (Eds.), *Information and communication technologies in tourism* (pp. 391–403). Springer.

Boes, K., Buhalis, D., & Inversini, A. (2016). Smart tourism destinations: Ecosystems for tourism destination competitiveness. *International Journal of Tourism Cities, 2*(2), 108–124. doi:10.1108/IJTC-12-2015-0032

Buhalis, D. (2020). Technology in tourism-from information communication technologies to etourism and smart tourism towards ambient intelligence tourism: A perspective article. *Tourism Review, 75*(1), 267–272. doi:10.1108/TR-06-2019-0258

Buhalis, D., & Amaranggana, A. (2014). Smart tourism destinations. In Z. Xiang & I. Tussyadiah (Eds.), *Information and communication technologies in tourism* (pp. 553–564). Springer-Verlag.

Buhalis, D., & Amaranggana, A. (2015). Smart tourism destinations enhancing tourism experience through personalisation of services. In I. Tussyadiah & A. Inversini (Eds.), *Information and communication technologies in tourism* (pp. 378–388). Springer.

Buonincontri, P., & Micera, R. (2016). The experience co-creation in smart tourism destinations: A multiple case analysis of European destinations. *Information Technology & Tourism, 16*(3), 285–315. doi:10.100740558-016-0060-5

Çelik, P., & Topsakal, Y. (2017). Akıllı turizm destinasyonları: Antalya destinasyonunun akıllı turizm uygulamalarının incelenmesi [Smart tourism destinations: review of smart tourism applications of Antalya destination]. *Seyahat ve Otel İşletmeciliği Dergisi, 14*(3), 149–166. doi:10.24010oid.369951

Chiappa, G. D., & Baggio, R. (2015). Knowledge transfer in smart tourism destinations: Analyzing the effects of a network structure. *Journal of Destination Marketing & Management*, *4*(3), 145–150. doi:10.1016/j.jdmm.2015.02.001

Coca-Stefaniak, J. A. (2019). Marketing smart tourism cities-a strategic dilemma. *International Journal of Tourism Cities*, *5*(4), 513–518. doi:10.1108/IJTC-12-2019-163

Dorcic, J., Komsic, J., & Markovic, S. (2019). Mobile technologies and applications towards smart tourism-state of the art. *Tourism Review*, *74*(1), 82–103. doi:10.1108/TR-07-2017-0121

Duran, G., & Uygur, S. M. (2019). Akıllı turizm destinasyonları kapsamında Ankara'nın akıllı turizm uygulamalarına yönelik bir araştırma [A research on Ankara's smart tourism applications in the scope of smart tourism destinations]. In *Proceedings of The Third International Congress on Future Tourism: Innovation, Entrepreneurship and Sustainability* (pp. 426-436). Mersin University Publications.

Erdem, A., Unur, K., & Şeker, F. (2019). Akıllı turizm destinasyonu olarak İstanbul'un değerlendirilmesi [Evaluation of Istanbul as a smart tourism destination]. In *Proceedings of International Congress on Digital Transformation in Tourism* (pp. 65-86). Düzce University Publications.

Erkmen, B., & Güler, E. G. (2020). Turizm ve dijitalleşme: 'Haskova-Edirne kültürel ve tarihi destinasyonlar projesi' örneği [Tourism and digitalization: 'Haskovo and Edirne – cultural and historical destinations project]. *Tourism and Recreation, 2*(1), 111-118.

Europe Commission. (2021). *European capitals of smart tourism.* https://smart-tourism-capital.ec.europa. eu/index_en

Femenia-Serra, F., & Ivars-Baidal, J. A. (2021). Do smart destinations really work? the case of Benidorm. *Asia Pacific Journal of Tourism Research*, *26*(4), 365–384. doi:10.1080/10941665.2018.1561478

Femenia-Serra, F., Neuhofer, B., & Ivars-Baidal, A. (2019). Towards a conceptualisation of smart tourists and their role within the smart destination scenario. *Service Industries Journal*, *39*(2), 109–133. doi:10.1080/02642069.2018.1508458

Gajdošík, T. (2018). Smart tourism: Concepts and insights from central Europe. *Czech Journal of Tourism*, *7*(1), 25–44. doi:10.1515/cjot-2018-0002

Gretzel, U. (2018). From smart destinations to smart tourism regions. *Journal of Regional Research*, *42*, 171–184.

Gretzel, U., Reino, S., Kopera, S., & Koo, C. (2015a). Smart tourism challenges. *Journal of Tourism*, *16*(1), 41–47.

Gretzel, U., Sigala, M., Xiang, Z., & Koo, C. (2015b). Smart tourism: Foundations and developments. *Electronic Markets*, *25*(3), 179–188. doi:10.100712525-015-0196-8

Gretzel, U., Werthner, H., Koo, C., & Lamsfus, C. (2015c). Conceptual foundations for understanding smart tourism ecosystems. *Computers in Human Behavior*, *50*, 558–563. doi:10.1016/j.chb.2015.03.043

Hunter, W. C., Chung, N., Gretzel, U., & Koo, C. (2015). Constructivist research in smart tourism. *Asia Pacific Journal of Information Systems*, *25*(1), 103–118. doi:10.14329/apjis.2015.25.1.105

Jasrotia, A., & Gangotia, A. (2018). Smart cities to smart tourism destinations: A review paper. *Journal of Tourism Intelligence and Smartness*, *1*(1), 47–56.

Johnson, A. G., & Samakovlis, I. (2018). A bibliometric analysis of knowledge development in smart tourism research. *Journal of Hospitality and Tourism Technology*, *10*(4), 600–623. doi:10.1108/JHTT-07-2018-0065

Jovicic, D. Z. (2019). From the traditional understanding of tourism destination to the smart tourism destination. *Current Issues in Tourism*, *22*(3), 276–282. doi:10.1080/13683500.2017.1313203

Kafa, N., Arıca, R., & Gök, N. S. (2020). Akıllı turizm araç ve uygulamalarına ilişkin turizm işletmesi yöneticilerinin görüşleri: Eskişehir üzerine nitel bir araştırma [Tourism managers opinions about smart tourism vehicles and applications: a qualitative research on Eskişehir]. *İşletme Araştırmaları Dergisi*, *12*(3), 2774-2787. doi:10.20491/isarder.2020.1007

Khan, S., Woo, M., Nam, K., & Chathoth, P. K. (2017). Smart city and smart tourism: A case of Dubai. *Sustainability*, *9*(12), 2279. doi:10.3390u9122279

Koo, C., Shin, S., Gretzel, U., Hunter, W. C., & Chung, N. (2016). Conceptualization of smart tourism destination competitiveness. *Asia Pacific Journal of Information Systems*, *26*(4), 561–576. doi:10.14329/apjis.2016.26.4.561

Li, Y., Hu, C., Huang, C., & Duan, L. (2017). The concept of tourism in the context of tourism information services. *Tourism Management*, *58*, 293–300. doi:10.1016/j.tourman.2016.03.014

Liberato, P., Alen, E., & Liberato, D. (2018). Smart tourism destination triggers consumer experience: The case of Porto. *European Journal of Management and Business Economics*, *27*(1), 6–25. doi:10.1108/EJMBE-11-2017-0051

Lopez de Avila, A. (2015, February). Smart destinations: xxı century tourism. In *Proceedings of the ENTER2015 Conference on Information and Communication Technologies in Tourism* (pp. 4-6), Academic Press.

Matos, A., Pinto, B., Barros, F., Martins, S., Martins, J., & Au-Yong-Oliveira, M. (2019). Smart cities and smart tourism: what future they bring? In Á. Rocha, H. Adeli, L. P. Reis, & S. Costanzo (Eds.), New knowledge in information systems and technologies. Springer.

Mehraliyev, F., Chan, I. C. C., Choi, Y., Köseoglu, M., & Law, R. (2020). A state-of-the-art review of smart tourism research. *Journal of Travel & Tourism Marketing*, *37*(1), 78–91. doi:10.1080/10548408.2020.1712309

Park, J. H., Lee, C., Yoo, C., & Nam, Y. (2016). An analysis of the utilization of facebook by local Korean governments for tourism development and the network of smart tourism ecosystem. *International Journal of Information Management*, *36*(6), 1320–1327. doi:10.1016/j.ijinfomgt.2016.05.027

Savić, J., & Pavlović, G. (2018). Analysis of factors of smart tourism development in Serbia. *Hotel and Tourism Management*, *6*(1), 81–91. doi:10.5937/menhottur1801081S

Shafiee, S., Ghatari, A. R., Hasanzadeh, A., & Jahanyan, S. (2019). Developing a model for sustainable smart tourism destinations: A systematic review. *Tourism Management Perspectives*, *31*, 287–300. doi:10.1016/j.tmp.2019.06.002

Şimşek, E., & Cinnioğlu, H. (2020). Akıllı turizm destinasyonlarındaki otellerin karekod kullanımı: İstanbul Smart Beyoğlu üzerine bir araştırma [The quick response code usage of hotels in smart tourism destinations: a research on Istanbul Smart Beyoglu]. *Uluslararası Yönetim İktisat ve İşletme Dergisi*, *16*(3), 675–690. doi:10.17130/ijmeb.798489

Ünal, A., & Bayar, S. B. (2020). Akıllı uygulamaları ve ürünleri kullanan turistlerin destinasyon seçim süreçleri: İstanbul örneği [Destination choice process of tourists using smart applications and products: the case of Istanbul]. *Uluslararası Sosyal Araştırmalar Dergisi*, *13*(70), 1066–1075. doi:10.17719/jisr.2020.4158

UNWTO. (2021). *Dijital transformation*. https://www.unwto.org/digital-transformation

Vasavada, M., & Padhiyar, J. (2016). "Smart tourism": Growth for tomorrow. *Journal of Research*, *1*(12), 55–61.

Wang, X., Li, X. R., Zhen, F., & Zhang, J. (2016). How smart is your tourist attraction?: Measuring tourist preferences of smart tourism attractions via a FCEM-AHP and IPA approach. *Tourism Management*, *54*, 309–320. doi:10.1016/j.tourman.2015.12.003

Xiang, Z., & Fesenmaier, D. R. (2017). Big data analytics, tourism design and smart tourism. In Z. Xiang & R. Fesenmaier (Eds.), *Analytics in smart tourism design: concepts and methods* (pp. 299–307). Springer. doi:10.1007/978-3-319-44263-1_17

Xiang, Z., Stienmetz, J., & Fesenmaier, D. R. (2021). Smart tourism design: Launching the annals of tourism research curated collection on designing tourism places. *Annals of Tourism Research*, *86*, 103154. doi:10.1016/j.annals.2021.103154

Yalçınkaya, P., Atay, L., & Korkmaz, H. (2018). An evaluation on smart tourism. *China-USA Business Review*, *17*(6), 308–315. doi:10.17265/1537-1514/2018.06.004

Zhu, W., Zhang, L., & Li, N. (2014). Challenges, function changing of government and enterprises in chinese smart tourism. In Z. Xiang & L. Tussyadiah (Eds.), *Information and communication technologies in tourism*. Springer.

KEY TERMS AND DEFINITIONS

E-Tourism: It is a form of tourism where virtual channels such as websites and smartphone applications are frequently used, especially in commercial relations between tourists and tourism businesses.

E-Tourist: It is the type of tourist who makes effective use of ICTs in the process of purchasing decision and while purchasing tourism products, during tourism experiences and in the evaluation process of tourism experiences.

Information and Communication Technologies (ICTs): It is the general name of technologic tools that provide access to virtual channels such as the internet and social media, which have made their profound effects felt in many areas, especially in the tourism sector, and other their life facilitators.

Smart Tourism: It is the type of tourism that requires the integration of many factors and components such as high-level physical and information technology infrastructure services, well-trained human resources, effective management understanding and leadership spirit, effective promotion and marketing practices, cooperation between stakeholders and environmental awareness.

Smart Tourism Destinations: These places can be defined as the touristic attraction areas where the concept of smart tourism is applied.

Smart Tourism Experience: It is the sum of the tourism experience that tourists get from the service they receive in smart tourism cities and/or destinations.

Smart Tourist: It is the type of tourist who demands smart tourism services, knows how to benefit from smart tourism services and actually benefits from these services.

Chapter 8
The Phenomenon of Value Co-Creation and Its Place in Air Transport

Fatma Selin Sak
Giresun University, Turkey

Özlem Atalık
Eskişehir Technical University, Turkey

Evrim Genç Kumtepe
Anadolu University, Turkey

ABSTRACT

It is known that businesses are looking for different ways to reach customers, both technologically and through employees, in order to protect their existing customers as well as to gain new customers. However, today, due to the personable approaches of services, there is a need to create a bond between the business and the customer. In this context, value is an original understanding that people have, and businesses aim to create value together by reaching more customers through personalized services. Thus, the importance of studies aimed at understanding this phenomenon based on multilateral profit relationship is increasing day by day. In the current study, the approach of creating value together is discussed, and the understanding of the creation of value together in air transportation operating in the service sector is examined.

*This book chapter is based on the doctoral dissertation entitled "The role of experience on the effect of customer value on the customer satisfaction: The case of Sabiha Gokcen International airport" by Fatma Selin Sak

DOI: 10.4018/978-1-7998-8306-7.ch008

INTRODUCTION

Co-creation emphasizes the common value creation between the manufacturer and the customer. The value of a product created together depends on a number of variables based on consumers' knowledge of the product. There are two conditions for creating the value together: (i) identification of a common problem by business and customers (Vega-Vazquez, Revilla-Camacho, & Cossio-Silva, 2013) and (ii) transparency of the business and customers' access to information about the product (Prahalad & Ramaswamy, 2004). Customer satisfaction is becoming an increasingly difficult phenomenon to achieve despite the intense efforts and high monetary expenditures of businesses. Consumers are becoming increasingly conscious, proactive, strengthened, connected and complex. Confident customers collaborate with the organization with the desire to create together. this only occurs by ensuring that the customer is motivated for creation according to the perceived level of ability, with feeling good or comfortable in the service role (McKee, Simmers, & Licata, 2006).

On the other hand, considering the air transport service process, an event that does not comply with the optimum flow of experience within a standard process such as security screening, check-in and baggage delivery, security screening for the transition to cleared areas, boarding, travel process, which starts at the entrance of the airport of passengers. When it occurs, this situation can cause both the perception of the entire process provided by the airport operator as unsuccessful and dissatisfaction with the airline operators. At this point, considering all the stakeholders (passengers, airlines, commercial enterprises, ground management, users, send-offs), in order to ensure passenger satisfaction, the co-creation of the processes in the airport flow allows the passenger to derive value from the most basic service, the flight itself.

In co-creation, involving passengers in the creation of travel arrangements helps personalize the service, creating a unique experience. Especially with the advent of the internet, passengers can organize their flights themselves (Grissemann & Stokburger-Sauer, 2012). This can also increase passenger satisfaction and ensure the formation of loyalty. In this direction, the aim of the study is to contribute to a better understanding by emphasizing the importance of the understanding of creating such an important value in air transport together with business and customer partnerships.

In the following parts of the study first, by referring to the concept of value in marketing, the customer role will be scrutinized as a result of the change in the concept of value today. Then the concept of creation together will be explained. In this context, it is seen that the concept of co-creation is used in the relevant literature in place of customer participation, co-production, common design concepts (Martínez-Cañas, Ruiz-Palomino, Linuesa-Langreo, & Blázquez-Resino, 2016; Gardner, 2019; Zhang, Lu, & Chen, 2018; Fernandes & Remelhe, 2016). Thus, it became necessary to explain the concepts mentioned in the study separately. In the last part of the study, the concept of creating value together is mentioned and its applications in air transport are included.

BACKGROUND

Concept of Value in Marketing

The main subject of marketing is a transaction. The transaction is the exchange of value between the two parties. Valuable things are not limited to goods, services and money; include other resources such as time, energy and emotions (Kotler, 1972) Marketing manages profitable customer relationships by engaging customers and has two purposes. First, attract new customers by promising superior value; the second is to maintain and grow existing customers by providing value and satisfaction. (Kotler & Armstrong, 2016, s. 29).

According to the updated definition of the American Marketing Association in 2013, "marketing is a set of institutions and processes for creating, communicating, delivering, and exchanging highly valued offerings for customers, buyers, partners, and society." (AMA, 2013).

In order to understand marketing, as seen in accepted definitions, the value must first be understood (Babin & James, 2010). In this context, when the marketing literature is examined, the importance of the concept of value has been recognized and it has been found that many researchers have been working on this subject. Use value, exchange value, aesthetic value, identity value, instrumental value, economic value, social value, shareholder value, symbolic value, functional value, utilitarian value, hedonic value, perceived value, community values, emotional value, expected value and brand value can be given as an example of different value concepts frequently used in marketing and consumer research (Karababa & Kjeldgaard, 2014). Although these differences have enriched the literature, they have also led to confusion of concepts (Sánchez-Fernández & Iniesta-Bonillo, 2007). In order to avoid this confusion, the value concept definitions of some authors that have become closer to each other are identified through literature review and shown in the Table 1.

Table 1. Conceptualization of value

Authors	Definitions
(Zeithaml, 1988)	The perceived value is the general assessment of the use of a product based on the consumer's perception of what is received and what is given in response. The value represents an exchange. What is taken and given varies from consumer to consumer.
(Flint, Woodruff, & Gardial, 1997)	A value judgment is a customers' assessment of the gap between all relevant benefits and sacrifices in a particular use case.
(Payne & Holt, 2001)	Value arises as a result of a preferential exchange relationship, such as benefits and gains, and the interaction between the customer and the product or service.
(Martinez-Hernandez, 2003)	The value is to ensure the satisfaction obtained from meeting the perceptions and expectations of customers regarding the benefits provided by the product/service and, on the other hand, to generate profits for the business.
(Kotler & Keller, 2006)	Value is a reflection of the tangible and abstract benefits and costs that customers perceive. The value can be seen as a combination of quality, service and price, called the "customer value trio".
(Oliver, 2010)	The value is a comparison of what is earned as a result of the use of the product (hedonic or improving performance, etc.) and the costs of obtaining it (financial, psychological or physical effort, etc.).
(Babin & James, 2010)	The concept of value encompasses giving resources such as money, time, opportunity, emotions, energy and image in return for obtaining factors that benefit such as quality, excitement, prestige, experience and comfort.

(Prepared by the Author)

In the studies carried out by the authors on different subjects, it is seen that the value is discussed in different contexts. In the literature, there are studies that examine value in the context of relational marketing (Ravald & Grönroos, 1996; Payne & Holt, 1999; Collins, 1999), perceived value (Sánchez-Fernández & Iniesta-Bonillo, 2007; Nambisan & Baron, 2009), customer value (Özgül, 2010; Woodruff,

1997; Holbrook, 2006; Flint, Woodruff, & Gardial, 1997), value co-creation behavior (Xie, Bagozzi, & Troye, 2008; Yi & Gong, 2013; Shamim & Ghazali, 2014; Sharma & Conduit, 2016; Ida, 2017).

The value addressed in the customer context is a personalized concept that differs from customer to customer while being effective in determining the behavior and preferences of the individual (Ravald & Grönroos, 1996). In their study, Sánchez-Fernández & Iniesta-Bonillo (2007) suggested that values and value are different concepts and, accordingly, personal values and perceived value have different meanings. The value is the result of an evaluation decision. On the other hand, the term values refer to the standards, rules, criteria, norms, objectives or ideals that form the basis of such an evaluation decision (Holbrook, 1999, s. 8).

In this context, when the customer value hierarchy that enables businesses to achieve success is examined, it is seen that the desired value consists of specific and measurable results related to preferences, characteristics and usage situations. Desired value arises when customers perceive how well or poorly a product performs when used. Businesses should learn about the use-case goals that customers want (or want to avoid) and the consequences of those goals. Because perceived value directly led to the formation of a sense of general satisfaction (Woodruff, 1997).

Woodruff (1997) has explained the concept of customer value that will ensure customer satisfaction. According to the author, customer value is the perceived preference of usage-based product features, quality-dependent performance, and results that facilitate (or prevent) the customer from achieving her goals and objectives.

Holbrook (2006), on the other hand, considers customer value in a broader perspective in the context of experience. This type of value is formed only by an interactive preference experience. Experience is the interaction between a highlighted object (e.g. a product) and a subject (e.g. a customer). Interaction is handled in three ways, comparatively, personally and situationally. The first involves comparisons between objects, the second involves the individual differences between subjects varying from one person to another, and the last one involves the binding nature of the situation in which the evaluation takes place.

In order to provide customer-appropriate products and services, different scales have been developed that form the set of values for revealing the values and behaviors that customers have. The most familiar of these is Rokeach's "Value List", which examines the values of American society (Williams, 1974). Mitchell then created the "Values and Lifestyle (VALS)" scale in 1983 (Mitchell, 1983). Similarly, Kahle's "Values List (LOV)" developed in the same year is an accepted study in the field (Kahle, 1983). Afterwards, Standford Research Institute made arrangements on the VALS scale and brought the VALS2 scale into the literature (Reynolds, 1985). The "Motivational value types" put forth by Schwartz (1992, 1994) were implemented in different countries (Schwartz, 1992; Schwartz, 1994).

Especially with the development of these scales, the issue of creating value for customers since the 1990s has started to attract significant attention in the management and marketing literature (Grönroos, 2008). Gummesson emphasizes that the value does not occur without interacting with a product and therefore it is not possible to distinguish between the manufacturer and the customer, and the value differs from customer to customer (2008).

For some, while creating an emotional interaction value, according to another, values do not occur without logical reasons. For some, emotional interactions can create a value, while for another, value does not occur without logical reasons (Gummesson, 2008). The value is determined not by the manufacturer's assumptions, but by the perception of the customer in the market. This perception can change over time (Chen, Batchuluun, & Batnasan, 2015). In this context, customer value is seen as an indicator of how successful the service has been over time (Babin & James, 2010).

Businesses will be able to assess whether they have sufficient resources through a mechanism in their value creation process with the proposed framework and guiding questions. These include methods such as designing and developing new products, manufacturing, logistics and demand forecasting. Similarly, businesses seeking to support customers' value creation can introduce these mechanisms using additional resources of the business in their value creation process. Value-added opportunities are only about identifying new ways to support the value creation processes of the customer or business. These can be accomplished by extracting customer data and then using that data to provide services to satisfy customers, or through joint production, joint development and joint design activities of businesses. As both businesses and customers begin to find innovative ways to support each other's value creation processes, the perspective of value creation can be expanded (Saarijärvi, Kannan, & Kuusela, 2013).

MAIN FOCUS OF THE CHAPTER

Value Co-Creation in Air Transport

Changing Paradigm of Value and Role of Customer

With the increase in internet usage and mobile devices supporting the internet, it is easier for the customer to access information whenever and wherever they want. Thanks to easier access to information, the search cost in the purchase decision has also become cheaper. Customers voluntarily write comments about goods or services on blogs, customer forums or through social media. Moreover, the value proposition presentation offered by the business has been transparently shared among customers, creating business models such as Trip Advisor, where it relies on travelers' feedback and comments. This move indicates a trend towards the customer-oriented market (Ayunia, 2013). The way businesses are now starting to have a dialogue with customers indicates that customers are gaining more and more power and control (Binkhorst & Dekker, 2009).

In this context, co-creation, which is one of the approaches that support the power of the customer, is considered one of the most important marketing paradigms today. According to this view, customers are no longer at the end of the value chain, but rather at the heart of the value creation process (Pongsa-kornrungsilp & Schroeder, 2011). On the other hand, with the changing marketing approach according to Prahalad & Ramaswamy (2004), who is the predecessor of the concept of creation, there is a process that provides double-sided satisfaction, not the kingdom of the customer. Accordingly, the customer should be allowed to personalize the service experience and this process should be provided jointly by the enterprise. In this case, although the product is the same, experiences differ and enrich according to the customers.

Considering the nature of the service, the competencies (knowledge and skills) of one party are offered for the benefit of the other (Vargo & Lusch, 2004). This approach emphasizes that value is co-created through a mutual exchange (Vargo, Maglio, & Akaka, 2008). As a matter of fact, in the service dominant logic, customers have an understanding of how producers create value for themselves, as well as what kind of value is created for them when they consume the service. (Ramaswamy & Gouillart, 2010). This situation, by adopting the service approach, provides a perspective on businesses to adjust their business strategies and marketing approaches according to the value creation based on customers' service consumption. (Grönroos, 2008).

Grönroos & Ravald (2011) emphasize the customer's standout role, indicating that since the customer is the one who wants the service to be in line with their expectations, the person who will contribute to the creation of the value should also be the customer. In this case, the customer must decide what value they want to create. For example, toothpaste is used not only to clean and brush teeth but also to have healthier and more beautiful smiles within the social environment (Grönroos ve Ravald, 2011: 8).

Ballantyne & Varey (2006) divided the activities that enable the creation of value for the customer into three categories: establishing relationships, communicating and having knowledge. Establishing relationships refers to providing support for the creation and implementation of information resources, communicating refers to improving relationships, and having knowledge refer to the knowledge necessary to improve the customer service experience, especially when created with dialogue and co-learning (Ballantyne & Varey, 2006). Accordingly, with the development of new technological solutions (such as digital TV, third generation mobile services), businesses are creating new ways for them to interact with their customers about creating innovative products, services and experiences together. For example, IKEA's approach has changed the logic in the service sector by rearranging activities in the traditional value chain. While IKEA designs and distributes the furniture, the customer assembles the product. Thus, the co-creation of value is achieved. In addition, as part of changes in customer preferences and lifestyles, it seems that customers have acted in a comparably more personal way over the past decade. This trend shows that customers want to create more personalized, experience-based and differentiated goods and services together (Payne, Storbacka, & Frow, 2008).

Pioneers of Co-Creation

Considering that co-creation is a component of customer participation, which is the premise of customer engagement, it becomes necessary to explain these concepts separately. It is striking that the concepts are often confused in the literature and are therefore used interchangeably.

Looking at the concept of customer engagement first, it is defined as processes, actions and interactions in which a service provider collaborates with existing or potential customers to learn about the market and improve organizational behavior (Matthing, Sanden, & Edvardsson, 2004). In their studies, the researchers discussed customer participation in the context of the interaction and non-interaction the customer establishes with businesses. Considering that customer engagement is a new and evolving concept, the importance of developing stronger customer relationships with engagement is increasingly recognized. (Kumar et al., 2010).

Accordingly, customer engagement should go beyond marketing function and better collaboration should be made in different parts of the business in managing different points of contact with the customer (Perkins & Fenech, 2014). There is also a need to investigate the extent to which the cognitive and emotional components of the engagement process work for different customer segments. In the study conducted by Bowden (2009), it is revealed that the participation process differs between first-time customers and experienced customers in terms of knowledge and interest levels.

According to Brodie et al. (2011), the concept of customer engagement replaces traditional concepts of involvement and co-creation, while customer experience becomes a must for customer engagement. On the other hand, in the customer engagement model established in the studies of Vivek, Beatty & Morgan (2012), involvement and co-production are seen as the precursors of customer engagement. The model describes the relationships between buyers, sellers, potential customers, current customers, consumers, business and society. On the other hand, it is also argued that customer engagement constitutes the phenomena of value, trust, emotional loyalty, word of mouth, loyalty and brand community engagement. Accordingly, when customers get a greater value than their expectations, they tend to engage more and participate in activities. This model revealed that involvement and customer participation have a significant impact on customer engagement.

Co-creation is about the extent to which the customer is involved in the production or delivery of the service. Thus, the common interests of both the customer and the business are mutually supported. Engagement is the perceived level of significance in the object based on internal needs, values and interests. Although engagement is a cognitive, emotional or motivational structure that perceives mental state or level of personal interest, it is not seen as a behavior. Engagement creates a larger outbound search, more depth of processing, more refinement, and increases in product trials. An engaged person can develop more positive attitudes towards a product, business or brand to which they are affiliated (Vivek, Beatty ve Morgan, 2012).

Co-creation is seen as a three-dimensional structure as business production, co-production and customer production. In business production, only the services offered by the business to the customer are included, while co-production is the case that both the business personnel and the customer perform the service together (Bendapudi & Leone, 2003 reported from Meuter ve Bitner, 1998). Customer production is the experience of emotional participation, self-service services, experience, self-selection, customer feedback (Payne, Storbacka, & Frow, 2008).

Co-production is divided into two as co-production and co-creation in the formation of basic services and value delivery. Co-production occurs when it is within the parameters defined by the business, and when customers integrate with their resources to produce something. In co-creation, customer involvement goes beyond pre-determined options and occurs spontaneously (Bolton & Saxena-Iyer, 2009). While co-creation starts with the contact of the customer with the business and ends with the final consumption phase; co-production occurs before the consumption phase, that is, during the production phase. Thus, production requires customers to participate in various activities such as design and similar activities that take place in one or more of the production stages (Etgar, 2008). Co-production is therefore a component of co-creation (Terblanche, 2014). According to Grönroos (2008), co-creation occurs when businesses offer the customer the opportunity to interact directly. In this way, businesses become facilitators that provide value creation. Co-production is the active role of the customer in the service delivery process, not only in the consumption phase but also in the production phase. Self-service technologies are a technology that increases customer interaction with businesses, which can be given as an example of co-production (Lin & Hsieh, 2011).

Be a sub-component of co-creation, co-production is divided into four dimensions in literature; information search, information sharing, responsible behavior and personal interaction (Ennew & Binks, 1999) (Yi & Gong, 2013; Ercsey, 2017; Shamim & Ghazali, 2015). Co-creation, on the other hand, is divided into two as participation behavior and citizenship behavior in Yi and Gong's (2013) studies. A total of eight dimensions of these components are then described. Information seeking, information sharing, responsible behavior, personal interaction is under the umbrella of participatory behavior, but feedback, advocacy, helping and tolerance are seen under citizenship behavior. In searching for information, customers try to understand the nature of the service and their role in the delivery process. Information seeking is the exchange of information and behavioral action in order to clarify the service needs of customers and to meet other cognitive needs. For example, customers are looking for information about service status or clarification of service parameters. The information sharing dimension implies that customers provide information to clarify their service expectations and obtain status (Kellogg, Youngdahl, & Bowen, 1997). Knowledge sharing reduces information uncertainty, allowing the client to understand and control the co-creation environments. Information sharing reduces information uncertainty, allowing the customer to understand and control their creative environment. It also enables clients to master their role as co-creators and integrate into the co-creation process (Yi & Gong, 2013). The active involvement of customers includes the necessity to inform employees about their needs they want to satisfy and to specify the features of the services they expect from the business. Responsible behavior occurs when customers accept their duties and responsibilities as partial employees. Because businesses see their customers as part of the service provided during the service process. This includes many elements that characterize the nature of the relationship, which as a requirement include factors such as trust, reliability, support, cooperation, flexibility and commitment. The last dimension, personal interaction, is about the absence of fear or threat in the relationship (Ennew & Binks, 1999).

The sub-dimensions of the citizenship component, the second component of co-creation, are listed below (Yi & Gong, 2013).

- Feedback; are recommendations provided by customers to employees and information that facilitates the improvement of service delivery in the long term.
- Advocacy; customers recommend businesses or employees to their family and friends.
- Help; is the willingness and support of customers to provide information to other customers. In this way, it contributes to the improvement of the service without the need for employees
- Tolerance; refers to customers who are still tolerant when service delivery does not meet the expectations of the individual.

It is important to keep production and value creation separate because there are different structures. Production includes the production of resources integrated by customers in their consumption or usage processes. Value creation is the process of creating value in the use of such resources. Therefore, the value is not produced, resources are produced about what value can be created. Likewise, there is a distinction between co-production and the co-creation of value. Due to the interactive nature of service activities, where production and consumption are partly simultaneous processes, customers are involved in this process by involving themselves in the production (Grönroos & Ravald, 2011).

Co-creation is the process in which products, services and experiences are jointly developed by businesses and their stakeholders, creating a whole new world of value (Ramaswamy, 2009). Especially in self-service types, co-creation and value-creation processes are involved. In the first one, the business and the customer are involved in the process of creating a joint output in order to reveal the product. In the second, the customer must use the technology to benefit from the output (Vargo, 2008). Thus, the common creative role of the customer is expanding with the increase in the education level of the customer, the development of technology, the spread of buy-it-yourself services and the availability of the internet everywhere (McColl-Kennedy et al.., 2009).

Defining Co-Creation

Co-creation, an old concept in the marketing literature (Grönroos, 2008), started to be widely used in 1986 when Kotler used the term "Producing consumer (prosumer) [1]" (Terblanche, 2014). Xie, Bagozzi & Troye (2008) discussed the co-creation process of value in the context of the customer being the producer-consumer.

When we consider today's changing conditions, it is seen that customers become producer-consumers with the including of services in the production process. When we consider today's changing conditions, it is seen that customers are involved in the service production process and become producers and consumers (Dedeoğlu, 2015). Thus, the concept of creating value has developed into "co-creation of value" between businesses and customers in the digital age we are in (Bettencourt, Lusch, & Vargo, 2014). This means that the customer creates value with the businesses in the use of the goods or services and includes not only monetary but also subjective evaluation of customers (Echeverri & Skålén, 2011).

Co-creation is seen as a function of direct or indirect interaction (Grönroos, 2008) and an attempt to build a radically changed relationship between the business and its customers (Zwick, Bonsu, & Darmody, 2008). When customers do not find co-creation valuable, they are less likely to accept it and therefore the benefits to the business are not recognized (Soltani, Jandaghi, & Forou, 2017).

Accordingly, the concept of creating together means creating mutual value and experience. Co-creation value is enhanced by the mutual activity of a consumer and a service provider through the establishment of different resources. In addition, customers do not accept business-generated experiences and want to shape these experiences both individually and with experts or other customers (Prahalad & Ramaswamy, 2000). The value is therefore used for customers' activities and interactions with service providers and other customers. In this context, together, creators emerge as customers who can apply their competencies by providing services for the benefit of other customers and themselves. These customers not only produce together but also work in partnership with businesses and other customers (Ida, 2017).

As can be seen, the concept of co-creation suggests that business activities are no longer limited to the business and that the client should at least rely on the labor force to ensure co-creation (Zwick, Bonsu, & Darmody, 2008). On the other hand, customers' participation in the production processes of the service increases as businesses try to reduce costs through customer engagement (McKee, Simmers, & Licata, 2006).

Contrary to Philip Kotler's old-school marketing view, which depends on Philip Kotler's famous "four Pss" for customer management along with cost advantage, the logic of creating together focuses on providing environments that free customers to produce and share products in a technical, social and cultural context (Zwick, Bonsu, & Darmody, 2008). Accordingly, co-creation is often based on the concepts of "new" or "experience" economics. There are two kinds of experience, passive participation and active participation. By participating in the customer creation process in uncovering the service, the customer plays a key role (Pine & Gilmore, 1998) and the customer exhibits a more active and even innovative behavior in producing the experience (Prebensen & Foss, 2011).

Co-creation refers to the process that results from the customer's use of the good or service rather than the output of the good or service (Payne, Storbacka, & Frow, 2008). Accordingly, co-creation behavior is defined as "a common, collaborative, simultaneous, missional process that generates value both materially and symbolically" (Galvagno & Dalli, 2014, s. 644). High-quality interactions that enable an individual customer to create unique experiences with the business are seen as a way to provide a new competitive advantage. Therefore, interactions that provide value to the parties must be co-created by both the business and the consumer (Prahalad & Ramaswamy, 2004; Kotler et al.., 2009, s.9). In fact, it is seen in the literature that co-creation is multilateral, but generally, two sides are emphasized in terms of business and customer (Bititci, Martinez, Albores, & Parung, 2004).

Co-Creation of Value Together in Air Transport Enterprises Operating in The Service Sector

Services are defined as the application of specific competencies (knowledge and skills) through jobs, processes and performances that benefit another business or the enterprise itself (Vargo & Lusch, 2004). In a service system, there is a "dynamic value creation configuration of resources" including people, organizations, shared knowledge and technologies (Spohrer et al., 2007). Services are viewed as a value creation perspective rather than a classification of market offers (Edvardsson, Gustafsson, & Roos, 2005).

In this context, service science emerges as an examination of the service systems that are formed as a result of the creation of resources (people, technology, businesses and shared information) and value together. Resources are important because they include resources that have certain rights (people and businesses), resources as qualifications (technology and shared information), physical assets (people and technology), and socially generated assets (businesses and shared information) (Maglio & Spohrer, 2008). Value is simply a factor that drives the development of the service system and can be measured by the system's compatibility or its ability to fit within its scope. (Vargo, Maglio, & Akaka, 2008).

During the service delivery of the business, the business should create as many customer contact points as possible while creating value using customer service. Only in this way is the creation of value supported and more opportunities to create value together. Contact points can be service activities such as call center, repair and maintenance support. According to the view of value in use, service providers cannot create value alone in planning, design and production processes. Customers create value when they exist in value creation processes, that is, when they use products when they need them in their daily activities (Grönroos, 2006).

Customer value creation is a customer-driven framework that helps businesses choose the best opportunities for growth by optimizing value creation between businesses and customers (Plaster & Alderman, 2006). This value is defined not in factories, but in the marketplace. Managers use market intelligence to make sense of how everyone in the business defines customer value and how this definition evolves over time. Customer focus and market knowledge are combined to create a functional organizational commitment to delivering superior value (Webster Jr., 1994). To clearly define the importance of creating together, these factors need to be explained on the basis of different perspectives of businesses and customers (Ayunia, 2013). The aim is to provide customer satisfaction and loyalty by adding more value to the basic product while ensuring that the business reaches its goals such as gaining profit (Ravald & Grönroos, 1996).

In the studies of Kuyucak & Şengür (2009), which deals with the stakeholders involved in the process of creating value for the passengers who are the end-users in the air transport industry, air traffic services, including the airport air and landside, catering, security, meteorology, the services provided by other suppliers such as fuel and the services of manufacturing and maintenance businesses, as well as the computerized reservation system where the tickets are purchased and the services provided by the agencies and ground service providers, airline companies are included in this chain. At this point, considering that all these services take place at airports, the importance and complex structure of airports should be understood in the value chain offered to end-users.

Customer value creation processes in air transport businesses are not traditionally like engineering processes. Value emerges as a result of dynamic, interactive, nonlinear and often unconscious processes. The importance of knowing the customer processes is important for the business to better understand where it should deliver the service. For example, a leading international airline company in the world has mapped how the onboard travel experience fits into the aggregate consumption process of premium customers. With the method called as shadowing technique, the friendliest employees of the airline company witnessed the process of the customer preparing to travel with the permission received from the customer. These employees came to the airport with the customers who were flying for business purposes, accompanied their travel, and spent time with them throughout the day, flying back together and dropping the passengers back to their homes. Thus, useful information was obtained and this information was used on subsequent flights (Payne, Storbacka, & Frow, 2008).

Liu, Fellows & Chan (2014), who examined the co-creation of value in an airport construction project, pointed out that customer and contractor (builder) cooperated in the project initiation phase through the value management meetings within the co-creation process as opposed to traditional procurement approaches.

According to Grönroos & Ravald (2011), the most effective example of the co-creation of value at the airport is the planning, development and placement of the automatic check-in system at an airport's terminal, allowing customers to obtain their own boarding pass.

For co-creation, the business provides a resource so that they build the embedded service together with the customers. In addition, it is ensured that value is created together with time saving and stress reduction.

From the point of view of service marketing and management, the process of creating together in the airport experience can take place in different ways, from the advantages that customers get from using technological equipment within the airport (mandatory check-in, security, processing without waiting in line for boarding, etc.), participating in exhibitions in the terminal, sharing airport experiences on social media, commenting and using airport entertainment systems (Wattanacharoensil, Schuckert, & Graham, 2016). In fact, according to Alexander & Jaakkola (2015), co-creation can be achieved by complying with airport security procedures or following instructions rather than coded behaviors in service encounters.

Different environments have been created to ensure co-creation within the terminals of Hongkong International Airport and Bangkok International Airport. Hongkong Airport offers self-service and mobile application services to its passengers. Thus, the experiences of the passengers are improved by establishing the values of "fast service", "time saving", "self-control", "sense of self-efficacy" and "anxiety reduction". For passengers, self-service technologies alleviate frustration and anxiety caused by airport processes. Bangkok Airport, on the other hand, uses social media effectively. It does this by using an icon symbolizing the airport to upload to social networking sites by promoting and photographing unique cultural artifacts representing its destination (Wattanacharoensil, Schuckert, & Graham, 2016).

In 2012, in partnership with Finnair Airlines and Helsinki Airport, a selection was made from among the ideas presented by 260 customers in order to create together with passengers. These ideas spread through social media such as Facebook and Twitter. As a result, "eco-friendly meat-free Monday" and "airport book swap" projects were implemented. First, passengers at Helsinki Airport were given the opportunity to make money by exchanging or selling the books they read. Afterwards, Finnair launched its best-selected vegetarian meal on its long-range flights. With these campaigns, the names of airlines and airport businesses have been announced more. In addition, enterprises have also enabled the campaigns to be successful with the participation of all parties by including their employees in the co-creation process (Jarvenpaa & Tuunainen, 2013).

In their study analyzing the relationships between co-production, co-creation of value and customer loyalty of the airline online check-in system, Chen and Wang (2016) have split the value of co-creation into three in the form of entertainment, economic and relationship value. Co-creation positively affects customer satisfaction by ensuring the joint production of the customers in three states of co-creation value. Furthermore, they determined that the value that positively affects customer satisfaction most during the self-service procurement is entertainment value.

For another example, in the Schiphol Airport 2018 annual report, managers stated that they conduct joint activities with airline businesses, travelers, residents, industry partners (air traffic, customs, etc.), government, financial stakeholders (banks, investors, partners), business partners (security company, tenants, contractors, etc.), employees, internet providers and information institutions in order to create the value together. They emphasized that with this cooperation, they have succeeded as operators in maintaining sustainability and security, having an expanding network structure, increasing the quality by improving customer experiences, and making restaurants, shopping and similar areas in line with customer expectations (Royal Schiphol Group, 2018, s. 22-23).

FUTURE RESEARCH DIRECTIONS

Value co-creation behavior is crucial in any industry where the customer exists. Thus, loyal customers can be created and business sustainability can be ensured. For this purpose, a conceptual study is presented for a comprehensive understanding of the concept of co-creation of value. In the study, sample applications for co-creation of value in the air transport sector are given. A detailed examination of the results of these applications in future studies may expand the contribution made to the theory. On the other hand, considering the current Covid-19 pandemic conditions, it can be discussed how the effort to create value together in the air transport sector is.

CONCLUSION

Co-creation of value is an approach inherently dominated by the notion of "make the product, then the customers will come" rather than "build with the customers and they are already there". Therefore, it is fair to say that co-creation is more of a win-more-win more approach as opposed to win-win cooperation (Ramaswamy & Gouillart, 2010).

The co-creation of value requires a paradigm shift, especially in the areas seen below (Ramaswamy, 2009):

- Beyond interactions in the system, as the focal point of value creation opportunities (WHERE).
- Beyond the competency base of the business and its suppliers, the place of value creation competence for individuals' networks and communities (customers and all other stakeholders inside and outside the business) (WHO).
- The basis for creating value for all concerned individuals in people's experience environments, beyond products and services (WHY).
- Assets and activities for participation platforms as a means of creating value (HOW).

Customer satisfaction is becoming an increasingly difficult phenomenon to achieve despite the intense efforts and high monetary expenditures of enterprises. Consumers are becoming increasingly conscious, proactive, strengthened, connected and complex. Confident customers collaborate with the organization with the desire to co-create. This happens only by ensuring that the client feels good or comfortable in the service role, as well as being motivated for creation, depending on the perceived ability level (McKee, Simmers, & Licata, 2006).

Co-creation in air transport is not only about creating things but also about interpreting and creating meaning (Ind & Coates, 2013). In this way, while operators take less risk, it is possible to design goods or services suitable for individuals. In the end, customer satisfaction increases with improved customer experience, while air transport businesses gain a competitive advantage (Delpechitre, Beeler-Connelly, & Chaker, 2018).

In this context, as in all other businesses, in order to create the behavior of co-create value in air transport operations, such as airlines and airports, it is necessary to first examine the demands, needs and expectations of the customers and act in accordance with the different perception of the value of each customer. Accordingly, it is more likely that value creation will be achieved with the encouragement of customers.

REFERENCES

Alexander, M., & Jaakkola, E. (2015). *Customer engagement behaviours and value co-creation*. Taylor & Francis Group.

AMA. (2013). *Definition of Marketing*. American Marketing Association. https://www.ama.org/AboutAMA/Pages/Definition-of-Marketing.aspx

Ayunia, S. (2013). *Measuring the unmeasured: An exploratory study of customer co-creation* (MSc Thesis). Delft University of Technology: Faculty of Technology, Policy, and Management.

Babin, B. J., & James, K. W. (2010). A brief retrospective and introspective on value. *European Business Review*, 22(5), 471–478. doi:10.1108/09555341011068895

Ballantyne, D., & Varey, R. J. (2006). Creating value-in-use through marketing interaction: The exchange logic of relating, communicating and knowing. *Marketing Theory*, 6(3), 335–348. doi:10.1177/1470593106066795

Bettencourt, L. A., Lusch, R. F., & Vargo, S. L. (2014). A service lens on value creation: Marketing's role in achieving strategic advantage. *California Management Review*, 57(1), 44–66. doi:10.1525/cmr.2014.57.1.44

Binkhorst, E., & Dekker, T. D. (2009). Agenda for co-creation tourism experience research. *Journal of Hospitality Marketing & Management*, 18(2-3), 311–327. doi:10.1080/19368620802594193

Bititci, U. S., Martinez, V., Albores, P., & Parung, J. (2004). Creating and managing value in collaborative networks. *International Journal of Physical Distribution & Logistics Management*, 34(3/4), 251–268. doi:10.1108/09600030410533574

Boeing. (2013). *Current Market Outlook 2013-2032*. Boeing Commercial: https://www.boeing.com/boeing/commercial/cmo/

Bolton, R., & Saxena-Iyer, S. (2009). Interactive services: A framework, synthesis and research directions. *Journal of Interactive Marketing, 23*(1), 91–104. doi:10.1016/j.intmar.2008.11.002

Bowden, J. H. (2009). The process of customer engagement: A conceptual framework. *Journal of Marketing Theory and Practice, 17*(1), 63–74. doi:10.2753/MTP1069-6679170105

Brodie, R. J., Hollebeek, L. D., Juric, B., & Ilic, A. (2011). Customer engagement: Conceptual domain, fundamental propositions, and implications for research. *Journal of Service Research, 14*(3), 252–271. doi:10.1177/1094670511411703

Chen, J. K., Batchuluun, A., & Batnasan, J. (2015). Services innovation impact to customer satisfaction and customer value enhancement in airport. *Technology in Society, 43*, 219–230. doi:10.1016/j.techsoc.2015.05.010

Dedeoğlu, A. Ö. (2015). Değişen pazaryerinde tüketici ve tüketimin rolüne ilişkin yeni yaklaşımlar: Ortak-üretim (co-production) ve ortak-yaratma (co-creation). *Ege Strategic Research Journal, 6*(2), 17–29.

Delpechitre, D., Beeler-Connelly, L. L., & Chaker, N. N. (2018). Customer value co-creation behavior: A dyadic exploration of the influence of salesperson emotional intelligence on customer participation and citizenship behavior. *Journal of Business Research, 92*, 9–24. doi:10.1016/j.jbusres.2018.05.007

Echeverri, P., & Skålén, P. (2011). Co-creation and co-destruction: A practice-theory based study of interactive value formation. *Marketing Theory, 11*(3), 351–373. doi:10.1177/1470593111408181

Edvardsson, B., Gustafsson, A., & Roos, I. (2005). Service portraits in service research: A critical review. *International Journal of Service Industry Management, 16*(1), 107–121. doi:10.1108/09564230510587177

Ennew, C. T., & Binks, M. R. (1999). Impact of participative service relationships on quality, satisfaction and retention: An exploratory study. *Journal of Business Research, 46*(2), 121–132. doi:10.1016/S0148-2963(98)00016-2

Etgar, M. (2008). A descriptive model of the consumer co-production process. *Journal of the Academy of Marketing Science, 36*(1), 97–108. doi:10.100711747-007-0061-1

Fernandes, T., & Remelhe, P. (2016). How to engage customers in co-creation: Customers' motivations for collaborative innovation. *Journal of Strategic Marketing, 24*(3-4), 311–326. doi:10.1080/0965254X.2015.1095220

Flint, D. J., Woodruff, R. B., & Gardial, S. F. (1997). Customer value change in industrial marketing relationships: A call for new strategies and research. *Industrial Marketing Management, 26*(2), 163–175. doi:10.1016/S0019-8501(96)00112-5

Galvagno, M., & Dalli, D. (2014). Theory of value co-creation: A systematic literature review. *Managing Service Quality, 24*(6), 643–683. doi:10.1108/MSQ-09-2013-0187

Gardner, D. (2019). *How Customer Participation Builds Trust in the Age of GDPR*. Marketing Profs: https://www.marketingprofs.com/articles/2019/40499/how-customer-participation-builds-trust-in-the-age-of-gdpr

Grissemann, U. S., & Stokburger-Sauer, N. E. (2012). Customer co-creation of travel services: The role of company support and customer satisfaction with the co-creation performance. *Tourism Management, 33*(6), 1483–1492. doi:10.1016/j.tourman.2012.02.002

Grönroos, C. (2006). Adopting a service logic for marketing. *Marketing Theory, 6*(3), 317–333. doi:10.1177/1470593106066794

Grönroos, C. (2008). Service logic revisited: Who creates value? And who co-creates? *European Business Review, 20*(4), 298–314. doi:10.1108/09555340810886585

Grönroos, C., & Ravald, A. (2011). Service as business logic: Implications for value creation and marketing. *Journal of Service Management, 22*(1), 5–22. doi:10.1108/09564231111106893

Gummesson, E. (2008). Extending the service-dominant logic: From customer centricity to balanced centricity. *Journal of the Academy of Marketing Science, 36*(1), 15–17. doi:10.100711747-007-0065-x

Holbrook, M. B. (1999). *Introduction to consumer value. In Consumer Value: A framework for analysis and research*. Routledge.

Holbrook, M. B. (2006). Consumption experience, customer value, and subjective personal introspection: An illustrative photographic essay. *Journal of Business Research, 59*(6), 714–725. doi:10.1016/j.jbusres.2006.01.008

Ida, E. (2017). The role of customers' involvement in value co-creation behaviour is value co-creation the source of competitive advantage? *Journal of Competitiveness, 9*(3), 51–66. doi:10.7441/joc.2017.03.04

Ind, N., & Coates, N. (2013). The meanings of co-creation. *European Business Review, 25*(1), 86–95. doi:10.1108/09555341311287754

Jarvenpaa, S. L., & Tuunainen, V. K. (2013). How Finnair socialized customers for service co-creation with social media. *MIS Quarterly Executive, 12*(3), 125–136.

Kahle, L. R. (1983). *Social Values and Social Change: Adaptation to Life in America*. Praeger.

Karababa, E., & Kjeldgaard, D. (2014). Value in marketing: Toward sociocultural perspectives. *Marketing Theory, 14*(1), 119–127. doi:10.1177/1470593113500385

Kellogg, D. L., Youngdahl, W. E., & Bowen, D. E. (1997). On the relationship between customer participation and satisfaction: Two frameworks. *International Journal of Service Industry Management, 8*(3), 206–219. doi:10.1108/09564239710185406

Kotler, P. (1972). A generic concept of marketing. *Journal of Marketing, 36*(2), 46–54. doi:10.1177/002224297203600209

Kotler, P., & Armstrong, G. (2016). *Principles of Marketing*. Pearson Education Limited.

Kotler, P., & Keller, K. L. (2006). *Marketing Management*. Pearson Prentice Hall.

Kuyucak, F., & Şengür, Y. (2009). Değer zinciri analizi: Havayolu işletmeleri için genel bir çerçeve. *KMU İİBF Dergisi*, (11), 132–147.

Lin, J.-S. C., & Hsieh, P.-L. (2011). Assessing the self-service technology encounters: Development and validation of SSTQUAL scale. *Journal of Retailing, 87*(2), 194–206. doi:10.1016/j.jretai.2011.02.006

Liu, A. M., Fellows, R., & Chan, I. (2014). Fostering value co-creation in construction: A case study of an airport project in India. *International Journal of Architecture, Engineering and Construction, 3*(2), 120–130.

Maglio, P. P., & Spohrer, J. (2008). Fundamentals of service science. *Journal of the Academy of Marketing Science, 36*(1), 18–20. doi:10.100711747-007-0058-9

Martínez-Cañas, R., Ruiz-Palomino, P., Linuesa-Langreo, J., & Blázquez-Resino, J. (2016). Consumer participation in co-creation: An enlightening model of causes and effects based on ethical values and transcendent motives. *Frontiers in Psychology, 7*(793). Advance online publication. doi:10.3389/fpsyg.2016.00793 PMID:27303349

Martinez-Hernandez, V. (2003). *Understanding Value Creation: The Value Matrix And The Value Cube* (Doctoral Thesis). University of Strathclyde.

Matthing, J., Sanden, B., & Edvardsson, B. (2004). New service development: Learning from and with customers. *International Journal of Service Industry Management, 15*(5), 479–498. doi:10.1108/09564230410564948

McKee, D., Simmers, C. S., & Licata, J. (2006). Customer self-efficacy and response to service. *Journal of Service Research, 8*(3), 207–220. doi:10.1177/1094670505282167

Mitchell, A. (1983). *The Nine American Lifestyles: Who We Are & Where We Are Going.* Warner.

Oliver, R. L. (2010). *Satisfaction: A Behavioral Perspective on the Consumer.* Routledge.

Payne, A., & Holt, S. (2001). Diagnosing customer value: Integrating the value process and relationship marketing. *British Journal of Management, 12*(2), 159–182. doi:10.1111/1467-8551.00192

Payne, A., Storbacka, K., & Frow, P. (2008). Managing the co-creation of value. *Journal of the Academy of Marketing Science, 36*(1), 83–96. doi:10.100711747-007-0070-0

Perkins, B., & Fenech, C. (2014). *The deloitte consumer review: The growing power consumers.* Deloitte.

Pine, J., & Gilmore, J. (1998). Welcome to the experience economy. *Harvard Business Review*, 97–105. PMID:10181589

Plaster, G., & Alderman, J. (2006). Customer value creation: A platform for profitable growth. *Charter Consulting*, 1-7.

Pongsakornrungsilp, S., & Schroeder, J. E. (2011). Understanding value co-creation in a co-consuming brand community. *Marketing Theory, 11*(3), 303–324. doi:10.1177/1470593111408178

Prahalad, C. K., & Ramaswamy, V. (2000). Co-opting customer competence. *Harvard Business Review, 78*(1), 79–87.

Prahalad, C. K., & Ramaswamy, V. (2004). Co-creation experiences: The next practice in value creation. *Journal of Interactive Marketing, 18*(3), 5–14. doi:10.1002/dir.20015

Prebensen, N. K., & Foss, L. (2011). Coping and co-creating in tourist experiences. *International Journal of Tourism Research, 13*(1), 54–67. doi:10.1002/jtr.799

Ramaswamy, V. (2009). Co-Creation of value – Towards an expanded paradigm of value creation. *Marketing Review St. Gallen, 26*(6), 11–17. doi:10.100711621-009-0085-7

Ramaswamy, V., & Gouillart, F. (2010). *Building the co-creative enterprise.* Harvard Business Review. https://www.researchgate.net/publication/47369356_Building_the_Co-Creative_Enterprise

Ravald, A., & Grönroos, C. (1996). The value concept and relationship marketing. *European Journal of Marketing, 30*(2), 19–30. doi:10.1108/03090569610106626

Reynolds, T. J. (1985). Implications for value research: A macro vs. micro perspective. *Psychology and Marketing, 2*(4), 297–305. doi:10.1002/mar.4220020408

Royal Schiphol Group. (2018). Value Creation Model. Annual Report 2018. Author.

Saarijärvi, H., Kannan, P. K., & Kuusela, H. (2013). Value co-creation: Theoretical approaches and practical implications. *European Business Review, 25*(1), 6–19. doi:10.1108/09555341311287718

Sánchez-Fernández, R., & Iniesta-Bonillo, M. (2007). The concept of perceived value: A systematic review of the research. *Marketing Theory Articles, 7*(4), 427–451. doi:10.1177/1470593107083165

Sharma, S., & Conduit, J. (2016). Cocreation culture in health care organizations. *Journal of Service Research, 19*(4), 438–457. doi:10.1177/1094670516666369

Soltani, M., Jandaghi, G., & Forou, P. (2017). Co-creation intention; presenting a model of antecedents and its impact on attitude toward the product (Case study in shatel company). *Iranian Journal of Management Studies, 10*(1), 143–174.

Terblanche, N. S. (2014). Some theoretical perspectives of co-creation and co-production of value by customers. *Acta Commercii, 14*(2), 1–8. doi:10.4102/ac.v14i2.237

Vargo, S. L. (2008). Customer Integration and Value Creation. *Journal of Service Research, 11*(2), 211–215. doi:10.1177/1094670508324260

Vargo, S. L., & Lusch, R. F. (2004). Evolving to a new dominant logic for marketing. *Journal of Marketing, 68*(1), 1–17. doi:10.1509/jmkg.68.1.1.24036

Vargo, S. L., Maglio, P. P., & Akaka, M. A. (2008). On value and value co-creation: A service systems and service logic perspective. *European Management Journal, 26*(3), 145–152. doi:10.1016/j.emj.2008.04.003

Vega-Vazquez, M., Revilla-Camacho, M. A., & Cossio-Silva, F. J. (2013). The value co-creation process as a determinant of customer satisfaction. *Management Decision, 51*(10), 1945–1953. doi:10.1108/MD-04-2013-0227

Vivek, S. D., Beatty, S. E., & Morgan, R. M. (2012). Customer engagement: Exploring customer relationships beyond purchase. *Journal of Marketing Theory and Practice, 20*(2), 127–145. doi:10.2753/MTP1069-6679200201

Wattanacharoensil, W., Schuckert, M., & Graham, A. (2016). An airport experience framework from a tourism perspective. *Transport Reviews*, *36*(3), 318–340. doi:10.1080/01441647.2015.1077287

Webster, F. E. Jr. (1994). Executing the new marketing concept. *Marketing Management*, *3*(1), 8–16.

Williams, R. M. (1974). The Nature of Human Values. by Milton Rokeach. *The Academy of Political Science*, *89*(2), 399–401.

Woodruff, R. B. (1997). Customer value: The next source for competitive advantage. *Journal of the Academy of Marketing Science*, *25*(2), 139–153. doi:10.1007/BF02894350

Xie, C., Bagozzi, R. P., & Troye, S. V. (2008). Trying to prosume: Toward a theory of consumers as co-creators of value. *Journal of the Academy of Marketing Science*, *36*(1), 109–122. doi:10.100711747-007-0060-2

Yi, Y., & Gong, T. (2013). Customer value co-creation behavior: Scale development and validation. *Journal of Business Research*, *66*(9), 1279–1284. doi:10.1016/j.jbusres.2012.02.026

Zeithaml, V. A. (1988). Consumer Perceptions of Price, Quality, and Value: A Means-End Model and Synthesis of Evidence. *Journal of Marketing*, *52*(3), 2–22. doi:10.1177/002224298805200302

Zhang, T., Lu, C., & Chen, P.-J. (2018). Engaging customers in value co-creation or co-destruction online. *Journal of Services Marketing*, *32*(1), 57–69. doi:10.1108/JSM-01-2017-0027

Zwick, D., Bonsu, S. K., & Darmody, A. (2008). Putting consumers to work: 'Co-creation' and new marketing govern-mentality. *Journal of Consumer Culture*, *8*(2), 163–196. doi:10.1177/1469540508090089

KEY TERMS AND DEFINITIONS

Co-Creation: It is any interaction between the customer and the business that will provide co-creation in the process of providing the service.

Co-Production: The product to be offered is produced together by the customer and the business within the scope of the production stage and the criteria determined by the business.

Customer Engagement: All actions, other than interactions and/or interactions with buyers, by including buyers in all processes in order to improve the business's goods or service processes.

Customer Participation: It is the extent to which the business and customers participate in the processes from the production stage of the goods or services to the after-sales services.

Customer Satisfaction: Customers meet their expectations by purchasing the product.

Value: It is the way an individual perceives his/her environment. The value obtained from the product, on the other hand, creates the gains of the customers by obtaining that product.

Value Co-Creation: In order to provide the benefit that customers expect by purchasing the product, they should act together with the businesses first.

ENDNOTE

[1] The concept of producing-consumer is a process rather than a single action (such as purchasing) and consists of the integration of physical activities, mental effort and socio-psychological experiences. People are involved in this process by providing inputs of money, time, labor and skills.

Section 3
Consumer Behaviour, Brand, and Digital Marketing

Chapter 9

Customer Brand Identification and Its Influence on Customer Loyalty in the Hotel Industry

Catarina Isabel Andrade Basílio
Estoril Higher Institute for Tourism and Hotel Studies, Portugal

Nuno Silva Gustavo
Estoril Higher Institute for Tourism and Hotel Studies, Portugal

ABSTRACT

Customer brand identification is described by the customer's perception and feeling about a brand. It brings value and meets the customer's needs. The four drivers of CBI are brand self-similarity, brand social benefits, brand identity, and memorable brand experiences. The purpose of this study is to understand the influence of CBI (and, consequently, its drivers) on customer loyalty and its perception of hotel brands. Although the importance of CBI has already been recognized in some studies, its effects on customer loyalty in the hospitality context are still relatively unexplored. A survey was used to understand and confirm that CBI and all four of its dimensions significantly influence customer loyalty. This means, in the hotel industry, customers tend to look for brands that are distinct from their competitors, have an identity of their own, and close to their values. It was also possible to conclude that the client tends to behave more favorably towards the brand, spreading positive word of mouth and recommending brands that meet CBI conditions.

INTRODUCTION

The hotel activity has an exceptionally competitive nature, either due to the growing level of an offer or the ease of reproducing its models, concepts and associated services (Mattila, 2006). This environment led to the need to look for new sources of differentiation and competitive advantages. The brand has become one of the main focuses globally for this purpose (Kayaman & Arasli, 2007; O'Neil & Mattila, 2010).

DOI: 10.4018/978-1-7998-8306-7.ch009

A strong brand represents an essential asset in this market context, with consequences regarding financial results. Other indicators, such as average price, occupancy rate, revenue and return on investment (ROI), also tend to have higher values. The brand also appears as a means of quality assurance and simplifies evaluating alternatives for the customer (O'Neill & Xiao, 2006).

Although the Customer Brand Identification (CBI) is an essential tool in defining a brand, it is still not mainly used in hotels (Leaniz & Rodriguez-de-Bolque, 2013). Consumers no longer buy branded services and products just for the sake of status and/or social status. The brand value, in some way, should contribute positively to their lives and relate to their concept of lifestyle (Sirgy & Su, 2000). This identification with the brand makes the customer use the product or service more and increases purchase frequency (Kuenzel & Halliday, 2010).

The main objective of this study is to understand the relationship between Customer Brand Identification and customer loyalty, starting by individually evaluating the behavior of the four dimensions of CBI.

Initially, a theoretical contextualization of each concept was carried out, which allowed the formulation of the hypotheses to be studied. Then, the methods used in the investigation, the structure of the survey, and procedures for evaluating the results were explained. Finally, the results were exposed and analyzed, and the conclusions presented.

LITERATURE REVIEW

Concept and Dimensions of Customer Brand Identification

Customer Brand Identification is understood by the customer's perception and feelings about a brand and how it brings value and encourages belonging (Lam S., Ahearne, Mullins, & Schillewaert, 2013). The CBI consists of four dimensions that can be organized into practical or cognitive dimensions. The dimensions of cognitive factors are brand self-similarity (Brand Self-Similarity - BSS) and brand identity (Brand Identity - BI). On the other hand, the Brand Social Benefits (BSB - brand social benefits) and Memorable Brand Experiences (MBE - consumer experiences) dimensions are mostly related to affective factors (Lam S. et al., 2013).

There are different focuses in the literature regarding this topic. Stokburger-Sauer, Ratneshwar, & Sen (2012) define CBI as the "union" of the customer with the brand, while, for example, Lam S., Ahearne, Hu, & Schillewaert (2010) focus on the definition of CBI from a perspective mainly psychological, that is, centered on feelings and their valuation of belonging. Others cover a more cognitive rather than affective perspective, arguing that the emotional factors of the relationship between a consumer and a brand should be analyzed separately from the consumer's identification with the brand (Bergami & Bagozzi, 2010; Stokburger-Sauer et al., 2012).

Creating a long-term relationship with customers begins by practicing marketing techniques that attract, develop, maintain, and improve the customer's relationship with the company (Kotler, Kartajaya, & Setiawan, 2017). In addition, companies must manage information about consumers to adopt more accurate practices and build a more robust commercial relationship. (Nastasoiu & Vandenbosch, 2018).

Satisfaction is understood as the feeling of pleasure or disappointment resulting from comparing the expectation of a product or service and its actual performance (Tsiros, Vikas, & Ross, 2004). According to several studies, quality is one of the priorities in the evaluation of service (El-Adly, 2019). This is defined by the ability of the characteristics and specifications of a product or service to satisfy customer needs, whether established or implied by the brand (Kotler, Kartajaya, & Setiawan, 2017).

Good CBI management can influence and increase customer satisfaction and, consequently, customer loyalty (He, Harris, & Li, 2005; Nam, Ekinci, & Whyatt, 2011; So, King, Sparks, & Wang, 2013), and amplifies the possibility of repurchasing the product (Ahearne, Bhattacharya, & Gruen, 2005).

Consumers do not buy brands just because of the way they work, but because the brand's value somehow contributes positively to their lives, and they express some personal concept (Sirgy, 1982). Although the CBI is an essential tool in defining a brand, this tool is still not widely used in hotels (Martínez & Rodríguez del Bosque, 2013).

Hypothesis I: There is a positive relationship between Customer Brand Identification and customer loyalty.

Since the CBI is composed of four dimensions with very different indicators, the analysis of this hypothesis is subordinated to the results obtained in hypotheses II, III, IV, and V.

Brand Self-Similarity

The identity of each person is formed by a set of beliefs and evaluations of each one regarding who and what they are (gender, age, ethnicity), abilities (mental and physical), values, history, roles, and social relationships (Elliot & Wattanasuwan, 1998).

Through its characteristics and the way, they relate to the customer, each brand also creates a personality (Kuenzel & Halliday, 2010). The meaning of each brand is developed through its image, which sustains and characterizes it in the minds of consumers (Keller, 2001)

For Keller (2001), the brand's meaning is constituted by brand performance and brand image. Performance encompasses the product or service itself as the primary influence on the customer experience, the WOM and what the company communicates about the product. The image is composed of extrinsic properties of the product or service. These two categories (performance and image) can reflect the brand's meaning directly from the consumer's experience or another type of contact, direct or indirect, such as advertising or WOM.

The personal definition of each one, according to Belch and Landon (1977), Dolich (1969), Sirgy (1982) and Hosany, Martin (2012), can be divided into four dimensions: Self-concept ("Me as I am"), Ideal Self-concept ("The Good Me"), Social Self-Concept and Ideal Social Self-Concept.

The Self-concept reflects the way each person is characterized. The Ideal Self-Concept is the way each person would want to be characterized. Social Self-Concept is represented by how consumers think others see them, and Ideal Social Self-Concept corresponds to how they would like to be seen (Belch, 1978; Landon, 1972; Dolich, 1969; Sirgy MJ, 1982; Hosany & Martin, 2012).

There is congruence in the personal image of the consumer when his/her self-concept corresponds to the image or personality of the product/service/brand (Aaker, 1999; Sirgy M.J., 1982; Sirgy & Su, 2000; Japutra, Ekinci, & Simkin, 2019). According to the theory of brand self-similarity, consumers will look for branded products or services that express their identity or their desired identity (Aaker, 1999; Ekinci, Sirakaya-Turk, & Preciado, 2013). In other words, people look for consistent situations and avoid situations that threaten their vision (Escalas & Bettman, 2003). According to Malär, Krohmer, Hoyer and Nyffenegger (2011), the greater the correspondence between real self-concept, ideal self-concept and brand image, the greater their emotional connection with the customer and their loyalty to the brand. For this reason, the following hypothesis is proposed:

Hypothesis II: The more the personality, meaning and self-concept of a hotel brand resemble the consumer, the greater its level of loyalty.

Brand Identity

Brand identity is a widely studied topic. It is defined in different ways by various authors, but, in essence, it encompasses all the characteristics that report the way of "being", "thinking" and the "behavior" of a brand (Buil, Catalán, & Martínez, 2016). According to the same authors, the brand identity directs the company towards its vision and objectives and essential towards the customer's perception.

Identity develops through several dimensions: culture, vision, personality, positioning, presentation/design, relationships, values, beliefs and other meanings represented by it (Mindrut, Manolica & Roman, 2015).

The brand personality passes to the customer through the logo, appearance, marketing, messages, actions, products, packaging, emotions, among others (Mindrut et al., 2015).

Brand awareness and brand equity are strongly linked to brand identity. When identity is adequate and there is high brand awareness, it automatically becomes associated with the satisfaction of specific needs and gains meaning. It also supports brand categorization and increases the possibility of finding it in a consumer's range of choice of products (Keller, 2001).

For situations where the consumer is not entirely dedicated to purchasing a product or service, the brand identity plays a crucial role, as the choices end up being seriously influenced by the distinction of the brand concerning the others (Keller, 2001). This situation happens when the consumer is not motivated to purchase (they are indifferent to any product or service) or when they do not have sufficient knowledge or experience with any brand in the category in question.

For So, King and Meng (2017), the essential characteristics for a brand's identity are prestige and distinction. A brand becomes more attractive the more significant its prestige and distinction in the market from other brands (He, Harris, & Li, 2005; Stokburger-Sauer, Ratneshwar, & Sen, 2012).

To be able to distinguish themselves, all the elements that make up a brand must be carefully selected with their specific importance to make it unique and original (Stokburger-Sauer et al., 2012). In addition, each one should have a role and reflection from the consumer's perspective and its marketing image. Through this management, emotional connections are eventually created with the consumer, increasing the probability of loyalty (Mindrut et al., 2015).

Prestige projects a specific organization positively and arises from the word of mouth (WOM) of people who have their opinion valued by others, that is, who are respected, admired, or popular (Bergami & Bagozzi, 2010). It is also defined by the know-how, specific attributes, and overall quality of the brand.

Prestige makes the customer feel that a particular brand appears to have a higher status than the others and may also reflect on their self-confidence when identifying with the brand (Ahearne, Bhattacharya & Gruen, 2005).

Hypothesis III: The more consumers identify the hotel brand as unique, prestigious and with high brand equity and awareness, the greater the level of customer loyalty.

Memorable Brand Experiences

Brands that can provide good experiences and transmit sentimental values to customers have greater chances of developing CBI, and finally, have better conditions for customer loyalty (Chaudhuri & Holbrook, 2001). Memorable Brand Experiences (MBE) involve perceptions of sensations, how the brand affects an individual and their participation in experiences (Schmitt, 2012).

Some brands manage to affect the customer effectively and personally, even if they are products or services that are not used regularly (Stokburger-Sauer, Ratneshwar & Sen, 2012). For Brakus, Schmitt, and Zarantonello (2009), the experience with a brand comprises the following four dimensions: sensory, affective, intellectual, and behavioral, the first being more important in services than in products.

The sensory dimension covers all the senses (touch, smell, sight, taste and hearing) that can be, in a way, provided by the brand (Hulten, 2011). They are essential elements to capture consumer interest (Brakus, Schmitt, & Zarantonello, 2009). They can come from sounds (such as music), smells (such as their perfumes), colors, shapes, designs, flavors, among others (Schmitt, 2012; Brakus, Schmitt, & Zarantonello, 2009). The multiple reproductions of these senses (for example, the use of the five senses simultaneously) is highlighted in the formation of brand equity and the improvement of the consumer experience by several authors (Hultén, Broweus, & Dijk, 2009; Hulten, 2011; Moreira, Fortes, & Santiago, 2017).

The emotions and feelings that brands reflect on customers make up the affective dimension and create an emotional relationship between the customer and the brand (Brakus, Schmitt, & Zarantonello, 2009). On the other hand, the intellectual dimension is in the analytical thinking or imagination about the brand, which draws the customer's attention. It translates into the curiosity projection of the brand's ability to solve problems and satisfy needs (Brakus, Schmitt, & Zarantonello, 2009).

Finally, the behavioral dimension is related to consumer attitudes and actions caused by the brand, involvement and related physical experiences (Brakus, Schmitt, & Zarantonello, 2009).

Thus, the following hypothesis is formulated:

Hypothesis IV: When a hotel brand provides memorable experiences that satisfy consumer needs, its loyalty level increases.

Brand Social Benefits

According to Stokburger-Sauer et al. (2012), Brand Social Benefits can be defined as an opportunity that a brand provides to foster positive social interactions, which eventually accentuate the CBI.

Any brand is associated with social and cultural characteristics originating from social groups that identify with each other and share the same commitment to a brand (Thompson, Rindfleisch, & Arsel, 2006). These characteristics develop a sense of belonging, whether in demographic, educational or occupational terms.

Brands serve as a form of expression of the desired personal identity and develop the customer's reputation through their community of members or direct interactions and relationships between themselves and consumers (Veloutsou, 2009).

This theory is motivated by the need for brands to have positive results resulting from interactions that satisfy consumers' social needs. In this way, brands help develop consumer self-esteem, help define their personality, and provide a place for everyone in society (Ellemers & Haslam, 2012; Popp & Woratschek, 2017).

Hypothesis V: The more community status and opportunities and social categorization a hotel brand provides, the greater the level of customer loyalty.

METHODS

For this study, it is essential to understand what the relationship between the CBI and customer loyalty is (a dimension that will be called in data analysis as CL), namely by reference to the four dimensions that compose it (BSS, BI, MBE and BSB), as well as emphasize some of the associated benefits.

The study of the CL dimension aims not only to ascertain the level of customer loyalty concerning the hotel brand but also to assess their perception, willingness to recommend and defend the brand against the CBI scenario.

First, based on the review of scientific production, indicators were determined for the different dimensions to be studied, as shown in Table 1.

Table 1. Dimensions and indicators for research

Dimensions	Indicators
H1: Brand Self-Similarity (BSS)	Brand Values; Meaning; Self-concept
H2: Brand Identity (BI)	Prestige, Attractiveness, Quality, Value
H3: Memorable Brand Experiences (MBE)	Satisfaction, Expectations, Stimuli
H4: Brand Social Benefits (BSB)	Social Relations, Sense of Belonging, Community and Social Identity
H5: Customer Brand Identification (CBI)	BSS, BI, MBE, BSB
CUSTOMER LOYALTY (CL)	Loyalty, Brand Defense, Recommendation

Using the snowball method, an online survey was launched from 19 to 30 July 2019, with the participation of 247 respondents. This distribution method is the most common way of collecting samples in qualitative studies and was only presented in Portuguese. This method also makes it possible to obtain a wide range of responses and cover a diverse population (Noy, 2007).

This survey consisted of 40 closed-ended questions, primarily referring to the respondent's degree of agreement with certain statements. A Likert scale from 1 to 5 was used, as it is the most common method for assessing the level of agreement. The extremes were "I completely disagree" and "I agree", and the intermediates "I disagree", "Indifferent" and "I agree".

For this survey, Google Forms was used, as it is a simple tool, but it allows the elaboration of several types of questions and the agglomeration of data that were later analyzed in SPSS.

In the first section, and because the objective is for the customer to focus on a single brand when answering the entire questionnaire, he is asked to name a brand where, preferably, he has already spent a stay. The chosen brand will not be relevant data for the investigation; it only provides consistency in the answers.

The survey was divided into six other sections. The first four refer to the dimensions of CBI, followed by a section dedicated to the assessment of customer perception and loyalty to the brand. For each indicator identified in Table 1, questions were appropriate based on their meanings interpreted in the literature review and other studies carried out so far.

In the end, some demographic data were also questioned, namely, gender, age, educational qualifications, occupation, marital status, income, and size of the household.

As for data analysis, first, a description of the variables under study was performed using frequency tables. Subsequently, Cronbach's alpha coefficients were calculated for the CL and CBI scales' dimensions to measure the reliability of the data. Next, to study the hypotheses, multiple linear regression models were created. These models measure the functional relationship between a dependent variable and at least one independent or explanatory variable. Finally, a decision tree was created that allowed the creation of user segments based on demographic variables and CBI dimensions.

RESULTS

Demographic Analysis

In Table 2, it is possible to observe the collected sociodemographic data considered most relevant to this investigation. Almost 70% of respondents are between the ages of 18 and 49, and another 25.9% are between 50 and 65. The vast majority are residents in the Autonomous Region of Madeira (81.4%). About 65.6% have at least a degree, and almost 30% have completed secondary or vocational education. As for their professional status, it is possible to verify that 68% of respondents are employed, and another 9% are student-workers, which means that 77.3% of respondents have a profession.

Table 2. Sociodemographic data

Variable	Option	n (%)
Gender	Male	89 (36%)
	Female	158 (64%)
Age	Under 18 years old	5 (2%)
	Between 18 and 29 years old	79 (32%)
	Between 30 and 49 years old	93 (37.7%)
	Between 50 and 65 years old	64 (25.9%)
	Greather than 65 years old	6 (2.4%)
Residence	Portugal	35 (14.2%)
	Região Autónoma da Madeira	201 (81.4%)
	Região Autónoma dos Açores	2 (0.8%)
	Foreign	9 (3.6%)
Education	Basic school	14 (5.7%)
	High school	71 (28.7%)
	Superior degree	124 (50.2%)
	Masters	27 (10.9%)
	Doctoral	11 (4.5%)
Occupation	Student	30 (12.1%)
	Working-student	23 (9.3%)
	Employed	168 (68%)
	Unemployed	9 (3.6%)
	Retired	17 (6.9%)

First, the correlation coefficients (since they allow establishing the degree of linear association between two numerical variables) of the indicators of each dimension about CL (Customer Loyalty) were analyzed. All indicators were shown to have a positive and significant correlation with CL (Table 3). For the entire study, data analysis with a 95% confidence interval was considered.

Table 3. Correlation coefficients of indicators in relation to CL

Dimension	Indicator	β	t	*p* value	$IC_{95\%}$ to β
Brand Self-Similarity	(Constant)	0.749	3.364	0.001	[0.310, 1.187]
	Brand values	0.185	3.145	0.002	[0.069, 0.301]
	Meaning	0.144	2.215	0.028	[0.016, 0.272]
	Self-concept	0.475	8.049	0.000	[0.359, 0.591]
Brand Identity	(Constant)	0.156	0.460	0.646	[-0.510, 0.821]
	Prestige	0.316	3.450	0.001	[0.136, 0.497]
	Attractiveness	0.239	2.530	0.012	[0.053, 0.424]
	Value	0.318	5.137	0.000	[0.196, 0.440]
Memorable Brand Experiences	(Constant)	-0.134	-0.459	0.647	[-0.709, 0.442]
	Satisfaction	0.382	4.771	0.000	[0.224, 0.540]
	Expectations	0.177	2.546	0.012	[0.040, 0.315]
	Stimuli	0.406	5.198	0.000	[0.252, 0.560]
Brand Social Benefits	(Constant)	1.515	9.424	0.000	[1.198, 1.832]
	Social Relations	0.274	4.916	0.000	[0.164, 0.384]
	Sense of Belonging	0.173	3.898	0.000	[0.086, 0.260]
	Community	0.144	3.498	0.001	[0.063, 0.226]
	Social Identity	0.095	2.544	0.012	[0.022, 0.169]

The correlation coefficients summarized in Table 4 show a relationship between the dimensions of CBI and customer loyalty (CL).

The brand identity (Brand Identity - BI), although it was the dimension that proved to be less influential in loyalty, it is still significant, with a moderate value (R=0.518 < 0.6). The remaining dimensions have strong, positive and significant correlation coefficients above 0.6.

This result is close to that of the authors Stokburger-Sauer, et al. (2012), who excluded the brand's prestige as essential for loyalty. Therefore, considering the indicators that make up the BI dimension and its results in customer loyalty, it is possible to validate Hypothesis III: The more the consumer identifies the hotel brand as unique, prestigious and with high brand equity and awareness, the more the consumer identifies the hotel brand as unique, prestigious and with high brand equity and awareness greater customer loyalty.

Table 4. Correlation coefficients between CL and CBI

		BSS	BI	MBE	BSB
CL	**R**	,754**	,518**	,752**	,721**
	p value	0.000	0.000	0.000	0.000
	n	247	247	175	247

Once confirmed that there is a correlation between CBI and CL, the effect of the first on the second is analyzed using the following theoretical model:

$$FDC = \beta_0 + \beta_1 \text{BSS} + {}^2{}_2 BI + \beta_3 MBE + \beta_4 BSB + \epsilon_i$$

However, during the validation of the previous model, the effect of the BI dimension was shown to be null. For this reason, a new model without this dimension was created. The final estimated model explains 70.8% (Table 5) of the variation in customer loyalty across the dimensions of the CBI, with an ANOVA p-value less than 0.05 (i.e., this model fits the data).

Table 5. Quality measures and fit of the estimated model

R	R²	Durbin Watson Test	ANOVA			
				SQ	F	p value
0.842	0.708	1.919	Regression	78.339	138.349	0.000
			Residual	32.276		

The MBE dimension is the one that most contributes to the variation in loyalty (Table 6). This dimension, for each value increased, contributes to the increase of 0.443 points in loyalty (CL). Thus, with 95% confidence, it can also be stated that, in samples from similar populations, if MBE increases by 1 point, then CL may increase between 0.273 and 0.613.

For this reason, hotel brands must invest hard in providing a unique experience, essentially seeking to refine all the client's senses (through smells, flavors, colors, shapes, designs, among), and in creating emotional and affective connections (Brakus et al., 2009). These are the factors that make a unique and memorable experience. In addition, however, customer satisfaction and management of expectations are vital for companies in the hotel market. Therefore, hypothesis IV is confirmed: When a hotel brand provides memorable experiences that satisfy the consumer's needs, the greater customer loyalty.

As for the BSS dimension, if it increases a value, it is expected that loyalty will increase, on average, by 0.246 values. However, in similar samples, this effect can vary between 0.089 and 0.402.

According to So et al. (2013), the self-similarity between the brand and the customer would increase their trust and perception of quality and value. In fact, in this investigation, Brand Self-Similarity was the dimension with the most significance for loyalty (Table 4). According to Tuskej, Golob and Podnar (2013), the most adjusted way to manage BSS is to determine the brand values according to its largest market segment (current or potential), adapting them over time to its evolution. It can, therefore, be said that the more the personality, meaning and self-concept of a hotel brand resembles the consumer, the greater the customer loyalty (Hypothesis II).

The estimated coefficient associated with Brand Social Benefits (BSB) is 0.299. If this dimension increases by one point, then loyalty is expected to increase by 0.299. This dimension was also shown to be significant for consumer loyalty. Stokburger-Sauer, et al. (2012) argued that fostering positive social interactions increases CBI and loyalty. These interactions can be created through events, co-creative marketing or other types of interaction between customers, whether physical or virtual (Stokburger-Sauer et al., 2012). Hypothesis V is then validated: The more status and opportunities of community and social categorization provide a hotel brand, the greater the customer's loyalty.

Finally, and because all hypotheses were confirmed, it can also be stated that: The more Customer Brand Identification, the greater the customer loyalty (Hypothesis I).

Table 6. Estimated coefficients for the model - CBI

	^{2}	t	*p* value	$IC_{95\%}$ to ^{2}
(Constant)	0.133	0.599	0.550	[-0.305, 0.570]
MBE	0.443	5.140	0.000	[0.273, 0.613]
BSS	0.246	3.091	0.002	[0.089, 0.402]
BSB	0.299	6.166	0.000	[0.203, 0.395]

Through the decision tree, it was possible to verify that, in this sample, the most loyal customers to the brand meet the following conditions: BSS greater than 4.4, aged equal to or greater than 30 years, and with MBE less than 4.8 or without experience. On the other hand, the most unfaithful customers have a BSS below 2.8, MBE below 3.2 or absent and BSB below 2.8.

Therefore, the most loyal customers were primarily adults who strongly resemble the brand and its values and had little or no experience with the brand (which could mean that they idealize a positive experience with the brand).

In this situation, the intellectual dimension appears in the model of brand experience dimensions by Brakus et al. (2009). According to this theory, the projection of curiosity concerning the brand and the needs it can satisfy increases its attractiveness and may attract the customer's attention.

On the other hand, for customers who do not develop self-likeness with the brand, have not had relevant experiences, and do not consider that the brand can provide social benefits, the average loyalty value is much lower.

CONCLUSION

Final Considerations

It can be considered that this investigation contributed significantly to the understanding of customer brand identification and customer loyalty. It was possible to conclude the different tools with which hotel brands can and should work to increase their attractiveness, improve their service and create conditions for the customer to repeat their experience with the brand.

The formation of a brand goes far beyond a name and a logo. This should have its meaning, its values and principles, characteristics (physical or immaterial), know-how and all the other aspects that will differentiate it from competitors in the market. The idea is to look for the necessary tools to create brand equity and brand awareness, that is, to create value for the customer and increase brand recognition in the market so that it is associated with quality, prestigious and unique service.

The concept of customer brand identification essentially aims to improve the customer's perception of the brand's value and all the benefits that it can provide. More than that, this investigation fulfilled the objective of understanding CBI's relationship with customer loyalty. The success of a hotel brand lies in creating a commitment between the client and the brand. This notion is considered more profitable than carrying out the marketing actions necessary to attract new customers and transmit more stability to the company in the market.

This study allowed us to validate that there is a positive and significant relationship between CBI and customer loyalty, a proposition that is by the conclusions drawn by several authors such as So, King, Sparks and Wang (2013) and Stokburger-Sauer, Ratneshwar and Sem (2012). In other words, and directly answering the starting question: in hospitality, when there is customer brand identification, the tendency is for the customer to be more likely to commit to the brand, increasing the loyalty rate.

This means that, in hotels, customers tend to look for brands that, in addition to satisfying their needs, also contribute positively to their lives, working as a form of expression and that have distinct characteristics that increase the value and quality of their experience.

In addition to increasing loyalty, it is equally important to note that the client tends to behave more favorably about the brand (brand advocacy), making them more likely to spread positive word-of-mouth and recommend the hotel brand to family and/or friends.

According to the specific objectives, it was also essential for this investigation to uniquely understand the CBI categories. Brand identity (BI), although the category that proved less influential in loyalty, is still quite significant. This conclusion is similar to that of the authors Stokburger-Sauer, Ratneshwar and Sen (2012), who excluded the brand's prestige as essential for loyalty. This indicator was, in fact, one of those with the lowest correlation values.

However, brand identity is composed of three other indicators: attractiveness, brand quality and value. Therefore, it can be said that the customer will be more likely to make their reservations at hotels with attractive brands, high brand awareness and brand equity. There should be a concern on hotel companies to provide quality service and appropriately suited to the price.

So, King, Sparks and Wang (2013) argued that the assimilation of the brand with the customer would increase their trust and perception of quality and value. In fact, in this investigation, Brand Self-Similarity was the category with the most significance for loyalty. This category is part of the identity created by the brand itself and the way it is disclosed to the customer. The customer creates an emotional connection with brands that are consistent with their identity or their desired identity. This principle is in line with investigations by Malär et al. (2011).

Next is the brand social benefits (BSB) category, which represents the ability to create social groups that identify and share the same commitment to the hotel brand. These groups allow the customer to create their social identity, integrate a community where they can develop social relationships, and, as a result, develop a sense of belonging to the brand. These interactions can be created through events, co-creative marketing or other types of interaction between customers, whether physical or virtual

(Stokburger-Sauer, Ratneshwar & Sen, 2012). All of this points to the conclusions of Stokburger-Sauer, Ratneshwar and Sen (2012), who argue that fostering positive social interactions increases CBI and, consequently, customer loyalty.

Finally, experience management, throughout the literature and especially in the case of services, emerges as a fundamental strategy for market differentiation and increased competitiveness. The memorable brand experiences (MBE) category was found to be very influential for customer loyalty. For this reason, hotel brands must invest hard in providing a unique experience, essentially seeking to refine all the client's senses (through smells, flavors, colors, shapes, designs, among others), and in creating emotional and affective connections (Brakus, Schmitt & Zarantonello, 2009). Therefore, it is essential to guarantee service and quality through, for example, qualified staff, adequately equipped and clean rooms, security and appropriate facilities.

In the elaboration of the decision tree, homogeneous groups and the expected loyalty of each group were observed. It was noticed that customers who do not identify with the brand have not had satisfactory experiences with the brand and do not consider that the brand provides social benefits and is, consequently, less likely to retain their loyalty. However, it is essential to point out that clients with the highest brand advocacy values identified with the brand are over 30 years old and have not had any experience with the brand. In this situation, the intellectual dimension may be at stake, which appears in the model of the brand experience dimensions by Brakus, Schmitt and Zarantonello (2009). According to this theory, the projection of curiosity concerning the brand and the needs it can satisfy increases its attractiveness and may attract the customer's attention.

Research Limitations

The survey was distributed online by a snowball, meaning that responses were given only by respondents who were volunteers and willing to participate in the study. Furthermore, the number of responses depends on the personal network size where the survey is shared. The more extensive the network, the larger the sample and vice versa. Due to the method in which it was distributed and, once again, because the sample depends on the author's network, this study was limited in demographic terms, with a large part of the sample residing in the Autonomous Region of Madeira.

In this investigation, consumer perceptions and behavior were assessed about brands chosen by the respondents themselves at the beginning of the survey. As a rule, respondents will have chosen a brand they know and for which they show, from the beginning, some preference, which may have caused higher averages and more evident correlations. For future investigations, it would be interesting to carry out this study applied to a specific brand, enabling the evaluation of customer interaction with brands that they do not know or have had little contact with.

Quantitative methods lead to the simplification or obfuscation of a complex universe. Using a qualitative method, for example, through interviews or honest answers, could promote a better understanding of consumer behavior and enrich the conclusions drawn in this investigation.

There are also limitations in analyzing data through regressions, especially for correlations between 0.3 and 0.7, for which the use of algorithms is suggested. Although regressions are a current and valid approach to achieving the research study objectives, alternative tests would help improve the quality and validity of the results.

Future Research

For this investigation, no type of hotel accommodation as specified. Future investigations would make sense to study customer perception and the consequences on loyalty for different market segments (e.g., luxury hotels vs. budget hotels), or even for other types of brands (of products or other services). It is an investigation that could also be replicated in different cultural contexts or with consumers with specific characteristics.

REFERENCES

Aaker, J. (1999). Self-esteem's moderation of self-congruity effects on brand loyalty. *Theoretical Economics Letters*, *7*(6), 45–57.

Ahearne, M., Bhattacharya, C., & Gruen, T. (2005). Antecedents and consequences of customer-company identification: Expanding the role of relationship marketing. *The Journal of Applied Psychology*, *90*(3), 574–585. doi:10.1037/0021-9010.90.3.574 PMID:15910151

Belch, G. (1978). Belief systems and the differential. *Advances in Consumer Research. Association for Consumer Research (U. S.)*, 320–325.

Bergami, M., & Bagozzi, R. (2010). Self-categorization, affective commitment and group self-esteem as distinct aspects of social identity in the organization. *British Journal of Social Psychology*, 555–577. PMID:11190685

Brakus, J., Schmitt, B., & Zarantonello, L. (2009). Brand experience: What Is It? How Is t Measured? Does It Affect Loyalty? *Journal of Marketing*, *73*(3), 52–68. doi:10.1509/jmkg.73.3.052

Buil, I., Catalán, S., & Martínez, E. (2016). The importance of corporate brand identity in business management: An application to the UK banking sector. *Business Research Quarterly*, *19*(1), 3–12. doi:10.1016/j.brq.2014.11.001

Chaudhuri, A., & Holbrook, M. (2001). The chain of effects from brand trust and brand affect to brand performance: The role of brand loyalty. *Journal of Marketing*, *65*(2), 81–93. doi:10.1509/jmkg.65.2.81.18255

Dolich, I. (1969). Congruence relationship between self-image and product brands. *JMR, Journal of Marketing Research*, *6*(1), 80–84. doi:10.1177/002224376900600109

Ekinci, Y., Sirakaya-Turk, E., & Preciado, S. (2013). Symbolic consumption of tourism destination brands. *Journal of Business Research*, *66*, 711-718.

El-Adly, M. (2019). Modelling the relationship between hotel perceived value, customer satisfaction, and customer loyalty. *Journal of Retailing and Consumer Services*, *50*, 322-332.

Ellemers, N., & Haslam, S. (2012). Social identity theory. Handbook of Theories of Social Psychology, 379-398.

Elliot, R., & Wattanasuwan, K. (1998). Consumption and the symbolic project of the self. *Consumer Research*, 17-20.

Escalas, J., & Bettman, J. (2003). You are what they eat the influence of reference groups on consumer connections to brands. *Journal of Consumer Psychology, 13*(3), 339–348. doi:10.1207/S15327663JCP1303_14

He, H., Harris, L., & Li, Y. (2005). Antecedents and consequences of customer-company identification: Expanding the role of relationship marketing. *The Journal of Applied Psychology*, 648–657. PMID:15910151

Hosany, S., & Martin, D. (2012). Self-image congruence in consumer behavior. *Journal of Business Research, 65*(5), 685–691. doi:10.1016/j.jbusres.2011.03.015

Hulten, B. (2011). Sensory marketing: The multi-sensory brand-experience concept. *European Business Review, 23*(3), 256–273. doi:10.1108/09555341111130245

Hultén, B., Broweus, N., & Dijk, M. (2009). *Sensory marketing.* Palgrave Macmillan. doi:10.1057/9780230237049

Japutra, A., Ekinci, Y., & Simkin, L. (2019). Self-congruence, brand attachment and compulsive buying. *Journal of Business Research, 99*, 456–463. doi:10.1016/j.jbusres.2017.08.024

Kayaman, R., & Arasli, H. (2007). Customer based brand equity: Evidence from the hotel industry. *Journal of Service Theory and Practice, 17*, 92–109.

Keller, K. (2001). *Building Customer-Based Brand Equity: A Blueprint for Creating Strong Brands.* Academic Press.

Kotler, P., Kartajaya, H., & Setiawan, I. (2017). *Marketing 4.0: Moving From Traditional to Digital.* Wiley.

Kuenzel, S., & Halliday, S. (2010). The chain of effects from reputation and brand personality congruence to brand loyalty: The role of brand identification. *Journal of Targeting, Measurement and Analysis for Marketing*, 167-176.

Lam, S., Ahearne, M., Hu, Y., & Schillewaert, N. (2010). Resistance to brand switching when a radically new brand is introduced: A social identity theory perspective. *Journal of Marketing, 74*(6), 6. doi:10.1509/jmkg.74.6.128

Lam, S., Ahearne, M., Mullins, R., & Schillewaert, N. (2013). Exploring the synamics of antecedents to consumer-brand identification with a new brand. *Journal of the Academy of Marketing Science, 41*(2), 234–252. doi:10.100711747-012-0301-x

Landon, E. (1972). Role of need for achievement in the perception of products: Proceedings of the American psychological association convention. *Journal of Consumer Research*, 741-7842. 10.1037/e611312012-119

Leaniz, P., & Rodriguez-de-Bolque, I. (2013). CSR and customer loyalty: The roles of trust, customer identification with the company and satisfaction. *International Journal of Hospitality Management*, 89–99.

Malär, L., Krohmer, H., Hoyer, W., & Nyffenegger, B. (2011). Emotional brand attachment and brand personality: The relative importance of the actual and the ideal self. *Journal of Marketing, 75*(4), 35–52. doi:10.1509/jmkg.75.4.35

Martínez, P., & Rodríguez del Bosque, I. (2013). CSR and customer loyalty: The roles of trust, customer identification with the company and satisfaction. *International Journal of Hospitality Management, 35*, 89–99. doi:10.1016/j.ijhm.2013.05.009

Mattila, A. (2006). How Affective Commitment Boosts Guest Loyalty (and Promotes Frequent-guest Programs). *The Cornell Hotel and Restaurant Administration Quarterly, 47*(2), 174–181. doi:10.1177/0010880405283943

Mindrut, S., Manolica, A., & Roman, C. (2015). Building brands identity. *Procedia Economics and Finance, 20*(15), 393–403. doi:10.1016/S2212-5671(15)00088-X

Moreira, A., Fortes, N., & Santiago, R. (2017). Influence of sensory stimuli on brand experience, brand equity and purchase intention. *Journal of Business Economics and Management, 18*(1), 68–83. doi:10.3846/16111699.2016.1252793

Nam, J., Ekinci, Y., & Whyatt, G. (2011). Brand equity, brand loyalty and consumer satisfaction. *Annals of Tourism Research, 38*(3), 1009–1030. doi:10.1016/j.annals.2011.01.015

Nastasoiu, A., & Vandenbosch, M. (2018). Competing with loyalty: How to design successful customer loyalty reward programs. *Business Horizons.*

O'Neill, J., & Xiao, Q. (2006). The Role of Brand Affiliation in Hotel Market Value. *Cornell Hospitality Quarterly, 47*(3), 210–223. doi:10.1177/0010880406289070

Popp, B., & Woratschek, H. (2017). Consumers' relationships with brands and brand communities - The multifaceted roles of identification and satisfaction. *Journal of Retailing and Consumer Services, 35*, 46–56. doi:10.1016/j.jretconser.2016.11.006

Schmitt, B. (2012). Brand insights from psychological and neurophysiological perspectives. *Journal of Consumer Psychology, 22*, 7–17. doi:10.1016/j.jcps.2011.09.005

Sirgy, M., & Su, C. (2000). Destination image, self-congruity, and travel behavior: Toward an integrative model. *Journal of Travel Research, 88*(4), 340–352. doi:10.1177/004728750003800402

Sirgy, M. J. (1982). Self-concept in consumer behavior: A critical review. *The Journal of Consumer Research, 9*(3), 287–300. doi:10.1086/208924

So, K., King, C., Hudson, S., & Meng, F. (2017). The missing link in building customer brand identification: The role of brand attractiveness. *Tourism Management, 59*, 640–651. doi:10.1016/j.tourman.2016.09.013

So, K., King, C., Sparks, B., & Wang, Y. (2013). The influence of customer brand identification on hotel brand evaluation and loyalty development. *International Journal of Hospitality Management, 34*(1), 31–41. doi:10.1016/j.ijhm.2013.02.002

Stokburger-Sauer, N., Ratneshwar, S., & Sen, S. (2012). Drivers of consumer-brand identification. *International Journal of Research in Marketing, 29*(4), 406–418. doi:10.1016/j.ijresmar.2012.06.001

Thompson, C., Rindfleisch, A., & Arsel, Z. (2006). Emotional branding and the strategic value of the doppelgänger brand image. *Journal of Marketing, 70*(1), 50–64. doi:10.1509/jmkg.70.1.050.qxd

Tsiros, M., Vikas, M., & Ross, W. (2004). The role of attributions in customer satisfaction: A reexamination. *The Journal of Consumer Research, 31*(2), 476–483. doi:10.1086/422124

Veloutsou, C. (2009). Brands as relationship facilitators in consumer markets. *Journal of Marketing, 9*, 127–130.

Ye, S., Li, J., Zeng, Z., & Hao, S. (2015). Research on the impact of social circles on self-brand connection: Regulation of self-awareness and brand value. *Open Journal of Business and Management, 3*(2), 339–348. doi:10.4236/ojbm.2015.32015

Chapter 10
Customer Relationship Management in Tourism in the Digitalization Process:
The Case of Turkey

İsmail Çalık

iD https://orcid.org/0000-0001-9815-5796

Gumushane University, Turkey

ABSTRACT

Thischapter aimed to explicate CRM concept along with its distinct dimensions. Following the explanation of the denotation, evolution, and types of the CRM concept, the benefits of CRM, success factors, and possible causes for downfall are discussed. Another section of the chapter considers the role and evolution of CRM in the digitization process. This part introduces the reader to the concepts of E-CRM and SCRM that arose during the process, as well as the success conditions and essential aspects of these approaches. This section examines the relationship between customer satisfaction and loyalty in the tourism sector, the impact of CRM on business performance, and CRM applications in the context of destination management. In the last part, CRM practices and approaches in Turkey were discussed in terms of destination management and tourism businesses, and some applications and modules employed in the digitalization process are included.

INTRODUCTION

Instead of traditional marketing approaches, the origin and advancement of the customer relationship management (CRM) idea are based on the relationship marketing approach, which sought to create, maintain, and develop relationships with all stakeholders, particularly customers (Gilbert, 1996). CRM techniques began to be discussed practice and in the literature in the mid-1990s, as information technologies were being used in sales and marketing applications (Payne and Flow, 2005). CRM, in its most generic definition, is an approach to enhance customer loyalty by providing tailored products

DOI: 10.4018/978-1-7998-8306-7.ch010

and services (Rigby, 2006). In the period from the 2000s to the present, the development of the CRM concept has also changed depending on digitalization and the concepts of eCRM and Social CRM have gained importance. Furthermore, the question of how destination management organizations or tourism businesses handle their social media platforms has become a critical part of success, depending on the impact of the social media on the tourism behavior of customers.

The CRM strategy in the tourism sector is consulted in a set of dimensions such as ensuring customer satisfaction and loyalty, loyalty programs offered by tourism businesses to guests, the effect of CRM on company performance and CRM strategy in destination management. On the other hand, with the effect of digitalization, the necessity of CRM in tourism has grown even more, and the gathering, appraisal, and integrating of customer data has become fundamental for company efficiency and customer satisfaction.

Turkey is a major tourist destination due to its tourism potential. Effective marketing and promotion approaches are regarded to be possible to generate the projected revenue from tourism. At this stage, implementing a CRM strategy in both destination management and tourism businesses will help to boost customer satisfaction and loyalty. The digital tourism strategy and the integrated CRM will play an important role in improving Turkey's competitiveness in tourism and increasing its profitability.

BACKGROUND

Definition, Evolution and Types of Customer Relationship Management Concept

The knowledge of marketing has evolved into a relationship-based understanding as a result of today's fierce competition circumstances. The concept of relationship marketing is based on the goal of establishing, developing, and maintaining long-term connections with customers. On looking at the theoretical framework of the relational marketing approach, it's noticeable that several practical techniques have been influenced by and inspired by it. CRM arose as a result of relationship marketing's evolution and adaptability to contemporary situations and practices.

CRM is one of the methodologies and strategies that aims to create and maintain good relationships with present and potential customers, as relationship marketing forecasts. In a fiercely competitive market, businesses strive to keep their market shares by maintaining their existing customers, and so uphold their market competitive advantages. Along with the protection of existing customers, the CRM approach is also the source of a number of implemented strategies regarding the increase in the market share by gaining new customers,

Customer relationship management (CRM) is the process of identifying customers who can be served efficiently and influencing interactions between the business and its consumers. The ultimate purpose of CRM is to maximize the existing and anticipated value of customers to the business (Kumar & Reinartz, 2006). CRM is the logical consequence of a company's integration with evolving and changing technology and organizational forms in light of the company's new and innovative marketing ideas, utilizing dynamic and up-to-date data (Boulding et al., 2006). Table 1 contains some definitions of customer relationship management.

Table 1. Definitions of CRM

CRM is a comprehensive strategy for acquiring, maintaining, and collaborating with select customers in order to provide superior value for both the organization and the customer.	Parvatiyar & Sheth (2000)
CRM is the process of establishing and maintaining long-term, mutually beneficial relationships with strategic customers.	Buttle (2001)
CRM is the process of better understanding the customer and better guiding the business within the framework of its expectations in all areas of contact with the customer.	Civelek (2016)
CRM refers to a company's strategy for gaining a better knowledge of and influencing customer behavior using appropriate communication technologies to improve customer acquisition, loyalty and profitability.	Swift (2001)
Customer relationship management (CRM) is the combination of technology and business procedures to suit the needs of customers.	Bose (2002)
CRM is to maintain and develop long-term relationships with customers in order to maximize profits.	Goel (2017)
CRM is a set of complex and interactive processes that aim to achieve the optimum balance between corporate investments and meeting customer needs in order to achieve maximum profits.	Schierholz et al., (2007)
CRM is a style of management that includes market research and data analysis to uncover customer needs, experiences, and other issues associated in order to improve business profitability.	Paas & Kuljen (2001)
CRM is an approach that allows companies to collect customer data quickly, identify their most valuable customers over time, and augment customer loyalty by offering personalized products and services,	Rigby (2006)
For different stakeholders, CRM means something completely different. CRM stands for customer relationship management and refers to the development of solutions that are tailored to the demands of specific customers. On the other hand, as for IT consultants, CRM means online analytical processing, and for customer interaction centers, it means complex and technical jargon.	Winer (2001)
People, processes, and technology are all components of CRM.	Chen & Popowich (2003)

As shown in a detailed manner in Table 1, there are some main issues that come out in the definitions of customer relationship management such as designing products in line with consumers' expectations, providing individualized products to customers, using a corporate approach to addressing customer behavior, organizing business operations towards customers' expectations, and so on and contributing to the profitability and efficiency of the business as a result of all these strategies.

Figure 1. Definition Processes of CRM
Source: (Payne & Frow, 2005, p. 168)

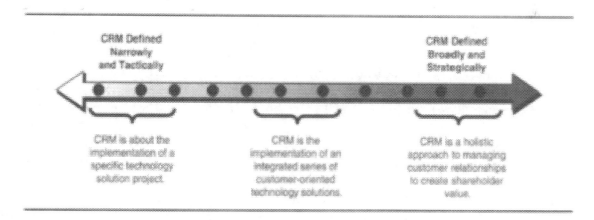

In Figure 1, the many points of view that evolved during the CRM definition processes are highlighted. CRM is characterized as a holistic customer relationship management devised to create company value in broad strategic definitions, while it is seen primarily as a technological solution application by businesses in narrow operational definitions.

After defining the customer relationship management concept, it may be beneficial to describe how it came to be. Changing customer needs, new demographic trends, and increasing customer diversity, differentiating customer behaviors (use of social media, use of mobile applications, etc.), the need for up-to-date customer data, customer's tendency to meet their needs quickly and efficiently, and intensified awareness of health and sustainability are just a few of the justifications as to why customer relationship management has developed in the historical process (Kumar & Reinartz, 2006).

While customer relationship management incorporates classic marketing principles, it broadens these concepts to include a new viewpoint on marketing. Companies began to develop innovative features, communication channels, and customer-friendly practices to suit customer expectations as a result of the paradigm shift that occurred in the early 1990s (Paas & Kuijlen, 2001). The main trends of the companies in the 150 years from the 1850s to the 2000s are given in the Figure 2. Customer relationship management is a relational marketing approach that was brought to the forefront in the 1990s and developed in the 2000s.

Figure 2. Firm Trends in the Last 150 Years
Source: (Bose, 2002, p. 90)

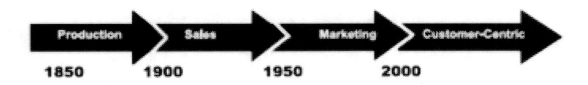

According to Bligh & Turk (2004:7), CRM began to be used firstly as a marketing tactic in the early 1990s to assist businesses improve their customer service methods. During this time, companies tended to use CRM to keep up with continuously changing demands and needs of buyers, markets, and competitors. On the other side, escalated usage of computers and the internet has resulted in customers having faster access to information and so changing their demands. Without a doubt, this predicament prompted businesses to build new customer techniques, and CRM began to emerge as a result.

Customer relationship management strategies have obviously evolved significantly from the 1990s to the 2020s. Companies have been employing CRM systems for the last 15-20 years to give more technologically advanced and high-performance services to their customers. CRM systems stand out because of their ability to acquire, analyze, and evaluate data on customer structures, thanks to advancements in information technology and web platforms. This technological advancement has given rise to a new philosophy in customer relations known as "e-customer" (Alokla et al., 2019). On the other side, the enterprise resource planning system (ERP), which consists of comprehensively integrated software sets and is used to manage and integrate all business functions for a company, was implemented and started to be used within the scope of CRM (Shehab et al., 2004). Finally, Today, CRM advancements represent a significant part in the growth of all software used by many organizations, particularly in the finance, tourism, mobile, and logistics industries. CRM strategies provide a greater emphasis on the customer than on the product, and the best way to operate a successful CRM program would be to get a balanced strategy that incorporates technology, process, and people (Chen & Popovich, 2003).

Along with new perspectives, marketing, management, information systems, e-commerce, technology, human resources management, and information management are all intertwined with customer relationship management. CRM appears to be based heavily on information systems and related applications to reach customers (Alokla et al., 2019). On the other hand, CRM was established and developed as a relationship marketing method (Ryals & Knox, 2001). CRM is indeed a set of methodologies for managing the organization's fundamental marketing, sales, service, and support operations, as well as customer connections. Customers' demands are also met through the use of information technology (IT) and information systems, which complement and incorporate the CRM process (Ngai, 2005).

Figure 3. Perspectives of CRM
Source: (Alokla et al., 2019, p.193)

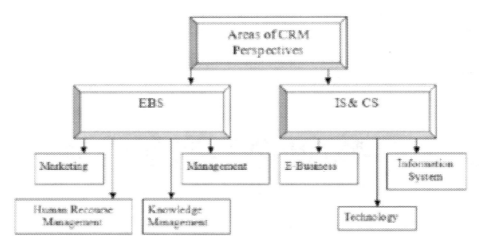

After clarifying the foundation of CRM and its evolution process, it is helpful to provide information on CRM types. Three different types of CRM are listed below (Rahimi et al., 2015):

- Operational CRM
- Collaborative CRM
- Analytic CRM

Operational *CRM*: Strengthening support processes ensures the CRM system's efficiency. It comprises marketing, sales, and service automation solutions (Schierholz et al., 2007). It recommends business processes and technologies that can help improve the efficiency of customer-oriented operations (Iriana & Buttle, 2007). It outlines how companies use automation to boost sales and customer service. Examples of operational CRM are call center and order processing systems, developing the online website, modifying the data collection and data management process, selecting and installing appropriate hardware and software, and establishing a customer database system (Kumar & Reinartz, 2006).

Collaborative *CRM*: Customer interaction points and communication channels are managed and synchronized by collaborative CRM systems (Schierholz et al., 2007). It uses collaborative services and infrastructures, managing any interaction between the company and its customers (Rahimi et al., 2015).

Analytic *CRM*: For a better knowledge of diverse consumer behaviors, analytic CRM systems store and assess information about them (Schierholz et al., 2007). According to Kelly (2000), the chief success criteria in analytical CRM are integration of application, data anatomy, multidimensionality, and selection of industry-specific methods.

Advantages of Customer Relations Management

CRM has transformed into one of today's modern most essential management strategies and the reasons why CRM emerged were listed by Duran (2002):

- Customer share has become notable, not market share,
- The concepts of customer satisfaction and customer loyalty gained importance,
- The value of existing customers was recognized, and retention efforts of these customers were needed,
- With the importance of one-on-one marketing, strategies to treat each customer according to their specific needs became necessary,
- Intense competitive environment,
- Mass marketing has become an increasingly expensive way of gaining customers,
- Developments experienced in communication technologies (web, e-mail, etc.) and database management systems.

The way for companies to build their future is to make use of successful CRM applications with the help of technology. By using customer data, it will be possible to analyze them in all aspects with CRM techniques. Customer data gathered by CRM might provide guidance to employees and guarantee effective communication with customers in so many other parts of the company, resulting in satisfied customer experiences (Kellen & Stefanczyk, 2002).

Another consequence of CRM activities for businesses is that they improve the performance of the company. Numerous studies have shown that CRM practices strengthen a company's performance (Boulding et al., 2006). A case study done by Ryals (2005) indicated that the implemented CRM measures resulted in a 270% increase in the firm's business profits. Srivanasan & Moorman (2005), conducted a research on a sample of 106 retail companies using the model analysis method, and concluded that CRM investments positively affected the company's performance.

Companies benefit from the CRM approach in terms of strategy development, value creation, and performance evaluation. CRM benefits disclose the company vision, create a competitive character, and segment the market in detail according to customer characteristics within the context of business and customer strategy. Besides, CRM delivers information systems, analysis tools, front and back office applications, and a meaningful data repository to businesses (Payne & Frow, 2005: 171). The conceptual framework of the CRM strategy and the benefits it provides to companies are displayed in Figure 4.

Figure 4. A Conceptual Framework for CRM Strategy
Source: (Payne & Frow, 2005, p.171)

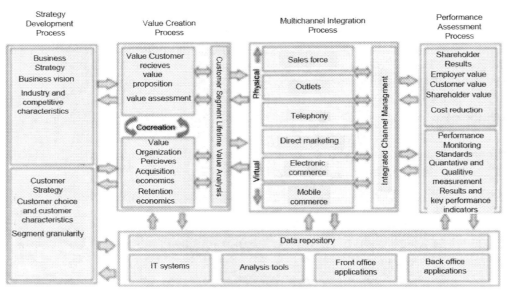

The following are the primary advantages of CRM solutions for businesses (Xu & Walton, 2005: 959; Swift, 2001: 28):

- Increasing customer satisfaction,
- Retention of current customers,
- Improving customer value,
- Providing strategic information to sales, marketing and finance departments,
- Obtaining new customers,

- Saving on company expenses,
- Reducing sales costs,
- Increasing customer productivity,
- Enhancing customer loyalty.

Understanding the relevance of the CRM strategy's criteria for success and potential reasons for failure could help make sure that the CRM process is carried out effectively and efficiently. Almotairi (2008: 5) explains the success factors of CRM as follows:

- Senior management support,
- Forming of organizational culture in which all employees are encouraged to share and learn about the new business structure and knowledge,
- Defining the CRM strategy and explaining it to the employees,
- Ensuring integration among departments,
- Skillful employees,
- Having principal information about customers,
- Managing the information technology network,
- Active participation of customers in the process,
- Defining CRM processes.

Along with the accomplishments of CRM process, there could be some disappointments owing to flaws that arise during the process. The reasons why this failure takes place are listed below (Chalmeta, 2006: 1017; Kumar & Reinartz, 2006).

- Regarding CRM as a purely technological change, and not accepting it as a new management approach,
- Company managements do not have enough information about the opportunities offered by CRM applications to companies and customers, and thus they do not supply support,
- Failing to create an effective customer relations system in the organizational culture,
- Not having a well-defined strategy and measurable company goals within the scope of CRM,
- Not redefining business processes,
- Obtaining low quality data and information,
- The organization's inability to manage change correctly,
- Not involving customers in CRM solution designs,
- Incompatibility between the CRM system and organizational processes.

Customer Relationship Management in the Digitalization Process

Since the late twentieth century, digitalization's progress, sometimes known as the "third industrial revolution," has permeated practically every sector of humanity, not only the technical realm. Digitalization, on the other hand, refers to the use of digital technologies to assist firms modify their business models and create new revenue and value-creating prospects (Happ & Ivancsó-Horváth, 2018). In addition to providing businesses with the opportunity to access the data created by the internet, digitization gives the opportunity to use the advantages of big data, cloud computing, internet of things and social software

(Reichstein & Härting, 2018). Digitalization has an impact on many aspects of business operations, encompassing business models, production methods, marketing channels, and employee job responsibilities. Organizations need to adapt their conventional management strategies to meet and engage with changes in market demand as a result of digital transformation (Galyarski & Mironova, 2021). Moreover, digital technology implementation in organizations and operations has resulted in substantial changes for businesses. These fundamental changes caused by digitalization in companies are presented below (Parviainen, 2017: 64):

- *Process stage:* It entails reducing conventional processes and implementing new digital tools and streamlining business processes accordingly,
- *Organization stage:* It means supporting consumers with innovative offerings and showcasing old services using new digital means by abandoning traditional practices,
- *Business area:* It refers to changing roles in the ecosystem and new value chains,
- *Social level:* The type of work and the means of influencing decision-making also change depending on the changing social structures.

Due to digital transformation, companies should pay attention to the following points in order to keep up with market variables where effective competitive mechanisms exist (Crittenden et al., 2019: 266):

- For the company, digitizing is an opportunity to be embraced,
- Types of digitization should be clearly understood,
- Evaluation of the current business model in order to identify the elements that need to change,
- Benefiting from new technologies within the company's own structure or available from the market,
- Researching digital ideas from different industries, companies or business networks and aligning them with the company's digitalization policy,
- Inspiring the digital change increasing the strengths of the company, creating new products and increasing customer value,
- Allocating resources for employee training in terms of facilitating adaptation to digitalization,
- Establishing a digital prioritization culture,
- Adapting the company to digital transformation quickly.

Customer relationship management has become increasingly consequential as the digitalization process has proceeded. Customer relationship management is one of the marketing strategies that helps businesses achieve long-term customer satisfaction and loyalty. Computerized reservation systems and global distribution systems have revolutionized the customer relations operation throughout the last 30 years. E-tourism and e-commerce applications have transformed and optimized the customer relationship management process as a result of this procedure (Rahimi et al., 2017).

There are eCRM and Social CRM concepts that need to be addressed in the context of CRM and digitalization. Electronic CRM (eCRM) is an approach for facilitating CRM implementations that focusses on internet or web-based communication involving companies and customers (Cherapanukom et al., 2021). Companies profit from eCRM, which merges technology and marketing components and coordinates consumers' online purchasing operations inside a transaction cycle to boost marketing capabilities (Alhaiou et al., 2009). In Figure 5, the basic conditions for the success of eCRM processes in hotel businesses are demonstrated. In organizational terms, these terms cover organizational readiness, customer service, knowledge management, technology support and social media. From the customer perspective, on the other side, it includes the quality of the rooms, the quality of the employees, hotel activities, restaurants and reservation processes (Cherapanukom et al., 2021).

Figure 5. Basic Success Conditions of e-CRM Processes in Hotels
Source: (Cherapanukom et al., 2021, p.306.)

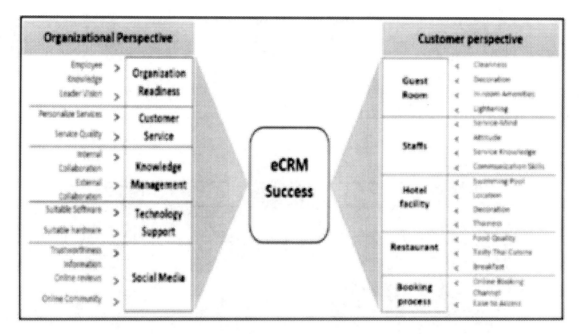

Chen & Chen (2004) illustrated the advantages of e-CRM techniques as follows:

• Rise in company revenues and profitability,
• Increase in customer satisfaction,
• Fast return on investments,
• Dissemination of positive word of mouth marketing among customers,
• Lower firm costs,
• Improved customer service,
• Higher employee productivity,
• Simplified business process,
• Lower marketing costs,
• Closer and more intimate communication management with customers,
• Increase in customer loyalty rates,
• Growth in customer depth and effectiveness,
• Better perception of customer requirements,
• Revealing customer profiles in a detailed way.

A further subject worthy of investigation in order to properly comprehend CRM in the digitalization process is social CRM. Social CRM, according to Greenberg (2010: 34), is defined as follows:

Social CRM is a business approach that entails using social media to communicate with customers in order to establish trust and brand loyalty. Social CRM is both a concept and a business approach for collaborating with customers in an accountable and interactive work environment with mutual information flow, supported by business rules, processes and socially.

Social CRM encompasses a broader perspective than standard CRM. The Social CRM strategy strives to make it easier for multiple stakeholders to communicate and collaborate in a large ecosystem (partners, customers, suppliers). Likewise, Social CRM advocates the importance of creating shared value among stakeholders and the necessity of integrating resources (Gamage et al., 2021). Greenberg (2010) presents the basic elements of the Social CRM strategy in Figure 6.

Figure 6. Primal Elements of SCRM Strategy
Source: (Greenberg, 2010, p.42)

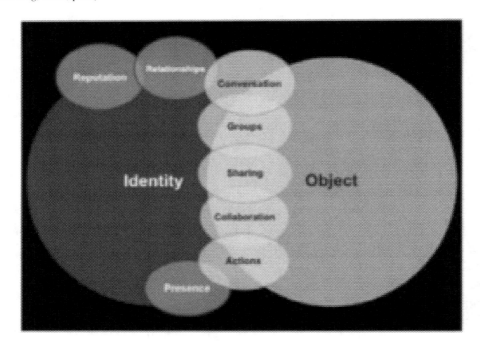

One of the cardinal elements of Social CRM understanding is the way you showcase your instant status on social media. Discovering how to reach customers when they are online is valuable. Uploading images and videos to social media and sending messages are examples of actions. Sharing on social media should be interpreted as sharing photographs and videos. Finally, when it comes to trust and reputation between people, mutual interaction is ensured, and thus, a relationship is established.

Customer Relationship Management in Tourism

Customer relationship management, it can be argued, plays a pivotal role in the tourist industry in managing primary and secondary customer relationships and converting these relationships into long-term relationships by boosting customer satisfaction. By soliciting travelers' feedback on the services, they experience from tourism businesses, it may be feasible to assess and upgrade existing services of tourism businesses. Customer satisfaction is boosted, and the foundations of long-term consumer relationships are constructed when services are modified based on customer feedback. Because of the substantial percentage of tourism destinations and tourism businesses that offer substitute products in the tourism industry, building long-term relationships with customers and nurturing a loyal customer base has become more crucial. As a result, one of the most powerful marketing methods for tourism businesses and destinations is customer relationship management.

As for the management of customer relations in the tourism sector, companies preserve records and customer databases on previous purchases and personal information in electronic media, which can be used by hotel, food and beverage businesses, and travel agencies. In addition, Tourism organizations might use websites, questionnaires, and other methods to assess the wishes, complaints, and views of their present consumers, and then formulate a service concept in response. It is one of the most strategically weighty actions for tourism businesses and tourist destinations to be able to generate lasting solutions, particularly for tourist wishes and complaints, in order to ensure long relationships with customers. Due to the surplus of substitute products in the tourism sector, touristic customers are able to quickly change their business or destination preferences. This circumstance emphasizes the need of efficient customer relationship management in the tourism industry, which would be based on a customer-centric approach.

Ensuring a healthy and reliable information flow is very eminent in terms of effectively managing customer relations in the tourism sector in the digitalization process. In addition, the existence of a successful digital marketing information system is critical for the maintenance of this information in tourism businesses. As a result, in order to respond to the requirements of tourism customers who want to have diverse experiences, it is vital to thoroughly understand and analyze their expectations. In this sense, it is very leading to have a strong and sustainable marketing information system and to manage and use this system in the best way. In addition, for tourism businesses, efficiently utilizing information and communication technology in the acquisition, protection, and flow of digital information about customers is paramount. Providing personalized service options to customers is among the issues that are gaining importance today to ensure that customers can have positive experiences in the decision process of purchasing touristic products and in after-sales services. In order to build the content of these customised service possibilities, businesses must acquire precise and reliable information about their customers. Therefore, the data obtained from customer relations in advance sheds light and guides businesses. To give an example of personalized service options, customers can visit the touristic product options in three dimensions in the virtual environment and choose accordingly. In another example within the scope of after-sales services, a customer who has a problem at the hotel he is staying in, the customer may be enabled to have a video call with the agency official via the live support line, then the customer's problem can be solved.

Customer Relationship Management (CRM), which is used to establish, develop, manage, maintain, and govern customer connections, is becoming increasingly serious in today's competitive environment. With CRM, hospitality firms may receive support from generating successful customer strategies, creating customer value, boosting customer loyalty, and enhancing profitability (Aktaş & Aksatan, 2012).

It is important for tourist industry stakeholders to be recognized by customers and to develop healthy communication in order to be a part of the tourist experience. Due to the extended usage of smart phones, the internet, and social media, traditional advertising and marketing tools have become digitalized, and digital marketing strategies have become the most robust component of customer relations (TÜRSAB et al, 2019).

Customer relationship management has become a basic element for the tourism industry, generating a massive amount of valuable information about customers. Customer relationship management offers tourism organizations never-before-seen chances for in-depth analysis and focusing on the customer-business relationship through using big data tools (Serrano, 2020).

Customer relationship management has been found to be significantly related to technology, destination management, firm performance, customer satisfaction, and cultural context in the tourism literature. Initially, CRM was only used as a technological software, neglecting the role of organizational factors (Rahimi et al., 2017). Hotels began to employ technology and multimedia information channels to develop interactions with customers once the internet's role in establishing relationships with customers grew significantly (Gilbert & Powell-Perry, 2001). Gilbert (1996) revealed that a five-stage systematic approach is needed to retain customers in the long run:

- Obtaining more information about the customer through database analysis,
- Developing the product and making it more attractive to the customer,
- Informing the customer about hotel services,
- Encouraging the customer to buy more regularly and to try different products,
- Making customer retention possible by developing different loyalty programs.

The literature additionally includes studies on customer satisfaction and loyalty in the context of CRM in tourism businesses. Barusman et al. (2020) conducted a study on hotel customers in Lampung, Indonesia and it has been determined that customer relationship management has been shown to have a major effect on customer satisfaction and loyalty. Furthermore, Swimberghe & Wooldridge (2014) conducted a study in food and beverage businesses and revealed that developing a productive CRM strategy in the workplace aids managers in increasing customer satisfaction and achieving corporate objectives. In a study conducted by Akter et al. (2021) in Saint Martin Islands, Customer relationship management practices in hotels have been found to have a favorable impact on tourist satisfaction and loyalty. According to Rahimi & Kozak (2017), especially in budget hotels, customers place more emphasis on basic tourist services and a comfortable accommodation experience rather than personalized products and services within the scope of CRM.

Another aspect of the discussion is the relationship between CRM strategy and the performance of tourism businesses. Ngo et al. (2018) stated that CRM applications bolstered small and medium-sized tourism businesses in improving their financial performance. Mohammed & Rashid (2012) emphasized the mediating role of marketing skills (planning and implementation) in the relationship between CRM dimensions and hotel performance in hotel businesses and suggested that hotels can raise their hotel performance and competitiveness by focusing on CRM dimensions and marketing capabilities. Mohammed et al. (2018) conducted research covering 447 hotel businesses operating in Malaysia, and in four main dimensions, the relationship between CRM technologies and organizational performance has been examined. The performance of CRM in organizations is influenced by the aspects of finance, customers, business processes, organizational learning, and growth, according to the research (Mohammed et al.,

2014). On the other hand, Soltani et al. (2018) emphasized that the relationships between organizational skill, customer orientation, information technologies and customer information management play a pivotal role in creating an effective CRM strategy.

Fyall et al. (2003) made several recommendations in the area of destination management. The author draws attention to promoting active engagement among tourists, creating a culture of coordination and cooperation in the destination, focusing on providing value in coordination with tourists, and building long-term relationships with customers. Vogh (2011) emphasizes that CRM study concentrated on destinations rather than tourism businesses, where CRM is widely used and investigated. CRM is mainly utilized in tourism destinations to build brand loyalty and generate repeat sales. CRM strategy and applications are used in the context of visitor relationship marketing in destination marketing corporations. The main advantages of this method in terms of destination marketing are as follows (Murdy & Pike, 2011: 1283).

- To have clear targets for acquiring and retaining visitors,
- To establish effective communication between departments,
- Top management's support for the success and deepen the visitor relations,
- To respond instantly to visitor requests,
- The employees' being sensitive and willingness to the visitor demands,
- To understand the needs of special visitors,
- Fast and timely realization of customer service,
- To Pay attention to all requests of private visitors,
- To educate employees in terms of the success and deepening of visitor relations,
- Organizational structure designed in the context of visitors' needs,
- To use sales/marketing experts in resource management processes,
- To establish and monitor performance standards according to visitors,
- To choose the human resources to manage visitor relations and the technological software and hardware to be used correctly,
- To maintain a comprehensive visitor database,
- To allocate time and financial resources to visitor relations,
- To provide personalized services to visitors.

Customer Relationship Management in Tourism in the Digitalization Process: The Case of Turkey

In this section of the book chapter, readers will learn about customer relationship management practices and strategies that have arisen in the Turkish tourism industry as a result of the digitalization process, as well as methods and procedures. The implementation of CRM initiatives in Turkey will be viewed from the perspective of destination management and tourism businesses.

Customer Relationship Management in Terms of Destination Management

According to tourism statistics, Turkey is one of the world's most popular tourist destinations, with roughly 45 million visitors and $34 billion in tourism revenue before Covid 19 (TÜRSAB, 2021). However, due to the influence of the Covid 19 pandemic phase, the number of visitors fell up to approximately 15 million people in 2020, and tourism revenues declined to $12 billion (Ministry of Culture and Tourism,

2021). With the completion of the Covid 19 pandemic, it is envisaged that tourism statistics would gain new momentum.

Tourism attractions are pertinent in today's digitalized world, but how and via which communication channels these attractions are advertised is considered essential. Destinations that construct strategies based on visitor expectations, needs, and needs, as well as destinations that adapt to the process, will be one step ahead of the competition at this moment. CRM strategy is also an approach that guides in which ways to interact with customers in destinations.

One of the destination management research put forward within the scope of digitalization in Turkish tourism is the report named *"Digitalization Roadmap in Tourism Sector"* prepared by the Association of Turkish Travel Agencies (TÜRSAB), Turkish Informatics Foundation (TBV) and ED Turkey. In the study, it is asserted that the performance improvement will be accomplished predominantly in the tourism industry, and organizations that can design creative products for their customers can help boost customer loyalty with the control and analysis of data collected throughout the customer's experience and the use of these results in decision-making mechanisms. Another crucial aspect of the paper is that technological transformation is an indispensable element for the implementation of CRM applications that center the tourism customer (TÜRSAB et al., 2019).

"Turkey Tourism Promotion and Development Agency" established on 15 July 2019 under the Ministry of Culture and Tourism focuses on making Turkey a brand and a centre of attraction in domestic and international tourism, as well as to communicate with tourists and carry out marketing activities domestically and internationally (TGA, 2021). In this context, the created "GoTurkey" portal provides information about facilities, destinations, cultural areas, natural areas, tourism types, activities for tourists who may visit Turkey (GoTurkey, 2021).

The smart city concept strives to address the requests and interests of visitors to the destination through collaboration and enhanced customer communication. In this sense, smart city digital products and services can be viewed as a destination CRM approach. In line with their expectations and interests for their travels, tourists anticipate major characteristics from destinations, such as the ability to plan their travels, search and compare information, make reservations, and share their experiences. As a consequence, the tourism industry now offers more detailed, adaptable, and personalized products, services, and experiences than ever before (Çelik & Topsakal, 2017). On the other hand, smart destinations that meet the above expectations of tourists come to the fore with features such as bringing together digital and real spaces, public-private consumer cooperation, government participation, creating creative and conscious people, and personalized services (Jovicic, 2017:280).

Within the context of digital tourism, Izmir Metropolitan Municipality and the Altındağ Municipality have completed projects that may assist in informing tourists and guaranteeing healthy communication with them. In this context, the "Izmir Digital Inventory" study was ended by the Izmir Metropolitan Municipality. The project consisted of the compilation of Turkey's first digital tourism encyclopedia, which included information and visuals on more than two thousand tourism areas from various sorts of tourism (Izmir Metropolitan Municipality, 2021). The smart tourism project called as "Smart Tourism Route Project, Altın Rota" prepared by Ankara Altındağ Municipality and supported by the Union of Municipalities of Turkey has been actualized. This initiative contributed to the creation of a smartphone application known as a digital tourism guide, which enables local and international visitors to alternate travel routes based on their location (Sabah Gazetesi, 2021). In the study conducted by Çelik & Topsakal (2017) in the sample of Antalya, it has been found to be at the beginning stage in terms of customer-oriented smart city applications.

Customer Relationship Management in Terms of Tourism Businesses

In terms of tourism businesses, CRM strategies are deemed primary for productivity, recognition, brand loyalty, ensuring customer satisfaction. In this section, firstly, the CRM strategies and practices of tourism businesses operating in the tourism sector in Turkey will be discussed.

Turkish Airlines is a company with powerful brand value in the context of CRM applications in Turkey. From past to present, the organization has implemented a number of high - level processes in order to assure client satisfaction and loyalty. Turkish Airlines (THY) has implemented a feedback system that allows the opinions of the guests regarding their travel experiences in order for its customers to have a comfortable and safe travel experience. the feedback evaluation procedure was performed in a transparent manner to ensure customer satisfaction (THY, 2021a). In a study by Madak & Salepcioğlu (2020), the satisfaction and loyalty of THY customers were investigated. According to the results of the research, the passenger satisfaction level of THY was found to be high in general. In addition, customer satisfaction level was measured to be high in the dimensions such as quick responding and solution creation ability, effectiveness of loyalty memberships, adequacy against customer problems and demands, ease of use of web pages and associated memberships. THY's "Smile and Miles" customer loyalty system involves award ticket issuance, flight class upgrades, mile transfer, and mile upgrade alternatives (THY, 2021b). According to Sarıışık & Batman (2014), participants using "Smile and Miles" declared that they prefer rewards and services indicated most such as award tickets, excess baggage allowance and seat guarantee in reservation.

THY was deemed worthy of many awards, especially in customer relations, operational and technical services. Some of these awards are *"Best Corporate Loyalty Program Award" (2018), "Operational Excellence Award" (2009), "Most Creative Travel Kit Award" (2018), "Airline with Best Program for Passengers Award" (2020), "Europe's Best Design Airline Award" (2019), "Most Punctual Airline Award"* (THY,2021c).

Different approaches and practices within the domain of CRM are also advantageous to hotel businesses. Many of these are data-driven marketing initiatives. Some examples of applications in this category are following the customer's stay frequency, sending congratulatory messages on special days, and informing about services and campaigns (Baykal & Ayyıldız, 2020). Customer loyalty programs, which are found among the CRM applications in hotels, have been broadly used by organizations in a variety of industries in recent years. Through these supply programs, businesses attempt to stimulate their long-term sales and profitability by focusing on customer loyalty (Uca Özer, 2015). In a study conducted by Uca Özer (2015) in 5-star hotels in Istanbul, Hotels primarily offer reward programs such as prizes, vouchers, and price reductions, according to research. The results of another study on the subject indicate that customer loyalty programs implemented by hotels have little or no impact on consumers' purchasing preferences. The same research alleged that differentiated and personalized loyalty programs in line with customers' priorities offer hotel managers the potential to gain serious customers in the market (Deloitte Türkiye, 2021).

Online hotel reviews and website content are included in the customer relationship management strategy of the hotels and they are used to ensure customer satisfaction and improve the customer communication systems. Responding to customers' complaints about the hotel in online environments may have a favorable impact on business performance and customer relations. Plus, positive customer comments, complaints and how complaints are answered also influence the demands of potential customers (Gürbüz & Ormankıran, 2020). The hotels' evaluating online complaints and making positive efforts to improve them are measures of how noteworthy a company's brand reputation is to them (Güzel, 2014). A research was conducted to reveal the purposes for which boutique hotel businesses operating in Turkey use their social media accounts. It has been identified that boutique hotels generally use Facebook, they do not benefit from experts in managing these pages. Also, the number of businesses that supply online reservations via Facebook was found to be low (Eryılmaz & Zengin, 2016).

Akyazı (2018) researched the contents shared by Top 10 tour companies operating in Turkey with the highest number of likes and followers on their twitter, instagram and facebook accounts. It was discovered that all companies' performance in terms of tweets and followers remained at a relatively low level. Furthermore, no posts concerning hotel promotions were found on social media accounts, according to the findings. In another study, the website contents of Group A travel agencies operating in Antalya were evaluated and remarkable outcomes were obtained. 82.6% of the websites contain product features and 66.7% have product information. However, only the contact information of the institution and the customer feedback form were included in the customer support and services within the scope of CRM. According to the results of the study, it has been shown that websites were being used for more informational purposes than for sales and customer service (Kutlu, 2020).

Akkuş & Çalışkan (2020) evaluated the current situation of social customer relationship management strategies of tourism businesses operating in Kastamonu. According to the findings, tourism organizations have a poor understanding of the definition of social customer relationship management. Besides, there is no software and strategy implemented by businesses related to this issue, and they were partially interested in social media activities. According to the results of another research on CRM activities in thermal hotel businesses by Bozok et al. (2014), management of customer relations departments does not exist in thermal hotel businesses, and such activities are handled by the front desk and senior management. Aksatan &Aktaş (2004) analyzed the CRM activities of small hospitality businesses operating in İzmir's Alaçatı town, and as a result of the research, it has been found that businesses are aware of the necessity and benefits of CRM, and they place more emphasis on the service component of CRM rather than the technology-supported dimension. Türker & Özaltın (2010), analyzed the CRM strategies of hotels according to their types and sizes and concluded that city hotels place a higher value on CRM than coastal hotels, and CRM strategies differ based on the managers' perspectives, not the size of the company.

In the hotel industry in Turkey, there are CRM modules that collect guest information such as guest comments, guest surveys, dynamic guest requests, reservations, daily events in a single center. (Elektra Opex, 2021). Technological elements such as using guest data in CRM systems in the digitalization process, matching the information in multi-channel customer relations applications, guest surveys and loyalty programs with the comments made about the hotel on online platforms are figured out with the assistance of expert CRM software (Webius Digital Agency, 2021).

Suggestions for Future Research

It is claimed that a comprehensive literature review is necessary to determine what aspects should be included in CRM strategies executed by tourism organizations and what hotel managers think about CRM applications. On the other hand, research about CRM in Turkish tourism literature revolves mostly around the analysis of guest comments and e-complaint types. For future researchers, it is recommended research should be conducted on the CRM strategies implemented by travel agencies and food and beverage businesses. Eventually, the prominence of CRM strategies in terms of destination management and marketing and research in the context of integration of destination data and customer data in the case of Turkey may promote the holistic approach of the CRM strategy.

CONCLUSION

The digitalized world has brought with it the introduction of CRM, eCRM, and Social CRM methodologies that envision the gathering, evaluation, and personalization of customer data, in addition to the traditional marketing approach. With the development of social media platforms, businesses offer tailored technological products and services to their customers in order to boost their efficiency and profitability and employ CRM modules predicated on quick and effective resolution of customer requests and complaints. In the tourism industry, especially institutionalized companies implement CRM solutions and benefit from customer experiences.

The majority of CRM studies in Turkish tourism literature are oriented on the examination of guest comments and other sorts of e-complaints (Güzel, 2014). It is encouraged that integrated studies with CRM and destination marketing be conducted in this environment.

There are, however, companies that provide excellent services, such as Elektra Opex and Webiusdigital within the scope of CRM modules in the Turkish tourism industry, more organizations that can deliver CRM software applications are needed.

There have been some genuine issues even in tour companies that are in the top 10 in terms of company volume in Turkey regarding the indicators such as shares, total number of likes, comments, number of followers and people followed on social media accounts of travel agencies (Akyazı, 2018). In this context, it can be said that travel agencies should involve CRM software and applications, particularly social media management.

Consequently, it is necessary to expand applications that can consolidate information in the context of smart tourism and smart cities in Turkey, as well as customer information. It is suggested that especially Municipal governments ought to have a CRM strategy, and tourism businesses that seek to stand out should employ CRM modules that incorporate data from social media instead of traditional loyalty programs.

REFERENCES

Akkuş, G., & Çalışkan, G. (2020). Destinasyon pazarlama faaliyetleri kapsamında yürütülen sosyal müşteri ilişkileri yönetiminin rolünü tespite yönelik nitel bir araştırma. *Elektronik Sosyal Bilimler Dergisi, 19*(76), 1984–1998.

Aksatan, M., & Aktaş, G. (2012). Küçük konaklama işletmelerinde müşteri ilişkileri yönetimi: Alaçatı örneği. *Anatolia: Turizm Araştırmaları Dergisi, 23*(2), 233–247.

Akyazı, E. (2018). Kurumsal itibar oluşturma ortamı olarak sosyal medya: Tur şirketlerinin sosyal medya hesapları üzerine bir araştırma. *Journal of Tourism Theory and Research, 4*(2), 87–97. doi:10.24288/jttr.415480

Almotairi, M. A. (2009). *A framework for successful CRM implementation* [Paper presentation]. *European and Mediterranean Conference on Information Systems*, İzmir, Turkey.

Alokla, M., Alkhateeb, M., Abbad, M., & Jaber, F. (2019). Customer relationship management: A review and classification. *Transnational Marketing Journal, 7*(2), 187–210. doi:10.33182/tmj.v7i2.734

Barusman, A. R. P., & Rulian, E. P. (2020). Customer satisfaction and retention and its impact on tourism in hotel industry. *Utopía y Praxis Latinoamericana, 25*(1), 117–126. doi:10.5281/zenodo.3774581

Baykal, M., & Ayyıldız, A. Y. (2020). Veri tabanlı pazarlama faaliyetlerinin müşteri sadakatine etkisi: Kuşadası'ndaki 4 ve 5 yıldızlı otel yöneticileri üzerine bir uygulama. *Journal of Tourism and Gastronomy Studies, 8*(2), 1247–1268. doi:10.21325/jotags.2020.606

Bligh, P., & Turk, D. (2004). *CRM Unplugged: Releasing CRM's Strategic Value*. John Wiley & Sons.

Bose, R. (2002). Customer relationship management: Key components for IT success. *Industrial Management & Data Systems, 102*(2), 89–97. doi:10.1108/02635570210419636

Boulding, W., Staelin, R., Ehret, M., & Johnston, W. J. (2005). A customer relationship management roadmap: What is known, potential pitfalls, and where to go. *Journal of Marketing, 69*(4), 155–166. doi:10.1509/jmkg.2005.69.4.155

Bozok, D., & Güven, Ö. Z. (2014). Termal konaklama işletmelerinde müşteri ilişkileri yönetimi (crm) üzerine bir araştırma: Frigya bölgesi örneği. *Dumlupınar Üniversitesi Sosyal Bilimler Dergisi, 41*, 131–140.

Buttle, F. (2001). The CRM value chain. *Marketing Business, 96*(2), 52–55.

Çelik, P., & Topsakal, Y. (2017). Akıllı turizm destinasyonları: Antalya destinasyonunun akıllı turizm uygulamalarının incelenmesi. *Seyahat ve Otel İşletmeciliği Dergisi, 14*(3), 149–166. doi:10.24010oid.369951

Chalmeta, R. (2006). Methodology for customer relationship management. *Journal of Systems and Software, 79*(7), 1015–1024. doi:10.1016/j.jss.2005.10.018

Chen, I. J., & Popovich, K. (2003). Understanding customer relationship management (CRM): People processes and technology. *Business Process Management Journal, 9*(5), 672–688. doi:10.1108/14637150310496758

Cherapanukom, V., Yanchinda, J., & Sangkakom, K. (2021). *Antecedents of eCRM success for hotel industry* [Paper presentation]. Conference on Electrical, Electronics, Computer and Telecommunication Engineering (IEEE), Cha-am, Thailand. 10.1109/ECTIDAMTNCON51128.2021.9425751

Civelek, A. (2016). Konaklama işletmelerinde müşteri ilişkileri yönetiminin işletme performansına etkisi: 5 yıldızlı oteller üzerine bir uygulama. *Selçuk Üniversitesi Sosyal Bilimler Meslek Yüksek Okulu Dergisi, 19*(2), 233–253.

Crittenden, A. B., Crittenden, V. L., & Crittenden, W. F. (2019). The digitalization triumvirate: How incumbents survive. *Business Horizons, 62*(2), 259–266. doi:10.1016/j.bushor.2018.11.005

Deloitte Türkiye. (2021). *Otellerde müşteri sadakatinin güçlendirilmesi*. https://www2.deloitte.com/tr/tr/pages/consumer-business/articles/restoration-in-hotel-loyalty.html

Duran, M. (2002). *CRM hakkında CRM: çok konuşulan ama az bilinen bir kavram*. http://danismend.com/kategori/altkategori/crm-hakkinda/

Elektra Opex. (2021). *Müşteri ilişkileri yönetimi modülü.* https://www.otelcrm.net/crm-yonetimi.html#

Eryılmaz, B., & Zengin, B. (2014). Butik otel işletmelerinin sosyal medya kullanımına yönelik bir inceleme: Facebook örneği. *Kastamonu Üniversitesi İktisadi ve İdari Bilimler Fakültesi Dergisi, 4*(2), 42–59.

Fyall, A., Callod, C., & Edwards, B. (2003). Relationship marketing: The challenge for destinations. *Annals of Tourism Research, 30*(3), 644–659. doi:10.1016/S0160-7383(03)00046-X

Galyarski, E., & Mironova, N. (2021). Digitalization and its impact on business processes. *Economics and Management, 18*(1), 81–89.

Gamage, T. C., Gnanapala, A., & Ashill, N. J. (2021). Understanding social customer relationship management adoption: Qualitative insights. *Journal of Strategic Marketing*, 1–25. doi:10.1080/0965254X.2021.1923056

Gilbert, D., & Powell-Perry, J. (2003). Exploring developments in web based relationship marketing within the hotel industry. *Journal of Hospitality & Leisure Marketing, 10*(3-4), 5–24. doi:10.1300/J150v10n03_02

Gilbert, D. C. (1996). Relationship marketing and airline loyalty schemes. *Tourism Management, 17*(8), 575–582. doi:10.1016/S0261-5177(96)00078-7

Goel, V., Singh, A., & Shrivastava, S. (2015). CRM: A winning approach for tourism sector. *International Journal of Engineering and Management Research, 5*(2), 321–325.

GoTurkey. (2021). *Türkiye experiences.* https://goturkiye.com/

Greenberg, P. (2010). *CRM at the speed of light: Social CRM strategies, tools, and techniques* (4th ed.). McGraw-Hill.

Gürbüz, E., & Ormankıran, G. A. (2020). Müşterilerin otel işletmelerine yönelik yorum ve şikâyetlerinin değerlendirilmesi. *Journal of Applied Tourism Research, 1*(1), 17–32.

Güzel, F. Ö. (2014). Marka itibarını korumada şikâyet takibi: Çevrimiçi seyahat 2.0 bilgi kanallarında bir uygulama. *Journal of Internet Applications and Management, 5*(1), 5–19. doi:10.5505/iuyd.2014.07108

Happ, E., & Ivancsó-Horváth, Z. (2018). Digital tourism is the challenge of future – a new approach to tourism. *"Dimitrie Cantemir" Christian University Knowledge Horizons – Economics, 10*(2), 9-16.

Iriana, R., & Buttle, F. (2007). Strategic, operational, and analytical customer relationship management: Attributes and measures. *Journal of Relationship Marketing, 5*(4), 23–42. doi:10.1300/J366v05n04_03

İzmir Belediyesi. (2021). *İzmir'in dijital turizm envanteri tamamlandı.* https://www.izmir.bel.tr/tr/Haberler/izmir-in-dijital-turizm-envanteri-tamamlandi/44533/156

Kellen, V., & Stefanczyk, K. (2002). Complexity, fragmentation, uncertainty, and emergence in customer relationship management. *Emergence, 4*(4), 39–50. doi:10.1207/S15327000EM0404_5

Kelly, S. (2000). Analytical CRM: The fusion of data and intelligence. *Interactive Marketing, 1*(3), 262–267. doi:10.1057/palgrave.im.4340035

Kültür ve Turizm Bakanlığı. (2021). *Turizm istatistikleri (Türkiye)* [Data Sets]. https://yigm.ktb.gov.tr/ Eklenti/81939,3103turizmistatistikleri2020-4pdf.pdf?0

Kumar, V., & Reinartz, W. (2006). *Customer relationship management concept, strategy, and tools* (3rd ed.). Springer-Verlag.

Kutlu, D. (2020). Antalya A grubu seyahat acentalarının web sitelerinin değerlendirilmesi. *Akademik Araştırmalar ve Çalışmalar Dergisi, 12*(23), 407–418.

Madak, S. S., & Salepçioğlu, M. A. (2020). Türk sivil havacılık sektöründe yolcu memnuniyeti ve sadakat ilişkisi: Türk havayolları örnek çalışması. *İstanbul Ticaret Üniversitesi Sosyal Bilimler Dergisi, 19*(37), 569-592.

Mohammed, A. A., & Rashid, B. (2012). Customer relationship management (CRM) in hotel industry: A framework proposal on the relationship among CRM dimensions, marketing capabilities, and hotel performance. *International Review of Management and Marketing, 2*(4), 220–230.

Mohammed, A. A., Rashid, B., & Tahir, S. (2014). Customer relationship management (CRM) technology and organization performance: Is marketing capability a missing link? An empirical study in the Malaysian hotel industry. *Asian Social Science, 10*(9), 197–212. doi:10.5539/ass.v10n9p197

Moudud-Ul-Huq, S., Akter, R., Mahmud, M. S., & Hasan, N. (2021). Impact of Customer Relationship Management on Tourist Satisfaction, Loyalty, and Retention: Saint Martin's Island. *International Journal of Customer Relationship Marketing and Management, 12*(3), 20–37. doi:10.4018/IJCRMM.2021070102

Murdy, S., & Pike, S. (2012). Perceptions of visitor relationship marketing opportunities by destination marketers: An importance-performance analysis. *Tourism Management, 33*(5), 1281–1285. doi:10.1016/j. tourman.2011.11.024

Ngai, E. W. T. (2005). Customer relationship management research (1992–2002): An academic literature review and classification. *Marketing Intelligence & Planning, 23*(6), 582–605. doi:10.1108/02634500510624147

Ngo, M. V., Pavelkova, D., Phan, Q. P. T., & Nguyen, N. V. (2018). Customer relationship management (CRM) in small and medium tourism enterprises: A dynamic capabilities perspective. *Tourism and Hospitality Management, 24*(1), 63–86. doi:10.20867/thm.24.1.11

Özer, S. U. (2015). İstanbul'da faaliyet gösteren beş yıldızlı otel işletmelerinin müşteri sadakat programlarının içerik analizi. *Ekonomi ve Yönetim Araştırmaları Dergisi, 4*(1), 134–157.

Paas, L., & Kuijlen, T. (2001). Towards a general definition of customer relationship management. *Journal of Database Marketing & Customer Strategy Management, 9*(1), 51–60. doi:10.1057/palgrave. jdm.3240058

Parvatiyar, A., & Sheth, J. N. (2000). Conceptual framework of customer relationship management. In *Proceedings of International Conference on Customer Relationship Management*. Management Development Institute Press.

Parviainen, P., Tihinen, M., Kääriäinen, J., & Teppola, S. (2017). Tackling the digitalization challenge: How to benefit from digitalization in practice. *International Journal of İnformation Systems and Project Management, 5*(1), 63–77. doi:10.12821/ijispm050104

Payne, A., & Frow, P. (2005). A strategic framework for customer relationship management. *Journal of Marketing, 69*(4), 167–176. doi:10.1509/jmkg.2005.69.4.167

Rahimi, R., Köseoglu, M. A., Ersoy, A. B., & Okumus, F. (2017). Customer relationship management research in tourism and hospitality: A state-of-the-art. *Tourism Review, 72*(2), 209–220. doi:10.1108/TR-01-2017-0011

Rahimi, R., & Kozak, M. (2017). Impact of customer relationship management on customer satisfaction: The case of a budget hotel chain. *Journal of Travel & Tourism Marketing, 34*(1), 40–51. doi:10.1080/10548408.2015.1130108

Rahimi, R., Nadda, V., & Wang, H. (2015). CRM in tourism: Customer relationship management (CRM). In R. Nilanjan (Ed.), *Emerging innovative marketing strategies in the tourism industry* (pp. 16–43). IGI Global. doi:10.4018/978-1-4666-8699-1.ch002

Reichstein, C., & Härting, R. (2018). Potantials of changing customer needs in a digital world – a conceptual model and recommendations for action in tourism. *Procedia Computer Science, 126*, 1484–1494. doi:10.1016/j.procs.2018.08.120

Rigby, D. K., Reichheld, F. F., & Schefter, P. (2002). Avoid the four perils of CRM. *Harvard Business Review, 80*(2), 101–109. PMID:11894676

Ryals, L. (2005). Making customer relationship management work: The measurement and profitable management of customer relationships. *Journal of Marketing, 69*(4), 252–261. doi:10.1509/jmkg.2005.69.4.252

Ryals, L., & Knox, S. (2001). Cross-functional issues in the implementation of relationship marketing through customer relationship management. *European Management Journal, 19*(5), 534–542. doi:10.1016/S0263-2373(01)00067-6

Sabah Gazetesi. (2021). *Başkentin ilk dijital turizm rehberi.* https://www.sabah.com.tr/ankara/2021/05/05/baskentin-ilk-dijital-turizm-rehberi

Sarışık & Batman. (2014). *Sık uçan yolcu programlarının müşteri sadakati üzerindeki etkisi: Thy miles&smiles uygulaması ve kullanıcıları örneği. In Uluslararası Türk Dünyası Sosyal Bilimler Kongresi.* Türk Dünyası Araştırmaları Vakfı Yayınları.

Schierholz, R., Kolbe, L. M., & Brenner, W. (2007). Mobilizing customer relationship management: A journey from strategy to system design. *Business Process Management Journal, 13*(6), 830–852. doi:10.1108/14637150710834587

Shehab, E. M., Sharp, M. W., Supramaniam, L., & Spedding, T. A. (2004). Enterprise resource planning: An integrative review. *Business Process Management Journal, 10*(4), 359–386. doi:10.1108/14637150410548056

Soltani, Z., Zareie, B., Milani, F. S., & Navimipour, N. J. (2018). The impact of the customer relationship management on the organization performance. *The Journal of High Technology Management Research, 29*(2), 237–246. doi:10.1016/j.hitech.2018.10.001

Srinivasan, R., & Moorman, C. (2005). Strategic firm commitments and rewards for customer relationship management in online retailing. *Journal of Marketing, 69*(4), 193–200. doi:10.1509/jmkg.2005.69.4.193

Swift, R. S. (2001). *Accelerating customer relationships: Using CRM and relationship technologies.* Prentice Hall Professional.

Swimberghe, K. R., & Wooldridge, B. R. (2014). Drivers of customer relationships in quick-service restaurants: The role of corporate social responsibility. *Cornell Hospitality Quarterly, 55*(4), 354–364. doi:10.1177/1938965513519008

Türk Hava Yolları (THY). (2021a). *Geri bildirim değerlendirme süreci.* https://www.turkishairlines.com/tr-int/bilgi-edin/musteri-iliskileri/geribildirim-degerlendirme-sureci/

Türk Hava Yolları (THY). (2021b). *Smile&miles müşteri sadakat programı içeriği.* https://www.turkishairlines.com/tr-int/miles-and-smiles/program-icerigi/

Türk Hava Yolları (THY). (2021c). *Ödüller.* https://www.turkishairlines.com/tr-int/basin-odasi/oduller/

Türker, A., & Özaltın, G. (2010). Konaklama işletmelerinde müşteri ilişkileri yönetimi: İzmir ili örneği. *Muğla Üniversitesi Sosyal Bilimler Enstitüsü Dergisi, 25*, 81–104.

Türkiye Turizm Tanıtım ve Geliştirme Ajansı (TGA). (2021). *Hakkında.* https://tga.gov.tr/hakkinda/

TÜRSAB, TBV, & ED Türkiye. (2019). *Turizm sektörü dijitalleşme yol haritası.* EY Türkiye Publishing.

TÜRSAB. (2021). *Turist sayısı ve turizm geliri (Türkiye)* [Data Sets]. https://www.tursab.org.tr/istatistikler/turist-sayisi-ve-turizm-geliri

Vogt, C. A. (2011). Customer relationship management in tourism: Management needs and research applications. *Journal of Travel Research, 50*(4), 356–364. doi:10.1177/0047287510368140

Webius Digital Agency. (2021). *CRM sistemlerinde misafir yorumlarının önemi.* https://webiusdigital.com/crm-misafir-yorumlarinin-onemi/

Winer, R. S. (2001). A framework for customer relationship management. *California Management Review, 43*(4), 89–105. doi:10.2307/41166102

Xu, M., & Walton, J. (2005). Gaining customer knowledge through analytical CRM. *Industrial Management & Data Systems, 105*(7), 955–972. doi:10.1108/02635570510616139

KEY TERMS AND DEFINITIONS

CRM in Destinations: Customer-friendly tourism solutions and applications that include flexible and personalized products and services and are compatible with digitalization processes in order to establish a long-term sustainable relationship with all stakeholders in the destinations.

CRM in Tourism Businesses: Applications containing personalized products and services compatible with digitalization developed by tourism enterprises in order to ensure efficiency, recognition, brand loyalty and profitability.

eCRM: İnternet-based techniques that focus on solving customer's requests and needs.

Social CRM: It is an approach that aims to gain the trust of customers by using social media tools and includes collaboration and experience sharing with all stakeholders in digital media.

Chapter 11
Digital Marketing as a Driver of Tourism:
Case Study in Paraty, Rio de Janeiro, Brazil

Gabriel Vieira Mendes Figueiredo
Pontifícia Universidade Católica de São Paulo, Brazil

João Pinheiro de Barros Neto
 https://orcid.org/0000-0002-5680-6658
Pontifícia Universidade Católica de São Paulo, Brazil

ABSTRACT

Brazil has enormous, underexplored tourism potential. To identify how digital marketing can boost tourism, the authors chose to examine the city of Paraty—a touristic microcosm of Brazil. Digital marketing is a low-cost marketing strategy that can reach potential tourists anywhere. Its use by tourism entrepreneurs has proven effective and able to generate significant return on investment. This exploratory study aimed to develop hypotheses. The authors used questionnaires and interviews to assess the perception of local tourism entrepreneurs regarding the affordances and advantages of digital marketing tools, techniques, and strategies. They found that entrepreneurs' adoption of digital marketing brought several benefits, including low investment costs and significant returns. However, the research revealed the need for training, mainly for small entrepreneurs to explore the numerous opportunities of the web in their businesses. Public authorities can also play a more leading role in combining and steering efforts to promote tourism.

INTRODUCTION

The tourism industry was one of the most impacted by the crisis triggered by the coronavirus, as social isolation was very cruel to the sector. Faced with such a delicate scenario, challenges were imposed, and companies had to adopt all kinds of strategies, many of them in the virtual world. Others, however, went even further, and began to offer a brand-new experience more suited to times of social distance. A

DOI: 10.4018/978-1-7998-8306-7.ch011

famous example was given by the Canadian Museum of Human Rights (https://humanrights.ca/), which now offers the experience "Explore the Museum from Home".

Through videos lasting 5 to 20 minutes, guided by collaborators, it is possible to discover the space and attractions as if it were a face-to-face visit.

However, in Brazil the situation was much worse because Brazilian tourism is mainly based on its natural beauty, a type of tourism that needs to be experienced. In addition, digitalization is reaching the main sectors of the Brazilian economy and tourism has not yet strongly adopted digital marketing strategies, much less opened up to the possibilities of hyper-personalization.

In this context, this chapter explores the affordances of digital marketing strategies to help increase the income of small and medium-sized tourism entrepreneurs in Paraty, in the state of Rio de Janeiro, Brazil.

Paraty is a famous tourist destination in Brazil due to its historical and cultural heritage, including colonial churches and buildings. In July 2019, Paraty was added to the UNESCO World Heritage List.

However, Paraty's immense tourism potential is still underexplored, given the lack of structured actions to promote tourism in a systematic fashion. Even the city's official website (http://www.paraty.com.br/) is a private initiative of a company based in São Paulo.

According to the World Tourism Organization (UNTWO, 2019), Brazil receives only around six million foreign visitors per year, ranking low in the list of top 50 destinations in the world.

No transparent information has been published in Paraty about the amount invested to leverage tourism through marketing. The local tourism department has not conducted any recent observation efforts, and we have seen a lack of professionalization in the industry. Because of this, online advertising for tourism has paled compared to what the city has to offer.

Based on social media and in-person visits to the city, our perception is that only the largest agencies have been engaged in digital marketing. Many locals and small business owners who live off tourism still lack an online presence and largely depend on the high season and word-of-mouth advertising to earn their income.

Thus, entrepreneurs need to act to promote their tourism businesses in a cheap but effective way. Social media and social networks, if well used, can have promising effects—not only for entrepreneurs themselves, but also for the city as a whole and nearby municipalities.

Considering the city's immense but underutilized tourism potential, this study explores whether small and medium-sized entrepreneurs could use digital marketing strategies to boost tourism and increase their income.

BACKGROUND

Digital Marketing

Marketing has evolved from product-driven (1.0 companies were focused on production and its portfolio; there was no glaring concern with brand building, market segmentation and personalization), to consumer-centric (2.0 market segmentation emerges with the objective of delimiting groups with common interests, and based on this filter, the proposal was to understand their concerns and propose customized solutions) to human-centric (3.0). In marketing 3.0, products, services, and business cultures ought to adopt and reflect human values to be successful. Such evolution happens to win the minds and hearts of consumers (Kotler, 2021).

The advancement of information and communication technologies (ICTs) and the accessibility to the web have created new possibilities for the development and growth of digital marketing. Today, digital marketing is a cornerstone of any marketing plan, used by successful companies to expand their reach and achieve desirable results (Gupta, 2018).

Currently, the complexities of using information technology in the tourism industry are already significant, with various applications throughout its production chain, including airlines, travel intermediaries, accommodation, food services, destinations, attractions, events, and entertainment. Tourists themselves are using technologies to support decision-making before the trip, during the trip, and at the destination (Benckendorff, Xiang & Sheldon, 2019).

Digital marketing currently involves using web technologies to reach and interact with existing and new audiences (Gabriel, Kiso, 2020). It has revolutionized all industries and changed the way companies reach customers.

The main difference between traditional and digital marketing is the latter's ability to monitor and track data on customer behavior, reactions, and preferences, as well as to verify the performance of digital marketing campaigns in real time.

Important transformations have been underway in the transition from traditional marketing to marketing 4.0, i.e., digital marketing. Society as a whole has changed due to connectivity. To succeed, entrepreneurs must now use the internet to leverage a new set of marketing metrics and practices, beginning with brand presentation and assimilation and culminating in full customer loyalty (Kotler, Kartajaya & Setiawan, 2017).

The latest development—marketing 5.0—will enable us to use technology to meet the needs of customers whose behavior has become more conscious. Social and environmental concerns have recently been forcing marketers to use artificial intelligence for marketing automation, agile marketing, and market segmentation. Marketing based on things like contextual technology, facial recognition, voice technology, virtual and augmented reality, Internet of Things (IoT), and blockchain will likely change the future of customer experience (Kotler, Kartajaya & Setiawan, 2021).

This study focuses on marketing 4.0—digital marketing—since marketing 5.0 is still incipient and out of reach for small and medium-sized Brazilian tourism entrepreneurs.

Digital Marketing and Tourism

In the tourism industry, the paradigm shift between traditional and digital marketing took place a few years ago and transformed the way companies reach actual and potential customers. To succeed digitally, tour operators now need to base their digital marketing campaigns on the quality of five strategies: Search Engine Optimization (SEO), email marketing, social media presence, content, and mobile device compatibility, which plays a crucial role (Kaur, 2017).

New technologies can contribute substantially to the development of tourism. The internet, for example, can make booking information and resources available to large numbers of tourists at relatively low costs. The web is also a communication tool between tourism providers, intermediaries, and tourists themselves. Tourist products and destinations are better advertised on the internet than on traditional media, such as old brochures and catalogs. ICTs allow direct, interactive relationships between tourism organizations and tourists. In terms of marketing, companies can build customer profiles and make personalized offers (Hojeghan & Esfangareh, 2011) .

The diffusion of digital channels, driven by the rapid development of ICTs, has bridged physical distances and deeply changed how people research, communicate, and shop. Companies have diversified their ways of interacting with customers and doing business. Several studies have shown the importance of exploring the dimension of persuasion, conversion, loyalty, and bonding of these new digital marketing tools (Magano & Cunha, 2020).

Although digital marketing is still developing, multiple studies have related it to tourism. Indeed, the digital revolution has brought new opportunities and posed threats to all businesses, including the tourism industry. Innovations involve cloud-based booking websites, information and experience sharing through digital platforms, and special offers designed to serve tourists in a personalized fashion. Thanks to globalization, the tourism market has gained access to detailed information about its customers and can closely monitor tourist behavior (Zsarnoczky, 2018, p. 1).

Digital media are key in promoting tourism, and increased tourist spending in turn boosts local residents' income. Increased tourist spending triggers a chain reaction: by looping through each cycle, it eventually disappears, but it produces a significant change in income (Watkins, Ziyadin, Imatayeva, Kurmangalieva, & Blembayeva, 2018).

Through digital marketing, tour operators can grant tourists immediate access to information, pictures, and videos of destinations, highlighting the qualities of tour packages through visual appeal and influencing customers' choice of destination. Decolar (www.decolar.com), for example, offers several packages and trips with easy payment and final value with taxes included and makes price comparisons for the customer.

Tourism companies promote their brand and reach potential customers by providing the best travel deals through various digital technologies, thus shaping the entire tourism industry. For example, CVC (www.cvc.com.br) is one of the most popular travel agencies in Brazil and offers flights and accommodation to various national and international destinations, in addition to several travel packages.

Digital marketing offers opportunities in terms of social media marketing, content marketing, mobile marketing (driven by people's access to the internet and mobile devices), and paid advertising, such as Facebook. This implies that digital marketing can reach individuals anywhere through creative content and targeted ads, helping increase the inflow of international tourists (Mkwizu, 2020).

Social media marketing—merely one among many avenues in digital marketing—requires understanding the social dynamics of the internet as a vast, extremely diverse, democratic space. It also requires adjusting marketing strategies and tactics to leverage the endless technological capabilities, cultures, and opportunities for interaction that have arisen in various media (Gretzel & Yoo, 2013).

Social media marketing campaigns are often perceived as cheap. However, if they are not carefully planned and executed, companies might miss the opportunity to engage tourist consumers more deeply and authentically, in far greater numbers and more consistently than through traditional media.

Social media marketing should not be used merely because it is cheaper and can be learned and executed in an autodidactic way. An amateur handling of the enormous potential of social media can be a costly mistake. Precisely because of its advantages, social media marketing must be thought through and used seriously and professionally.

Consumer expectations have been increasingly high in social media, and negative feedback can spread quickly. Social media marketing is a dynamic field, as new technologies and advertising models constantly emerge. This means that the social media landscape continues to change and that social media marketing strategies must be continually adjusted to new, often fleeting realities.

The pandemic forced companies to reinvent opportunities and thus find the most diverse applications for digital marketing: inbound marketing (techniques to gain the interest of an audience through the development and sharing of content, aiming to connect with people in a direct way and creating a lasting relationship); mobile marketing (specific actions to impact mobile device users, whether they are cell phones, tablets, notebooks, smart watches, GPS connected to the car); content marketing (to engage and engage users to connect with the product or service without necessarily trying the solution); social media marketing (Instagram, WhatsApp and Facebook), among others, because the universe of digital marketing literally has no more limits (Larrossa, 2021).

These various modalities of digital marketing allow tour operators to think about how to deliver more value and better experiences for a richer and more profitable trip for tourists. The smartphone is an indispensable travel companion for all tourists and during a trip it has proved to be an excellent tool to look for directions, find restaurants, read tips, and book hotels. In short, digital marketing not only sells, but it also makes life easier for tourists.

Indeed, digitization appears in all walks of life. Digital tourism represents a paradigm shift due to the emergence of digital marketing tools and techniques, which can help local companies—and destinations more broadly—become more competitive in the tourism market (Happ & Ivancsó-Horváth, 2018, p. 15).

Tourism in Brazil: Opportunities and Limitations

By defining tourism as the act of moving to discover the new, we can allude to the nomadic origin of humans. Moving is inherent to our species, and we owe much to our ancestors' explorations. According to Ito (2008, p.124), "driven by economic factors, ancient peoples embarked on exploratory journeys to conquer lands and riches", which parallels the so-called adventure tourism.

Amaral Junior (2008) wrote that, soon after being built around 2700 B.C., the Egyptian pyramids already attracted religious—or simply curious—visitors, a primitive form of what we now call tourism.

Internal and external tourism relate tourists' place of origin and destination. When a tourist comes from abroad, the welcoming country is referred to as the host (Hudson & Hudson, 2020).

Tourism is crucial for host countries, given the economic flow it sparks. However, Rabahy (2020) noted that, in 2019, Brazil welcomed only 0.47% of international tourists. That is a meager number, especially if we consider Brazil's continental dimensions and compare it against other destinations, such as Europe (which welcomes 51% of tourists), Asia and the Pacific (24%), and North America (10%).

In any industry, stimulating entrepreneurs represents an effective alternative to ensure better living conditions for people and boost the national economy. Each enterprise creates new jobs and opportunities for those who have trouble finding work—from the youngest seeking their first job to elders who wish or need to continue working (Barros Neto, 2018, p. 144).

Brazil, like Paraty, offers countless tourist options: religious, cultural, historical, and adventure tourism, ecotourism, beaches, and forests, among others. Paraty represents a microcosm of Brazil, whose enormous tourism potential is largely underexplored. The causes of this underutilization, however, are not addressed in this study. We focus on development opportunities through digital marketing strategies for tourism entrepreneurs.

Digital Marketing Tools and Strategies

Marketing is broadly understood as any and all actions generated in the market with at least one objective. As an organizational function, marketing is a "set of processes that involve creating, communicating, and delivering value to customers, such as customer relations and management, to benefit the organization and its audience" (Kotler & Keller, 2006).

Starting in the 1990s, the consolidation of the internet and the emergence of e-commerce revolutionized businesses. Computers became less complex and were integrated into business and domestic life, which facilitated managing and interacting with thousands of online customers. Considering this complex, disputed, and difficult market created by numerous societal changes, developing a clear, integrated strategy for business, branding, marketing, and communication is pivotal (Ranpersad, Souza, & Nunes, 2012, p. 180).

With the COVID-19 pandemic, many services went fully online, from the first commercial contact to delivery—as in the case of banks. However, although virtual tourism exists, tourism still largely relies on in-person visits.

This is where digital marketing comes in, as a "set of communication actions carried out through the web, such as through mobile phones, tablets, and laptops, to advertise and sell products and services quickly and effectively" (Assad, 2016, p. 29).

Digital marketing has actually become an umbrella term for all advertising or promotion strategies and actions that operate through media and web channels, including websites, blogs, social media, video platforms, and forums.

Considering digital marketing as a system within a set of strategies, tools, and actions, we must identify some of its key concepts.

Branding goes far beyond a logo, a name, and a slogan. As a core element of a company's relations with customers, branding "represents the perceptions and feelings of consumers regarding a product and its performance, including what the product or service means to consumers" (Kotler & Armstrong, 2007, p. 210).

In this sense, creating a structured branding process is vital for a brand to consolidate in the market and bond with the public, building emotion and connection. Branding actions are critical if the product or service is to meet customer expectations.

SEO is a linchpin in digital marketing strategy, as it constitutes an "aggregate of all the work necessary to produce a great volume of successful references from search engines, web directories, and other websites, with the ultimate goal of popularizing a website" (Jerkovic, 2010, p. 20). In other words, SEO aims to popularize a website in search engines.

In addition, using stories to convey messages and feedback allows the intended strategy to be better understood through narratives. Stories bring to light valuable contributions experienced in work processes (Knaflic, 2019).

Brands have increasingly used storytelling to captivate their target audience, as organizations expect a level of consumption and acknowledge the need to influence customers' thoughts.

The use of storytelling has become common in several areas, for example, Itaú (https://www.itau.com.br), a large Brazilian bank, has been adopting storytelling with the intention of showing the company as a "friend" of the customer, not a traditional financial institution. In its campaign, Itaú told the story of the character Hilário (https://vimeo.com/31776366), someone struggling to save money. The bank used Hilário's story to give tips on budget-conscious use and engage the customer with its brand.

In tourism, storytelling is even stronger, as every tourist place has stories to tell, and in every trip, there are situations that can turn into memorable stories. Furthermore, stories can be told by residents, tourists, or tourism agents. These are stories with a lot of potential to promote tourist destinations, because in fact, storytelling has the power to inform, persuade, move, and promote support and initiatives in society (Manosso, Ruiz & Nakatani, 2020).

Understanding the concepts of organic and paid traffic is also crucial for planning digital marketing strategies focused on increasing engagement and in-person visiting, among other goals. Traffic refers to internet users who can visit the company's website or its social media, or simply view content of interest.

Organic traffic has no immediate cost: organic visitors reach the business website through search engines. Because of this, businesses must invest in content marketing strategies by producing optimized content that helps people find the company online more easily.

In paid traffic, businesses must pay for visitors to get to the company's website. They do so by purchasing ads containing keywords with links to the company's website. Thus, investing in paid media can boost website visits and sales.

Whether organic or paid, traffic strategies are key to boost the enterprise in the market, thus increasing traffic and the likelihood of sales.

Copywriting is a content production strategy aimed at convincing the reader to perform a specific action. It is a persuasive text that uses triggers to arouse interest and generate sales (Ferreira, 2018).

Seeing copywriting as a strategy is vital for business success because good writing turns contact with the audience into action and builds relationships.

Social media have become part of the lives of billions worldwide, so the impact of these networks on business is immense. Social media presence has become an indispensable digital marketing strategy.

In social media, people register personal data and use their profiles to relate to others, publish, and communicate. Companies also create profiles to gain access to users and connect with customers and potential customers to grow their businesses.

It is therefore critical for tourism organizations to invest in digital marketing and use strategies to attract customers—including foreigners—and increase revenues.

METHODS

Paraty, a coastal city in Rio de Janeiro, Brazil, is 236 km away from the state capital. With around 38,000 inhabitants, the city is a nationally famous tourist destination (Gaspar & Gaspar, 2021).

Paraty had its heyday during the Brazilian colonial period under the rule of Portugal (from 1530 to 1822). It was a key port of export of gold coming from the state of Minas Gerais. As the gold trade ended, Paraty faced decline and isolation. However, locals thank the city's loss of relevance for the preservation of its customs and traditions—which rendered Paraty a prominent tourist destination.

Since the 18th century, Paraty has also been known for the artisanal production of pinga (a typical Brazilian sugarcane liquor). Apart from having a rich historical heritage of sacred art and churches, the city is famous for its uneven streets and well-preserved 18th to 19th-century architecture, which we observed during our visit to the city.

We chose Paraty for this exploratory study because it represents a microcosm of the Brazilian tourist landscape and because of our ease of access to the city. We came from São Paulo, 330 km away.

Data were collected on-site through questionnaires and interviews. Collection was conducted between September 4 and September 9, 2020, by one of the researchers. This researcher travelled to Paraty after five months of lockdown due to the COVID-19 pandemic.

This researcher's on-site observations were also used to build this chapter. Observation is widely used in the social sciences as "a data collection technique that obtains information by using the senses to grasp certain aspects of reality" (Diehl & Tatim, 2012).

As a research technique, observation allows us to collect data on behaviors and attitudes and obtain information not included in interview scripts and questionnaires.

Because our on-site research took place shortly after the reopening of trade and tourism, information collection was somewhat difficult. Businesses were undergoing an adaptation phase, and entrepreneurs were busy adjusting to the new protocols.

On the positive side, we were able to observe the shortcomings and weaknesses of the local tourism industry. This was useful for our conclusions and recommendations.

Quantitative Research

In our visit to Paraty, questionnaires were distributed to tourism-related establishments. Two days later, as agreed, we returned to those businesses to collect the forms. Eighteen valid answers were obtained, 10 of them from women and 8 from men. Table 1 shows respondents' ages.

Table 1. Age group of respondents

Age	18–22	23–27	28–32	33–37	38–42	43–47	48–52
Respondents	5.6%	5.6%	11.1%	16.7%	38.9%	16.7%	5.6%

Source: (Research, 2020).

While staying in Paraty, our researcher noticed that boat tours were an extremely competitive business, as tourists could choose from countless boats online or on-site at the city pier, near the historic center.

Among the digital channels used by entrepreneurs to communicate with the audience, Instagram stood out: 100% of respondents used it. Facebook was just behind (89%), followed by the businesses' own websites (78%), and finally by WhatsApp (only 6%).

This showcases the importance of a good communication and social media management strategy, especially concerning Instagram and Facebook. In addition to sharing invaluable assets for companies, such as public attention and consumer data, these platforms are communication channels for creating and maintaining consumer-brand relationships.

The digital marketing strategy most used by respondents was social media management and content production (83% adherence).

Another highlight was the use of each business own website (61% adherence). Besides being an excellent source of traffic and revenue, the business website is an alternative to intermediaries, such as Booking.com. This is something to be analyzed carefully by entrepreneurs, as it can be a great strategy for reducing costs, avoiding intermediary fees, generating revenue, and obtaining valuable data about users browsing on the website.

Table 2. Digital marketing strategies used by respondents

Strategy	All Options	Branding	Storytelling	Google Ads	Facebook Ads	Social Media
Percent	6%	22%	28%	50%	50%	83%

Source: (Research, 2020).

Only 6% said they use or have used all strategies at some point, which suggests that these organizations have not yet reached maturity when it comes to integrating digital marketing strategies.

We also sought to understand whether entrepreneurs were developing digital marketing internally, by themselves, or choosing to hire specialized services. A total of 72.20% reported having hired professional services related to digital marketing (i.e., support by consultants, digital agencies, or specialists), while 27.80% denied having used any such service.

We also asked about the existence of company employees responsible for both designing and executing digital marketing strategies. While 61.1% of entrepreneurs reported having at least one such employee, 38.9% reported having none.

Table 3 shows businesses' investments in digital marketing. These findings suggest companies pay little attention to the matter, even by Brazilian standards.

Table 3. Investments in digital marketing (in Brazilian reais)

Amount (BRL)	<500	501–2000	2001–3000	>3000	No investment ever made
Respondents	22.2%	22.2%	27.8%	5.6%	22.2%

Source: (Research, 2020); (USD 1.00 = BRL 5.497 as of April 24, 20211).

All 14 respondents (77.8%) who invested in digital marketing said they obtained a positive return that made the expense worthwhile.

Of those 14, 46.1% reported a return on investment above 50%, as shown in Table 4. This result is significant, indicating that leveraging digital marketing helped increase the income of entrepreneurs.

Table 4. Return on investment in digital marketing

Return	1%–10%	11%–20%	21%–30%	31%–40%	41%–50%	>50%
Respondents	15.4%	15.4%	7.7%	7.7%	7.7%	46.1%

Source: (Research, 2020).

Table 5 shows that digital marketing also positively affected the number of tourists. A total of 35.7% of respondents who invested in digital marketing strategies and tools reported a 21%–30% customer growth, and 64.30% saw a 21%–40% growth.

Table 5. Customer growth after investments in digital marketing

Growth	1%–10%	11%–20%	21%–30%	31%–40%	41%–50%	>50%
Respondents	14.3%	7.1%	35.7%	28.6%	7.1%	7.2%

Source: (Research, 2020).

In addition to the 18 questionnaires, three interviews were conducted with local entrepreneurs willing to contribute to the research.

Interviews

The first interviewee had been working in the tourism industry since 2013. On weekends and holidays, he offered his boat, with passenger capacity up to eight people, for rent on the Paraty Mirim beach. The interviewee considered himself an entrepreneur because he had "fought hard" to conquer his principal asset—the boat. He offered customized tours and predefined itineraries through the city's main beaches and islands.

However, for the interviewee, boat tours merely represented supplemental income. He largely earned his living from construction, and he did not advertise his services in any way.

Because he was unaware of any digital marketing strategy, his business had limited growth, solely relying on tourist flow and word-of-mouth among beach visitors.

The second interviewee had been an inn administrator for six years. The inn was considered large by local standards. She performed different functions in the company, from managing teams to developing and executing digital marketing strategies. She claimed to take on the burden of such functions due the lack of service providers who actually understood digital marketing and said she felt uncomfortable outsourcing the company's marketing.

The interviewee had been using several digital marketing strategies for three years. Her strategies included the use of Booking.com (an intermediary). To avoid dependence on this platform, she studied digital marketing on her own by watching YouTube videos.

She learned how to build a website through Wix.com and adopted paid traffic strategies via Facebook Ads and Google Ads. With the help of a co-worker, a journalism major, she began using copywriting to develop ads and content for the business website and social media.

The marketing strategies they used to leverage sales revolved around branding, content creation, social media management, SEO, and paid traffic.

The inn also offered receptive tourism, focusing on customers coming from countries such as England, the Netherlands, and Germany. The inn used digital marketing strategies, mainly paid ads, to reach such audience.

According to the interviewee, the company exceeded its goal by 300% thanks to digital marketing. This encouraged her to increasingly invest in this type of strategy, using partnerships with influencers, livestreams, and data-driven decision-making to offer tourists a full experience.

The third interviewee had been engaged in tourism in Paraty for about 30 years. Owner of a large receptive tourism agency, he had his own fleet of vehicles and vessels and over 100 employees.

He reported having three full-time employees dedicated to developing and executing the company's marketing strategies. He hired a consultant to map opportunities for improvement, such as changes to the website for SEO purposes and upgrades in branding strategy for deeper, data-driven customer understanding.

Besides using e-commerce to sell tour packages and tickets, the interviewee said he manages social media—like Instagram, Facebook, and Pinterest—and uses paid Google Ads and Facebook Ads to reach audiences abroad.

He deemed digital marketing crucial to the success of his company but stressed that the support of the operation itself and customer service as a whole were decisive as well. In fact, he noted that without good service, investing in marketing could be a trap, as constant customer ratings of the company would be made public. Seeking a full customer experience has thus become increasingly important.

Both quantitative data and qualitative interviews emphasized the importance of adopting digital marketing tools and strategies for the development of businesses, especially small enterprises.

Observations

Our stay in Paraty revealed the impact of the COVID-19 pandemic in some of the tourist establishments. Most businesses shut down on March 19, 2020 and did not reopen until August 9, 2020— a five-month interruption. When they reopened, businesses had to work at 50% of their capacity. According to entrepreneurs, this severely hampered cash flow management.

Another pandemic-related obstacle was having to deal with a reduced product inventory, mainly cleaning and food items for tourists. This is because uncertainty around the number of tourists visiting the city post-lockdown made it impossible to purchase larger volumes of products. Consequently, bargaining power was reduced and variable costs increased.

We also noticed that reopening businesses required investments: the purchase of personal protective equipment and other items was mandatory due to sanitary protocols, and communication expenses were needed to let customers know they were welcome again.

After the lifting of restrictions in Paraty, a feeling of suppressed demand emerged in the tourism industry: businesses that used digital marketing saw the demand for lodging increase substantially on weekends, while weekdays remained weak. Room occupancy averaged 28% on weekdays and 50% on weekends. Such numbers can be considered excellent, since the maximum occupancy as per the protocols was 50%.

The Municipal Tourism Department of Paraty has not carried out observations to record how many inns, hotels, tourism agencies, self-employed workers, or other tourist businesses exist in the city.

Paraty also lacks a press office to publish good news that attract tourists. Bad news, in contrast, are not properly controlled and responded. The State Tourism Department of Rio de Janeiro has promoted no campaigns aimed at tourism.

Despite being a key industry—accounting for a significant share of the local economy— tourism is evidently underappreciated in Paraty. As a result, a group of entrepreneurs has come together and organized to play many of the typical roles of tourism promotion, normally performed by public authorities. The group has conducted research, actions, and protocol development to help boost the industry in Paraty. However, they have not adopted digital marketing actions in a systemic, structured fashion.

The COVID-19 pandemic sparked a wave of layoffs in the tourism industry. In some places, up to 50% of the workforce were fired without any local government action to mitigate the negative consequences of the lockdown. When businesses reopened, they began to re-hire and strove to meet protocol requirements.

Our quantitative data showed that local tourism entrepreneurs were not entirely unfamiliar with digital marketing. However, their use of it was incipient and usually nonprofessional.

Indeed, most local tour operators were small, with few to no resources or technology. They mostly used smartphones to message customers and other entrepreneurs via WhatsApp.

We found a business, large by local standards (over 100 employees), with a clearly coordinated marketing team effort. Using analytics to strengthen branding and understand customer profiles, they often adopted new actions based on tourists' expectations, which resulted mainly in new attractions and tours.

This company invested in organic and paid traffic because they saw this strategy as relevant to the success and growth that, pandemic aside, had been taking place. This company's use of digital marketing was more professional and mature. In addition to producing content for social media, they used Facebook Ads and Google Ads to reach the target audience and access important data on tourists, which they used to develop specific actions. Storytelling and copywriting were also part of the company's digital marketing plan.

SEO and the business website were key in business operations and in attracting foreign customers, thus leveraging receptive tourism. By analyzing data from the increased customer and potential customer traffic on the business website, the agency also boosted its revenues and sustainable development.

Our quantitative and qualitative data and our observations suggest that using and investing in digital marketing brings several positive transformations for tourism companies, whatever their size. Such results promote business growth and development more than mere survival.

SOLUTIONS AND RECOMMENDATIONS

Based on the present case study, we saw that small and medium tourism entrepreneurs in Brazil are starting to explore digital marketing to sell more, however, they are still far from adopting and adapting digitalization to hyper-personalized marketing with obvious benefits for all interested parties.

We have seen that typical tourism entrepreneurs in Brazil still practice artisanal tourism, are unaware of the simplest digital marketing tools and do not even imagine the ample opportunities they may have if they adopt more current practices of this type of marketing, which are very common in many places and learning them is not so difficult.

When asked about the return on investment in digital marketing, participants made it clear that executing strategies was crucial for the development of enterprises.

By using digital marketing tools and strategies, even small local businesses can arrive at new sales channels and attract tourists from all over the world without having to pay fees to intermediary platforms, such as Booking.com. Despite being important for businesses, intermediaries deduce a high fee from each booking made on the platform, thus decreasing net profit margin.

Developing websites and applying digital marketing provides payoffs with low investment, since entrepreneurs themselves can build and maintain such platforms.

All digital marketing efforts are designed, structured, and implemented in digital channels—from websites to messaging applications. Far from rocket science, digital marketing is simply a new form of marketing adapted to online media. Online media, in turn, have also adapted to function as a means of communication, advertising, and even sales—even if they were not designed for such purposes.

A relevant possibility would be that of training tourism entrepreneurs in basic and advanced courses on digital marketing and its tools, techniques, and strategies. Traditional courses on people management, financial management, and foreign languages—common in training and development programs for entrepreneurs offered by government agencies—would also be beneficial.

The data and observations strongly emphasized the need for entrepreneurial education and training for host communities. This would make them aware of the importance of preserving their cultural heritage and the benefits of the tourist flow. Such training should also spotlight technological trends that can be leveraged —especially digital marketing—to increase tourist flow and raise residents' standard of living through tourism.

It would be important not only for governments to provide training, but also lines of credit for those who, once trained, show real interest in digitizing their business and move forward along the path of hyper-personalization, something practically unknown by tourism operators in Paraty. Considering that this is one of the most sought-after tourist destinations in Brazil, it can be inferred that the situation in the rest of the country is the same or even worse.

From a practical point of view, it is strongly recommended that tourism entrepreneurs in Paraty quickly adopt digital marketing strategies, as it is possible to get to know them and even train themselves through videos widely available on Youtube.

It is suggested that lawmakers and public authorities study the possibility of adopting even fiscal incentives to accelerate the adoption of digital marketing by tourist entrepreneurs, at first, and as soon as possible, more sophisticated strategies such as hyper-personalization of experiences for tourists. We believe that this suggestion is most likely useful to several other Brazilian municipalities, in addition to Paraty.

Entrepreneurs from different industries in Paraty could also build solutions by coming together. This would enable businesses to deliver a full experience to tourists, making them more likely to return and recommend tourism in Paraty to multiple acquaintances. This coming together could take the form of cooperatives or associations since the guidance expected from the government is insufficient.

For small and medium tourism companies in Paraty, mass campaigns may even be new, but in today's marketing world, this is a strategy that has been losing more and more efficiency, even in digital channels such as email and social networks.

Today's marketing is replacing massification with personalized strategies, which create unique experiences for customers. Although it seems complex for those who have not even entered the digital world, personalization is not only applicable to large companies, but it can also be practiced by companies of various sizes and segments (Spina, 2019).

Therefore, the case we studied shows that there is a long way to go by small entrepreneurs in the city of Paraty before reaching personalization, and even more so to adhere to hyper personalization.

FUTURE RESEARCH DIRECTIONS

An exploratory study does not allow for generalizations. Instead, it builds hypotheses to be tested and checked in more targeted research. Therefore, a promising next step would be to collect large amounts of data (big data and analytics) and share information with entrepreneurs and public entities. This could facilitate the adoption of common digital marketing strategies and enable strategic decisions based on concrete information.

According to two of the largest entrepreneurs we interviewed, using digital marketing made their businesses more mature. They accessed various data, which allowed them to better understand their audience and sales and communication channels. Data-driven decision-making made digital marketing more professional within organizations and sparked company growth.

The need for a more proactive role by the local tourism department—to conduct studies such as observations and collect relevant data on the number of lodging facilities, tourism agencies, businesses, etc.—points to a promising line of research. Such research could investigate government participation in fostering a better experience for tourists.

Another suggestion would be to assess the potential of digital marketing to leverage tourism aimed at more diverse audiences—perhaps even specifically addressing minorities through focused strategies.

Further research could evaluate collaboration between industry players and other sectors to ultimately deliver a better experience for Paraty visitors. This could be valuable because we identified a certain reluctance by some players to hire digital marketing service providers for business development.

By addressing an evolving technology and the conditions observed in Paraty, this study paves the way for broader reflections on the future of tourism— not only in Paraty, but also in Brazil as a whole.

In an increasingly dynamic, competitive, technological world, transformations in the global economy and society bring new and challenging demands for everyone. However, they also bring great potential for tourism. Brazil's inherent suitability for tourism manifests in its natural, cultural, and artistic riches—all well represented in Paraty.

Researchers must shed light on what is needed to ensure long-term, continuous, sustainable development. In the face of competition in the international market, which is likely to intensify significantly after the COVID-19 pandemic, research must address the strategy Brazilian tourism should follow to compete on an equal footing with international players.

This study also indicates some other important research endeavors, such as defining the best development model for tourism in Brazil, discovering opportunities available to Brazilian companies, and examining existing threats to Brazilian tourism entrepreneurs.

Finally, researchers should seek answers to the major challenge of promoting an active, competitive insertion of Brazilian tourism in the digital economy of the fourth industrial revolution.

CONCLUSION

Albeit exploratory, this study suggests that digital marketing strategies and tools used by tourism entrepreneurs contribute to the growth of the industry. This process involves branding, using highly targeted ads, which can reach Brazilians as well as foreigners, developing websites and blogs, and boosting organic traffic with SEO.

Based on our data collection from participants, the tourism industry encompasses non-professionalized tourist entrepreneurs whose businesses represent supplemental income. This implies a strong need for training, not only in business management but also in digital marketing.

Unthinkable until just a few decades ago (Webber, 2013), space tourism has started to become a reality: the first space tourists have already purchased tickets for millions of dollars. Considering that, this study is relevant in showing how Brazilian tourism entrepreneurs still face many hardships and are far removed from technologies and strategies that could greatly benefit Brazilian tourism and foreign tourists.

In the participants' opinion, digital marketing really is a promising tool—not as a silver bullet for business, but mainly as a complement to strategies for attracting new customers and maintaining business relationships to deliver the best possible experience.

Finally, we recommend adopting digital marketing as a strategy to better advertise quality tourist itineraries in Paraty. This would help increase the number of national and international tourists, boost the income of entrepreneurs, and create jobs for community members. To do so, Brazilian tourism entrepreneurs need training both in digital tools and in business management.

REFERENCES

Amaral, J. B., Jr. (2008). O Turismo na periferia do capitalismo: a revelação de um cartão postal. Tese de Doutorado Ciências Sociais. São Paulo: Pontifícia Universidade Católica de São Paulo - PUC SP.

Assad, N. (2016). *Marketing de conteúdo: como fazer sua empresa decolar no meio digital*. Atlas.

Barros Neto, J. P. (2018). *Administração: fundamentos de administração empreendedora e competitiva*. Atlas.

Benckendorff, P. J., Xiang, Z., & Sheldon, P. J. (2019). *Tourism information technology*. CABI Tourism Texts. doi:10.1079/9781786393432.0000

Diehl, A. A., & Tatim, D. C. (2012). *Pesquisa em ciências sociais aplicadas: métodos e técnicas*. Pearson.

Ferreira, G. (2018). *Copywriting: palavras que vendem milhões*. DVS.

Gabriel, M., & Kiso, R. (2020). *Marketing na era digital: conceitos, plataformas e estratégias*. Atlas.

Gaspar, E., & Gaspar, R. (2021). *Informações úteis*. Fonte: PARATI.COM.BR: http://www.paraty.com.br/index.asp

Gretzel, U., & Yoo, K.-H. (2013). Premises and promises of social media marketing in tourism. In *The Routledge handbook of tourism marketing* (pp. 491–504). Routledge.

Gupta, G. (2018). Inclusive Use of Digital Marketing in Tourism Industry. In Information Systems Design and Intelligent Applications. Advances in Intelligent systems and Computing (pp. 411-419). Singapure: Springer.

Happ, E., & Ivancsó-Horváth, Z. (2018). Digital tourism is the challenge of future – a new approach to tourism. *Knowledge Horizons - Economics, 10*, 9-16.

Hojeghan, S. B., & Esfangareh, A. N. (2011). Digital economy and tourism impacts, influences and challenges. In *The 2nd International Geography Symposium GEOMED2010* (pp. 308-316). Kemer: Elsevier Ltd. 10.1016/j.sbspro.2011.05.136

Hudson, L., & Hudson, S. (2020). *Marketing para turismo, hospitalidade e eventos: uma abordagem global e digital*. Senac.

Ito, C. A. (2008). *Evolução histórica do turismo e suas motivações*. Tópos.

Jerkovic, J. G. (2010). *SEO: Técnicas essenciais para aumentar a visibilidade na web*. Novatec.

Kaur, G. (2017). *The importance of digital marketing in the tourism industry*. International Journal of Research - Granthaalayah. doi:10.29121/granthaalayah.v5.i6.2017.1998

Knaflic, C. N. (2019). *Storytelling com dados: um guia sobre visualização de dados para profissionais de negócios*. Alta Books.

Kotler, P. (2021). *Marketing para o século XXI: como criar, conquistar e dominar mercados*. Alta Books.

Kotler, P., & Armstrong, G. (2007). *Princípios de marketing*. Pearson.

Kotler, P., Kartajaya, H., & Setiawan, I. (2017). *Marketing 4.0*. Sextante.

Kotler, P., Kartajaya, H., & Setiawan, I. (2021). *Marketing 5.0: technology for humanity*. John Wiley & Sons.

Kotler, P., & Keller, K. L. (2006). *Administração de marketing: a bíblia do marketing*. Prentice Hall.

Larrossa, L. (2021). *Instagram, WhatsApp e Facebook para Negócios: Como ter lucro através dos três principais canais de venda*. São Paulo: DVS.

Magano, J., & Cunha, M. N. (2020). Digital marketing impact on tourism in Portugal: A quantitative study. *African Journal of Hospitality, Tourism and Leisure*, 1–19.

Manosso, F. C., Ruiz, T. C. D., & Nakatani, M. S. M. (2020). A aplicação do Storytelling nas pesquisas em Turismo: Uma Revisão Bibliométrica, Sistemática e Integrativa da Literatura. *Revista de Turismo Contemporâneo*, 8(2), 337–358. doi:10.21680/2357-8211.2020v8n2ID16465

Mkwizu, K. H. (2020). *Digital marketing and tourism: opportunities for Africa*. International Hospitality Review.

Rabahy, W. A. (2020). Análise e perspectivas do turismo no Brasil. Revista Brasileira de Pesquisa em Turismo, pp. 1-13.

Ranpersad, H., Souza, G. d., & Nunes, J. (2012). Construção de marca bem-sucedida nas micro, pequenas e medidas empresas: o passo a passo para a construção de uma marca. In *J. P. Barros Neto, Manual do empreendedor: de micro a pequenas empresas* (pp. 177–205). Qualitymark.

Spina, F. (2019). *Personalização: quem fala com todos não fala com ninguém, personalize seu marketing digital*. DVS.

UNTWO. (2019). World tourism barometer. World Tourism Organization.

Watkins, M., Ziyadin, S., Imatayeva, A., Kurmangalieva, A., & Blembayeva, A. (2018). Digital tourism as a key factor in the development of the economy. In Economic Annals-XXI (pp. 40-45). Kiev: Institute of Society Transformation. doi:10.21003/ea.V169-08

Webber, D. (2013). Space tourism: Its history, future, and importance. *Acta Astronautica*, 92(2), 138–143. doi:10.1016/j.actaastro.2012.04.038

Zsarnoczky, M. (2018). The digital future of the tourism & hospitality industry. Boston Hospitality Review, 1-9.

ADDITIONAL READING

Bragança, J. O. (2012). *Paraty: minhas fotos*. Capivara.

Cotrim, C. R. M. (2012). *Villa de Paraty*. Capivara.

Jain, G., Paul, J., & Shrivastava, A. (2021). Hyper-personalization, co-creation, digital clienteling and transformation. *Journal of Business Research*, *124*, 12–23. doi:10.1016/j.jbusres.2020.11.034

Saraceni, S. (2006). *Estação Paraty*. Geração Editorial.

Wirth, K., & Sweet, K. (2020). *One-to-One personalization in the age of machine learning: harnessing data to power great customer experiences*. BookBaby.

ENDNOTE

[1]   https://economia.uol.com.br/cotacoes/cambio/

Chapter 12
Importance–Performance Analysis of Tourism Destination Attractiveness:
Technology and Other Influencing Factors

João Ferreira do Rosário
 https://orcid.org/0000-0003-2524-8523
Escola Superior de Comunicação Social, Instituto Politécnico de Lisboa, Portugal

Maria de Lurdes Calisto
CiTUR, Portugal

Ana Teresa Machado
Escola Superior de Comunicação Social, Instituto Politécnico de Lisboa, Portugal

Nuno Gustavo
Estoril Higher Institute for Tourism and Hotel Studies, Portugal

ABSTRACT

This chapter presents an importance-performance analysis to evaluate the ability of a destination's attributes to attract tourists through tourism stakeholder perceptions. In this case, one of Europe's larger destination cities, Lisbon, was considered. It departs from the proposition that tourists are not the most knowledgeable about a destination while the evaluation of a destination's competitiveness from the supply side perspective is scarce. This stakeholder feedback approach to identifying a destination's attributes to attract tourists showed that only 7 of the 40 attributes (five of them related to accessibility and technological infrastructures as municipality responsibility) fall in the IPA grid Concentrate Here quadrant, results that are consistent with the recently received Best City Destination and Best City Break World Travel Awards. This research shows the relevance of multiple stakeholders' feedback to evaluate a city's attributes, including the feedback about the city's need to improve its technological offer through an integrated digital strategy.

DOI: 10.4018/978-1-7998-8306-7.ch012

INTRODUCTION

The tourism sector, with its increasing economic importance, has gained relevance in academic research (Leask, 2016), with substantial gains in terms of scientific knowledge and decision-making support tools. With the growth of world tourism and the growing rivalry amongst destinations, achieving destination competitiveness is a central feature of tourism policy and academic debate. The knowledge about a destination's competitive position, including its weaker and stronger attributes, is vital to governments and market players (Dwyer, Forsyth, & Rao, 2000) since it is critical for its success (Dwyer & Kim, 2003) and (Mangion, Durbarry, & Sinclair, 2005).

According to Ritchie & Crouch (2003), destination competitiveness refers to 'its ability to increase tourism expenditure, to increasingly attract visitors, while providing them with satisfying, memorable experiences, and to do so in a profitable way, while enhancing the well-being of destination residents and preserving the natural capital of the destination for future generations.' A pitfall is that competitiveness is hard to measure (Gooroochurn & Sugiyarto, 2005) and few models have been created to evaluate the competitiveness of a destination (Lee, Choi, & Breiter, 2013). There are some examples of these efforts, such as the case of Hassan (2000) competitiveness model considering sustainable tourism, Kozak (2002) benchmarking approach to tourism competitiveness, and Dwyer & Kim (2003) model to allow comparison between countries and tourism industries. It is also the case of Ritchie & Crouch (2003) model with a sustainable tourism perspective, and Gomezelj & Mihalič (2008) study of the De Keyser–Vanhove model and the Integrated Model of Destination Competitiveness, as applied to Korea and Australia. However, this kind of analysis can present problems (Dwyer, Cvelbar, Edwards, & Mihalic, 2012), such as the combination of very different attributes in a single index; the difficulty of obtaining a multi-destination assessment by tourists through a questionnaire, which may also bias the response based on the degree of sympathy for the country; and the evaluation of different destinations based on the same attributes (Dwyer & Kim, 2003).

IMPORTANCE-PERFORMANCE ANALYSIS MODEL

The importance-performance analysis (IPA) model was created by Martilla & James (1977) as a business research methodology to help management decisions, based on the concepts of choice models of multiple attributes. It helps investment allocation decisions to maintain and improve consumer satisfaction, with a first application in the vehicle industry marketing. The objective of the IPA model is to make data interpretation accessible and to suggest relevant measures to improve competitiveness, based on the optimization of the allocation of resources among the various attributes analyzed (Abalo, Varela, & Manzano, 2007).

In the traditional IPA technique, data from customer satisfaction surveys or service quality surveys (Cronin & Taylor, 1992) are utilized to construct a two-dimensional grid. In this grid, the x-axis depicts the attribute importance, and the y-axis the attribute performance (satisfaction or service quality). The mean of performance and importance divides the grid into four quadrants, identifying areas of high or low attribute performance combined with high or low attribute importance. The grid (Table 1) provides managers with information on the aspects that (I) require additional investment as they are underperforming; aspects that (II) are performing well but need continued investment, aspects that (III) are of low priority and require little investment, and aspects that (IV) are at risk of overinvestment as they are of small importance to customers (Coghlan, 2012).

Table 1. IPA grid

		Low	High
Importance	High	**I** **Concentrate here** (Increase resources)	**II** **Keep up the Good Work** (Sustain resources)
	Low	**III** **Low Priority** (No change in resources)	**IV** **Potential Overkill** (Curtail Resources)
			Performance

(Martilla & James, 1977)

Martilla & James (1977) presented several clues when applying this analysis, such as:

- . The importance of deciding what attributes to measure. In tourism, when applying this analysis to a specific location, we must choose the attributes that are relevant for the competitiveness of the location;
- . In the questionnaire, group all questions about attributes importance and group all questions about attributes performance, to avoid the importance evaluation to influence the performance evaluation of the attributes;
- . The positioning of the vertical and horizontal axis is a matter of judgment, the aim is to identify relative and not absolute levels of importance and performance. Usually, the middle position of a 5 or 7-point Likert scale is used to divide the grid;
- . The use of median as a measure of central tendency, while is preferable to means in scales like the referred above, can be analyzed together with the mean. If the results are close, the mean have more information to work with;
- . The analysis of the importance-performance grid must be made from the top to the bottom of the grid, considering each attribute in order of its relative importance.

Importance-Performance Analysis Questions and Issues

The objective of the IPA model is to make data interpretation accessible and to suggest relevant measures to improve competitiveness, based on the optimization of the allocation of resources among the various attributes analyzed (Abalo et al., 2007). But the application of this methodology raised some questions and issues, showing that the IPA methodology is applied in a less structured way.

Seven basic questions were proposed about how IPA can be pursued (Lai & Hitchcock, 2015). The authors concluded, considering their research sample, that researchers applied different methodologies regarding each question, as presented in Table 2.

Table 2. Importance-performance analysis questions and issues

Question	IPA Research
What attributes?	Their own and/or borrowed from other studies.
Which Likert Scale?	Often 5 or 7-point Likert scales. In the more recent research, 7-point.
Which sample size?	At least 10 for each question, often around 20.
Convenience or probability sampling?	Random is more frequent.
Factor Analysis? EFA or CFA?	Around 20% use EFA. CFA is rare.
The t-test in difference calculation between Importance and Performance or just results presentation? Need difference calculation?	Around 20% of the studies use the t-test.
Use of I-P mapping? And how?	Around 90% use the I-P mapping, with the data-centered approach more common.

(Lai & Hitchcock, 2015)

For the quadrants mapping to be the most correct considering the IPA aim of discriminating between the attributes to identify performance gaps and priorities for strategy development, the center of the IPA model grid choice is critical. Most researchers use the mean values of observed real values (Oh, 2001), while others use the data mean or the center of the Likert scale (Bacon, 2003). Bacon (2003), in his research about the best model to predict improvement priorities (between scale-centered quadrant model, the data-centered quadrant model, or the diagonal line model) and the best method for assessing Importance (direct ratings, simple correlations or multiple regression coefficients) concluded that the diagonal line model and direct measures of importance are the best in predicting improvement priorities. In the diagonal line over the IPA grid method, all attributes above an upward sloping 45°line stand for points where importance exceeds performan. In this case, they stand for high priorities for improvement or market opportunities. The attributes below the diagonal line represent the opposite, satiated needs. All attributes over the line have the same importance and performance results, and the same priority for improvement (Hawes & Rao, 1985).

But is possible to use stricter importance and performance standards and therefore, by setting the crosshair intersection above the neutral point, 3 for a 5-Likert scale or 4 for a 7-Likert scale, that will allow more exigence in the evaluation and a clearer sign to choose the attribution of limited resources. With different criteria, such as scale means or actual means, the discrimination between satisfaction and dissatisfaction can be quite different (Sever, 2015).

(Sever, 2015) discussed additional issues in IPA presented by researchers, namely the missing precision and consistency of the Importance definition (Dwyer et al., 2012); how the IPA doesn't distinguish between attributes in each quadrant, that can be near thresholds or far from them, while offering the same investment suggestion (Tarrant & Smith, 2002) and how to interpret the attributes near to the discriminating thresholds, because a small change in attribute position can change the quadrant position and proposed investment decision, were Wu & Shieh (2009) proposed the use of confidence interval to keep the validity of the research when variability is present. These authors suggested the use of a different IPA model, which additionally includes the measure of statistical variance.

(Feng, Mangan, Wong, Xu, & Lalwani, 2014) considered the relevance of the gap analysis between importance and performance as more helpful in improving a resource allocation strategy, compared to merely using IPA or gap analysis.

Considering the sample size, the rule of thumb in social science surveys can be adequate for IPA surveys. The minimum acceptable sample size usually is 100 completed questionnaires, 200 participants are considered adequate and samples of 300–400 participants offer a balance between statistical reliability and logistical feasibility (Sarantakos, 2013; Simpson, Patroni, Teo, Chan, & Newsome, 2019; Tsang, Royse, & Terkawi, 2017; Weston & Gore, 2006). (Lai & Hitchcock, 2015) in their research sample observed around 20 completed questionnaires for each question.

Bruyere, Rodriguez, & Vaske (2002) concluded that sample segmentation allows for more precise predictors of improvement priorities, by the identification of distinct user groups with different consumer profiles. The authors concluded that at an aggregate level the results of the importance-performance analysis could lead to a strategy, while segmented results lead to another strategy and that the IPA with segmentation can offer more information to help managers in the search for a single strategy that appeases multiple user groups.

IMPORTANCE-PERFORMANCE ANALYSIS IN TOURISM

While there exists research on the feedback of tourists (Morgan, M., Lugosi, P., & Ritchie, 2010) using different methodologies (Pearce & Benckendorff, 2006), the IPA model (Martilla & James, 1977) was extended to research fields such as tourism (Evans & Chon, 1989) and (Oh, 2001), and is nowadays used to evaluate tourism locations and help to measure their competitiveness considering the worldwide competition for tourists and the need to attract them. The model results help in the optimization of the allocation of resources among the attributes of the tourist sector (Abalo et al., 2007) to increase the competitiveness of a tourist destination. The wide application of the technique is due to its recognized advantages (Sever, 2015; Sörensson & von Friedrichs, 2013), allowing researchers and practitioners alike to understand destination performance and to formulate strategies for improvements in the products / services offer (Bi, Liu, Fan, & Zhang, 2019)

Despite some criticism (Busacca & Arbore, 2011) of the IPA model that has emerged over the years since its development, the model allows a rigorous competitive analysis of a tourist destination and has been widely applied to tourism, as demonstrated by (Lai & Hitchcock, 2015). The application of the IPA model to the tourism industry is recurrent in the last decades, starting with the work of Crompton & Duray (1985) and several extensions of the model have emerged over the years (Guizzardi & Stacchini, 2017). In the tourism field, the IPA has been applied with both concepts of satisfaction, the school of thought that considers satisfaction (or dissatisfaction) as the difference (positive or negative) between previous expectations and later experience (Parasuraman, Zeithaml, & Berry, 1985) and the school of thought that identifies satisfaction as the answer from consumer to perceived performance (Tse & Wilton, 1988).

(Azzopardi & Nash, 2013) analyzed the choice between the direct and indirect measurement of the Importance, since, while a multidimensional concept, it can be biased by self-report measures. That bias includes social bias or tourist fatigue bias, which can lead to lower engagement with the questionnaire and can make the respondent evaluate as very important all attributes in the questionnaire, rating all of them with high values (Abalo et al., 2007). As an alternative to try to avoid some of the problems presented above, some authors recommend indirect measurement, using statistical tools such as correlation estimation, multivariate regression measurement, and conjoint analysis (Chu, 2002), (Matzler, Sauerwein, & Heischmidt, 2003). The limitations of the indirect measurement are the strict assumptions underlying the statistical procedures (Chu, 2002), (Matzler et al., 2003). Other authors consider that tourist respondent's bias, like social bias, is not strong enough to make direct measurement inferior to indirect measurement (Sanbonmatsu, Kardes, Houghton, Ho, & Posavac, 2003). Some authors recommend data collection through different tourism stakeholders, a method used in similar research related to the tourism sector. For these authors, the recipient of the questionnaire should be the one who knows best the studied market, which is not necessarily the tourist who visit it, avoiding some of the bias problems found in tourist questionnaires (Bacon, 2003) and (Dwyer, Cvelbar, Edwards & Mihalic, 2012).

Considering the attributes choices, while some IPA research use well-developed attributes deriving from previous studies (Tonge & Moore, 2007), some authors remember that if the Importance measurement doesn't reflect the specific characteristics of the research target, the implications for the study in terms of validity can be serious (Azzopardi & Nash, 2013). (Lai & Hitchcock, 2015) recommended that researchers should develop their own unique set of attributes for the study they are undertaking. (Oh, 2001) considered that the choice of the right attributes for the IPA model is relevant to obtain the best management decisions, because they will be made considering the relevant attributes. The factor analysis made over the chosen attributes results more commonly in factors with three to five attribute factors.

In the last few years many empirical studies in the field of tourism were made using the IPA model, such as analysis of tourist sites by the sea, namely in Croatia (Vodeb & Rudež, 2017); analysis of tourist sites with sea activities, namely in Japan (Kwon, Chung, Yoon, & Kwon, 2017); analysis of inland tourist sites or cities, notably in Serbia (Djeri, Stamenković, Blešić, Milićević, & Ivkov, 2018), international perceptions of a country, like Taiwan, as a tourist destination (Jeng, Snyder, & Chen, 2019), streetscapes at a tourism destination, like in Indonesia (Patandianan & Shibusawa, 2020), types of regions (mountain, spa, and wine) such as present in the Czech Republic (Rašovská, Kubickova, & Ryglová, 2020), etc., etc. The attributes selected were usually are a mix of attributes created for the analysis of the specific location, combined with more generic attributes that are common for several kinds of locations, like accommodation or shopping facilities.

Considering the application of the IPA methodology to tourism research (Table 3), Azzopardi & Nash (2013) explained the four quadrants of the IPA grid.

Table 3. The IPA grid: application to tourism research

Quadrant (I): High importance and Low performance (concentrate here)	**Quadrant (II): High importance and High performance (keep up the good work)**
While we can see key success attributes to competitiveness, they fail to satisfy the tourist's perceived level of performance, considering the importance they give these attributes. These are attributes that have significant weaknesses and are a threat to competitiveness. They must have the highest priority in resource allocation and management efforts.	These attributes have high importance for tourists and also high performance, offering a competitive advantage that must be maintained. It shows that resources are effectively applied. The investment must be kept or even enhanced, to improve the competitive advantage in these critical attributes.
Quadrant (III): Low importance and Low performance (low priority)	**Quadrant (IV): Low importance and High performance (possible overkill)**
The attributes in this quadrant cannot be seen as key success attributes. Their low performance is not a competitive issue, as tourists see them as minor weaknesses. They are not priorities in resource allocation. They are the first ones to have their resources cut if needed, to reallocate to other attributes, like attributes in quadrant I.	Attributes that have an overperformance and that receive resources above their needs, considering that their low importance has a minimum impact on competitiveness. Resources allocated to attributes in this quadrant must be relocated to attributes where additional resources are needed.

(Azzopardi and Nash, 2013)

Further Importance-Performance Analysis Research Models in Tourism

In recent years, new research has been made with the aim of improving the Importance-Performance Analysis (IPA) method applied to tourism activity.

Enright & Newton (2004) presented a joint approach using both, Tourism Destination Competitiveness (TDC) and Importance-Performance Analysis (IPA) models. Soler & Gemar, (2019) while considering the joint method as useful, presented some warnings about the results obtained, showing that museums and galleries, while usually receiving large investments, received low importance in their research. The authors advised that the conclusion that these attributes could be a wasted effort must be cautiously taken, but evaluated positively this joint approach.

(Bi et al., 2019) proposed a methodology for conducting importance-performance analysis (IPA) through online reviews, composed of three stages "(1) mining useful information from online reviews, (2) estimating each attribute's performance and importance, and (3) constructing IPA plot, where the latent Dirichlet allocation (LDA), the improved one-vs-one strategy based support vector machine (IOVO-SVM) and the ensemble neural network-based model (ENNM) are respectively used". The authors concluded that the proposed methodology could obtain effective analysis results with lower cost and shorter time, allowing also a large-scale survey. It also allows evaluation of competitive companies in different periods, while being limited to the fake reviews problem.

(Soler & Gemar, 2019) proposed another model, the asymmetric impact-performance analysis (AIPA). This model combines the Penalty–Reward Contrast Analysis (PRCA) and the IPA, using the three factors of consumer satisfaction theory to analyze these patterns (Albayrak & Caber, 2013). It also presents an evaluation of the key attributes to increase the user's overall satisfaction (Caber, Albayrak, & Loiacono, 2013). The authors concluded that the AIPA model can consider other aspects that may cause dissatisfaction, like the urban environment in their research, whose attributes have the potential to cause dissatisfaction in a client. Like (Barnes, Mattsson, & Sørensen, 2014), (Soler & Gemar, 2019) consider that holistic management of a customer's brand experience in the destination "is a key factor in customer satisfaction with the destination, and in the intention to return and recommend."

(Wullur & Samehe, 2020) used in their research a combination of the Importance Performance Analysis (IPA) approach and the decision making and evaluation laboratory (DEMATEL) technique. This methodology allows the consideration of causal relation among some attributes and the calculation of the direct and indirect influence relationship between attributes, and the level of dominance of each attribute. If there exists a cause-and-effect relationship between an attribute and others, the level of importance of that attribute will be greater and the attribute needs to get more priority (Chen, Wu, Li, & Wang, 2018)

THE IMPORTANCE-PERFORMANCE ANALYSIS APPLIED TO LISBON CITY

While several applications of the Importance-Performance Analysis have been made with developments of the IPA model combining different research methodologies, in this chapter, we present the application of the Importance / Performance Analysis (Martilla & James, 1977) to one of Europe's pre-pandemic fastest-growing destination cities, Lisbon. This research aims to obtain insights about the relevance of attributes influencing Lisbon city tourism competitiveness, and what is the performance of the city in these attributes. While there is already an IPA study considering the tourist's feedback about Portugal

(Padma, 2016), to the best of our knowledge, this is the first research made considering the tourism stakeholder's perspectives for this destination.

This study contributes both to academia and practice. This research reveals the relevance of a multiple stakeholder approach to evaluate the destination's competitiveness attributes, as most research is based on the opinion of travelers. It also offers Lisbon's destination managers and other stakeholders, information about the attributes that contribute to the evaluation and the choice of the city of Lisbon as a tourist destination. The results can also help the investment allocation decisions by different players, private and public, in the city's tourism sector.

METHODOLOGY

Research Procedures

Lisbon's competitiveness research was made from the perspective of tourism stakeholders – tour operators, travel agencies, hotels, restaurants, museums, and other operators, following several steps:

- Several attributes were defined considering similar empiric research and other topics discussed in the literature;
- A questionnaire was developed to collect the tourism stakeholders perceptions, regarding the importance of a set of attributes and the performance of Lisbon as a tourism destination regarding each of those attributes;
- Confirmatory factor analysis was applied to each attribute category considered;
- Finally, the importance-performance and gap analyses were made.

Questionnaire Design

In the questionnaire design we included a mix of specific attributes to reflect the characteristics of Lisbon (Azzopardi & Nash, 2013), (Lai & Hitchcock, 2015), with attributes deriving from previous studies (Tonge & Moore, 2007), considering that the choice of the proper attributes for the IPA model is relevant to obtain the best management decisions (Oh, 2001)

Following the recommendation above, the attributes in the questionnaire were firstly listed considering a review of earlier research in the same destination category – city destination. The list of attributes was then updated considering the feedback from Turismo de Portugal, the Portuguese governmental organization that aims to dynamize the tourism sector in Portugal. This process resulted in 40 attributes considering the following areas: city environment, accommodation, restaurants, cultural and natural attractions, activities and events, shopping, accessibility, and infrastructures. The questionnaire asks respondents about their perceived importance for each of the 40 attributes and the perceived performance of the city of Lisbon on the same attributes, using a 7-point Likert scale (lower importance (1) to higher importance (7); and, lower performance (1) to higher performance (7)). As the survey was directed to tourism operators, the only profile information we considered relevant, keeping the respondent's anonymity, was the organization's category and location in the city of Lisbon.

Before the dissemination of the questionnaire, a preliminary trial with 16 operators was made. From their feedback, we only needed to make residual wording changes in the explanation of two questions.

Data Collection and Analysis

An online questionnaire was developed, and the respective link was sent by email to tourism stakeholders in the city of Lisbon, with the contacts collected from industry databases available from Turismo de Portugal, obtaining a sample of 127 stakeholders.

Data analysis was made using Excel with the Real Statistics Resource Pack Release 6.2 (Zaiontz C., 2019) add-in. Confirmatory factor analyses using the Principal Component Extraction, the Kaiser-Meyer-Olkin (KMO) measure of sampling adequacy, and the Bartlett's test of the sphericity significance level and the Cronbach's alpha were conducted to examine internal consistency reliability and validity of the latent variables (categories of attributes).

A set of descriptive statistics was calculated - including median, mean, and standard deviation, for importance and performance scores of the 40 attributes and also importance and performance scores of the categories of attributes obtained through Confirmatory Factor Analysis. The Shapiro-Wilk test for the distribution normality was applied. Parametric (t-test) and non-parametric (Wilcoxon and Mann–Whitney) tests were also applied to the attributes and categories of attributes.

The gap analysis, considering the difference between the evaluation of the attributes´ importance scores and the attributes performance scores (Bacon, 2003), (Feng et al., 2014) was made, with the application of the Mann-Whitney test to the results.

IPA scale-centered and data-centered quadrants grids and diagonal line model grids (Lai & Hitchcock, 2015) were applied for all attributes (variables) and also for the categories of attributes (latent variables obtained through factor analysis).

RESULTS

Sample Characterization

In what concerns the tourism stakeholder categories, accommodation (hotels, apartment hotels, B&B, guest houses, hostels, and other accommodation companies) represent more than 40% of the sample. Tourism animation companies and travel agencies represent almost 35% of the respondents. Restaurants are also a relevant category, with near 12% of the sample (Table 4).

Table 4. Sample distribution by type of tourism stakeholder

Category	Absolut frequency	Relative frequency
Hotel or Apartment Hotel	33	25.98%
Tourist animation company	26	20.47%
Travel agency	17	13.39%
Restaurant	15	11.81%
Bed & Breakfast and other	15	11.81%
Disco	6	4.72%
Hostel	5	3.94%
Pub	4	3.15%
Tourism transportation	2	1.57%
Other	4	3.15%

If one considers the distribution of companies throughout the city, the sample covers almost all neighborhoods in Lisbon (see Figure 1), except for Beato (east side near Tagus river) and Santa Clara (north of Lisbon) (Table 5).

Figure 1. Lisbon's neighborhoods
Source: Lisboa Municipality

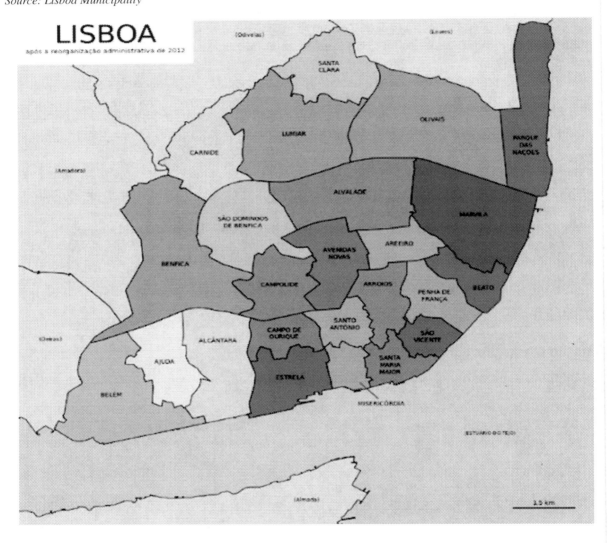

The neighborhoods with the higher frequencies of responses are generally the ones with more tourism stakeholders through the city, as these are the neighborhoods that are more often visited by tourists (Table 5).

Table 5. Sample distribution by neighborhood in Lisbon

Lisbon's neighborhoods	Absolut frequency	Relative frequency
Santa Maria Maior	19	14.96%
Avenidas Novas	16	12.60%
Misericórdia	12	9.45%
Alcântara	10	7.87%
Arroios	10	7.87%
Santo António	8	6.30%
Benfica	7	5.51%
Alvalade	6	4.72%
Belém	6	4.72%
Campo de Ourique	6	4.72%
Areeiro	4	3.15%
São Domingos de Benfica	4	3.15%
Parque das Nações	3	2.36%
Campolide	2	1.57%
Estrela	2	1.57%
Lumiar	2	1.57%
Marvila	2	1.57%
Olivais	2	1.57%
Penha de França	2	1.57%
São Vicente	2	1.57%
Ajuda	1	0.79%
Carnide	1	0.79%
Beato	0	0.00%
Santa Clara	0	0.00%

Reliability and Validity Analysis of Attributes

The seven factors (categories of attributes) and the results of the confirmatory analysis are shown in Table 6. The Cronbach's alpha ranged from 0.82 to 0.94 (in the scale of importance) and from 0.84 to 0.95 (in the scale of performance) showing considerable reliability. Each of the seven factors using Bartlett's test of sphericity has a significance level of less than 0.05. In what concerns the KMO, all results are near or above 0.80, apart from the Cultural and Natural Attractions category, which in any case shows a result of 0.64, considering the importance and 0.77 considering performance.

Table 6. Results of reliability and validity tests

	Importance			Performance		
	Cronbach α	KMO	Bartlett Sig.	Cronbach α	KMO	Bartlett Sig.
City Environment	0.87	0.85	0.00	0.91	0.89	5.13
Accommodation (all types)	0.85	0.80	0.00	0.89	0.81	5.80
Restaurants	0.89	0.80	0.00	0.94	0.87	5.50
Cultural and Natural Attractions	0.94	0.85	0.00	0.95	0.86	5.51
Activities and Events	0.82	0.64	0.00	0.84	0.77	5.25
Shopping	0.88	0.79	0.00	0.93	0.82	5.35
Accessibility and Infrastructures	0.92	0.86	0.00	0.93	0.87	4.33

Importance-Performance Analysis

We will now analyze the results of the importance and performance scores for the attributes and categories of attributes.

Importance of the Attributes for Lisbon's Attractiveness

The median scores of importance range from 5 to 7, with mean scores between 4.86 and 6.44, and both median and mean having a statistically significant result (non-parametric Wilcoxon test of median > 4 and parametric t-test of mean > 4 in a 7-Likert scale) for all attributes considered (Table 7). These results suggest that tourism stakeholders in Lisbon consider all 40 attributes important to Lisbon's tourism attractiveness.

The attribute with the highest importance level is safety (feeling of security during the stay) with a median of 7 and a mean of 6.44. Quality and cleanliness of accommodation and food quality in restaurants have a median of 7 and a mean of 6.37. Value for money for accommodation has a median of 7 and a mean of 6.21, and warmth and friendliness of the local population a median of 7 and a mean of 6.15. Two of the attributes are related to the activity of the tourism stakeholders themselves, namely accommodation and restaurants, while the other two are related to social attributes of the city - offering a safe environment, warmth and friendliness.

The attributes considered less important (but still with impact in Lisbon attractiveness) are car parking availability (median of 5 and mean of 4.86; concentration of tourists (median of 5 and mean 5.09) and resting atmosphere in the city (low bustle, excitement, city noise) with a median of 5 and a mean of 5.15. The respondents consider that the concentration of tourists and the resting atmosphere aren't yet key factors in Lisbon tourism attractiveness, having similar evaluation about car parking availability.

Performance of Lisbon in Each Attribute

Although performance variables have a lower mean than their respective importance with the exception of housing type diversity (hotels, hostels, local housing, etc.), almost all have a 'positive' (more than 4) evaluation (Table 7). The median scores of the performance of Lisbon in each attribute range from 4 to 6 with a mean between 3.98 and 5.85.

Three attributes, public transport accessibility (passengers with special needs), car parking availability, and technological infrastructures availability (Internet access offered by the Lisbon municipality) have a median and mean without a statistically significant result higher than 4 (in a 7-Likert scale, non-parametric Wilcoxon test of median > 4 and parametric t-test of mean >4), showing a lower performance perception for these three attributes.

The attribute with the highest performance is warmth and friendliness of the local population with a median of 6 and a mean of 5.85, while quality and cleanliness of accommodation (median of 6 and mean 5.69) and food quality in restaurants (median of 6 and mean of 5.61) also have good performance perceptions, with 2nd and 3rd highest scores.

The three attributes with the higher performance perception scores correspond respectively to the 5th, 2nd, and 3rd attributes in terms of importance. The three most important attributes, safety (feeling of security during the stay)], quality and cleanliness of accommodation and food quality of restaurants rank respectively in 8th, 2nd, and 3rd in performance results.

Considering the "technological infrastructures availability", the offer in shopping malls, shops, public transports, etc. is considered more important and with better performance than the municipality offer, wi-fi in the streets for instance. Considering these results we can conclude that respondents consider tourists already using their telecommunications supplier Internet offer and that the use of wi-fi is expected to be higher in the locations like the described.

As such, from the tourism stakeholder feedback we can consider that Lisbon city has the most important attributes with positive performance perceptions, contributing to the city's competitiveness.

Importance and Performance of Categories of Attributes

In what concerns the importance and performance scores of attributes categories (Table 7, bold rows), the mean ranges between 5.53 (activities and events) and 6.03 (restaurants) for importance, with statistically significant median and mean results of higher than 4. The attributes categories performance has a mean between 4.39 (accessibility and infrastructure) and 5.49 (accommodation), all having median and mean with statistically significant results higher than 4.

Stakeholders consider as the three more important attributes categories the restaurants, accommodation, and cultural and natural attractions, respectively with the 2nd, 1st, and 3rd performance scores. The less important attribute category is activities and events, which also have the lowest performance.

The worst performance attribute category, that is 5th in importance evaluation, is Accessibility and Infrastructures, mainly due to the lower performance of "public transport accessibility", "car parking availability" and also the "technological infrastructures availability (Lisbon municipality offer)", which show the need of improvement of the city technological infrastructures.

These results show that the categories of attributes that are considered as having more importance in Lisbon attractiveness also have better performance evaluations.

Table 7. Importance-performance scores and gap

Attributes and Categories of Attributes	Importance			Performance			Gap		
	Mean	SD	p-value	Mean	SD	p-value	Mean Diff.	SD	p-value
City Environment	**5,74**	**1,16**	**0,00**	**5,04**	**1,33**	**0,00**	**-0,70**	**1,28**	**0,00**
Street cleaning	5,87	1,55	0,00	4,57	1,87	0,00	-1,31	1,76	0,00
Safety	6,44	1,17	0,00	5,45	1,47	0,00	-0,99	1,46	0,00
Resting atmosphere	5,15	1,63	0,00	4,63	1,71	0,00	-0,52	1,81	0,01
Warmth and friendliness of local population	6,15	1,22	0,00	5,85	1,19	0,00	-0,30	1,25	0,01
Concentration of tourists	5,09	1,37	0,00	4,87	1,66	0,00	-0,22	1,70	0,44
Police support	5,57	1,44	0,00	4,82	1,56	0,00	-0,75	1,75	0,00
Medical-hospital support	5,50	1,51	0,00	4,97	1,55	0,00	-0,54	1,66	0,00
Accommodation (all offer)	**5,89**	**0,96**	**0,00**	**5,49**	**1,18**	**0,00**	**-0,40**	**1,09**	**0,01**
Quality and Cleanliness	6,37	1,10	0,00	5,69	1,35	0,00	-0,68	1,25	0,00
Variety of available services	5,74	1,18	0,00	5,54	1,31	0,00	-0,20	1,43	0,29
Unique characteristics	5,43	1,39	0,00	5,18	1,43	0,00	-0,25	1,55	0,14
Housing type diversity	5,57	1,24	0,00	5,60	1,30	0,00	0,03	1,51	0,62
Value for money	6,21	1,14	0,00	5,27	1,55	0,00	-0,94	1,59	0,00
Restaurants	**6,03**	**1,01**	**0,00**	**5,39**	**1,29**	**0,00**	**-0,65**	**1,22**	**0,00**
Menu options	5,38	1,21	0,00	5,31	1,31	0,00	-0,07	1,44	0,74
Service Quality	6,11	1,16	0,00	5,24	1,49	0,00	-0,87	1,54	0,00
Cuisine Diversity	5,53	1,17	0,00	5,37	1,30	0,00	-0,16	1,31	0,42
Food Quality	6,37	1,15	0,00	5,61	1,46	0,00	-0,76	1,42	0,00
Value for money	6,13	1,22	0,00	5,28	1,50	0,00	-0,85	1,55	0,00
Cultural and Natural Attractions	**5,79**	**1,11**	**0,00**	**5,26**	**1,33**	**0,00**	**-0,53**	**1,14**	**0,00**
Monuments Attractivity	5,98	1,07	0,00	5,53	1,43	0,00	-0,45	1,19	0,01
Museums Attractivity	5,84	1,22	0,00	5,38	1,49	0,00	-0,46	1,30	0,01
Nature Attractions	5,91	1,19	0,00	5,47	1,38	0,00	-0,43	1,35	0,01
Cultural options variety	5,61	1,31	0,00	5,31	1,41	0,00	-0,30	1,36	0,12
Monuments and Museums value for money	5,72	1,40	0,00	5,06	1,62	0,00	-0,67	1,76	0,00
Cultural options value for money	5,72	1,39	0,00	5,09	1,59	0,00	-0,64	1,70	0,00
Tour costs (bus) value for money	5,73	1,37	0,00	4,84	1,68	0,00	-0,89	1,83	0,00
Activities and Events	**5,53**	**1,01**	**0,00**	**5,03**	**1,21**	**0,00**	**-0,50**	**1,00**	**0,00**
Outdoor Recreation Variety	5,58	1,24	0,00	4,98	1,39	0,00	-0,61	1,11	0,00
Evening Entertainment Variety	5,49	1,23	0,00	5,24	1,42	0,00	-0,25	1,30	0,25
Evening entertainment value for money	5,43	1,34	0,00	4,79	1,61	0,00	-0,65	1,70	0,00
Variety of Special Events / Festivals	5,63	1,16	0,00	5,08	1,43	0,00	-0,55	1,22	0,00
Shopping	**5,78**	**1,10**	**0,00**	**5,16**	**1,38**	**0,00**	**-0,62**	**1,22**	**0,00**
Service Cordiality	5,77	1,36	0,00	5,22	1,55	0,00	-0,55	1,48	0,00
Store Variety	5,46	1,23	0,00	5,20	1,43	0,00	-0,25	1,34	0,24

Continued on following page

Table 7. Continued

Attributes and Categories of Attributes	Importance			Performance			Gap		
	Mean	SD	p-value	Mean	SD	p-value	Mean Diff.	SD	p-value
Offer Quality	5,94	1,20	0,00	5,17	1,47	0,00	-0,77	1,44	0,00
Value for money	5,83	1,25	0,00	5,02	1,58	0,00	-0,81	1,61	0,00
Accessibility and Infrastructures	**5,76**	**1,23**	**0,00**	**4,39**	**1,59**	**0,00**	**-1,36**	**1,42**	**0,00**
Tourism centers availability and help provided	5,84	1,51	0,00	4,59	1,81	0,00	-1,25	1,79	0,00
Public transport information	5,80	1,43	0,00	4,40	1,81	0,01	-1,40	1,77	0,00
Public transport accessibility	5,83	1,56	0,00	4,12	1,97	0,25	-1,72	1,97	0,00
Public transport network density (number of stops), distance to public transport stop	5,67	1,46	0,00	4,39	1,85	0,01	-1,28	1,77	0,00
Individual transport availability (taxi, uber or similar)	5,87	1,28	0,00	5,39	1,45	0,00	-0,47	1,50	0,00
Car parking availability	4,86	1,85	0,00	3,98	2,01	0,45	-0,88	2,32	0,00
Technological infrastructures availability (Internet access, etc.) (Lisbon municipality offer)	5,77	1,46	0,00	4,13	1,96	0,24	-1,65	2,08	0,00
Technological infrastructures availability (Internet access, etc.) (Shopping centers, shops, transports, etc.)	6,00	1,34	0,00	4,94	1,76	0,00	-1,06	1,77	0,00

Gap Analysis

Gap analysis concerns the difference between performance and importance means for each attribute or attribute category (Bacon, 2003), (Feng et al., 2014). A negative value shows that the performance in an attribute or attribute category is lower than the importance that is given to it, presenting a potential situation to improve their performance.

Considering each of the 40 attributes, not all have statistically significant gaps, meaning that for these attributes their performance and importance have similar evaluations (Table 7). The larger negative gaps are -1.72 for public transport accessibility (passengers with special needs), - 1.65 for technological infrastructures availability (Internet access offered by Lisbon Municipality), and -1.40 for public transport information (schedules, etc.). Eight of the attributes, while with a negative gap, these gaps are not statistically significant.

The results show again the importance of improvement of the technological infrastructures by Lisbon municipality to achieve a better performance in a truly relevant attribute for a location tourism (and business) attractivity. We must remember that one of the reasons why the Web Summit is now in Lisbon and not Dublin was the problems with the technological infrastructures like Wi-Fi access that could not fail in this kind of event. "The conference moved to Lisbon in 2016, citing the limitations of size and infrastructure in Dublin, where it had begun its life in 2009" (O'Leary, 2020).

The only attribute with a positive gap, but not statistically significant, is housing type diversity (hotels, hostels, local housing, etc.).

For the categories of attributes all gaps are negative, but not statistically significant negative values. The differences range from -1.36 in accessibility and infrastructures to -0.40 in accommodation, as shown in Table 7.

Importance-Performance Analysis Grid

The importance and performance scores of all attributes and latent variables (categories of attributes) were applied to an IPA grid, considering both scale-centered and data-centered techniques (Bacon, 2003) with the diagonal model line in all grids (Hawes & Rao, 1985).

In the scale-centered analysis only the car parking availability, with a 'negative' performance mean of 3.98 and the lowest importance score, although higher than 4 (4.86), is in quadrant I (concentrate here). All other attributes are in quadrant II (Keep up the good work).

For the data-centered IPA grids applied to the attributes (Chart 1), the importance mean is 5.75, and the performance mean is 5.06 and for the data-centered grids of categories of attributes (Chart 2), the importance mean is 5.79 and the performance mean is 5.11, presenting more exigent IPA grids than the scale-centered.

Figure 2. Importance-performance grid - attributes (data-centered)

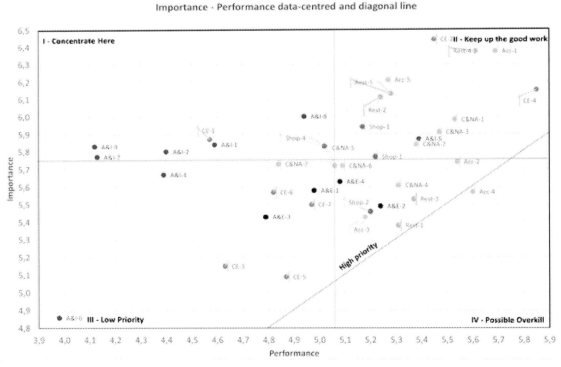

As expected, since it has a positive gap, accommodation (housing categories) is the only attribute below the diagonal line, meaning that the respondents consider that Lisbon has a good accommodation offer considering hotels, hostels, local housing, etc.

The 40 attributes are distributed throughout the four quadrants, with seven of them (the lowest number of attributes in one quadrant) in quadrant I (concentrate here) and 9 in quadrant III (low priority)., 13 in quadrant II (keep with good work) or quadrant III (low priority). The quadrant IV (possible overkill) has 11 attributes.

Considering Quadrant I, concentrate here, one of the attributes concerns the city environment (street cleaning), and the other concerns shopping (value for money). All other five related to accessibility and infrastructures, including the availability of tourism centers (Lisbon has 5, including one in the airport and another one in the international train station), public transport information (schedules, etc., that are present in the bus and subway stations and internet), public transport accessibility (transportation for passengers with special needs), technological infrastructures availability (internet access offered by Lisbon Municipality (inexistent as a Lisbon offer but some municipality buildings have it)), and technological infrastructures availability (internet access available in shopping centers, shops, transports (bus, subway, airport), etc. (much more common and faster in these days)). One should notice that only one of the five technological infrastructure availability attributes in this quadrant is a partial private-sector responsibility, Internet access, etc. (shopping centers, shops, transports, etc.).

As such, the IPA model shows both attributes that consider the "technological infrastructure availability" in Quadrant I, "Concentrate here", with a need of investment to improve the Performance considering the Importance of these attributes.

In the opposite quadrant IV (Possible overkill), there are 11 attributes of all categories except accessibility and infrastructures. The accommodation has three of the five attributes in this quadrant, showing that there is a perception of a good Lisbon accommodation offer.

There are nine attributes of four categories, in quadrant III (Low priority). Considering the category City Environment, the attributes are Policing (police visibility, level of support if needed)] and Medical-hospital support (hospitals, health centers, medical staff, emergency (112)), Resting atmosphere (low bustle, excitement, city noise) and the Concentration of tourists. Lisbon resting atmosphere and tourist concentration, while in this quadrant, have importance scores to show at least some concern because they are close to the data mean, but it is expected to be less concerning in a pós-pandemic Lisbon. Also, the NHS investment made with the pandemic will stay and improve the performance perception about medical-hospital support. The other attributes are Public transport network density ((number of stops, distance to public transport stop) that are improving like the subway investment in more stations through the city to be made in the following years. Even the car parking public and private offers are increasing. The other ones, Cultural and Natural Attractions (Tour costs (bus) value for money) and Activities and Events (Evening entertainment value for money) are private-sector decisions while Activities and Events (Outdoor Recreation Variety (Physical Activity Equipment, Cycle Tracks, Bicycles, etc.)) had large investments by the Lisbon municipality in the recent years.

Quadrant II (keep with good work) has 13 attributes, the highest number of attributes in one quadrant, showing that Lisbon is doing well regarding attractiveness as a tourism destination.

In the categories of attributes data-centered IPA grid (Chart 2), there are no categories of attributes in quadrant I (concentrate here), three categories of attributes are in quadrant III (low priority), namely City Environment, Activities and Events and Accessibility and Infrastructure (due to lower Importance of some of these category attributes but with the lowest Performance of all categories), and two categories of variables are in quadrant II (keep up the good work). Restaurants and Accommodation. Cultural and Natural Attractions and Shopping are in quadrant IV (possible overkill). As such, we can consider these results as globally positive indicators for Lisbon's competitiveness as a tourist attraction.

Figure 3. Importance-performance grid – categories of attributes (data-centered)

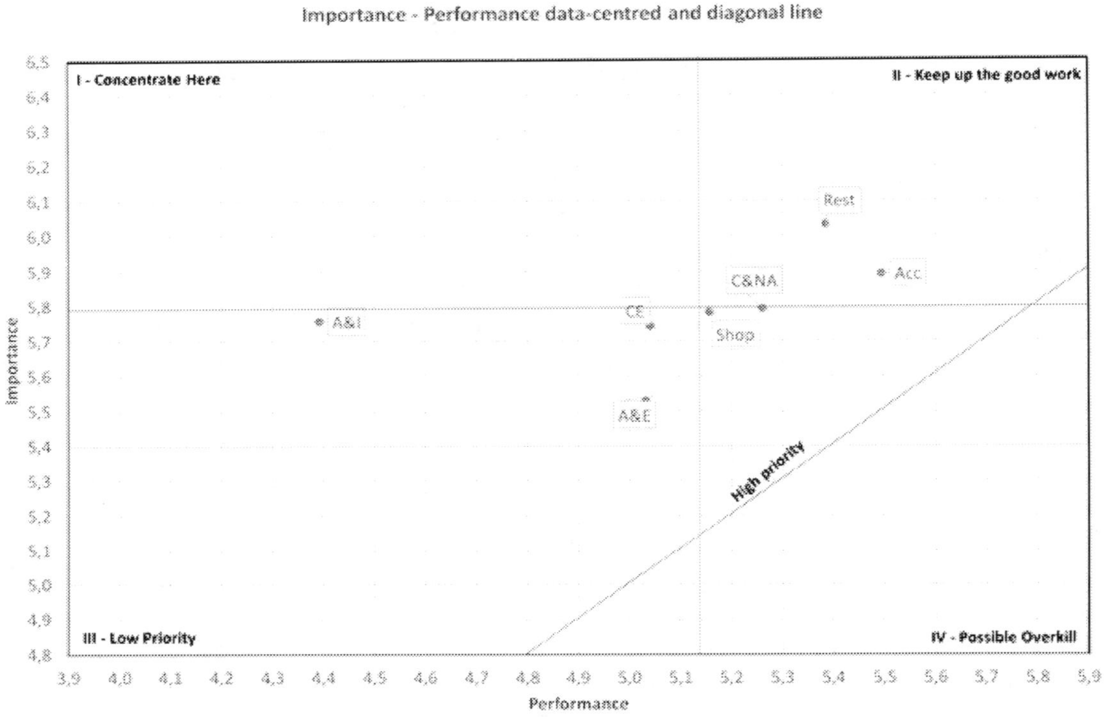

CONCLUSIONS, LIMITATIONS, AND FUTURE RESEARCH

This research aims at assessing Lisbon's competitiveness to attract tourists using the importance-performance analysis (IPA) based on the perceptions of tourism stakeholders working in several areas of tourism business in Lisbon, like hotels, restaurants, travel agencies, and others, whose activity depends on the tourist's attraction to the city.

The results reveal that all 40 attributes studied are considered as important, while globally there exists a positive perception of the city attributes performance.

. In terms of performance, the lowest score of performance was car parking availability, with also the lowest importance score for this attribute, because it is not expected that tourists that visit Lisbon will use a car often. Other two attributes with low performance to be considered as in need of improvement are public transport accessibility (passengers with special needs) and technological infrastructure availability (Internet access offered by Lisbon Municipality), even if in the last situation the offer by the private-sector locations and public transports can help in that gap. These results show a need for attention for these two attributes, even if not having a negative (below 4) evaluation. Both attributes are municipality responsibility.

On the IPA data-centered grids, only seven of the 40 attributes are in quadrant I (concentrate here), five of these being in the accessibility and infrastructures category with four of them as municipality responsibilities, and nine in quadrant III (low priority), with four of them being in the accessibility and infrastructures category and four of them being in the city environment category, with the majority also a municipality responsibility.

Regarding the gap analysis (the difference between performance and importance), importance scores are higher than the performance scores for all attributes except accommodation type diversity (hotels, hostels, local housing, etc.)] where the performance mean is slightly higher than the importance mean. The higher negative mean difference is for public transport accessibility (passengers with special needs), attribute with also the second lower mean, 4.12, showing the attention needed to this attribute by Lisbon municipality.

We are now in a huge technological change with the implementation of the fifth generation technology standard for cellular networks, the 5G and a new generation of Wi-Fi technology, Wi-Fi 6. Considering 5G versus Wi-Fi 6, they are considered to complement each other in different environments, with 5G more in outdoor networks and Wi-Fi-6 in indoor networks (Cisco, 2020).

Regarding Lisbon, while the private sector at the beginning of 2021 started the implementation of the 5G tests, the first one within a Football stadium (A Bola, 2021), museums, and public transport systems bus (Carris) and subway (Metro) already have Wi-Fi connection that is expected to be updated with new technologies like the Wi-Fi 6 (Dinheiro Vivo, 2020).

Lisbon Municipality is preparing investment to have a Wi-Fi network covering the city without any details regarding the technology options considering the complementarity of 5G and Wi-Fi 6 technologies. The strategy must consider also the EU Roaming legislation, update at the beginning of 2021 (European Comission, 2021), that allows any EU citizen to have in a country they visit the same costs and features of the communications plan they have at home, increasing the probability that the tourist will have greater use of their own operator data services.

In terms of the attribute's categories, none is in quadrant I (concentrate here) and three of these (City Environment, Activities and Events and Accessibility and Infrastructure) are in quadrant III (low priority), due to the explained reasons.

These results are coherent with the recent year's tourism World Travel Awards, such as the World's Leading City Break Destination 2020, Europe's Leading City Tourist Board 2020, World's Leading City Break Destination 2019, Europe's Leading City Break Destination 2019, Europe's Leading City Tourist Board 2019, World's Leading City Break Destination 2018, World's Leading City Destination 2018 and Europe's Leading City Destination 2018.

This research has limitations that must be addressed in future research. The most relevant one is the sample size, which is lower than advised in the methodology literature concerning IPA.

Considering the attributes near the discriminating thresholds, further analysis can be made with the use of confidence intervals to keep the validity of the research (Wu & Shieh, 2009).

Additional attributes could also be used, considering other characteristics of a location's attractiveness for tourists.

Notwithstanding, there are practical and theoretical implications of these results. From the practitioners' point of view, results are useful to obtain efficient investment public policies by destination managers such as the Lisbon municipality or even the Portuguese government, as they are for the decision-making of all categories of Lisbon tourism stakeholders.

From an academic standpoint, this chapter addresses will increase of the literature regarding the application of the IPA model using data from tourism stakeholders, revealing the relevance of a multiple stakeholder approach to identifying a destination's attributes for competitiveness, following some authors conclusions that the recipient of the questionnaire should be the one who knows best the studied market, which is not necessarily the tourist who visit it, avoiding some of the bias problems found in tourist questionnaires (Bacon, 2003) and (Dwyer, Cvelbar, Edwards & Mihalic, 2012).

Further research should complement these results with the perception of tourists regarding the same attributes. This research can also offer insights about eventual differences between the tourism stakeholder's perceptions and the tourist's perceptions in terms of attributes importance and performance, following the research of authors like (Bacon, 2003) and (Dwyer, Cvelbar, Edwards & Mihalic, 2012).

Further statistical analysis could also be useful, using different statistical tools like logistic regression to assess which attribute contribute to the tourist decision about Lisbon as a travel destination. Also benchmarking analysis, comparing different destination cities throughout Europe through a common set of attributes, can be a relevant line of research.

REFERENCES

Abalo, J., Varela, J., & Manzano, V. (2007). Importance values for Importance-Performance Analysis: A formula for spreading out values derived from preference rankings. *Journal of Business Research*, *60*(2), 115–121. doi:10.1016/j.jbusres.2006.10.009

Albayrak, T., & Caber, M. (2013). The symmetric and asymmetric influences of destination attributes on overall visitor satisfaction. *Current Issues in Tourism*, *16*(2), 149–166. doi:10.1080/13683500.2012.682978

Azzopardi, E., & Nash, R. (2013). A critical evaluation of importance-performance analysis. *Tourism Management*, *35*, 222–233. doi:10.1016/j.tourman.2012.07.007

Bacon, D. R. (2003). A Comparison of Approaches to Importance-Performance Analysis. *International Journal of Market Research*, *45*(1), 1–15. doi:10.1177/147078530304500101

Barnes, S. J., Mattsson, J., & Sørensen, F. (2014). Destination brand experience and visitor behavior: Testing a scale in the tourism context. *Annals of Tourism Research*, *48*, 121–139. doi:10.1016/j.annals.2014.06.002

Bi, J. W., Liu, Y., Fan, Z. P., & Zhang, J. (2019). Wisdom of crowds: Conducting importance-performance analysis (IPA) through online reviews. *Tourism Management, 70*(March), 460–478. doi:10.1016/j.tourman.2018.09.010

Bola, A. (2021, April 9). *A BOLA - Estádio da Luz é o primeiro a receber tecnologia 5G em Portugal (Benfica).* Retrieved June 29, 2021, from https://www.abola.pt/nnh/2021-04-09/benfica-estadio-da-luz-e-o-primeiro-a-receber-tecnologia-5g-em-portugal/885908

Bruyere, B. L., Rodriguez, D. A., & Vaske, J. J. (2002). Enhancing Importance-Performance Analysis Through Segmentation Brett. *Journal of Travel & Tourism Marketing*, *12*(1), 63–80. doi:10.1300/J073v12n01_05

Busacca, B., & Arbore, A. (2011). Rejuvenating importance-performance analysis. *Journal of Service Management*, *22*(3), 409–429. doi:10.1108/09564231111136890

Caber, M., Albayrak, T., & Loiacono, E. T. (2013). The Classification of Extranet Attributes in Terms of Their Asymmetric Influences on Overall User Satisfaction: An Introduction to Asymmetric Impact-Performance Analysis. *Journal of Travel Research*, *52*(1), 106–116. doi:10.1177/0047287512451139

Chen, C.-Y., Wu, T.-S., Li, M.-L., & Wang, C.-T. (2018). Integration of Importance - Performance Analysis and Fuzzy Dematel. *International Journal of Computer Science and Information Technologies*, *10*(3), 19–38. doi:10.5121/ijcsit.2018.10302

Chu, R. (2002). Stated-importance versus derived-importance customer satisfaction measurement. *Journal of Services Marketing*, *16*(4), 285–301. doi:10.1108/08876040210433202

Cisco. (2020, April). *5 Things to Know About Wi-Fi 6 and 5G - Cisco*. Retrieved June 29, 2021, from https://www.cisco.com/c/m/en_us/solutions/enterprise-networks/802-11ax-solution/nb-06-5-things-WiFi6-5G-infograph-cte-en.html

Coghlan, A. (2012). Facilitating reef tourism management through an innovative importance-performance analysis method. *Tourism Management*, *33*(4), 767–775. doi:10.1016/j.tourman.2011.08.010

Crompton, J. L., & Duray, N. A. (1985). An Investigation of the Relative Efficacy of Four Alternative Approaches to Importance-Performance Analysis. *Journal of the Academy of Marketing Science*, *13*(4), 69–80. doi:10.1007/BF02737200

Cronin, J. J. Jr, & Taylor, S. A. (1992). Measuring Service Quality: A Reexamination and Extension. *Journal of Marketing*, *56*(3), 55–68. doi:10.1177/002224299205600304

Dinheiro Vivo. (2020, June 17). *Lisboa quer rede wi-fi gratuita pela cidade*. Retrieved June 29, 2021, from https://www.dinheirovivo.pt/empresas/lisboa-quer-rede-wi-fi-gratuita-pela-cidade-12695714.html

Djeri, L., Stamenković, P., Blešić, I., Milićević, S., & Ivkov, M. (2018). An importance-performance analysis of destination competitiveness factors: Case of Jablanica district in Serbia. *Economic Research-Ekonomska Istrazivanja*, *31*(1), 811–826. doi:10.1080/1331677X.2018.1456351

Dwyer, L., Cvelbar, L. K., Edwards, D., & Mihalic, T. (2012). Fashioning a destination tourism future: The case of Slovenia. *Tourism Management*, *33*(2), 305–316. doi:10.1016/j.tourman.2011.03.010

Dwyer, L., Forsyth, P., & Rao, P. (2000). The price competitiveness of travel and tourism: A comparison of 19 destinations. *Tourism Management*, *21*(1), 9–22. doi:10.1016/S0261-5177(99)00081-3

Dwyer, L., & Kim, C. (2003). Destination competitiveness: Determinants and indicators. *Current Issues in Tourism*, *6*(5), 369–414. doi:10.1080/13683500308667962

Enright, M. J., & Newton, J. (2004). Tourism destination competitiveness: A quantitative approach. *Tourism Management*, *25*(6), 777–788. doi:10.1016/j.tourman.2004.06.008

European Comission. (2021, February 24). *Commission proposes new Regulation to ensure free roaming*. Retrieved June 29, 2021, from https://ec.europa.eu/commission/presscorner/detail/en/IP_21_653

Evans, M. R., & Chon, K.-S. (1989). Formulating and Evaluating Tou Rism Policy Using Importance-Performance Analysis. *Hospitality Education and Research Journal, 13*(3), 203–213. doi:10.1177/109634808901300320

Feng, M., Mangan, J., Wong, C., Xu, M., & Lalwani, C. (2014). Investigating the different approaches to importance-performance analysis. *Service Industries Journal, 34*(12), 1021–1041. doi:10.1080/02642069.2014.915949

Gomezelj, D. O., & Mihalič, T. (2008). Destination competitiveness-Applying different models, the case of Slovenia. *Tourism Management, 29*(2), 294–307. doi:10.1016/j.tourman.2007.03.009

Gooroochurn, N., & Sugiyarto, G. (2005). Competitiveness indicators in the travel and tourism industry. *Tourism Economics, 11*(1), 25–43. doi:10.5367/0000000053297130

Guizzardi, A., & Stacchini, A. (2017). Destinations strategic groups via Multivariate Competition-based IPA. *Tourism Management, 58*, 40–50. doi:10.1016/j.tourman.2016.10.004

Hassan, S. S. (2000). Determinants of market competitiveness in an environmentally sustainable tourism industry. *Journal of Travel Research, 38*(3), 239–245. doi:10.1177/004728750003800305

Hawes, J. M., & Rao, C. P. (1985). Using importance — Performance analysis to develop health care marketing strategies. *Journal of Health Care Marketing, 5*(4), 19–25. http://widgets.ebscohost.com/prod/customerspecific/ns000290/authentication/index.php?url=https%3A%2F%2Fsearch.ebscohost.com%2Flogin.aspx%3Fdirect%3Dtrue%26AuthType%3Dip%2Ccookie%2Cshib%2Cuid%26db%3Dbth%26AN%3D6850675%26lang%3Dpt-pt%26site%3Deds-live%26sco PMID:10275156

Jeng, C. R., Snyder, A. T., & Chen, C. F. (2019). Importance–performance analysis as a strategic tool for tourism marketers: The case of Taiwan's Destination Image. *Tourism and Hospitality Research, 19*(1), 112–125. doi:10.1177/1467358417704884

Kozak, M. (2002). Comparative analysis of tourist motivations by nationality and destinations. *Tourism Management, 23*(3), 221–232. doi:10.1016/S0261-5177(01)00090-5

Kwon, J., Chung, T., Yoon, S. H., & Kwon, K. B. (2017). Importance and Satisfaction of Destination Attraction for Water-Based Tourism in Jeju Island. *Asian Social Science, 13*(10), 1. doi:10.5539/ass.v13n10p1

Lai, I. K. W., & Hitchcock, M. (2015). Importance-performance analysis in tourism: A framework for researchers. *Tourism Management, 48*, 242–267. doi:10.1016/j.tourman.2014.11.008

Leask, A. (2016). Visitor attraction management: A critical review of research 2009–2014. *Tourism Management, 57*, 334–361. doi:10.1016/j.tourman.2016.06.015

Lee, J., Choi, Y., & Breiter, D. (2013). An Exploratory Study of Convention Destination Competitiveness from the Attendees' Perspective: Importance-Performance Analysis and Repeated Measures of Manova. *Journal of Hospitality & Tourism Research (Washington, D.C.), 40*(5), 589–610. doi:10.1177/1096348013515913

Mangion, M. L., Durbarry, R., & Sinclair, M. T. (2005). Tourism competitiveness: Price and quality. *Tourism Economics, 11*(1), 45–68. doi:10.5367/0000000053297202

Martilla, J. A., & James, J. C. (1977). Importance-Performance Analysis. *Journal of Marketing, 41*(1), 77–79. doi:10.1177/002224297704100112

Matzler, K., Sauerwein, E., & Heischmidt, K. A. (2003). Importance-performance analysis revisited: The role of the factor structure of customer satisfaction. *Service Industries Journal, 23*(2), 112–129. doi:10.1080/02642060412331300912

Morgan, M., Lugosi, P., & Ritchie, J. B. (Eds.). (2010). The tourism and leisure experience: Consumer and managerial perspectives. Channel View Publication.

O'Leary, N. (2020, December 15). *Portugal stands by €11m annual fee to host Web Summit.* Retrieved June 29, 2021, from https://www.irishtimes.com/business/technology/portugal-stands-by-11m-annual-fee-to-host-web-summit-1.4436786

Oh, H. (2001). Revisiting importance – performance analysis. *Tourism Management, 22*(6), 617–627. doi:10.1016/S0261-5177(01)00036-X

Padma, P. (2016). Strategic quadrants and service quality: Tourist satisfaction in Portugal. *The Quality Management Journal, 23*(2), 57–70. doi:10.1080/10686967.2016.11918471

Parasuraman, A., Zeithaml, V. A., & Berry, L. L. (1985). A Conceptual Model Service Its Quality and Implications for Future Research. *Research Paper, 49*(4), 41–50. doi:10.1016/S0148-2963(99)00084-3

Patandianan, M. V., & Shibusawa, H. (2020). Importance and performance of streetscapes at a tourism destination in Indonesia: The residents' perspectives. *Frontiers of Architectural Research, 9*(3), 641–655. doi:10.1016/j.foar.2020.05.006

Pearce, P., & Benckendorff, P. (2006). Journal of Quality Assurance in Hospitality & Tourism Benchmarking, Usable Knowledge and Tourist Attractions. *Journal of Quality Assurance in Hospitality & Tourism, 7*(1–2), 29–52. doi:10.1300/J162v07n01_03

Rašovská, I., Kubickova, M., & Ryglová, K. (2020). Importance–performance analysis approach to destination management. *Tourism Economics.* Advance online publication. doi:10.1177/1354816620903913

Ritchie, J. R. B., & Crouch, G. I. (2003). *The Competitive Destination: A Sustainable Tourism Perspective.* CABI Pub. Retrieved from https://books.google.pt/books?id=yvydAwAAQBAJ

Sanbonmatsu, D. M., Kardes, F. R., Houghton, D. C., Ho, E. A., & Posavac, S. S. (2003). Overestimating the Importance of the Given Information in Multiattribute Consumer Judgment. *Journal of Consumer Psychology, 13*(3), 289–300. doi:10.1207/S15327663JCP1303_10

Sarantakos, S. (2013). *Social Research* (4th ed.). Palgrave Macmillian. doi:10.1007/978-1-137-29247-6

Sever, I. (2015). Importance-performance analysis: A valid management tool? *Tourism Management, 48*, 43–53. doi:10.1016/j.tourman.2014.10.022

Simpson, G. D., Patroni, J., Teo, A. C. K., Chan, J. K. L., & Newsome, D. (2019). Importance-performance analysis to inform visitor management at marine wildlife tourism destinations. *Journal of Tourism Futures, 6*(2), 165–180. doi:10.1108/JTF-11-2018-0067

Soler, I. P., & Gemar, G. (2019). Factors that affect the perception of a tourist resource's value: The case of the Caminito del Rey. *Tourism & Management Studies, 15*(3), 7–16. doi:10.18089/tms.2019.150301

Sörensson, A., & von Friedrichs, Y. (2013). An importance-performance analysis of sustainable tourism: A comparison between international and national tourists. *Journal of Destination Marketing & Management, 2*(1), 14–21. doi:10.1016/j.jdmm.2012.11.002

Tarrant, M. A., & Smith, E. K. (2002). The use of a modified importance-performance framework to examine visitor satisfaction with attributes of outdoor recreation settings. *Managing Leisure, 7*(2), 69–82. doi:10.1080/13606710210137246

Tonge, J., & Moore, S. A. (2007). Importance-satisfaction analysis for marine-park hinterlands: A Western Australian case study. *Tourism Management, 28*(3), 768–776. doi:10.1016/j.tourman.2006.05.007

Tsang, S., Royse, C. F., & Terkawi, A. S. (2017). Guidelines for developing, translating, and validating a questionnaire in perioperative and pain medicine. *Saudi Journal of Anaesthesia, 11*(5), 80. Advance online publication. doi:10.4103ja.SJA_203_17 PMID:28616007

Tse, D. K., & Wilton, P. C. (1988). Models of Consumer Satisfaction Formation: An Extension. *JMR, Journal of Marketing Research, 25*(2), 204–212. doi:10.1177/002224378802500209

Vodeb, K., & Rudež, H. N. (2017). Which attributes are important to tourists in a mature seaside destination? A case of Opatija in Croatia. *Tourism (Zagreb), 65*(3), 267–279. doi:10.1016/j.addr.2005.07.002

Weston, R., & Gore, P. A. Jr. (2006). A Brief Guide to Structural Equation Modeling. *The Counseling Psychologist, 34*(5), 719–751. Advance online publication. doi:10.1177/0011000006286345

Wu, H. H., & Shieh, J. I. (2009). The development of a confidence interval-based importance-performance analysis by considering variability in analyzing service quality. *Expert Systems with Applications, 36*(3 PART 2), 7040–7044. doi:10.1016/j.eswa.2008.08.055

Wullur, M., & Samehe, V. (2020). Importance Performance Analysis using Dematel: A Case Study on Tourist Destination Attributes in Manado Indonesia. *SHS Web of Conferences, 76*, 01024. 10.1051hsconf/20207601024

Zaiontz, C. (2019). *Real Statistics Using Excel*. www.real-statistics.com

Chapter 13

Living Room Instead of Hotel Room:
The Underlying Motivation of Peer-to-Peer Booking in Airbnb and Hotels

Artur Martea

Estoril Higher Institute for Tourism and Hotel Studies, Portugal

ABSTRACT

The chapter explores shared accommodation platforms such as Airbnb and the primary motivations for its customers. This research will be based on the deductive process, which is focused on primary and secondary research. This research aims to analyze the motivation towards either the Airbnb platform or traditional hotel from different perspectives, such as economic, environmental, and social. Additionally, after secondary data research, the questionnaire has been constructed to understand the main concepts of the P2P platform and its customers' needs. The investigation tried to notice what are the motivations which drive individuals to use P2P accommodation service. Through the survey, it was possible to see the motivations mainly related to the economic factor and environmental. Primarily due to the lower price of Airbnb, there is a more significant intent to book through this specific platform.

INTRODUCTION

Economic transformations have characterized the 21st century. After major historical events, the world economy intensified its revival by giant steps, cooperation between countries, technological development and favorable economic policies. One of those significant changing concepts that influence modern industries is collaborative consumption, later called sharing economy (Felson & Spaeth, 1978). The tourism and hospitality sector has seen an enormous shift in travel and changing patterns of tourism consumption based on alliances with the sharing economy.

It is also essential to mention the influence of digital solutions in the hospitality sector, driving profound changes in consumer behavior based on the sharing economy boom (Juul, 2017). As well, Marketing was an essential factor for P2P platform growth. For instance, moving from Marketing 1.0

DOI: 10.4018/978-1-7998-8306-7.ch013

to 4.0 was a massive step into getting closer to consumers and reducing the costs from traditional marketing to digital. Kotler et al. (2017) stated that Marketing 4.0 combines online and offline interaction between companies and customers. Additionally, it is about balancing machine-to-machine connectivity with human-to-human.

Moreover, millennials, or Generation Y, are the primary influencers of all industries. They are characterized as the segment of consumers for whom collaborative consumption is most appealing, as a means of providing access to products, services and resources without the necessity of purchasing or owning them (Hwang & Griffiths, 2017). The different perceptions over ownership and the empathy towards sustainability issues changed consumerism completely, making sharing services more and more popular.

Regarding the hotel industry, the most significant impact has been made with the appearance of online sharing accommodation providers such as Airbnb. Looking back at history, the primary motivation for bringing the service on the market was not the lack of accommodation on the supply curve, but the high price of the Hotel service, which could not allow people to use it. The demand to have a similar Hotel service but affordable made Airbnb's service overgrow.

In 2008, the born year of Airbnb, people just started to understand the sharing economy concept. The P2P service was being noticed not only in shared accommodations but also in the car-sharing industry. The whole concept of traveling has been changed from the traditional hotel stay and all included packages to a new way of traveling. They are being defined and targeted as novelty-seeking travelers (Guttentag, 2015). The analysis of the phenomenon will be limited to a specific territory, Lisbon, Portugal.

Everything started with the Great Recession, which has hit the country in 2008 and had a significant impact on all major industries. The horrific economic crisis led to the collapse of hotel operations, being severely affected overnight stays falling and recovering only in 2013 (Cushman & Wakefield, 2017). This is one of the most critical factors that made Airbnb, part of the shared economy, proliferate on the market. It was not only about the consumer side but also the buy-to-let side investment.

The evolution and effects of shared accommodation systems can be analyzed thoroughly only after having the concrete definition of the most important terms. Sharing economy is a relatively new term not used much in the current scientific literature. The sharing economy or collaborative economy describes a business model that builds on sharing resources between individuals through P2P services, allowing customers to access goods when needed (Böckmann, 2013). After the appearance of short-term rental accommodations, those were qualified as part of the sharing economy as being created according to the same business model. Airbnb claims to be part of the sharing or collaborative economy, where digital platforms allow the exchange of underused goods and services, potentially implying a more sustainable form of consumption (Dredge & Gyimóthy, 2015). Far behind the sustainability factor, Airbnb has many other reasons that made its growth so impactful for the Hotel Industry.

For Generation Y, people born in 1981-1994/6, popular media users with high access to information and high frequency of travel, the idea to stay in a host accommodation seems engaging and innovative. People seek to choose the shared accommodation type in city breaks due to extra income, openness and a high level of interest in getting to know the area from the locals' perspective (Leask, Fyall & Barron, 2014). The growth of tourism in Lisbon, Portugal, has been credited lately to the city's focus on developing cultural tourism and private sectors' increasing investments in real estate. In the recent studies, in the Greater Lisbon area (a metropolitan area covering 18 municipalities), there are currently 360 hotel establishments offering 31.500 accommodation units. According to Airbnb.com's official stats for 2017, there are around 20.000 rooms available with a capacity to accommodate 50.000 people, and the number continues to increase.

According to the study conducted in July 2017, in the peak month of traveling, most prices fall between 60$ and 104$ per night, depending on the accommodation type, which is cheaper than an actual hotel stays. The simple search of the same room, same period, in the same area (Commerce Square, Lisbon) show a double price of 225$ (Cunha, 2017). However, many Hoteliers and industry analysts perceive Airbnb as a threat. Many others consider Airbnb not significant. As Guttentag and Smith (2017) stated, the skeptics see Airbnb as inconsequentially small, and besides that, Worldwide Hilton's CEO has commented that it is tough for Airbnb to replicate what they are doing. However, as mentioned in (Zervas et al., 2017), Airbnb can affect hotel room revenue through lower occupancy rates, decreased hotel room prices, or a combination of these two factors, but did not impact revenue per available room (RevPAR), suggesting hotels were reducing rates to maintain occupancy. It has been proved in (Guttentag et al., 2017) research that (Swig, 2014) a hospitality consultant who looked at San Francisco hotel occupancy rates from early 2014 and found weekday rates to be up and weekend rates to be down, which he suggested was due to Airbnb and other similar companies because weekend occupancies are driven more by leisure travelers, who are more likely to use Airbnb.

In the present time, this approach to the economy has been explored by modern research studies mainly to the extent of where the origin is and how it can replace traditional accommodation during hotel trips. There are several literature sources since 2010 which analyze in-depth the first discussed questions. Still, there is a gap in the works researching the cause and consequences of the phenomenon in the hotel industry. This work contributes to the investigation of the shared accommodation system and how people's choice to use it changes or not the growth and evolution of hotel giants on the market.

LITERATURE REVIEW

Shared Economy in Tourism and Hospitality

Recent studies of P2P platforms have helped people share and use underutilized resources on a large scale upon payment, giving rise to the new phenomenon called sharing economics (Roma, Panniello & Lo Nigro, 2019). In other words, under the sharing economy model, everyone can become a service provider by using specific underutilized resources. Additionally, as Roma et al. (2019) mentioned, excellent examples of platforms enabling sharing economies are Airbnb and Couchsurfing for hospitality or Uber and BlaBlaCar in the automotive industry.

This unique and novel characteristic of using underutilized resources owned by many individuals translates into a competitive price offered by sharing economy platforms, thus making them a real threat to cope with the traditional industries. According to Ernst & Young (2018), sharing economy is a socio-economic ecosystem built around sharing human and physical resources.

While sharing economy activities can fall into four categories, namely recirculation of goods, increased utilization of durable assets, exchange of services and sharing of productive assets, sharing business presents two significant challenges: a) own goods or provide services that they provide to customers, usually short-term; b) create P2P platforms connecting providers or hosts with users (Lim, 2020).

Sharing assets is an old practice in human societies. The so-called "sharing economy" is much more recent, as it involves matching people who want to share assets via online platforms, potentially at a global scale, using personal computers, tablets and smartphones (Gata, 2015).

The term "rent" is nowadays becoming the new "owner." The fundamental question is why an individual needs to own a unique place if that could be rented property or vehicle at a lower price. This change is getting more accessible by online services or platforms such as Airbnb, which helps people share their rooms or real places. BlaBlaCar, another platform for sharing rides with travelers. The firms help allocate resources where they are needed and charge a small percentage in return (Böckmann, 2013).

In tourism and hospitality, the sector has become one of the pioneering sectors of the sharing economy, allowing visitors and residents to share their homes, cars, meals and local expertise (Cheng, 2016). Juul (2017) stated that sharing economy is not limited to tourism and can be found in many social and economic activities, although tourism has been one of the sectors most impacted.

From Marketing 1.0 to 4.0

The term web 1.0 emerged from the research around the development of Web 2.0. Before that, the researcher usually referred to Web 1.0 as Electronic Commerce or E-Business Lytras et al., (2009).

Additionally, Borges (2009) says that Marketing 1.0 is being characterized as being intrusive, interruptive and a style of one-way shouting at our customers (outbound marketing), where 2.0 Marketing is being characterized as being part more of conversations, collaborations, communities and WOM (word of mouth). In other words, Kotler et al. (2010) define marketing 2.0 as a customer-oriented era. The reason is that the customer defines the product value. Customers became well informed and they can quickly and independently compare several similar products. Each customer is unique in their preferences; therefore, Marketers have the intention to touch their hearts and mind.

Subsequently, Marketing 3.0 was born, where the aim was not only to satisfy consumers' needs but also to approach their needs. Companies practicing 3.0 marketing had more essential missions, visions and values to contribute to the world. As seen in Kotler et al. (2010), marketing 3.0 believes that consumers are complete human beings whose other needs and hopes should never be neglected. Therefore, Marketing 3.0 complements emotional marketing with human spirit marketing. "Entry into the era of Marketing 3.0 will make the algorithms to work for us and also instead of us, suggesting, simplifying and offering tailor-made solutions" Tarabasz, (2013, p.127). Thus, the term AI (Artificial Intelligence) ceases to be an abstraction, which becomes a part of everyday life.

Additionally, as Tabasz (2013) stated, if this barrier is crossable, as supposed by 2030, then web 4.0 is also known as the intelligent Web or Meta Web. An excellent example of 4.0 characteristics is seen in the work of Ungerman, Dedkova & Gurinova (2018). They describe the philosophy of Industry 4.0 will lead to a considerable reduction of manual workers and a high demand for well-educated people. In addition to that, there is an assumption of reducing the costs associated with the 4.0 marketing. The responses in Ungerman et al. (2018) showed that there are still no clear responses that an increase in costs will occur, as some of the businesses stated that they had observed some reductions in their costs. Time plays a significant role in this whole process. Thus, in the short term, thanks to the introduction of Marketing 4.0, these are costs that, in the long run, will lead to reductions. It is said that entry of this period will permit total merging of humans with technologies, allowing for complete remote equipment operation and treating machinery as living creatures (Ungerman et al., 2018).

In this transitional era, a new marketing approach is required. Thus, marketing 4.0 has been created as the natural outgrowth of marketing 3.0 (Kotler et al., 2017). Marketing 4.0 is a marketing approach that combines online and offline interaction between companies and customers. In this era, only digital interaction is not sufficient. Additionally, offline touch represents a massive differentiation in the online world.

Moreover, finally, Marketing 4.0 is about balancing machine-to-machine connectivity with human-to-human. This is done to improve marketing productivity. Nowadays, clients are no longer mass buyers with physical needs. As said in Kotler et al., 2017 "mind-heart and spirit, they are fully formed human beings."

New Business Models in Hospitality: From Traditional to P2P Models

Sharing economy and collaborative consumption are new concepts born from Web 2.0 and mobile technology, constituting the core of intelligent tourism cities, albeit sharing economy is one of the most representative business ecosystems (Yi, Yuan & Yoo, 2020).

Zervas et al. (2017) investigated how the entry of Airbnb influenced the local hospitality industry and the unemployment rate in the tourism industry. Most studies showed that the prevalence of P2P rental platforms significantly hurt the performance of the hotels (Liang, Schuckert, Law & Chen, 2020).

Many people believe that the sharing economy is an exciting alternative for consumers due to its economic benefits (ex. Low prices), which was considered necessary, especially after the global economic crisis Tussyadiah (2015). However, Botsman & Rogers (2011) argue that collaborative consumption is driven not by economic factors. Additionally, Tussyadiah (2015) affirms that consumers are aware of the pressure that overconsumption can influence our environment. She also believes that collaborative consumption will continue to grow even after the global economy is recovered. Thus, sharing is a way of reducing environmental concerns, the renewed belief in the importance of the community and these factors move consumers towards the practice of sharing and openness.

There are four primary vital factors why people tend to use P2P accommodations. Guttentag (2016) suggests that consumers use P2P due to their economic and experiential values. Tussyadiah (2016) believes that three more factors motivate people to use P2P platforms: Sustainability, community and economic benefits.

The sharing economy was facilitated by the appearance of an online platform entered with force into the hotel market. The growth of new business models of P2P platforms opened new opportunities for tourist destinations, such as increasing the revenue of locals and offering new jobs. However, it also represents a challenge for tourist destinations and management issues and the companies in the hotel sector that still follow the traditional business model (Tussyadiah & Zach, 2015).

The new models, such as the case of P2P platforms, were able to respond to changing consumers and their preferences, which raised concerns about their impact on the traditional industry. Spending on accommodation is one of the significant budgets for tourists. Chattopadhyay & Mitra (2020) states that Airbnb offers several benefits than traditional hotels. As an example, the average room price offered in the shared accommodation of Airbnb is usually less than that of the hotels in the majority of cities. Additionally, the travelers enjoy a better experience because of the vast features offered by the hosts and those matched with their desired rentals. This is the reason why Airbnb is seen as a significant threat to traditional hotel accommodation.

As seen in other studies of Botsman & Rogers (2010); Gansky (2010), the emergence of the sharing economy was advantaged by changing consumer attitudes and behaviors and their consumer practices, usually resulting from economic and social pressures, such as the feeling of community and desire for more sustainable forms of consumption. Thus, P2P platforms will satisfy specific consumer needs with lower prices that hotels cannot satisfy: lower prices, richer social experiences and more sustainable travel. Sigala (2014) states that collaborative commerce is growing fast. It disrupts traditional value chains and threatens companies set aside while consumers are connecting and buying from each other. Moreover, Tussyadiah & Zach (2016) said that Airbnb served 17 million guests worldwide, a 350% increase from 2010. The growth of Airbnb as a P2P platform is far higher than publicly traded hotel chains, such as Marriott and Wyndham, at 8% and 6%, respectively.

The Impacts of Airbnb on Hotels

Although several studies have investigated the effects of Airbnb on the hotel industry, these studies have reported mixed results, which, in the context of the following limitation of these formative studies leave a significant gap in the literature on this emerging phenomenon (Dogru et al., 2019, p.29).

There are numerous research studies about Airbnb's impact on the hotel industry. For example, Zervas et al. (2017); Signal et al. (2018); found that Airbnb growth affects the hotel industry economically. However, Dogru et al. (2020) found that Airbnb has little or no negative impact on the hotel industry. He showed that Airbnb does not affect hotel room demand and revenues in major U.S. hotel markets.

The success of these platforms with consumers and their potential growth triggered a growing concern about the negative impact that the hotel industry could cause (Heo, 2016). This new business model affects the market's competitiveness as tourists start to exchange hotel rooms for P2P accommodation. A study based on the impacts caused by Airbnb on the Texas hotel market found that a 1% increase in the number of Airbnb supply decreased hotel revenues by 0,05% Zervas et al., (2017). Moreover, Zervas et al. (2017) found that it mainly as economy hotels that are substituted for the Airbnb accommodation since these are more similar to the characteristics of P2P accommodation. Kaplan & Nadler (2015) believes that beyond the impact on the lodging sector, proponents of Airbnb argue that it has a positive economic impact in the broader hospitality such as (Restaurant, pubs, attractions) through increases in income and job creation. Blal et al. (2018, p.86) "found that all Airbnb listings do not impact the growth of the RevPar (Revenue per available room) albeit the average price of the Airbnb offer is positively associated with patterns of hotel sales performance."

Additionally, the most exciting finding was that the satisfaction of the Airbnb users is negatively associated with the hotel performance patterns. In other words, Airbnb directly impacts hotel performance Blal et al. (2018). Generally, Airbnb's entrance into the lodging market as a disruptive innovation forces other existing firms to adapt to Airbnb and consumer demands for personalized experience Tussyadiah (2016).

Another idea of why people chose Airbnb rather than hotel rooms because the hosts have fixed costs of the rent and utilities and minimal labor cost and untaxed extra income gained through letting Li & Tabari (2019). Additionally, a strong point mentioned in previous work is that Airbnb can adjust the prices in peak times, thus limiting hotels' pricing power.

According to a San Francisco Financial Times report, customers reduced their stay in a hotel from 79% to 40%, thanks to Airbnb.

However, besides all of the positive impacts of Airbnb on the tourism economy, there are still mixed opinions about the impact of Airbnb on the Hotel industry. For instance, Airbnb still lacks security services. According to (Li & Tabari, 2019), somebody who has been staying in Airbnb property in the US has been robbed and murdered, and a man in Britain raped a CouchSurfing guest from Hong Kong in 2009. In Contrast, Guttentag (2015) referred that Airbnb operates parallel with the conventional accommodation sector and thus does not "take a slice of the pie."

METHODOLOGY

The main objective of this study is to define the consumer motivation of choosing shared accommodation during traveling rather than the traditional hotel stay. It will provide a deep insight into the consumer behavior approach and enhance the understanding of the mentioned concepts as shared economy, shared accommodation, hotel operation, consumer behavior. The study's objective is to define what lacks in the hotel industry and what features made the Airbnb service grow hugely compared to the first one. As the author of this work will combine primary research and secondary research, there will be an addition to the overall available knowledge about the industries.

To this end, a questionnaire was applied to users of the Airbnb platform. After a test was done on a small number of individuals, an online questionnaire through Google forms was shared through social media, in particular Portuguese groups only on Facebook. Additionally, the survey took place the whole month of April 2020. The questionnaire afterward was exported to Excel, and then all data introduced into SPSS. Later on, variables were defined, and specific tables and charts developed will be seen further in the study.

The questionnaire was 100% anonymous as the questions included personal data, such as age, income and level of education. Furthermore, it has aimed to cover answers from residents of Portugal who already used the Airbnb platform. Given the circumstances, it was decided to conduct an online format questionnaire to cover a more significant number of responses. The online questionnaire was designed, so it orders not to take more than five minutes to complete and obtain as much information as possible in the given time. Google forms were used due to its simplistic tool.

The questionnaire was used to target Portuguese people rather than those living in Portugal or abroad. Due to the modern world and social media, it was easier to target a specific group. Different groups from Facebook were used, such as Portugueses em Londres, Emigrants Portugueses. This specific questionnaire was divided into different dimensions. The reason for that is easier to define the primary motivators of the Airbnb platform. Each dimension will include specific questions which will be a part of that dimension. For example, the economic dimension will include questions regarding the product's price and its quality versus price perception.

Moving on to the social factor, that will analyze the possible new interactions with people thanks to the usage of the P2P accommodation platform and maybe living new experiences while using this specific accommodation type. Another dimension is satisfaction. In this part, the questions were based on the overall satisfaction of the customers and their willingness to recommend the platform to others due to their excellent stay. In other words, if their stay exceeded their needs, what are the chances that they will recommend the platform to other people. The questionnaire also had the consumers' behavior dimension, which was often seen in other authors' studies. This dimension aimed to analyze customers' behavior regarding few aspects such as previous customer reviews, level of knowledge of the Airbnb platform and how often they use other accommodation platforms. The present questionnaire has 23 questions. The questions were mainly related to the motivational factors of using the Airbnb platform.

In this survey, there were five multiple-choice questions regarding socio-demographic characteristics of the respondents regarding their gender, age, annual income, occupation and highest educational grade.

Subsequently, the survey had four multiple-choice questions: "What channel is used while booking accommodation?"; "What are (would be) the reasons for not using the online booking platforms?"; "Comparing to other platforms, how would you describe your experience with Airbnb?"; "What influenced you to book through Airbnb?". There are two direct answer questions: "Do you know about Airbnb"; and "Have you ever stayed in Airbnb." Two multiple-choice grid questions with a scale from 1 to 4: "What factors made you book through Airbnb? Please rate these attributes to your importance from one to four (1-Very important, 2- Important, 3-not important, 4-indifferent)"; and "If you were to change from Airbnb to hotels, what would be the reason for it? Please rate these attributes to your importance from one to four (1-Very important, 2- Important, 3-not important, 4-indifferent)". Finally, nine questions which include a scale from 1 to 5: "Airbnb allows me to know local customs/experience"; "Airbnb allows me to have more interaction with locals"; "Airbnb allows knowing new people"; "Airbnb is cheaper than staying in another type of accommodation"; "I have access to good quality accommodation at a low price"; "I have access to unique and traditional apartments"; "I trust previous guests reviews while making a decision"; I will recommend Airbnb to others" and "Airbnb makes me travel more."

CASE STUDY: AIRBNB IN LISBON, PORTUGAL

Current Situation of Airbnb in Lisbon

According to the INE (Instituto Nacional de Estatística, 2018), the Metropolitan Area of Lisbon, after the 2011 census, showed 2 821 876 inhabitants in 18 towns around. However, Lisbon City has only 506 654 inhabitants in an area of 100,1 km 2, according to (Pordata 2018). As mentioned in (insideairbnb, 2018), there are approximately 16.230 listings on the Airbnb platform in the city of Lisbon, where 74,8% represents entire properties, 24% private rooms and only 1% of shared room properties. The municipality of Lisbon consists of 24 "freguesias" (Administrative divisions of the city) were Santo Antonio, Misericórdia, São Vicente, Alcântara, Santa Maria Maior and Belem are the most crowded ones and under significant tourism pressure. Joseph Zadeh, who was the ninth employee to join Airbnb after opening, has been interview by the "Visão" magazine and he stated that Airbnb is now focused on delivering to their customers' Experiences with locals, as this is the tendency of the upcoming years.

Additionally, he says that people are searching for more and more interaction with the locals, which has led them to introduce experiences with locals (Vânia, August 2017). Accordingly, to Conceição (2019), Portugal is placed in the top 10 largest markets for the platform, just ahead of Germany and China. The impact generated by tourists that booked through Airbnb in 2016 exceeded 2 Billion euros. However, the leading countries are the United States, followed by France and Spain. In retrospect, Portuguese tourists who booked through Airbnb spent on average € 115 per day. In this context, tourists spent 41% of the expenses in their neighborhoods. However, some Airbnb critics argue that these platforms increase home prices by restricting long-term home rentals' supply, intensifying local affordability issues (Lee, 2016). In this way, they present unfair competition to short-term lodging such as Hotels. 88% of the guest that has chosen to stay with Airbnb rather than the hotel was because they wanted to feel "like locals" Almeida & Ramos, (2016.)

Additionally, half of the guests in Portugal have stayed in Lisbon: 433 000 guests, while the average monthly earnings for a typical host is 530 Euro (Almeida & Ramos, 2016). The local Portuguese statistics are not representative due to their calculation of local accommodations. In their statistics, only nine or more beds are included in the statistics calculations (INE, 2016). This means that the total number of local accommodations is much higher than 13,7%.

Possible Implication in Evolution of Airbnb for Lisbon's Inhabitants

The idea of sharing economy has emerged in different digital platforms such as Airbnb, Uber, Booking. In this case, Airbnb has that concept of mediation between peers and for that to happen, they charge the hosts a percentage. By acting as a mediator, Airbnb assumes no labor-related responsibility (Saturnino & Sousa, 2019). This is why any hosts who are using the Airbnb platform act as independent53 workers and Airbnb avoids any legal commitments. According to Portuguese law (Decree-Law No. 128-2014), every establishment Airbnb, or Hostels or any other which is included in this sector declare the profits, pay social security contribution as a self-employed worker and comply with the renting regulations such as having a fire hazard system, running hot and cold water, among others. This means that the Portuguese Government already acknowledges hosts and Airbnb (Saturino et al., 2019). We cannot deny the positive impact it has on people's lives; however, we should consider the negative impacts.

Several European countries understood the negative effect of tourism and the massification of Airbnb and have put forward measures to mitigate their problems. As stated in (Moreira, 2019), Amsterdam will stop promoting the city as a tourist destination. Madrid decided to limit 10 thousand apartments to local accommodation (Lisbon already has almost 20 thousand). The ban was recently introduced in Berlin as only a 90 nights per year limit per property per owner. This shows already a significant evolution of the sharing economy in big cities and the Government's contribution to keeping it under control. To keep every host interested in using the platform, Airbnb created new ways of attracting people and recognition programs for the host. As stated in (Airbnb n.d), it is a way of earning more money by attracting people with the host's status (Super host) and coupons for other Airbnb stays for the future.

Additionally, to be more competitive in the hospitality market, Airbnb has implemented more critical features for the business. According to (https://www.airbnb.co.uk/new), the new features include different packages: Family, Work, Honeymoon, Wedding, Social Stays, Dinner party, One of a kind and Group getaway. When you book from a collection, you can expect a highly-rated home with all the essentials for the type of trip you are taking–from equipped kitchens for families to Wi-Fi and self-check-in for work trips. Airbnb+ are those properties with high-quality, well-equipped homes with hosts known for great reviews and attention to detail. These types of properties are verified in person. Additionally, the most significant difference between Hotels and Airbnb that the reviews are based not only on properties but also the over way around. Super guest a new concept of educating the consumers about taking care of the property as their own.

Perceptions of Lisbon's Inhabitants towards Airbnb

In the age of e-commerce, every industry is involved in online sales and hospitality and tourism are no exception (Schuckert, Liu & Law, 2015). Hotels and local accommodation have an essential thing in common. Hotels, be they luxury or best value properties, use OTA (online Travel Agencies) or direct bookings. After consumption, customers give feedback online and such online reviews have become increasingly important. The same method uses the Airbnb platform, direct on-site bookings and after each stay, both host and the guest can give their feedback about the stay. These kinds of actions are fast up-to-date and have become word of mouth (Schuckert et al., 2015). Word-of-mouth has been recognized as a crucial driver of product sales. WOM may also be a reliable source of information about the quality of experience goods (i.e., products that cannot be easily characterized before consumption) (Li & Hitt, 2018). According to Saturino et al. (2019), some Portuguese hosts have different positions about Airbnb in the community. A female host confirms that the main reason for hosting their apartment is an increase in their income. However, the same host confirms that she is considering a new way of travel meet the tourist from around the world and sharing experiences with them. Another opinion about hosting a house is that the host feels like a self-employer and Airbnb is a partner. The male host confirms that he could do it alone, but it will not have the same impact as working with Airbnb. Local accommodations are an integral part of hospitality. However, very little research has been carried on the type of local housing in concrete. The reason for this fact seems to lie in the fact that this is a very recent tourist typology generated by fundamental changes in the way of doing tourism (Perloiro, 2016). Despite this, in the last years, many studies have focused on local accommodations, especially Airbnb (Guttentag, 2013).

DATA ANALYSIS

Descriptive Statistics

Sociodemographic Variables

The study collected a total of 248 valid responses. Proceeding to the socio-demographic analysis of the survey, we can see a high percentage of females (71%), then (28,6%) were males, with 0,4% preferring not to disclose their gender.

More than half of the respondents were a part of the younger generation, with ages between 18 and 28 years old (57,7%), ages between 29 and 39 years old (29.0%). A smaller percentage were between 40 and 49 years old (9,7%), between 50-59 years old (3,2%) and over 70 years old (0,4%).

Concerning occupation, 42,3% were employed, 21,4% students, 16,1% working students, 10,1% unemployed, 8,5% entrepreneurs, 0,8% retired and 0,4% to others.

Regarding educational qualifications, the majority of respondents possesses a bachelor's degree, which constitutes 38,7%, then straight after bachelor's degree another considerable number of respondents showed 34,3% of Masters' degree, 21,4% had 12th grade or equivalent studies, 3,6% had Ph.D., an equal number of AP degree and up to 9th grade which is 0,8% and only 0,4% of respondents had their college finished.

Finally, the last question about the socio-demographic profile of respondents was about their annual income. It appears that 31,9% of respondents had an income between 10 000 and 20 000 €. Another high percentage of respondents had up to 10 000 €, which is 28,6%. Consequently, 18,5% had between 20 000 – 35 000 €, then 9,7% had 35 000 – 50 000 €, and 7,3% enjoyed an income of more than 50 000€ and only 4,0% showed no income.

Consumer Behavior

The questionnaire also included questions about the habits of consumers' behavior. The first question addressed the channel used to book accommodation. It was found that the majority book through official websites in alliance with intermediate websites (52,4%), 21,4% book only through official websites and

16,5% book only through intermediate websites. A lower percentage has been observed while booking through official websites in alliance with intermediate websites and online travel agencies (2,8%). The same percentage has been seen while booking in alliance with official websites with intermediate websites and through telephone, constituting 2,8% respectively. A total of 2,4% of respondents is booking through intermediate websites in alliance with online travel agencies only, 0,8% choose to book through intermediate websites together with telephone, only 0,4% book through official websites in alliance with online travel agencies and 0,4% choose to book only through online travel agencies.

Concerning the reasons for not booking through online booking, platforms could be seen as the following factors: Majority (40,3%) said they have no concerns and do use online booking platforms no matter what. A total of 30,2% of respondents claimed they are concerned about their safety/privacy, 16,5% said they do not trust the platforms in terms of paying, 5,6% answered that they prefer face-to-face contact with the responsible person, 3,6% have little experience using the internet, nine respondents showed the same percentage of 0,4% which means single individuals that are concerned about following factors: Asking for special price; Better prices and cancelation policies while booking direct; Cancelation policies; knowing the owner; Might be higher; Not having images of the rooms available or information about parking and Wi-Fi; Other people or agencies responsible for organizing the travel; Price and the last is Royalty program.

Respondents have been asked if they know about the Airbnb platform. Almost everyone has answered that they know the platform, which constitutes (99,2%) and only (0,8%) claimed they do not know this platform.

Respondents have been asked if they have used the platform. If they choose as an answer that they have been using before, the respondents were taken to the next question; if they choose "NO," they have been taken to submit the form. The majority claimed that they stayed before in Airbnb (83,1%) of respondents, another 16,9% answered that they never used it before.

The following question was about the usage of the platform. The majority of respondents answered that they rarely use Airbnb, which is 38,3%, another 31,6% said they often are using the platform, while 21,4% said they sometimes use the platform, 8,7% always use the platform and the missing values are the ones which never used Airbnb before.

Social and Economical

The next question refers to price, and how important is it to everyone who is booking, excluding the 42 individuals who has never stayed in Airbnb following results are obtained: Very important (68,4%), Important (30,1%) and only 1,5% said the price is not an important factor while booking through Airbnb.

The next variable is the environmental one and the importance of choosing the platform. In this case, 41,7% answered that it is an important factor, and 30,1% said it is a very important factor while booking through Airbnb. Another 17,5% answered that it is not important, and only 10,7% claimed it is indifferent.

From the local experience point of view, 44,2% stated it is an important factor, and 31,6% indicated it is a very important factor. Only 18,0% answered that it is not an important factor, and 6,3% claimed to be indifferent about the local experience.

The household amenities showed the following results: 48,5% choose this factor as important, 33,5% very important, 13,6% not important and only 4,4% found it indifferent.

The localization was considered as a factor of booking through the Airbnb platform, where majority choose it as a very important factor (57,3%), 32,0% as an important factor, 8,7% as a not important factor and only 1,9% said it is indifferent.

Regarding factors was contributing to the local community, 43,7% selected not important factor, 24,3% important, another 22,8% as indifferent and only 9,2% as a very important factor.

Following the last variable, the following result was obtained for using a non-touristic place: 42,2% as a not important factor at all, 28,6% as an important factor, 16,5% were indifferent and 12,6% as a very important price.

As the last variable of this question, the author chose easiness of booking through the Airbnb platform. Respondents answered that it is an important factor (44,7%), 42,2% answered as a very important factor, only 9,7% as a not important factor and 3,4% indifferent.

The following question is part of a social dimension, which allows studying more in-depth consumer behavior. This question allowed respondents to choose more than one factor, which made it more apparent what influenced them to book the accommodation with the platform. The highest number of respondents choose only friends and family, which constitutes 19,4%, a slightly lower percentage was combining word of mouth with friends and family (18,9%). Another factor considered was word of mouth, which had 10,7%, for a convenient package we could see only 9,7%, then 7,3% have answered other reasons which made them book through Airbnb. Word of mouth in alliance with convenient package had 5,3%, word of mouth with advertising showed 4,9%, friends or family with the advertising had a slightly smaller percentage which is 4,4%, the same percentage as word of mouth together with friends or family and convenient package. It is seen 3,9% for another factors. Advertising and convenient package consist only of 1,9%, only 1,0% have chosen the mix of every factor and 0,5% word of mouth with advertising and convenient package.

The next question brings the consumer to answer, which would be the factors that influence them to go from Airbnb to hotel. The first factor is price, which showed the following results: the majority answered it is very important (58,3%), 32,5% answered as an important factor, whereas 6,8% answered as not important and only 2,4% indifferent.

The next factor of the same question was staff interaction, and the respondents answered that it is an important factor (42,2%), 30,6% as a very important factor, while 16,5% as a non-important factor and 10,7% chose indifferently.

As for localization, 42,2% of respondents found it a very important factor, 41,3% as an important factor, and a percentage of 10,7% as a non-important factor and only 5,8% indifferent about localization.

In terms of facilities, a significant percentage of respondents found it as a very important factor (49,5%), 42,2% found it important, while only 5,3% found it as a not important and 2,9% indifferent.

The last factor considered in this question is the cleanliness of the hotel. The majority of respondents answered that this is a very important factor (59,7%), 35,0% answered that it is important, a very few respondents answered that it is not important only (2,9%) and 2,4% indifferent about it.

Satisfaction

The following questions will be reflecting their agreement about the statements. The first statement was if Airbnb allows consumers to know the local customs/culture better, and in this order following results were obtained: 39,8% Agree with the statement, 39,3% are neutral about that, 11,2% strongly agree, 7,8% disagree, and only 1,9% strongly disagree.

The following statement was "Airbnb allows me to have more interactions with locals". Here, we have the next presented results from the respondents: 37,4% are neutral, 33,0% agree with the statement, 13,1% disagree, 12,1% strongly agree and only 4,4% strongly disagree.

Another Likert scale question was about knowing new people, where 35,0% answered neutral about that, 33,0% they agree with the statement than another 15,0% disagree, 10,7% strongly agree and 6,3% strongly disagree.

For the following affirmation, it is seen a higher number of respondents who agree with the statement "Airbnb is cheaper than another type of accommodation" (43,2%) agree, 27,2% strongly agree, 18,0% neutral, then 9,2% disagree and only 2,4% strongly disagree.

For the following statement, which is "I have access to good quality accommodation at a low price", we have a higher level of respondents who agreed with it, which is 54,4%, 20,4% strongly agree, additionally, in this statement, there are no answers of strongly disagree, it is seen 18,9% of neutral answers and only 6,3% disagree.

From the following statement, it is seen that half of the respondents answered as they agree that "I have access to unique and traditional apartments" (50,0%), 25,2% are neutral about it, 17,0% strongly agree with the affirmation and then 6,8% disagree and only 1,0% completely disagree.

When respondents have been asked if Airbnb makes them travel more, we have obtained the following results: 33% were neutral, 26,7% disagree with the statement, a smaller number of respondents answered that they agree (22,3%), 10,2% strongly disagree and, in the end, 7,8% of respondents strongly agree with it.

The last question of the questionnaire was about the overall experience with the Airbnb platform. The primary purpose of this question was to understand how the consumer's stay was finally, and if it was at a high level, or in other words, if subconscious, the experience with Airbnb was better than another type of accommodations. Respectively here we see that majority of respondents respond that it is excellent (58,3%), 34,0% said it is neutral, only 4,9% poor and 2,9% claimed they never used another platform besides Airbnb.

Data Analysis

All questions from the questionnaire were divided into sections according to the dimension, which was further analyzed. After obtaining the survey answers in the questionnaire, the results were analyzed. In order to achieve a better understanding of the data, it was needed to do a comparative analysis between some of the variables.

During the literature review, it was found that consumers are generally attracted by numerous factors while choosing their accommodation. One of the most common factors was the price or economic factor of the individuals while making a booking. In order to verify this fact, two tests will be carried out.

The first one is Bartlett's test and Kaiser-Meyer-Olkin (KMO). Bartlett's test will verify if there is a strong correlation for the factorial analysis to be done. On the other hand, the KMO test will measure the adequacy of using the factorial analysis. For the validation of the tests, Bartlett's example needs to have a significant p-value lower than 0,05, and KMO should have index ranges from 0 to 1, with 0.6 suggested as the minimum value for good factor analysis.

As can be seen in table 1, there is a low significance level, precisely 000, which is strong evidence against the hypothesis.

Table 1. KMO and Bartlett's test

KMO		0,978
Bartlett's test	Approx. Chi-Square	11721,44
	Df	406
	Sig.	0,000

The following table shows the extracted components (5). The components explain nearly 79% of the variability in the original 23 variables, so you can considerably reduce the complexity of the data set by using these components with only 21% loss. In addition, SPSS selected higher than 1, representing quality scores of the data set and representing a decisive factor of statistical analysis.

Table 2. Principal component analysis

Component	Initial Eigenvalues			Extraction Sums of Squared Loadings		
	Total	% of Variance	Cumulative %	Total	% of Variance	Cumulative %
1	21.614	63.6	63.6	21.614	63.6	63.6
2	1.705	5.1	68.6	1.705	5.1	68.6
3	1.284	3.8	72.4	1.284	3.8	72.4
4	1.230	3.6	76.0	1.230	3.6	76.0
5	1.036	3.1	79.0	1.036	3.1	79.0

The table contains component loadings that show a correlation between variables and components because these are possible correlation values range from -1 to +1; as you can see by the footnote provided by SPSS, five components were extracted, the five components that had an Eigenvalue greater than 1.

It is vital to highlight that four variables were removed during component matrix analysis because they were interfering with the study. The factors removed are: Q.3(What is your occupation?); Q.6(What channel is used while making a booking?) Q.7(What are, would be the factors for not using online booking platforms?) Q.8(Do you know about Airbnb?). In the attached rotation component matrix table 10, we can see that from 5 components, we removed three due to significantly less relationship with the items.

Component 1 has a strong relationship with Q.9(Have you ever stayed in Airbnb?), Q.11 (What factors made you book through Airbnb? Please rate these attributes in order to your importance from one to four (1-Very important, 2- Important, 3-not important, 4-indifferent), Q.20(I trust the previous guests' reviews while making a decision), Q.18(I have access to suitable quality accommodation at a low price), Q.13(If you were to change from Airbnb to hotels, what would be the reason for it? Please rate these attributes in order to your importance from one to four (1-Very important, 2- Important, 3-not important, 4-indifferent), Q.19(I have access to unique and traditional apartments), Q.23(Comparing to other platforms, how would you describe your experience with Airbnb?), Q.14(Airbnb allows me to know the local customs/experience), Q.21(I will recommend Airbnb to others), Q.17(Airbnb is cheaper than staying in another type of accommodation), Q.15(Airbnb allows me to have more interactions with locals), Q.16(Airbnb allows knowing new people), Q.22(Airbnb makes me travel more), Q.10(How often do you use Airbnb?), Q.12(What influenced you to book through Airbnb? You can choose more than one.); [factor loading more than 0.5].

Component 2 has a stronger relationship with items Q.2(What is your age?), Q.5 (What is your annual income?), Q.4 (What is your higher educational level?).

The investigated relationship examines the content of the items with high loadings from each factor to see if they fit together conceptually and can be named. For example, the relation between component 1'high loading and related variables emphasizes motivation for use and generally consumer behavior approach while the second component emphasizes socio-demographic aspect.

CONCLUSION

Final Considerations

Sharing economy is a concept that emerged at the beginning of the 21st century and it is shaping industries across the whole world. Sharing economy became popular once with digitalization and technology innovation, thus featuring available assets. Sharing assets is an old practice in human history, although the so-called "sharing economy" is a recent name, which involves matching people who want to share via online platforms (Gata, 2015).

During the analysis through an online survey, it was found that 71% of respondents were females and 28,6% were males. Thus, it was found that 99% of respondents knew about the Airbnb platform; however, only 83% have stayed in this type of accommodation. Also, it can be stated that the results were biased because it was considered a big gap between the gender of the respondents. This is due to that females are considerably more active on social media than males.

The main question is why an individual should own something if that could be rented (ex. property, vehicle) and at a lower price. Thanks to online platforms and in this case, Airbnb especially, which help people to share their rooms or entire apartments.

Not only in Portugal, but worldwide P2P platforms and especially Airbnb has managed to open new business opportunities for individuals. People nowadays can be their bosses and run a small property business due to the newly emerged P2P platforms.

The secondary research results revealed that four main factors are influencing people to use P2P platforms accommodations. Guttentag (2016) suggests that people use Airbnb due to their economic and experiential values. It was also observed that there are three more factors that motivate people to use P2P platforms: Sustainability, community and economic benefits. One of the research questions was the environmental factor, which was validated. As well as in the secondary research, it was found that 88% of hosts around the world incorporate green practicing into hosting. Comparing to the hotel industry, Airbnb has used less water, less waste and drain less energy.

Additionally, the main subject concerning using the P2P platform was the economic factor. However, people do not use Airbnb no matter their economic situation. This means that if people would have more money, there is a probability that they will not be using Airbnb as much as someone who is affected by the high prices of hotel rooms, for example.

It is important to highlight that customers after staying in P2P accommodation were more likely to recommend it to others due to their previous great experience. Coming back to the study's objective, it is important to mention that Airbnb has potentially increased the economic impact on the wider hospitality such as (restaurants, pubs, attractions) and this was through increases in income and job opportunities.

Regarding Airbnb in Portugal, it is important to mention that Airbnb has placed Portugal in the top 10 countries that demonstrated a direct economic impact from the platform regarding lost income. Some Portuguese hosts have different positions about Airbnb in the community. The majority confirms that the main reason is due to an increase in their income. Few people stated that they feel like self-employer and that Airbnb is some partner. However, they are sure that it would not have the same outcome renting their property if it would be through the Airbnb platform.

As the study's main objective was to determine why people tend to use Airbnb instead of hotels, the first conclusion that can be drawn is that the price is an enormous motivator for people. Therefore, consumers are attracted by a good price of the P2P platforms, also observed in Guttentag (2016).

Regarding environmental issues concerning P2P platforms, few ideas have shown that CO_2 emissions of the Airbnb platform are much more reduced than hotel industry (Skjelvik et al., 2017). Additionally, in studies carried by Tussyadiah (2015); Botsman & Rogers (2011), it was found that consumers usually are aware of the environmental impact and that overconsumption can negatively influence our environment. Thus, people think about the environment while booking through the P2P platform.

Another aspect was considered while studying the literature review: the intention to be closer to locals. The social factor is as well a base concept of Airbnb, as the focus of Airbnb is to deliver a local experience and to live like a local.

Lastly, to assess if people will recommend the platform to others due to their great experience, results suggest people tend to use Airbnb again.

To conclude, Airbnb is still very well positioned in the hospitality industry, where the price is still the main motivator for people to use the platform. However, it is important to keep in mind other aspects guiding the consumers to use P2P instead of hotels.

Research Limitations

In a majority of scientific research, the conclusion has had to face certain limitations. Consumers' needs are changing rapidly. Technology is changing all of the industries as well as hospitality. Thus, barriers to entry into the business are minimal. This paper was based on quantitative research, which implies that the answers to the question are only valid for that specific group of people. Therefore, it is not possible to generalize the perception and opinions based only on the questionnaire answers. In other words, the respondents that participated in this study could be biased. The reason for that is that the majority are Portuguese nationals and thus the economic factor could be different if the respondents would have been German or some other nationalities. Secondly, the questionnaire was online-based, which could create potential problems in terms of understanding. In other words, respondents could not clarify any doubts that might arise. In addition, the questionnaire was created in English, which could create few problems or be misunderstood by the respondents. Thus, qualitative research using interviews could have been a great tool to analyze consumers' views and potential hosts. Lastly, the lack of updated research studies on the Airbnb topic concerning the Hotel industry is somewhat limited. Consequently, various internet sources which might have a lower level of credibility were used while completing this paper.

Future Research

Throughout this research, a few topics could serve for future research investigation:

1. In-depth analysis of top 10 Airbnb cities, with detailed information of Average Daily Rate of the properties, number of bookings, the reason for booking through a P2P platform.
2. The impact of Airbnb on a specific destination, whether the platform is used as a primary source of accommodation or mainly as a disturbing factor for the hotel industry. As mentioned before, studies that after could be analyzed compared with hotel graphs of overnight stays, arrivals, daily rates, among others. This will help estimate where Airbnb is impacting the existing hotels in the specific territory.

Therefore, the dimensions of consumer behavior could be analyzed more in-depth to have a more extensive understanding of this phenomenon. In this context, brand loyalty or quality of service could be taken into consideration.

Moreover, another topic would be analyzing the connection between different economic factors and brand loyalty or social factors. This, in the end, would give a bigger picture of consumer behavior, especially in hospitality. In the end, it is recommended to understand what hotels are inventing in order to cope with the new P2P platforms. From strategies to communicate with consumers through different channels. As the sharing economy is developing fast and all are becoming digital, the traditional hotel industry should become as well much more innovative.

REFERENCES

Almeida, L., & Ramos, D. (2016). Tourism Porto and North of Portugal – Case Study Concerning Private Accommodation. *The 5th Jubilee International Scientific Congress. Global Tourism Challenges in 21st century*, 1-6.

Blal, I., Singal, M., & Templin, J. (2018). Airbnb's effect on hotel sales growth. *International Journal of Hospitality Management, 73*, 85–92. doi:10.1016/j.ijhm.2018.02.006

Borges, B. (2009). *Bridging the gap between seller and buyer through social media marketing. Marketing 2.0*. Wheatmark.

Botsman, R., & Rogers, R. (2011). *What's Mine is Yours: The Rise of Collaborative*. Collins.

Chattopadhyay, M., & Kumar, S. (2020). What Airbnb host listings influence peer-to-peer tourist accommodation price. *Journal of Hospitality & Tourism Research (Washington, D.C.), 44*(4), 1–27102. doi:10.1177/1096348020910211

Chen, C., & Chang, Y. (2018). The importance of marketer-generated content to peer-to-peer property rental platforms: Evidence from Airbnb. *Telematics and Informatics, 35*(84), 1-11.

Cheng, M. (2016). Sharing economy: A review and agenda for future research. *International Journal of Hospitality Management, 57*, 60–70. doi:10.1016/j.ijhm.2016.06.003

Cunha, J. M. (2017). *Airbnb is Lisbon's largest "hotel" José Maria Cunha*. Medium. Accessed 10th May, 2020. from https://medium.com/@zemariacunha/airbnb-is-lisbons-largest-hotelfc00a0c5ff7b

Dogru, T., Mody, M., & Suess, C. (2019). Adding evidence to the debate: Quantifying Airbnb's disruptive impact on ten key hotel markets. *Tourism Management, 72,* 27–38. doi:10.1016/j.tourman.2018.11.008

Dogru, T., Mody, M., Suess, C., McGinley, S., & Line, D. N. (2020). The Airbnb paradox: Positive employment effects in the hospitality industry. *Tourism Management, 77,* 1–12. doi:10.1016/j.tourman.2019.104001

Dredge, D. & Gyimóthy, S. (2015) The collaborative economy and tourism: Critical perspectives, questionable claims and silenced voices. *Tourism Recreation Research, 40*(3). doi:10.1080/02508281.2015.1086076

Ernst & Young LLP. (2018,). *The rise of the sharing economy*. Accessed 23 May 2020 from: http://sharehub.kr/wp-content/uploads/2015/11/e1a7c1d73dfae19dcfa0.pdf

Felson, M., & Spaeth, J. L. (1978). Community structure and collaborative consumption. *The American Behavioral Scientist, 21*(4), 614–624. doi:10.1177/000276427802100411

Gansky, L. (2010). *The mesh: Why the future of business is sharing*. Penguin Group.

Gata, J. E. (2015). *The sharing economy, competition and regulation*. Competition Policy International Europe Column.

Guttentag, D. (2015). Airbnb: Disruptive innovation and the rise of an informal tourism accommodation sector. *Current Issues in Tourism, 18*(12), 1192–1217. doi:10.1080/13683500.2013.827159

Guttentag, D., Smith, S., Potwarka, L., & Havitz, M. (2017). Why Tourists Choose Airbnb: A Motivation-Based Segmentation Study. *Journal of Travel Research, 57*(1), 1–18.

Heo, C. (2016). Sharing economy and prospects in tourism research. *Annals of Tourism Research, 58,* 156–170. doi:10.1016/j.annals.2016.02.002

Inside Airbnb. (n.d.). *Inside Airbnb: Lisbon. Adding data to the debate*. Accessed 8th January, 2020, from: http://insideairbnb.com/lisbon/?neighbourhood=neighbourhood_group%7CLisboa&filterEntireHomes=false&filterHighlyAvailable=false&filterRecentReviews=false&filterMultiListings=false

Instituto Nacional de Estatistica. (2018). *Statistical Yearbook of Área Metropolitana de Lisboa, 104.*

Kaplan, R. A. & Nadler M. L. (2015). Airbnb: A case study in occupancy regulation and taxation. *University of Chicago Law Review, 82,* 103-115.

Kotler, P., Kartajaya, H., & Setiawan, I. (2010). *From products to customer to human Spirit, Marketing 3.0*. John Wiley and Sons. doi:10.1002/9781118257883

Kotler, P., Kartajaya, H., & Setiawan, I. (2017). *Marketing 4.0 – Moving from traditional to digital*. John Wiley and Sons.

Lee, D. (2016). How Airbnb short-term rentals exacerbate Los Angeles's affordable housing crisis: Analysis and policy recommendations. *Harvard Law & Policy Review, 50*(6), 229–253.

Li, L., & Tabari, S. (2019). Impact of Airbnb on customers' behavior in the UK hotel industry. *Tourism Analysis, 24*(1), 13–26. doi:10.3727/108354219X15458295631891

Li, X., & Hitt, L. (2018). Self-Selection and Information Role of online Product Reviews. *Information Systems Research, 19*(4), 456–474. doi:10.1287/isre.1070.0154

Liang, S., Schuckert, M., Law, R., & Chen, C. (2020). The importance of marketer-generated content to peer-to-peer property rental platforms: Evidence from Airbnb. *International Journal of Hospitality Management, 84,* 1–11. doi:10.1016/j.ijhm.2019.102329

Lim, W. M. (2020). The sharing economy: A marketing perspective. *Australasian Marketing Journal, 28*(3), 4–13. doi:10.1016/j.ausmj.2020.06.007

Lytras, M. D., Damiani, E., & Ordóñez de Pablos, P. (Eds.). (2009). Web 2.0 The Business Model. Springer.

Moreira, R. S. (2019). Já não cabem mais Airbnb em Lisboa. *O Jornal Económico.* Acessed 19th May, 2020 from: https://jornaleconomico.sapo.pt/noticias/ja-nao-cabem-mais-airbnb-em-lisboa-451783

Perloiro, T. (2016). *O impacto do alojamento local na reabilitaçãoo urbana em Lisboa* (Master's degree thesis). Instituto Superior Técnico, Lisboa, Portugal.

Roma, P., Panniello, U., & Lo Nigro, G. (2019). Sharing economy and incumbents' pricing strategy: The impact of Airbnb on the hospitality industry. *International Journal of Production Economics, 214,* 17–29. doi:10.1016/j.ijpe.2019.03.023

Saturnino, R., & Souse, H. (2019). Hosting as a lifestyle: The case of Airbnb digital platform and Lisbon hosts. *The Open Journal of Sociopolitical Studies, 12*(3), 794-818.

Schuckert, M., Liu, X., & Law, R. (2015). Hospitality and tourism online reviews. Recent trends and future directions. *Journal of Travel & Tourism Marketing, 32*(5), 608–621. doi:10.1080/10548408.2014.933154

Sigala, M. (2014). Collaborative commerce in tourism: Implication for research and industry. *Current Issues in Tourism, 20*(4), 346-355.

Skjelvik, J., Erlandsen, A., & Haavardsholm, O. (2017). *Environmental impact and potential of the sharing economy.* Nordic Council of Ministers. Accessed 27 March 2020, from: https://norden.diva-portal.org/smash/get/diva2:1145502/FULLTEXT01.pdf

Swig, R. (2014, August 29). *Alt-accommodation impact felt in San Francisco.* Hotel News Now. Accessed 20th April, 2020, from: https://www.hotelnewsnow.com/Articles/23683/Alt-accommodationimpact-felt-in-San-Francisco

Tarabasz, A. (2013). The reevaluation of communication in customer approach- towards marketing 4.0. *International Journal of Contemporary Management, 12*(4), 124–134.

Tussyadiah, L. (2015). An exploratory study on drivers and deterrents of collaborative consumption in travel. In L. Tussyadiah & A. Inversini (Eds.), *Information and Communication Technologies in Tourism* (pp. 1–13). Springer.

Tussyadiah, L. (2016). Factors of satisfaction and intention to use peer-to-peer accommodation. *International Journal of Hospitality Management*, *55*, 70–80. doi:10.1016/j.ijhm.2016.03.005

Tussyadiah, L., & Zach, F. (2015). Hotels vs. Peer-to-Peer Accommodation Rentals: Text Analytics of Consumer Reviews in Portland, Oregon. Travel and Tourism Research Association.

Ungerman, O., Dedkova, J., & Gurinova, K. (2018). The impact of marketing innovation on the competitiveness of enterprises in the context of the industry 4.0. *Journal of Competitiveness*, *10*(2), 132–148. doi:10.7441/joc.2018.02.09

Yi, J., Yuan, G., & Yoo, G. (2020). The effect of the perceived risk on the adoption of the sharing economy in the tourism industry: The case of Airbnb. *Business Computer Science*, *57*(1), 1–11. doi:10.1016/j.ipm.2019.102108

Zervas, G., Proserpio, D., & Byers, J. (2017). The rise of sharing economy: Estimating the impact of Airbnb on the hotel industry. *JMR, Journal of Marketing Research*, *54*(5), 1–45. doi:10.1509/jmr.15.0204

Chapter 14
The Hierarchization of Product Attributes:
Hotel Managers in the Decision and Purchasing Processes of Consumers – The Case of Outbound Markets of Porto

Inês Guerra Alves

Estoril Higher Institute for Tourism and Hotel Studies, Portugal

ABSTRACT

This study aims to investigate which hotels' attributes are most valued by the guests of the main markets of Porto. The guests' knowledge, preferences, and needs are crucial data that impact customer satisfaction. As a people-to-people industry, the hotel industry must consider the heterogeneity of its markets and invest in improving its services, considering the aspects they value. However, is the heterogeneity pronounced that much? Or are there any similarities between markets? Guests do not have similar satisfaction levels, so to guarantee the best experience for the most significant number of customers, these should be studied by market segments, once individual study would be impracticable. Through the comments made on the Booking.com, following the assumption that guests comment on what they value, the attributes that guests of different nationalities refer to Porto hotels have been collected. From the analysis of all the collected data, it can be concluded that all the main markets' value attributes and the fundamental differences are based on the hierarchy of these attributes.

INTRODUCTION

The primary objective of any company is profit. The hotel industry is related to the activity of hotels providing, in addition to accommodation, a considerable amount of complementary services, to meet the individual needs of their consumers, the guests (Dubcová et al., 2013), so that loyalty and consumption, so that the hotel achieves the intended profit. Customer loyalty resulting from customer satisfaction is an essential factor in improving results, especially corporate profit (Wolsfold et al., 2016; Djekic et al., 2016).

DOI: 10.4018/978-1-7998-8306-7.ch014

All the transformations that have been felt with the globalization effect, and in particular the evolution concerning transport, which shorten distances and bring countries closer, have had an impact on the hotel industry, which has increasingly become a global service, that is, its "competitive set" is no longer a local scale, but a global scale. In addition to the competition, which must be overcome to achieve the primary objective, globalization creates the need to know the new customers that come up with it and their needs, as, increasingly, the country of origin of the guests is diversified and your preferences and needs as well.

Knowing potential customers and understanding the extent to which tourists from different places, whether countries or regions, resemble or differ in terms of preferences and attitudes is an advantage for hoteliers (Ozdipciner et al., 2012) that seek to satisfy the needs of their customers, to be a preference when making a purchase decision, to gain loyalty and to obtain good word-of-mouth advertising. Companies that can anticipate and recognize their customers' needs show better results than those that do not (Almsalam, 2014). The theory that hotel management decisions should start with guests' understanding to generate a feeling of satisfaction is defended by several managers (Lu et al., 2015). Therefore, identifying what is relevant for customers becomes of utmost importance for hotel managers (Albayrak & Caber, 2015).

The theme of customer satisfaction is a recurrent subject in current literature. The significant increase in competition in the hotel sector means that hoteliers need to stand out and make a difference in the market. However, it is not enough to make a difference. It is necessary that this difference is perceived and valued by consumers and seeks to satisfy their needs. Tourists are increasingly looking to personalize their trips, taking into account their needs. The impersonal system in which "mass tourism" operates is no longer sufficient for more experienced travelers, who seek to customize the tourist experience to their needs and preferences (Dwyer, 2015).

In the current global market, tourism companies are increasingly striving to increase customer satisfaction through their products and services, following the premise that customer satisfaction is one of the most relevant antecedents of companies' financial performance (Albayrak & Caber, 2015) since the dissatisfaction caused by the low quality of the service is considered a cost of non-quality (WHDP, 2014).

Data collected through an online source is reliable, as customers tend to rely more on an online assessment, where people feel more comfortable expressing their praise and criticism of the products and services provided to them (Lee et al., 2013). Increasingly, online reviews are used as a means of knowledge of hotels by tourists. These are one of the sources of information used in the purchase decision process by consumers. That is, a dissatisfied customer will not be just a non-loyal customer but also a customer who will negatively influence a large number of people in your purchasing process. Therefore, it is essential to work on this source of information to take into account the positive and negative aspects pointed out to the hotel to improve it so that a negative comment is compensated in the future with positive comments about the) same attribute(s). This will demonstrate concern for guests' comfort and well-being and consideration for their opinion. A quality improvement will increase satisfaction, which will be converted into an increase in the results of the hotel company (Eshtetie et al., 2016).

Today, information about customers and their preferences is accessible to any hotelier. Online reviews are an excellent source of information that offers hoteliers the opportunity to know the point of view of various customers and potential customers from different countries and with different needs, allowing them to invest in improving their services based on a specific base. Solid and grounded as to the improvements that must be made (Khozaei, 2016). Improvements are all the more effective when attributes that should be improved are identified (Lin et al., 2009).

In a globalized world, where the hotel industry is a sector vulnerable to this globalization, the need to adapt to new realities is imminent. Guests cannot receive homogeneous treatment, as they have different preferences, needs, past experiences and goals, and these differences are increasingly noticed by the different cultures that stay in a hotel at the same time. The focus on customer satisfaction thus becomes more complex since the factors that lead to this satisfaction do not have a global standard, leaving the hotel industry from being focused on "mass tourism" to become a personalized experience (Ueltschy et al., 2007). Therefore, it is crucial to know the customers and which aspects of the hotel they value most so that hoteliers can invest more in a particular attribute depending on the person in front of them, seeking to maximize their satisfaction.

This study seeks to take the customer as a starting point, but the main challenge will be to help hoteliers more efficiently achieve the objective that all companies propose profit.

Among several possible market segments to analyze, namely gender, trip purpose, trip duration, income, age, education level, among others, the market segment chosen in this study is the culture. of the guest (Ozdipciner et al., 2012). Cultural differences and their impact on many aspects of human behavior have been studied with some frequency (Hofstede et al., 2010). However, its impact on the hotel industry is still an understudied matter.

Given this problem, the study's main objective is to inform hoteliers which aspects and attributes, depending on their nationality and consequently culture, guests most seek and value during their stay, so that they can improve their offer and attract a more significant number of tourists.

To delimit the study to obtain more relevant conclusions, hotels in the city of Porto in 2017 were defined as the object of the sample. The city of Porto is experiencing tourist growth, being a preferred destination for a number at a time. The most significant number of tourists from different parts of the world, having already been recognized on several occasions. It was considered pertinent that the study is carried out based on the hotels of a destination that is still growing and getting to know its tourists.

Considering this market segment, it is essential to know what we intend to analyze, and in this case, the analysis will focus on the factors that impact customer satisfaction, given their national culture. After defining the intended analysis, the objects that will allow the analysis to be carried out are defined - the attributes, and where the information is taken from - online reviews.

Considering the factors mentioned above, the question that arises and that the study intends to resolve is: "Which attributes do most hotel guests in the city of Porto value during the decision process, depending on the issuing outbound market?

LITERATURE REVIEW

Customer Satisfaction in Hospitality

As a result of increasing globalization, the competitive environment is growing, and one of the main current objectives of organizations is the maintenance and satisfaction of customers (Pizam et al., 2013) to make the company sustainable and profitable (Farooq, 2016). Customer loyalty associated with their satisfaction is crucial in improving results and mainly corporate profits (Worsfold et al., 2016). Customer orientation is essential for the survival of companies, allowing them to achieve the goal of customer satisfaction and retention (Djekic et al., 2016). The knowledge of the needs and desires of a specific market segment, through the search for continuous feedback from customers, allows us to anticipate complaints and not go after losses, with this concept of customer orientation being presented by Vavra (1997). A satisfied customer has a strong tendency to re-consume a particular product or service and recommend it to friends and family. The result will be customer loyalty and retention (Eshtetie et al., 2016).

The main factors that influence customer satisfaction are desires, expectations, emotions, quality perceived by the customer, price, perceived value, and the company's image that supplies the product (Tinoco & Ribeiro, 2007). After several years of studies on the subject, several theories and models were created to identify customer satisfaction factors. According to the Three Factors of Customer Satisfaction Theory, customer satisfaction is not a one-dimensional concept. This means that the opposite of dissatisfaction is not necessarily satisfaction. This theory divides the factors into basics, excitement/enthusiasm and performance. The primary factors can create dissatisfaction if they are not present, but they do not mean satisfaction when fulfilled. In turn, excitement/enthusiasm factors increase overall customer satisfaction (OCS). When present, these attributes are highly valued. However, if they are not present, they do not cause a feeling of dissatisfaction. The third factor is the performance of attributes.

The relationship between this and the OCS is presented as symmetric. When the performance of these attributes is high, they provoke a feeling of satisfaction. However, if the performance level is low, they cause customer dissatisfaction (Albayrak & Caber, 2015). There are several ways to analyze the attributes that influence satisfaction.

On the other hand, many authors argue that this is not true and that the relationship is asymmetric, such as Hui, Zhao, Fan and Au in 2004, Kano, Seraku, Takahashi and Tsuji in 1984 and Slevitch and Oh in 2010, that is, the negative performance of an attribute may have a more significant influence on the OCS than its positive performance, as suggested in the Three Factors of Customer Satisfaction Theory (Albayrak & Caber, 2015). Thus, the primary attributes are critical when performance is low and are indifferent when performance is high. In turn, the excitement/enthusiasm attributes are critical when performance is high and are indifferent to OCS when performance is low (Deng et al., 2008).

Parasuraman, Zeithaml and Berry defined *service quality* as the difference between the expectations created regarding the service received and the customer's perception of the delivered service (Parasuraman et al., 1988). For Salazar, Costa and Rita (2010), quality is defined by the consumer. As such, it is essential to constantly seek information on the expectations and perceptions of customers and those who are not, providing the latter with information about the competition and the way forward: improving the quality-of-service results in an improvement in the level of guest satisfaction and an increase in profits (Eshtetie et al., 2016). The strategy developed with a view to this improvement, to be effective, must be based on the identification and selection of specific quality attributes that need this improvement (Lin et al., 2009).

The concern with this aspect of service quality is mainly due to the concept of "non-quality cost", which is summed up in the monetary and reputation costs that error in the provision of service or product offer cause. A dissatisfied customer may not always express themselves to the organization, but, on average, they transmit their dissatisfaction to at least nine people, on the other hand, a satisfied customer will pass the word to only three people about the excellent experience (W.H.D.P, 2014).

According to Lockwood (1994), three benefits can be derived from service quality. Customer Satisfaction, since the superior quality of service, increases its competitiveness by improving its reputation, increasing repeat sales and reducing the number of dissatisfied customers who do not foretell themselves but do not repeat the service. Productivity or Profitability allows you to reduce wasted resources on low-quality products/services, optimizing operations and reducing costs. Furthermore, benefits in terms of Human Resources, as employees who provide high-quality service feel motivated and improve their performance (Branco et al., 2010).

In short, the concern and measurement of service quality allow any company to improve and determine whether services are good or bad and whether customers are satisfied or not (Eshtetie, Seyoum, & Hussen Ali, 2016).

Like the concept of satisfaction associated with other services, according to Lu, Berchoux, Marek and Chen (2015), a satisfied guest feels that the value of the service he received is equal to or greater than the price.

In the study conducted by Lu et al (2015), the hotel managers who were interviewed argued that a satisfied customer repeats the hotel stay. This level of satisfaction is only reached when customers find in the hotel what they are looking for, and it offers services that meet their needs and correspond to their expectations.

The hotel sector is increasingly a highly competitive global industry, with a growing demand for innovative products beyond traditional concepts (Kandampully & Suhartanto, 2000). The competitive environment in the sector, because of the economic situation, technological developments and globalization, has changed the importance of service quality and has led market agents to adopt new approaches to maximize customer satisfaction based on service quality (Eshtetie et al., 2016), following the premise that the former is the primary antecedent of the hotel's financial performance (Anderson & Mittla, 2000).

Studying and understanding the customer is crucial to success in the hospitality industry (Goeldner et al., 2000). Many hotel managers defend that all management decisions must start with the guest's understanding, always following the policy most likely to generate a higher level of satisfaction among guests (Lu et al., 2015). Identifying the attributes of the hotel product or service that are most relevant to the guest's pleasure becomes of utmost importance for hotel managers (Albayrak & Caber, 2015).

Five aspects influence guest satisfaction, the service, the guest himself, the guest's nationality, the hotel and the destination. In their study, the authors identified hotels as the biggest influencers on customer satisfaction, with the hotel's location, cleanliness and quality of rooms as the main influencing aspects (Radojevic et al., 2017). From the perspective of Reuland et al. (1985), the influencing factors of customer satisfaction are grouped into three categories, the material product, which in the case of restaurants is limited to food and drink, the behavior of the staff, who are in permanent contact with guests and, finally, the environment, that is, the building, the decoration, the furniture.

Understanding the customer's motivations is of utmost importance. The benefits of this understanding can manifest through the hotel's physical characteristics and services, as well as in the way it interacts with potential customers through its advertising and public relations materials (Lu et al., 2015). Companies that can anticipate and recognize their customers' needs obtain more significant results than those that do not seek to know what customers are looking for (Almsalam, 2014). In addition, features such as convenient location, quality of service, reputation, and friendliness of the staff are essential aspects of hotels and significantly impact customer satisfaction (Dolnicar & Otter, 2003).

Hospitality Attributes

Hotel products are made up of specific characteristics, services and requirements that we call attributes. For the most part, hotel products are presented in tangible and intangible attributes, attributes that are highly interconnected and have a significant impact on guest quality assessment (Alzaid & Soliman, 2002). However, tangible attributes are more influential in global satisfaction since these elements are more easily modified and renewed (Albayrak et al., 2010), and these can be evaluated and measured (Maric et al., 2016). The tangibility of hotel products concerns the external appearance of the facilities, the conditions of the accommodation and the restaurant, and the equipment, staff and physical characteristics of hotel services (Maric et al., 2016). Therefore, this study is understood as an attribute of the hotel product that may influence customer satisfaction during their stay related to the hotel.

The importance of attributes is not identical for all guests; it depends on several variables. According to Rhee and Yang (2015), the requirements sought by tourists can vary depending on the purpose of the stay, its duration and the people traveling, whether it is a trip with family, friends or colleagues.

Whether or not they are spending their money, all hotel guests always have high expectations for their stay. This is because they are always looking for the best service, service and comfort, and, according to Rhee and Yang (2015), they assess the hotel according to six critical attributes, such as value, location, sleep quality, rooms, cleanliness and service, some being more critical than others depending on the guest.

These attributes, due to their relevance for tourists, necessarily affect hotel room rates. The number of stars in a hotel is what has the most significant impact on the rate and the ratings given by customers since they are both quality indexes for tourists (Castro et al., 2016).

According to Maric, Maric and Dimitrovsku (2016), studies published on the subject show that the attributes that most influence hotel choice are cleanliness, location, price, safety, quality of service and hotel reputation. However, room cleanliness, safety and staff efficiency are the most critical hotel attributes (Atkinson, 1988).

In their study, Stringman and Gerdes (2010) analyzed the contents of reviews about hotels. Comments containing the words "staff", "price", "airport," and "center" are the most frequent in the comments with the highest ranking. In the case of guests who give lower ratings, the most used words are "bed" and noise", which can be associated with the attributes "room" and "sleep quality", respectively. In turn, cleanliness is mentioned equally regardless of the score given to the hotel (Stringam & Gerdes, 2010).

Location

Location is considered the most objective attribute of a hotel, as it is a stable characteristic and is the same for all hotel guests, regardless of the room they stay in or the dish they order at the restaurant (Radojevic et al., 2017).

This, along with cleanliness, is a criterion whose value is easier to predict based on the market segment (Radojevic et al., 2017). Naturally, location becomes critical for tourists looking for a place close to the places they want to visit, or, in the case of business travelers, close to the place of their meetings (Rhee & Yang, 2015). This convenience of location is usually associated with easy parking, accessibility to the airport and proximity to public transport (Dolnicar & Otter, 2003), and its classification is often influenced by the destination, namely size, dispersion of points of interest and distribution of hotels (Radojevic et al., 2017).

In a pre-booking moment, when tourists choose the place of their stay, location is a factor that has a significant influence and, as such, is a determining factor in room rates. For example, in Lisbon, distance to the center and accessibility to the airport are variables that explain the difference between fares. However, the latter is not as relevant due to the excellent transport infrastructure that the city itself offers (Castro et al., 2016).

Once at the destination, the location attribute loses its importance for hotel guests since the choice of the hotel was made in advance, and guests are already aware of its location vis-à-vis points of interest (Rhee & Yang, 2015).

Room

The hotels' main product is the rooms, which are mostly an objective criterion, although less than the location, since in addition to the material characteristics, there are also aesthetics that depend on the customer's taste (Radojevic et al., 2017).

This attribute is possibly the most critical aspect for guests coming from a long trip. Guests traveling for tourism or business will not spend most of their stay in their room. However, when they stay in the room, they want to make sure they have the greatest possible comfort (Rhee & Yang, 2015).

The attribute "Room" is constituted by the size of the room, the arrangement and comfort, and the size of the bathroom (Dolnicar & Otter, 2003). However, delimiting the factors that influence the classification of this attribute is complex due to the variety of styles, amenities and amenities that exist in different hotel rooms, and, therefore, Rhee and Yang (2015) assume that the customer evaluates the overall quality of the room taking into account the level of satisfaction that you got from experience during your stay.

Comfort

The search for comfort is seen as a fundamental human behavior, and as such, it is to be expected that this is an essential attribute in the hotel industry (Spake et al., 2003).

Comfort is the second most important attribute in the hotel product after personalization. When referring to comfort, this encompasses physical comfort and psychological comfort, which are essential in the clients' stay, although physical comfort plays a slightly more critical role than psychological comfort (Ariffin & Maghzi, 2012).

Physical comfort is essentially determined by the quality of hotel services or by the physical environment. As such, luxury hotels, according to Rhee and Yang (2015), present a greater possibility of offering a higher degree of physical comfort compared to the budget they have available.

Service

Any business starts and ends with a service. However, sometimes this attribute is neglected by those who provide it, due to the physical and psychological wear of the function (tiredness) and the difficulty involved in interacting with people, and the company ends up not meet the minimum standards required by customers (Rhee & Yang, 2015).

In hotel terms, the attribute "Service" encompasses factors such as friendly staff, professionalism or quality of service and 24-hour room service (Dolnicar & Otter, 2003). This attribute is usually associated with interactions between the customer and the hotel team, including reception, room service, cleaning and restaurant staff, and this interaction can directly affect the level of satisfaction with the hotel service (Rhee & Yang, 2015). According to Radojevic, Stanisic and Stanic (2017), service is the only attribute where national identity plays an important role.

The service appears as the third most important attribute for the guest. Guests are made to feel welcome in a hotel when they are greeted warmly upon arrival. Therefore, all hotels must ensure a warm welcome upon arrival (Ariffin & Maghzi, 2012). Kuo (2007) also argues that the interaction between staff and guests is a critical factor in customer satisfaction, namely the ability to solve problems, empathy, offering a service with taste and friendship.

Given the importance of this attribute in guest satisfaction and evaluation, all staff must be aware of the importance of customer orientation, especially employees who interact directly with them (Maric et al., 2016).

Cleaning

Cleanliness is an essential attribute for any business, and the hotel industry is no exception (Rhee & Yang, 2015). However, the evaluation made by guests to this attribute is influenced both by the hotel and by the personality and taste of the person who evaluates it, since they have specific standards of cleanliness and, sometimes, by the destination (Radojevic et al., 2017).

When cleaning in the hotel industry, room and bathroom cleaning is indicated as the most important. However, cleaning common areas, such as the lobby, corridors, elevators and restaurants, also influences the impression that guests get from the cleanliness of the hotel (Rhee & Yang, 2015).

Value

Value is an attribute that is difficult to explain, and according to Radojevic, Stanisic and Stanic (2017), it has low importance in the choice of the hotel but great importance in the choice of destination.

The difficulty in interpreting this attribute is because it is perceived differently depending on the guest. Thus, on the one hand, it can be interpreted only by evaluating the price, but on the other hand, it can be perceived as a quality-price comparison, that is, what benefits it enjoys (facilities, service, amenities, among others) against the value money that dispenses (Rhee & Yang, 2015).

The attribute "Value" includes the stay price, the monetary value, discounts, the breakfast offer and free Wi-Fi access. These factors were referred to by the authors as components of the "Value" attribute, as they are frequently referenced by studies that already existed on the subject (Dolnicar & Otter, 2003). Following this definition, the authors, Rhee and Yang (2015), based their study on the assumption that the attribute "Value" is interpreted as the understanding by customers that they are earning more than what they are paying for their stay at the hotel.

Technology

The technology attribute is relatively recent; however, it increasingly presents a position of relevance for guests (Njite & Schaffer, 2017), especially for younger generations, such as Millenials (Generation Y) and Digital Natives (Generation Z).

Interaction with guests, check-in and check-out processes and communication increasingly depend on technology, with investment in technology being a constant concern for hotel directors so that guests can enjoy the best service, as technological trends are constantly evolving (Njite & Schaffer, 2017).

In their study, Njite and Schaffer (2017) concluded that guests expect this attribute to be a standard feature among hotels. For example, access to Wi-Fi is something guests take for granted.

Sleep Quality

The attribute "Sleep Quality" presents some complexity as it encompasses different factors, such as the bedroom, bed comfort, noise and ambient temperature, impacting both positively and negatively (Rhee & Yang, 2015). Nevertheless, this is an attribute that is given considerable relevance by tourists when evaluating their stay (Liu et al., 2013).

Online Reviews

The sample of this study will be taken from the Online Reviews present on Booking.com. As such, in order to substantiate this choice of population, it is crucial to understand what Online Reviews are, what can influence these reviews, namely the impact that cultural differences have, and what are the motivations that lead a consumer of a product, in of a hotel product, posting reviews, whether positive or negative, on an online platform. The significant growth in Internet use has led to the increased popularity of reviews, which appear on social networks generated by consumers (Ayeh et al., 2016). The growing use of e-commerce websites to purchase goods and services has made the Internet the sales channel of excellence in many sectors, namely the tourism sector (Ogut & Cezar, 2012). According to the study by Bughin et al. (2010), between 20% to 50% of purchase decision-making is influenced by eWOM (electronic Word-of-Mouth), revealing it as an essential source of information for consumers. Online reviews allow consumers to have a perception of the product before its purchase, considering the opinion of other consumers, and leading to a lower (higher) expectation about the product if the evaluation made by customers who have already enjoyed the product or service is low (high) (Ogut & Cezar, 2012).

The importance of online reviews can be analyzed from different perspectives. For example, it can be seen from the perspective of the customer and the uncertainty in the purchase of the service, in the case of the hotel sector, and from the perspective of the hotelier, both in terms of marketing that is done for the hotel product when there are positive reviews about the product, as well as in the perspective of continuous improvement of the service, taking into account less positive comments (Rhee & Yang, 2015).

According to Anderson (2014), around 88% of consumers trust online reviews and personal recommendations equally, noting that the percentage of people who, at the time of booking, is influenced by online reviews has been increasing. In the tourism sector, the dependence on this type of information is significant since, due to the intangible and heterogeneous characteristics associated with the tourism product, it is not easy to assess it before its consumption (Xie et al., 2016). In addition, through online review platforms, guests share their experiences, whether positive or negative, to alert not only potential future consumers but also in the hope that there will be an improvement in the quality of hotel service (Rhee & Yang, 2015).

Currently, the use of mobile devices when booking trips increases the use of Online Reviews (OR) in the decisions that are necessary to take when planning a trip (PwC, 2015).

According to several authors, the purchase intention on the part of potential customers can be directly influenced by OR, and as such, they play a role as a source of consumer information (Dou et al., 2012). The importance that this source currently exerts is justified by the fact that consumers increasingly tend to trust the evaluations of other consumers to the detriment of the information provided by the service or product providers, as it is considered more independent and reliable (Kardon, 2007; PwC, 2015).

In their study, Constantinides and Holleschovsky (2016) confirmed that 60% of their sample frequently uses OR when deciding to purchase a particular product or service. However, the influence on the decision only occurs when there is high consumer confidence in OR.

Trust in the OR may depend on several factors. According to Zhao, Wang, Guo and Law (2015), there are six characteristics of an OR that influence the impact it can have on decision making, they are the usefulness, that is, if the comment highlights factors that are important to the potential customer; the knowledge of who writes the OR; the date the assessment was made; the number of comments that exist about the product or service, whether the comment is positive or negative, and the details that the comment conveys (Zhao et al., 2015). A high volume of OR about a given hotel can become a significant influencer in the act of booking, as it significantly increases the quality of ratings (Xie et al., 2014) and the reliability of the reviews, given that different people present themselves the same opinion about a particular characteristic, the element of risk is removed (Kirby, 2000).

According to Zhao, Wang, Guo and Law (2015), it is standard for a hotel with a low rating to convey a clear low-value proposition to the potential customer, which considerably reduces the probability of booking. (Zhao et al., 2015). Nevertheless, et al. (2011), as a conclusion of their study, state that a 10% increase in the travel OR index would increase bookings by more than 5% (Ye et al., 2011). For Vermeulen and Seegers (2009), just the fact that the hotel is exposed to OR increases the consideration by potential consumers (Vermeulen & Seegers, 2009).

However, the impact of ORs is not linear and also depends on the profile of each one. For example, in the study guided by Helversen, Abramczuk, Kopec and Nielek (2018), they concluded that product rankings strongly influence young adults and that between two the same products, the one that gets a higher ranking is the one most frequently chosen by this age group.

Still, in this follow-up of the profile of the potential consumer, the evaluations referring to hotels with Food & Beverage (F&B) help to minimize uncertainties in decision-making by consumers. Consumers regardless of their culture. However, cultures that are more averse to uncertainty tend to take more account of online reviews made by customers than cultures more willing to take risks, as is the case of American culture compared to Singapore society (Ayeh et al., 2016).

The reasons that lead potential consumers to seek information in ORs can be diverse, the most commonly mentioned being the reduction of uncertainty. Constantinides and Holleschovsky (2016) divide the motivations for seeking OR into four categories, information behavior, risk reduction, seeking quality and social participation.

For potential consumers, OR platforms, such as Booking.com and TripAdvisor, increase market transparency, reducing purchase risk (Constantinides & Holleschovsky, 2016), and potential guests increasingly seek to make well-founded decisions, based on feedback from previous guests (Bickart & Schindler, 2001), since, according to Chen et al. (2015) and Jin and Phuna (2015), consumers consider the images shared by hotels as untrustworthy.

In addition to the motivations presented by Constantinides and Holleschovsky (2016), point to the reduction of research time and purchase effort as other factors that motivate the search for information through ORs.

It is also important to note that not all reviews have the same impact on those looking for information about a particular hotel. In the opinion of Han et al. (2016), the ratings of the global review indexes (GRI) are not sufficiently clarifying, and as such, it is necessary to read the comments, thus having a more significant impact on the decision.

Comments can be two-fold. That is, they can be positive or negative. Positive comments should provide recommendations for potential guests, and negative ones identify problems and share ways to avoid them (Markham-Bagnera & S., 2016). In the study by Liu and Park (2015), the results showed that positive ORs are considered more beneficial than negative ones, this is justified by the fact that the client already has a pre-decision preference and seeks to increase the credibility of that decision. On the other hand, Purnawirawan et al. (2015) argue that the negative ORs have a more significant impact on attitudes, possibly presenting a more significant weight at the time of decision than the positive ORs (Lee et al., 2008).

ORs are a beneficial source of information for most travelers (Gretzel & Yoo, 2008), and most of them only resort to ROs after choosing their destination to find a place to stay (Cox et al., 2009). Therefore, understanding how and when these reviews, present online and carried out by previous guests, impact travelers' intention to book is critical for hotels to optimize e-WOM as a marketing tool (Zhao et al., 2015).

ORs are not just a means of communication between customers who have already used the service and those who intend to do so in the future. Increasingly, ORs are seen as a tool in understanding customer behavior, as they are a source of information about their opinions, feelings and needs (Li et al., 2012).

ORs are an advantage for hoteliers, as they allow them to see if hotels are meeting guests' expectations, identify possible gaps in the provision of services and initiate a process of improvements to ensure customer satisfaction (PwC, 2015; Baka, 2016).

Numerous advantages can be taken from these platforms by hoteliers. The comments and ratings shared on these platforms about the hotel product provide the hotelier with information that allows him to innovate and develop his product, to improve and personalize the service, having as a starting point the consumers themselves, to this process Gustavo (, 2012), titled it "co-creation" (Gustavo, 2012; Jahandideh et al., 2014). According to Radojevic, Stanisic and Stanic (2017), online assessments made by customers become a new source of information in the study of customer satisfaction, as it holds specific and detailed information about services in various tourist destinations.

Authors Neirotti, Raguseo and Paolucci (2016) state that hotels highly rated on the OR platforms should explore the information that can be taken from the comments to increase their booking potential.

METHODS

The research method took place in three moments: pre-analysis, material exploration and treatment of the obtained results and interpretation. At first, pre-analysis, the choice of documents corresponds to the choice of hotels from which the comments were taken. The second moment, the exploration of the material corresponds to the formulation of the database. Finally, the third moment, treatment of the obtained results and interpretation, consists of the treatment of the raw results to become relevant and valid. It can be simple statistical operations (percentage) or more complex (factorial analysis) transformed into information transferred to tables, graphs, figures or models.

In the data collection process, it was first decided which population to draw the sample from. The choice fell on the city of Porto since there is more excellent knowledge about this city, and this facilitates the interpretation of some comments and because it is a growing city in terms of tourism and there are few studies on tourists and guests in the city in question. The data collection method consisted of a manual collection of comments made by hotel guests on the Booking.com platform during 2017 and their interpretation. Comments that are not made in Portuguese, French, English and Spanish were translated using Google Translate. After collecting the comments, a table will be created that will be used in the data analysis. This table will consider variables that may influence the comments and attributes mentioned: month in which the comment was made, hotel typology, hotel category and guest nationality.

After identifying the variables considered relevant for the study and interpreting the comment to adapt it to the general attributes. Initially, they were just identified the sub-attributes, but due to the number of sub-attributes collected (364 sub-attributes), the need arose to group these sub-attributes into more generic attributes to obtain more significant data.

Reviews of 9 hotels chosen at random, located in Porto or Vila Nova de Gaia, were analyzed. Of the nine hotels used in the sample, four belong to a hotel chain and five are independent, and two are from each two-star, three-star and four-star category and three from the five-star category. The analysis of another independent hotel compared to the hotels included in a hotel chain is since few relevant comments in the independent 5-star hotels were compared to the comments collected in the other categories and typologies. At the end of the analysis, the number of comments relevant to the survey does 3911 reviews, of which 684 reviews from two-star hotels, 1317 reviews from three-star hotels, 1002 reviews from four-star hotels and 906 reviews from luxury hotels five stars.

RESULTS

Sample

As mentioned in previous chapters, the data from this investigation were taken from the Booking.com platform, where the comments made by guests who stayed in the city of Porto in 2017 can be found.

Figure 1. Total comments from the main outbound markets

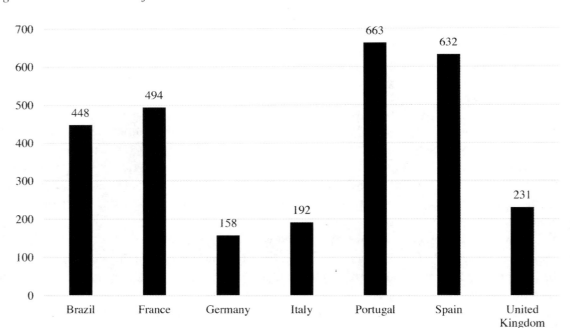

The sample consists of 3911 comments made by guests of different nationalities who have stayed in the selected hotels. Of these reviews, as can be seen in Graph 2, most are related to 3-star hotels, and the category with the lowest value of reviews is 2-star hotels, with 684 reviews.

In the main inbound markets, confirming the trend of the data presented by INE, there are more comments from Portuguese guests, followed by Spanish and French guests (Figure 1).

Data Analysis

Through the analysis of the collected sample, it can be concluded that the Booking.com platform is used mainly by European guests, which, although they are the main markets in the city of Porto, represent 77% of the sample, making the comparative conclusions between continents less significant. Still, concerning the sample, we can conclude that 3 and 4-star hotels receive a much higher number of comments than other hotels.

Regarding the analysis of the results in the approach of the relative weight of the mention of attributes in the comments according to nationality, the main conclusions drawn in global terms are that there are four attributes highlighted for the main issuing markets, they are, the "Breakfast", the "Location", the "Staff" and the "Room". What differentiates the nationalities from each other is that the importance of each of these attributes is different, although the "Room" is the most relevant for all of them. At the second level of importance, the Italian, Spanish and Brazilian nationalities have a similar attribute, the "Location", the French, Portuguese and British nationality the "Staff" attribute, and the German nationality, without parallel with any other nationality in the issuing markets, presents "Breakfast" as the second attribute in the hierarchy of the most valued attributes.

Objectively and individually, the main conclusions drawn from the analysis of the main issuing markets will be presented, according to the most relevant attributes for each nationality (Figure 2).

Figure 2. Hierarchy of the main outbound markets (number of mentions)

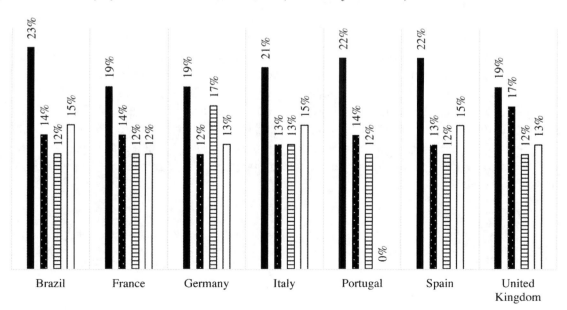

The hierarchy of the most critical attributes for the German guests in the sample is in the following order: (1) Room (2) Breakfast (3) Location (4) Staff. When booking German guests, hotel managers should pay attention to the room conditions in the first instance, not neglecting, however, attention to breakfast aspects and the behavior of the staff in the presence of a German guest. However, aspects related to location cannot be improved and can only be covered with reasonable indications by the staff regarding the best routes to destinations. This hierarchy can vary depending on the characteristics of the hotel, namely, in 4-star hotels where breakfast is more important for German guests.

For the Brazilian guest, the hierarchy of attributes is as follows: (1) Room, (2) Location, (3) Staff, (4) Breakfast. Once again, the room should be the hotelier's primary concern when checking in with a Brazilian guest. However, the behavior of the Staff will also be very relevant to the satisfaction of these customers. These values may register some differences depending on the category and type of hotel, namely in 5-star hotels where location loses importance to the detriment of the staff attribute.

The British guest hierarchy follows this order: (1) Room, (2) Staff, (3) Location, (4) Breakfast. Therefore, it is concluded that for the British guest, attributes related to the Staff should be taken into account almost as much as the attributes related to the room, since they present similar percentages in the results. As with guests of other nationalities, the hierarchy can change depending on the type and category of the hotel, and it is concluded that the importance of breakfast decreases in 5-star hotels.

Similar to the Brazilian hierarchy, the Spanish guest presents in its hierarchy the following order: (1) Room, (2) Location, (3) Staff and (4) Breakfast. When making a purchase decision, the Spanish guest will be particularly concerned with aspects of the location, which cannot be changed. For this reason, your room must always be to your liking during your stay, as it is the most crucial attribute for you to ensure your satisfaction. Aspects related to the Staff only start to be relevant from the 3-star category onwards, and aspects related to breakfast are more relevant in independent hotels.

Guests of French origin present the following order in their hierarchy: (1) Room, (2) Staff, (3) Breakfast, (4) Location. The room and its conditions should also focus on the hotelier's concern when receiving French guests and the Staff's behavior, which gains even more importance in 5-star hotels. Location is primarily considered by guests booking lower category hotels.

According to the results obtained, Italian guests present the following hierarchy of the most relevant attributes: (1) Room, (2) Location, (3) Breakfast and Staff. When booking an Italian guest in Porto, hoteliers must provide a comfortable, clean room with the necessary equipment to ensure customer satisfaction. Furthermore, aspects related to breakfast and Staff are of equal importance and should also be considered when improving services to increase Italian customer satisfaction.

Finally, the Portuguese guest has the following hierarchy: (1) Room, (2) Staff, (3) Breakfast. Except for guests from the main outbound markets in the city of Porto, this guest does not have the "Location" attribute in its hierarchy. That is, the main attributes for the customer are subject to improvement by the hotelier. It is also concluded that aspects related to Staff become more significant for Portuguese guests in 4 and 5-star hotels.

CONCLUSION

Discussion

This last chapter of the study is intended to present the answer that appears in the initial chapter, and which serves the purpose of the investigation: "What attributes do most hotel guests in the city of Porto value during the decision process, depending on the issuing market?"

The present investigation aimed to approach a current and pertinent theme for the hotel universe. After analyzing several investigations already carried out, it can be concluded that the improvement of the product offered, customer satisfaction, and the heterogenization of the needs of hotel product customers are topics addressed by several authors. These themes represent one of the current and past concerns of the hotel industry, the attraction of customers and their loyalty. However, this concern is currently on a larger scale, thanks to the significant increase in competition caused by globalization and the significant increase in online reviews that began to impact consumer purchase decision-making.

In order to answer the initial question, some assumptions were established, some of which were defended by authors mentioned in the investigation. The first assumption is based on the fact that a guest only includes in the comments he writes on an online platform the relevant aspects, whether positive or negative. The second assumption is that an individual's culture determines what he pays attention to and ignores. That is, it determines what is valued by each individual (Hall, 1976). Finally, the third assumption of the investigation is that customer satisfaction follows a weighted compensatory model presented. Therefore, the attributes have different importance for guests, and therefore, it is possible to make a hierarchy of hotel attributes (Pizam et al., 2013).

The conclusions are drawn from the second approach. According to nationality, the relative weight of the attributes presents in the comment according to nationality will be expected to be similar to the previous ones. However, the main differences lie in the fact that, although mentioned a lot by Germans, the room and staff are mentioned by less than 50% of guests, with a greater emphasis on Location and Breakfast. Like Spaniards and Italians, most Brazilian guests mention aspects related to the room and location in their comments, revealing aspects that should be considered if guests of these nationalities are hosted. However, Brazilian guests present first in the hierarchy, the fourth, and the Italians and Spaniards. Most British guests mention aspects related to the staff, location and room in their comments, in this hierarchical order, and these attributes must be considered, and the hotel must focus on training its staff so that they register the better approach to these customers. Most French guests are concerned with room and staff characteristics, being the only one of the main issuing markets that do not present its hierarchy, the location. Finally, it can also be concluded that the Portuguese guest is the only one who does not present a significant number of comments about a specific product, thus making it the most complex to analyze and satisfy.

After analyzing the results, other questions can be answered. First, it is concluded that there is a similarity in the relevant attributes, but there are differences in their order. However, Spanish and Italian nationality guests show similar results in terms of valuing the room and location, also answering the question of similarities between Latino guests. British and French guests also have similarities, being the only ones in which the staff attribute is valued by more than 50% of the guests in the sample.

As for the differences and similarities between guests from eastern and western countries, we can conclude that there are. For example, Asians value location above all other attributes and Europeans value bedrooms, while Americans (Western countries) and Oceanic (Eastern countries) value the same attributes, although Americans rank fourth and oceanic first in the hierarchy. The localization.

Additionally, there is an attribute that can be considered transversal to the guests' nationalities, the "Room". This is since this is the main product of the hotel and because it has several characteristics that can be analyzed and evaluated, superior to any other attribute.

Overall, the results show that the staff becomes more relevant to customers in higher categories, replacing "Location," which is more important to guests in lower categories. Furthermore, when comparing high season and low season, location is more relevant in high season, losing importance in low season. It is thus concluded that the "Location" attribute is the most vulnerable to the variables considered, even though it is mentioned by most guests from the main issuing markets in their comments.

Finally, regarding the main differences between the two analyses, in theoretical terms, is that the analysis of the number of mentions of the attributes allows us to understand the importance in terms of the characteristics that the attribute presents, that is, if it has many mentions, it may mean that it has many features that can be mentioned in the reviews, and the more features mentioned this means, the more critical it will be to the guest. Nevertheless, on the other hand, the analysis of the number of comments that have the attribute present allows complementing the previous analysis, i.e., knowing that specific attributes are essential, will they be necessary for most guests of a particular nationality? Therefore, from the results of the analysis, we were able to conclude that the attributes "Breakfast" and "Staff" are not as relevant for most of the main issuing markets as the first analysis would seem, although they have many mentioned characteristics and therefore become critical for some guests of a particular nationality.

Comparing the results of this investigation with previous studies, the conclusions of this study show some similarities with studies such as those by Radojevic, Stanisic and Stanic (2017), which mention "Location", "Staff" and "Room" as the main valued attributes by the guests. Furthermore, this study seems to be aligned with Albayrak and Caber (2015), who mention the relevance of the attributes "F&B", "Staff" and "Room", and Maric (2016), which mentions the attributes "Room" and "Staff" that, in general, are mentioned by guests as crucial in their satisfaction. On the other hand, the conclusions are antagonistic to the conclusions presented by Ramanathan and Ramanathan (2011). They mention that the attributes most valued by the British are "Quality/Price" and "Maintenance", "Cleanliness" and "Security" as two of the most relevant attributes for guests (Atkinson, 1988), and the time difference must be considered.

In conclusion, given the results presented, it is possible to conclude that the guest culture of the main outbound markets influences the ranking of the attributes most valued by guests. However, some attributes are essential for most guests, although the level of importance is distinguished.

Limitations

During the study, some limitations were detected that could influence the results, which could improve future investigations. The first limitation detected is that there are attributes, such as the price of the stay, which is not mentioned before booking because it is defined before booking. The same could happen with the location. However, there is proximity to the hotel that is only visible during the stay. The second limitation resides in the fact that the sample only contains one hotel of each typology/category, which can influence the attributes mentioned by the characteristics of the hotels. The third limitation detected is that European guests mainly use the platform used as a source of information. Although it was chosen because the main outbound markets are European, it does not allow analyzing emerging markets nor making meaningful comparisons of the guests from different continents. The last limitation detected is related to the platform from which the data were collected, which does not allow considering other variables that can influence the hierarchy of the most valued attributes, such as age group and travel motivations.

Future Directions

As a proposal for future investigations and considering the limitations that the study presents, it would be interesting to compare what hoteliers consider to be the attributes most valued by guests according to their nationality and what guests claim to value. Alternatively, as an alternative to researching the main markets, prepare a study on the markets growing in tourism in Porto, trying to overcome the limitations that this study presents.

REFERENCES

Albayrak, T., Caber, M., & Aksoy, S. (2010). Relationships of the tangible and intangible elements of tourism products with overall customer satisfaction. International Journal of Trade. *Economics and Finance, 1*(2), 140–143.

Albayrak, T. & Caber, M. (2015). *Prioritisation of the hotel attributes according to their influence on satisfaction: A comparison of two techniques.* Academic Press.

Almsalam, S. (2014). The Effects of Customer Expectation and Perceived Service Quality on Customer Satisfaction. *International Journal of Business and Management Invention, 3*(8), 79–84.

Alzaid, A. A., & Soliman, A. A. (2002). Service quality in Riyadh's Elite hotels: Measurement and evaluation. *King Saud University Journal, 14*(2), 83–103.

Anderson, E. W., Fornell, C., & Lehmann, D. R. (1994). Customer Satisfaction, Market Share, and Profitability: Findings from Sweden. *Journal of Marketing, 58*(3), 53–56.

Anderson, E. W., & Mittla, V. (2000). Strengthening the Satisfaction-Profit Chain. *Journal of Service Research, 3*(2), 107–120. doi:10.1177/109467050032001

Anderson, M. (2014). *Local consumer review survey 2014.* Available at: https://searchengineland.com/88-consumers-trust-online-reviews-muchpersonal-recommendations-195803

Ariffin, A., & Maghzi, A. (2012). A preliminary study on customer expectations of hotel hospitality: Influences of personal and hotel factors. *International Journal of Hospitality Management, 31*(1), 191–198. doi:10.1016/j.ijhm.2011.04.012

Atkinson, A. (1988). Answering the eternal question: what does the customer want? *The Cornell Hotel and Restaurant Administration Quarterly, 29*(2), 12-14.

Ayeh, J., Au, N., & Law, R. (2016). Investigating cross-national heterogeneity in the adoption of online hotel reviews. *International Journal of Hospitality Management, 55*, 142–153. doi:10.1016/j.ijhm.2016.04.003

Baka, V. (2016). The becoming of user-generated reviews: Looking at the past to understand the future of managing reputation in the travel sector. *Tourism Management*, *53*, 148–162. doi:10.1016/j.tourman.2015.09.004

Bickart, B., & Schindler, R. (2001). Internet forums as influential sources of consumer information. *Journal of Interactive Marketing*, *15*(3), 31–40. doi:10.1002/dir.1014

Branco, G., Ribeiro, J., & Tinoco, M. (2010). Determinantes da satisfação e atributos da qualidade em serviços de hotelaria. *Prod*, *20*(4), 576–588. doi:10.1590/S0103-65132010005000057

Bughin, J., Doogan, J., & Vetvik, O. (2010). *A new way to measure word-of-mouth marketing*. Available at: https://www.mckinsey.com/business-functions/marketing-and-sales/ourinsights/a-new-way-to-measure-word-of-mouth-marketing

Castro, C., Fereira, F., & Fereira, F. (2016). Trends in hotel pricing: Identifying guest value hotel attributes using the cases of Lisbon and Porto. *Worldwide Hospitality and Tourism Themes*, *8*(6), 691–698. doi:10.1108/WHATT-09-2016-0047

Chen, C., Nguyen, B., Klaus, P., & Wu, M. (2015). Exploring electronic word-of-mouth (eWOM) in the consumer purchase decision-making process: The case of online holidays – evidence from United Kingdom (UK) consumers. *Journal of Travel & Tourism Marketing*, *32*(8), 953–970. doi:10.1080/10548408.2014.956165

Constantinides, E., & Holleschovsky, N. (2016). *Impact of Online Product Reviews on Purchasing Decisions*. SCITEPRESS. doi:10.5220/0005861002710278

Cox, C., Burgess, S., Sellitto, C., & Buultjens, J. (2009). The role of user-generated content in tourists' travel planning behavior. *Journal of Hospitality Marketing & Management*, *17*(4), 743–764. doi:10.1080/19368620903235753

Deng, W. J., Kuo, Y. F., & Chen, W. C. (2008). Revised importance–performance analysis: Threefactor theory and benchmarking. *Service Industries Journal*, *28*(1), 37–51. doi:10.1080/02642060701725412

Djekic, I., Kane, K., Tomic, N., Kalogianni, E., Rocha, A., Zamioudi, L., & Pacheco, R. (2016). Cross-cultural consumer perceptions of service quality in restaurants. *Nutrition & Food Science*, *46*(6), 827–843. doi:10.1108/NFS-04-2016-0052

Dolnicar, S., & Otter, T. (2003). Which hotel attributes matter? A review of previous and a framework for future research. Academic Press.

Dou, X., Walden, J. A. L. S., & Lee, J. Y. (2012). Does source matter? Examining source effects in online product reviews. Computers in Human Behavior, 1555-1563.

Dubcová, A., Petrikovie, J. & Šolcavá, L. (2013). Globalization and the hotel industry in Slovakia. *Annals of the University of Bucharest: Geography Series, 62*.

Dwyer, L. (2015). Globalization of tourism: Drivers and outcomes. *Tourism Recreation Research*, *40*(3), 326–339. doi:10.1080/02508281.2015.1075723

Eshtetie, S., Seyoum, W., & Hussen Ali, S. (2016). Service Quality and Customer Satisfaction in Hospitality Industry: The Case of Selected Hotels in Jimma Town, Ethiopia. *Global Journal of Management and Business Research, 16*(5).

Farooq, M. S. (2016). *Social Support and Entrepreneurial Skills as Antecedents of Entrepreneurial Behaviour*. Universiti Malaysia Sarawak.

Goeldner, C. R., Ritchie, J. R. B., & MacIntosh, R. W. (2000). *Tourism: Principles, Practices Philosophies* (8th ed.). John Wiley & Sons, Inc.

Gretzel, U., & Yoo, K. (2008). *Use and Impact of Online Travel Reviews*. doi:10.1007/978-3-211-77280-5_4

Gustavo, N. (2012). Modelos e Processos de Gestão em Negócios Turísticos. Tendências num contexto em mudança. *Revista Turismo & Desenvolvimento, 17/18*, 671–685.

Hall, E. (1976). *Beyond Culture*. Anchor Books/Doubleday.

Han, H. J., Mankad, S., Gavirneni, N., & Verma, R. (2016). What guests really think of your hotel: Text analytics of online customer reviews. *Cornell Hospitality Report, 16*(2), 1–19.

Helversen, B., Abramczuk, K., Kopec, W., & Nielek, R. (2018). Influence of consumer reviews on online purchasing decisions in older and younger adults. *Decision Support Systems, 113*, 1–10. doi:10.1016/j.dss.2018.05.006

Hofstede, G., Hofstede, G., & Minkov, M. (2010). Dimensions of National Cultures. In *Intercultural Cooperation and Its Importance for Survival* (pp. 53–296). McGraw-Hill.

Jahandideh, B., Golmohammadi, A., Meng, F., O'Gorman, K. D., & Taheri, B. (2014). Cross-cultural comparison of Chinese and Arab consumer complaintbehavior in the hotel context. *International Journal of Hospitality Management, 41*, 67–76. doi:10.1016/j.ijhm.2014.04.011

Jin, S. V., & Phua, J. (2015). Making reservations online: The impact of consumer-written and system-aggregated user-generated content (UGC) In travel booking websites on consumers' behavioral intentions. *Journal of Travel & Tourism Marketing, 33*(1), 1–17.

Kandampully, J., & Suhartanto, D. (2000). Customer loyalty in the hotel industry: The role of customer satisfaction and image. *International Journal of Contemporary Hospitality Management, 12*(6), 346–351. doi:10.1108/09596110010342559

Kardon, B. (2007). They're saying nasty things. *Marketing News, 41*(20), 30.

Khozaei, M. (2016). The study of factors affecting customer's satisfaction with the three star hotels in Dubai. International Journal of Advanced Engineering. *Management Science, 2*(2), 21–24.

Kirby, C. (2000). *Everyone's a critic: Web sites hope online reviews of products lead to online buying*. Available at: https://www.sfgate.com/business/article/EVERYONE-S-A-CRITIC-Web-siteshopeon-line-2782075.php

Kuo, C. (2007). The importance of hotel employee service attitude and satisfaction of international tourists. *Service Industries Journal, 27*(8), 1073–1085. doi:10.1080/02642060701673752

Lee, J., Lee, J.-N., & Tan, B. C. Y. (2013). The contrasting attitudes of reviewer and seller in electronic word-of-mouth: A communicative action theory perspective. *Asia Pacific Journal of Information Systems*, *23*(3), 105–129. doi:10.14329/apjis.2013.23.3.105

Lee, J., Park, D., & Han, I. (2008). The effect of negative online consumer reviews on product attitude: An information processing view. *Electronic Commerce Research and Applications*, *7*(3), 341–352. doi:10.1016/j.elerap.2007.05.004

Li, H., Ye, Q., & Law, R. (2012). Determinants of Customer Satisfaction in the Hotel Industry: An Application of Online Review Analysis. *Asia Pacific Journal of Tourism Research*, 119–108.

Lin, S. P., Chan, Y. H., & Tsai, M. C. (2009). A transformation function corresponding to IPA and gap analysis. *Total Quality Management & Business Excellence*, *20*(8), 829–846. doi:10.1080/14783360903128272

Liu, S., Law, R., Rong, J., Li, G., & Hall, J. (2013). Analyzing changes in hotel customers' expectations by trip mode. *International Journal of Hospitality Management*, *34*, 359–371. doi:10.1016/j.ijhm.2012.11.011

Liu, Z., & Park, S. (2015). What makes a useful online review? Implication for travel product websites. *Tourism Management*, *47*, 140–151. doi:10.1016/j.tourman.2014.09.020

Lu, C., Berchoux, C., Marek, M., & Chen, B. (2015). Service quality and customer satisfaction: Qualitative research implications for luxury hotels. *International Journal of Culture, Tourism and Hospitality Research*, *9*(2), 168–182. doi:10.1108/IJCTHR-10-2014-0087

Maric, D. M. V., Maric, R., & Dimitrovski, D. (2016). Analysis of Tangible and Intangible HotelnService Quality Components. *Industrija*, *44*(1), 7–25. doi:10.5937/industrija1-8437

Markham-Bagnera, S. (2016). *An examination of online ratings on performance indicators: An analysis of the Boston hotel market*. Iowa State University.

Neirotti, P., Raguseo, E. & Paolucci, E. (2016). Are customers' reviews creating value in the hospitality industry? Exploring the moderating effects of market positioning. *International Journal of Information Management, 36*(6), 1133-1143.

Njite, D., & Schaffer, J. (2017). Revisiting Attributes: How Important Is Green in the Consumer Selection of Hotel Rooms? *International Journal of Hospitality & Tourism Administration*, *18*(2), 219–244. doi:10.1080/15256480.2016.1263168

Ogut, H., & Cezar, A. (2012). *Prosumer motivations for electronic word-of-mouth communication behaviors*. Procedia.

Ozdipciner, N., Li, X., & Uysal, M. (2012). Cross-cultural differences in purchase decision-making criteria. *International Journal of Culture, Tourism and Hospitality Research*, *4*(4), 340–351.

Pizam, A., Shapoval, V., & Ellis, T. (2013). Customer satisfaction and its measurement in hospitality enterprises: A revisit and update. *International Journal of Contemporary Hospitality Management*, *28*(1), 2–35. doi:10.1108/IJCHM-04-2015-0167

PwC. (2015). *Online Reputations: Why hotel reviews matter and how hotels respond*. PwC.

Radojevic, T., Stanisic, N., & Stanic, N. (2017). Inside the Rating Scores: A Multilevel Analysis of the Factors Influencing Customer Satisfaction in the Hotel Industry. *Cornell Hospitality Quarterly*, *58*(2), 134–164. doi:10.1177/1938965516686114

Reuland, R., Coudrey, J., & Fagel, A. (1985). Research in the field of hospitality. *International Journal of Hospitality Management*, *4*(4), 141–146. doi:10.1016/0278-4319(85)90051-9

Rhee, H., & Yang, S. (2015). Does hotel attribute importance differ by hotel? Focusing on hotel star-classifications and customers' overall ratings. *Computers in Human Behavior*, *50*, 576–587. doi:10.1016/j.chb.2015.02.069

Salazar, A., Costa, J., & Rita, P. (2010). A service quality evaluation scale for the hospitality sector: Dimensions, attributes and behavioural intentions. *Worldwide Hospitality and Tourism Themes*, *2*(4), 383–397. doi:10.1108/17554211011074047

Spake, D., Beatty, S., Brockman, B., & Crutchfield, T. (2003). Consumer comfort in service relationships: Measurement and importance. *Journal of Service Research*, *5*(4), 316–332. doi:10.1177/1094670503005004004

Stringam, B. B., & Gerdes, J. J. Jr. (2010). An analysis of word-of-mouse ratings and guest comments of online hotel distribution sites. *Journal of Hospitality Marketing & Management*, *19*(7), 773–796. doi:10.1080/19368623.2010.508009

Tinoco, M. A. & Ribeiro, J. L. (2007). Uma nova abordagem para a modelagem das relações entre os determinantes da satisfação dos clientes de serviços. *Revista Produção, 17*(3).

Ueltschy, L. C., Laroche, M., Eggert, A., & Bindl, U. (2007). Service quality and satisfaction: An international comparison of professional services perceptions. *Journal of Services Marketing*, *21*(6), 410–423. doi:10.1108/08876040710818903

Vavra, T. G. (1997). *Improving Your Measurement of Customer Satisfation: A Guide to Creating, Conducting, Analyzing, and Reporting Customer Satisfaction Measurement Programs*. Academic Press.

Vermeulen, I., & Seegers, D. (2009). Tried and tested: The impact of online hotel reviews on consumer consideration. *Tourism Management*, *30*(1), 123–127. doi:10.1016/j.tourman.2008.04.008

W.H.D.P. (2014). Relationship between Service Quality and Customer Relationship in sir Lankan hotel industry. *International Journal of Scientific and Research Publications*, 2-8.

Worsfold, K., Fisher, R., McPhail, R., Francis, M., & Thomas, A. (2016). Satisfaction, value and intention to return in hotels. *International Journal of Contemporary Hospitality Management*, *28*(11), 2570–2588. doi:10.1108/IJCHM-04-2015-0195

Xie, K. L., Chen, C., & Wu, S. (2016). Online consumer review factors affecting offline hotel popularity: Evidence from TripAdvisor. *Journal of Travel & Tourism Marketing*, *33*(2), 211–223. doi:10.1080/10548408.2015.1050538

Xie, K. L., Zhang, Z., & Zhang, Z. (2014). The business value of online consumer reviews and management response to hotel performance. *International Journal of Hospitality Management*, *43*, 1–12. doi:10.1016/j.ijhm.2014.07.007

Ye, Q., Law, R., Gu, B., & Chen, W. (2011). The influence of user-generated content on traveler behavior: An empirical investigation on the effects of e-word-of-mouth to hotel online bookings. *Computers in Human Behavior*, *27*(2), 634–639. doi:10.1016/j.chb.2010.04.014

Zhao, X., Wang, L., Guo, X., & Law, R. (2015). The influence of online reviews to online hotel booking intentions. *International Journal of Contemporary Hospitality Management*, *27*(6), 1343–1364. doi:10.1108/IJCHM-12-2013-0542

Chapter 15
The Importance of Online Reputation Management in Four- and Five-Star Hotes:
Case of Lisbon

Catarina Silva
Estoril Higher Institute for Tourism and Hotel Studies, Portugal

Miguel Belo
Estoril Higher Institute for Tourism and Hotels Studies, Portugal

ABSTRACT

In recent years, online reputation management has become increasingly crucial in the hotel industry, as online reviews have become one of the most critical factors in choosing accommodation. Consequently, hotels have adapted themselves to this new reality and define strategies focused on online reputation management, whose primary goal is to monitor and correct unwanted situations verified on the internet. Regarding its importance, several investigations about online reputation management have been made, but mostly about their impact on consumer satisfaction and decision-making. This investigation shows that hotels in Lisbon adopt adequate strategies in both four and five-star hotels, and their classification (star rating) did not influence the strategies chosen by them. Additionally, hotels with the same classification have similar strategies, in contrast to some investigations in the literature. Finally, the method of data collection chosen for the current investigation was the online survey, since it allows the collection of a significant volume of data in a short period.

INTRODUCTION

The present investigation aims to answer the following starting question: "What are the strategies adopted by the four and five-star hotels in the city of Lisbon, given the importance of online reputation

DOI: 10.4018/978-1-7998-8306-7.ch015

management in the hotel industry?". Once the hotels' strategies are known, it is intended to analyze each category's behavior and understand if the hotel classification influences the chosen approaches.

Considering the review of the existing literature on the subject, it is observed that most studies focus mainly on the consumer (Lee & Blum, 2015; Diana-Jens & Ruibal, 2015; Xie, So & Wang, 2017), particularly on what refers to the impact of online reputation and online reviews on their satisfaction (Picazo-Vela, 2009; Li, Ye & Law., 2013; Gu & Ye, 2014; Berezina, Bilgihan, Cobanoglu & Okumus, 2016) and decision-making (Litvin, Goldsmith & Pan, 2008; Vermeulen & Seegers, 2009; Levy, Duan & Boo, 2013; Melián-González, Bulchand-Gidumal & López-Valcárcel, 2013; Rose & Blodgett, 2016). Thus, the present investigation aims to focus on the view of hotels and analyze their behavior in this area.

Nevertheless, some studies in the literature portray the impacts of reputation on the performance of hotels (Diana-Jens & Ruibal, 2015; Xie et al., 2017) and equally (and similarly to this research) the management of responses to online reviews, according to some indicators (Lee & Blum, 2015; Liu, Schuckert & Law, 2015; Xie, Zhang, Zhang, Singh & Lee, 2016; Aureli & Supino, 2017; Xie et al., 2017).

Lisbon (Metropolitan Area) choice was since there were no similar studies in this region and because it has significant international recognition84 as a destination of excellence in Portugal. For example, the Portuguese capital was recently considered the "Best City Break Destination in the World" by the World Travel Awards (Público, 2017).

Concerning four and five-star hotels, the choice fell on the two highest categories as they focus more on face-to-face interactions and provide highly individualized and personalized service to their customers, which may contrast with the communications made in the online panorama (Park & Allen, 2013). Also, proper online reputation management is more expected in higher category hotels (Xie et al., 2016).

Finally, this article is divided into five main points, namely: literature review, methodology, results and discussion, conclusion and implications of the investigation.

LITERATURE REVIEW

Online Reputation Management

Inserted in the online world, companies are currently a click away from millions of people, becoming the topic of reputation (and respective management) increasingly crucial in the success of organizations. This issue can act for or against companies, making it crucial to adopt appropriate strategies.

Thus, online reputation management consists of "monitoring the media, detecting relevant content, analyzing what people say about an entity and, if necessary, interacting with consumers" (Amigó, Artils, Gonzalo, Spina, Liu & Corujo, 2010, p.1). Although this management is focused on online reviews, it was decided to focus this research on this element as it is an aspect that assumes significant importance in the hotel industry. This situation can be proven in a study by the World Tourism Organization (2014), which found that 69% of respondents said that online reviews were extremely important for the hotel.

As a source of reliable information in the consumer's eyes (Lee, 2009; Sparks, Perkins & Buckley, 2013), online reviews allow you to create an even more positive image about the hotel and shape its reputation (Campbell, 2015). If, on the one hand, positive online reviews allow to increase reserves and market share (Torres, Singh & Robertson-Ring, 2015), negative ones lead, on the contrary, to reputational damage and consequent drop in revenue (Sparks & Browning, 2011; Vermeulen & Seegers, 2009).

Whether positive or negative, online reviews are "an opportunity for the hotel to start a conversation and create a connection with the guest" (Mayer, 2015, p. 7).

Regarding how hotels manage their online reputation, it appears that response management is an open text, publicly disclosed online and intended to respond to online consumer reviews (Xie et al., 2017), and it has been the object of study in the literature (Sorensen, 2012; Park & Allen, 2013; Liu et al., 2015).

Concerning this research, we intend to analyze some of the leading indicators focused on response management, namely: response to online reviews, response source, response time, monitoring frequency, and response approaches.

Monitoring Online Reputation

Considering the importance of social media, namely online review websites, it is crucial to understand how long hoteliers have monitored their online presence and how often they do so. This process allows them to access information about the market and the hotel's current situation at no cost (Hills & Cairncross, 2011). In fact, according to Baka (2016), online monitoring reputation on websites such as TripAdvisor is already part of the daily routine of some hotels.

Regarding the start of monitoring, Aureli and Supino (2017) found that most of the hotels surveyed (60%) started this process three or more years ago, followed by those that started two years ago (18%), one year ago (17%) and finally six months (5%). In contrast, in a guide on best practices for managing online reviews presented by Barsky and Frame (2009), the authors mentioned a study carried out by Market Metrix and TripAdvisor that found that around 85% of hotels had no strategies for monitoring, respond and act on online reviews. Also, Levy et al. (2013) stated that hotel managers do not provide any guidelines for monitoring and responding to online reviews.

Regarding the frequency of monitoring, Aureli and Supino (2017) observed that most hotels monitored this process every week (47%), followed by those that did daily (33%), fortnightly (9%), monthly (6%) and quarterly (5%).

On the other hand, Lee and Blum (2015) analyzed the regularity with which hotels monitored and responded to online reviews in addition to the speed of response. In this study, it was interesting to observe that the hotels that responded in less time did not have a regular strategy, while those with a regular monitoring strategy had a longer response time.

The absence, or relatively little involvement of hotels monitoring your online reputation can be due to several factors - the lack of interest in knowing what consumers think about the hotel, the existence of older generation hoteliers who, consequently, do not have as much knowledge and skills to use the new one's technologies and, finally, the excessive consumption of time and resources that this process can take (Aureli & Supino, 2017).

The Approach to Responding to Online Review

Response management should focus on responding to both negative and positive online reviews. Responding to positive feedback allows consumers to feel that they are being listened to and that hotel management takes their opinions into account (Xie et al., 2017). Responding to negative reviews online can lead to higher satisfaction levels as the hotel publicly describes its problem-solving policy (Xie, Zhang & Zhang, 2014). On this topic, Liu et al. (2015) found that providing a sincere response to the dissatisfied consumer makes them feel better and more willing to revisit the establishment without spreading negative feedback. Also, for Sparks and Bradley (2014), the response to online reviews reduces the probability of readers having negative and/or wrong perceptions about the hotel in question.

Although significant these days, it was observed in some investigations that hotels had response rates well below expectations. Park and Allen (2013) stated that apart from hotels rarely responding to online reviews, using entirely different strategies when they do. On the other hand, Liu et al. (2015) concluded in their study that there is no direct relationship between the response rate and the class of hotels. Aureli and Supino (2017) found that two- and three-star hotels are less active in response management than higher categories. Also, about this study, the authors observed that 44% of respondents said they responded to both positive and negative online reviews, 32% never responded to any online review, 23% responded only to negatives, and only 1% was dedicated to responding only to positives.

Lee and Blum (2015) concluded that the response rates to online reviews in most of the hotels analyzed were low and primarily focused on the positives. Still, the four- and five-star rated hotels had the highest response rate to negative feedback. Park and Allen (2013) also contributed to this theme and analyzed four hotels (two five-star and the other two four-star) concerning their procedure for responding to online reviews. The authors concluded that, in general, hotels follow different approaches from each other.

On the other hand, and defending the response to positive reviews online, ReviewPro (2011) made some suggestions to encourage hoteliers to respond to positive feedback considering the following steps: 1) thanks 2) reinforce the positive aspects mentioned; 3) congratulate the hotel staff on their excellent performance; 4) invite the customer to come back, promoting new services. In addition to these suggestions, ReviewPro (2011) also states that hoteliers should be brief, show empathy, personalize each answer and avoid repetition.

Sparker (2015) also mentioned that hoteliers should take this opportunity to question the customer about possible improvements to be implemented in the establishment. Smith (2016) noted that companies should invite consumers to revisit the establishment and share feedback in other channels.

About negative online reviews, these should be a priority (ReviewPro, 2011; Lee & Blum, 2015), and the steps should translate into a thank you, an apology, an explanation of corrective actions and a suggestion to contact the offline hotel channels for further clarification (ReviewPro, 2011; Chuang, Cheng, Chang & Yang, 2012; Baker, 2016). It is also important to emphasize that the answer must be given a calmly and considered tone, avoiding abusive and furious answers that will only further damage the hotel's reputation (ReviewPro, 2011).

Other recommendations include never questioning the legitimacy of the reviewer, even suspecting that it is a false review (ReviewPro, 2011), avoiding generic responses (ReviewPro, 2011; Min, Lim & Magnini, 2014; Benjamin, Kriss & Egelman, 2016; Campbell, 2016), pay attention that the response content does not contain expressions that the customer does not understand (ReviewPro, 2011) and do not resort to discounts or any other type of compensation to solve the problem (ReviewPro, 2011; Campbell, 2016).

Overall, an appropriate response approach is essential, but taking on a prevention strategy is even more accurate. To this end, it is crucial that hoteliers create an organizational culture that fosters the importance of online reputation, sharing examples of positive and negative reviews about the hotel online in training and training sessions (ReviewPro, 2011; Sparker, 2015).

Response Time Management to Online Reviews

The response time to an online review is simply the period between the period marked by the posting of the online review by the consumer and the period in which he received a response from the hotel. Once again, the existing literature is unclear regarding the ideal response time to each type of online review. Xie et al. (2017), for example, observed in their study an average response time of about fifteen days, while Sparks and Bradley (2014) found a period between one to three days.

Speed-of-response studies are much more associated with negative than positive feedback, and it is easy to see why. According to the theory of service recovery (Andreassen, 2000 op cit. Xie et al., 2017), the speed with which managers respond to service failures is crucial. In the online world, this situation is even more pertinent as online reviews are exposed to many people, and the lack of response may lead to believe that the hotel is not dealing correctly with consumer complaints. Although hotel managers must respond immediately to online complaints (Levy et al., 2013), it was found that more extended responses are easily forgiven in higher category hotels when compared to lower categories (Xie et al., 2017). Sparks, So and Bradley (2016) demonstrated that quick responses to negative online reviews improve reliability and consumer concerns. Aureli and Supino (2017) also defended that sincere and quick responses allow the recovery of consumer loyalty and the hotel's reputation in general.

The literature presents some indications about the ideal response time, but only regarding online reviews in general terms or only about negative ones. ReviewPro (2017) states that online reviews, in general, should be answered within three to five days (considering a 40% response rate), although Revinate (2014) advocates that this period should not exceed 24 hours.

Staff Involvement in Online Reputation Management

Although little is discussed in the literature (Sparks et al., 2016; Xie et al., 2017), the person responsible for managing responses can be one of the most critical information in the customer's assessment of the hotel (Xie et al., 2017). A wrong choice in this area is even considered one of the main mistakes in online reputation management (Murphy, 2016).

Lee and Blum (2015) identified that positions respond to more and less online reviews in their research. Regarding those with a more significant presence in the management of 89 responses, it was concluded that the leading positions were General Manager, Guest Services Supervisor, Public Relations Supervisor and Social Media team member. On the contrary, those responsible for the lowest number of responses were the Director of Sales, Assistant Front Office Manager and the Hotel Manager.

The importance of the response source may be related to the credibility and reliability perceived by the consumer. On this topic, Sparks et al. (2016) concluded in their research that consumers consider responses from senior positions more trustworthy. However, other investigations point to the fact that responses from senior positions are only crucial for some types of hotels. This was observed in the study by Xie et al. (2017) in which it was found that responses from senior positions were only crucial for hotels classified as "Budget traveler hotels" (one star), "mid-market economy hotels" (two stars) and "full-service hotels" (three stars), while for the hotels "above-average hotels" (four stars) and "luxury hotels" (five stars) the responses from top-tier managers were the most recommended.

Although most studies mention only internal staff in response management, it appears that sometimes, and mostly in larger hotels, those responsible for hotel management decide to transfer some (or all) responsibility to an external company using outsourcing. Even so, Aureli and Supino (2017) found in their research that hotel managers rarely choose to transfer this responsibility to external companies. Most of the hotels surveyed in the study stated that they intended to manage the question of responses to online reviews through internal employees of the organization, albeit sometimes with the help of a professional consultant. Sparks and Bradley (2014) also defended that hotels, exceptionally the most luxurious and larger ones, can use outsourcing strategies to monitor the entire online reputation of the hotel, but the management of responses is always the responsibility of the hotel itself.

METHODS

To achieve the objectives of the present investigation, a questionnaire survey on online reputation management (QUHLGRO) was implemented in four and five-star hotels in the Metropolitan Area of Lisbon. The universe of the study was defined as a total of 142 units (41 five-star and 101 four-star) (Turismo de Portugal, 2017). Due to various limitations, the questionnaire was made available online to 113 hotels, whose characteristics of the sample were translated into four and five-star hotels in Lisbon and with a presence, at least, on the online Booking channel. It was decided to administer this survey online and not in person due to administrative and time limitations. Regarding the characteristics of the questionnaire, it was simple, of reduced duration and communicated in advance to the respondent, with closed and mandatory questions mostly sent via email, LinkedIn and the hotel's official Facebook page.

To test the receptivity of the questionnaire with the selected hotels, a pre-test phase was carried out between July 5, 2017, and July 12, 2017, during which the questionnaire was sent to 20 hotels included in the sample. At the end of the pre-test phase with a positive response, the questionnaire was then sent to the remaining hotels in the sample, remaining available until August 22, 2017, when 88 responses were recorded. Compared to the universe understudy, this value allowed obtaining a confidence level of 95% with a margin of error of 6.5%. Subsequently, the statistical treatment was carried out using the SPSS (Statistical Package for Social Science) program.

RESULTS AND DISCUSSION

Regarding the first variable analyzed based on the data collected (QUHLGRO, 2017), it was found that most of the hotels participating in the study belonged to the four-star category (70.5%), while only 29.5% were translated into five-star hotels (Figure 1).

Figure 1. Hotels' category

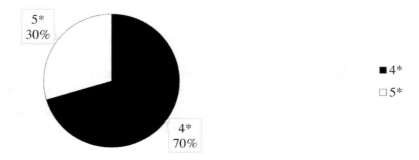

After identifying the participating hotels based on their classification, how they were distributed online was analyzed. Based on graph 2, it can be seen that Booking was the only online channel chosen by all participants, although it was found that all five-star hotels also selected channels such as TripAdvisor, Expedia/Hotels.com and their website. In four-star hotels, in addition to 91 Booking, most channels selected were also the own website (96.8%), Expedia/Hotels.com (95.2%) and TripAdvisor (90.3%)

Figure 2. Online channels

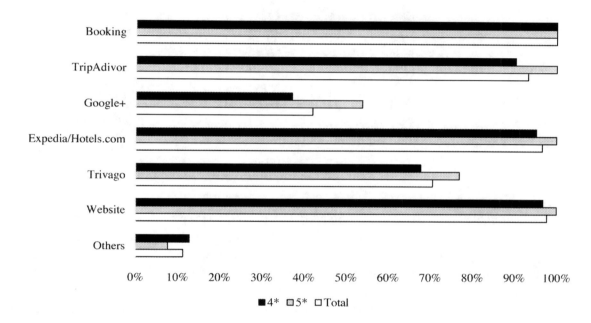

Regarding the hotel's current rating on the Booking channel, Figure 3 shows that, regardless of the category, most respondents knew its rating, with only one five-star hotel not knowing its value. It was also found that the hotels had good rating levels, verifying that most five-star hotels had a rating between the values "9-10" while in four-stars the most significant percentage92 (53.2%) was observed in the values "7-8", although 45.2% presented a value of "9-10". The lowest value recorded was a rating from 5 to 6, but it was only observed in 1.1% of the responses obtained, namely in a five-star hotel.

Figure 3. The current rating of hotels on the booking channel

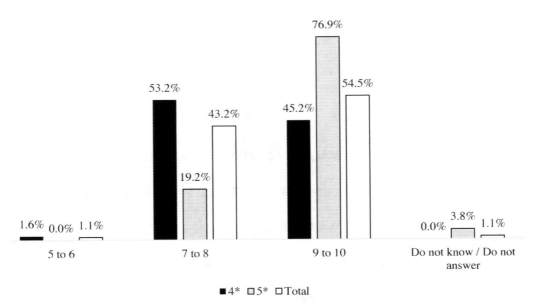

After analyzing the rating issue, it was observed that, in both categories, the majority of respondents said they used software to support online reputation management, with a significant emphasis on the ReviewPro software (figure 4). Although with little significant weight, it was found that 12.7% of participants mentioned other software, such as Availpro, RateTiger and Power BI. It should also be noted that N=55 was found in the representative graphics of the software and, consequently, the absence of 33 responses. This situation is due to non-applicable answers (n/a), taking into account the skip logic questions present in the questionnaire.

Figure 4. The use of online reputation management support software and related software used

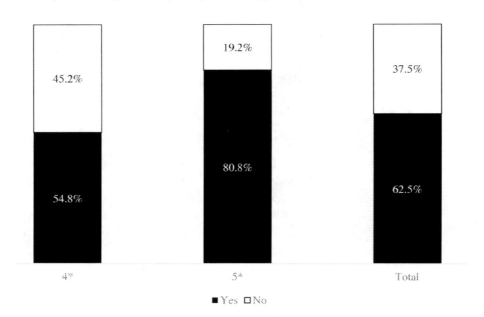

Although some of the issues mentioned above reveal, in part, the importance that participating hotels attribute to the component of online reputation, it was decided to question the hotels on this topic directly. Based on Graph 5, it was found that in both categories, the majority of participants stated that in the hotel with which they collaborate, the theme of online reputation was considered a critical element (87.1% in four-star hotels and 88, 5% in hotels of five). The remaining options had very little weight, and any of the respondents did not choose the option "not at all important". Once the issue of importance has been analyzed, it becomes crucial to understand whether or not hotels are monitoring their online reputation and analyzing how long this monitoring has been carried out.

Figure 5. The current rating of hotels on the booking channel

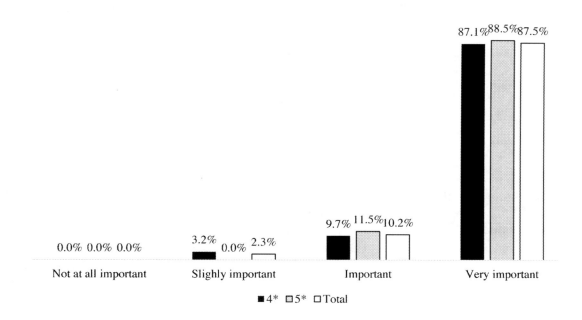

Regarding Figure 6, it is observed that, regardless of the category, the hotels surveyed stated that they had been monitoring their online reputation for three years (61.3% in four-star hotels and 61.5% in five-star hotels). Although with a less significant weight, it was found that all five-star hotels claimed to monitor their reputation, although with different starting periods. It was found that 26.9% of respondents had been doing this monitoring for two years, 7.7% for six months and finally 3.8% for a year. Concerning four-star hotels, it was observed that 19.4% of the participants stated that the hotel had been monitoring this for two years, 9.7% for one year and, finally, 3.2% for six years months, with the remaining 6.5% being hotels that confirmed not performing this task.

Figure 6. Monitoring online reputation

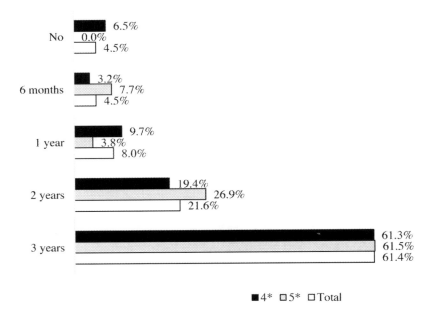

■4* □5* □Total

Regarding the frequency of monitoring (Figure 7), it was once again found similar behavior in the two categories, as most participants mentioned that this monitoring was done daily (62.1% in four-star hotels and 69 .2% in five-star hotels), followed by those that do it weekly (29.3% in four-star hotels and 26.9% in five-star hotels) and, finally, monthly (8.6% in hotels four stars and 3.8% for five). Therefore, regarding this analysis and the one carried out previously, it is possible to conclude that most hotels, regardless of category, present an adequate strategy in monitoring their online reputation. However, monitoring online reputation can (and should) involve monitoring online reviews in the various online channels that enable the publication of feedback by consumers. Thus, it became crucial for this investigation to analyze whether or not hotels responded to online reviews and, if they did, to realize95 if the response was given to all types, to know who was responsible for this task, in which online channels were answered, what the response time was, and finally, the response approaches depending on their type.

Figure 7. The frequency of online reputation monitoring

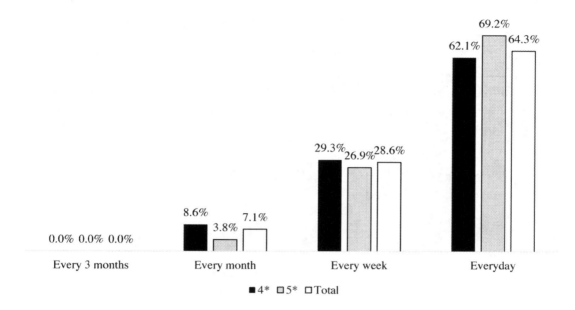

Considering Figure 8, it is possible to conclude that, once again and regardless of the hotel category, most respondents stated that they collaborate with response to online reviews, with a significant value of 90.3% in both the categories.

Figure 8. Monitoring and responding to online reviews

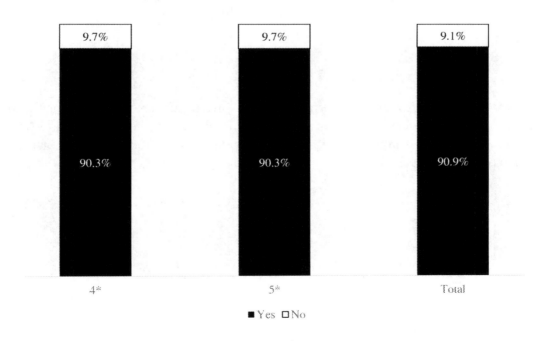

Regarding the answer source (Figure 9), the respondents had a diversity of answers, with no agreement between the two hotel categories. In four-star hotels, it was observed that the predominant position (although not the majority) was the General Manager (28.6%), followed by the Hotel Manager and the Marketing &96 Public Relations Team (both with 21.4% of the responses) and finally the Front Office Supervisor (16.1%). Concerning five-star rated hotels, the position that stood out the most was the Marketing & Public Relations Team (41.7%), followed by the General Manager (29.2%), Front Office Supervisor (12.5%) and with only 4.2% of responses, the Hotel Manager. In any of the categories, it should be noted that any of the respondents did not select the option referring to the external/outsourcing company.

Figure 9. The person responsible for responding to online reviews

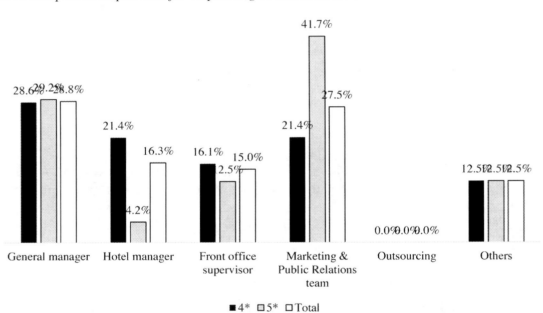

Returning to one of the first analyses carried out in this investigation, namely on online channels, it was found that most of these channels allowed response management by hotels. Thus, through Figure 10, it was found that more than 90% of respondents, regardless of classification, stated that the hotel responded to online reviews in more than one online channel.

Figure 10. Number of online channels managed under online reputation

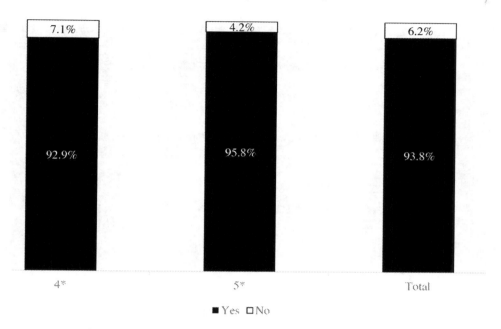

Regarding the chosen channels (Figure 11), Booking was selected by all four-star hotels under analysis, although the same situation was not verified in five-star hotels (95.7%). Considering four-star hotels, the channels that followed Booking were namely TripAdvisor (90.4%), Expedia/Hotels.com (71.2%), own website (51.9%) and, with a weightless significance, Google+ (23.1%) and Trivago (9.6%). Regarding five-star hotels, it was observed that Booking and TripAdvisor were the most selected online channels and, interestingly, with the same relevance (95.7%), followed by Expedia/Hotels.com (69.6%) and finally Trivago, Google+ and its website (all with 30.4% of responses).

Still, regarding the response to online reviews, it was found through figure 12 that, regardless of the hotel category, the vast majority of respondents (85.7% in four-star hotels and 95.8% in five-star hotels) stated that they responded to both online reviews (positive and negative). Regarding this analysis, it is also important to emphasize that hotels that did not respond to both types of online reviews chose to respond to negatives rather than positives.

Now particularizing each of the types of online reviews, it became necessary to carry out an individualized analysis considering the approach and response time. Starting with the positives (Graph 13), it is possible to observe that half of the four-star hotels responded to this type of online review within a week, compared to five-star hotels that mainly responded in one day (60.9%). The latter also found that about a third of respondents said that the hotel responded within a week, and only 4.3% mentioned two weeks. In four-star hotels, the remaining 50% of respondents said that the hotel responded to this type of online review within one day (27.1%), two weeks (18.8%) and one month (4.2%). It is important to note that five-star hotels did not mention any response period longer than two weeks.

Figure 11. Online channels where hotels respond to online reviews

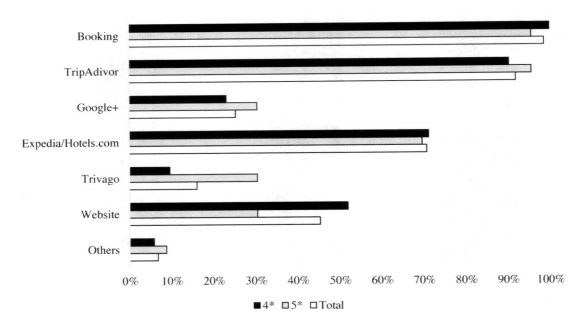

Figure 12. Typology of answered online reviews

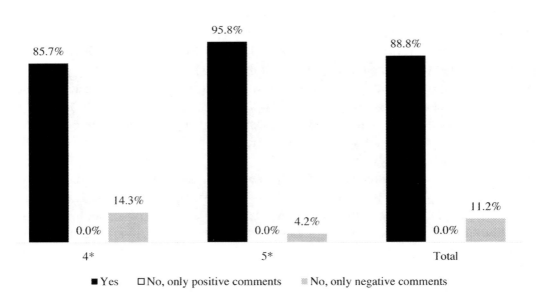

Figure 13. Response time to positive reviews online

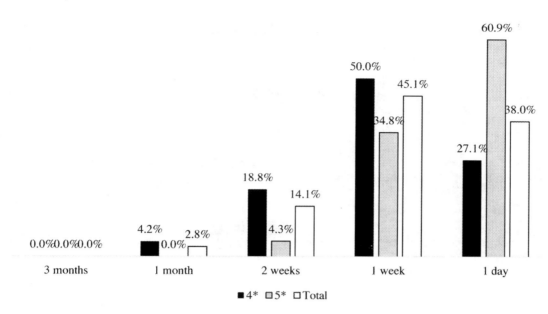

Regarding the response approaches to positive online reviews (figure 14), the most selected approach by both hotels (50.0% in four-star hotels and 47.8% in five-star hotels) was the one that was translated in a "personalized thank you, reinforce the positive aspects, congratulate the staff, encourage the return, publicize services"2. Regarding the following approaches, the two categories of hotels only showed similar results regarding the less selected approach, which consisted of "responding in a personalized way, reinforcing the positive aspects, inviting the customer to come back and sharing the feedback"3 (10.4% in four-star hotels and only 4.3% in five-star hotels). For other approaches, 2 Text changed due to character limitation in SPSS. Original text: "Thank you for the comment in a personalized way, re-inforce the positive aspects mentioned, congratulate all the staff and invite the customer to come back, disclosing new services and facilities 3 Text changed due to the limitation of characters in SPSS. Original text: "Respond in a personalized way, reinforce the positive aspects, invite the customer to return and also share your feedback on other online platforms" 21.7% of four-star hotels and 22.9% of rated hotels five chose the "thank you in a personalized way, reinforce the positive aspects, invite the customer to come back and ask for recommendations" approach. It is important to emphasize that the three strategies mentioned above translate into the most appropriate approaches, taking into account the literature review. The last approach is the least good approach as it encourages generic responses and is selected by 26.1% of the five-star hotels and by 16.7% of the four-star hotels.

Figure 14. The approach to responding to positive reviews online

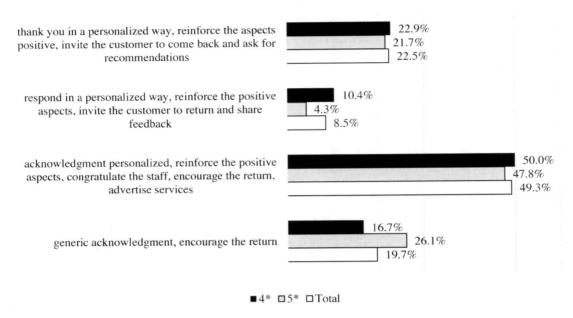

Moving on to the analysis of negative online reviews (figure 15), a similar situation to the one pre-viously observed was verified. Regarding the response time, it was found that in four-star hotels, the most mentioned option was the response given within one week (46.4%), followed by one day (41.1%), two weeks (10.7%) and one month (1.8%). Regarding five-star hotels, the overwhelming majority of participants (79.2%) reported that the response to this type of online review was given in just one day, followed by responses within a week (20.8%).

Figure 15. Response time to negative reviews online

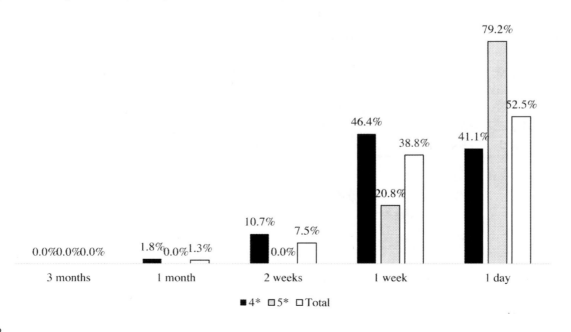

Regarding the response approaches, it was observed that the management of responses to negative reviews online turns out to be more complex than responding to positive ones, as there was a diversity of responses. Still, and considering figure 16, it was observed that the approach that consisted of "apologizing, accepting the error, describing the solutions to be implemented and providing a direct offline contact" was the most mentioned in four and five-star hotels (62.5% and 83.3%, respectively). According to the literature review, this approach is the only reasonable approach present in the questionnaire, thus revealing that most hotels in both categories end up following the adequate strategy possible about managing responses to negative online reviews.

Regarding the remaining approaches, it was found that 19.6% of the four-star hotels and only 4.2% of the five-star hotels chose the approach that translated into "responding in a generic way and with just an apology". About the approach that advocated "apologizing and offering some compensation (voucher, discount)", it was concluded that four-star hotels had a higher percentage than five-star hotels (8.9% and 7, 5%, respectively). It is also important to emphasize that four-star hotels have a more significant number of other approaches described by respondents, although with a tiny percentage (8.9%). This percentage in five-star hotels was 8.3%. Finally, the approach that advocated "responding immediately, without thinking, adopting a defensive posture and attacking the consumer" was not selected by any participants.

Based on the analysis carried out above, it is possible to conclude that most of the hotels analyzed, regardless of their category, present an adequate strategy for managing responses to positive and negative reviews online. The only exception was found in the response time in four-star hotels, which should ideally be just one day (mainly regarding the response to negative reviews online).

Figure 16. The approach to responding to negative reviews online

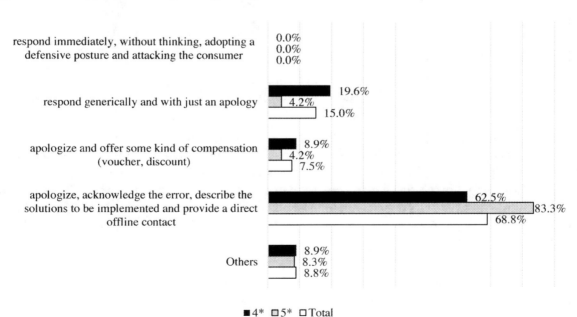

Finally, one of the last questions refers to satisfaction with the current online reputation management strategy (Figure 17). Regarding this analysis, it was observed that none of the hotel categories managed to reach at least 50% of the responses to the "very satisfied" option, even though 42.3% of the responses were found in five-star hotels and about one-third (33.9%) in four-star hotels. For 54.8% of the four-star hotels and 46.2% of the five-star ones, the participants of this research102 mentioned being satisfied. About the lowest levels of satisfaction, only 8.1% of respondents inserted in four-star hotels and 11.5% in five-star hotels, revealed to be dissatisfied with the hotel's current strategy. Finally, it is essential to mention that no five-star hotel under review mentioned being satisfied with this component.

Figure 17. Satisfaction with the current online reputation management strategy

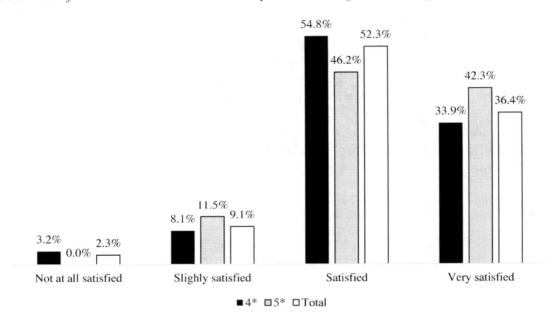

On the issue of education and training (figure 18), it can be seen that, regardless of the hotel category, most respondents said they used both types of online reviews in staff training actions (79.0% in four-star hotels and 80.8% in those with a five-star rating). Regarding the other alternatives, there was a very little weight of those who only used negative reviews online (4.8% in four-star hotels and 7.7% in five-star hotels) and positive (which was only observed in hotels five-star ratings). The absence of online reviews, in general, was found in 16.1% of four-star rated hotels and only 7.7% in five-star hotels.

Figure 18. The current rating of hotels on the booking channel

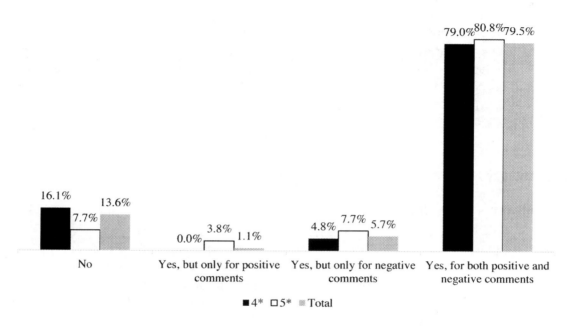

Figure 19. The factors for improving online reputation management strategy

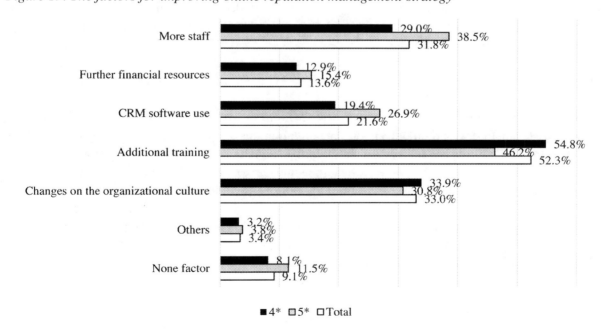

Finally, and although most participants are, at least, satisfied with the hotel's current online reputation management strategy, it was observed (figure 19) that the most mentioned factor for improving the current strategy was the implementation of more training and training actions, both in four-star hotels (54.8%) and in five-star hotels (46.2%). Other equally important factors translated into the change in organizational culture (33.0%), the need for more staff (31.8%), the use of CRM software (21.6%) and the need for more financial resources (13.6%). Furthermore, it should be noted that only 11.5% of five-star hotels and 8.1% of four-star hotels considered that there was no factor for improving the management of online reputation.

CONCLUSION

Discussion

In this last point of this article, it is considered that, based on the results obtained, we can answer the initial question formulated: "What are the strategies adopted by the four and five-star hotels in the city of Lisbon, given their importance the management of online reputation in hospitality?"

In a general view, Lisbon is a city that has been gaining more prominence worldwide due to its beauty, climate, gastronomy, and rich culture.

On the topic of online reputation, it was found that this is a subject that has been gaining more and more critical in the hotel world, although some studies have revealed some non-conformity among hotels in the strategies adopted, not forgetting that most investigations are centered on the consumer's perspective.

Although it was expected that the hotels analyzed in this investigation would present very different strategies from each other, the case of Lisbon turned out to be a good surprise. Considering the literature review and the results obtained in this investigation, it is concluded that most hotels consider this topic to be very important in their daily lives and that the adopted procedures are reflected in an adequate strategy.

Some examples of these procedures include using online reputation management support software, regularly monitoring reputation, responding to all types of online reviews (in an appropriate and personalized way), prioritizing responding to online reviews with a negative connotation, and assigning this responsibility only to internal hotel staff.

Given the procedures mentioned above, it was found that most of the hotels under review said they were, at least, satisfied with their current online reputation management strategy, although the need for more training and training in this area was highlighted, among other improvements factors.

In general, this investigation concluded that the hotels under analysis in the city of Lisbon have, for the most part, adequate strategies in managing their online reputation and that there is a very similar behavior within each category. Concerning the comparison between the two categories under analysis, only discrepancies were found about the speed of response, although this did not translate into a problematic case. Thus, it is possible to conclude that the hotel classification did not influence the strategies adopted by the hotels in this investigation.

Implications

Although with some limitations, this investigation allowed us to analyze the theme of online reputation in hotels in the city of Lisbon, which had not yet been the subject of research in this area. It was also an investigation that aimed to encompass the negative and positive online reviews in order to contradict the majority of existing studies in the literature that focused mainly on the analysis of complaints management and online reviews of a negative nature (Levy et al., 2013; Rose & Blodgett, 2016).

Therefore, this is considered an investigation that can help hotels better to understand the current situation of the Lisbon hotel industry, as it allows us to observe the main approaches and strategies for managing online reputation and the leading procedures for responding to online reviews. This greater awareness of the current situation in Lisbon regarding the importance of managing online reputation can lead to a change in behavior on the part of hotels that do not have the most appropriate strategies or even those that intend to improve their establishment.

It is also believed that this research may serve as a reference for future research, whether it is an expansion of what has been analyzed here or simply searching for new themes centered on this theme.

REFERENCES

Amigó, E., Artiles, J., Gonzalo, J., Spina, D., Liu, B., & Corujo, A. (2010). *WePS-3 Evaluation Campaign: Overview of the Online Reputation Management Task*. CEUR-WS.

Aureli, S., & Supino, E. (2017). Online Reputation Monitoring: An Exploratory Study on Italian Hotel Managers. *International Journal of Hospitality & Tourism Administration, 18*(1), 84–109. doi:10.1080/15256480.2016.1264903

Baka, V. (2016). The becoming of user-generated reviews: Looking at the past to understand the future of managing reputation in the travel sector. *Tourism Management, 53*, 148–162. doi:10.1016/j.tourman.2015.09.004

Baker, J. (2016). *How To Respond To Positive and Negative Reviews*. Disponível em: https://www.vendasta.com/blog/how-to-respond-reviews-good-bad

Barsky, J., & Frame, C. (2009). *Handling Online Reviews: Best Practices*. Disponível em: https://cdn.tripadvisor.com/pdfs/ExpertTips_HandlingOnlineReviews.pdf

Benjamin, B., Kriss, P., & Egelman, C. (2016). Responding to Social Media Reviews: The Benefits of Digital Customer Dialogue. Medallia Institute. Disponível em https://go.medallia.com/rs/medallia/images/WP-Best-Western-Social

Berezina, K., Bilgihan, A., Cobanoglu, C., & Okumus, F. (2016). Understanding Satisfied and Dissatisfied Hotel Customers: Text Mining of Online Hotel Reviews. *Journal of Hospitality Marketing & Management, 25*(1), 1–24. doi:10.1080/19368623.2015.983631

Campbell, C. (2015). *How Online Reviews and Reputation Can Support Your Social Media Strategy*. Disponível em: https://www.socialmediatoday.com/marketing/reviewtrackers/2015-09-30/howonlinereviews-and-reputation-can-support-your-social-media

Campbell, C. (2016). *Respond to Negative Reviews Like These Business Owners*. Disponível em: https://www.reviewtrackers.com/respond-negative-reviews/

Chuang, S., Cheng, Y., Chang, C., & Yang, S. (2012). The effect of service failure types and service recovery on customer satisfaction: A mental accounting perspective. *Service Industries Journal, 32*(2), 257–271. doi:10.1080/02642069.2010.529435

Diana-Jens, P., & Ruibal, A. (2015). La reputación online y su impacto en la política de precios de los hoteles. *Cuadernos de Turismo, 36*(36), 129–155. doi:10.6018/turismo.36.230911

Gu, B., & Ye, Q. (2014). First Step in Social Media: Measuring the Influence of Online Management Responses on Customer Satisfaction. *Production and Operations Management, 23*(4), 570–582. doi:10.1111/poms.12043

Hills, J., & Cairncross, G. (2011). Small accommodation providers and UGC web sites: Perceptions and practices. *International Journal of Contemporary Hospitality Management, 23*(1), 26–43. doi:10.1108/09596111111101652

Lee, H. & Blum, S. (2015). How hotel responses to online reviews differ by hotel rating: an exploratory study. *Worldwide Hospitality and Tourism Themes, 7*(3), 242-250.

Lee, S. (2009). How do online reviews affect purchasing intention? *African Journal of Business Management, 3*(10), 576–581.

Levy, S., Duan, W., & Boo, S. (2013). An Analysis of One-Star Online Reviews and Responses in the Washington, D.C., Lodging Market. *Cornell Hospitality Quarterly, 54*(1), 49–63. doi:10.1177/1938965512464513

Li, H., Ye, Q., & Law, R. (2013). Determinants of Customer Satisfaction in the Hotel Industry: An Application of Online Review Analysis. *Asia Pacific Journal of Tourism Research, 18*(7), 784–802. doi:10.1080/10941665.2012.708351

Litvin, S., Goldsmith, R., & Pan, B. (2008). Electronic word-of-mouth in hospitality and tourism management. *Tourism Management, 29*(3), 458–468. doi:10.1016/j.tourman.2007.05.011

Liu, X., Schuckert, M., & Law, R. (2015). Can Response Management Benefit Hotels? Evidence from Hong Kong Hotels. *Journal of Travel & Tourism Marketing, 32*(8), 1069–1080. doi:10.1080/10548408.2014.944253

Mayer, N. (2015). *Online reputations Why hotel reviews matter and how hotels respond.* PWC.

Melián-González, S., Bulchand-Gidumal, J., & López-Valcárcel, B. (2013). Online Customer Reviews of Hotels: As Participation Increases, Better Evaluation Is Obtained. *Cornell Hospitality Quarterly, 54*(3), 274–283. doi:10.1177/1938965513481498

Min, H., Lim, Y., & Magnini, V. (2014). Factors Affecting Customer Satisfaction in Responses to Negative Online Hotel Reviews: The Impact of Empathy, Paraphrasing and Speed. *Cornell Hospitality Quarterly, 56*(2), 223–231. doi:10.1177/1938965514560014

Murphy, C. (2016). *5 Hotel Online Reputation Mistakes You Might Be Making.* Disponível em: https://www.revinate.com/blog/2016/08/5-hotel-onlinereputationmistakes-might-making/

Observatório. (2017). *Observatório do Turismo de Lisboa – Dados de novembro 2017.* Disponível em: https://www.visitlisboa.com/sites/default/files/2018- 01/RTL168-OBS.pdf

Park, S., & Allen, J. (2013). Responding to Online Reviews: Problem Solving and Engagement in Hotels. *Cornell Hospitality Quarterly, 54*(1), 64–73. doi:10.1177/1938965512463118

Picazo-Vela, S. (2009). The Effect of Online Reviews on Customer Satisfaction: An Expectation Disconfirmation Approach. *AMCIS 2009 Doctoral Consortium.*

Publico. (2017). *Portugal eleito melhor destino no mundo.* Disponível em: https://www.publico.pt/2017/12/10/fugas/noticia/portugal-eleito-melhor-destinodomundo-1795505

ReviewPro. (2011). *How to Respond to Online Reviews.* Disponível em: https://www.reviewpro.com/wp-content/uploads/pdf/en-guide-responding-reviews.pdf

Revinate. (2014). *Responding to Online Reviews: A Guide for Hoteliers.* Disponível em: https://www.revinate.com/resource/responding-online-reviewsguidehoteliers/

Rose, M. & Blodgett, J. G. (2016). Should Hotels Respond to Negative Online Reviews? *Cornell Hospitality Quarterly, 57*(4), 396-410.

Smith, D. (2016). *How to Respond to Positive Reviews.* Available at: https://www.vendasta.com/blog/how-to-respond-to-positive-reviews

Sorensen, N. (2012). *Management Response to Online Complaints.* Tese de Licenciatura, Modul Viena University.

Sparker, B. (2015). *How to Respond to Positive Reviews.* Disponível em: https://www.reviewtrackers.com/respond-positive-reviews/

Sparks, B., & Bradley, G. (2014). A "Triple A" Typology of Responding to Negative Consumer-generated Online Reviews. *Journal of Hospitality & Tourism Research (Washington, D.C.), 41*(6), 1–27.

Sparks, B., & Browning, V. (2011). The impact of online reviews on hotel booking intentions and perception of trust. *Tourism Management, 32*(6), 1310–1323. doi:10.1016/j.tourman.2010.12.011

Sparks, B., Perkins, H., & Buckley, R. (2013). Online travel reviews as persuasive communication: The effects of content type, source, and certification logos on consumer behaviour. *Tourism Management, 39*, 1–9. doi:10.1016/j.tourman.2013.03.007

Sparks, B., So, K., & Bradley, G. (2016). Responding to negative online reviews: The effects of hotel responses on customer inferences of trust and concern. *Tourism Management, 53*, 74–85. doi:10.1016/j.tourman.2015.09.011

Torres, E., Singh, D., & Robertson-Ring, A. (2015). Consumer reviews and the creation of booking transaction value: Lessons from the hotel industry. *International Journal of Hospitality Management, 50*, 77–83. doi:10.1016/j.ijhm.2015.07.012

Turismo de Portugal. (2017). *TravelBi.* Disponível em: http://travelbi.turismodeportugal.pt/pt-pt/bi/Paginas/PowerBI/Oferta-Hoteleira.aspx

Vermeulen, I. E., & Seegers, D. (2009). Tried and tested: The impact of online hotel reviews on consumer consideration. *Tourism Management, 30*(1), 123–127. doi:10.1016/j.tourman.2008.04.008

World Tourism Organization. (2014). *Online Guest Reviews and Hotel Classification Systems – An Integrated Approach.* UNWTO.

Xie, K., Zhang, Z., Zhang, J., Singh, A., & Lee, S. (2016). Effects of managerial response on consumer eWOM and hotel performance: Evidence from TripAdvisor. *International Journal of Contemporary Hospitality Management, 28*(9), 2013–2034. doi:10.1108/IJCHM-06-2015-0290

Xie, K. L., So, K. K., & Wang, W. (2017). Joint effects of management responses and online reviews on hotel financial performance: A data-analytics approach. *International Journal of Hospitality Management, 62*, 101–110. doi:10.1016/j.ijhm.2016.12.004

Xie, K. L., Zhang, Z., & Zhang, Z. (2014). The business value of online consumer reviews and management response to hotel performance. *International Journal of Hospitality Management, 43*, 1–12. doi:10.1016/j.ijhm.2014.07.007

Compilation of References

Aaker, J. (1999). Self-esteem's moderation of self-congruity effects on brand loyalty. *Theoretical Economics Letters, 7*(6), 45–57.

Abalo, J., Varela, J., & Manzano, V. (2007). Importance values for Importance-Performance Analysis: A formula for spreading out values derived from preference rankings. *Journal of Business Research, 60*(2), 115–121. doi:10.1016/j. jbusres.2006.10.009

Adobe. (2014). *2014 Mobile Consumer Survey Results.* https://www.mycustomer.com/sites/default/files/attachments/ Adobe%20mobile_survey_report_ie%5B1%5D%5B1%5D.pdf

Ağraş, S., Ayyıldız, A., & Aktürk, E. (2020). Akıllı turizmin Türkiye'deki büyük şehirlerde uygulanabilirliği: İstanbul örneği [Applicability of smart tourism in major cities in Turkey: The case of Istanbul]. *Bartın Üniversitesi İktisadi ve İdari Bilimler Fakültesi Dergisi, 11*(21), 207–231.

Ahani, A., Nilashi, M., Ibrahim, O., Sanzogni, L., & Weaven, S. (2019). Market segmentation and travel choice prediction in Spa hotels through TripAdvisor's online reviews. *International Journal of Hospitality Management, 80*, 52–77. doi:10.1016/j.ijhm.2019.01.003

Ahearne, M., Bhattacharya, C., & Gruen, T. (2005). Antecedents and consequences of customer-company identification: Expanding the role of relationship marketing. *The Journal of Applied Psychology, 90*(3), 574–585. doi:10.1037/0021-9010.90.3.574 PMID:15910151

Akkuş, G., & Çalışkan, G. (2020). Destinasyon pazarlama faaliyetleri kapsamında yürütülen sosyal müşteri ilişkileri yönetiminin rolünü tespite yönelik nitel bir araştırma. *Elektronik Sosyal Bilimler Dergisi, 19*(76), 1984–1998.

Akman, E., Karaman, A. S., & Kuzey, C. (2020). *Visa trial of international trade: evidence from support vector machines and neural networks.* Https://Doi.Org/10.1080/23270012.2020.1731719 doi:10.1080/23270012.2020.1731719

Aksatan, M., & Aktaş, G. (2012). Küçük konaklama işletmelerinde müşteri ilişkileri yönetimi: Alaçatı örneği. *Anatolia: Turizm Araştırmaları Dergisi, 23*(2), 233–247.

Akyazı, E. (2018). Kurumsal itibar oluşturma ortamı olarak sosyal medya: Tur şirketlerinin sosyal medya hesapları üzerine bir araştırma. *Journal of Tourism Theory and Research, 4*(2), 87–97. doi:10.24288/jttr.415480

Al Shehhi, M., & Karathanasopoulos, A. (2020). Forecasting hotel room prices in selected GCC cities using deep learning. *Journal of Hospitality and Tourism Management, 42*, 40–50. doi:10.1016/j.jhtm.2019.11.003

Albayrak, T. & Caber, M. (2015). *Prioritisation of the hotel attributes according to their influence on satisfaction: A comparison of two techniques.* Academic Press.

Albayrak, T., & Caber, M. (2013). The symmetric and asymmetric influences of destination attributes on overall visitor satisfaction. *Current Issues in Tourism, 16*(2), 149–166. doi:10.1080/13683500.2012.682978

Albayrak, T., Caber, M., & Aksoy, S. (2010). Relationships of the tangible and intangible elements of tourism products with overall customer satisfaction. International Journal of Trade. *Economics and Finance, 1*(2), 140–143.

Alexander, M., & Jaakkola, E. (2015). *Customer engagement behaviours and value co-creation.* Taylor & Francis Group.

Ali, A. M., Joshua Thomas, J., & Nair, G. (2021). *Academic and Uncertainty Attributes in Predicting Student Performance.* Springer. doi:10.1007/978-3-030-68154-8_72

Ali, A., & Frew, A. (2013). *Information and communication technologies for sustainable tourism.* Routledge. doi:10.4324/9780203072592

Alkhayrat, M., Aljnidi, M., & Aljoumaa, K. (2020). A comparative dimensionality reduction study in telecom customer segmentation using deep learning and PCA. *Journal of Big Data, 7*(1), 1–23. doi:10.1186/s40537-020-0286-0

Almeida, L., & Ramos, D. (2016). Tourism Porto and North of Portugal – Case Study Concerning Private Accommodation. *The 5th Jubilee International Scientific Congress. Global Tourism Challenges in 21st century*, 1-6.

Almotairi, M. A. (2009). *A framework for successful CRM implementation* [Paper presentation]. *European and Mediterranean Conference on Information Systems*, İzmir, Turkey.

Almsalam, S. (2014). The Effects of Customer Expectation and Perceived Service Quality on Customer Satisfaction. *International Journal of Business and Management Invention, 3*(8), 79–84.

Alokla, M., Alkhateeb, M., Abbad, M., & Jaber, F. (2019). Customer relationship management: A review and classification. *Transnational Marketing Journal, 7*(2), 187–210. doi:10.33182/tmj.v7i2.734

Alzaid, A. A., & Soliman, A. A. (2002). Service quality in Riyadh's Elite hotels: Measurement and evaluation. *King Saud University Journal, 14*(2), 83–103.

AMA. (2013). *Definition of Marketing.* American Marketing Association. https://www.ama.org/AboutAMA/Pages/Definition-of-Marketing.aspx

Amaral, J. B., Jr. (2008). O Turismo na periferia do capitalismo: a revelação de um cartão postal. Tese de Doutorado Ciências Sociais. São Paulo: Pontifícia Universidade Católica de São Paulo - PUC SP.

Amigó, E., Artiles, J., Gonzalo, J., Spina, D., Liu, B., & Corujo, A. (2010). *WePS-3 Evaluation Campaign: Overview of the Online Reputation Management Task.* CEUR-WS.

Anderson, M. (2014). *Local consumer review survey 2014.* Available at: https://searchengineland.com/88-consumers-trust-online-reviews-muchpersonal-recommendations-195803

Anderson, E. W., Fornell, C., & Lehmann, D. R. (1994). Customer Satisfaction, Market Share, and Profitability: Findings from Sweden. *Journal of Marketing, 58*(3), 53–56.

Anderson, E. W., & Mittla, V. (2000). Strengthening the Satisfaction-Profit Chain. *Journal of Service Research, 3*(2), 107–120. doi:10.1177/109467050032001

Arat, T., & Dursun, G. (2016). Seyahat ve Konaklama Tercihi Açısından Sosyal Paylaşım Sitelerinin Kullanımı. *Selçuk Üniversitesi Sosyal Bilimler Meslek Yüksekokulu Dergisi, 19*(41), 112-128.

Ardito, L., Cerchione, R., Vecchio, P. D., & Reguseo, E. (2019). Big data in smart tourism: Challenges, issues and opportunities. *Current Issues in Tourism, 22*(15), 1805–1809. doi:10.1080/13683500.2019.1612860

Arefieva, V., Egger, R., & Yu, J. (2021). A machine learning approach to cluster destination image on Instagram. *Tourism Management, 85*, 104318. doi:10.1016/j.tourman.2021.104318

Ariffin, A., & Maghzi, A. (2012). A preliminary study on customer expectations of hotel hospitality: Influences of personal and hotel factors. *International Journal of Hospitality Management, 31*(1), 191–198. doi:10.1016/j.ijhm.2011.04.012

Assad, N. (2016). *Marketing de conteúdo: como fazer sua empresa decolar no meio digital.* Atlas.

Ataman, H. (2018). *Akıllı turizm ve akıllı destinasyonlar: Edremit Körfezi'ne yönelik bir uygulama* [Smart tourism and smart destinations: an application intended for the Gulf of Edremit] [Unpublished master dissertation]. Balikesir University Institute of Social Sciences, Department of International Trade and Marketing, Balikesir, Turkey.

Atar, A. (2019). Dijital Dönüşüm ve Turizme Etkileri. M. Sezgin, S. Özdemir Akgül, & A. Atar. In *Turizm 4.0 (Dijital Dönüşüm)* (pp. 100–111). Detay.

Atkinson, A. (1988). Answering the eternal question: what does the customer want? *The Cornell Hotel and Restaurant Administration Quarterly, 29*(2), 12-14.

Aureli, S., & Supino, E. (2017). Online Reputation Monitoring: An Exploratory Study on Italian Hotel Managers. *International Journal of Hospitality & Tourism Administration, 18*(1), 84–109. doi:10.1080/15256480.2016.1264903

Ayeh, J., Au, N., & Law, R. (2016). Investigating cross-national heterogeneity in the adoption of online hotel reviews. *International Journal of Hospitality Management, 55*, 142–153. doi:10.1016/j.ijhm.2016.04.003

Ayunia, S. (2013). *Measuring the unmeasured: An exploratory study of customer co-creation* (MSc Thesis). Delft University of Technology: Faculty of Technology, Policy, and Management.

Ayyıldız, A. Y., & Ayyıldız, T. (2020). Pazarlama fırsatı olarak akıllı turizm: Kuşadası örneği [Smart tourism as a marketing opportunity: the case of Kuşadası]. *Business & Management Studies: An International Journal, 8*(1), 599–623. doi:10.15295/bmij.v8i1.141

Azis, N., Amin, M., Chan, S., & Aprilia, C. (2020). How smart tourism technologies affect tourist destination loyalty. *Journal of Hospitality and Tourism Technology, 11*(4), 603–625. doi:10.1108/JHTT-01-2020-0005

Azzopardi, E., & Nash, R. (2013). A critical evaluation of importance-performance analysis. *Tourism Management, 35*, 222–233. doi:10.1016/j.tourman.2012.07.007

Babin, B. J., & James, K. W. (2010). A brief retrospective and introspective on value. *European Business Review, 22*(5), 471–478. doi:10.1108/09555341011068895

Bacon, D. R. (2003). A Comparison of Approaches to Importance-Performance Analysis. *International Journal of Market Research, 45*(1), 1–15. doi:10.1177/147078530304500101

Bahar, M., Yüzbaşıoğlu, N., & Topsakal, Y. (2019). Akıllı Turizm ve Süper Akıllı Turist Kavramları Işığında Geleceğin Turizm Rehberliğine Bakış. *Journal of Travel and Tourism Research, 14*, 72–93.

Baka, V. (2016). The becoming of user-generated reviews: Looking at the past to understand the future of managing reputation in the travel sector. *Tourism Management, 53*, 148–162. doi:10.1016/j.tourman.2015.09.004

Baker, J. (2016). *How To Respond To Positive and Negative Reviews.* Disponível em: https://www.vendasta.com/blog/how-to-respond-reviews-good-bad

Ballantyne, D., & Varey, R. J. (2006). Creating value-in-use through marketing interaction: The exchange logic of relating, communicating and knowing. *Marketing Theory, 6*(3), 335–348. doi:10.1177/1470593106066795

Barnes, D., & Hinton, M. (2007). Searching for e-business performance measurement system. *The Electronic Journal of Information System, 10*(1), 134–142.

Barnes, S. J., Mattsson, J., & Sørensen, F. (2014). Destination brand experience and visitor behavior: Testing a scale in the tourism context. *Annals of Tourism Research, 48*, 121–139. doi:10.1016/j.annals.2014.06.002

Barros Neto, J. P. (2018). *Administração: fundamentos de administração empreendedora e competitiva*. Atlas.

Barsky, J., & Frame, C. (2009). *Handling Online Reviews: Best Practices*. Disponível em: https://cdn.tripadvisor.com/pdfs/ExpertTips_HandlingOnlineReviews.pdf

Bartik, A. W., Bertrand, M., Cullen, Z., Glaeser, E. L., Luca, M., & Stanton, C. (2020). The impact of COVID-19 on small business outcomes and expectations. *Proceedings of the National Academy of Sciences*. 10.1073/pnas.2006991117

Barusman, A. R. P., & Rulian, E. P. (2020). Customer satisfaction and retention and its impact on tourism in hotel industry. *Utopía y Praxis Latinoamericana, 25*(1), 117–126. doi:10.5281/zenodo.3774581

Baykal, M., & Ayyıldız, A. Y. (2020). Veri tabanlı pazarlama faaliyetlerinin müşteri sadakatine etkisi: Kuşadası'ndaki 4 ve 5 yıldızlı otel yöneticileri üzerine bir uygulama. *Journal of Tourism and Gastronomy Studies, 8*(2), 1247–1268. doi:10.21325/jotags.2020.606

Belanche, D., Casaló, L. V., Flavián, C., & Schepers, J. (2020). Service robot implementation: A theoretical framework and research agenda. *Service Industries Journal, 40*(3-4), 203–225. doi:10.1080/02642069.2019.1672666

Belch, G. (1978). Belief systems and the differential. *Advances in Consumer Research. Association for Consumer Research (U. S.)*, 320–325.

Benckendorff, P. J., Xiang, Z., & Sheldon, P. J. (2019). *Tourism information technology*. Cabi. doi:10.1079/9781786393432.0000

Benckendorff, P., Moscardo, G., & Pendergast, D. (2010). *Tourism and Generation Y*. CABI Publishing.

Bengio, Y., Simard, P., & Frasconi, P. (1994). Learning Long-Term Dependencies with Gradient Descent is Difficult. *IEEE Transactions on Neural Networks, 5*(2), 157–166. doi:10.1109/72.279181 PMID:18267787

Benjamin, B., Kriss, P., & Egelman, C. (2016). Responding to Social Media Reviews: The Benefits of Digital Customer Dialogue. Medallia Institute. Disponível em https://go.medallia.com/rs/medallia/images/WP-Best-Western-Social

Bennane, Y., & Haouata, S. (2019, April). L'industrie touristique en évolution: De l'ère des opérateurs à l'ère des agrégateurs touristiques. In *Congrès international sur le tourisme et le développement durable*. Destinations et Produits Touristiques, Compétitivité et Innovation.

Berezina, K., Bilgihan, A., Cobanoglu, C., & Okumus, F. (2016). Understanding Satisfied and Dissatisfied Hotel Customers: Text Mining of Online Hotel Reviews. *Journal of Hospitality Marketing & Management, 25*(1), 1–24. doi:10.1080/19368623.2015.983631

Bergami, M., & Bagozzi, R. (2010). Self-categorization, affective commitment and group self-esteem as distinct aspects of social identity in the organization. *British Journal of Social Psychology*, 555–577. PMID:11190685

Bettencourt, L. A., Lusch, R. F., & Vargo, S. L. (2014). A service lens on value creation: Marketing's role in achieving strategic advantage. *California Management Review, 57*(1), 44–66. doi:10.1525/cmr.2014.57.1.44

Bi, J. W., Liu, Y., Fan, Z. P., & Zhang, J. (2019). Wisdom of crowds: Conducting importance-performance analysis (IPA) through online reviews. *Tourism Management, 70*(March), 460–478. doi:10.1016/j.tourman.2018.09.010

Bi, J.-W., Han, T.-Y., & Li, H. (2020). *International tourism demand forecasting with machine learning models: The power of the number of lagged inputs.* Https://Doi.Org/10.1177/1354816620976954 doi:10.1177/1354816620976954

Bickart, B., & Schindler, R. (2001). Internet forums as influential sources of consumer information. *Journal of Interactive Marketing, 15*(3), 31–40. doi:10.1002/dir.1014

Bigne, E., Ruiz, C., Cuenca, A., Perez, C., & Garcia, A. (2021). What drives the helpfulness of online reviews? A deep learning study of sentiment analysis, pictorial content and reviewer expertise for mature destinations. *Journal of Destination Marketing & Management, 20*, 100570. doi:10.1016/j.jdmm.2021.100570

Bi, J. W., Li, H., & Fan, Z. P. (2021). Tourism demand forecasting with time series imaging: A deep learning model. *Annals of Tourism Research, 90*, 103255. doi:10.1016/j.annals.2021.103255

Bilgihan, A., Smith, S., Ricci, P., & Bujisic, M. (2016). Hotel guest preferences of in-room technology amenities. *Journal of Hospitality and Tourism Technology, 7*(2), 118–134. doi:10.1108/JHTT-02-2016-0008

Binkhorst, E., & Dekker, T. D. (2009). Agenda for co-creation tourism experience research. *Journal of Hospitality Marketing & Management, 18*(2-3), 311–327. doi:10.1080/19368620802594193

Bititci, U. S., Martinez, V., Albores, P., & Parung, J. (2004). Creating and managing value in collaborative networks. *International Journal of Physical Distribution & Logistics Management, 34*(3/4), 251–268. doi:10.1108/09600030410533574

Blal, I., Singal, M., & Templin, J. (2018). Airbnb's effect on hotel sales growth. *International Journal of Hospitality Management, 73*, 85–92. doi:10.1016/j.ijhm.2018.02.006

Bligh, P., & Turk, D. (2004). *CRM Unplugged: Releasing CRM's Strategic Value.* John Wiley & Sons.

Boeing. (2013). *Current Market Outlook 2013-2032.* Boeing Commercial: https://www.boeing.com/boeing/commercial/cmo/

Boes, K., Buhalis, D., & Inversini, A. (2015). Conceptualising Smart Tourism Destination Dimensions. In A. I. I. Tussyadiah (Ed.), *Information and communication technologies in tourism 2015* (pp. 391–403). Springer International Publishing.

Boes, K., Buhalis, D., & Inversini, A. (2015). Conceptualising smart tourism destination dimensions. In I. Tussyadiah & A. Inversini (Eds.), *Information and communication technologies in tourism* (pp. 391–403). Springer.

Boes, K., Buhalis, D., & Inversini, A. (2016). Smart tourism destinations: Ecosystems for tourism destination competitiveness. *International Journal of Tourism Cities, 2*(2), 108–124. doi:10.1108/IJTC-12-2015-0032

Boffey, D. (2021). *3D printing: Dutch couple become Europe's first inhabitants of a 3D-printed house.* https://www.theguardian.com/technology/2021/apr/30/dutch-couple-move-into-europe-first-fully-3d-printed-house-eindhoven

Bola, A. (2021, April 9). *A BOLA - Estádio da Luz é o primeiro a receber tecnologia 5G em Portugal (Benfica).* Retrieved June 29, 2021, from https://www.abola.pt/nnh/2021-04-09/benfica-estadio-da-luz-e-o-primeiro-a-receber-tecnologia-5g-em-portugal/885908

Bolton, R., & Saxena-Iyer, S. (2009). Interactive services: A framework, synthesis and research directions. *Journal of Interactive Marketing, 23*(1), 91–104. doi:10.1016/j.intmar.2008.11.002

Borges, B. (2009). *Bridging the gap between seller and buyer through social media marketing. Marketing 2.0.* Wheatmark.

Bose, R. (2002). Customer relationship management: Key components for IT success. *Industrial Management & Data Systems, 102*(2), 89–97. doi:10.1108/02635570210419636

Botsman, R., & Rogers, R. (2011). *What's Mine is Yours: The Rise of Collaborative.* Collins.

Boulding, W., Staelin, R., Ehret, M., & Johnston, W. J. (2005). A customer relationship management roadmap: What is known, potential pitfalls, and where to go. *Journal of Marketing, 69*(4), 155–166. doi:10.1509/jmkg.2005.69.4.155

Bowden, J. H. (2009). The process of customer engagement: A conceptual framework. *Journal of Marketing Theory and Practice, 17*(1), 63–74. doi:10.2753/MTP1069-6679170105

Boz, H. (2015). *Balıkesir Üniversitesi Sosyal Bilimler Enstitüsü Anabilim Dalı. In Turistik ürün satın alma karar sürecinde itkiselliğin rolü: Psikonörobiyokimyasal analiz.* Doktora Tezi.

Boz, H., Arslan, A., & Koç, E. (2017). Neuromarketing aspect of tourism pricing psychology. *Tourism Management Perspectives, 23*, 119–128. doi:10.1016/j.tmp.2017.06.002

Bozok, D., & Güven, Ö. Z. (2014). Termal konaklama işletmelerinde müşteri ilişkileri yönetimi (crm) üzerine bir araştırma: Frigya bölgesi örneği. *Dumlupınar Üniversitesi Sosyal Bilimler Dergisi, 41*, 131–140.

Brakus, J., Schmitt, B., & Zarantonello, L. (2009). Brand experience: What Is It? How Is t Measured? Does It Affect Loyalty? *Journal of Marketing, 73*(3), 52–68. doi:10.1509/jmkg.73.3.052

Branco, G., Ribeiro, J., & Tinoco, M. (2010). Determinantes da satisfação e atributos da qualidade em serviços de hotelaria. *Prod, 20*(4), 576–588. doi:10.1590/S0103-65132010005000057

Brennen, J. S., & Kreiss, D. (2016). Digitalisation. *The international encyclopedia of communication theory and philosophy*, 1-11.

Brodie, R. J., Hollebeek, L. D., Juric, B., & Ilic, A. (2011). Customer engagement: Conceptual domain, fundamental propositions, and implications for research. *Journal of Service Research, 14*(3), 252–271. doi:10.1177/1094670511411703

Bruyere, B. L., Rodriguez, D. A., & Vaske, J. J. (2002). Enhancing Importance-Performance Analysis Through Segmentation Brett. *Journal of Travel & Tourism Marketing, 12*(1), 63–80. doi:10.1300/J073v12n01_05

Bughin, J., Doogan, J., & Vetvik, O. (2010). *A new way to measure word-of-mouth marketing.* Available at: https://www.mckinsey.com/business-functions/marketing-and-sales/ourinsights/a-new-way-to-measure-word-of-mouth-marketing

Buhalis, D. (2003). *E-Tourism: Information Technology for Strategic Tourism Management.* London: Financial Times / Prentice-Hall.

Buhalis, D., & Amaranggana, A. (2015). Smart Tourism Destinations Enhancing Tourism Experience Through Personalisation of Services. In Information and Communication Technologies in Tourism 2015. Springer. doi:10.1007/978-3-319-14343-9_28

Buhalis, D. (2000). Marketing the competitive destination of the future. *Tourism Management, 21*(1), 97–116. doi:10.1016/S0261-5177(99)00095-3

Buhalis, D. (2000). Tourism and Information Technologies: Past, Present and Future. *Tourism Recreation Research, 25*(1), 41–58. doi:10.1080/02508281.2000.11014899

Buhalis, D. (2020). Technology in tourism-from information communication technologies to etourism and smart tourism towards ambient intelligence tourism: A perspective article. *Tourism Review, 75*(1), 267–272. doi:10.1108/TR-06-2019-0258

Buhalis, D., & Amaranggana, A. (2014). Smart tourism destinations enhancing tourism experience through personalisation of services. In I. Tussyadiah & A. Inversini (Eds.), *Information and communication technologies in tourism 2015* (pp. 377–389). Springer.

Buhalis, D., & Amaranggana, A. (2014). Smart tourism destinations. In Z. Xiang & I. Tussyadiah (Eds.), *Information and communication technologies in tourism* (pp. 553–564). Springer-Verlag.

Buhalis, D., & Amaranggana, A. (2015). Smart tourism destinations enhancing tourism experience through personalisation of services. In I. Tussyadiah & A. Inversini (Eds.), *Information and communication technologies in tourism* (pp. 378–388). Springer.

Buhalis, D., & Foerste, M. (2015). SoCoMo marketing for travel and tourism: Empowering co-creation of value. *Journal of Destination Marketing & Management, 4*(3), 151–161. doi:10.1016/j.jdmm.2015.04.001

Buhalis, D., & Law, R. (2008). Progress in information technology and tourism management: 20 years on and 10 years after the internet-the state of etourism research. *Tourism Management, 29*(4), 609–623. doi:10.1016/j.tourman.2008.01.005

Buhalis, D., & Leung, R. (2018). Smart hospitality—Interconnectivity and interoperability towards an ecosystem. *International Journal of Hospitality Management, 71*, 41–50. doi:10.1016/j.ijhm.2017.11.011

Buhalis, D., & O'Connor, P. (2005). Information Communication Technology Revolutionizing Tourism. *Tourism Recreation Research, 30*(3), 7–16. doi:10.1080/02508281.2005.11081482

Buil, I., Catalán, S., & Martínez, E. (2016). The importance of corporate brand identity in business management: An application to the UK banking sector. *Business Research Quarterly, 19*(1), 3–12. doi:10.1016/j.brq.2014.11.001

Buonincontri, P., & Micera, R. (2016). The experience co-creation in smart tourism destinations: A multiple case analysis of European destinations. *Information Technology & Tourism, 16*(3), 285–315. doi:10.100740558-016-0060-5

Busacca, B., & Arbore, A. (2011). Rejuvenating importance-performance analysis. *Journal of Service Management, 22*(3), 409–429. doi:10.1108/09564231111136890

Buttle, F. (2001). The CRM value chain. *Marketing Business, 96*(2), 52–55.

Caber, M., Albayrak, T., & Loiacono, E. T. (2013). The Classification of Extranet Attributes in Terms of Their Asymmetric Influences on Overall User Satisfaction: An Introduction to Asymmetric Impact-Performance Analysis. *Journal of Travel Research, 52*(1), 106–116. doi:10.1177/0047287512451139

Çakmak, T. F., & Demirkol, Ş. (2017). Teknolojik Gelişmelerin Turist Rehberliği Mesleğine Etkileri Üzerine Bir Swot Analizi. *Bingöl Üniversitesi Sosyal Bilimler Enstitüsü Dergisi, 7*, 221-235.

Calheiros, A. C., Moro, S., & Rita, P. (2017). Sentiment Classification of Consumer-Generated Online Reviews Using Topic Modeling. *Journal of Hospitality Marketing & Management, 26*(7), 675–693. doi:10.1080/19368623.2017.1310075

Campbell, C. (2015). *How Online Reviews and Reputation Can Support Your Social Media Strategy.* Disponível em: https://www.socialmediatoday.com/marketing/reviewtrackers/2015-09-30/howonlinereviews-and-reputation-can-support-your-social-media

Campbell, C. (2016). *Respond to Negative Reviews Like These Business Owners.* Disponível em: https://www.reviewtrackers.com/respond-negative-reviews/

Cankurt, S. (2016). Tourism demand forecasting using ensembles of regression trees. *2016 IEEE 8th International Conference on Intelligent Systems, IS 2016 - Proceedings*, 702–708. 10.1109/IS.2016.7737388

Card, J. A., Chen, C. Y., & Cole, S. T. (2003). Online Travel Products Shopping: Differences between Shoppers and Nonshoppers. *Journal of Travel Research, 42*(2), 133–139. doi:10.1177/0047287503257490

Carter, E. (2017). *Social Media, Mobile, and Travel: Like, Tweet, and Share Your Way Across the Globe.* https://www.webfx.com/blog/social-media/social-media-mobile-travel/

Castro, C., Fereira, F., & Fereira, F. (2016). Trends in hotel pricing: Identifying guest value hotel attributes using the cases of Lisbon and Porto. *Worldwide Hospitality and Tourism Themes, 8*(6), 691–698. doi:10.1108/WHATT-09-2016-0047

Çelik, E. (2020). Osmanlı Topraklarına Yeni Bir Gezi Türü: 19. ve 20. Yüzyılda Cruise Gezileri. *Cumhuriyet Tarihi Araştırmaları Dergisi, 16*(32), 401–430.

Çelik, P., & Topsakal, Y. (2017). Akıllı turizm destinasyonları: Antalya destinasyonunun akıllı turizm uygulamalarının incelenmesi [Smart tourism destinations: review of smart tourism applications of Antalya destination]. *Seyahat ve Otel İşletmeciliği Dergisi, 14*(3), 149–166. doi:10.24010oid.369951

Chalmeta, R. (2006). Methodology for customer relationship management. *Journal of Systems and Software, 79*(7), 1015–1024. doi:10.1016/j.jss.2005.10.018

Chang, Y. C., Ku, C. H., & Chen, C. H. (2020). Using deep learning and visual analytics to explore hotel reviews and responses. *Tourism Management, 80*, 104129. doi:10.1016/j.tourman.2020.104129

Chathoth, P. K., Ungson, G. R., Harrington, R. J. & Chan, E. S. (2016). Co-creation and higher order customer engagement in hospitality and tourism services. *International Journal of Contemporary Hospitality Management, 28*(2), 222-245.

Chathoth, P. K., Ungson, G. R., Harrington, R. J., & Chan, E. S. W. (2016). Co-creation and higher order customer engagement in hospitality and tourism services. *International Journal of Contemporary Hospitality Management, 28*(2), 222–245. doi:10.1108/IJCHM-10-2014-0526

Chattopadhyay, M., & Kumar, S. (2020). What Airbnb host listings influence peer-to-peer tourist accommodation price. *Journal of Hospitality & Tourism Research (Washington, D.C.), 44*(4), 1–27102. doi:10.1177/1096348020910211

Chaudhuri, A., & Holbrook, M. (2001). The chain of effects from brand trust and brand affect to brand performance: The role of brand loyalty. *Journal of Marketing, 65*(2), 81–93. doi:10.1509/jmkg.65.2.81.18255

Chen, C., & Chang, Y. (2018). The importance of marketer-generated content to peer-to-peer property rental platforms: Evidence from Airbnb. *Telematics and Informatics, 35*(84), 1-11.

Chen, C., Nguyen, B., Klaus, P., & Wu, M. (2015). Exploring electronic word-of-mouth (eWOM) in the consumer purchase decision-making process: The case of online holidays – evidence from United Kingdom (UK) consumers. *Journal of Travel & Tourism Marketing, 32*(8), 953–970. doi:10.1080/10548408.2014.956165

Chen, C.-Y., Wu, T.-S., Li, M.-L., & Wang, C.-T. (2018). Integration of Importance - Performance Analysis and Fuzzy Dematel. *International Journal of Computer Science and Information Technologies, 10*(3), 19–38. doi:10.5121/ijcsit.2018.10302

Cheng, M. (2016). Sharing economy: A review and agenda for future research. *International Journal of Hospitality Management, 57*, 60–70. doi:10.1016/j.ijhm.2016.06.003

Chen, I. J., & Popovich, K. (2003). Understanding customer relationship management (CRM): People processes and technology. *Business Process Management Journal, 9*(5), 672–688. doi:10.1108/14637150310496758

Chen, J. K., Batchuluun, A., & Batnasan, J. (2015). Services innovation impact to customer satisfaction and customer value enhancement in airport. *Technology in Society, 43*, 219–230. doi:10.1016/j.techsoc.2015.05.010

Cheraghalizadeh, R., & Tümer, M. (2017). The effect of applied resources on competitive advantage in hotels: Mediation and moderation analysis. *Journal of Hospitality and Tourism Management, 31*, 265–272. doi:10.1016/j.jhtm.2017.04.001

Cherapanukom, V., Yanchinda, J., & Sangkakom, K. (2021). *Antecedents of eCRM success for hotel industry* [Paper presentation]. Conference on Electrical, Electronics, Computer and Telecommunication Engineering (IEEE), Cha-am, Thailand. 10.1109/ECTIDAMTNCON51128.2021.9425751

Chien, G. C. L., & Law, R. (2003). The impact of the severe acute respiratory syndrome on hotels: A case study of Hong Kong. *International Journal of Hospitality Management, 22*(3), 327–332. doi:10.1016/S0278-4319(03)00041-0 PMID:32287842

Chitungo, I., Mhango, M., Mbunge, E., Dzobo, M., Musuka, G., & Dzinamarira, T. (2021, November 2). Utility of telemedicine in sub-Saharan Africa during the COVID-19 pandemic. A rapid review. *Human Behavior and Emerging Technologies*, hbe2.297. Advance online publication. doi:10.1002/hbe2.297

Chuang, S., Cheng, Y., Chang, C., & Yang, S. (2012). The effect of service failure types and service recovery on customer satisfaction: A mental accounting perspective. *Service Industries Journal, 32*(2), 257–271. doi:10.1080/026420 69.2010.529435

Chung, N., & Koo, C. (2015). The Use of Social Media in Travel Information Search. *Telematics and Informatics, 32*(2), 215–229. doi:10.1016/j.tele.2014.08.005

Chu, R. (2002). Stated-importance versus derived-importance customer satisfaction measurement. *Journal of Services Marketing, 16*(4), 285–301. doi:10.1108/08876040210433202

Çiçek, E., Pala, U., & Özcan, S. (2013). Destinasyon Tercihlerinde Web Sitelerinin Önemi: Yerli Turistler Üzerine Bir Araştırma. *Sosyoteknik Sosyal ve Teknik Araştırmalar Dergisi, 3*(5), 1–14.

Cilliers, E. J. (2017). The Challange of Teaching Generation Z. *The International Journal of Social Sciences (Islamabad), 3*(1), 188–198.

Cisco. (2020, April). *5 Things to Know About Wi-Fi 6 and 5G - Cisco*. Retrieved June 29, 2021, from https://www.cisco.com/c/m/en_us/solutions/enterprise-networks/802-11ax-solution/nb-06-5-things-WiFi6-5G-infograph-cte-en.html

Civelek, A. (2016). Konaklama işletmelerinde müşteri ilişkileri yönetiminin işletme performansına etkisi: 5 yıldızlı oteller üzerine bir uygulama. *Selçuk Üniversitesi Sosyal Bilimler Meslek Yüksek Okulu Dergisi, 19*(2), 233–253.

Cleverciti. (2021). *9 European smart tourism destinations to watch and learn from*. https://www.cleverciti.com/en/resources/blog/9-european-smart-tourism-destinations-to-watch-and-learn-from

Coca-Stefaniak, J. A. (2019). Marketing smart tourism cities-a strategic dilemma. *International Journal of Tourism Cities, 5*(4), 513–518. doi:10.1108/IJTC-12-2019-163

Coghlan, A. (2012). Facilitating reef tourism management through an innovative importance-performance analysis method. *Tourism Management, 33*(4), 767–775. doi:10.1016/j.tourman.2011.08.010

Constantinides, E., & Holleschovsky, N. (2016). *Impact of Online Product Reviews on Purchasing Decisions*. SCITEPRESS. doi:10.5220/0005861002710278

Conyette, M. (2015). 21 Century Travel using Websites, Mobile and WearableTechnology Devices. *Athens Journal of Tourism, 2*(2), 105–116. doi:10.30958/ajt.2-2-3

Çöp, S., İbiş, S., & Kızıldemir, Ö. (2020). Seyahat Motivasyonlarının X, Y ve Z Kuşaklarına Göre Farklılıklarının İncelenmesi Üzerine Bir Araştırma. *Uluslararası Toplum Araştırmaları Dergisi, 16*(30), 2530–2550.

Costa, A., & Gonçalves, B. (2018). *Assistentes Pessoais Inteligentes com Reconhecimento de Voz*. Instituto Superior Tecnico.

Cox, C., Burgess, S., Sellitto, C., & Buultjens, J. (2009). The role of user-generated content in tourists' travel planning behavior. *Journal of Hospitality Marketing & Management, 17*(4), 743–764. doi:10.1080/19368620903235753

Creswell, J. W. (2014). *Research design: Qualitative, quantitative, and mixed methods approaches* (4th ed.). SAGE Publications, Inc.

Crittenden, A. B., Crittenden, V. L., & Crittenden, W. F. (2019). The digitalization triumvirate: How incumbents survive. *Business Horizons, 62*(2), 259–266. doi:10.1016/j.bushor.2018.11.005

Crivellari, A., & Beinat, E. (2020). LSTM-Based Deep Learning Model for Predicting Individual Mobility Traces of Short-Term Foreign Tourists. *Sustainability 2020, 12*(1), 349. doi:10.3390/su12010349

Crompton, J. L., & Duray, N. A. (1985). An Investigation of the Relative Efficacy of Four Alternative Approaches to Importance-Performance Analysis. *Journal of the Academy of Marketing Science, 13*(4), 69–80. doi:10.1007/BF02737200

Cronin, J. J. Jr, & Taylor, S. A. (1992). Measuring Service Quality: A Reexamination and Extension. *Journal of Marketing, 56*(3), 55–68. doi:10.1177/002224299205600304

Cunha, J. M. (2017). *Airbnb is Lisbon's largest "hotel" José Maria Cunha.* Medium. Accessed 10th May, 2020. from https://medium.com/@zemariacunha/airbnb-is-lisbons-largest-hotelfc00a0c5ff7b

Dabija, D.-C., Bejan, B. M., & Tipi, N. (2018). Generation X Versus Millenials Communication Behaviour on Social Media When Purchasing Food Versus Tourist Services. *Ekonomie a Management, 21*(1), 191–205. doi:10.15240/tul/001/2018-1-013

Dahlman, E. (2018). *What Is 5G? Em: 5G NR: the Next Generation Wireless Access Technology.* Academic Press. Elsevier.

Dan, W., Park, S., & Fesenmaier, D. R. (2012). The Role of Smartphones in Mediating the Touristic Experience. *Journal of Travel Research, 51*(4), 371–387. doi:10.1177/0047287511426341

de l'Architecture, C. (2021). *Visite de la grotte de Lascaux 1/1, le jumeau virtuel À partir du 8 juillet 2021.* https://www.citedelarchitecture.fr/fr/evenement/visite-de-la-grotte-de-lascaux-11-le-jumeau-virtuel

Dedeoğlu, A. Ö. (2015). Değişen pazaryerinde tüketici ve tüketimin rolüne ilişkin yeni yaklaşımlar: Ortak-üretim (co-production) ve ortak-yaratma (co-creation). *Ege Strategic Research Journal, 6*(2), 17–29.

Del Chiappa, G., Alarcón-Del-Amo, M.-D.-C., & Lorenzo-Romero, C. (2016). Internet and User-Generated Content Versus High Street Travel Agencies: A Latent Gold Segmentation in the Context of Italy. *Journal of Hospitality Marketing & Management, 25*(2), 197–217. doi:10.1080/19368623.2014.1001933

Del Chiappa, G., & Baggio, R. (2015). Knowledge transfer in smart tourism destinations: Analyzing the effects of a network structure. *Journal of Destination Marketing & Management, 4*(3), 145–150. doi:10.1016/j.jdmm.2015.02.001

Del Vecchio, P., & Passiante, G. (2017). Is tourism a driver for smart specialization? Evidence from Apulia, an Italian region with a tourism vocation. *Journal of Destination Marketing & Management, 6*(3), 163–165. doi:10.1016/j.jdmm.2016.09.005

Deloitte Türkiye. (2021). *Otellerde müşteri sadakatinin güçlendirilmesi.* https://www2.deloitte.com/tr/tr/pages/consumer-business/articles/restoration-in-hotel-loyalty.html

Deloitte. (2020). *The end of an era: Rethink what's normal. Portuguese Hospitality Atlas 2020 – 15th edition.* https://www2.deloitte.com/content/dam/Deloitte/pt/Documents/AtlasHotelaria/ATLAS2020_en.pdf

Deloitte. (2021). *The future of hospitality: Re-engaging consumers post pandemic.* https://www2.deloitte.com/content/dam/Deloitte/ca/Documents/consumer-industrial-products/ca-future-of-hospitality-pov-aoda-en.pdf

Delpechitre, D., Beeler-Connelly, L. L., & Chaker, N. N. (2018). Customer value co-creation behavior: A dyadic exploration of the influenceof salesperson emotional intelligence on customer participation andcitizenship behavior. *Journal of Business Research, 92*, 9–24. doi:10.1016/j.jbusres.2018.05.007

Deng, W. J., Kuo, Y. F., & Chen, W. C. (2008). Revised importance–performance analysis: Threefactor theory and benchmarking. *Service Industries Journal, 28*(1), 37–51. doi:10.1080/02642060701725412

DESI. (2020). *European Commission, Digital Economy and Society Index Thematic Chapters*. https://innogrowth.org/wp-content/uploads/2020/07/DESI-2020.pdf

Diana-Jens, P., & Ruibal, A. (2015). La reputación online y su impacto en la política de precios de los hoteles. *Cuadernos de Turismo, 36*(36), 129–155. doi:10.6018/turismo.36.230911

Dias, A. L., González-Rodríguez, M. R., & Patuleia, M. (2021). Retaining tourism lifestyle entrepreneurs for destination competitiveness. *International Journal of Tourism Research, 23*(4), 701–712. Advance online publication. doi:10.1002/jtr.2436

Diehl, A. A., & Tatim, D. C. (2012). *Pesquisa em ciências sociais aplicadas: métodos e técnicas*. Pearson.

Dinheiro Vivo. (2020, June 17). *Lisboa quer rede wi-fi gratuita pela cidade*. Retrieved June 29, 2021, from https://www.dinheirovivo.pt/empresas/lisboa-quer-rede-wi-fi-gratuita-pela-cidade-12695714.html

Dinnie, K. (2008). *Nation branding. Concepts, issues, practice*. Butterworth-Heinemann.

Djekic, I., Kane, K., Tomic, N., Kalogianni, E., Rocha, A., Zamioudi, L., & Pacheco, R. (2016). Cross-cultural consumer perceptions of service quality in restaurants. *Nutrition & Food Science, 46*(6), 827–843. doi:10.1108/NFS-04-2016-0052

Djelassi, S., Diallo, M. F., & Zielke, S. (2018). How self-service technology experience evaluation affects waiting time and customer satisfaction? A moderated mediation model. *Decision Support Systems, 111*, 1–10. doi:10.1016/j.dss.2018.04.004

Djeri, L., Stamenković, P., Blešić, I., Milićević, S., & Ivkov, M. (2018). An importance-performance analysis of destination competitiveness factors: Case of Jablanica district in Serbia. *Economic Research-Ekonomska Istrazivanja, 31*(1), 811–826. doi:10.1080/1331677X.2018.1456351

Dogru, T., Mody, M., & Suess, C. (2019). Adding evidence to the debate: Quantifying Airbnb's disruptive impact on ten key hotel markets. *Tourism Management, 72*, 27–38. doi:10.1016/j.tourman.2018.11.008

Dogru, T., Mody, M., Suess, C., McGinley, S., & Line, D. N. (2020). The Airbnb paradox: Positive employment effects in the hospitality industry. *Tourism Management, 77*, 1–12. doi:10.1016/j.tourman.2019.104001

Dolich, I. (1969). Congruence relationship between self-image and product brands. *JMR, Journal of Marketing Research, 6*(1), 80–84. doi:10.1177/002224376900600109

Dolnicar, S., & Otter, T. (2003). Which hotel attributes matter? A review of previous and a framework for future research. Academic Press.

Dolot, A. (2018). *The Characteristics of Generation Z. E-mentor*. Warsaw School of Economics.

Dombey, O. (2004). The effects of SARS on the Chinese tourism industry. *Journal of Vacation Marketing, 10*(1), 4–10. doi:10.1177/135676670301000101

Dong, H. (n.d.). *The Application of Artificial Neural Network, Long short-term Memory Network and Bidirectional Long short-term Memory Network in the Grades Prediction*. Academic Press.

Dorcic, J., Komsic, J., & Markovic, S. (2019). Mobile technologies and applications towards smart tourism-state of the art. *Tourism Review, 74*(1), 82–103. doi:10.1108/TR-07-2017-0121

Dou, X., Walden, J. A. L. S., & Lee, J. Y. (2012). Does source matter? Examining source effects in online product reviews. Computers in Human Behavior, 1555-1563.

Dredge, D. & Gyimóthy, S. (2015) The collaborative economy and tourism: Critical perspectives, questionable claims and silenced voices. *Tourism Recreation Research, 40*(3). doi:10.1080/02508281.2015.1086076

Dredge, D., Phi, G., Mahadevan, R., Meehan, E., & Popescu, E. S. (2018). *Digitalisation in Tourism: In-depth analysis of challenges and opportunities. Virtual Tourism Observatory.* Aalborg University.

Dubcová, A., Petrikovie, J. & Šolcavá, L. (2013). Globalization and the hotel industry in Slovakia. *Annals of the University of Bucharest: Geography Series, 62.*

Dube, K., Nhamo, G., & Chikodzi, D. (2020). COVID-19 cripples global restaurant and hospitality industry. *Current Issues in Tourism*, 1–5.

Dubey, A. K., & Jain, V. (2019). Comparative Study of Convolution Neural Network's Relu and Leaky-Relu Activation Functions. *Lecture Notes in Electrical Engineering, 553*, 873–880. doi:10.1007/978-981-13-6772-4_76

Duffy, B. R. (2003). Anthropomorphism and the social robot. *Robotics and Autonomous Systems, 42*(3-4), 177–190. doi:10.1016/S0921-8890(02)00374-3

Dunn, J. C. (2008). *A Fuzzy Relative of the ISODATA Process and Its Use in Detecting Compact Well-Separated Clusters.* Https://Doi.Org/10.1080/01969727308546046 doi:10.1080/01969727308546046

Duran, M. (2002). *CRM hakkında CRM: çok konuşulan ama az bilinen bir kavram.* http://danismend.com/kategori/altkategori/crm-hakkinda/

Duran, G., & Uygur, S. M. (2019). Akıllı turizm destinasyonları kapsamında Ankara'nın akıllı turizm uygulamalarına yönelik bir araştırma [A research on Ankara's smart tourism applications in the scope of smart tourism destinations]. In *Proceedings of The Third International Congress on Future Tourism: Innovation, Entrepreneurship and Sustainability* (pp. 426-436). Mersin University Publications.

Duthion, B., & Mandou, C. (2016). *L'innovation dans le tourisme: culture numérique et nouveaux modes de vie.* De Boeck Supérieur.

Dwyer, L. (2015). Globalization of tourism: Drivers and outcomes. *Tourism Recreation Research, 40*(3), 326–339. doi:10.1080/02508281.2015.1075723

Dwyer, L., Cvelbar, L. K., Edwards, D., & Mihalic, T. (2012). Fashioning a destination tourism future: The case of Slovenia. *Tourism Management, 33*(2), 305–316. doi:10.1016/j.tourman.2011.03.010

Dwyer, L., Forsyth, P., & Rao, P. (2000). The price competitiveness of travel and tourism: A comparison of 19 destinations. *Tourism Management, 21*(1), 9–22. doi:10.1016/S0261-5177(99)00081-3

Dwyer, L., & Kim, C. (2003). Destination competitiveness: Determinants and indicators. *Current Issues in Tourism, 6*(5), 369–414. doi:10.1080/13683500308667962

EC. (2021). *European Commission, European Capitals of Smart Tourism.* https://smart-tourism-capital.ec.europa.eu/european-capitals-smart-tourism_en#about-the-award

Echeverri, P., & Skålén, P. (2011). Co-creation and co-destruction: A practice-theory based study of interactive value formation. *Marketing Theory, 11*(3), 351–373. doi:10.1177/1470593111408181

Eck, N. J. v., & Waltman, L. (2009). Vosviewer: A Computer Program for Bibliometric Mapping. *Econometrics: Computer Programs & Software eJournal.*

Edvardsson, B., Gustafsson, A., & Roos, I. (2005). Service portraits in service research: A critical review. *International Journal of Service Industry Management, 16*(1), 107–121. doi:10.1108/09564230510587177

Egghe, L., & Rousseau, R. (2002). Co-citation, bibliographic coupling and a characterization of lattice citation networks. *Scientometrics, 55*(3), 349–361. doi:10.1023/A:1020458612014

Ekinci, Y., Sirakaya-Turk, E., & Preciado, S. (2013). Symbolic consumption of tourism destination brands. *Journal of Business Research, 66*, 711-718.

El-Adly, M. (2019). Modelling the relationship between hotel perceived value, customer satisfaction, and customer loyalty. *Journal of Retailing and Consumer Services, 50*, 322-332.

Elektra Opex. (2021). *Müşteri ilişkileri yönetimi modülü.* https://www.otelcrm.net/crm-yonetimi.html#

Ellemers, N., & Haslam, S. (2012). Social identity theory. Handbook of Theories of Social Psychology, 379-398.

Elliot, R., & Wattanasuwan, K. (1998). Consumption and the symbolic project of the self. *Consumer Research*, 17-20.

Elujide, I., Fashoto, S. G., Fashoto, B., Mbunge, E., Folorunso, S. O., & Olamijuwon, J. O. (2021). Application of deep and machine learning techniques for multi-label classification performance on psychotic disorder diseases. *Informatics in Medicine Unlocked, 23*, 100545. doi:10.1016/j.imu.2021.100545

Emerald Publishing. (2020). *Driverless cars and their impact on our future.* https://www.emeraldgrouppublishing.com/opinion-and-blog/driverless-cars-and-their-impact-our-future

Encalada, L., Boavida-Portugal, I., Cardoso Ferreira, C., & Rocha, J. (2017). Identifying tourist places of interest based on digital imprints: Towards a sustainable smart city. *Sustainability, 9*(12), 2317. doi:10.3390u9122317

Endüstri40. (2019). *Endüstri Mitleri ve Kavram Yanılgıları.* https://www.endustri40.com/endustri-4-0-mitleri-ve-kavram-yanilgilari/

Engizek, N., & Sekerkaya, A. (2016). X ve Y Kuşak Kadınlarının Karar Verme Tarzları Bakımından İncelenmesi. *Mustafa Kemal Üniversitesi Sosyal Bilimler Enstitüsü Dergisi, 13*, 242–271.

Ennew, C. T., & Binks, M. R. (1999). Impact of participative service relationships on quality, satisfaction and retention: An exploratory study. *Journal of Business Research, 46*(2), 121–132. doi:10.1016/S0148-2963(98)00016-2

Enright, M. J., & Newton, J. (2004). Tourism destination competitiveness: A quantitative approach. *Tourism Management, 25*(6), 777–788. doi:10.1016/j.tourman.2004.06.008

Erdem, A., Unur, K., & Şeker, F. (2019). Akıllı turizm destinasyonu olarak İstanbul'un değerlendirilmesi [Evaluation of Istanbul as a smart tourism destination]. In *Proceedings of International Congress on Digital Transformation in Tourism* (pp. 65-86). Düzce University Publications.

Erkmen, B., & Güler, E. G. (2020). Turizm ve dijitalleşme: 'Haskova-Edirne kültürel ve tarihi destinasyonlar projesi' örneği [Tourism and digitalization: 'Haskovo and Edirne – cultural and historical destinations project]. *Tourism and Recreation, 2*(1), 111-118.

Ernst & Young LLP. (2018,). *The rise of the sharing economy.* Accessed 23 May 2020 from: http://sharehub.kr/wp-content/uploads/2015/11/e1a7c1d73dfae19dcfa0.pdf

Eryılmaz, B., & Zengin, B. (2014). Butik otel işletmelerinin sosyal medya kullanımına yönelik bir inceleme: Facebook örneği. *Kastamonu Üniversitesi İktisadi ve İdari Bilimler Fakültesi Dergisi, 4*(2), 42–59.

Escalas, J., & Bettman, J. (2003). You are what they eat the influence of reference groups on consumer connections to brands. *Journal of Consumer Psychology, 13*(3), 339–348. doi:10.1207/S15327663JCP1303_14

Escobar, S. D., & Margherita, E. G. (2021). Outcomes of Smart Tourism Applications On-site for a Sustainable Tourism: Evidence from Empirical Studies. In A. M. A. Musleh Al-Sartawi (Ed.), *The Big Data-Driven Digital Economy: Artificial and Computational Intelligence* (pp. 271–283). Springer International Publishing. doi:10.1007/978-3-030-73057-4_21

Eshtetie, S., Seyoum, W., & Hussen Ali, S. (2016). Service Quality and Customer Satisfaction in Hospitality Industry: The Case of Selected Hotels in Jimma Town, Ethiopia. *Global Journal of Management and Business Research, 16*(5).

Espino-Rodríguez, T. F., & Padrón-Robaina, V. (2005). A resource-based view of outsourcing and its implications for organizational performance in the hotel sector. *Tourism Management, 26*(5), 707–721. doi:10.1016/j.tourman.2004.03.013

Etgar, M. (2008). A descriptive model of the consumer co-production process. *Journal of the Academy of Marketing Science, 36*(1), 97–108. doi:10.100711747-007-0061-1

E-Travel Marketing India. (2015). *Annual Report 2015 E-Travel Marketing India: A Path to Purchase*. Octane Marketing Private Limited. Retrieved from https://octaneresearch.in/research/e-travel-marketing-india/

EU (2019). *Initiative of European Capital of Smart Tourism. Guide for Applicants*. SmartTourismCapital.eu

EU (2020). *Compendium of Best Practices '2019-2020 European Capital of Smart Tourism Competitions'*. Report commissioned by European Union and prepared by Scholz & Friends Agenda Berlin GmbH European Office.

Europe Commission. (2021). *European capitals of smart tourism*. https://smart-tourism-capital.ec.europa.eu/index_en

European Comission. (2021, February 24). *Commission proposes new Regulation to ensure free roaming*. Retrieved June 29, 2021, from https://ec.europa.eu/commission/presscorner/detail/en/IP_21_653

European Commission. (2019). *Annual report on European SMEs 2018/2019 Research & Development and Innovation by SMEs*. https://op.europa.eu/en/publication-detail/-/publication/cadb8188-35b4-11ea-ba6e-01aa75ed71a1/language-en

European Travel Commission. (2020). *Study on Generation Z Travellers*. Brussel: ETC Market Intelligence.

Evans, M. R., & Chon, K.-S. (1989). Formulating and Evaluating Tou Rism Policy Using Importance-Performance Analysis. *Hospitality Education and Research Journal, 13*(3), 203–213. doi:10.1177/109634808901300320

Farooq, M. S. (2016). *Social Support and Entrepreneurial Skills as Antecedents of Entrepreneurial Behaviour*. Universiti Malaysia Sarawak.

Fashoto, S. G., Mbunge, E., Ogunleye, G., & den Burg, J. Van. (2021). *Implementation of machine learning for predicting maize crop yields using multiple linear regression and backward elimination*. https://mjoc.uitm.edu.my

Fashoto, S. G., Mbunge, E., Ogunleye, G., & den Burg, J. Van. (2021). *Implementation of machine learning for predicting maize crop yields using multiple linear regression and backward elimination*. Retrieved from https://mjoc.uitm.edu.my

Felson, M., & Spaeth, J. L. (1978). Community structure and collaborative consumption. *The American Behavioral Scientist, 21*(4), 614–624. doi:10.1177/000276427802100411

Femenia-Serra, F., & Ivars-Baidal, J. A. (2021). Do smart destinations really work? the case of Benidorm. *Asia Pacific Journal of Tourism Research, 26*(4), 365–384. doi:10.1080/10941665.2018.1561478

Femenia-Serra, F., Neuhofer, B., & Ivars-Baidal, A. (2019). Towards a conceptualisation of smart tourists and their role within the smart destination scenario. *Service Industries Journal, 39*(2), 109–133. doi:10.1080/02642069.2018.1508458

Feng, M., Mangan, J., Wong, C., Xu, M., & Lalwani, C. (2014). Investigating the different approaches to importance-performance analysis. *Service Industries Journal, 34*(12), 1021–1041. doi:10.1080/02642069.2014.915949

Fernandes, T., & Remelhe, P. (2016). How to engage customers in co-creation: Customers' motivations for collaborative innovation. *Journal of Strategic Marketing, 24*(3-4), 311–326. doi:10.1080/0965254X.2015.1095220

Ferreira, G. (2018). *Copywriting: palavras que vendem milhões.* DVS.

Ferreira, J. J. M., Fernandes, C. I., & Ratten, V. (2016). A co-citation bibliometric analysis of strategic management research. *Scientometrics, 109*(1), 1–32. doi:10.100711192-016-2008-0

Flint, D. J., Woodruff, R. B., & Gardial, S. F. (1997). Customer value change in industrial marketing relationships: A call for new strategies and research. *Industrial Marketing Management, 26*(2), 163–175. doi:10.1016/S0019-8501(96)00112-5

Foray, D., Goddard, J., Beldarrain, X. G., Landabaso, M., McCann, P., Morgan, K., . . . Ortega-Argilés, R. (2012). Guide to research and innovation strategies for smart specialisations. Brussels: S3P-European Union.

Fotiadis, A., Polyzos, S., & Huan, T. C. T. C. (2021). The good, the bad and the ugly on COVID-19 tourism recovery. *Annals of Tourism Research, 87*, 103117. doi:10.1016/j.annals.2020.103117 PMID:33518847

Future Foundation. (2016). *Millennial Traveller Report: Why Millennials Will Shape.* https://www.thinktur.org/media/Expedia-Millennial-Traveller-Report.pdf

Fyall, A., Callod, C., & Edwards, B. (2003). Relationship marketing: The challenge for destinations. *Annals of Tourism Research, 30*(3), 644–659. doi:10.1016/S0160-7383(03)00046-X

Gabriel, M., & Kiso, R. (2020). *Marketing na era digital: conceitos, plataformas e estratégias.* Atlas.

Gajdošík, T. (2018). Smart tourism: Concepts and insights from central Europe. *Czech Journal of Tourism, 7*(1), 25–44. doi:10.1515/cjot-2018-0002

Galvagno, M., & Dalli, D. (2014). Theory of value co-creation: A systematic literature review. *Managing Service Quality, 24*(6), 643–683. doi:10.1108/MSQ-09-2013-0187

Galyarski, E., & Mironova, N. (2021). Digitalization and its impact on business processes. *Economics and Management, 18*(1), 81–89.

Gamage, T. C., Gnanapala, A., & Ashill, N. J. (2021). Understanding social customer relationship management adoption: Qualitative insights. *Journal of Strategic Marketing*, 1–25. doi:10.1080/0965254X.2021.1923056

Gansky, L. (2010). *The mesh: Why the future of business is sharing.* Penguin Group.

Gardner, D. (2019). *How Customer Participation Builds Trust in the Age of GDPR.* Marketing Profs: https://www.marketingprofs.com/articles/2019/40499/how-customer-participation-builds-trust-in-the-age-of-gdpr

Garín-Muñoz, T., Perez-Amaral, T., & Lopez, R. (2020). Consumer engagement in e-Tourism: Micro-panel data models for the case of Spain. *Tourism Economics, 26*(6), 853–872. doi:10.1177/1354816619852880

Garrigos-Simon, F. J., Narangajavana-Kaosiri, Y., & Lengua-Lengua, I. (2018). Tourism and sustainability: A bibliometric and visualization analysis. *Sustainability, 10*(6), 1976.

Gaspar, E., & Gaspar, R. (2021). *Informações úteis.* Fonte: PARATI.COM.BR: http://www.paraty.com.br/index.asp

Gata, J. E. (2015). *The sharing economy, competition and regulation*. Competition Policy International Europe Column.

Gaur, A., & Kumar, M. (2018). A systematic approach to conducting review studies: An assessment of content analysis in 25 years of IB research. *Journal of World Business*, *53*(2), 280–289. doi:10.1016/j.jwb.2017.11.003

Gbenga, S., Member, F., & Sani, S. (n.d.). *Design and Implementation of MOLP Problems with Fuzzy Objective Functions Using Approximation and Equivalence Approach*. Academic Press.

Gelter, J., Lexhagen, M., & Fuchs, M. (2020). A meta-narrative analysis of smart tourism destinations: Implications for tourism destination management. *Current Issues in Tourism*, 1–15. doi:10.1080/13683500.2020.1849048

Ghosal, A., Nandy, A., Das, A. K., Goswami, S., & Panday, M. (2020). A Short Review on Different Clustering Techniques and Their Applications. *Advances in Intelligent Systems and Computing*, *937*, 69–83. doi:10.1007/978-981-13-7403-6_9

Giglio, S., Bertacchini, F., Bilotta, E., & Pantano, P. (2019). Using social media to identify tourism attractiveness in six Italian cities. *Tourism Management*, *72*, 306–312. doi:10.1016/j.tourman.2018.12.007

Gilbert, D. C. (1996). Relationship marketing and airline loyalty schemes. *Tourism Management*, *17*(8), 575–582. doi:10.1016/S0261-5177(96)00078-7

Gilbert, D., & Powell-Perry, J. (2003). Exploring developments in web based relationship marketing within the hotel industry. *Journal of Hospitality & Leisure Marketing*, *10*(3-4), 5–24. doi:10.1300/J150v10n03_02

Giudici, E., Dettori, A., & Caboni, F. (2017). Neurotourism: Futuristic Perspective or Today's Reality? In *20th Excellence in Services International Conference* (pp. 335-346). Academic Press.

Glänzel, W. (2003). *Bibliometrics as a research field: A course on theory and application of bibliometric indicators*. Course Handouts.

Goeldner, C. R., Ritchie, J. R. B., & MacIntosh, R. W. (2000). *Tourism: Principles, Practices Philosophies* (8th ed.). John Wiley & Sons, Inc.

Goel, V., Singh, A., & Shrivastava, S. (2015). CRM: A winning approach for tourism sector. *International Journal of Engineering and Management Research*, *5*(2), 321–325.

Gomezelj, D. O., & Mihalič, T. (2008). Destination competitiveness-Applying different models, the case of Slovenia. *Tourism Management*, *29*(2), 294–307. doi:10.1016/j.tourman.2007.03.009

Gonçalves, L., Patrício, L., Teixeira, J. G., & Wunderlich, N. V. (2020). Understanding the customer experience with smart services. *Journal of Service Management*, *31*(4), 1–22. doi:10.1108/JOSM-11-2019-0349

Gonzalez, R., Gasco, J., & Llopis, J. (2019). ICTs in hotel management: A research review. *International Journal of Contemporary Hospitality Management*, *31*(9), 3583–3609. doi:10.1108/IJCHM-07-2017-0470

González-Reverté, F., Díaz-Luque, P., Gomis-López, J. M., & Morales-Pérez, S. (2018). Tourists' risk perception and the use of mobile devices in beach tourism destinations. *Sustainability*, *10*(2), 413. doi:10.3390u10020413

Gooroochurn, N., & Sugiyarto, G. (2005). Competitiveness indicators in the travel and tourism industry. *Tourism Economics*, *11*(1), 25–43. doi:10.5367/0000000053297130

Gössling, S., Scott, D., & Hall, C. M. (2021). Pandemics, tourism and global change: A rapid assessment of COVID-19. *Journal of Sustainable Tourism*, *29*(1), 1–20. doi:10.1080/09669582.2020.1758708

GoTurkey. (2021). *Türkiye experiences*. https://goturkiye.com/

Greenberg, P. (2010). *CRM at the speed of light: Social CRM strategies, tools, and techniques* (4th ed.). McGraw-Hill.

Gretzel, U., Ham, J., & Koo, C. (2018). Creating the city destination of the future: the case of smart Seoul. In Managing Asian Destinations. Perspectives on Asian Tourism (pp. 199-214). Singapore: Springer. doi:10.1007/978-981-10-8426-3_12

Gretzel, U. (2018). From smart destinations to smart tourism regions. *Journal of Regional Research, 42*, 171–184.

Gretzel, U. (2020). Guiding principles for good governance of the smart destination. *Travel and Tourism Research Association: Advancing Tourism Research Globally, 42*, 1–10.

Gretzel, U., Fesenmaier, D. R., Fromica, S., & O'Leary, J. T. (2006). Searching for the future: Challenges faced by destination marketing organizations. *Journal of Travel Research, 45*(1), 116–126. doi:10.1177/0047287506291598

Gretzel, U., Fesenmaier, D. R., & O'Leary, J. T. (2006). The Transformation of Consumer Behaviour. D. Buhalis, & C. Costa. In *Tourism Business Frontier* (pp. 1–18). Elsevier. doi:10.1016/B978-0-7506-6377-9.50009-2

Gretzel, U., Fuchs, M., Baggio, R., Hoepken, W., Law, R., & Neidhardt, J. (2020). e-Tourism Beyond COVID-19: A call for transformative research. *Journal of Information Technology & Tourism, 43*, 1–21.

Gretzel, U., & Jamal, T. (2009). Conceptualizing the creative tourist class: Technology, mobility, and tourism experiences. *Tourism Analysis, 14*(4), 471–481. doi:10.3727/108354209X12596287114219

Gretzel, U., Koo, C., Sigala, M., & Xiang, Z. (2015). Special issue on smart tourism: Convergence of information technologies, experiences, and theories. *Electronic Markets, 25*(3), 175–177. doi:10.100712525-015-0194-x

Gretzel, U., Reino, S., Kopera, S., & Koo, C. (2015a). Smart tourism challenges. *Journal of Tourism, 16*(1), 41–47.

Gretzel, U., Sigala, M., Xiang, Z., & Koo, C. (2015b). Smart tourism: Foundations and developments. *Electronic Markets, 25*(3), 179–188. doi:10.100712525-015-0196-8

Gretzel, U., Werthner, H., Koo, C., & Lamsfus, C. (2015). Conceptual foundations for understanding smart tourism ecosystems. *Computers in Human Behavior, 50*, 558–563. doi:10.1016/j.chb.2015.03.043

Gretzel, U., & Yoo, K. (2008). *Use and Impact of Online Travel Reviews.* doi:10.1007/978-3-211-77280-5_4

Gretzel, U., & Yoo, K.-H. (2013). Premises and promises of social media marketing in tourism. In *The Routledge handbook of tourism marketing* (pp. 491–504). Routledge.

Grissemann, U. S., & Stokburger-Sauer, N. E. (2012). Customer co-creation of travel services: The role of company support and customer satisfaction with the co-creation performance. *Tourism Management, 33*(6), 1483–1492. doi:10.1016/j.tourman.2012.02.002

Grönroos, C. (2006). Adopting a service logic for marketing. *Marketing Theory, 6*(3), 317–333. doi:10.1177/1470593106066794

Grönroos, C. (2008). Service logic revisited: Who creates value? And who co-creates? *European Business Review, 20*(4), 298–314. doi:10.1108/09555340810886585

Grönroos, C., & Ravald, A. (2011). Service as business logic: Implications for value creation and marketing. *Journal of Service Management, 22*(1), 5–22. doi:10.1108/09564231111106893

Gu, B., & Ye, Q. (2014). First Step in Social Media: Measuring the Influence of Online Management Responses on Customer Satisfaction. *Production and Operations Management, 23*(4), 570–582. doi:10.1111/poms.12043

Guizzardi, A., Pons, F. M. E., Angelini, G., & Ranieri, E. (2021). Big data from dynamic pricing: A smart approach to tourism demand forecasting. *International Journal of Forecasting, 37*(3), 1049–1060. doi:10.1016/j.ijforecast.2020.11.006

Guizzardi, A., & Stacchini, A. (2017). Destinations strategic groups via Multivariate Competition-based IPA. *Tourism Management, 58*, 40–50. doi:10.1016/j.tourman.2016.10.004

Gülmez, M., Kavacık, S. Z., Kaçmaz, Y. Y., & Özyurt, P. M. (2014). Turistlerin Turizme Yönelik İnternet Kullanım Alışkanlıkları Üzerine Bir Araştırma. *Turizm ve Araştırma Dergisi, 3*(1), 5–18.

Gummesson, E. (2008). Extending the service-dominant logic: From customer centricity to balanced centricity. *Journal of the Academy of Marketing Science, 36*(1), 15–17. doi:10.100711747-007-0065-x

Gupta, G. (2018). Inclusive Use of Digital Marketing in Tourism Industry. In Information Systems Design and Intelligent Applications. Advances in Intelligent systems and Computing (pp. 411-419). Singapure: Springer.

Gürbüz, E., & Ormankıran, G. A. (2020). Müşterilerin otel işletmelerine yönelik yorum ve şikâyetlerinin değerlendirilmesi. *Journal of Applied Tourism Research, 1*(1), 17–32.

Gursoy, D. (2020). *Covid-19 Research for Hospitality Industry: Customer Sentiments. COVID-19 Study 5 Report: Restaurant and Hotel Industry, Washington State.* School of Hospitality Business Management.

Gursoy, D., & Chi, C. G. (2020). Effects of COVID-19 pandemic on hospitality industry: Review of the current situations and a research agenda. *Journal of Hospitality Marketing & Management, 29*(5), 527–529. doi:10.1080/1936862 3.2020.1788231

Gustavo, N. (2012). Modelos e Processos de Gestão em Negócios Turísticos. Tendências num contexto em mudança. *Revista Turismo & Desenvolvimento, 17/18,* 671–685.

Gustavo, N. (2018). Trends in Hospitality Marketing and Management: facing the 21st century challenges. In L. Cagica & P. Isaías (Eds.), *Handbook of Research on Entrepreneurship and Marketing for Global Reach in the Digital Economy* (pp. 311–337). IGI Global. doi:10.4018/978-1-5225-6307-5

Gustavo, N., & Belo, M. (2019). O Novo Ambiente Competitivo dos Negócios Turísticos. In *Tourfly. Inovação e Futuro: Contributos para o Desenho da Oferta Turística na Área Metropolitana de Lisboa* (pp. 35–55). ESHTE – Escola Superior de Hotelaria e Turismo do Estoril.

Guttentag, D. (2015). Airbnb: Disruptive innovation and the rise of an informal tourism accommodation sector. *Current Issues in Tourism, 18*(12), 1192–1217. doi:10.1080/13683500.2013.827159

Guttentag, D., Smith, S., Potwarka, L., & Havitz, M. (2017). Why Tourists Choose Airbnb: A Motivation-Based Segmentation Study. *Journal of Travel Research, 57*(1), 1–18.

Güzel, F. Ö. (2014). Marka itibarını korumada şikâyet takibi: Çevrimiçi seyahat 2.0 bilgi kanallarında bir uygulama. *Journal of Internet Applications and Management, 5*(1), 5–19. doi:10.5505/iuyd.2014.07108

Habegger, B., Hasan, O., Brunie, L., Bennani, N., Kosch, H., & Damiani, E. (2014). Personalization vs. privacy in big data analysis. *International Journal of Big Data,* 25–35. doi:10.29268tbd.2014.1.1.3

Haddouche, H., & Salomone, C. (2018). Generation Z And The Tourist Experience: Tourist Stories And Use Of Social Networks. *Journal of Tourism Futures, 4*(1), 69–79. doi:10.1108/JTF-12-2017-0059

Hall, C. M. (2019). Constructing sustainable tourism development: The 2030 agenda and the managerial ecology of sustainable tourism. *Journal of Sustainable Tourism, 27*(7), 1044–1060. doi:10.1080/09669582.2018.1560456

Hall, C. M., Scott, D., & Gössling, S. (2020). Pandemics, transformations and tourism: Be careful what you wish for. *Tourism Geographies, 22*(3), 1–22. doi:10.1080/14616688.2020.1759131

Hall, E. (1976). *Beyond Culture.* Anchor Books/Doubleday.

Han, H. J., Mankad, S., Gavirneni, N., & Verma, R. (2016). What guests really think of your hotel: Text analytics of online customer reviews. *Cornell Hospitality Report, 16*(2), 1–19.

Hao, J.-X., Wang, R., Law, R., & Yu, Y. (2021). How do Mainland Chinese tourists perceive Hong Kong in turbulence? A deep learning approach to sentiment analytics. *International Journal of Tourism Research*, *23*(4), 478–490. doi:10.1002/jtr.2419

Happ, E., & Ivancsó-Horváth, Z. (2018). Digital tourism is the challenge of future – a new approach to tourism. *"Dimitrie Cantemir" Christian University Knowledge Horizons – Economics, 10*(2), 9-16.

Happ, E., & Ivancsó-Horváth, Z. (2018). Digital tourism is the challenge of future – a new approach to tourism. *Knowledge Horizons - Economics, 10*, 9-16.

Hassan, S. S. (2000). Determinants of market competitiveness in an environmentally sustainable tourism industry. *Journal of Travel Research*, *38*(3), 239–245. doi:10.1177/004728750003800305

Hawes, J. M., & Rao, C. P. (1985). Using importance — Performance analysis to develop health care marketing strategies. *Journal of Health Care Marketing*, *5*(4), 19–25. http://widgets.ebscohost.com/prod/customerspecific/ns000290/authentication/index.php?url=https%3A%2F%2Fsearch.ebscohost.com%2Flogin.aspx%3Fdirect%3Dtrue%26AuthType%3Dip%2Ccookie%2Cshib%2Cuid%26db%3Dbth%26AN%3D6850675%26lang%3Dpt-pt%26site%3Deds-live%26sco PMID:10275156

Helversen, B., Abramczuk, K., Kopec, W., & Nielek, R. (2018). Influence of consumer reviews on online purchasing decisions in older and younger adults. *Decision Support Systems*, *113*, 1–10. doi:10.1016/j.dss.2018.05.006

Henderson, J. C., & Ng, A. (2004). Responding to crisis: Severe acute respiratory syndrome (SARS) and hotels in Singapore. *International Journal of Tourism Research*, *6*(6), 411–419. doi:10.1002/jtr.505

Heo, C. (2016). Sharing economy and prospects in tourism research. *Annals of Tourism Research*, *58*, 156–170. doi:10.1016/j.annals.2016.02.002

He, Q., Meadows, M., Angwin, D., Gomes, E., & Child, J. (2020). Strategic Alliance Research in the Era of Digital Transformation: Perspectives on Future Research. *British Journal of Management*, *31*(3), 589–617. doi:10.1111/1467-8551.12406

Hernández-Méndez, J., & Muñoz-Leiva, F. (2015). What type of online advertising is most effective for eTourism 2.0? An eye tracking study based on the characteristics of tourists. *Computers in Human Behavior*, *50*, 618–625. doi:10.1016/j.chb.2015.03.017

Higgins-Desbiolles, F. (2020). Socialising tourism for social and ecological justice after COVID-19. *Tourism Geographies*, *22*(3), 610–623. doi:10.1080/14616688.2020.1757748

Hills, J., & Cairncross, G. (2011). Small accommodation providers and UGC web sites: Perceptions and practices. *International Journal of Contemporary Hospitality Management*, *23*(1), 26–43. doi:10.1108/09596111111101652

Hochreiter, S., & Schmidhuber, J. (1997). Long Short-Term Memory. *Neural Computation*, *9*(8), 1735–1780. doi:10.1162/neco.1997.9.8.1735 PMID:9377276

Hofstede, G., Hofstede, G., & Minkov, M. (2010). Dimensions of National Cultures. In *Intercultural Cooperation and Its Importance for Survival* (pp. 53–296). McGraw-Hill.

Hojeghan, S. B., & Esfangareh, A. N. (2011). Digital economy and tourism impacts, influences and challenges. In *The 2nd International Geography Symposium GEOMED2010* (pp. 308-316). Kemer: Elsevier Ltd. 10.1016/j.sbspro.2011.05.136

Höjer, M., & Wangel, J. (2015). Smart sustainable cities: definition and challenges. In *ICT innovations for sustainability* (pp. 333–349). Springer. doi:10.1007/978-3-319-09228-7_20

Holbrook, M. B. (1999). *Introduction to consumer value. In Consumer Value: A framework for analysis and research.* Routledge.

Holbrook, M. B. (2006). Consumption experience, customer value, and subjective personal introspection: An illustrative photographic essay. *Journal of Business Research*, *59*(6), 714–725. doi:10.1016/j.jbusres.2006.01.008

Hollenstein, H. (2004). Determinants of the adoption of Information and Communication Technologies (ICT); an empirical analysis based on firm-level data for the Swiss business sector. *Structural Change and Economic Dynamics*, *15*(3), 315–342. doi:10.1016/j.strueco.2004.01.003

Hong, W.-C. (2009). Global Competitiveness Measurement for the Tourism Sector. *Current Issues in Tourism*, *12*(2), 105–132. doi:10.1080/13683500802596359

Höpken, W., Eberle, T., Fuchs, M., & Lexhagen, M. (2020). *Improving Tourist Arrival Prediction: A Big Data and Artificial Neural Network Approach.* Https://Doi.Org/10.1177/0047287520921244 doi:10.1177/0047287520921244

Hosany, S., & Martin, D. (2012). Self-image congruence in consumer behavior. *Journal of Business Research*, *65*(5), 685–691. doi:10.1016/j.jbusres.2011.03.015

Huang, C. D., Goo, J., Nam, K., & Yoo, C. W. (2017). Smart Tourism Technologies in Travel Planning: The Role of Exploration. *Information & Management*, *54*(6), 757–770. doi:10.1016/j.im.2016.11.010

Hudson, L., & Hudson, S. (2020). *Marketing para turismo, hospitalidade e eventos: uma abordagem global e digital.* Senac.

Hulten, B. (2011). Sensory marketing: The multi-sensory brand-experience concept. *European Business Review*, *23*(3), 256–273. doi:10.1108/09555341111130245

Hultén, B., Broweus, N., & Dijk, M. (2009). *Sensory marketing.* Palgrave Macmillan. doi:10.1057/9780230237049

Hung, K. K. C., Mark, C. K. M., Yeung, M. P. S., Chan, E. Y. Y., & Graham, C. A. (2018). The role of the hotel industry in the response to emerging epidemics: A case study of SARS in 2003 and H1N1 swine flu in 2009 in Hong Kong. *Globalization and Health*, *14*(1), 1–7. doi:10.118612992-018-0438-6 PMID:30482214

Hunter, W. C., Chung, N., Gretzel, U., & Koo, C. (2015). Constructivist research in smart tourism. *Asia Pacific Journal of Information Systems*, *25*(1), 103–118. doi:10.14329/apjis.2015.25.1.105

Huovila, A., Bosch, P., & Airaksinen, M. (2019). Comparative analysis of standardized indicators for Smart sustainable cities: What indicators and standards to use and when? *Cities (London, England)*, *89*, 141–153. doi:10.1016/j.cities.2019.01.029

Hysa, B., Karasek, A., & Zdonek, I. (2021). Social Media Usage by Different Generations as a Tool for Sustainable Tourism Marketing in Society 5.0 Idea. *Sustainability*, *13*(3), 2–27. doi:10.3390u13031018

Iannacci, J. (2018). Internet of Things (IoT); Internet of Everything (IoE); Tactile Internet; 5G – A (Not So Evanescent) Unifying Vision Empowered by EH-MEMS (Energy Harvesting MEMS) and RF-MEMS (Radio Frequency MEMS). *Sensors and Actuators. A, Physical*, *272*, 187–198. doi:10.1016/j.sna.2018.01.038

Ida, E. (2017). The role of customers' involvement in value co-creation behaviour is value co-creation the source of competitive advantage? *Journal of Competitiveness*, *9*(3), 51–66. doi:10.7441/joc.2017.03.04

India Brand Equity Foundation. (2021). *Indian Tourism & Hospitality Sector Report.* A report Published by Indian Brand Equity Foundation (IBEF). Retrieved from https://www.ibef.org/download/Tourism-and-Hospitality-February2021.pdf

Ind, N., & Coates, N. (2013). The meanings of co-creation. *European Business Review*, *25*(1), 86–95. doi:10.1108/09555341311287754

Inside Airbnb. (n.d.). *Inside Airbnb: Lisbon. Adding data to the debate.* Accessed 8th January, 2020, from: http://insideairbnb.com/lisbon/?neighbourhood=neighbourhood_group%7CLisboa&filterEntireHomes=false&filterHighlyAvailable=false&filterRecentReviews=false&filterMultiListings=false

Institute of Internal Auditors (IIA). (2019). *Global Perspectives and Insights. 5G e a Quarta Revolução Industrial, EUA.* Institute of Internal Auditors.

Instituto Nacional de Estatística (INE). (2020). *Atividade Turística: Dezembro 2020.* https://www.ine.pt/xportal/xmain?xpid=INE&xpgid=ine_destaques&DESTAQUESdest_boui=415204526&DESTAQUESmodo=2

Instituto Nacional de Estatistica. (2018). *Statistical Yearbook of Área Metropolitana de Lisboa, 104.*

Ip, C., Leung, R., & Law, R. (2011). Progress and development of information and communication technologies in hospitality. *International Journal of Contemporary Hospitality Management, 23*(4), 533–551. doi:10.1108/09596111111130029

Iriana, R., & Buttle, F. (2007). Strategic, operational, and analytical customer relationship management: Attributes and measures. *Journal of Relationship Marketing, 5*(4), 23–42. doi:10.1300/J366v05n04_03

Ismagilova, E., Hughes, L., Dwivedi, Y. K., & Raman, K. R. (2019). Smart cities: Advances in research—An information systems perspective. *International Journal of Information Management, 47,* 88–100. doi:10.1016/j.ijinfomgt.2019.01.004

Ito, C. A. (2008). *Evolução histórica do turismo e suas motivações.* Tópos.

Ivanov, S. (2020). The impact of automation on tourism and hospitality jobs. *Information Technology & Tourism, 22,* 205-215.

Ivanov, S., & Webster, C. (2017). Adoption of robots, artificial intelligence and service automation by travel, tourism and hospitality companies – a cost-benefit analysis. Sofia University "St. Kliment Ohridski".

Ivanov, S., Webster, C., & Berezina, K. (2017). Adoption of robots and service automation by tourism and hospitality companies. *Revista Turismo & Desenvolvimento, 27/28,* 1501–1517.

Ivanov, S., Webster, C., & Seyyedi, P. (2018). Consumers' attitudes towards the introduction of robots in accommodation establishments. *Tourism (Zagreb), 66*(3), 302–317.

Ivars-Baidal, J. A., Celdrán-Bernabeu, M. A., Femenia-Serra, F., Perles-Ribes, J. F., & Giner-Sánchez, D. (2021). Measuring the progress of smart destinations: The use of indicators as a management tool. *Journal of Destination Marketing & Management, 19,* 100531. doi:10.1016/j.jdmm.2020.100531

Ivars-Baidal, J. A., Celdrán-Bernabeu, M. A., Mazón, J.-N., & Perles-Ivars, Á. F. (2019). Smart destinations and the evolution of ICTs: A new scenario for destination management? *Current Issues in Tourism, 22*(13), 1581–1600. doi:10.1080/13683500.2017.1388771

Ivars-Baidal, J. A., Vera-Rebollo, J. F., Perles-Ribes, J., Femenia-Serra, F., & Celdrán-Bernabeu, M. A. (2021). Sustainable tourism indicators: What's new within the smart city/destination approach? *Journal of Sustainable Tourism,* 1–24. doi:10.1080/09669582.2021.1876075

İzmir Belediyesi. (2021). *İzmir'in dijital turizm envanteri tamamlandı.* https://www.izmir.bel.tr/tr/Haberler/izmir-in-dijital-turizm-envanteri-tamamlandi/44533/156

Jahandideh, B., Golmohammadi, A., Meng, F., O'Gorman, K. D., & Taheri, B. (2014). Cross-cultural comparison of Chinese and Arab consumer complaintbehavior in the hotel context. *International Journal of Hospitality Management, 41,* 67–76. doi:10.1016/j.ijhm.2014.04.011

Japutra, A., Ekinci, Y., & Simkin, L. (2019). Self-congruence, brand attachment and compulsive buying. *Journal of Business Research*, *99*, 456–463. doi:10.1016/j.jbusres.2017.08.024

Jaremen, D. E., Jędrasiak, M., & Rapacz, A. (2016). The Concept of Smart Hotels as an Innovation on the Hospitality Industry Market – Case Study of Puro Hotel in Wrocław. *Economic Problems of Tourism*, *36*, 65–75. doi:10.18276/ept.2016.4.36-06

Jarvenpaa, S. L., & Tuunainen, V. K. (2013). How Finnair socialized customers for service co-creation with social media. *MIS Quarterly Executive*, *12*(3), 125–136.

Jasrotia, A., & Gangotia, A. (2018). Smart cities to smart tourism destinations: A review paper. *Journal of Tourism Intelligence and Smartness*, *1*(1), 47–56.

Jeng, C. R., Snyder, A. T., & Chen, C. F. (2019). Importance–performance analysis as a strategic tool for tourism marketers: The case of Taiwan's Destination Image. *Tourism and Hospitality Research*, *19*(1), 112–125. doi:10.1177/1467358417704884

Jeong, M., Lee, M., & Nagesvaran, B. (2016). Employees' use of mobile devices and their perceived outcomes in the workplace: A case of luxury hotel. *International Journal of Hospitality Management*, *57*, 40–51. doi:10.1016/j.ijhm.2016.05.003

Jerkovic, J. G. (2010). *SEO: Técnicas essenciais para aumentar a visibilidade na web*. Novatec.

Jiang, Y. & Wen, J. (2020). Effects of COVID-19 on hotel marketing and management: A perspective article. *International Journal of Contemporary of Hospitality Management*, 1-17.

Jiang, M., & Fan, X. (2020). *Retinamask: A Face Mask Detector*. ArXiv.

Jiao, X., Li, G., & Chen, J. L. (2020). Forecasting international tourism demand: A local spatiotemporal model. *Annals of Tourism Research*, *83*, 102937. doi:10.1016/j.annals.2020.102937

Jin, S. V., & Phua, J. (2015). Making reservations online: The impact of consumer-written and system-aggregated user-generated content (UGC) In travel booking websites on consumers' behavioral intentions. *Journal of Travel & Tourism Marketing*, *33*(1), 1–17.

Johnson, A. G., Rickly, J. M., & McCabe, S. (2021). Smartmentality in Ljubljana. *Annals of Tourism Research*, *86*, 103094. doi:10.1016/j.annals.2020.103094

Johnson, A. G., & Samakovlis, I. (2018). A bibliometric analysis of knowledge development in smart tourism research. *Journal of Hospitality and Tourism Technology*, *10*(4), 600–623. doi:10.1108/JHTT-07-2018-0065

Joo, Y., & Tan, T.-B. (2020). *Smart cities in Asia: an introduction*. doi:10.4337/9781788972888

Jovicic, D. Z. (2019). From the traditional understanding of tourism destination to the smart tourism destination. *Current Issues in Tourism*, *22*(3), 276–282. doi:10.1080/13683500.2017.1313203

Juvan, E., & Dolnicar, S. (2014). The attitude–behaviour gap in sustainable tourism. *Annals of Tourism Research*, *48*, 76–95. doi:10.1016/j.annals.2014.05.012

Juvan, E., & Dolnicar, S. (2017). Drivers of pro-environmental tourist behaviours are not universal. *Journal of Cleaner Production*, *166*, 879–890. doi:10.1016/j.jclepro.2017.08.087

Kafa, N., Arıca, R., & Gök, N. S. (2020). Akıllı turizm araç ve uygulamalarına ilişkin turizm işletmesi yöneticilerinin görüşleri: Eskişehir üzerine nitel bir araştırma [Tourism managers opinions about smart tourism vehicles and applications: a qualitative research on Eskişehir]. *İşletme Araştırmaları Dergisi, 12*(3), 2774-2787. doi:10.20491/isarder.2020.1007

Kahle, L. R. (1983). *Social Values and Social Change: Adaptation to Life in America.* Praeger.

Kalipe, G., Gautham, V., & Behera, R. K. (2018). Predicting Malarial Outbreak using Machine Learning and Deep Learning Approach: A Review and Analysis. *Proceedings - 2018 International Conference on Information Technology, ICIT 2018*, 33–38. 10.1109/ICIT.2018.00019

Kamińska, A. (2018). *The application of methods of social network analysis in bibliometrics and webometrics. Measures and tools.* Academic Press.

Kandampully, J., Bilgihan, A., & Zhang, T. (2016). Developing a people-technology hybrids model to unleash innovation and creativity: The new hospitality frontier. *Journal of Hospitality and Tourism Management, 29*, 154–164. doi:10.1016/j.jhtm.2016.07.003

Kandampully, J., & Suhartanto, D. (2000). Customer loyalty in the hotel industry: The role of customer satisfaction and image. *International Journal of Contemporary Hospitality Management, 12*(6), 346–351. doi:10.1108/09596110010342559

Kang, M., & Schuett, M. A. (2013). Determinants Of Sharing Travel Experiences in Social Media. *Journal of Travel & Tourism Marketing, 30*(1-2), 93–107. doi:10.1080/10548408.2013.751237

Kanjanasupawan, J., Chen, Y. C., Thaipisutikul, T., Shih, T. K., & Srivihok, A. (2019). Prediction of tourist behaviour: Tourist visiting places by adapting convolutional long short-Term deep learning. *Proceedings of 2019 International Conference on System Science and Engineering, ICSSE 2019*, 12–17. 10.1109/ICSSE.2019.8823542

Kansakar, P., Munir, A., & Shabani, N. (2019). Technology in the Hospitality Industry: Prospects and Challenges. *IEEE Consumer Electronics Magazine, 8*(3), 60–65. doi:10.1109/MCE.2019.2892245

Kaplan, R. A. & Nadler M. L. (2015). Airbnb: A case study in occupancy regulation and taxation. *University of Chicago Law Review, 82*, 103-115.

Karababa, E., & Kjeldgaard, D. (2014). Value in marketing: Toward sociocultural perspectives. *Marketing Theory, 14*(1), 119–127. doi:10.1177/1470593113500385

Karakan, H. İ. (2020). Y Kuşağı ve Turizm. Ç. Ertaş, & B. Kanca. In *Turizmin Geleceği: Yeni Deneyimler* (pp. 33–52). Detay.

Kardon, B. (2007). They're saying nasty things. *Marketing News, 41*(20), 30.

Kattara, H. S., & El-Said, O. A. (2014). Customers' preferences for new technology-based self-services versus human interaction services in hotels. *Tourism and Hospitality Research, 13*(2), 67–82. doi:10.1177/1467358413519261

Kaur, G. (2017). *The importance of digital marketing in the tourism industry.* International Journal of Research - Granthaalayah. doi:10.29121/granthaalayah.v5.i6.2017.1998

Kaushik, A. K., & Kumar, V. (2018). Investigating consumers' adoption of SSTs – a case study representing India's hospitality industry. *Journal of Vacation Marketing, 24*(3), 275–290. doi:10.1177/1356766717725560

Kayaman, R., & Arasli, H. (2007). Customer based brand equity: Evidence from the hotel industry. *Journal of Service Theory and Practice, 17*, 92–109.

Kellen, V., & Stefanczyk, K. (2002). Complexity, fragmentation, uncertainty, and emergence in customer relationship management. *Emergence, 4*(4), 39–50. doi:10.1207/S15327000EM0404_5

Keller, K. (2001). *Building Customer-Based Brand Equity: A Blueprint for Creating Strong Brands.* Academic Press.

Kellogg, D. L., Youngdahl, W. E., & Bowen, D. E. (1997). On the relationship between customer participation and satisfaction: Two frameworks. *International Journal of Service Industry Management, 8*(3), 206–219. doi:10.1108/09564239710185406

Kelly, S. (2000). Analytical CRM: The fusion of data and intelligence. *Interactive Marketing, 1*(3), 262–267. doi:10.1057/palgrave.im.4340035

Keskin, K., & Küçükali, U. F. (2017). Sanallaşmanın Toplum Hayatına Etkileri. *İnsan ve Toplum Bilimleri Araştırmaları Dergisi, 6*(1), 396-418.

Kessler, M. M. (1963). Bibliographic coupling between scientific papers. *American Documentation, 14*(1), 10–25. doi:10.1002/asi.5090140103

Khan, S., Woo, M., Nam, K., & Chathoth, P. K. (2017). Smart city and smart tourism: A case of Dubai. *Sustainability, 9*(12), 2279. doi:10.3390u9122279

Khanzode, C. A., & Sarode, R. (2016). Evolution of the world wide web: from web 1.0 to 6.0. *International Journal of Digital Library Services, 6*(2), 1-11.

Khorsand, R., Rafiee, M., & Kayvanfar, V. (2020). Insights into TripAdvisor's online reviews: The case of Tehran's hotels. *Tourism Management Perspectives, 34*, 100673. doi:10.1016/j.tmp.2020.100673

Khozaei, M. (2016). The study of factors affecting customer's satisfaction with the three star hotels in Dubai. International Journal of Advanced Engineering. *Management Science, 2*(2), 21–24.

Kim, B. Y. & Oh, H. (2004). How do hotel firms obtain a competitive advantage? *International Journal of Contemporary Hospitality Management, 16*, 65-71.

Kim, D., & Kim, S. (2017). The role of mobile technology in tourism: Patents, articles, news, and mobile tour app reviews. *Sustainability, 9*(11), 2082. doi:10.3390u9112082

Kim, S. S., Chun, H., & Lee, H. (2005). The effects of SARS on the Korean hotel industry and measures to overcome the crisis: A case study of six Korean five-star hotels. *Asia Pacific Journal of Tourism Research, 10*(4), 369–377. doi:10.1080/10941660500363694

Kim, S. S., Kim, J., Badu-Baiden, F., Giroux, M., & Choi, Y. (2021). Preference for robot service or human service in hotels? Impacts of the COVID-19 pandemic. *International Journal of Hospitality Management, 93*, 102795. doi:10.1016/j.ijhm.2020.102795

Kirby, C. (2000). *Everyone's a critic: Web sites hope online reviews of products lead to online buying.* Available at: https://www.sfgate.com/business/article/EVERYONE-S-A-CRITIC-Web-siteshopeonline-2782075.php

Kline, S., Almanza, B., & Neal, J. (2014). Hotel guest room cleaning: a systematic approach. In B. Almanza, R. Ghiselli, & K. Mahmood (Eds.), *Food Safety: Researching the Hazard in Hazardous Foods* (pp. 303–322). CRC Press Taylor and Francis.

Knaflic, C. N. (2019). *Storytelling com dados: um guia sobre visualização de dados para profissionais de negócios.* Alta Books.

Kon, B. (2017). *Humanica. Kuşakları Anlamak ve Yönetmek.* https://www.humanica.com.tr/kusaklari-anlamak-yonetmek/

Koo, C., Shin, S., Gretzel, U., Hunter, W. C., & Chung, N. (2016). Conceptualization of smart tourism destination competitiveness. *Asia Pacific Journal of Information Systems, 26*(4), 561–576. doi:10.14329/apjis.2016.26.4.561

Kornova, G., & Loginova, E. (2019). Service opportunities in the development of the hospitality services market in terms of the new industrialization. *Advances in Social Science, Education and Humanities Research, 240*, 496-499.

Kotler, P. (1972). A generic concept of marketing. *Journal of Marketing, 36*(2), 46–54. doi:10.1177/002224297203600209

Kotler, P. (2021). *Marketing para o século XXI: como criar, conquistar e dominar mercados.* Alta Books.

Kotler, P., & Armstrong, G. (2007). *Princípios de marketing.* Pearson.

Kotler, P., & Armstrong, G. (2016). *Principles of Marketing.* Pearson Education Limited.

Kotler, P., Kartajaya, H., & Setiawan, I. (2010). *From products to customer to human Spirit, Marketing 3.0.* John Wiley and Sons. doi:10.1002/9781118257883

Kotler, P., Kartajaya, H., & Setiawan, I. (2017). *Marketing 4.0 – Moving from traditional to digital.* John Wiley and Sons.

Kotler, P., Kartajaya, H., & Setiawan, I. (2017). *Marketing 4.0.* Sextante.

Kotler, P., Kartajaya, H., & Setiawan, I. (2017). *Marketing 4.0: Moving From Traditional to Digital.* Wiley.

Kotler, P., Kartajaya, H., & Setiawan, I. (2021). *Marketing 5.0: technology for humanity.* John Wiley & Sons.

Kotler, P., & Keller, K. L. (2006). *Administração de marketing: a bíblia do marketing.* Prentice Hall.

Kotler, P., & Keller, K. L. (2006). *Marketing Management.* Pearson Prentice Hall.

Kozak, M. (2002). Comparative analysis of tourist motivations by nationality and destinations. *Tourism Management, 23*(3), 221–232. doi:10.1016/S0261-5177(01)00090-5

Krippendorff, K. (2018). *Content analysis: An introduction to its methodology.* Sage publications.

Król, K. (2020). Evolution of online mapping: From Web 1.0 to Web 6.0. *Geomatics, Landmanagement and Landscape, 1,* 33–51. doi:10.15576/GLL/2020.1.33

Kuenzel, S., & Halliday, S. (2010). The chain of effects from reputation and brand personality congruence to brand loyalty: The role of brand identification. *Journal of Targeting, Measurement and Analysis for Marketing,* 167-176.

Kulshrestha, A., Krishnaswamy, V., & Sharma, M. (2020). Bayesian BILSTM approach for tourism demand forecasting. *Annals of Tourism Research, 83,* 102925. doi:10.1016/j.annals.2020.102925

Kültür ve Turizm Bakanlığı. (2021). *Turizm istatistikleri (Türkiye)* [Data Sets]. https://yigm.ktb.gov.tr/Eklenti/81939,3103turizmistatistikleri2020-4pdf.pdf?0

Kumar, V., & Reinartz, W. (2006). *Customer relationship management concept, strategy, and tools* (3rd ed.). Springer-Verlag.

Kuo, C. (2007). The importance of hotel employee service attitude and satisfaction of international tourists. *Service Industries Journal, 27*(8), 1073–1085. doi:10.1080/02642060701673752

Kuo, C.-M., Chen, L.-C., & Tseng, C.-Y. (2017). Investigating an innovative service with hospitality robots. *International Journal of Contemporary Hospitality Management, 29*(5), 1–44. doi:10.1108/IJCHM-08-2015-0414

Kutlu, D. (2020). Antalya A grubu seyahat acentalarının web sitelerinin değerlendirilmesi. *Akademik Araştırmalar ve Çalışmalar Dergisi, 12*(23), 407–418.

Kuyucak, F., & Şengür, Y. (2009). Değer zinciri analizi: Havayolu işletmeleri için genel bir çerçeve. *KMU İİBF Dergisi,* (11), 132–147.

Kwon, J., Chung, T., Yoon, S. H., & Kwon, K. B. (2017). Importance and Satisfaction of Destination Attraction for Water-Based Tourism in Jeju Island. *Asian Social Science, 13*(10), 1. doi:10.5539/ass.v13n10p1

Lai, I. K. W., & Hitchcock, M. (2015). Importance-performance analysis in tourism: A framework for researchers. *Tourism Management, 48*, 242–267. doi:10.1016/j.tourman.2014.11.008

Lakatos, E. M., & Marconi, M. A. (2017). *Metodologia do Trabalho Científico* (4th ed.). Editora Atlas.

Lam, S., Ahearne, M., Hu, Y., & Schillewaert, N. (2010). Resistance to brand switching when a radically new brand is introduced: A social identity theory perspective. *Journal of Marketing, 74*(6), 6. doi:10.1509/jmkg.74.6.128

Lam, S., Ahearne, M., Mullins, R., & Schillewaert, N. (2013). Exploring the synamics of antecedents to consumer-brand identification with a new brand. *Journal of the Academy of Marketing Science, 41*(2), 234–252. doi:10.100711747-012-0301-x

Landon, E. (1972). Role of need for achievement in the perception of products: Proceedings of the American psychological association convention. *Journal of Consumer Research*, 741-7842. 10.1037/e611312012-119

Lanka, E., Lanka, S., Rostron, A. & Singh, P. (n.d.). Why We Need Qualitative Research in Management. *Revista de Administração Contemporânea. Journal of Contemporary Administration, 25*(2), 1-8.

Larrossa, L. (2021). *Instagram, WhatsApp e Facebook para Negócios: Como ter lucro através dos três principais canais de venda*. São Paulo: DVS.

Law, R., Buhalis, D., & Cobanoglu, C. (2014). Progress on information and communication technologies in hospitality and tourism. *International Journal of Contemporary Hospitality Management, 26*(5), 727–750. doi:10.1108/IJCHM-08-2013-0367

Law, R., Leung, R., & Buhalis, D. (2009). Information technology applications in hospitality and tourism: A review of publications from 2005-2007. *Journal of Travel & Tourism Marketing, 26*(5/6), 599–623. doi:10.1080/10548400903163160

Law, R., Li, G., Fong, D. K. C., & Han, X. (2019). Tourism demand forecasting: A deep learning approach. *Annals of Tourism Research, 75*, 410–423. doi:10.1016/j.annals.2019.01.014

Leaniz, P., & Rodriguez-de-Bolque, I. (2013). CSR and customer loyalty: The roles of trust, customer identification with the company and satisfaction. *International Journal of Hospitality Management*, 89–99.

Leask, A. (2016). Visitor attraction management: A critical review of research 2009–2014. *Tourism Management, 57*, 334–361. doi:10.1016/j.tourman.2016.06.015

Lee, H. & Blum, S. (2015). How hotel responses to online reviews differ by hotel rating: an exploratory study. *Worldwide Hospitality and Tourism Themes, 7*(3), 242-250.

Lee, C. K., Song, H. J., Bendle, L. J., Kim, M. J., & Han, H. (2012). The impact of nonpharmaceutical interventions for 2009 H1N1 influenza on travel intentions: A model of goal-directed behavior. *Tourism Management, 33*(1), 89–99. doi:10.1016/j.tourman.2011.02.006 PMID:32287736

Lee, D. (2016). How Airbnb short-term rentals exacerbate Los Angeles's affordable housing crisis: Analysis and policy recommendations. *Harvard Law & Policy Review, 50*(6), 229–253.

Lee, J., Choi, Y., & Breiter, D. (2013). An Exploratory Study of Convention Destination Competitiveness from the Attendees' Perspective: Importance-Performance Analysis and Repeated Measures of Manova. *Journal of Hospitality & Tourism Research (Washington, D.C.), 40*(5), 589–610. doi:10.1177/1096348013515913

Lee, J., Lee, J.-N., & Tan, B. C. Y. (2013). The contrasting attitudes of reviewer and seller in electronic word-of-mouth: A communicative action theory perspective. *Asia Pacific Journal of Information Systems, 23*(3), 105–129. doi:10.14329/apjis.2013.23.3.105

Lee, J., Park, D., & Han, I. (2008). The effect of negative online consumer reviews on product attitude: An information processing view. *Electronic Commerce Research and Applications*, *7*(3), 341–352. doi:10.1016/j.elerap.2007.05.004

Lee, S. (2009). How do online reviews affect purchasing intention? *African Journal of Business Management*, *3*(10), 576–581.

Lee, T. H., Jan, F.-H., & Yang, C.-C. (2013). Conceptualizing and measuring environmentally responsible behaviors from the perspective of community-based tourists. *Tourism Management*, *36*, 454–468. doi:10.1016/j.tourman.2012.09.012

Lee, Y., Leeb, S., & Kim, D.-Y. (2021). Exploring hotel guests' perceptions of using robot assistants. *Tourism Management Perspectives*, *37*, 100781. doi:10.1016/j.tmp.2020.100781

Le, H., Ho, Lee, & Jung. (2019). Application of Long Short-Term Memory (LSTM) Neural Network for Flood Forecasting. *Water (Basel)*, *11*(7), 1387. doi:10.3390/w11071387

LeHub. (2017): *Connaisses-vous la nouvelle definition du marketing?* https://lehub.laposte.fr/dossiers/connaissez-vous-nouvelle-definition-marketing

Leung, R., & Law, R. (2005). An analysis of information technology publications in leading hospitality journals. *FIU Hospitality Review*, *23*(2), 55–65.

Levy, S., Duan, W., & Boo, S. (2013). An Analysis of One-Star Online Reviews and Responses in the Washington, D.C., Lodging Market. *Cornell Hospitality Quarterly*, *54*(1), 49–63. doi:10.1177/1938965512464513

Lew, A. (2020). *How to Create a Better Post-COVID-19 World*. https://medium.com/new-earth-consciousness/creating-a-better-post-covid-19-world-36b2b3e8a7ae

Liang, S., Schuckert, M., Law, R., & Chen, C. (2020). The importance of marketer-generated content to peer-to-peer property rental platforms: Evidence from Airbnb. *International Journal of Hospitality Management*, *84*, 1–11. doi:10.1016/j.ijhm.2019.102329

Liberato, P., Alen, E., & Liberato, D. (2018). Smart tourism destination triggers consumer experience: The case of Porto. *European Journal of Management and Business Economics*, *27*(1), 6–25. doi:10.1108/EJMBE-11-2017-0051

Li, H., Hu, M., & Li, G. (2020). Forecasting tourism demand with multisource big data. *Annals of Tourism Research*, *83*, 102912. doi:10.1016/j.annals.2020.102912

Li, H., Ye, Q., & Law, R. (2012). Determinants of Customer Satisfaction in the Hotel Industry: An Application of Online Review Analysis. *Asia Pacific Journal of Tourism Research*, 119–108.

Li, J., Xu, L., Tang, L., Wang, S., & Li, L. (2018). Big data in tourism research: A literature review. *Tourism Management*, *68*, 301–323. doi:10.1016/j.tourman.2018.03.009

Li, L., & Tabari, S. (2019). Impact of Airbnb on customers' behavior in the UK hotel industry. *Tourism Analysis*, *24*(1), 13–26. doi:10.3727/108354219X15458295631891

Lim, W. M. (2020). The sharing economy: A marketing perspective. *Australasian Marketing Journal*, *28*(3), 4–13. doi:10.1016/j.ausmj.2020.06.007

Lin, J.-S. C., & Hsieh, P.-L. (2011). Assessing the self-service technology encounters: Development and validation of SSTQUAL scale. *Journal of Retailing*, *87*(2), 194–206. doi:10.1016/j.jretai.2011.02.006

Lin, S. P., Chan, Y. H., & Tsai, M. C. (2009). A transformation function corresponding to IPA and gap analysis. *Total Quality Management & Business Excellence*, *20*(8), 829–846. doi:10.1080/14783360903128272

Litvin, S., Goldsmith, R., & Pan, B. (2008). Electronic word-of-mouth in hospitality and tourism management. *Tourism Management*, *29*(3), 458–468. doi:10.1016/j.tourman.2007.05.011

Liu, A. M., Fellows, R., & Chan, I. (2014). Fostering value co-creation in construction: A case study of an airport project in India. *International Journal of Architecture, Engineering and Construction*, *3*(2), 120–130.

Liu, S., Law, R., Rong, J., Li, G., & Hall, J. (2013). Analyzing changes in hotel customers' expectations by trip mode. *International Journal of Hospitality Management*, *34*, 359–371. doi:10.1016/j.ijhm.2012.11.011

Liu, X., Schuckert, M., & Law, R. (2015). Can Response Management Benefit Hotels? Evidence from Hong Kong Hotels. *Journal of Travel & Tourism Marketing*, *32*(8), 1069–1080. doi:10.1080/10548408.2014.944253

Liu, Z., & Park, S. (2015). What makes a useful online review? Implication for travel product websites. *Tourism Management*, *47*, 140–151. doi:10.1016/j.tourman.2014.09.020

Li, X., & Hitt, L. (2018). Self-Selection and Information Role of online Product Reviews. *Information Systems Research*, *19*(4), 456–474. doi:10.1287/isre.1070.0154

Li, X., Law, R., Xie, G., & Wang, S. (2021). Review of tourism forecasting research with internet data. *Tourism Management*, *83*, 104245. doi:10.1016/j.tourman.2020.104245

Li, Y., & Cao, H. (2018). Prediction for Tourism Flow based on LSTM Neural Network. *Procedia Computer Science*, *129*, 277–283. doi:10.1016/j.procs.2018.03.076

Li, Y., Hu, C., Huang, C., & Duan, L. (2017). The concept of tourism in the context of tourism information services. *Tourism Management*, *58*, 293–300. doi:10.1016/j.tourman.2016.03.014

Lo, A., Cheung, C., & Law, R. (2006). The survival of hotels during disaster: A case study of Hong Kong in 2003. *Asia Pacific Journal of Tourism Research*, *11*(1), 65–80. doi:10.1080/10941660500500733

Lopatovska, I. (2018). Talk to me: Exploring user interactions with the Amazon Alexa. *Journal of Librarianship and Information Science*, 1–14.

López de Ávila, A. (2015). *Informe destinos turísticos inteligentes: construyendo el futuro*. Technical report. https://www.segittur.es/opencms/export/sites/segitur/.content/galerias/descargas/proyectos/Libro-Blanco-Destinos-Tursticos-Inteligentes-ok es.pdf

Lopez de Avila, A. (2015, February). Smart destinations: xxi century tourism. In *Proceedings of the ENTER2015 Conference on Information and Communication Technologies in Tourism* (pp. 4-6), Academic Press.

López, J., Pérez, D., Zalama, E., & Gómez-García-Bermejo, J. (2014). BellBot. A hotel assistant system based on mobile robots. *International Journal of Advanced Robotic Systems*, 1–11.

Lu, C., Berchoux, C., Marek, M., & Chen, B. (2015). Service quality and customer satisfaction: Qualitative research implications for luxury hotels. *International Journal of Culture, Tourism and Hospitality Research*, *9*(2), 168–182. doi:10.1108/IJCTHR-10-2014-0087

Lukanova, G., & Galina, I. (2019). Robots, Artificial Intelligence and Service Automation in Hotels. In E. P. Limited (Ed.), *Robots, Artificial Intelligence, and Service Automation in Travel, Tourism, and Hospitality* (pp. 157–183). Emerald Publishing Limited. doi:10.1108/978-1-78756-687-320191009

Luo, Y., He, J., Mou, Y., Wang, J., & Liu, T. (2021). Exploring China's 5A global geoparks through online tourism reviews: A mining model based on machine learning approach. *Tourism Management Perspectives*, *37*, 100769. https://doi.org/10.1016/j.tmp.2020.100769

Luo, Y., & Xu, X. (2021). Comparative study of deep learning models for analyzing online restaurant reviews in the era of the COVID-19 pandemic. *International Journal of Hospitality Management*, *94*, 102849. doi:10.1016/j.ijhm.2020.102849 PMID:34785843

Luque Gil, A. M., Zayas Fernández, B., & Caro Herrero, J. L. (2015). The Smart Tourism Destination and the Territorial Intelligence: Problems and opportunities. *Investigaciones Turísticas*, (10), 1–25.

Luttrell, R., & McGrath, K. (2015). Millenials: Who are they? Where have they been? Where are they going? In *The Millenial Mindset: Unraveling Fact From Fiction* (pp. 3–21). Rowman & Littlefield.

Lv, S. X., Peng, L., & Wang, L. (2018). Stacked autoencoder with echo-state regression for tourism demand forecasting using search query data. *Applied Soft Computing*, *73*, 119–133. doi:10.1016/j.asoc.2018.08.024

Lytras, M. D., Damiani, E., & Ordóñez de Pablos, P. (Eds.). (2009). Web 2.0 The Business Model. Springer.

Lyu, S., & Hwang, J. (2015). Are The Days of Tourist Information Centers Gone? Effects of the Ubiquitous Information Environment. *Tourism Management*, *48*, 54–63. doi:10.1016/j.tourman.2014.11.001

Madak, S. S., & Salepçioğlu, M. A. (2020). Türk sivil havacılık sektöründe yolcu memnuniyeti ve sadakat ilişkisi: Türk havayolları örnek çalışması. *İstanbul Ticaret Üniversitesi Sosyal Bilimler Dergisi*, *19*(37), 569-592.

Magano, J., & Cunha, M. N. (2020). Digital marketing impact on tourism in Portugal: A quantitative study. *African Journal of Hospitality, Tourism and Leisure*, 1–19.

Maglio, P. P., & Spohrer, J. (2008). Fundamentals of service science. *Journal of the Academy of Marketing Science*, *36*(1), 18–20. doi:10.100711747-007-0058-9

Majhi, S. K. (2019). Fuzzy clustering algorithm based on modified whale optimization algorithm for automobile insurance fraud detection. *Evolutionary Intelligence*, *14*(1), 35–46. doi:10.1007/S12065-019-00260-3

Malär, L., Krohmer, H., Hoyer, W., & Nyffenegger, B. (2011). Emotional brand attachment and brand personality: The relative importance of the actual and the ideal self. *Journal of Marketing*, *75*(4), 35–52. doi:10.1509/jmkg.75.4.35

Mangion, M. L., Durbarry, R., & Sinclair, M. T. (2005). Tourism competitiveness: Price and quality. *Tourism Economics*, *11*(1), 45–68. doi:10.5367/0000000053297202

Manosso, F. C., Ruiz, T. C. D., & Nakatani, M. S. M. (2020). A aplicação do Storytelling nas pesquisas em Turismo: Uma Revisão Bibliométrica, Sistemática e Integrativa da Literatura. *Revista de Turismo Contemporâneo*, *8*(2), 337–358. doi:10.21680/2357-8211.2020v8n2ID16465

Maric, D. M. V., Maric, R., & Dimitrovski, D. (2016). Analysis of Tangible and Intangible HotelnService Quality Components. *Industrija*, *44*(1), 7–25. doi:10.5937/industrija1-8437

Markham-Bagnera, S. (2016). *An examination of online ratings on performance indicators: An analysis of the Boston hotel market*. Iowa State University.

Martilla, J. A., & James, J. C. (1977). Importance-Performance Analysis. *Journal of Marketing*, *41*(1), 77–79. doi:10.1177/002224297704100112

Martínez-Cañas, R., Ruiz-Palomino, P., Linuesa-Langreo, J., & Blázquez-Resino, J. (2016). Consumer participation in co-creation: An enlightening model of causes and effects based on ethical values and transcendent motives. *Frontiers in Psychology*, *7*(793). Advance online publication. doi:10.3389/fpsyg.2016.00793 PMID:27303349

Martinez-Hernandez, V. (2003). *Understanding Value Creation: The Value Matrix And The Value Cube* (Doctoral Thesis). University of Strathclyde.

Martínez-Román, J. A., Tamayo, J. A., Gamero, J., & Romero, J. E. (2015). Innovativeness and business performances in tourism SMEs. *Annals of Tourism Research*, *54*, 118–135. doi:10.1016/j.annals.2015.07.004

Martino, F., & Spoto, A. (2006). Social Network Analysis: A brief theoretical review and further perspectives in the study of Information Technology. *PsychNology Journal*, *4*, 53–86.

Masco, J. (2017). The Crisis in Crisis. *Current Anthropology*, *58*(S15), S65–S76.

Matos, A., Pinto, B., Barros, F., Martins, S., Martins, J., & Au-Yong-Oliveira, M. (2019). Smart cities and smart tourism: what future they bring? In Á. Rocha, H. Adeli, L. P. Reis, & S. Costanzo (Eds.), New knowledge in information systems and technologies. Springer.

Matthing, J., Sanden, B., & Edvardsson, B. (2004). New service development: Learning from and with customers. *International Journal of Service Industry Management*, *15*(5), 479–498. doi:10.1108/09564230410564948

Mattila, A. (2006). How Affective Commitment Boosts Guest Loyalty (and Promotes Frequent-guest Programs). *The Cornell Hotel and Restaurant Administration Quarterly*, *47*(2), 174–181. doi:10.1177/0010880405283943

Matzler, K., Sauerwein, E., & Heischmidt, K. A. (2003). Importance-performance analysis revisited: The role of the factor structure of customer satisfaction. *Service Industries Journal*, *23*(2), 112–129. doi:10.1080/02642060412331300912

Ma, Y., Xiang, Z., Du, Q., & Fan, W. (2018). Effects of user-provided photos on hotel review helpfulness: An analytical approach with deep leaning. *International Journal of Hospitality Management*, *71*, 120–131. https://doi.org/10.1016/j.ijhm.2017.12.008

Mayer, N. (2015). *Online reputations Why hotel reviews matter and how hotels respond*. PWC.

Mbunge, E., Makuyana, R., Chirara, N., & Chingosho, A. (n.d.). Fraud Detection in E-Transactions using Deep Neural Networks-A Case of Financial Institutions in Zimbabwe Cite this paper Fraud Detection in E-Transactions using Deep Neural Networks-A Case of Financial Institutions in Zimbabwe. *International Journal of Science and Research, 17*(2). doi:10.21275/ART20176804

Mbunge, E., Vheremu, F., & Kajiva, K. (2017). A Tool to Predict the Possibility of Social Unrest Using Sentiments Analysis-Case of Zimbabwe Politics 2017-2018. *International Journal of Science and Research, 6*. doi:10.21275/ART20177198

Mbunge, E. (2020). Integrating emerging technologies into COVID-19 contact tracing: Opportunities, challenges and pitfalls. *Diabetes & Metabolic Syndrome*, *14*(6), 1631–1636. doi:10.1016/j.dsx.2020.08.029 PMID:32892060

Mbunge, E., Jiyane, S., & Muchemwa, B. (2022). Towards emotive sensory Web in virtual health care: Trends, technologies, challenges and ethical issues. *Sensors International*, *3*, 100134. doi:10.1016/j.sintl.2021.100134

Mbunge, E., Simelane, S., Fashoto, S. G., Akinnuwesi, B., & Metfula, A. S. (2021). Application of deep learning and machine learning models to detect COVID-19 face masks - A review. *Sustainable Operations and Computers*, *2*, 235–245. doi:10.1016/j.susoc.2021.08.001

McCrindle, M. (2018). *The ABC of XYZ: Understanding the Global Generations*. McCrindle Research.

McKee, D., Simmers, C. S., & Licata, J. (2006). Customer self-efficacy and response to service. *Journal of Service Research*, *8*(3), 207–220. doi:10.1177/1094670505282167

McKinsey. (2020). *Beyond coronavirus: The path to the next normal*. https://www.mckinsey.com/industries/healthcare-systems-and-services/our-insights/beyond-coronavirus-the-path-to-the-next-normal

Mehraliyev, F., Chan, I. C. C., Choi, Y., Köseoglu, M., & Law, R. (2020). A state-of-the-art review of smart tourism research. *Journal of Travel & Tourism Marketing*, *37*(1), 78–91. doi:10.1080/10548408.2020.1712309

Melián-González, S., Bulchand-Gidumal, J., & López-Valcárcel, B. (2013). Online Customer Reviews of Hotels: As Participation Increases, Better Evaluation Is Obtained. *Cornell Hospitality Quarterly*, *54*(3), 274–283. doi:10.1177/1938965513481498

Melián-González, S., Gutiérrez-Taño, D., & Bulchand-Gidumal, J. (2019). Predicting the intentions to use chatbots for travel and tourism. *Current Issues in Tourism*, 1–19.

Meng, Y. (2020). *The hospitality way of survival after Covid-19 crisis*. Retrieved from the École Hôtelière de Lausanne website: https://hospitalityinsights.ehl.edu/hospitality-covid19-crisis

Merricks, W. J. (2019). Politicising smart cities standards. In C. Coletta, L. Evans, L. Heaphy, & R. Kitchin (Eds.), *Creating smart cities* (pp. 33–48). Routledge.

Meuter, M. L., Ostrom, A. L., Roundtree, R. I., & Bitner, M. J. (2000). Self-Service Technologies: Understanding Customer Satisfaction with Technology-Based Service Encounters. *Journal of Marketing*, *64*(3), 50–64. doi:10.1509/jmkg.64.3.50.18024

Miah, S. J., Vu, H. Q., Gammack, J., & McGrath, M. (2017). A Big Data Analytics Method for Tourist Behaviour Analysis. *Information & Management*, *54*(6), 771–785. doi:10.1016/j.im.2016.11.011

Milán-García, J., Uribe-Toril, J., Ruiz-Real, J. L., & de Pablo Valenciano, J. (2019). Sustainable Local Development: An Overview of the State of Knowledge. *Resources*, *8*(1), 31. doi:10.3390/resources8010031

Militante, S. V., & Dionisio, N. V. (2020). Deep Learning Implementation of Facemask and Physical Distancing Detection with Alarm Systems. *Proceeding - 2020 3rd International Conference on Vocational Education and Electrical Engineering: Strengthening the Framework of Society 5.0 through Innovations in Education, Electrical, Engineering and Informatics Engineering, ICVEE 2020*. 10.1109/ICVEE50212.2020.9243183

Mindrut, S., Manolica, A., & Roman, C. (2015). Building brands identity. *Procedia Economics and Finance*, *20*(15), 393–403. doi:10.1016/S2212-5671(15)00088-X

Min, H., Lim, Y., & Magnini, V. (2014). Factors Affecting Customer Satisfaction in Responses to Negative Online Hotel Reviews: The Impact of Empathy, Paraphrasing and Speed. *Cornell Hospitality Quarterly*, *56*(2), 223–231. doi:10.1177/1938965514560014

Mitchell, A. (1983). *The Nine American Lifestyles: Who We Are & Where We Are Going*. Warner.

Mkwizu, K. H. (2020). *Digital marketing and tourism: opportunities for Africa*. International Hospitality Review.

Mohammed, A. A., & Rashid, B. (2012). Customer relationship management (CRM) in hotel industry: A framework proposal on the relationship among CRM dimensions, marketing capabilities, and hotel performance. *International Review of Management and Marketing*, *2*(4), 220–230.

Mohammed, A. A., Rashid, B., & Tahir, S. (2014). Customer relationship management (CRM) technology and organization performance: Is marketing capability a missing link? An empirical study in the Malaysian hotel industry. *Asian Social Science*, *10*(9), 197–212. doi:10.5539/ass.v10n9p197

Mohd-Any, A. A., Winklhofer, H., & Ennew, C. (2014). Measuring Users' Value Experience on a Travel Website (e-Value): What Value Is Cocreated by the User? *Journal of Travel Research*, *54*(4), 496–510. doi:10.1177/0047287514522879

Moreira, R. S. (2019). Já não cabem mais Airbnb em Lisboa. *O Jornal Económico*. Acessed 19th May, 2020 from: https://jornaleconomico.sapo.pt/noticias/ja-nao-cabem-mais-airbnb-em-lisboa-451783

Moreira, A., Fortes, N., & Santiago, R. (2017). Influence of sensory stimuli on brand experience, brand equity and purchase intention. *Journal of Business Economics and Management*, *18*(1), 68–83. doi:10.3846/16111699.2016.1252793

Morgan, M., Lugosi, P., & Ritchie, J. B. (Eds.). (2010). The tourism and leisure experience: Consumer and managerial perspectives. Channel View Publication.

Morosan, C., & DeFranco, A. (2016). It's About Time: Revisiting UTAUT2 to Examine Consumers' Intentions to Use NFC Mobile Payments in Hotels. *International Journal of Hospitality Management*, *53*, 17–29. doi:10.1016/j.ijhm.2015.11.003

Mostafa, L. (2020). Machine Learning-Based Sentiment Analysis for Analyzing the Travelers Reviews on Egyptian Hotels. *Advances in Intelligent Systems and Computing*, *1153*, 405–413. doi:10.1007/978-3-030-44289-7_38

Moudud-Ul-Huq, S., Akter, R., Mahmud, M. S., & Hasan, N. (2021). Impact of Customer Relationship Management on Tourist Satisfaction, Loyalty, and Retention: Saint Martin's Island. *International Journal of Customer Relationship Marketing and Management*, *12*(3), 20–37. doi:10.4018/IJCRMM.2021070102

Mubarak, A. A., Cao, H., & Ahmed, S. A. M. (2021). Predictive learning analytics using deep learning model in MOOCs' courses videos. *Education and Information Technologies*, *26*(1), 371–392. doi:10.100710639-020-10273-6

Mullis, M. (2018). *Generational Travel Differences: 4 Insights And 4 Surprises*. https://www.wexinc.com/insights/blog/wex-travel/generational-travel-differences/

Murdy, S., & Pike, S. (2012). Perceptions of visitor relationship marketing opportunities by destination marketers: An importance-performance analysis. *Tourism Management*, *33*(5), 1281–1285. doi:10.1016/j.tourman.2011.11.024

Murphy, C. (2016). *5 Hotel Online Reputation Mistakes You Might Be Making*. Disponível em: https://www.revinate.com/blog/2016/08/5-hotel-onlinereputationmistakes-might-making/

Murphy, H. C., Chen, M.-M., & Cossutta, M. (2016). An Investigation of Multiple Devices and Information Sources Used in the Hotel Booking Process. *Tourism Management*, *52*, 44–51. doi:10.1016/j.tourman.2015.06.004

Naidoo, P., Ramseook-Munhurrun, P., Seebaluck, N., & Janvier, S. (2015). Investigating the Motivation of Baby Boomers For Adventure Tourism. *Social and Behavioral Sciences*, *175*, 254–251. doi:10.1016/j.sbspro.2015.01.1197

Nakanishi, J. (2018). *Can a Humanoid Robot Engage in Heartwarming Interaction Service at a Hotel?* ACM. doi:10.1145/3284432.3284448

Nam, J., Ekinci, Y., & Whyatt, G. (2011). Brand equity, brand loyalty and consumer satisfaction. *Annals of Tourism Research*, *38*(3), 1009–1030. doi:10.1016/j.annals.2011.01.015

Nastasoiu, A., & Vandenbosch, M. (2018). Competing with loyalty: How to design successful customer loyalty reward programs. *Business Horizons*.

Nayyar, A., Mahapatra, B., Le, D., & Suseendran, G. (2018). Virtual Reality (VR) & Augmented Reality (AR) technologies for tourism and hospitality industry. *IACSIT International Journal of Engineering and Technology*, *7*(2.21), 156–160. doi:10.14419/ijet.v7i2.21.11858

Neirotti, P., Raguseo, E. & Paolucci, E. (2016). Are customers' reviews creating value in the hospitality industry? Exploring the moderating effects of market positioning. *International Journal of Information Management, 36*(6), 1133-1143.

Ngai, E. W. T. (2005). Customer relationship management research (1992–2002): An academic literature review and classification. *Marketing Intelligence & Planning*, *23*(6), 582–605. doi:10.1108/02634500510624147

Ngo, M. V., Pavelkova, D., Phan, Q. P. T., & Nguyen, N. V. (2018). Customer relationship management (CRM) in small and medium tourism enterprises: A dynamic capabilities perspective. *Tourism and Hospitality Management*, *24*(1), 63–86. doi:10.20867/thm.24.1.11

Nicolás, E. S. (2020, April 22). EU pledges help, as tourism faces €400bn hit. *EU Observer*. https://euobserver.com/coronavirus/148137

Nikoli, G., & Lazakidou, A. (2019). The Impact of Information and Communication Technology on the Tourism Sector. *Almatourism-Journal of Tourism, Culture and Territorial Development*, *10*(19), 45–68.

Nilashi, M., Yadegaridehkordi, E., Ibrahim, O., Samad, S., Ahani, A., & Sanzogni, L. (2019a). Analysis of Travelers' Online Reviews in Social Networking Sites Using Fuzzy Logic Approach. *International Journal of Fuzzy Systems*, *21*(5), 1367–1378. doi:10.1007/S40815-019-00630-0

Nilashi, M., Bagherifard, K., Rahmani, M., & Rafe, V. (2017). A recommender system for tourism industry using cluster ensemble and prediction machine learning techniques. *Computers & Industrial Engineering*, *109*, 357–368. doi:10.1016/j.cie.2017.05.016

Nilashi, M., Samad, S., Ahani, A., Ahmadi, H., Alsolami, E., Mahmoud, M., Majeed, H. D., & Abdulsalam Alarood, A. (2021). Travellers decision making through preferences learning: A case on Malaysian spa hotels in TripAdvisor. *Computers & Industrial Engineering*, *158*, 107348. doi:10.1016/j.cie.2021.107348

Nilashi, M., Yadegaridehkordi, E., Ibrahim, O., Samad, S., Ahani, A., & Sanzogni, L. (2019b). Analysis of Travelers' Online Reviews in Social Networking Sites Using Fuzzy Logic Approach. *International Journal of Fuzzy Systems*, *21*(5), 1367–1378. https://doi.org/10.1007/s40815-019-00630-0

Njite, D., & Schaffer, J. (2017). Revisiting Attributes: How Important Is Green in the Consumer Selection of Hotel Rooms? *International Journal of Hospitality & Tourism Administration*, *18*(2), 219–244. doi:10.1080/15256480.2016.1263168

Noone, B., & Robson, S. (2014). Using Eye Tracking to Obtain a Deeper Understanding of What Drives Online Hotel Choice. *Cornell Hospitality Report*, *14*(18). www.chr.cornell.edu

O'Leary, N. (2020, December 15). *Portugal stands by €11m annual fee to host Web Summit*. Retrieved June 29, 2021, from https://www.irishtimes.com/business/technology/portugal-stands-by-11m-annual-fee-to-host-web-summit-1.4436786

O'Neill, J., & Xiao, Q. (2006). The Role of Brand Affiliation in Hotel Market Value. *Cornell Hospitality Quarterly*, *47*(3), 210–223. doi:10.1177/0010880406289070

Observatório. (2017). *Observatório do Turismo de Lisboa – Dados de novembro 2017*. Disponível em: https://www.visitlisboa.com/sites/default/files/2018- 01/RTL168-OBS.pdf

OECD. (2020). *Main Science and Technology Indicators, Volume 2020 Issue 1*. OECD.

OECD. (2020). *OECD Tourism Trends and Policies 2020, Chapter 2, Preparing tourism services for the digital future*. https://www.oecd-ilibrary.org/sites/f528d444-en/index.html?itemId=/content/component/f528d444-en

Ogut, H., & Cezar, A. (2012). *Prosumer motivations for electronic word-of-mouth communication behaviors*. Procedia.

Oh, H. (2001). Revisiting importance – performance analysis. *Tourism Management*, *22*(6), 617–627. doi:10.1016/S0261-5177(01)00036-X

Okumus, B., & Bilgihan, A. (2014). Proposing a Model to Test Smartphone Users' Intention to Use Smart Applications When Ordering Food in Restaurants. *Journal of Hospitality and Tourism Technology*, *5*(1), 31–49. doi:10.1108/JHTT-01-2013-0003

Olifer, N., & Olifer, V. (2006). *Computer Networks, Principles, Technologies and Protocol for Network Design.* John Wiley and Sons Ltd.

Oliver, R. L. (2010). *Satisfaction: A Behavioral Perspective on the Consumer.* Routledge.

Organisation for Economic Co-operation and Development (OECD). (2021). *Rebuilding tourism for the future: COVID-19 policy responses and recovery.* https://www.oecd-ilibrary.org/social-issues-migration-health/rebuilding-tourism-for-the-future-covid-19-policy-responses-and-recovery_bced9859-en

Ostrom, A. L., Parasuraman, A., Bowen, D. E., Patrício, L., Voss, C. A., & Lemon, K. (2015). Service research priorities in a rapidly changing context. *Journal of Service Research, 18*(2), 127–159. doi:10.1177/1094670515576315

Özdemir Akgül, S., & Sezgin, M. (2019). Konaklama İşletmelerinde Yeni Bir Yaklaşım Nöroturizm: Yerli ve Yabancı Turist Algısı Üzerine Bir Araştırma. *Journal of Recreation and Tourism Research*, 70-80.

Ozdipciner, N., Li, X., & Uysal, M. (2012). Cross-cultural differences in purchase decision-making criteria. *International Journal of Culture, Tourism and Hospitality Research, 4*(4), 340–351.

Özer, S. U. (2015). İstanbul'da faaliyet gösteren beş yıldızlı otel işletmelerinin müşteri sadakat programlarının içerik analizi. *Ekonomi ve Yönetim Araştırmaları Dergisi, 4*(1), 134–157.

Paas, L., & Kuijlen, T. (2001). Towards a general definition of customer relationship management. *Journal of Database Marketing & Customer Strategy Management, 9*(1), 51–60. doi:10.1057/palgrave.jdm.3240058

Padma, P. (2016). Strategic quadrants and service quality: Tourist satisfaction in Portugal. *The Quality Management Journal, 23*(2), 57–70. doi:10.1080/10686967.2016.11918471

Palumbo, F., Dominici, G., & Basile, G. (2014). The Culture on the Palm of Your Hand: How to Design a User Oriented Mobile App for Museums. In Management of cultural products: e-relationship marketing and accessibility perspectives (pp. 224-243). IGI Global.

Pamukçu, H., & Tanrısever, C. (2019). Turizm Endüstrisinde Dijital Dönüşüm. M. Sezgin, S. Özdemir Akgül, & A. Atar. In *Turizm 4.0 (Dijital Dönüşüm)* (pp. 2–22). Detay.

Pan, B., & Zhang, L. (2016). An Eyetracking Study on Online Hotel Decision Making: The Effects of Images and Umber of Options. *Travel and Tourism Research Association: Advancing Tourism Research Globally, 27.*

Pan, S.-Y., Gao, M., Kim, H., Shah, K. J., Pei, S.-L., & Chiang, P.-C. (2018). Advances and challenges in sustainable tourism toward a green economy. *The Science of the Total Environment, 635*, 452–469. doi:10.1016/j.scitotenv.2018.04.134 PMID:29677671

Papadopoulos, N., & Hamzaoui-Essoussi, L. (2015). Place Images and Nation Branding in the African Context: Challenges, Opportunities, and Questions for Policy and Research. *Africa Journal of Management, 1*(1), 54–77. doi:10.1080/23322373.2015.994423

Parasuraman, A., Zeithaml, V. A., & Berry, L. L. (1985). A Conceptual Model Service Its Quality and Implications for Future Research. *Research Paper, 49*(4), 41–50. doi:10.1016/S0148-2963(99)00084-3

Park, S. (2018). *Comparing Self-Service Technologies and Human Interaction Services in the Hotel Industry* (Masters Thesis). University of Central Florida.

Park, E., Park, J., & Hu, M. (2021). Tourism demand forecasting with online news data mining. *Annals of Tourism Research, 90*, 103273. doi:10.1016/j.annals.2021.103273

Park, J. H., Lee, C., Yoo, C., & Nam, Y. (2016). An analysis of the utilization of facebook by local Korean governments for tourism development and the network of smart tourism ecosystem. *International Journal of Information Management*, *36*(6), 1320–1327. doi:10.1016/j.ijinfomgt.2016.05.027

Park, S., & Allen, J. (2013). Responding to Online Reviews: Problem Solving and Engagement in Hotels. *Cornell Hospitality Quarterly*, *54*(1), 64–73. doi:10.1177/1938965512463118

Parvatiyar, A., & Sheth, J. N. (2000). Conceptual framework of customer relationship management. In *Proceedings of International Conference on Customer Relationship Management*. Management Development Institute Press.

Parviainen, P., Tihinen, M., Kääriäinen, J., & Teppola, S. (2017). Tackling the digitalization challenge: How to benefit from digitalization in practice. *International Journal of İnformation Systems and Project Management*, *5*(1), 63–77. doi:10.12821/ijispm050104

Patandianan, M. V., & Shibusawa, H. (2020). Importance and performance of streetscapes at a tourism destination in Indonesia: The residents' perspectives. *Frontiers of Architectural Research*, *9*(3), 641–655. doi:10.1016/j.foar.2020.05.006

Patin, S. (2020). *Les enjeux du numérique en sciences sociales et humaines: vers un Homo numericus?* https://hal.archives-ouvertes.fr/hal-03173567

Payne, A., & Frow, P. (2005). A strategic framework for customer relationship management. *Journal of Marketing*, *69*(4), 167–176. doi:10.1509/jmkg.2005.69.4.167

Payne, A., & Holt, S. (2001). Diagnosing customer value: Integrating the value process and relationship marketing. *British Journal of Management*, *12*(2), 159–182. doi:10.1111/1467-8551.00192

Payne, A., Storbacka, K., & Frow, P. (2008). Managing the co-creation of value. *Journal of the Academy of Marketing Science*, *36*(1), 83–96. doi:10.100711747-007-0070-0

Pearce, P., & Benckendorff, P. (2006). Journal of Quality Assurance in Hospitality & Tourism Benchmarking, Usable Knowledge and Tourist Attractions. *Journal of Quality Assurance in Hospitality & Tourism*, *7*(1–2), 29–52. doi:10.1300/J162v07n01_03

Pellegrin, H. (2018). *Cirkwi: L'agrégateur de données spécifiques au Tourisme.* https://www.tom.travel/2018/03/07/cirkwi-lagregateur-de-donnees-specifiques-tourisme/

Peltomäk, S. M. (2015). *Crises in the Tourism Industry and Their Effects on Different* (Master Thesis). HAAGA-HELIA University of Applied Sciences.

Pencarelli, T. (2020). The digital revolution in the travel and tourism industry. *Information Technology & Tourism*, *22*(3), 455–476. doi:10.100740558-019-00160-3

Pérez, Y. P., & Barreiro, D. B. (2019). Using big data to measure tourist sustainability: Myth or reality? *Sustainability*, *11*(20).

Perianes-Rodriguez, A., Waltman, L., & van Eck, N. J. (2016). Constructing bibliometric networks: A comparison between full and fractional counting. *Journal of Informetrics*, *10*(4), 1178–1195. doi:10.1016/j.joi.2016.10.006

Perkins, B., & Fenech, C. (2014). *The deloitte consumer review: The growing power consumers.* Deloitte.

Perloiro, T. (2016). *O impacto do alojamento local na reabilitaçãoo urbana em Lisboa* (Master's degree thesis). Instituto Superior Técnico, Lisboa, Portugal.

Phillips, C. A., & Langston, M. A. (2019). A robustness metric for biological data clustering algorithms. *BMC Bioinformatics*, *20*(15), 1–8. doi:10.1186/S12859-019-3089-6

Picazo-Vela, S. (2009). The Effect of Online Reviews on Customer Satisfaction: An Expectation Disconfirmation Approach. *AMCIS 2009 Doctoral Consortium.*

Piccialli, F., Giampaolo, F., Casolla, G., Di Cola, V. S., & Li, K. (2020). A Deep Learning approach for Path Prediction in a Location-based IoT system. *Pervasive and Mobile Computing, 66,* 101210. doi:10.1016/j.pmcj.2020.101210

Pillai, S. G., Kavitha, H., Seo, W. S., & Kim, W. G. (2021). COVID-19 and hospitality 5.0: Redefining hospitality operations. *International Journal of Hospitality Management, 94*(3). Advance online publication. doi:10.1016/j.ijhm.2021.102869

Pine, J., & Gilmore, J. (1998). Welcome to the experience economy. *Harvard Business Review,* 97–105. PMID:10181589

Pinillos, R., Marcos, S., Feliz, R., Zalama, E., & Gómez-García-Bermejo, J. (2016). Long-term assessment of a service robot in a hotel environment. *Robotics and Autonomous Systems, 79,* 1–60. doi:10.1016/j.robot.2016.01.014

Piteira, M., Aparicio, M., & Costa, C. J. (2019). A Ética na Inteligência Artificial: Desafios. Institute of Electrical and Electronics Engineers.

Pizam, A., Shapoval, V., & Ellis, T. (2013). Customer satisfaction and its measurement in hospitality enterprises: A revisit and update. *International Journal of Contemporary Hospitality Management, 28*(1), 2–35. doi:10.1108/IJCHM-04-2015-0167

Plaster, G., & Alderman, J. (2006). Customer value creation: A platform for profitable growth. *Charter Consulting,* 1-7.

Polese, F., Botti, A., Grimaldi, M., Monda, A., & Vesci, M. (2018). Social innovation in smart tourism ecosystems: How technology and institutions shape sustainable value co-creation. *Sustainability, 10*(1), 140. doi:10.3390u10010140

Polyzos, S., Samitas, A., & Spyridou, A. E. (2020). *Tourism demand and the COVID-19 pandemic: an LSTM approach.* Https://Doi.Org/10.1080/02508281.2020.1777053 doi:10.1080/02508281.2020.1777053

Pongsakornrungsilp, S., & Schroeder, J. E. (2011). Understanding value co-creation in a co-consuming brand community. *Marketing Theory, 11*(3), 303–324. doi:10.1177/1470593111408178

Ponomariov, B. L., & Boardman, P. C. (2010). Influencing scientists' collaboration and productivity patterns through new institutions: University research centers and scientific and technical human capital. *Research Policy, 39*(5), 613–624. doi:10.1016/j.respol.2010.02.013

Popat, K. A., & Sharma, P. (2013). Wearable Computer Applications. *International Journal of Engineering and Innovative Technology, 3*(1), 213–217.

Popp, B., & Woratschek, H. (2017). Consumers' relationships with brands and brand communities - The multifaceted roles of identification and satisfaction. *Journal of Retailing and Consumer Services, 35,* 46–56. doi:10.1016/j.jretconser.2016.11.006

Porter, M. E., & Heppelmann, J. E. (2014). How smart, connected products are transforming competition. *Harvard Business Review, 92*(11), 64–88.

Pradhan, M. K., Oh, J., & Lee, H. (2018). Understanding travelers' behavior for sustainable smart tourism: A technology readiness perspective. *Sustainability, 10*(11), 4259. doi:10.3390u10114259

Prahalad, C. K., & Ramaswamy, V. (2000). Co-opting customer competence. *Harvard Business Review, 78*(1), 79–87.

Prahalad, C. K., & Ramaswamy, V. (2004). Co-creation experiences: The next practice in value creation. *Journal of Interactive Marketing, 18*(3), 5–14. doi:10.1002/dir.20015

Prebensen, N. K., & Foss, L. (2011). Coping and co-creating in tourist experiences. *International Journal of Tourism Research, 13*(1), 54–67. doi:10.1002/jtr.799

Publico. (2017). *Portugal eleito melhor destino no mundo.* Disponível em: https://www.publico.pt/2017/12/10/fugas/noticia/portugal-eleito-melhor-destinodomundo-1795505

PwC. (2015). *Online Reputations: Why hotel reviews matter and how hotels respond.* PwC.

Rabahy, W. A. (2020). Análise e perspectivas do turismo no Brasil. Revista Brasileira de Pesquisa em Turismo, pp. 1-13.

Radojevic, T., Stanisic, N., & Stanic, N. (2017). Inside the Rating Scores: A Multilevel Analysis of the Factors Influencing Customer Satisfaction in the Hotel Industry. *Cornell Hospitality Quarterly, 58*(2), 134–164. doi:10.1177/1938965516686114

Rahimi, R., Köseoglu, M. A., Ersoy, A. B., & Okumus, F. (2017). Customer relationship management research in tourism and hospitality: A state-of-the-art. *Tourism Review, 72*(2), 209–220. doi:10.1108/TR-01-2017-0011

Rahimi, R., & Kozak, M. (2017). Impact of customer relationship management on customer satisfaction: The case of a budget hotel chain. *Journal of Travel & Tourism Marketing, 34*(1), 40–51. doi:10.1080/10548408.2015.1130108

Rahimi, R., Nadda, V., & Wang, H. (2015). CRM in tourism: Customer relationship management (CRM). In R. Nilanjan (Ed.), *Emerging innovative marketing strategies in the tourism industry* (pp. 16–43). IGI Global. doi:10.4018/978-1-4666-8699-1.ch002

Ramaswamy, V., & Gouillart, F. (2010). *Building the co-creative enterprise.* Harvard Business Review. https://www.researchgate.net/publication/47369356_Building_the_Co-Creative_Enterprise

Ramaswamy, V. (2009). Co-Creation of value – Towards an expanded paradigm of value creation. *Marketing Review St. Gallen, 26*(6), 11–17. doi:10.100711621-009-0085-7

Ranpersad, H., Souza, G. d., & Nunes, J. (2012). Construção de marca bem-sucedida nas micro, pequenas e medidas empresas: o passo a passo para a construção de uma marca. In *J. P. Barros Neto, Manual do empreendedor: de micro a pequenas empresas* (pp. 177–205). Qualitymark.

Rascouet, A. (2019). *French 'Flying Man' Succeeds in Cross-Channel Attempt.* https://www.bloomberg.com/news/articles/2019-08-04/french-flying-man-finally-succeeds-in-cross-channel-attempt

Rašovská, I., Kubickova, M., & Ryglová, K. (2020). Importance–performance analysis approach to destination management. *Tourism Economics.* Advance online publication. doi:10.1177/1354816620903913

Ravald, A., & Grönroos, C. (1996). The value concept and relationship marketing. *European Journal of Marketing, 30*(2), 19–30. doi:10.1108/03090569610106626

Reed, D. (2019). *Most Travelers, Including Baby Boomers, Are Cool With Digital Travel Technology, But Younger Ones Crave More.* https://www.forbes.com/sites/danielreed/2019/11/05/a-large-majority-of-travelers-including-baby-boomers-are-cool-with-digital-travel-technology-but-younger-travelers-crave-even-more/?sh=4740dfdc22d0

Reichstein, C., & Härting, R. (2018). Potantials of changing customer needs in a digital world – a conceptual model and recommendations for action in tourism. *Procedia Computer Science, 126*, 1484–1494. doi:10.1016/j.procs.2018.08.120

Renjith, S., Sreekumar, A., & Jathavedan, M. (2019). Evaluation of partitioning clustering algorithms for processing social media data in tourism domain. *2018 IEEE Recent Advances in Intelligent Computational Systems, RAICS 2018*, 127–131. doi:10.1109/RAICS.2018.8635080

Renjith, S., Sreekumar, A., & Jathavedan, M. (2020a). An extensive study on the evolution of context-aware personalized travel recommender systems. *Information Processing & Management, 57*(1), 102078. https://doi.org/10.1016/J.IPM.2019.102078

Renjith, S., Sreekumar, A., & Jathavedan, M. (2020b). Performance evaluation of clustering algorithms for varying cardinality and dimensionality of data sets. *Materials Today: Proceedings, 27*, 627–633. https://doi.org/10.1016/J.MATPR.2020.01.110

Reuland, R., Coudrey, J., & Fagel, A. (1985). Research in the field of hospitality. *International Journal of Hospitality Management, 4*(4), 141–146. doi:10.1016/0278-4319(85)90051-9

Revfine. (2019). *Key Digital Trends in the Hospitality Industry*. https://www.revfine.com/digital-trends-hospitality-industry/

ReviewPro. (2011). *How to Respond to Online Reviews*. Disponível em: https://www.reviewpro.com/wp-content/uploads/pdf/en-guide-responding-reviews.pdf

Revinate. (2014). *Responding to Online Reviews: A Guide for Hoteliers*. Disponível em: https://www.revinate.com/resource/responding-online-reviewsguidehoteliers/

Reynolds, T. J. (1985). Implications for value research: A macro vs. micro perspective. *Psychology and Marketing, 2*(4), 297–305. doi:10.1002/mar.4220020408

Rhee, H., & Yang, S. (2015). Does hotel attribute importance differ by hotel? Focusing on hotel star-classifications and customers' overall ratings. *Computers in Human Behavior, 50*, 576–587. doi:10.1016/j.chb.2015.02.069

Ribes, J. F. P., & Baidal, J. I. (2018). Smart sustainability: A new perspective in the sustainable tourism debate. *Investigaciones Regionales-Journal of Regional Research*, (42), 151–170.

Rigby, D. K., Reichheld, F. F., & Schefter, P. (2002). Avoid the four perils of CRM. *Harvard Business Review, 80*(2), 101–109. PMID:11894676

Ritchie, J. R. B., & Crouch, G. I. (2003). *The Competitive Destination: A Sustainable Tourism Perspective*. CABI Pub. Retrieved from https://books.google.pt/books?id=yvydAwAAQBAJ

Rodriguez, M. Z., Comin, C. H., Casanova, D., Bruno, O. M., Amancio, D. R., Costa, L. da F., & Rodrigues, F. A. (2019). Clustering algorithms: A comparative approach. *PLoS One, 14*(1), e0210236. https://doi.org/10.1371/JOURNAL.PONE.0210236

Romanazzi, S., Petruzzellis, L., & Iannuzzi, E. (2011). "Click & experience. Just virtually there." The Effect of a Destination Website on Tourist Choice: Evidence from Italy. *Journal of Hospitality Marketing & Management, 20*(7), 791–813. doi:10.1080/19368623.2011.605037

Romão, J., & Neuts, B. (2017). Territorial capital, smart tourism specialization and sustainable regional development: Experiences from Europe. *Habitat International, 68*, 64–74. doi:10.1016/j.habitatint.2017.04.006

Roma, P., Panniello, U., & Lo Nigro, G. (2019). Sharing economy and incumbents' pricing strategy: The impact of Airbnb on the hospitality industry. *International Journal of Production Economics, 214*, 17–29. doi:10.1016/j.ijpe.2019.03.023

Rose, M. & Blodgett, J. G. (2016). Should Hotels Respond to Negative Online Reviews? *Cornell Hospitality Quarterly, 57*(4), 396-410.

Rosenbaum, M. S., Ramirez, G. C., Campbell, J., & Klaus, P. (2021). The product is me: Hyper-personalized consumer goods as unconventional luxury. *Journal of Business Research, 129*, 446–454. doi:10.1016/j.jbusres.2019.05.017

Royal Schiphol Group. (2018). Value Creation Model. Annual Report 2018. Author.

Ruel, H., & Njoku, E. (2020). AI redefining the hospitality industry. *Journal of Tourism Futures.*

Rust, R. T., & Huang, M.-H. (2014). The service revolution and the transformation of marketing science. *Marketing Science, 33*(2), 206–221. doi:10.1287/mksc.2013.0836

Rutty, M., Gössling, S., Scott, D., & Hall, C. M. (2015). The global eff ects and impacts of tourism: an overview. In S. G. C. M. Hall & D. Scott (Eds.), *The Routledge handbook of tourism and sustainability* (pp. 36–63). Routledge.

Ryals, L. (2005). Making customer relationship management work: The measurement and profitable management of customer relationships. *Journal of Marketing, 69*(4), 252–261. doi:10.1509/jmkg.2005.69.4.252

Ryals, L., & Knox, S. (2001). Cross-functional issues in the implementation of relationship marketing through customer relationship management. *European Management Journal, 19*(5), 534–542. doi:10.1016/S0263-2373(01)00067-6

Saarijärvi, H., Kannan, P. K., & Kuusela, H. (2013). Value co-creation: Theoretical approaches and practical implications. *European Business Review, 25*(1), 6–19. doi:10.1108/09555341311287718

Sabah Gazetesi. (2021). *Başkentin ilk dijital turizm rehberi.* https://www.sabah.com.tr/ankara/2021/05/05/baskentin-ilk-dijital-turizm-rehberi

Sahadev, S., & Islam, N. (2005). Why hotels adopt ICTs: A study on the ICT adoption propensity of hotels in Thailand. *International Journal of Contemporary Hospitality Management, 17*(5), 391–401. doi:10.1108/09596110510604814

Salazar, A., Costa, J., & Rita, P. (2010). A service quality evaluation scale for the hospitality sector: Dimensions, attributes and behavioural intentions. *Worldwide Hospitality and Tourism Themes, 2*(4), 383–397. doi:10.1108/17554211011074047

Salwani, I. S., Marthandan, G., Norzaidi, M. D., & Chong, S. C. (2009). E- Commerce usage and business performance in the Malaysian tourism sector: Empirical analysis. *Information Management & Computer Security, 17*(2), 166–185. doi:10.1108/09685220910964027

Sanbonmatsu, D. M., Kardes, F. R., Houghton, D. C., Ho, E. A., & Posavac, S. S. (2003). Overestimating the Importance of the Given Information in Multiattribute Consumer Judgment. *Journal of Consumer Psychology, 13*(3), 289–300. doi:10.1207/S15327663JCP1303_10

Sánchez-Fernández, R., & Iniesta-Bonillo, M. (2007). The concept of perceived value: A systematic review of the research. *Marketing Theory Articles, 7*(4), 427–451. doi:10.1177/1470593107083165

Sánchez-Medina, A. J., & C-Sánchez, E. (2020). Using machine learning and big data for efficient forecasting of hotel booking cancellations. *International Journal of Hospitality Management, 89,* 102546. doi:10.1016/j.ijhm.2020.102546

Sarantakos, S. (2013). *Social Research* (4th ed.). Palgrave Macmillian. doi:10.1007/978-1-137-29247-6

Sarı Çallı, D. (2015). Uluslararası Seyahatlerin Tarihi Gelişimi ve Son Seyehat Trendleri Doğrultusunda Türkiye'nin Konumu. *Turizm ve Araştırma Dergisi, 4*(1), 5–28.

Sarışık & Batman. (2014). *Sık uçan yolcu programlarının müşteri sadakati üzerindeki etkisi: Thy miles&smiles uygulaması ve kullanıcıları örneği. In Uluslararası Türk Dünyası Sosyal Bilimler Kongresi.* Türk Dünyası Araştırmaları Vakfı Yayınları.

Sarı, Y. (2003). *Bölgesel Düzeyde Hazırlanan Web Sitelerinin Turizm Talebine Etkisinin Araştırılması: Muğla Bölgesinde Bir Uygulama. Doktora Tezi.* Muğla Üniversitesi, Sosyal Bilimler Enstitüsü, İktisat Ana Bilim Dalı.

Sarı, Y., & Kozak, M. (2005). Turizm Pazarlamasında İnternetin Etkisi: Destinasyon Web Siteleri İçin Bir Model Önerisi. *Akdeniz İ.İ.B.F. Dergisi, 9,* 248–27.

Sassmannshausen, S. P., & Volkmann, C. (2018). The scientometrics of social entrepreneurship and its establishment as an academic field. *Journal of Small Business Management*, *56*(2), 251–273. doi:10.1111/jsbm.12254

Saturnino, R., & Souse, H. (2019). Hosting as a lifestyle: The case of Airbnb digital platform and Lisbon hosts. *The Open Journal of Sociopolitical Studies*, *12*(3), 794-818.

Savić, J., & Pavlović, G. (2018). Analysis of factors of smart tourism development in Serbia. *Hotel and Tourism Management*, *6*(1), 81–91. doi:10.5937/menhottur1801081S

Scaglione, M., Schegg, R., & Murphy, J. (2009). Website adoption and sales performance in Valais' hospitality industry. *Technovation*, *29*(1), 625–631. doi:10.1016/j.technovation.2009.05.011

Schierholz, R., Kolbe, L. M., & Brenner, W. (2007). Mobilizing customer relationship management: A journey from strategy to system design. *Business Process Management Journal*, *13*(6), 830–852. doi:10.1108/14637150710834587

Schmitt, B. (2012). Brand insights from psychological and neurophysiological perspectives. *Journal of Consumer Psychology*, *22*, 7–17. doi:10.1016/j.jcps.2011.09.005

Schuckert, M., Liu, X., & Law, R. (2015). Hospitality and tourism online reviews. Recent trends and future directions. *Journal of Travel & Tourism Marketing*, *32*(5), 608–621. doi:10.1080/10548408.2014.933154

Scott, D., Gössling, S., Hall, C. M., & Peeters, P. (2016). Can tourism be part of the decarbonized global economy? The costs and risks of alternate carbon reduction policy pathways. *Journal of Sustainable Tourism*, *24*(1), 52–72.

Scott, D., Hall, C. M., & Gössling, S. (2016). A review of the IPCC Fifth Assessment and implications for tourism sector climate resilience and decarbonization. *Journal of Sustainable Tourism*, *24*(1), 8–30.

Seemiller, G. (2017). *Generation Z: Educating and Engaging the Next Generation of Students*. https://journals.sagepub.com/doi/pdf/10.1002/abc.21293

Serrat, O. (2009). *Social Network Analysis*. Academic Press.

Sever, I. (2015). Importance-performance analysis: A valid management tool? *Tourism Management*, *48*, 43–53. doi:10.1016/j.tourman.2014.10.022

Seyitoğlu, F., & Ivanov, S. (2020). A conceptual framework of the service delivery system design for hospitality firms in the (post-)viral world: The role of service robots. *International Journal of Hospitality Management*, *91*, 1–10. doi:10.1016/j.ijhm.2020.102661 PMID:32952262

Shafiee, S., Ghatari, A. R., Hasanzadeh, A., & Jahanyan, S. (2019). Developing a model for sustainable smart tourism destinations: A systematic review. *Tourism Management Perspectives*, *31*, 287–300. doi:10.1016/j.tmp.2019.06.002

Sharma, G. D., Thomas, A., & Paul, J. (2021). Reviving tourism industry post-COVID-19: A resilience-based framework. *Tourism Management Perspectives*, *37*, 100786. https://doi.org/10.1016/j.tmp.2020.100786

Sharma, S., & Conduit, J. (2016). Cocreation culture in health care organizations. *Journal of Service Research*, *19*(4), 438–457. doi:10.1177/1094670516666369

Shehab, E. M., Sharp, M. W., Supramaniam, L., & Spedding, T. A. (2004). Enterprise resource planning: An integrative review. *Business Process Management Journal*, *10*(4), 359–386. doi:10.1108/14637150410548056

Shell. (2021). *Video ads of Shell Oil Company in Turkey for sustainable contactless technologies*. https://www.shell.com.tr/suruculer/engin-akyurek-shellde-kalitesinin-verdigi-guvenle-shell-hep-ileride.html

Shen, S., Sotiriadis, M., & Zhou, Q. (2020). Could smart tourists be sustainable and responsible as well? The Contribution of Social Networking Sites to Improving Their Sustainable and Responsible Behavior. *Sustainability*, *12*(4), 1470. doi:10.3390u12041470

Sigala, M. (2014). Collaborative commerce in tourism: Implication for research and industry. *Current Issues in Tourism*, *20*(4), 346-355.

Sigala, M. (2003). Developing and Benchmarking Internet Marketing Strategies in the Hotel Sector in Greece. *Journal of Hospitality & Tourism Research (Washington, D.C.)*, *27*(4), 375–401. doi:10.1177/10963480030274001

Sigala, M. (2020). Tourism and COVID-19: Impacts and implications for advancing and resetting industry and research. *Journal of Business Research*, *117*, 312–321. doi:10.1016/j.jbusResearch2020.06.015

Sigalat-Signes, E., Calvo-Palomares, R., Roig-Merino, B., & García-Adán, I. (2020). Transition towards a tourist innovation model: The smart tourism destination: Reality or territorial marketing? *Journal of Innovation & Knowledge*, *5*(2), 96–104. doi:10.1016/j.jik.2019.06.002

Simpson, G. D., Patroni, J., Teo, A. C. K., Chan, J. K. L., & Newsome, D. (2019). Importance-performance analysis to inform visitor management at marine wildlife tourism destinations. *Journal of Tourism Futures*, *6*(2), 165–180. doi:10.1108/JTF-11-2018-0067

Şimşek, E., & Cinnioğlu, H. (2020). Akıllı turizm destinasyonlarındaki otellerin karekod kullanımı: İstanbul Smart Beyoğlu üzerine bir araştırma [The quick response code usage of hotels in smart tourism destinations: a research on Istanbul Smart Beyoglu]. *Uluslararası Yönetim İktisat ve İşletme Dergisi*, *16*(3), 675–690. doi:10.17130/ijmeb.798489

Sirgy, M. J. (1982). Self-concept in consumer behavior: A critical review. *The Journal of Consumer Research*, *9*(3), 287–300. doi:10.1086/208924

Sirgy, M., & Su, C. (2000). Destination image, self-congruity, and travel behavior: Toward an integrative model. *Journal of Travel Research*, *88*(4), 340–352. doi:10.1177/004728750003800402

Skift. (2019). *Travel Marketing Across Generations in 2020: Reaching Gen Z, Gen X, Millennials, and Baby Boomers.* https://skift.com/2019/12/11/travel-marketing-across-generations-in-2020-reaching-gen-z-gen-x-millennials-and-baby-boomers/

Skjelvik, J., Erlandsen, A., & Haavardsholm, O. (2017). *Environmental impact and potential of the sharing economy.* Nordic Council of Ministers. Accessed 27 March 2020, from: https://norden.diva-portal.org/smash/get/diva2:1145502/FULLTEXT01.pdf

Smith, D. (2016). *How to Respond to Positive Reviews.* Available at: https://www.vendasta.com/blog/how-to-respond-to-positive-reviews

Sobaih, A. E., Elshaer, I., Hasanein, A. M., & Abdelaziz, A. S. (2021). Responses to COVID-19: The role of performance in the relationship between small hospitality enterprises' resilience and sustainable tourism development. *International Journal of Hospitality Management*, *94*, 102824. doi:10.1016/j.ijhm.2020.102824

So, K., King, C., Hudson, S., & Meng, F. (2017). The missing link in building customer brand identification: The role of brand attractiveness. *Tourism Management*, *59*, 640–651. doi:10.1016/j.tourman.2016.09.013

So, K., King, C., Sparks, B., & Wang, Y. (2013). The influence of customer brand identification on hotel brand evaluation and loyalty development. *International Journal of Hospitality Management*, *34*(1), 31–41. doi:10.1016/j.ijhm.2013.02.002

Soler, I. P., & Gemar, G. (2019). Factors that affect the perception of a tourist resource's value: The case of the Caminito del Rey. *Tourism & Management Studies*, *15*(3), 7–16. doi:10.18089/tms.2019.150301

Soltani, M., Jandaghi, G., & Forou, P. (2017). Co-creation intention; presenting a model of antecedents and its impact on attitude toward the product (Case study in shatel company). *Iranian Journal of Management Studies*, *10*(1), 143–174.

Soltani, Z., Zareie, B., Milani, F. S., & Navimipour, N. J. (2018). The impact of the customer relationship management on the organization performance. *The Journal of High Technology Management Research*, *29*(2), 237–246. doi:10.1016/j.hitech.2018.10.001

Sop, S. A. (2018). Nöropazarlama Yaklaşımının Turizm Araştırmalarındaki Konumu Üzerine Kavramsal Bir Değerlendirme. In *The Second International Congress on Future of Tourism Innovation, Entrepreneurship and Sustainability* (pp. 318-324). Mersin: Mersin Üniversitesi Yayınları.

Sorensen, N. (2012). *Management Response to Online Complaints*. Tese de Licenciatura, Modul Viena University.

Sörensson, A., & von Friedrichs, Y. (2013). An importance-performance analysis of sustainable tourism: A comparison between international and national tourists. *Journal of Destination Marketing & Management*, *2*(1), 14–21. doi:10.1016/j.jdmm.2012.11.002

Spake, D., Beatty, S., Brockman, B., & Crutchfield, T. (2003). Consumer comfort in service relationships: Measurement and importance. *Journal of Service Research*, *5*(4), 316–332. doi:10.1177/1094670503005004004

Sparker, B. (2015). *How to Respond to Positive Reviews*. Disponível em: https://www.reviewtrackers.com/respond-positive-reviews/

Sparks, B., & Bradley, G. (2014). A "Triple A" Typology of Responding to Negative Consumer-generated Online Reviews. *Journal of Hospitality & Tourism Research (Washington, D.C.)*, *41*(6), 1–27.

Sparks, B., & Browning, V. (2011). The impact of online reviews on hotel booking intentions and perception of trust. *Tourism Management*, *32*(6), 1310–1323. doi:10.1016/j.tourman.2010.12.011

Sparks, B., Perkins, H., & Buckley, R. (2013). Online travel reviews as persuasive communication: The effects of content type, source, and certification logos on consumer behaviour. *Tourism Management*, *39*, 1–9. doi:10.1016/j.tourman.2013.03.007

Sparks, B., So, K., & Bradley, G. (2016). Responding to negative online reviews: The effects of hotel responses on customer inferences of trust and concern. *Tourism Management*, *53*, 74–85. doi:10.1016/j.tourman.2015.09.011

Spina, F. (2019). *Personalização: quem fala com todos não fala com ninguém, personalize seu marketing digital*. DVS.

Srinivasan, R., & Moorman, C. (2005). Strategic firm commitments and rewards for customer relationship management in online retailing. *Journal of Marketing*, *69*(4), 193–200. doi:10.1509/jmkg.2005.69.4.193

Starĉević, S., & Konjikušić, S. (2018). Why Millenials as Digital Travelers Transformed Marketing Strategy in Tourism Industry. In *The Third International Scientific Conference, Tourism in Function of Development of the Republic of Serbia: Tourism in the Era of Digital Transformation* (pp. 221-240). Vrnjačka Banja.

Stephen, F. G., Olumide, O., & Jacob, G. A. (2013). Application of Data Mining Technique for Fraud Detection in Health Insurance Scheme Using Knee-Point K-Means Algorithm. *Australian Journal of Basic and Applied Sciences*, *7*(8), 140–144.

Stokburger-Sauer, N., Ratneshwar, S., & Sen, S. (2012). Drivers of consumer-brand identification. *International Journal of Research in Marketing*, *29*(4), 406–418. doi:10.1016/j.ijresmar.2012.06.001

Stringam, B. B., & Gerdes, J. J. Jr. (2010). An analysis of word-of-mouse ratings and guest comments of online hotel distribution sites. *Journal of Hospitality Marketing & Management*, *19*(7), 773–796. doi:10.1080/19368623.2010.508009

Sun, Y., Song, H., Jara, A. J., & Bie, R. (2016). Internet of things and big data analytics for smart and connected communities. *IEEE Access: Practical Innovations, Open Solutions, 4*, 766–773. doi:10.1109/ACCESS.2016.2529723

Swarbrooke, J., & Horner, S. (2002). *O Comportamento Do Consumidor no Turismo* (1st ed.). Aleph.

Sweetescape. (2019). *Gen X, Millennials, and Gen Z: Travel Habits of the Generations.* https://www.sweetescape.com/en/blog/ideas/travel-habits

Swift, R. S. (2001). *Accelerating customer relationships: Using CRM and relationship technologies.* Prentice Hall Professional.

Swig, R. (2014, August 29). *Alt-accommodation impact felt in San Francisco.* Hotel News Now. Accessed 20th April, 2020, from: https://www.hotelnewsnow.com/Articles/23683/Alt-accommodationimpact-felt-in-San-Francisco

Swimberghe, K. R., & Wooldridge, B. R. (2014). Drivers of customer relationships in quick-service restaurants: The role of corporate social responsibility. *Cornell Hospitality Quarterly, 55*(4), 354–364. doi:10.1177/1938965513519008

Szromek, A. R., Hysa, B., & Karasek, A. (2019). The Perception of Overtourism from the Perspective. *Sustainability, 11*(24), 2–19. doi:10.3390u11247151

Tabassum, S., Pereira, F., Fernandes, S., & Gama, J. (2018). Social network analysis: An overview. *Wiley Interdisciplinary Reviews. Data Mining and Knowledge Discovery, 8*(5), e1256. doi:10.1002/widm.1256

Taecharungroj, V., & Mathayomchan, B. (2019). Analysing TripAdvisor reviews of tourist attractions in Phuket, Thailand. *Tourism Management, 75*, 550–568. https://doi.org/10.1016/J.TOURMAN.2019.06.020

Tanasic, B. R. (2017). Impact of Sensory Branding On The Decision-Making Process of Tourism Product Purchase. *Journal of Research in Engineering and Innovation,* 109-125.

Tan, E. M.-Y., Goh, D. H.-L., Theng, Y.-L., & Foo, S. (2007). An Analysis of Services for the Mobile Tourist. In *The International Conference on Mobile Technology, Applications and Systems* (pp. 490-494). 10.1145/1378063.1378142

Tanti, A., & Buhalis, D. (2016). *Connectivity and the Consequences of Being (Dis)connected.* Information and Communication Technologies in Tourism. doi:10.1007/978-3-319-28231-2_3

Tarabasz, A. (2013). The reevaluation of communication in customer approach- towards marketing 4.0. *International Journal of Contemporary Management, 12*(4), 124–134.

Tarrant, M. A., & Smith, E. K. (2002). The use of a modified importance-performance framework to examine visitor satisfaction with attributes of outdoor recreation settings. *Managing Leisure, 7*(2), 69–82. doi:10.1080/13606710210137246

Taş, M., Akkaşoğlu, S., & Akyol, C. (2018). Turizm İşletmelerinde Bilgi Sistemi Kullanımı Kapsamında Seyahat Acentesi Web Sitelerinin İncelenmesi. *Akademik Bakış Dergisi,* 207-221.

Terblanche, N. S. (2014). Some theoretical perspectives of co-creation and co-production of value by customers. *Acta Commercii, 14*(2), 1–8. doi:10.4102/ac.v14i2.237

Tew, P. J., Lu, Z., Tolomiczenko, G., & Gellatly, J. (2008). SARS: Lessons in strategic planning for hoteliers and destination marketers. *International Journal of Contemporary Hospitality Management, 20*(3), 332–346. doi:10.1108/09596110810866145

Thinkdigital. (2020). https://www.thinkdigital.travel/talking-to-gen-z/

Thompson, C., Rindfleisch, A., & Arsel, Z. (2006). Emotional branding and the strategic value of the doppelgänger brand image. *Journal of Marketing, 70*(1), 50–64. doi:10.1509/jmkg.70.1.050.qxd

Tinoco, M. A. & Ribeiro, J. L. (2007). Uma nova abordagem para a modelagem das relações entre os determinantes da satisfação dos clientes de serviços. *Revista Produção, 17*(3).

Tonge, J., & Moore, S. A. (2007). Importance-satisfaction analysis for marine-park hinterlands: A Western Australian case study. *Tourism Management, 28*(3), 768–776. doi:10.1016/j.tourman.2006.05.007

Torres, E., Singh, D., & Robertson-Ring, A. (2015). Consumer reviews and the creation of booking transaction value: Lessons from the hotel industry. *International Journal of Hospitality Management, 50*, 77–83. doi:10.1016/j.ijhm.2015.07.012

Tsai, C. F., Chen, K., Hu, Y. H., & Chen, W. K. (2020). Improving text summarization of online hotel reviews with review helpfulness and sentiment. *Tourism Management, 80*, 104122. https://doi.org/10.1016/j.tourman.2020.104122

Tsang, S., Royse, C. F., & Terkawi, A. S. (2017). Guidelines for developing, translating, and validating a questionnaire in perioperative and pain medicine. *Saudi Journal of Anaesthesia, 11*(5), 80. Advance online publication. doi:10.4103ja.SJA_203_17 PMID:28616007

Tse, A. C. B., So, S., & Sin, L. (2006). Crisis management and recovery: How restaurants in Hong Kong responded to SARS. *International Journal of Hospitality Management, 25*(1), 3–11. doi:10.1016/j.ijhm.2004.12.001

Tse, D. K., & Wilton, P. C. (1988). Models of Consumer Satisfaction Formation: An Extension. *JMR, Journal of Marketing Research, 25*(2), 204–212. doi:10.1177/002224378802500209

Tsiros, M., Vikas, M., & Ross, W. (2004). The role of attributions in customer satisfaction: A reexamination. *The Journal of Consumer Research, 31*(2), 476–483. doi:10.1086/422124

Turismo de Portugal. (2017). *TravelBi.* Disponível em: http://travelbi.turismodeportugal.pt/pt-pt/bi/Paginas/PowerBI/Oferta-Hoteleira.aspx

Turismo de Portugal. (2020a). *Travel BI.* Available at: https://travelbi.turismodeportugal.pt/pt-pt/Paginas/PowerBI/hospedes.aspx

Turismo Portugal. (2020b). *Selo "Clean & Safe". Empreendimentos Turísticos. Requisitos a cumprir.* Turismo de Portugal.

Türk Hava Yolları (THY). (2021a). *Geri bildirim değerlendirme süreci.* https://www.turkishairlines.com/tr-int/bilgi-edin/musteri-iliskileri/geribildirim-degerlendirme-sureci/

Türk Hava Yolları (THY). (2021b). *Smile&miles müşteri sadakat programı içeriği.* https://www.turkishairlines.com/tr-int/miles-and-smiles/program-icerigi/

Türk Hava Yolları (THY). (2021c). *Ödüller.* https://www.turkishairlines.com/tr-int/basin-odasi/oduller/

Türker, A., & Özaltın, G. (2010). Konaklama işletmelerinde müşteri ilişkileri yönetimi: İzmir ili örneği. *Muğla Üniversitesi Sosyal Bilimler Enstitüsü Dergisi, 25*, 81–104.

Türkiye Turizm Tanıtım ve Geliştirme Ajansı (TGA). (2021). *Hakkında.* https://tga.gov.tr/hakkinda/

TÜRSAB, TBV, & ED Türkiye. (2019). *Turizm sektörü dijitalleşme yol haritası.* EY Türkiye Publishing.

TÜRSAB. (2021). *Turist sayısı ve turizm geliri (Türkiye)* [Data Sets]. https://www.tursab.org.tr/istatistikler/turist-sayisi-ve-turizm-geliri

Tussyadiah, I. P., & Park, S. (2018). Consumer Evaluation of Hotel Service Robots. *Information and Communication Technologies in Tourism*, 308-320.

Tussyadiah, L., & Zach, F. (2015). Hotels vs. Peer-to-Peer Accommodation Rentals: Text Analytics of Consumer Reviews in Portland, Oregon. Travel and Tourism Research Association.

Tussyadiah, I. P., & Fesenmaier, D. R. (2009). Mediating the tourist experiences Access to Places via Shared Videos. *Annals of Tourism Research, 36*(1), 24–40. doi:10.1016/j.annals.2008.10.001

Tussyadiah, L. (2015). An exploratory study on drivers and deterrents of collaborative consumption in travel. In L. Tussyadiah & A. Inversini (Eds.), *Information and Communication Technologies in Tourism* (pp. 1–13). Springer.

Tussyadiah, L. (2016). Factors of satisfaction and intention to use peer-to-peer accommodation. *International Journal of Hospitality Management, 55*, 70–80. doi:10.1016/j.ijhm.2016.03.005

Ueltschy, L. C., Laroche, M., Eggert, A., & Bindl, U. (2007). Service quality and satisfaction: An international comparison of professional services perceptions. *Journal of Services Marketing, 21*(6), 410–423. doi:10.1108/08876040710818903

Ünal, A., & Bayar, S. B. (2020). Akıllı uygulamaları ve ürünleri kullanan turistlerin destinasyon seçim süreçleri: İstanbul örneği [Destination choice process of tourists using smart applications and products: the case of Istanbul]. *Uluslararası Sosyal Araştırmalar Dergisi, 13*(70), 1066–1075. doi:10.17719/jisr.2020.4158

Ungerman, O., Dedkova, J., & Gurinova, K. (2018). The impact of marketing innovation on the competitiveness of enterprises in the context of the industry 4.0. *Journal of Competitiveness, 10*(2), 132–148. doi:10.7441/joc.2018.02.09

United Nations World Tourism Organization (UNWTO). (2021). *UNWTO World Tourism Barometer and Statistical Annex, January 2021.* https://www.e-unwto.org/DOI/abs/10.18111/wtobarometereng.2021.19.1.1?journalCode=wtobarometereng

United Nations. (2020). *Shared responsibility, global solidarity: Responding to the socio-economic impacts of COVID-19.* https://unsdg.un.org/sites/default/files/2020-03/SG-Report-Socio-Economic-Impact-of-Covid19.pdf

UNTWO. (2019). World tourism barometer. World Tourism Organization.

UNWTO. (2021). *Dijital transformation.* https://www.unwto.org/digital-transformation

UNWTO. (2021). *Sustainable Development.* https://www.unwto.org/sustainable-development

van Eck, N. J., & Waltman, L. (2010). Software survey: VOSviewer, a computer program for bibliometric mapping. *Scientometrics, 84*(2), 523–538. doi:10.100711192-009-0146-3 PMID:20585380

Vargo, S. L. (2008). Customer Integration and Value Creation. *Journal of Service Research, 11*(2), 211–215. doi:10.1177/1094670508324260

Vargo, S. L., & Lusch, R. F. (2004). Evolving to a new dominant logic for marketing. *Journal of Marketing, 68*(1), 1–17. doi:10.1509/jmkg.68.1.1.24036

Vargo, S. L., Maglio, P. P., & Akaka, M. A. (2008). On value and value co-creation: A service systems and service logic perspective. *European Management Journal, 26*(3), 145–152. doi:10.1016/j.emj.2008.04.003

Vasavada, M., & Padhiyar, J. (2016). "Smart tourism": Growth for tomorrow. *Journal of Research, 1*(12), 55–61.

Vavra, T. G. (1997). *Improving Your Measurement of Customer Satisfation: A Guide to Creating, Conducting, Analyzing, and Reporting Customer Satisfaction Measurement Programs.* Academic Press.

Vecchio, P. D., Mele, G., Ndou, V., & Secundo, G. (2018). Creating value from Social Big Data: Implications for Smart Tourism Destinations. *Information Processing & Management, 54*(5), 847–860. doi:10.1016/j.ipm.2017.10.006

Vega-Vazquez, M., Revilla-Camacho, M. A., & Cossio-Silva, F. J. (2013). The value co-creation process as a determinant of customer satisfaction. *Management Decision, 51*(10), 1945–1953. doi:10.1108/MD-04-2013-0227

Veloso, B., Leal, F., Malheiro, B., & Burguillo, J. C. (2019). On-line Guest Profiling and Hotel Recommendation. *Electronic Commerce Research and Applications*, *34*, 2–33. doi:10.1016/j.elerap.2019.100832

Veloutsou, C. (2009). Brands as relationship facilitators in consumer markets. *Journal of Marketing*, *9*, 127–130.

Vendrell-Herrero, F., Gomes, E., Bustinza, O. F., & Mellahi, K. (2018). Uncovering the role of cross-border strategic alliances and expertise decision centralization in enhancing product-service innovation in MMNEs. *International Business Review*, *27*(4), 814–825. doi:10.1016/j.ibusrev.2018.01.005

Verma, A., & Shukla, V. (2019). Analyzing the influence of IoT in Tourism Industry. *International Conference on Sustainable Computing in Science, Technology & Management*, 2083-2093. 10.2139srn.3358168

Vermeulen, I., & Seegers, D. (2009). Tried and tested: The impact of online hotel reviews on consumer consideration. *Tourism Management*, *30*(1), 123–127. doi:10.1016/j.tourman.2008.04.008

Vilelas, J. (2017). *Investigação. O processo de Construção do Conhecimento* (2nd ed.). Edições Sílabo.

Vivek, S. D., Beatty, S. E., & Morgan, R. M. (2012). Customer engagement: Exploring customer relationships beyond purchase. *Journal of Marketing Theory and Practice*, *20*(2), 127–145. doi:10.2753/MTP1069-6679200201

Vivion, N. (2016). *What stats reveal about travel behaviors by generation.* https://www.sabre.com/insights/what-stats-reveal-about-travel-behaviors-by-generation/

Vodeb, K., & Rudež, H. N. (2017). Which attributes are important to tourists in a mature seaside destination? A case of Opatija in Croatia. *Tourism (Zagreb)*, *65*(3), 267–279. doi:10.1016/j.addr.2005.07.002

Vogt, C. A. (2011). Customer relationship management in tourism: Management needs and research applications. *Journal of Travel Research*, *50*(4), 356–364. doi:10.1177/0047287510368140

W.H.D.P. (2014). Relationship between Service Quality and Customer Relationship in sir Lankan hotel industry. *International Journal of Scientific and Research Publications*, 2-8.

Wang, X., Li, X. R., Zhen, F., & Zhang, J. (2016). How smart is your tourist attraction?: Measuring tourist preferences of smart tourism attractions via a FCEM-AHP and IPA approach. *Tourism Management*, *54*, 309–320. doi:10.1016/j.tourman.2015.12.003

Wasserman, S., Faust, K., Press, C. U., Granovetter, M., Cambridge, U. o., & Iacobucci, D. (1994). *Social Network Analysis: Methods and Applications*. Cambridge University Press. doi:10.1017/CBO9780511815478

Watkins, M., Ziyadin, S., Imatayeva, A., Kurmangalieva, A., & Blembayeva, A. (2018). Digital tourism as a key factor in the development of the economy. In Economic Annals-XXI (pp. 40-45). Kiev: Institute of Society Transformation. doi:10.21003/ea.V169-08

Wattanacharoensil, W., Schuckert, M., & Graham, A. (2016). An airport experience framework from a tourism perspective. *Transport Reviews*, *36*(3), 318–340. doi:10.1080/01441647.2015.1077287

Webber, D. (2013). Space tourism: Its history, future, and importance. *Acta Astronautica*, *92*(2), 138–143. doi:10.1016/j.actaastro.2012.04.038

Webius Digital Agency. (2021). *CRM sistemlerinde misafir yorumlarının önemi.* https://webiusdigital.com/crm-misafir-yorumlarinin-onemi/

Webster, F. E. Jr. (1994). Executing the new marketing concept. *Marketing Management*, *3*(1), 8–16.

Wen, J., Wang, W., Kozak, M., Liu, X., & Hou, H. (2020). Many brains are better than one: The importance of interdisciplinary studies on COVID-19 in and beyond tourism. *Tourism Recreation Research*.

Wen, Z., Huimin, G., & Kavanaugh, R. R. (2005). The impacts of SARS on the consumer behaviour of Chinese domestic tourists. *Current Issues in Tourism*, 8(1), 22–38. https:// DOI.org/10.1080/13683500508668203

Weston, R., & Gore, P. A. Jr. (2006). A Brief Guide to Structural Equation Modeling. *The Counseling Psychologist*, 34(5), 719–751. Advance online publication. doi:10.1177/0011000006286345

White, M. D., & Marsh, E. E. (2006). Content analysis: A flexible methodology. *Library Trends*, 55(1), 22–45. doi:10.1353/lib.2006.0053

Wiharto, W., & Suryani, E. (2020). The Comparison of Clustering Algorithms K-Means and Fuzzy C-Means for Segmentation Retinal Blood Vessels. *Acta Informatica Medica*, 28(1), 42. https://doi.org/10.5455/AIM.2020.28.42-47

Williams, K. C., & Page, R. A. (2011). Marketing to the Generations. *Journal of Behavioral Studies in Businesses*, 3(1), 36–53.

Williams, R. M. (1974). The Nature of Human Values. by Milton Rokeach. *The Academy of Political Science*, 89(2), 399–401.

Wilson, S., & Laing, R. (2018). *Wearable Technology: Present and Future*. University of Leeds.

Winer, R. S. (2001). A framework for customer relationship management. *California Management Review*, 43(4), 89–105. doi:10.2307/41166102

Woodruff, R. B. (1997). Customer value: The next source for competitive advantage. *Journal of the Academy of Marketing Science*, 25(2), 139–153. doi:10.1007/BF02894350

World Economic Forum. (2019). *Outbreak readiness and business impact protecting lives and livelihoods across the global economy*. http://www3.weforum.org/docs/WEF HGHI_Outbreak_Readiness_Business_Impact.pdf

World Tourism Organization. (2011). *Technology in Tourism*. https://www.e-unwto.org/doi/pdf/10.18111/9789284414567

World Tourism Organization. (2014). *Online Guest Reviews and Hotel Classification Systems – An Integrated Approach*. UNWTO.

World Tourism Organization. (2019). *The Future of Work and Skills Development in Tourism – Policy Paper*. UNWTO.

World Travel & Tourism Council (WTTC). (2018). *Travel & tourism economic impact 2018 Portugal*. https://www.sgeconomia.gov.pt/ficheiros-externos-sg/wttc_portugal2018-pdf.aspx

World Travel & Tourism Council (WTTC). (2020). *Global economic impact & trends 2020*. https://wttc.org/Portals/0/Documents/Reports/2020/Global%20Economic%20Impact%20Trends%202020.pdf?ver=2021-02-25-183118-360

Worsfold, K., Fisher, R., McPhail, R., Francis, M., & Thomas, A. (2016). Satisfaction, value and intention to return in hotels. *International Journal of Contemporary Hospitality Management*, 28(11), 2570–2588. doi:10.1108/IJCHM-04-2015-0195

Wu, H. H., & Shieh, J. I. (2009). The development of a confidence interval-based importance-performance analysis by considering variability in analyzing service quality. *Expert Systems with Applications*, 36(3 PART 2), 7040–7044. doi:10.1016/j.eswa.2008.08.055

Wu, H.-C., & Cheng, C.-C. (2018). Relationships between technology attachment, experiential relationship quality, experiential risk and experiential sharing intentions in a smart hotel. *Journal of Hospitality and Tourism Management*, 37, 42–58.

Wullur, M., & Samehe, V. (2020). Importance Performance Analysis using Dematel: A Case Study on Tourist Destination Attributes in Manado Indonesia. *SHS Web of Conferences, 76*, 01024. 10.1051hsconf/20207601024

Xiang, Z., Dan, W., O'Leary, J., & Fesenmaier, D. R. (2015a). Adapting to the Internet: Trends in Travelers' Use of the Web for Trip Planning. *Journal of Travel Research, 54*(4), 511–527. doi:10.1177/0047287514522883

Xiang, Z., & Fesenmaier, D. R. (2017). Big data analytics, tourism design and smart tourism. In Z. Xiang & R. Fesenmaier (Eds.), *Analytics in smart tourism design: concepts and methods* (pp. 299–307). Springer. doi:10.1007/978-3-319-44263-1_17

Xiang, Z., & Gretzel, U. (2010). Role of Social Media in Online Travel Information Search. *Tourism Management, 31*(2), 179–188. doi:10.1016/j.tourman.2009.02.016

Xiang, Z., Magnini, V. P., & Fesenmaier, D. R. (2015b). Information Technology and Consumer Behavior in Travel and Tourism: Insights From Travel Planning Using the Internet. *Journal of Retailing and Consumer Services, 22*, 244–249. doi:10.1016/j.jretconser.2014.08.005

Xiang, Z., Stienmetz, J., & Fesenmaier, D. R. (2021). Smart Tourism Design: Launching the annals of tourism research curated collection on designing tourism places. *Annals of Tourism Research, 86*, 103154. doi:10.1016/j.annals.2021.103154

Xiang, Z., Wober, K., & Fesenmaier, D. R. (2008). Representation of the online tourism domain in search engines. *Journal of Travel Research, 47*(2), 137–150. doi:10.1177/0047287508321193

Xie, C., Bagozzi, R. P., & Troye, S. V. (2008). Trying to prosume: Toward a theory of consumers as co-creators of value. *Journal of the Academy of Marketing Science, 36*(1), 109–122. doi:10.100711747-007-0060-2

Xie, G., Qian, Y., & Wang, S. (2021). Forecasting Chinese cruise tourism demand with big data: An optimized machine learning approach. *Tourism Management, 82*, 104208. doi:10.1016/j.tourman.2020.104208

Xie, K. L., Chen, C., & Wu, S. (2016). Online consumer review factors affecting offline hotel popularity: Evidence from TripAdvisor. *Journal of Travel & Tourism Marketing, 33*(2), 211–223. doi:10.1080/10548408.2015.1050538

Xie, K. L., So, K. K., & Wang, W. (2017). Joint effects of management responses and online reviews on hotel financial performance: A data-analytics approach. *International Journal of Hospitality Management, 62*, 101–110. doi:10.1016/j.ijhm.2016.12.004

Xie, K. L., Zhang, Z., & Zhang, Z. (2014). The business value of online consumer reviews and management response to hotel performance. *International Journal of Hospitality Management, 43*, 1–12. doi:10.1016/j.ijhm.2014.07.007

Xie, K., Zhang, Z., Zhang, J., Singh, A., & Lee, S. (2016). Effects of managerial response on consumer eWOM and hotel performance: Evidence from TripAdvisor. *International Journal of Contemporary Hospitality Management, 28*(9), 2013–2034. doi:10.1108/IJCHM-06-2015-0290

Xu, M., & Walton, J. (2005). Gaining customer knowledge through analytical CRM. *Industrial Management & Data Systems, 105*(7), 955–972. doi:10.1108/02635570510616139

Yalçınkaya, P., Atay, L., & Korkmaz, H. (2018). An evaluation on smart tourism. *China-USA Business Review, 17*(6), 308–315. doi:10.17265/1537-1514/2018.06.004

Yamashita, R., Nishio, M., Do, R. K. G., & Togashi, K. (2018). Convolutional neural networks: An overview and application in radiology. *Insights Into Imaging, 9*(4), 611–629. Advance online publication. doi:10.100713244-018-0639-9 PMID:29934920

Ye, Q., Law, R., Gu, B., & Chen, W. (2011). The influence of user-generated content on traveler behavior: An empirical investigation on the effects of e-word-of-mouth to hotel online bookings. *Computers in Human Behavior*, *27*(2), 634–639. doi:10.1016/j.chb.2010.04.014

Ye, S., Li, J., Zeng, Z., & Hao, S. (2015). Research on the impact of social circles on self-brand connection: Regulation of self-awareness and brand value. *Open Journal of Business and Management*, *3*(2), 339–348. doi:10.4236/ojbm.2015.32015

Yi, J., Yuan, G., & Yoo, G. (2020). The effect of the perceived risk on the adoption of the sharing economy in the tourism industry: The case of Airbnb. *Business Computer Science*, *57*(1), 1–11. doi:10.1016/j.ipm.2019.102108

Yi, Y., & Gong, T. (2013). Customer value co-creation behavior: Scale development and validation. *Journal of Business Research*, *66*(9), 1279–1284. doi:10.1016/j.jbusres.2012.02.026

Yoo, C., Kwon, S., Na, H., & Chang, B. (2017). Factors affecting the adoption of gamified smart tourism applications: An integrative approach. *Sustainability*, *9*(12), 2162. doi:10.3390u9122162

Yu, C.-E. (2019). Humanlike robots as employees in the hotel industry: Thematic content analysis of online reviews. *Journal of Hospitality Marketing & Management*, *29*(1), 22–38.

Yücel, A., & Coşkun, P. (2018). Nöropazarlama Literatür İncelemesi. *Fırat Üniversitesi Sosyal Bilimler Dergisi*, 157-177.

Yu, J., Seo, J., & Hyun, S. S. (2021). Perceived hygiene attributes in the hotel industry: Customer retention amid the COVID-19 crisis. *International Journal of Hospitality Management*, *93*, 102768. doi:10.1016/j.ijhm.2020.102768

Zaiontz, C. (2019). *Real Statistics Using Excel*. www.real-statistics.com

Zeithaml, V. A. (1988). Consumer Perceptions of Price, Quality, and Value: A Means-End Model and Synthesis of Evidence. *Journal of Marketing*, *52*(3), 2–22. doi:10.1177/002224298805200302

Zeng, D., Tim, Y., Yu, J., & Liu, W. (2020). Actualizing big data analytics for smart cities: A cascading affordance study. *International Journal of Information Management*, *54*, 102156. doi:10.1016/j.ijinfomgt.2020.102156

Zervas, G., Proserpio, D., & Byers, J. (2017). The rise of sharing economy: Estimating the impact of Airbnb on the hotel industry. *JMR, Journal of Marketing Research*, *54*(5), 1–45. doi:10.1509/jmr.15.0204

Zhang, B., Li, N., Shi, F., & Law, R. (2020). *A deep learning approach for daily tourist flow forecasting with consumer search data*. Https://Doi.Org/10.1080/10941665.2019.1709876 doi:10.1080/10941665.2019.1709876

Zhang, Y., Li, G., Muskat, B., & Law, R. (2020). *Tourism Demand Forecasting: A Decomposed Deep Learning Approach*. Https://Doi.Org/10.1177/0047287520919522 doi:10.1177/0047287520919522

Zhang, T., Lu, C., & Chen, P.-J. (2018). Engaging customers in value co-creation or co-destruction online. *Journal of Services Marketing*, *32*(1), 57–69. doi:10.1108/JSM-01-2017-0027

Zhao, X., Wang, L., Guo, X., & Law, R. (2015). The influence of online reviews to online hotel booking intentions. *International Journal of Contemporary Hospitality Management*, *27*(6), 1343–1364. doi:10.1108/IJCHM-12-2013-0542

Zhu, W., Zhang, L., & Li, N. (2014). Challenges, function changing of government and enterprises in chinese smart tourism. In Z. Xiang & L. Tussyadiah (Eds.), *Information and communication technologies in tourism*. Springer.

Zsarnoczky, M. (2018). The digital future of the tourism & hospitality industry. Boston Hospitality Review, 1-9.

Zsarnoczky, M. (2018). The Digital Future of the Tourism & Hospitality Industry. *Boston Hospitality Review*, 1-9.

Zsarnoczky, M. (2018, Spring). The Digital Future of the Tourism & Hospitality Industry. *Boston Hospitality Review*, 1-9.

Zupic, I., & Čater, T. (2015). Bibliometric methods in management and organization. *Organizational Research Methods, 18*(3), 429–472. doi:10.1177/1094428114562629

Zwick, D., Bonsu, S. K., & Darmody, A. (2008). Putting consumers to work: 'Co-creation' and new marketing governmentality. *Journal of Consumer Culture, 8*(2), 163–196. doi:10.1177/1469540508090089

About the Contributors

Nuno Gustavo holds a PhD in Tourism, Leisure and Culture, completed in 2011 in the University of Coimbra. He is Assistant Professor at the Estoril Higher Institute for Tourism and Hotel Studies (ESHTE) since 2002, collaborating with several institutions on both international and national levels, such as Oporto Católica University, Grenoble Graduate School of Business, Eduardo Mondlane University - ESHTI, Lúrio University, Cape Verde Institute for Tourism and Hotel Studies and the University of Coimbra. His main areas of interest are focused on strategic and operations management and marketing of tourism and hospitality businesses. He has edited 2 books, published 19 book chapters and 10 articles in specialized journals, collaborating with 20 fellow researchers and receiving 4 awards. The curriculum also shows the development of several projects in the field of tourism and hospitality in Portugal, Mozambique and Cape Verde. He is also a member of the Editorial Board (Review Board Member) of the Journal of Hospitality and Tourism Management.

Luísa Carvalho held a PhD in Management in University of Évora – Portugal. Professor of Management on Department of Economics and Management, Institute Polytecnic of Setubal– Portugal. Guest professor in international universities teaches in courses of master and PhDs programs. Researcher at CEFAGE (Center for Advanced Studies in Management and Economics) University of Evora – Portugal. Author of several publications in national and international journals, books and book chapters.

* * *

Boluwaji Akinnuwesi is a professor in the Department of Computer Science in University of Swaziland. Teaches course in Computer Science. Research interest is in Software Engineering with emphasis in System Design Methodology, Software Testing and Performance Evaluation. Presently applies the system development methodologies in his research works in Health Informatics where he makes use of Deep and Machine Learning techniques to develop Expert Systems and Decision Support system for differential diagnoses of diseases. His publications are in these areas and he has developed a number of software frameworks for solving real life problems.

Ozlem Atalik is a Assoc. Professor in the Aeronautical and Astronautical Faculty at the Eskisehir Technical University. Atalik completed her Ph.D. at Anadolu University and his undergraduate studies at Anadolu University. Her research interests lie in the area of airline marketing, customer relationship management and service marketing.

João Barros Neto is a Post-Doctor, Doctor in Sociology and Master in Administration: Organization and Human Resources from the Pontifical Catholic University of São Paulo - PUC SP (Brazil), Specialist in Administration from EAESP / FGV and Bachelor in Administration. Professor in the area of People Management in the Administration Course at PUC SP. Coordinator of the Extension Course in Leadership and Positive Leadership at PUC SP / COGEAE. He published 35 books as an author, co-author and organizer. Professional administrator for over 38 years with experience in management and leadership of small, medium and large public and private organizations, member of the groups of Excellence of the Regional Administration Council of São Paulo (GEGIES and GEPAD).

Catarina Basílio holds a Bachelor's Degree in Management from Iscte Business School and a Master's Degree in Hotel Management at Estoril Higher Institute for Tourism and Hotel Studies (ESHTE), completed in 2019.

İsmail Çalık is a lecturer at Gümüşhane University, Faculty of Tourism, Department of Tourism Management and Vice Dean at the same faculty. Çalık's research areas are sustainable tourism, intangible cultural heritage and tourism, occupational health and safety in tourism, tourism and traditional handicrafts and halal tourism. Çalık has many books and articles on Gümüşhane province and the Eastern Black Sea Region.

Maria de Lurdes Calisto holds a Ph.D. in Management, awarded by the University of Évora. She is a researcher (integrated) at CiTUR - Center for Applied Research in Tourism and a collaborator at CEFAGE - Center for Studies and Advanced Training in Management and Economics of the University of Évora. Develops research in Business and Management, areas in which she supervises doctoral thesis and several master dissertations. Her research interests are innovation management, intrapreneurial behaviour, corporate entrepreneurship, business strategy, and strategic marketing, particularly in tourism and hospitality companies. She participates as a researcher and project manager in several research projects and has been awarded competitive research grants. Has several publications with global book editors and scientific journals and is frequently invited as a reviewer. She is also frequently invited as a lecturer with Portuguese and foreign universities.

Tonderal Chiremba holds a BSc (majoring in Computer Science and Mathematics) from the University of Eswatini. His research areas include machine learning and applied mathematics.

Dinesh Dhankhar holds the position of Senior Assistant Professor in Department of Tourism & Hotel Management, Kurukshetra University, Kurukshetra with doctoral degree in the subject. He has ten years of teaching experience with number of publications.

Stephen G. Fashoto is currently a Senior Lecturer in the Department of Computer Science in University of Swaziland, Kwaluseni, Swaziland. He was also a Lecturer in the Department of Computer Science in Redeemer's University, Ede, Osun State, Nigeria between 2007 and 2014. He obtained his B.Sc. (Honours) in Computer Science & Mathematics and MSc in Computer Science both from the University of Port Harcourt, Nigeria and PhD in Computer Science from University of Ilorin, Nigeria. He has over 15 years of teaching and research experience at the university. His research interests are in Computer Science Education, Machine Learning, and Computational Intelligence, Health informatics,

Data mining, and application of optimization techniques. He is the Chair of the Computational Intelligence and Health Informatics Research Group in the Department of Computer Science at the University of Eswatini.

João Carlos Ferreira do Rosário holds a Ph.D. in Management awarded by Instituto Superior de Economia e Gestão (Universidade de Lisboa) and is Marketing Professor-Adjunct at Escola Superior de Comunicação Social (ESCS)-Instituto Politécnico de Lisboa, Portugal. Coordinator of Advertising and Marketing Department and Coordinator of the ESCS Research Line "Communication, Strategies, and Creativity". Member of the ESCS Technical-Scientific Council. Professor of Marketing and Management courses at graduation and master's degrees. Research fellow at CiTUR - Center for Applied Research in Tourism, with published scientific articles, communications, and book chapters in the Marketing, Tourism and Information and Communication Technologies research areas. Scientific journals editor and reviewer and scientific conferences and books reviewer. Portuguese coordinator of trans-European academic projects such as Businet HedCom, Businet International Trade Mission, REVE-IP, and IP ISTAR-DOT-Erasmus. Project coordinator of IPL-IDICA Research Projects.

Gabriel Figueiredo graduated in Business Administration from the Pontifical Catholic University of São Paulo. He has experience in startup's and multinationals, between bank and industry, working with sales, customer service, business intelligence and marketing. He has worked in the leadership of intrapreneurial projects, focusing on data and reverse logistics. Researcher interested in digital marketing and strategic planning.

Evrim Genç Kumtepe is a full professor in the Open Education Faculty at Anadolu University, Turkey. Dr. Genc Kumtepe holds a BSc. degree in Agricultural Engineering from Ankara University in the field of Aquaculture and received her masters and doctorate degrees in the Program of Science Education at Florida State University (FSU), USA. She has also a minor degree from the Program of Measurement and Statistics at FSU. Her primary research interests focus on science and technology in education, distance science education, and interaction and communication issues in science. She is the head of Continuing Education Department and serves as a coordinator for Internship and Practicum Courses of the Faculty. Dr. Genc Kumtepe has published many research papers in journals, edited book chapters, book chapters and conference proceedings. She has been involved in a number of local and international research projects over the years.

Nuno Gustavo holds a PhD in Tourism, Leisure and Culture, completed in 2011 in the University of Coimbra. He is Assistant Professor at the Estoril Higher Institute for Tourism and Hotel Studies (ESHTE) since 2002, collaborating with several institutions on both international and national levels, such as Oporto Católica University, Grenoble Graduate School of Business, Eduardo Mondlane University - ESHTI, Lúrio University, Cape Verde Institute for Tourism and Hotel Studies and the University of Coimbra. His main areas of interest are focused on strategic and operations management and marketing of tourism and hospitality businesses. He has edited 2 books, published 19 book chapters and 10 articles in specialized journals, collaborating with 20 fellow researchers and receiving 4 awards. The curriculum also shows the development of several projects in the field of tourism and hospitality in Portugal, Mozambique and Cape Verde. He is also a member of the Editorial Board (Review Board Member) of the Journal of Hospitality and Tourism Management.

Merve İşçen studied bachelor at Burdur Mehmet Akif Ersoy University, Department of Accomodation Management. She is a master's student at Izmir Katip Celebi University, Department of Tourism Management. She is studying for a master's thesis on the perception of service quality in green hotels under the supervision of the same chapter's first author in this book. English knowledge is B2 level. She has studies on tourist guides' perceptions of mobile applications, visitor experiences for cave tourism, and occupational health and safety in accommodation businesses. Her research interests are neuromarketing and digitalization in tourism and tourist behaviour.

Ana Teresa Machado holds a Ph.D. in Management/Digital Marketing, completed in 2011 in the Lisbon School of Economics and Management. She is an Assistant Professor at the School of Communication and Media Studies since 1983 and coordinator of the master's degree in advertising and marketing since 2018. Her main areas of interest are focused on strategic marketing and digital marketing & communication. She has participated in six research projects and several international and scientific conferences and published articles in specialized journals. She is also a member of the Scientific Board of the Tourism & Management Studies Journal.

Clara Madeira is a Master Fellowship at COMEGI, at the Universidade Lusíada - Norte. Her research interests fall on the topics of strategic development and management, consumer behavior, sustainability, and the environment. She holds both a Master's from the University of Porto and a Degree from the University of Lisbon in Economics.

Carlos Martins is a Ph.D. in Management in 2012 by Lusiada University - Lisbon; Master in Management in 1993 by ISEG – University of Lisbon, and Degree in Management and Public Administration in 1984 by ISCSP (Lisbon - Portugal). He is an Assistant Professor at Universidade Lusíada Porto, and at the Polytechnic Institute of Maia.

Elliot Mbunge is a Lecturer in the Department of Computer Science at the University of Eswatini (formerly University of Swaziland, Kwaluseni, Eswatini (formerly Swaziland). He is a holder of B.Sc, M.Sc and currently pursuing his PhD in the field of Information Technology with Durban University of Technology, South Africa. He is a Member of Computational Intelligence and Health Informatics Research Group in the Department of Computer Science at the University of Eswatini.

Andile Metfula is a Senior Lecturer and the Head of the Computer Science Department housed under the Faculty of Science and Engineering in University of Eswatini (formerly the University of Swaziland), Kwaluseni, Eswatini (formerly Swaziland). He has a PhD from the University of Cape Town (South Africa), MSc from Rensselaer Polytechnic Institute (USA) and BSc from the University of Swaziland (now the University of Eswatini). His passion is in Information Systems and Innovation. In the past few years, his team in the Department has been able to organize the first-ever ICT Fair in the country.

Benhildah Muchemwa is studying BSc in Information Technology at the University of Eswatini. Her research areas include machine learning, data science and mobile health.

Murat Ödemiş completed his PhD at Gazi University Institute of Social Sciences, Department of Tourism Management, his Master's degree from Gazi University Institute of Educational Sciences,

Department of Tourism Management Education, and his BS degree from Bolu Abant İzzet Baysal University, School of Tourism and Hotel Management, Department of Tourism Management and Hotel Management. In 2015, he started his academic life as an Instructor at Gumushane University, Faculty of Tourism. As of 2019, Asst. Prof. Dr. As a member, he continues to work at Gumushane University, Faculty of Tourism. Research areas; strategic management in tourism enterprises, sustainable tourism, cultural tourism and tourism marketing. The author has served as a referee in national and international journals.

Paula Rodrigues holds a Ph.D. in Management, in the Faculty of Economics at the University of Porto, Portugal. She is an Associate Professor in Brand Management at the School of Economics and Management, Lusíada University - North, Portugal. Since 1995, she teaches Brand Management, Consumer Behaviour, Econometrics, statistics, and Quantitative Methods at the Universidade Lusíada - Norte. She has published several scientific papers, chapters, and books. Her on-going research projects concern consumer-brand relationships in the field of luxury, tourism and hospitality, and consumer goods.

Fatma Selin Sak received her bachelor's degree from the Department of Civil Air Transportation Management in 2010 and her master's degree from the department of aviation management in 2015 with her thesis "Analyzing the profiles and preferences of airline passengers traveling for holiday purposes with geographical information systems: Antalya example". It is understood that he graduated from Anadolu University, Institute of Social Sciences, Department of Civil Aviation Management in 2020 with his thesis "The role of experience in the effect of customer value co-creation behavior on customer satisfaction: the example of Sabiha Gökçen Airport". Besides having sector experience in the field of Civil Aviation, he also has various studies on airline and airport marketing.

Lakhvinder Singh is doctorate in Tourism and working as Assistant Professor of Tourism in Government College, Kaithal (Haryana), India with more than 5 years of teaching experience. He has nearly 40 research publications in his credit. He is in the Editorial/Advisory Board of different Journals of International and National repute. His areas of interest include tourist behavior, tourism marketing, tourism impact, culture & religious tourism, e-tourism and ICT in tourism.

Nil Sonuç She is an assistant professor at İzmir Katip Çelebi University, Faculty of Tourism. Bachelor at Dokuz Eylül University, Tourism Management (Education in English & French). 4th year of bachelor & Master at Université de Savoie, in Chambéry/France at "Masters of European Hospitality Management". Internship in Guadeloupe. Master thesis in French on Sustainable Tourism Development in Guadeloupe. PhD in Tourism Management, Dokuz Eylül University, İzmir, Turkey. PhD thesis on Social Tourism in İzmir. Pedagogical Formation at Dokuz Eylul University, for teaching English. Licensed tour guide in French & English. Since 2007 teaches tourism at universities in İzmir & taught at European Universities, Belgium, Germany, Italy, Portugal & Denmark by Erasmus Teaching Exchange. Publications on sustainability and tourism, sustainable tourism marketing, environmental and social sustainability of tourism, sustainable tourism product and planning, accessible tourism, digitalisation and tourism, wellness tourism, gender in tourism guidance, yoga tourism, destinations in Turkey and Europe, slow tourism, western European cuisine, bar management, mythology, tourism and hospitality management, tourism education, cultural heritage and tourism. Research interests: Publishing in French, qualitative research, multidisciplinary tourism studies on neuro-tourism, wellness, well-being, psychology, digitalisation, cultural heritage and inclusion, social tourism, tour guiding, sustainable tourism.

Ana Sousa is a Post-Doctoral Fellowship at COMEGI, of the University Lusíada and an Associate Researcher at GOVCOPP of the University of Aveiro. She holds a PhD in Marketing and Strategy from the University of Minho, Portugal. She holds a Master in Marketing and Business Administration and a Degree in Business Management from ISAG - European Business School, and a Degree in Psychology from the University of Porto. Her research interests are Consumer-brand relationships in the field of luxury, Tourism and hospitality, Place Branding and Cultural Heritage.

Index

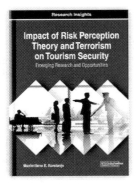
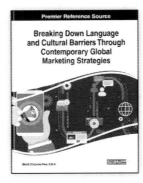

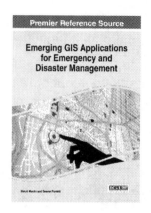   

IGI Global Author Services

Providing a high-quality, affordable, and expeditious service, IGI Global's Author Services enable authors to streamline their publishing process, increase chance of acceptance, and adhere to IGI Global's publication standards.

Benefits of Author Services:

- **Professional Service:** All our editors, designers, and translators are experts in their field with years of experience and professional certifications.
- **Quality Guarantee & Certificate:** Each order is returned with a quality guarantee and certificate of professional completion.
- **Timeliness:** All editorial orders have a guaranteed return timeframe of 3-5 business days and translation orders are guaranteed in 7-10 business days.
- **Affordable Pricing:** IGI Global Author Services are competitively priced compared to other industry service providers.
- **APC Reimbursement:** IGI Global authors publishing Open Access (OA) will be able to deduct the cost of editing and other IGI Global author services from their OA APC publishing fee.

Author Services Offered:

English Language Copy Editing
Professional, native English language copy editors improve your manuscript's grammar, spelling, punctuation, terminology, semantics, consistency, flow, formatting, and more.

Scientific & Scholarly Editing
A Ph.D. level review for qualities such as originality and significance, interest to researchers, level of methodology and analysis, coverage of literature, organization, quality of writing, and strengths and weaknesses.

Figure, Table, Chart & Equation Conversions
Work with IGI Global's graphic designers before submission to enhance and design all figures and charts to IGI Global's specific standards for clarity.

Translation
Providing 70 language options, including Simplified and Traditional Chinese, Spanish, Arabic, German, French, and more.

Hear What the Experts Are Saying About IGI Global's Author Services

"Publishing with IGI Global has been an amazing experience for me for sharing my research. The strong academic production support ensures quality and timely completion." – **Prof. Margaret Niess, Oregon State University, USA**

"The service was very fast, very thorough, and very helpful in ensuring our chapter meets the criteria and requirements of the book's editors. I was quite impressed and happy with your service." – **Prof. Tom Brinthaupt, Middle Tennessee State University, USA**

Learn More or Get Started Here:

For Questions, Contact IGI Global's Customer Service Team at cust@igi-global.com or 717-533-8845

www.igi-global.com

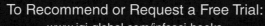